TEACHINGS AND COMMENTARIES

on the

BOOK of MORMON

ALSO BY ED J. PINEGAR

Latter-day Commentary on the Old Testament
(with Richard J. Allen)
The Ultimate Missionary Companion
Latter-day Commentary on the New Testament
Lengthen Your Shuffle

ALSO BY RICHARD J. ALLEN

Latter-day Commentary on the Old Testament
(with Ed J. Pinegar)

* * * *

available in book
or book on cassette format
from Covenant

TEACHINGS AND COMMENTARIES

on the

BOOK *of* MORMON

ED J. PINEGAR *and* RICHARD J. ALLEN

Covenant

Published by Covenant Communications, Inc.
American Fork, Utah

Copyright © 2003 by Ed J. Pinegar and Richard J. Allen
Cover image *Mormon Abridging the Plates* by Tom Lovell © by Intellectual Reserve, Inc. Courtesy of the Museum of Church History and Art
Cover and book design © 2003 by Covenant Communications, Inc.

Printed in Canada
First Printing: September 2003

10 09 08 07 06 05 04 03   10 9 8 7 6 5 4 3 2 1

ISBN 1-59156-296-1

TABLE OF CONTENTS

CHAPTER ONE

"THE KEYSTONE *of* OUR RELIGION"

TITLE PAGE TO THE BOOK OF MORMON, THE TESTIMONY OF THREE WITNESSES,
THE TESTIMONY OF EIGHT WITNESSES, TESTIMONY OF THE PROPHET JOSEPH SMITH

*"I told the brethren [the twelve Apostles] that the Book of Mormon
was the most correct of any book on earth, and the keystone of our religion,
and a man would get nearer to God by abiding by its precepts, than by any other book."*
—JOSEPH SMITH, *HISTORY OF THE CHURCH OF JESUS CHRIST
OF LATTER-DAY SAINTS*, 7 VOLS., 4:461.

THEMES *for* LIVING

The Book of Mormon: Divine Agenda of Hope
The Book of Mormon: Another Testament of Jesus Christ
The Book of Mormon: A Compass for Our Time

INTRODUCTION

The Book of Mormon, to use the words of President Ezra Taft Benson, is "one of the most significant gifts given to the world in modern times" ("The Book of Mormon—Keystone of Our Religion," *Ensign*, Nov. 1986, 4). The bestowal of this magnificent gift by the Lord as part of the latter-day Restoration—this "marvelous work and a wonder" foreseen by the prophet Isaiah (2 Ne. 27:26)—is in essence a profound act of divine love and mercy. Among the earliest verses of the Book of Mormon is this promise: "But behold, I, Nephi, will show unto you that the tender mercies of the Lord are over all those whom he hath chosen, because of their faith, to make them mighty even unto the power of deliverance" (1 Ne. 1:20). Some thousand years later the prophet Moroni, in sealing up the record for future generations, gave utterance once again to the central theme of the Lord's loving mercy to His children: "Behold, I would exhort you that when ye shall read these things, if it be wisdom in God that ye should read them, that ye would remember how merciful the Lord hath been unto the children of men, from the creation of Adam even down until the time that ye shall receive these things, and ponder it in your hearts" (Moro. 10:3).

Thus the Book of Mormon is one of the Lord's gifts of love to the world in the latter days to inspire hope, strengthen testimonies, establish truth, and unfold a sure course of advancement through a modern landscape fraught with the stumbling blocks of pride, godless materialism, immorality, and even terrorism. The Book of Mormon, "Another Testament of Jesus Christ," contains what Moroni called "the fulness of the everlasting Gospel" (JS—H 1:34), designed to prepare mankind for the second advent of the Savior. It is a beacon of inspiration that reflects to a hungering and benighted world the glory of the Atonement and the radiance of God's plan for the redemption, salvation, and eternal life of His children. Truly the prophet/historian Mormon caught the essence of the book's supernal significance in bringing to pass the Lord's covenant plan of love and mercy ordained from the foundations of the world: "For the eternal purposes of the Lord shall roll on, until all his promises shall be fulfilled" (Morm. 8:22). The Book of Mormon is the latter-day guidebook for understanding the Lord's covenant promises and learning to live in accordance with the divine dictum: "Therefore I would that ye should be perfect even as I, or your Father who is in heaven is perfect" (3 Ne. 12:48).

1. THE BOOK OF MORMON: DIVINE AGENDA OF HOPE

THEME. The Book of Mormon is a compelling appeal to all of us as God's children to bring our lives into harmony with gospel principles. If we respond to that divine invitation, then a glorious hope is kindled in our hearts, dispelling all doubt and opening up a certain pathway of spiritual deliverance founded on the testimony of the Savior, Jesus Christ, as Redeemer and author of our salvation.

> *"Which is to show unto the remnant of the House of Israel what great things the Lord hath done for their fathers; and that they may know the covenants of the Lord, that they are not cast off forever—And also to the convincing of the Jew and Gentile that JESUS is the CHRIST, the ETERNAL GOD, manifesting himself unto all nations"* (Book of Mormon title page).

> *"And I also remember that thou hast said that thou hast prepared a house for man, yea, even among the mansions of thy Father, in which man might have a more excellent hope; wherefore man must hope, or he cannot receive an inheritance in the place which thou hast prepared"* (Ether 12:32).

> *"And the remission of sins bringeth meekness, and lowliness of heart; and because of meekness and lowliness of heart cometh the visitation of the Holy Ghost, which Comforter filleth with hope and perfect love, which love endureth by diligence unto prayer, until the end shall come, when all the saints shall dwell with God"* (Moro. 8:26).

MOMENT OF TRUTH. Picture the scene: The prophet/historian Moroni, sole representative of his people upon the earth, surrounded by the devastating effects of indescribable carnage at the hands of the prevailing Lamanites—themselves reduced to vicious interfaction warring and butchery—commits to an earthly vault the sacred engraved chronicle made at the hands of a long sequence of the Lord's prophets, he being the last. "And my father also was killed by them, and I even remain alone to write the sad tale of the destruction of my people. But behold, they are gone, and I fulfil the commandment of my father. And whether they will slay me, I know not. Therefore I will write and hide up the records in the earth; and whither I go it mattereth not" (Morm. 8:3–4).

In this scene of impenetrable darkness, Moroni refused to permit his soul to be overcome with gloom or resignation, for he was motivated by a divine assurance. He looked forward with prophetic eye to the time when the sacred records would come forth again through the power of God unto the salvation of mankind: "And blessed be he that shall bring this thing to light [i.e., Joseph Smith]; for it shall be brought out of darkness unto light, according to the word of God; yea, it shall be brought out of the earth, and it shall shine forth out of darkness, and come unto the knowledge of the people; and it shall be done by the power of God" (Morm. 8:16).

Just as the Book of Mormon is an inspired abridgement of multiple records generated according to divine design, Moroni's title page for the book is an inspired summary of the book's stated fourfold purpose: (1) to bring forward the evidence of the Lord's great dealings with His people of former times, (2) to illuminate the covenant process of salvation, (3) to show that the Lord's people can have hope and are not cast adrift without anchor and guidance, and (4) to present a further glorious witness that Jesus is the Christ.

MODERN PROPHETS SPEAK

Joseph Smith:

> Take away the Book of Mormon and the revelations, and where is our religion? We have none. (History of the Church of Jesus Christ of Latter-day Saints, 7 vols., 2:52; hereafter cited as *HC*)

Gordon B. Hinckley:

> Without reservation I promise you that if you will prayerfully read the Book of Mormon, regardless of how many times you previously have read it, there will come into your hearts an added measure of the Spirit of the Lord. There will come a strengthened resolution to walk in obedience to his commandments, and there will come a stronger testimony of the living reality of the Son of God. . . . (*Teachings of Gordon B. Hinckley* [Salt Lake City: Deseret Book, 1997], 41, 44)

ILLUSTRATIONS FOR OUR TIME

"The Greatest Book in the World." Shortly after writing my contribution for this section on a Sunday afternoon, I went to a local hospital to visit one of the high priests in the ward. He was a stalwart brother (not yet seventy years old) who had been suffering for many months with a malady that had caused him constant, excruciating pain. Observing his state of affairs, I could only shake my head at this misery and ask if he needed anything—reading materials perhaps. No, he assured me. He was well provided for. Of special comfort was his favorite book, the Book of Mormon. He told me he had read this sacred scripture some thirty or forty times since his mission as a young elder. "It is the greatest book in the world," he stated emphatically. "Any time I am down, I reach for this book and read from its pages.

I say a little prayer beforehand and it always picks me up." Thus he declared thankfully that the Book of Mormon was his principal written source of hope and solace in the world.

Truly the Book of Mormon is the Lord's means of hope, ordained of Him to "speak out of the ground" and "whisper out of the dust" in these latter days as a means of lifting our spirits unto salvation (see Isa. 29:4). Through God's blessing, hope may prevail over modern despair, just as light prevails over darkness. Moroni, quoting his father Mormon, puts it in perspective: "And again, my beloved brethren, I would speak unto you concerning hope. How is it that ye can attain unto faith, save ye shall have hope? And what is it that ye shall hope for? Behold I say unto you that ye shall have hope through the atonement of Christ and the power of his resurrection, to be raised unto life eternal, and this because of your faith in him according to the promise. Wherefore, if a man have faith he must needs have hope; for without faith there cannot be any hope" (Moro. 7:40–42).

And so it is: the Book of Mormon stands as a beacon of hope along a mortal pathway frequently marked by challenges to our endurance and by trials of our faith. As Nephi stated: 'Wherefore, ye must press forward with a steadfastness in Christ, having a perfect brightness of hope, and a love of God and of all men. Wherefore, if ye shall press forward, feasting upon the word of Christ, and endure to the end, behold, thus saith the Father: Ye shall have eternal life" (2 Ne. 31:20). (Allen)

The Book of Hope. The goodness of God comes to us through His Word, Jesus Christ. Our Savior lived and died for us and worked out the infinite Atonement that we might live again in the presence of our Father, if we but heed the word. Knowledge of the word, as it has been given us through the Book of Mormon and through our holy prophets, works upon the minds and hearts of men—it provides hope, it brings about an increase of the love of God, and it increases our faith and enables us to exercise more faith. In short, it causes change (see Alma 31:5).

Alma preached to the people at Zarahemla, saying, "Behold, he changed their hearts; yea, he awakened them out of a deep sleep, and they awoke unto God. Behold, they were in the midst of darkness; nevertheless, their souls were illuminated by the light of the everlasting word; yea, they were encircled about by the bands of death, and the chains of hell, and an everlasting destruction did await them" (Alma 5:7).

We can begin to see the power and the blessing of the word of God in our lives. We can discern with greater clarity the correlation between the Word—even Jesus Christ—on the one hand, and His printed word, the word of God, on the other. Our lives are illuminated by the teachings of the scriptural record, which bears witness of the divinity of the Father and His Son. In this very way the Book of Mormon has saved my life and has blessed our family continually as we have searched it during family scripture study. It is not only the key to our religion—it is our key to eternal life (see 1 Ne. 8:15). As we heed the scriptural counsel, we have hope for life eternal. We see the blessings of obedience: "And inasmuch as ye shall keep my commandments, ye shall prosper, and shall be led to a land of promise; yea, even a land which I have prepared for you; yea, a land which is choice above all other lands" (1 Ne. 2:20). This phrase or one similar to it occurs thirteen times in the Book of Mormon. (Pinegar)

2. THE BOOK OF MORMON: ANOTHER TESTAMENT OF JESUS CHRIST

THEME. On 7 April 1829, Oliver Cowdery began his labors as a scribe to assist Joseph Smith in the translation of the Book of Mormon. The Lord's instruction to both of them at that time sheds light on one of the principal doctrines of the kingdom, namely, the doctrine of witnessing:

> *"And now, behold, I give unto you, and also unto my servant Joseph, the keys of this gift, which shall bring to light this ministry; and in the mouth of two or three witnesses shall every word be established"* (D&C 6:28; see also 2 Cor. 13:1).

Thus the Book of Mormon stands beside the Bible as an additional witness to the divinity of Jesus Christ, the author of salvation.

MOMENT OF TRUTH. Looking back over the annals of God's dealing with His children in the western world, Moroni perceived the central purpose of the Book of Mormon as "the convincing of the Jew and Gentile that JESUS is the CHRIST, the ETERNAL GOD, manifesting himself unto all nations" (Book of Mormon title page). According to President Ezra Taft Benson, "The Book of Mormon is the keystone in our witness of Jesus Christ, who is Himself the cornerstone of everything we do. It bears witness of His reality with power and clarity. Unlike the Bible, which passed through generations of copyists, translators, and corrupt religionists who tampered with the text, the Book of Mormon came from writer to reader in just one inspired step of translation. Therefore, its testimony of the Master is clear, undiluted, and full of power" ("The Book of Mormon—Keystone of Our Religion," *Ensign*, Nov., 1986, 5). Just as Moroni added his illuminating summary pronouncement as a title page for the ancient record before committing it to the ground, the Church in 1982 added the crowning words "Another Testament of Jesus Christ" to the title of this restored sacred scripture, thus underscoring in bold terms the central purpose of the book.

Furthermore, Moroni, like Nephi before him, was given power to look forward prophetically to the day when this new witness of Christ would itself be confirmed and substantiated by men called to view the plates and testify of their divine origin: "And behold, ye [Joseph Smith] may be privileged that ye may show the plates unto those who shall assist to bring forth this work; And unto three shall they be shown by the power of God; wherefore they shall know of a surety that these things are true. And in the mouth of three witnesses shall these things be established; and the testimony of three, and this work, in the which shall be shown forth the power of God and also his word, of which the Father, and the Son, and the Holy Ghost bear record—and all this shall stand as a testimony against the world at the last day" (Ether 5:2–4; cf. 2 Ne. 11:3; 27:12–14). Thus three special witnesses were called and empowered by divine decree in 1829 to see the sacred plates at the hand of Moroni and hear the voice of the Lord declaring the truth of the record (see D&C 17; *HC,* 1:52–59). Moreover, eight additional witnesses were allowed to handle the plates in accordance with Nephi's promises that "the Lord God will proceed to bring forth the words of the book; and in the mouth of as many witnesses as seemeth him good will he establish his word; and wo be unto him that rejecteth the word of God!" (2 Ne. 27:14).

MODERN PROPHETS SPEAK

Joseph Smith:

> The boldness of my plans and measures can readily be tested by the touchstone of all schemes, systems, projects, and adventures—truth; for truth is a matter of fact; and the fact is, that by the power of God I translated the Book of Mormon from hieroglyphics, the knowledge of which was lost to the world, in which wonderful event I stood alone, an unlearned youth, to combat the worldly wisdom and multiplied ignorance of eighteen centuries, with a new revelation, which (if they would receive the everlasting Gospel,) would open the eyes of more than eight hundred millions of people, and make "plain the old paths," wherein if a man walk in all the ordinances of God blameless, he shall inherit eternal life; and Jesus Christ, who was, and is, and is to come, has borne me safely over every snare and plan laid in secret or openly, through priestly hypocrisy, sectarian prejudice, popular philosophy, executive power, or law-defying mobocracy, to destroy me. (*HC,* 6:74)

ILLUSTRATIONS FOR OUR TIME

The Names and Titles of the Savior. When we give heed to the word, we can begin to understand and appreciate the Atonement. The Book of Mormon is filled with plain and precious teachings about our Savior. Note from the following how intricately the Book of Mormon weaves into its sacred tapestry references to Christ:

> The Book of Mormon contains not only a great variety of names and titles for Jesus, but also many thousands of personal pronouns that refer to him. . . . The pronouns that have reference to God are interspersed throughout the Book of Mormon text, mingled with his 101 names and titles.

> Beyond the use of deific names, titles, and pronouns in the Nephite record, wit-
> nesses of Jesus appear in the form of symbols, presented through such figures of speech
> as metaphor, simile, synecdoche, metonymy, implication, and personification.
> Metaphors of Christ, for example, are common in the book and include Moses' brazen
> serpent (1 Nephi 17:41; Helaman 8:14–15), "keeper of the gate" (2 Nephi 9:41),
> "Lamb of God" (1 Nephi 10:10), "the light and the life of the world" (3 Nephi
> 9:18), "Son of Righteousness" (3 Nephi 25:2), foundation stone (Jacob 4:15–16),
> "the truth of the world" (Ether 4:12), and "rock" and "true vine" (1 Nephi 15:15).
> (Donald W. Parry, *Expressions of Faith: Testimonies of Latter-day Saint Scholars,* ed.
> Susan Easton Black [Salt Lake City: Deseret Book, 1996], 217–19).

The word ties everything to Christ. Christ, then, is the fulfillment of the word. The printed word
teaches us that Jesus is the Christ, the Son of the living God; and it should root us to Him (see Hel.
5:12). The Book of Mormon is a great testament—the true witness—that Jesus is the true and living
Christ. (Pinegar)

The Limbs of the Sycamores. In front of the elegant older chapel we once attended in our home ward
are several majestic sycamore trees. With their massive gray-brown dappled branches projecting
broadleaf foliage on all sides, they form a protective canopy of comfort and shade. I often wondered,
walking past those trees, how the gigantic limbs, suspended horizontally almost parallel to the ground,
could remain solidly in place under so much weight. Then I remembered reading years earlier about a
little secret of nature explained by scientists like Buckminster Fuller, namely, the tetrahedron. Nature
uses the tetrahedron (or four-sided pyramid) as the basis of much of the organic architecture of natural products, such as plants and trees. It was that miraculous tetrahedral construction buried within that
kept the sycamore limbs in place. Why is the tetrahedron so strong? Because it is formed of four equi-
lateral triangles—each one singularly rigid and fixed. We imitate the two-dimensional triangular construct in the girders and joists of our buildings. But it is the three-dimensional tetrahedron that presents one of the most efficient and effective manifestations of strength found in nature.

The Book of Mormon is like a three-dimensional tetrahedron. Moroni gave expression to the strength
of the book in his introductory title page when he identified the four key dimensions of this scriptural powerhouse: "Which is to show unto the remnant of the House of Israel what great things the Lord
hath done for their fathers; and that they may know the covenants of the Lord, that they are not cast
off forever—And also to the convincing of the Jew and Gentile that JESUS is the CHRIST, the ETER-
NAL GOD, manifesting himself unto all nations."

Thus the agenda of the whole work can be summarized in four points: (1) To preserve and present great
stories from the past concerning the Lord's loving mercy to His children, (2) to teach great and sacred
covenants for the present, (3) to engender great hope for the future (i.e., that we are not "cast off forever"), and (4) to build all of this upon the sure foundation of the Savior, the great Redeemer. This

fourfold agenda is the key to the book's vitality. This scriptural mission of power captures the wonder of the Book of Mormon, as its influence is felt across the span of time and across its noble pages from first to last. Like the branches of the sycamore trees, this book extends protection and comfort to grateful recipients among every nation, kindred, tongue, and people who are willing to apply Moroni's promise to let the Spirit confirm its truth (see Moro. 10:3–5).

Over the years as a teacher I have often utilized this fourfold summary to communicate the simplicity and power of the Book of Mormon to my fellow learners. Several years ago one of our good neighbors, a skilled cabinetmaker, fashioned a series of small wooden tetrahedrons according to the cardboard construct I had developed as a teaching aid. It was a joy to present these beautifully finished models to several students in an institute class my wife and I taught recently when they completed the assignment to read the Book of Mormon in its entirety. It was our hope that they would use these small wooden models as a reminder of what Jacob promised to future readers about cultivating hope in Christ: "For, for this intent have we written these things, that they may know that we knew of Christ, and we had a hope of his glory many hundred years before his coming; and not only we ourselves had a hope of his glory, but also all the holy prophets which were before us" (Jacob 4:4).

It is into the assembly of such majestic witnesses that the holy scriptures beckon us. In the ennobling pattern of righteous living unfolded within the pages of the word of God, we can find strength to sustain our lives with purpose and hope. In particular, the Book of Mormon offers us another powerful testament of Jesus Christ, another radiating witness of His divinity and Saviorhood, another comforting assurance that we can, through obedience, return to His presence and that of the Father when our mortal journey is through. (Allen)

3. THE BOOK OF MORMON: A COMPASS FOR OUR TIME

THEME. Through the grace of God, a manifold array of prophets from the distant past focused their discerning eye on our day and laid out a road map of truth aligned specifically with our modern needs. They described enduring paths through the highways and byways of a largely godless society. The Book of Mormon is a compass and a guide for the faithful in modern times. Moroni, the last of the ancient compilers, addressed his words directly and emphatically to latter-day readers: "Behold, I speak unto you as if ye were present, and yet ye are not. But behold, Jesus Christ hath shown you unto me, and I know your doing" (Morm. 8:35). Knowing that so many servants of God over the ages have been mindful of our challenges and anxiously engaged in providing the precise counsel for returning home should give us a continual feeling of gratitude for their sacrifices on our behalf.

"For behold, it is as easy to give heed to the word of Christ, which will point to you a straight course to eternal bliss, as it was for our fathers to give heed to this compass, which would point unto them a straight course to the promised land" (Alma 37:44).

MOMENT OF TRUTH. The prophet Nephi, first contributor to the Book of Mormon, like Moroni, the last, knew that he was writing for compatriots who would be living in a future day. His deepest motivation was to persuade others to believe in Christ and follow the gospel plan, for he knew that thereby, and only thereby, could lasting happiness be achieved: "Wherefore, for this cause hath the Lord God promised unto me that these things which I write shall be kept and preserved, and handed down unto my seed, from generation to generation, that the promise may be fulfilled unto Joseph, that his seed should never perish as long as the earth should stand. Wherefore, these things shall go from generation to generation as long as the earth shall stand; and they shall go according to the will and pleasure of God; and the nations who shall possess them shall be judged of them according to the words which are written. For we labor diligently to write, to persuade our children, and also our brethren, to believe in Christ, and to be reconciled to God; for we know that it is by grace that we are saved, after all we can do" (2 Ne. 25:21–23).

What a singular experience for modern readers to peruse the pages of a sacred book whose compilers, acting under inspiration, were speaking directly to them. Moroni knew the conditions that would prevail at the time of the Restoration, of which the publication of the Book of Mormon was one of the earliest manifestations: "And no one need say they [the records] shall not come, for they surely shall, for the Lord hath spoken it; for out of the earth shall they come, by the hand of the Lord, and none can stay it; and it shall come in a day when it shall be said that miracles are done away; and it shall come even as if one should speak from the dead" (Morm. 8:26).

MODERN PROPHETS SPEAK

Joseph F. Smith:

> I note your remarks in relation to reading the Book of Mormon and the Doctrine and Covenants, and I heartily approve of your views. No man can be an efficient missionary of this church unless he is familiar with these books. And the more familiar he is with them, the more capable will he be to discharge the duties of his ministry. Indeed, I think sometimes that we neglect too much the advocacy of the Book of Mormon. In the early days of the church, it was the preaching of the Book of Mormon and the proof of its existence or coming forth, as found in the Bible, that made converts to the church. It was as necessary then to prove our authority by the Bible as it is now, but it seems to me that to show the world from the Bible that the Book of Mormon, or such a book as it is, was to

come forth in the latter days, is a strong argument for our cause. It is a great mistake to set aside or ignore the word of God as revealed in the latter days in preaching this gospel to the world. Of course it is not always wise to feed the people with strong meat at first, but one of the foundation stones of the church in the latter day is the revelation of the Book of Mormon and the restoration of the Gospel it contains, as also the visions and revelations given to the Prophet Joseph Smith. To be ashamed of these is to be ashamed of our ministry, to dodge these facts is to fail in the spirit of our ministry. In my opinion these things should be preached and then substantiated by the accepted version of the old Bible. (Comp. Hyrum M. Smith and Scott G. Kenney, *From Prophet to Son: Advice of Joseph F. Smith to His Missionary Sons,* [Salt Lake City: Deseret Book, 1981], 69–70)

ILLUSTRATIONS FOR OUR TIME

A Covert From Storm and From Rain. As an institute instructor, I was privileged not long ago to study the Book of Mormon with a number of choice young singles. They reflected a spirit of sincere inquiry and a genuine desire to serve the Lord. The material was presented in the context of the Book of Mormon being an inspired road map to guide our footsteps in the latter days, just as President Ezra Taft Benson had counseled: "We must make the Book of Mormon a center focus of study [as] it was written for our day. The Nephites never had the book; neither did the Lamanites of ancient times. It was meant for us. Mormon wrote near the end of the Nephite civilization. Under the inspiration of God, who sees all things from the beginning, he abridged centuries of records, choosing the stories, speeches, and events that would be most helpful to us. . . . If they saw our day and chose those things which would be of greatest worth to us, is not that how we should study the Book of Mormon? We should constantly ask ourselves, 'Why did the Lord inspire Mormon (or Moroni or Alma) to include that in his record? What lesson can I learn from that to help me live in this day and age?'" ("The Book of Mormon—Keystone of Our Religion," *Ensign,* Nov. 1986, 6).

Those questions were answered for us dramatically by an event that occurred shortly after the commencement of the institute class that year—the terror attack of 11 September 2001. Like everyone in the nation, we were shocked by the devastating upheaval wrought upon our way of life by evil forces. Could there be any security and peace after such a revolutionary shift in the status quo? And then we read together from the words of Isaiah that Nephi had included in his record: "And the Lord will create upon every dwelling-place of mount Zion, and upon her assemblies, a cloud and smoke by day and the shining of a flaming fire by night; for upon all the glory of Zion shall be a defense. And there shall be a tabernacle for a shadow in the daytime from the heat, and for a place of refuge, and a covert from storm and from rain" (2 Ne. 14:5–6; cf. Isa. 4:5–6).

One of the students later wrote a letter expressing how the Book of Mormon, and specifically that passage from Isaiah, had been a blessing and a guide at a time of challenge: "When I consider 2 Nephi 14:5–6, I can't help but think of our nation's recent events. In a time when evil is so apparent and terror so present, I have asked myself where I might find refuge or safety. Right now I live far from the 'Holy Places' of my youth, namely with my family and dear friends. But even so far away, I can find refuge in many places, like Institute. After a hectic day at work, where my attention is distracted by so many busy, yet less important things, I am glad to have Institute as a refuge, a place to associate with other saints, to feel the Spirit, and to study the word of God. It has truly been a blessing, 'a covert from storm and from rain.'" Thus the Book of Mormon, once again, was confirmed as a spiritual road map for our day. (Allen)

Applying the Word with Power. We have mentioned how Alma likened the word of Christ to the Liahona. The word of God literally gives direction to our lives. Nephi expressed this principle in another way: "Angels speak by the power of the Holy Ghost; wherefore, they speak the words of Christ. Wherefore, I said unto you, feast upon the words of Christ; for behold, the words of Christ will tell you all things what ye should do" (2 Ne. 32:3). This is a sobering promise: not some of the things, not most of the things, but all things that we should do can come to us through the words of Christ, because they have power to change our lives. Nothing compares to the virtue of the word of God. When man lives by every word that proceeds forth from the mouth of God, it becomes our compass for life—a personal Liahona.

We learn from the Doctrine and Covenants the following: "Learn of me, and listen to my words." Then what happens? We walk in the meekness of His Spirit and will have peace in Him (D&C 19:23). The direction in our lives comes from adhering to the word of God.In visiting with Elder Bruce R. McConkie when I was a young man, I asked him why he said that the "fulness of the gospel" was not in the Book of Mormon. He said to me, "Oh, Ed, my brother, you don't understand. You see, the fulness of the gospel is in the lives of the people as they live the gospel teachings from the Book of Mormon." That was the day I began to understand that the word of God becomes powerful in our lives only as we apply it. We then recognize that the words of Christ will tell us all things we should do (see 2 Ne. 32:3); we recognize that it is the will of the Lord, the mind of the Lord, the word of the Lord, the voice of the Lord, and the power of God unto salvation (see D&C 68:4–6); we realize that the word of God will cause men to do good more than anything else (see Alma 31:5); we recognize what Nephi was trying to teach us:

> And I did read many things unto them which were written in the books of Moses; but that I might more fully persuade them to believe in the Lord their Redeemer I did read unto them that which was written by the prophet Isaiah; for I did liken all scriptures unto us, that it might be for our profit and learning." (1 Ne. 19:23)

Then all scriptures are for our profit and learning—our compass for living. We take all scriptures personally that may apply to our lives. The word of God is for us to live today. The fulness of the gospel is in our lives as we live the word of God.
A method to apply the word of God might be simply stated in steps:

1. Read the scriptures carefully.
2. Ponder them as they relate to you.
3. Write down each scripture reference and the main idea that is there.
4. Write a personal statement on how you're going to live this scripture.

I can, I must, I shall, I will—these first-person commitment statements will make the scriptures live in your life. Nephi taught another great lesson:

> And it came to pass that I, Nephi, said unto my father: I will go and do the things which the Lord hath commanded, for I know that the Lord giveth no commandments unto the children of men, save he shall prepare a way for them that they may accomplish the thing which he commandeth them." (1 Ne. 3:7)

Here are some examples of applying scripture directly to our lives:

I can keep the commandments because the Lord will help me by preparing a way.
I will pray today or I will keep the commandment of the fast on fast Sunday.
I will live worthy of the Spirit that I might have direction in my life.

As a Book of Mormon teacher at Brigham Young University and the Orem, Utah Institute, I had my students do applications with each reading assignment. It changed lives. To this day students will come up and tell me about their application booklet. One student did over 1,375 in one semester. Needless to say, the applications to life from the Book of Mormon gave inspiration and direction for their lives. (Pinegar)

SUMMARY

Truly the Book of Mormon is a divine agenda of hope, an inspired additional testament of Jesus Christ, and a precise compass for our time. "And the angel spake unto me, saying: These last records, which thou hast seen among the Gentiles, shall establish the truth of the first, which are of the twelve apostles of the Lamb, and shall make known the plain and precious things which have been taken away from them; and shall make known to all kindreds, tongues, and people, that the Lamb of God is the Son of the Eternal Father, and the Savior of the world; and that all men must come unto him, or they cannot be saved. And they must come according to the words which shall be established by the mouth of the Lamb; and the words of the Lamb shall be made known in the records of thy seed, as well as in the records of the twelve apostles of the Lamb; wherefore they both shall be established in one; for there is one God and one Shepherd over all the earth" (1 Ne. 13:40–41).

"The words of the Lamb" in the Book of Mormon convey in undefiled purity the essence of the everlasting gospel of truth and peace. The Lord's own testimony of this work confirms its divine origin and purpose: "And gave unto [Joseph Smith] commandments which inspired him; And gave him power from on high, by the means which were before prepared, to translate the Book of Mormon; Which contains a record of a fallen people, and the fulness of the gospel of Jesus Christ to the Gentiles and to the Jews also; Which was given by inspiration, and is confirmed to others by the ministering of angels, and is declared unto the world by them—Proving to the world that the holy scriptures are true, and that God does inspire men and call them to his holy work in this age and generation, as well as in generations of old; Thereby showing that he is the same God yesterday, today, and forever. Amen" (D&C 20:7–12).

Should we not with gratitude search this work continually and derive from it the intended blessings and spiritual sustenance prepared for us by a loving and merciful God? Should we not heed the counsel of latter-day prophets by making the Book of Mormon a daily source of inspiration? The Lord clearly warned us not to be forgetful in this regard: "And this condemnation resteth upon the children of Zion, even all. And they shall remain under this condemnation until they repent and remember the new covenant, even the Book of Mormon and the former commandments which I have given them, not only to say, but to do according to that which I have written—That they may bring forth fruit meet for their Father's kingdom; otherwise there remaineth a scourge and judgment to be poured out upon the children of Zion. For shall the children of the kingdom pollute my holy land? Verily, I say unto you, Nay" (D&C 84:56–59).

The Lord sees all. He discerns our needs with perfect understanding. He is aware of our struggles: "For as the heavens are higher than the earth, so are my ways higher than your ways, and my thoughts than your thoughts" (Isa. 55:9). Accordingly, He prepared the Book of Mormon as a spiritual shield and bolster for His Saints in the latter days, and as a clarion call for all nations to feast at the banquet table of spiritual truth. Every word, every phrase, every story has meaning and significance for us as a means to increase our faith and courage to endure to the end. The Lord wants to elevate our perspective, to show us the merciful plan that will enable us, through the blessing of His Spirit, to traverse the landscape of mortal life successfully. As He told Joseph Smith: "Behold, there are many things engraven upon the plates of Nephi which do throw greater views upon my gospel; therefore, it is wisdom in me that you should translate this first part of the engravings of Nephi, and send forth in this work" (D&C 10:45). Is it not therefore beholden upon us all to apply these "greater views" diligently, with grateful hearts and minds for such a magnificent gift from God?

CHAPTER TWO

"ALL THINGS ACCORDING *to* HIS WILL"

1 NEPHI 1–7

*"Prepare ye to follow the way of the Lord. That is what this church is all about—
to help us to prepare to follow the way of the Lord, to walk in obedience to
His commandments, to get into our lives the spirit of His work,
to come to know Him and to love Him, and to seek to do His will.
Prepare ye to follow the way of the Lord."*

—GORDON B. HINCKLEY, *TEACHINGS OF GORDON B. HINCKLEY*
(SALT LAKE CITY: DESERET BOOK, 1997), 470.

THEMES *for* LIVING

"Goodly" Parents Teach Their Children
There Is Safety in Following the Lord's Counsel
The Scriptures: An Indispensable Road Map for the Journey of Life
Discipleship Always Means Willing Alignment with God's Decrees
Prophetic Mission: Preserving and Conveying the Word of God
Obedience Is the Pathway to Vitality; Murmuring Is the Pathway to Death

INTRODUCTION

Mortality affords each one of us the opportunity to demonstrate our willingness to keep the commandments of the Lord and to "do all things according to his will" (1 Ne. 7:12) by exercising our faith in Him. That is the test of our earthly experience (see 1 Ne. 3:7). We should be valiant in submitting to all things in all humility, thus overcoming pride and the natural man (see Mosiah 3:19). The Lord's example was supreme, as the sacred record reveals: "And he went a little further, and fell on his face, and prayed, saying, O my Father, if it be possible, let this cup pass from me: nevertheless not as I will, but as thou wilt . . . He went away again the second time, and prayed, saying, O my Father, if this cup may not pass away from me, except I drink it, thy will be done" (Matt. 26:39, 42).

When we keep the commandments and submit to the will of our Heavenly Father, we will enjoy the extraordinary blessing of having His Spirit always with us (see D&C 20:77, 79; Moro. 4:3; 5:2). Through obedience in heeding the promptings of the Spirit and honoring the covenant principles, we will be "favored of the Lord" (1 Ne. 1:1; Mosiah 10:13; Alma 48:20; Ether 1:34). That is one of the pervasive and overarching themes of the Book of Mormon.

1. "GOODLY" PARENTS TEACH THEIR CHILDREN

THEME. In accordance with the pattern of heaven, parents have the fundamental mission of teaching their children the truths of salvation. The Lord Himself instigated this solemn process through personal and angelic instruction to Adam and Eve (see Moses 5:5–11), who in turn made all things known unto their children, including the plan of redemption (see Moses 5:12). In our day the Lord has ordained and commanded anew that parents should teach their children righteousness (see D&C 68:25–28). *The Family: A Proclamation to the World* provides the most recent prophetic and apostolic articulation of this commandment: "Husband and wife have a solemn responsibility to love and care for each other and for their children. 'Children are an heritage of the Lord' (Ps. 127:3). Parents have a sacred duty to rear their children in love and righteousness, to provide for their physical and spiritual needs, to teach them to love and serve one another, to observe the commandments of God and to be law-abiding citizens wherever they live. Husbands and wives—mothers and fathers—will be held accountable before God for the discharge of these obligations." Again and again the Book of Mormon reinforces the importance of this parental theme.

MOMENT OF TRUTH. Picture this: Nephi, the great prophet/scribe of ancient America, looks back over thirty years of experience to revisit the pathways of trial and dislocation, opportunity and spiritual discovery, traversed by his family since the time they left their homeland. From the beginning, Nephi had always been careful to keep a record of his people, but now the Lord has commanded him to augment the chronicle with "other plates" on which he was to preserve "many things . . . which are good in my sight, for the profit of thy people" (2 Ne. 5:30). Always the obedient servant, Nephi complies readily with this commandment: "And I engraved that which is pleasing unto God. And if my people are pleased with the things of God they will be pleased with mine engravings which are upon these plates" (2 Ne. 5:32).

It is instructive to note the content of the first sentence that Nephi records under inspiration from the Lord. The very first sentiment that he recaptures from his spiritual memory bank is a reference to his parents and his home-based learning experience: "I, Nephi, having been born of goodly parents, therefore I was taught somewhat in all the learning of my father" (1 Ne. 1:1). Nephi conveys to his readership from the very first strokes of his spiritual chronicle his sense of home and his gratitude for parental guidance. This moment of truth reminds us of the solemn duty of parents to love and instruct their children. Innate within the role of a mother and father in Zion is to teach their children the gospel of Jesus Christ and to walk uprightly before the Lord. And so it was also in the days of Lehi, as the following statement confirms:

> A significant difference between Babylon, the city of the devil, and Zion, the city of God, is in the way they approach the responsibility to teach the children. In Zion, education will be the responsibility of parents and the Church. The ancient Israelites were expected to teach their sons and daughters everything possible or available to know God and man and the universe around them. Besides that, each boy was to be taught a trade or means of making a living, and every girl was to be taught all those things upon which the preservation of life and society and home are dependent. The teaching of a trade was usually the father's direct duty, and trades tended to be passed down from father to son. The wealthy often hired tutors for their children or sent them to a local school taught by available masters.

> A careful study of the Book of Mormon will show that the responsibility for supporting and promoting education among the Nephites was in the home and that it remained in the home. (Glenn L. Pearson and Reid E. Bankhead, *Building Faith with the Book of Mormon* [Salt Lake City: Bookcraft, 1986], 77–78)

MODERN PROPHETS SPEAK

Brigham Young:

> We should never permit ourselves to do anything we are not willing to see our children do. We should set them an example that we wish them to imitate. (*Discourses of Brigham Young*, sel, and comp. John A. Widtsoe [Salt Lake City: Deseret Book, 1954] 208)

ILLUSTRATIONS FOR OUR TIME

Teaching by Example. One day I had my two youngest sons in tow on a tour of a used-car lot. I fingered a fender and kicked a tire, turning to find my boy imitating me exactly. Brett, age five, was just withdrawing his toe from a kick when Cory, age three, tested the tire in an identical manner. At first I laughed. Then I realized soberly how very real the game of follow-the-leader can be. They had no idea why their father had done this—they merely followed suit. Many years later, President Thomas S. Monson verbalized exactly what I had felt that day:

> As parents, we should remember that our lives may be the book from the family library which the children most treasure. Are our examples worthy of emulation? Do we live in such a way that a son or a daughter may say, "I want to follow my dad," or "I want to be like my mother"? Unlike the book on the library shelf, the covers of which shield its contents, our lives cannot be closed. Parents, we truly are an open book in the library of learning in our homes. ("Dedication Day," *Ensign,* Nov. 2000, 65)

As parents we are teachers in word and in deed. There are many planned teaching moments, such as family prayer, family scripture time, family home evening, family council, and family interviews. There are also innumerable unplanned teaching opportunities. We should realize that we are teaching through our lives every moment of every day. (Pinegar)

A Father's Example. Even before my wife's father had gone to his eternal reward, my wife often spoke to me about her vivid childhood memories of seeing him reading and pondering the scriptures. This image of her father faithfully broadening his spiritual understanding through the word of God is an enduring source of inspiration and comfort to her. She remembers fondly the frequent times when he noticed her there, watching him, and called her to his side to read a passage to her—most often from the Book of Mormon—and share his feelings about it. "Is that not beautiful?" he would say, often with a tear in his eye. This made a lasting impression on his daughter.

How many of us present a similar image to our children and others who may be watching? How many of us teach by example the principle of enlarging our souls and seeking after pure intelligence through the word of God? "Search the scriptures," the Lord said, "for in them ye think ye have eternal life: and they are they which testify of me" (John 5:39). How many of us contemplate that in the act of sincerely searching the scriptures, we might well serve as an object lesson to those who search for the correct way to search, who seek after the most productive way to seek? Often the greatest lessons are taught more through the doing than the saying. We as parents and grandparents should live worthy of such opportunities. (Allen)

Likening the Scriptures to Our Lives

1 Nephi 1:1—Nephi was born of goodly parents who taught him the gospel.

Application—We as parents must honor our sacred duty and teach our children the gospel (D&C 68: 25–28).

2. THERE IS SAFETY IN FOLLOWING THE LORD'S COUNSEL.

THEME. What greater overseer of our travels could there be than the Lord? What greater road map than His divine decrees? A righteous branch of the house of Joseph had to be established in the promised land; therefore, it was imperative that Lehi and his family leave Jerusalem and settle in a new land according to the Lord's will.

"Therefore, I would that ye should know, that after the Lord had shown so many marvelous things unto my father, Lehi, yea, concerning the destruction of Jerusalem, behold he went forth among the people, and began to prophesy and to declare unto them concerning the things which he had both seen and heard. And it came to pass that the Jews did mock him because of the things which he testified of them; for he truly testified of their wickedness and their abominations; and he testified that the things which he saw and heard, and also the things which he read in the book, manifested plainly of the coming of a Messiah, and also the redemption of the world. And when the Jews heard these things they were angry with him; yea, even as with the prophets of old, whom they had cast out, and stoned, and slain; and they also sought his life, that they might take it away. But behold, I, Nephi, will show unto you that the tender mercies of the Lord are over all those whom he hath chosen, because of their faith, to make them mighty even unto the power of deliverance." (1 Ne. 1:18–20)

For behold, it came to pass that the Lord spake unto my father, yea, even in a dream, and said unto him: Blessed art thou Lehi, because of the things which thou hast done; and because thou hast been faithful and declared unto this people the things which I commanded thee, behold, they seek to take away thy life. And it came to pass that the Lord commanded my father, even in a dream, that he should take his family and depart into the wilderness. And it came to pass that he was obedient unto the word of the Lord, wherefore he did as the Lord commanded him." (1 Ne. 2:1–3)

MOMENT OF TRUTH. Lehi's generation was involved in the flux of momentous happenings in the kingdoms of Israel and Judah. The great prophet Isaiah had made his monumental pronouncements only a century earlier (740–701 B.C.) in concert with the righteous initiatives of the somewhat younger religious and political reformer Hezekiah, king of Judah from 715 to 686 B.C. Lehi himself was almost surely an eyewitness in his younger years to the celebrated reform efforts of King Josiah, under whose reign (641 to 610 B.C.) the temple was restored and a book of the Mosaic law was rediscovered, causing much excitement among the faithful (see 2 Kgs. 22–23; 2 Chr. 34–35).

But the broad reformation was still not sufficient to spiritually transform a largely corrupt and idolatrous people. There were still wicked political leaders during these times, and many prophets, including Jeremiah (another of Lehi's contemporaries), were empowered of the Lord to warn the people with clarity and sharpness. The message of prophecy was clear: the people had to repent or the city of Jerusalem would be destroyed. Lehi, himself courageously active among the prophetic ranks, prayed earnestly on behalf of his people. A vision was opened unto him concerning the coming of our beloved Savior Jesus Christ and of the imminent destruction of Jerusalem. Many would be carried away captive into Babylon. Lehi preached and prophesied to no avail. The people mocked him and sought to take away his life. Therefore, the Lord spoke to Lehi and commanded him to take his family into the wilderness.

We, like Lehi, have moments of truth in our lives when we must seek refuge in the Lord. He will lead and guide us to safety, no matter what the outside circumstances. He will nurture us and bless us according to our needs (see Alma 7:11–12). We would be wise to remember that there is always safety in following the Lord and His commandments.

MODERN PROPHETS SPEAK

Boyd K. Packer:
> Elijah was warned to flee from the presence of the king. He went eastward and hid by the brook Cherith, and there the ravens fed him. Eventually the brook dried up. Thus Elijah himself was not immune from the trials the Lord had caused him to call forth upon the people by sealing the heavens so there would be no rain. This too illustrates a principle that members of the Church should consider. In later years the Lord counseled his disciples to stay in the world, even though they were to be not of the world. A life of righteousness does not necessarily lift from any soul the trials and difficulties, suffering and concerns of life. But the righteous do have some protection and blessings, and there is power working in their behalf. (*The Holy Temple* [Salt Lake City: Bookcraft, 1980], 104)

ILLUSTRATIONS FOR OUR TIME

Wilford Woodruff:

> I have occupied considerable space in referring to those peculiar circumstances which have attended me during life, and to sum the matter up it stands thus:—I have broken both legs—one in two places—both arms, my breastbone and three ribs, and had both ankles dislocated. I have been drowned, frozen, scalded and bit by a mad dog—have passed through several severe fits of sickness, and encountered poison in its worst forms—have landed in a pile of railroad ruins—have barely been missed by passing bullets, and have passed through a score of other hairbreadth escapes.

> It has appeared miraculous to me, that with all the injuries and broken bones which I have had, I have not a lame limb, but have been enabled to endure the hardest labor, exposures and journeys—have often walked forty, fifty, and on one occasion, sixty miles in a day. The protection and mercy of God has been over me, and my life thus far has been preserved; for which blessings I feel to render the gratitude of my heart to my Heavenly Father, praying that the remaining of my days may be spent in his service and in the building up of his kingdom. (As told in *Best-Loved Stories of the LDS People,* ed. Jack M. Lyon, Linda Ririe Gundry, and Jay A. Parry [Salt Lake City: Deseret Book, 1997], 319)

Likening the Scriptures to Our Lives

1 Nephi 2:1–3—Lehi was a righteous man. He received promptings from the Lord because of his obedience and was commanded to leave Jerusalem. Thus his family was preserved.

Application—There are blessings awaiting us as we follow the counsel of the Lord, for He blesses us immediately (see D&C 82:10).

3. THE SCRIPTURES: AN INDISPENSABLE ROAD MAP FOR THE JOURNEY OF LIFE

THEME. Lehi was commanded to obtain the brass plates before undertaking the journey to the promised land. It was important that Lehi have the genealogy of his fathers, the written language of his forebears, and the recorded word of God—all of which were contained on the brass plates.

> *"And it came to pass that he spake unto me, saying: Behold I have dreamed a dream, in the which the Lord hath commanded me that thou and thy brethren shall return to Jerusalem. For behold, Laban hath the record of the Jews and also a genealogy of my fore-*

fathers, and they are engraven upon plates of brass. Wherefore, the Lord hath command-
ed me that thou and thy brothers should go unto the house of Laban, and seek the records,
and bring them down hither into the wilderness." (1 Ne. 3:2–4)

"And behold, it is wisdom in God that we should obtain these records, that we may pre-
serve unto our children the language of our fathers; And also that we may preserve unto
them the words which have been spoken by the mouth of all the holy prophets, which have
been delivered unto them by the Spirit and power of God, since the world began, even
down unto this present time." (1 Ne. 3:19–20)

MOMENT OF TRUTH. During Lehi's time, the custodian of the priceless chroni-cles of God's dealings with His people, preserved on plates of brass, was an unscrupu-lous official in Jerusalem named Laban. Following Lehi's instructions to his sons to go to Laban's house and get the plates, Laman and Lemuel began to murmur. The younger Nephi became favored of the Lord because he didn't murmur. Out of this recorded event comes the oft-quoted statement of Nephi: "I will go and do the things which the Lord hath commanded, for I know that the Lord giveth no commandments unto the children of men, save he shall prepare a way for them that they may accom-plish the thing which he commandeth them" (1 Ne. 3:7).

The Lord is our strength. He will provide a way if we will but do our part. We must persevere even as Nephi did following the failure of both attempts to get the plates, being threatened even unto death, and being beaten by his brothers. An angel appeared and chastised Laman and Lemuel, informing them that the Lord would deliver Laban into their hands, and still Laman and Lemuel murmured because they had doubt. Nephi's faith was evident as he explained that the Lord could do all things, of which the preservation of the Israelites at the Red Sea was one example. A great truth then comes forth to those who believe and trust in the Lord: "And I was led by the Spirit, not knowing beforehand the things which I should do" (1 Ne. 4:6).

MODERN PROPHETS SPEAK

Heber J. Grant:

> Laban stole their wealth and tried to destroy them. Nephi's brethren commenced to murmur again, and they took a rod and beat him with it. As they did so an angel of the Lord stood before them, and he commanded them to go up again, promising that God should deliver Laban into their hands. I call the attention of the young men and young ladies to this, for I have heard many of them say, "Oh, if I could only see an angel, I would believe and forever be faithful." The seeing of an angel amounts to nothing, unless you are keeping the commandments of God. No soon-

er had the heavenly messenger departed than these elder brethren, who were lacking in faith and did not keep the commandments of God, commenced to murmur, and instead of having faith in the promises of the angel, they said unto Nephi, "How is it possible that the Lord will deliver Laban into our hands? Behold, he is a mighty man, and he can command fifty, yea, even he can slay fifty: then, why not us?" Did this discourage Nephi? Did he lack faith? No; he believed in the promises of the angel of God, and he said unto them, "Let us go up again unto Jerusalem, and let us be faithful in keeping the commandments of the Lord; for behold He is mightier than all the earth, then why not mightier than Laban and his fifty, yea, or even than his tens of thousands?" They went up and were successful. (*CR,* Oct. 1900, 34)

ILLUSTRATIONS FOR OUR TIME

The Lord Is in Charge. In 1 Nephi 4:6, Nephi said, "And I was led by the Spirit, not knowing beforehand the things which I should do." That didn't mean that Nephi hadn't studied or prayed or worked. He had already been righteous up to this point. But at that moment he didn't know what to do. You will probably have the same thing happen to you. You'll say, "Oh Father," and at that moment when you pray, "What should I do?" then all of a sudden the words will come. You'll find yourself testifying to others, when questions arise, "And by the power of the Spirit, I testify to you that what I have said is true, and I know it's true because the Lord bore witness to me that it's true." You will bear your testimony with power, and then you'll wonder, "How did I do that?" Remember, the Lord is in charge!

When you teach with power, you teach the mind and the will of God. You speak by the Spirit, and the Spirit speaks the word of Christ, which is the mind and the will of God (see D&C 68:4). Do you remember what was happening about the time of Alma 17:2–3? Alma had gone one way and the sons of Mosiah had gone another way, and they met up again as the sons of Mosiah were traveling toward the land of Zarahemla. Alma must have said something like, "Oh Ammon, Omner, Himni, and Aaron, it's so good to see you," and no doubt they exchanged embraces and hugs. Then Alma said that what added to his joy was that his friends had "waxed strong in the knowledge of the truth" and "they were men of sound understanding." Why? Because "they had searched the scriptures diligently, that they might know the word of God." But this was not all. They'd also "given themselves to much prayer and fasting," so that when they spoke, they spoke by revelation and by prophecy, "with the power and authority of God." (Pinegar)

Priceless Heritage. On my shelf of books at home is a set of the four standard works bound in black leather. The pages are frayed and the bindings are worn from over fifty years of continual use. These scriptures accompanied me on my mission as a young elder to Germany. They were again my companion during a second sojourn in Europe to officiate with the Brigham Young University Study Abroad. They accompanied me yet again during the years my wife and I spent in Maryland while I was active in university service. This set of scriptures has moved with us wherever we have gone. These books will always occupy a place of honor on my shelf, even though they have been in "retirement" for a few years due to the advent of newer editions of the scriptures that include expanded annotations and Topical Guide.

What is so special about this particular set of scriptures? This set was given to me by my mother. In fact, the triple combination, beginning with the Book of Mormon, bears a personal handwritten notation with the date May 20, 1948—the day she passed away unexpectedly while giving birth to my younger brother. This set of scriptures was the last gift she gave to me, the first being life itself. Similar sets of scriptural treasure were presented to my younger brother and my older sister.

What greater gifts can a mother give to her children than mortal life itself, to begin with, and then, subsequently, nurture in gospel truth leading to eternal life? There is no more indispensable road map for life's journey than the scriptures. Just as the Lord commanded Lehi to return and obtain the brass plates before commencing his journey to the promised land, we, too, must never be without the priceless guide of God's sure word, as Paul observed: "And take the helmet of salvation, and the sword of the Spirit, which is the word of God" (Eph. 6:17). (Allen)

Likening the Scriptures to Our Lives

1 Nephi 3:20; 1 Nephi 5:21—The words of our prophets are recorded in the holy scriptures; they are the commandments of the Lord.

Application—We are to live by every word that proceeds forth from the mouth of God. By keeping the commandments, we will find that the Spirit will always be with us.

4. DISCIPLESHIP ALWAYS MEANS WILLING ALIGNMENT WITH GOD'S DECREES

THEME. What does one do when commanded by God to pursue a course normally inimical to one's deepest drives and values? Nephi learned the answer to this paradox when he was constrained by the Spirit to kill Laban for the purpose of preserving the sacred record for an entire nation. He learned that the Spirit will direct us in all things. Sometimes it is so difficult that we need to be taught by the Spirit concerning our specific instructions. We simply need confirmation that any discomfort arises from the natural man, or unfamiliarity, rather than divinely driven conscience. Such was the case in regard to Nephi taking Laban's life.

> *"And it came to pass that I was constrained by the Spirit that I should kill Laban; but I said in my heart: Never at any time have I shed the blood of man. And I shrunk and would that I might not slay him." (1 Ne. 4:10)*

MOMENT OF TRUTH. As Nephi faced the awesome challenge of taking a human life by divine commandment, he must have reflected on sentiments similar to those found in Hosea. "Who is wise, and he shall understand these things? Prudent, and he shall know them? For the ways of the Lord are right, and the just shall walk in them: but the transgressors shall fall therein." (Hosea 14:9) His former obedience and teachable humility helped him recognize the Spirit's voice of superior wisdom.

When we understand and appreciate a doctrine, principle, or commandment by the Spirit, it is easier to accept and live such things. We witness this all the time in teaching, whether in the mission field, in our quorums and classes, or in our homes.

MODERN PROPHETS SPEAK

Joseph Smith, Jr.:

> We cannot keep all the commandments without first knowing them, and we cannot know them all, or more than we now know unless we comply with or keep those we have already received. That which is wrong under one circumstance, may be, and often is, right under another.

> God said, "Thou shalt not kill"; at another time He said "Thou shalt utterly destroy." This is the principle on which the government of heaven is conducted—by revelation adapted to the circumstances in which the children of the kingdom are placed. Whatever God requires is right, no matter what it is, although we may not see the reason thereof till long after the events transpire. . . .

> Everything that God gives us is lawful and right. (*The Teachings of Joseph Smith,* ed. Larry E. Dahl and Donald Q. Cannon [Salt lake City: Bookcraft, 1997], 575)

ILLUSTRATIONS FOR OUR TIME

Extra Copies. President Thomas S. Monson recently remarked, "I know of no experience more sweet or feeling more precious than to heed a prompting only to discover that the Lord has answered another person's prayer through you" ("Peace, Be Still," *Ensign,* Nov. 2002, 55). He relates the following story of how a series of inspired decisions helped bless the lives of all concerned in this story:

> While attending the annual meetings of the Boy Scouts of America in 1971, I took with me several copies of the *New Era,* that I might share with officials of Scouting this excellent publication. As I opened the package, I found that my secretary, for no accountable reason, had given me two extra copies of the June issue, an issue that featured temple mar-

riage. I left the two copies in the hotel room and, as planned, distributed the other copies.

On the final day of the conference, I had no desire to attend the scheduled luncheon but felt compelled to return to my room. The telephone was ringing as I entered. The caller introduced herself as Sister Knotts. She asked if I could provide a blessing for her ten-year-old daughter. I agreed readily, and she indicated that she and her husband, their daughter, and their son would come immediately to my hotel room. As I waited, I prayed for help. The applause of the convention was replaced by the peace of prayer.

Then came the knock at the door and the privilege of meeting a choice Latter-day Saint family. Ten-year-old Deanna walked with the aid of crutches. Cancer had required the amputation of her left leg. Her clothing was clean, her countenance radiant, her trust in God unwavering. A blessing was provided. Mother and son knelt by the side of the bed, while the father and I placed our hands on tiny Deanna. We were directed by the Spirit of God. We were humbled by its power.

I felt the tears course down my cheeks and tumble upon my hands as they rested on the head of that beautiful child of God. I spoke of eternal ordinances and family exaltation. The Lord prompted me to urge this family to enter the holy temple of God. At the conclusion of the blessing, I learned that such a temple visit was planned for that very summer. Questions pertaining to the temple were asked. I heard no heavenly voice, nor did I see a vision. Yet there came to me a certain statement: "Refer to the *New Era*." I looked to the dresser, and there were the two copies of the temple issue of the *New Era*. One was given to Deanna. One was provided to her parents. Each was reviewed and read.

The Knotts family said farewell, and once again the room was still. A prayer of gratitude came easily and, once more, the resolve to provide a place for prayer. (Thomas S. Monson, *Inspiring Experiences That Build Faith: From the Life and Ministry of Thomas S. Monson* [Salt Lake City: Deseret Book, 1994], 115–16) (Pinegar)

The Coat. On several occasions as a young boy, I can recall my father telling me the story about "the coat." He had been saving for a considerable length of time to buy a heavy winter coat for my mother so that she would have added protection against the stark Canadian weather. Finally the coat fund had grown to a sufficient size and the time was at hand. As he sat one Sunday with the family in sacrament meeting, he was pondering the planned gift and thinking of the joy it would bring to his wife.

As it turned out, the program that day centered on missionary work and the sacrifices that the Saints are called upon to make in order to carry the gospel message to others. My father's thoughts then shifted to a certain older couple in town—two fine and stalwart members who were preparing to go on a mission. Being of modest means, they were struggling to gather together resources for their mission, and the local Church leaders had sent word requesting the support of local Saints. My father could not suppress an idea that came into his mind: he had the impression that he should donate those funds (several hundred dollars—a goodly sum in those days) for the benefit of the missionary couple and their service to the Lord. But how would his wife feel about the shift in plans? Surely she would be supportive and have faith that a way would be prepared to obtain a coat at a later time. He had stated over and over again to his family that Nephi was one of his great scriptural heroes, and if Nephi had the faith to do as the Lord commanded (1 Ne. 3:7), then should not he exercise faith as well?

He proceeded to donate the entire coat fund to the Church for the benefit of the missionary couple. Thus they were able to go on the Lord's errand. As it turned out, they were soon called upon as part of their missionary service to preside over a branch of the Church that was struggling to achieve greater unity. Their efforts succeeded admirably, and the branch prospered under their leadership. My father later commented that it was a source of great satisfaction to him to know that the coat was having such a positive influence in building the kingdom of God. As for my mother, an opportunity presented itself eventually to obtain a fine coat for her after all—and thus all were served well.

Many years later, as a member of a branch presidency at the Missionary Training Center, I noted with admiration that many of the young missionaries had sacrificed temporal opportunities of various kinds—in some cases valuable and even irretrievable athletic scholarships—to respond to missionary calls. They were putting the Lord first when confronted with a choice. In my own experience I have noted repeatedly that blessings flow from making such choices in favor of the Lord. During one period of my life, I found that my testimony was strengthened immeasurably when I willingly accepted a call to serve as a bishop, even though it meant that the completion of the graduate degree I was pursuing at the time would need to be postponed for a while. But everything eventually worked out, as always, "in the due time of the Lord" (D&C 138:56). The opportunity to participate actively in building the kingdom of God was the pearl of great price—not to be exchanged for any professional pursuit. As the Savior taught during His ministry: "But seek ye first the kingdom of God and his righteousness, and all these things shall be added unto you" (3 Ne. 13:33; cf. JST Matt. 6:33). (Allen)

Likening the Scriptures to Our Lives

1 Nephi 3:7; 1 Nephi 4:6; 1 Nephi 4:18—The Lord provides a way for us to keep his commandments. He will lead us by His Spirit . . . and we can do challenging things as directed.

Application—We must never forget that the Lord will provide a way for us to keep the commandments. We must trust in Him (see Prov. 3:5–6) for His Spirit will surely lead us (see 2 Nephi 32:5), and we can do hard things in the strength of the Lord (see Alma 26:11–12).

5. PROPHETIC MISSION: PRESERVING AND CONVEYING THE WORD OF GOD

THEME. Among the greatest gifts God has given to mankind is the gift of His scriptural word, granted as a loving endowment to build faith, secure obedience, and open the gateway to immortality and eternal life. The mission of prophets is to preserve this scriptural word and convey it to God's children.

> *"And it mattereth not to me that I am particular to give a full account of all the things of my father, for they cannot be written upon these plates, for I desire the room that I may write of the things of God. For the fulness of mine intent is that I may persuade men to come unto the God of Abraham, and the God of Isaac, and the God of Jacob, and be saved. Wherefore, the things which are pleasing unto the world I do not write, but the things which are pleasing unto God and unto those who are not of the world. Wherefore, I shall give commandment unto my seed, that they shall not occupy these plates with things which are not of worth unto the children of men." (1 Ne. 6:3–6)*

MOMENT OF TRUTH. Nephi was commanded of the Lord to make plates and to engrave thereon the record of his people and the record of his father—including his and Lehi's prophecies—that he might persuade men to come unto Christ and "for other wise purposes, which purposes are known unto the Lord" (1 Ne. 19:3). The scriptures are the words of our Savior Jesus Christ, and all scriptures testify of Christ. They are testaments or witnesses of our Savior. We are to live by every word that proceeds from the mouth of God (see D&C 84:43–46); they were written to invite all to come unto Christ and be perfected in Him (see Moro. 10:32). Alma used the word of God to reclaim the Zoramites to the cause of Christ (see Alma 31:5), and we must use them for similar purposes in our service to the Lord. We are to open our mouths (D&C 33:8–11) and warn our neighbors (D&C 88:81). The purpose of this dispensation is to invite all to come unto Christ.

MODERN PROPHETS SPEAK

Bruce R. McConkie:

> John, who bore testimony of Jesus, did so for one reason and one reason only: he was seeking to persuade men to believe in Christ, to come unto him, to accept him as the Son of God, and to be saved by obedience to the laws and ordinances of his gospel. When John baptized for the remission of sins, he was not seeking disciples who would follow him, except as he guided them to the one who should come after. Indeed, the very remission of sins that he promised could not come until they received the Holy Ghost—the baptism of fire—which burns sin and evil out of a human soul as though by fire. John's whole purpose was to persuade his disciples to follow, not himself, but the Lord Jesus whose witness he was. (*The Mortal Messiah: From Bethlehem to Calvary*, 4 vols. [Salt Lake City: Deseret Book, 1979–1981], 1:438)

ILLUSTRATIONS FOR OUR TIME

Delighting in the Word of God. Remember that before others can sense the power and divinity of the Book of Mormon for themselves, they must sense it in us. We must delight in the word of God. We must love the Book of Mormon. We must feast upon its words.

When the Book of Mormon becomes delicious to you, you will sparkle. You will be excited. When others ask you why, you will say, "Oh, I just read this part here; it is so good I can hardly wait to tell you!" If you don't feel that way, others won't feel that way. Now perhaps you can begin to understand why one precious half-hour every day is spent supping from the pages of this book of books. Learn to love the book, and you'll not only love to live its teachings yourself, but you'll love to teach it.

President Benson said, "I would particularly urge you to read again and again the Book of Mormon and ponder and apply its teachings" (Come, Listen to a Prophet's Voice [Salt Lake City: Deseret Book, 1990], 3). Isn't that interesting? Ponder and apply its teachings. I try to do that every day. I ponder the scriptures every night, and then apply a scripture in my life every day, even recording it in my journal. This daily application of scriptures can absolutely change our lives.

I taught the Book of Mormon at Brigham Young University for sixteen years, and I was always astounded when I would talk about something in class and a student would observe, "Oh, I read that once."

"Oh, you read it once?" I would reply. "Well, I teach this book every year and find things I've never even seen before. And you've read it once?"

So, we had an assignment. I gave extra credit to students who read 2 Nephi 9 or Enos for thirty days in a row before going to bed. A student once asked me: "Why? Why do we need to read it every day? I mean, I'll get it after just a night or two."

"You just read it and see," I answered.

Well, one day I was walking to class, and all of a sudden this young man was waiting for me by the door. He literally leapt upon me, gave me a hug and said, "Oh, Brother Ed, Brother Ed, it's true, it's true!"

I said, "I know it's true."

"I understand what you mean now," he said. "I read Enos, and on the twenty-first day something happened inside. I wanted everybody to be converted. Brother Ed, I'm thinking of checking out of school and going on my mission today."

"Can't you just wait two more weeks until the semester ends?" I asked.

This young man fell in love with the Book of Mormon because he did what the prophet said, again and again and again, and then he applied it in his life. Until we apply it to our lives, we will not delight in it. We will not enjoy this feeling. We will not be enthusiastic about it. We'll say, "Yeah, I read the book this morning." But when we love it, we'll live it because we apply it.

Nephi understood this principle: "For my soul delighteth in the scriptures, and my heart pondereth them" (2 Ne. 2:15). President Benson also understood: "Reread the Book of Mormon so that we might more fully come unto Christ, be committed to him, centered in him, and consumed in him" ("Come Unto Christ," *Ensign,* Nov. 1987, 87).

When Christ comes into our lives, we are born of God, and we'll also be strengthened through the Book of Mormon. If we are conscientious in our study of the Book of Mormon, we will not be susceptible to Satan's enticings. I promise you that if you'll earnestly and prayerfully ponder and steadfastly read the Book of Mormon and live it, the adversary will have no effect upon you. And unless you do that, you will not be strong.

Why is this? How do we become spiritually strong? How do we grow in faith? The answer is always the same: The word of God applied in our lives makes us strong. It makes our spirits strong; our spirits grow in strength when we sup from the pages of the Book of Mormon. There is power in the book that begins to flow into our lives the moment we begin to seriously study the Book of Mormon. We will find greater power to resist temptation. We will find the power to avoid deception. We will find the power to stay on the straight and narrow path. These are promises President Benson has given us.

If we truly delight in the word, we are worthy to be instruments in the Lord's hands. And then we will know that the power of the word is the greatest power to change people's lives. (See Alma 31:5.)

Based upon my experiences as a missionary and a mission president, I have learned that we convert people like us. What we are is what our converts want to be. If our light is strong, they will see Christ in us.

The Savior said, "Behold, I am the light which ye shall hold up, that which ye have seen me do, behold, ye see that I have prayed unto my father and ye all have witnessed" (3 Ne. 18:24). In other words, the light that we have, the light that we possess, the light that we hold up, is our conversion to Christ. So it's natural that others like what we like, that they want to do what we do. If we are rooted in the Book of Mormon, that's what they will want to have. If we are not rooted to the Book of Mormon, chances are they will be rooted to something else, and when the whistling winds of the world come by, all of a sudden they will wither and even die. It's that precious; it's that critical.

When we truly delight in the word, our ability to motivate others to read the Book of Mormon will be enhanced significantly. In other words, when we delight, they'll be delighted. Every day, we should have a goal to place so many copies of the Book of Mormon. (Pinegar)

Likening the Scriptures to Our Lives

1 Nephi 6:4–5—Preserving the word of God is for the intent of inviting all to come unto Christ. This is pleasing unto God and those not of the world.

Application—We must come to understand that the word is not only sacred but precious to our lives, for it brings us to Christ, for the Word is in fact Jesus Christ (see John 1:1–14; Rev. 19:13).

6. OBEDIENCE IS THE PATHWAY TO VITALITY; MURMURING IS THE PATHWAY TO DEATH

THEME. The Lord's commandments are always given to improve and edify the Saints as they seek to build the kingdom of God. Following His commandments is the key to "peace in this world, and eternal life in the world to come" (D&C 39:23). In opposition to that, obeying reluctantly or, worse, allowing the spirit of dissension and murmuring to short-circuit obedience altogether is the sure pathway to decline, "captivity and death" (2 Ne. 2:27).

> *"And it came to pass that the Lord commanded him that I, Nephi, and my brethren, should again return unto the land of Jerusalem, and bring down Ishmael and his family into the wilderness. And it came to pass that I, Nephi, did again, with my brethren, go forth into the wilderness to go up to Jerusalem. And it came to pass that we went up unto the house of Ishmael, and we did gain favor in the sight of Ishmael, insomuch that we did speak unto him the words of the Lord. And it came to pass that the Lord did soften the heart of Ishmael, and also his household, insomuch that they took their journey with us down into the wilderness to the tent of our father." (1 Ne. 7:2–5)*

MOMENT OF TRUTH. The Lord commanded Lehi to send his sons back to Jerusalem once again to seek a partnership with Ishmael's family for the journey to the promised land. Once again, obedience was the opportunity to enter the pathway of vitality, for this action would allow Lehi's sons to take Ishmael's daughters to wife, that they might have posterity.

Laman and Lemuel did not murmur on the long trek back to Jerusalem but again took up murmuring upon their return. Nephi admonished them to remember that they had seen an angel, that they had been delivered out of the hands of Laban, and that if they were faithful they could obtain a land of promise. Alternately, they could remain in Jerusalem and perish. Laman and Lemuel became angry and bound Nephi. Nephi prayed for strength, and the bands were loosed. Some of Ishmael's family pled for Nephi. Laman and Lemuel were touched and asked for forgiveness. Nephi frankly forgave them.

MODERN PROPHETS SPEAK

Russell M. Nelson:

> Lehi told his sons to return once again to Jerusalem, this time to get Ishmael and his family. Perhaps each young man felt a bit better about it this time, knowing that there was the possibility he might be rewarded with one of the daughters of Ishmael to become his wife. This rugged discipline was but a prologue to Lehi's family's going subsequently all the way across what we now know as the Saudi Arabian Peninsula to its southeastern shore, where ships were to be built. And this challenge was but prelude to their ultimate destiny—to go across ocean waters to the promised land.
>
> In fact, much of scriptural history reports requirements of the Lord's prophets and people to go to their particular proving grounds. (*The Power within Us* [Salt Lake City: Deseret Book, 1988], 17–18)

ILLUSTRATIONS FOR OUR TIME

Faith and Prayers of a Mother

Lucy Mack Smith:

> On the first of August [1834], Joseph and Hyrum returned [from Zion's Camp]. They were overjoyed to meet us again in health, more especially on account of the perils which they had passed through during their absence. Joseph and Hyrum sat down beside me, each holding one of my hands in his, while they related the following story:
>
> > "When we started on our journey, we made arrangements to have everyone made as comfortable as possible; but the sufferings which are incident to such an excursion made some of the brethren discontented, and they began to murmur against us, saying, The Lord never required them to take such a tiresome journey, and that it was folly for them to suffer such fatigue and inconvenience just to gratify us. We warned them, in the name of the Lord, to stop their murmuring; for, if they did not, the displeasure of the Almighty would be manifested in judgments in their midst. But many of

them paid no attention to what we said, until one morning when they went out to harness up their horses, and found them all so lame as to be unable to travel. We then told them that this was a curse which had come upon them because of transgression; but, if they would repent, it might be removed—if not, a greater curse would come upon them. They believed what we said and repented of their folly. . . . It was not long, however, till the spirit of dissension arose again. . . .

"Soon after arriving at the point of destination, the cholera broke out in our midst; the brethren were so violently attacked that it seemed impossible to render them any assistance. They immediately sent for us to lay hands on them, but we soon discovered that this, also, was a judgment from the Almighty; for, when we laid our hands upon them, in the name of the Lord, the disease immediately fastened itself upon us and in a few minutes we were in awful agony. We made signals to each other . . . in order to join in prayer to God that he would deliver us from this dreadful influence. . . . We were hardly able to stand upon our feet, and we feared that we should die in that western wilderness without the privilege of blessing our children, or giving them one word of parting counsel. We . . . fell upon our knees and cried unto the Lord that he would deliver us from this awful calamity, but we arose worse than before. We kneeled down the second time, and when we commenced praying the cramp seized us, gathering the cords in our arms and legs in bunches and operating equally severe throughout our system. We still besought the Lord, with all our strength, to have mercy upon us, but all in vain. It seemed as though the heavens were sealed against us. . . . We then kneeled down the third time, concluding never to rise to our feet again until one or the other should get a testimony that we should be healed; and that the one who should get the first intimation of the same from the Spirit, should make it known to the other."

They stated further, that after praying some time the cramp began to release its hold; and, in a short time, Hyrum sprang to his feet and exclaimed, "Joseph, we shall return to our families. I have had an open vision, in which I saw mother kneeling under an apple tree; and she is even now asking God, in tears, to spare our lives, that she may again behold us in the flesh. The Spirit testifies, that her prayers, united with ours, will be answered."

"Oh, my mother!" said Joseph, "how often have your prayers been the means of assisting us when the shadows of death encompassed us." (Lucy Mack Smith, *History of Joseph Smith,* ed. Preston Nibley [Salt Lake City: Bookcraft, 1958], 227–29)

Likening the Scriptures to Our Lives

1 Ne. 7:9–13—Obedience is the test of life (see Abr. 3:25; D&C 98:14). Nephi chooses this pathway. Laman and Lemuel hearken not to the word of the Lord and forget what great things the Lord had done for them and are left without the Spirit; thus they murmur and seek Nephi's life.

Application—Let us learn that there is only one way back to the presence of the Lord, and that is to align ourselves with the principles, commandments, and laws of heaven. If we exercise faith (see 1 Ne. 10:17), love (see D&C 76:116), and obedience (see D&C 20:77–79), the Spirit will lead us.

SUMMARY

We learn in the beginning of this magnificent record that the test of mankind is always before us. Will we choose to obey the will of the Lord and receive the blessings of heaven or lose the blessings through disobedience? The key is to learn vicariously from the scriptures. Not only can we apply positive principles to our lives, we can also learn to avoid trials and tribulations by doing the will of God, knowing full well that earth life is full of afflictions. Surely this is the clarion principle: "Thy will be done" (see Matt. 6:10; 26:42; 3 Ne. 13:10; Moses 4:2).

It is in accordance with this principle that "goodly" parents teach their children the truths of salvation, just as Lehi and Sariah taught Nephi and his siblings. Our families obtain refuge and safety through following the Lord's counsel as reflected in the scriptures, for they constitute an indispensable road map for the journey of life. By aligning ourselves willingly with God's decrees—no matter how difficult and challenging—we take upon ourselves the essence of discipleship. From the beginning of time, God's prophets have preserved and conveyed the word of God with unmistakable clarity to God's children, that they might indeed understand and cultivate the qualities of true discipleship.

When it comes to the principle of "Thy will be done," there are only two choices: obedience is the pathway to vitality; murmuring is the pathway to death. This is, indeed, the pervasive message of the Book of Mormon. Just six years after this sacred text was published and sent into the world, the Prophet Joseph Smith again sounded the all-encompassing theme of obedience in the dedicatory prayer for the Kirtland Temple: "Help thy servants to say, with thy grace assisting them: Thy will be done, O Lord, and not ours" (D&C 109:44).

CHAPTER THREE

THE VISION *of* THE TREE *of* LIFE

1 NEPHI 8–11; 12:16–18; 15

"The tree of life: Figuratively, the tree from which the faithful pick the fruit of eternal life. To eat thereof is to inherit eternal life in the kingdom of God. Of his vision of the tree of life, Lehi said: 'I beheld a tree, whose fruit was desirable to make one happy. And it came to pass that I did go forth and partake of the fruit thereof; and I beheld that it was most sweet, above all that I ever before tasted. Yea, and I beheld that the fruit thereof was white, to exceed all the whiteness that I had ever seen. And as I partook of the fruit thereof it filled my soul with exceeding great joy; wherefore, I began to be desirous that my family should partake of it also; for I knew that it was desirable above all other fruit' (1 Ne. 8:10–11)."
—BRUCE R. MCCONKIE, *DOCTRINAL NEW TESTAMENT COMMENTARY*, 3 VOLS. (SALT LAKE CITY: BOOKCRAFT, 1965–1973), 3:447.

THEMES *for* LIVING

Symbols That Inspire Goodness—The Meaning of Lehi's Vision
The Typology of Travelers in the Vision of the Tree of Life
The Power in Pondering

INTRODUCTION

The tree of life vision is a marvelous symbolic representation of man's search for eternal life. Within every mortal breast is planted that divine spark of illumination—the "Spirit of Christ," as Moroni described it—leading toward that which is noble and good (see Moro. 7:16). On the basis of the invitation to rise toward one's spiritual potential, humankind is granted the choice to come to Christ and partake of the fruit of divine love. As part of the mortal experience, individuals are faced with daunting trials and temptations along the way. Will they nevertheless choose the right? Lehi's vision reveals the bitter truth of what happens when mortal decision-making falls short of the mark. Not all mortals hold to the iron rod of the word of God, that sure and true pathway leading to salvation and eternal life. Some travelers desist in grasping the iron rod from the outset. Some hold to it but pander to choices and distractions that draw them off course. Some hold to the rod long enough to attain the tree of life but then choose to fall back again, thus relinquishing the glorious gift of redemption, immortality, and eternal life that was within their grasp.

And yet there is hope, for Lehi also sees the other side of the picture. There are those who, given the choice, embrace valiantly the course of righteous obedience on their trek toward the tree of life. Despite all the distractions encountered along the mortal pathway, they are able to reach the tree and savor its matchless fruit, both tree and fruit being a representation of the love of God, even the gift of His beloved Son for the salvation of humankind. As we cling to the word of God—which is in effect an expression of "the merits, and mercy, and grace of the Holy Messiah," or higher Word (2 Ne. 2:8)—it will become our director or Liahona for life (see Alma 37:37–47). By continually nurturing the word with faith, diligence, and patience, we will enable it to take root in our hearts and we will come to partake of the fruit of eternal life and joy unspeakable (see Alma 32:40–43).

1. SYMBOLS THAT INSPIRE GOODNESS— THE MEANING OF LEHI'S VISION

THEME. Understanding and applying the interpretation of the symbols in the vision of the tree of life brings meaning and spiritual nourishment to our lives.

> *"And it came to pass that I beheld a tree, whose fruit was desirable to make one happy. And it came to pass that I did go forth and partake of the fruit thereof; and I beheld that it was most sweet, above all that I ever before tasted. Yea, and I beheld that the fruit thereof was white, to exceed all the whiteness that I had ever seen. And as I partook of*

the fruit thereof it filled my soul with exceedingly great joy; wherefore, I began to be desirous that my family should partake of it also; for I knew that it was desirable above all other fruit." (1 Ne. 8:10–12)

MOMENT OF TRUTH. As the prophet Lehi, spokesperson of the Lord's will, tarried in the wilderness with his family, he reported experiencing a remarkable spiritual event: "Behold, I have dreamed a dream; or, in other words, I have seen a vision" (1 Ne. 8:2). What he saw with prophetic insight was a dynamic scene that instilled in him two diametrically opposite emotions—one of joy on behalf of his righteous sons, Sam and Nephi, and one of fear on behalf of Laman and Lemuel, whose attitude and behavior were scarcely in keeping with divine mandate (see 1 Ne. 8:3–4). Lehi unfolded for his family the details of the memorable tree of life vision that has become one of the most celebrated and compelling statements of the gospel plan, and the consequences of mortal choice, in all of holy writ.

The tree of life vision encompasses a multiplicity of symbols that invite informed interpretation and greater understanding based on the keys given in the scriptures themselves. This greater understanding leads in turn to daily applications, based on faith, that promote increased goodness and righteousness in life.

MODERN PROPHETS SPEAK

Jeffrey R. Holland:

> The reader finds the first manifestation of the symbolic Christ in the vision of the Tree of Life, which Lehi documented in 1 Nephi 8 and which was further explained in the vision that Nephi received shortly thereafter. In Lehi's dream, "after many hours of darkness" (consider the darkness of an existence bereft of the Light of the World), he came upon a large and spacious field in which he saw "a tree, whose fruit was desirable to make one happy."

> After partaking of the fruit, Lehi declared, "I beheld that it was most sweet, above all that I ever before tasted. Yea, and I beheld that the fruit thereof was white, to exceed all the whiteness that I had ever seen.

> "And as I partook of the fruit thereof it filled my soul with exceedingly great joy" (1 Nephi 8:12). . . .

> Thus, at the very outset of the Book of Mormon, in its first fully developed allegory, Christ is portrayed as the source of eternal life and joy, the living evidence of divine love, and the means whereby God will fulfill his covenant with the house of Israel and indeed the entire family of man, returning them to all their eternal prom-

ises. (*Christ and the New Covenant: The Messianic Message of the Book of Mormon* [Salt Lake City: Deseret Book, 1997], 159–162)

ILLUSTRATIONS FOR OUR TIME

The Spiritual Forest. The landscape of the scriptural record is marked with numberless oases of living trees that symbolize the vitality of the gospel in the lives of mortal travelers. This spiritual forest—from the trees of dual significance in the Garden of Eden, to the tree of life in Lehi's immortal dream, to Alma's unfolding tree of faith—offers to the believer an enduring shelter of truth and righteousness and the promise of "the greatest of all the gifts of God" (1 Ne. 15:36), even divine love (1 Ne. 11:25).

The word "tree" is used 428 times in the scriptures. "Tree of life" itself occurs approximately 29 times. Few images in the scriptures awaken in the hearts of truth seekers more reverence and awe than the image of the noble tree, the unfailing emblem of enduring growth, timeless strength, and towering majesty. Jeremiah, Lehi's immediate contemporary, extended the image of the tree by applying it to the person directly: "Blessed is the man that trusteth in the Lord, and whose hope the Lord is. For he shall be as a tree planted by the waters, and that spreadeth out her roots by the river, and shall not see when heat cometh, but her leaf shall be green." (Jer. 17:7–8). Similarly, Lehi's younger contemporary, Ezekiel, wrote of his vision of the temple of God, which issues forth a stream of healing water to sustain trees and growth on either side (Ezek. 47:7–9), surely a further manifestation of God's spiritual nourishment active in the lives of the Saints. A similar image is reflected again by John in his vision of the tree of life in the midst of the paradise of God (see Rev. 2:7; 22:2, 14).

Again and again the image of the tree seeks to awaken in our souls a sense of spiritual potential—from the allegory of the olive trees as a likeness of Israel's unfolding and destiny (Jacob 5), to the images of Zion's "branches" extending around the world, to the very substance of Zion's organizational structure itself (i.e., poles and stakes of wood that support the canopy of spiritual refuge), and, yes, to the very essence of the wooden cross of the Atonement itself. All of these tree-related emblems come back to one thing: the love of God manifested through the blessings of the gospel of Jesus Christ.

For all of us there are trees of significance standing there somewhere in the record of our lives, some of which we may have planted and nourished personally. There is no dearth of models to reflect on. We come back repeatedly to that Sacred Grove where the boy Joseph received the first messages about the Restoration and learned firsthand about the actuality of the living Father and Son. We remember with respect the story of President Hinckley's venerated walnut tree that became the podium for the new Conference Center, from which emanates continual truth about the "tree of life."

My wife recounts her vivid childhood memory of a cherished willow tree, visible from her bedroom window, through whose limbs she could see in her mind's eye, season after season, the temple of God standing nearby as a symbol of everlasting life. For her, the willow tree was part of a spiritual forest that offers peace and hope. I can recall with satisfaction the towering ash tree in the backyard of my child-hood home in whose upper branches we boys had constructed a tree house of some complexity where we could retreat to ponder and think about things from a higher perspective. In our home today, we still have on display a sculpture of the Holy Family beautifully carved from linden wood by an Austrian artist we met one year—a tree-based symbol of Christ's birth.

There is value in walking through the spiritual forest of your life and in contemplating the blessings of God embodied in the imagery of those special trees that reflect His love and remind us of the promise: "To him that overcometh will I give to eat of the tree of life, which is in the midst of the paradise of God" (Rev. 2:7). (Allen)

A Decision of Glory. The vision of the tree of life portrays realities. As real as the love of God is, so are temptations, so are the people involved in the struggle for their spiritual lives. Consider the following success story from Marion D. Hanks and our desire to be among those who partake of the fruit of the tree and do not fall away:

Marion D. Hanks:

Let me give you a headline of an experience not unfamiliar to many of you. Some of you have made a different answer already I suppose. A fine girl whom we'll call Gerry, which wasn't her name, was invited by her other high school associates, she being a freshman, to attend a social which was to be the year's introduction of the freshmen girls of high social level to this particular group. Gerry went, thrilled. She had a natural desire to be appreciated and popular; she wanted to succeed. Her mother was equally pleased because the girls who had invited her were fine girls so far as she knew. She had a new dress, was all pretty and ready when they called. She went to the place and found that she, after a little time, was the only one in the whole room not smoking. This surprised her because some of the girls she knew to be from homes of Latter-day Saint affiliation, some active ones. She felt a little out of place, wondered whether it wouldn't be appropriate to just hold a cigarette though she never had.

But she put that away and was uncomfortable and yet able to associate to an extent, when the next step occurred. A sixteen-year-old girl broke out a case of champagne her dad had been thoughtful enough to provide, and they all began to drink it. Pretty soon, Gerry discovered that almost literally she was on one side of the room and they on the other. I don't want to suggest she felt very good about it, or noble, or heroic, or like Joan of Arc; she felt terrible. She was under a kind of pressure and with influences she was not used to. She wanted to succeed; she didn't want to be, right in the beginning, characterized as one who was foolish or prudish or ridiculous. She stood and thought, considered holding a glass—this wouldn't hurt—then decided she couldn't do that. And almost literally, I repeat, found herself isolated from them to the point that finally, in accompaniment to their jeers and sneers and laughter, she left the place, walked all the way down the canyon, got home sobbing and disconsolate, heartbroken.

Her mother talked to her for a time and then invited me to. I told her the story of Lehi's vision; do you remember it? Just a point or two. Lehi had a vision of a great tree on which was fruit more desirable than any other fruit in the world. You had to get to it by way of a path alongside of which ran a rod of iron. There were mists of darkness coming up to obscure the path from a big chasm running alongside. Across the chasm was a large and spacious building filled with people dressed in the most impressive finery, having a real big time pointing their fingers at and laughing at the people across the chasm who had eaten the fruit and knew the value of it, it being the tree of the love of God or the tree of life. Well, I talked to her a little, told her I was not a prophet and didn't pretend to be, but that I would be willing, knowing that life is made of not one decision but a lot of them, yet to tell her that in my opinion the decision she had just made was an heroic and a great one, and that the day would come when, with a husband worthy of her and children whom she loved as she then could not understand she would love them, she would kneel down and thank God for the decisions of that hour. Well, that day came. (in Leon R. Hartshorn, comp., *Outstanding Stories by General Authorities,* 3 vols. [Salt Lake City: Deseret Book, 1970–1973], 1:111–12) (Pinegar)

Likening the Scriptures to Our Lives

1 Nephi 15:36—The fruit of the tree is precious and desirable to make one happy. It is the most precious gift from God.

Application—Let us seek this fruit by holding to the iron rod and staying on the strait and narrow path and by enduring to the end to receive this gift, the gift of eternal life (see D&C 14:7).

2. THE TYPOLOGY OF TRAVELERS IN THE VISION OF THE TREE OF LIFE

THEME. In seeking eternal life, one must get on the straight and narrow path, hold to the iron rod, and press forward steadfastly to partake of the tree of life. It takes great effort and perseverance to remain among the faithful and obedient and avoid casting one's lot with those fellow travelers who fail to reach out and grab hold of the iron rod, or having once chosen it, still fall by the wayside or reject the fruit of God's love.

"And I also beheld a strait and narrow path, which came along by the rod of iron, even to the tree by which I stood; and it also led by the head of the

fountain, unto a large and spacious field, as if it had been a world. And I saw numberless concourses of people, many of whom were pressing forward, that they might obtain the path which led unto the tree by which I stood. And it came to pass that they did come forth, and commence in the path which led to the tree. And it came to pass that there arose a mist of darkness; yea, even an exceedingly great mist of darkness, insomuch that they who had commenced in the path did lose their way, that they wandered off and were lost." (1 Ne. 8:20–23)

MOMENT OF TRUTH. Lehi's vision of the tree of life is both a supernal allegory of God's plan of loving redemption and a template for application in one's immediate life. What Lehi saw in prophetic vision had its source in the highest reaches of the spiritual firmament, yet it had enormous utility as a compass for the real experiences of the moment. Lehi was wise enough to see that his vision had meaning not just in concept and principle, but especially when applied to himself, his wife, and his family. So it must be with us all. The tree of life is not an abstract model to be admired like a tapestry, but a road map that becomes a stunning self-revelation when we hold it up as a mirror in which to see ourselves and determine our position before God.

In the vision of the tree of life, we are granted a clear view of the types of people ever present on the mortal landscape and the different and distinct strategies that each of these groups might elect in their quest for their perception of a fulfilling lifestyle.

MODERN PROPHETS SPEAK

Ezra Taft Benson:

> Satan is waging war against the members of the Church who have testimonies and are trying to keep the commandments. . . .

> When we read of the spreading curse of drugs, or read of the pernicious flood of pornography and immorality, do any of us doubt that these are the forbidden paths and rivers of filthiness Lehi described? . . .

> In his dream, Lehi saw an iron rod which led through the mist of darkness. He saw that if people would hold fast to that rod, they could avoid the rivers of filthiness, stay away from the forbidden paths, stop from wandering in the strange roads that lead to destruction. Later his son Nephi clearly explained the symbolism of the iron rod. When Laman and Lemuel asked, "What meaneth the rod of iron?" Nephi answered, "It was the word of God; and [note this promise] whoso would hearken

unto the word of God, and hold fast unto it, they would never perish; neither could the temptations and the fiery darts of the adversary overpower them unto blindness, to lead them away to destruction." (1 Ne. 15:23–24). Not only will the word of God lead us to the fruit which is desirable above all others, but in the word of God and through it we can find the power to resist temptation, the power to thwart the work of Satan and his emissaries. . . .

My dear brethren, this is an answer to the great challenge of our time. The word of God, as found in the scriptures, in the words of living prophets, and in personal revelation, has the power to fortify the Saints and arm them with the Spirit so they can resist evil, hold fast to the good, and find joy in this life. ("The Power of the Word," *Ensign,* May 1986, 79–80)

ILLUSTRATIONS FOR OUR TIME

A Father's Blessing. Many years ago, on the eve of getting married and starting a family of my own, I asked my father to give me a father's blessing. This being a patriarchal prerogative, he prepared himself during a long period of fasting and prayer and then bestowed upon my head a wonderful blessing containing many words of personal encouragement and counsel, somewhat in the spirit of Lehi's famous dream. At the conclusion of the blessing, he stated something that can be readily shared with others because of its universal application: "And now, my beloved son, as you journey forth into the uncertain world, reach up your hands to the lap of God. And if you will do this He will lead you, He will guide you, save and exalt you in the Eternal Worlds."

Just as the prophet Lehi had received wisdom from on high in the form of a panoramic vision intended for all mankind, so my own father had received inspiration to give counsel to his son in a unique and effective way. Often truth is conveyed more readily in the form of imagery or stories with symbolic power, and thus Lehi's vivid dream has served to bless the lives of countless millions who seek guidance in traversing a mortal landscape fraught with temptations and distractions of all kinds. Similarly, fathers and mothers can tell uplifting stories to their children and grandchildren, seeking inspiration from on high to find the most effective imagery for expressing true principles in such a way that the rising generation will more readily make choices that bless and enlighten. (Allen)

Likening the Scriptures to Our Lives

1 Nephi 8:12—Lehi, as with all faithful parents, found great joy in the partaking of the fruit. Immediately thereafter his first desire was to get his family to partake.

Application—We must never forget that our joy and rejoicing is in our posterity, our families. Families are eternal. Our roles within these families are eternal. They never change. It is our eternal duty as well as our eternal joy to magnify our stewardships within our families (see Mosiah 4:14–15).

3. THE POWER IN PONDERING

THEME. The power of meditating and pondering brings eternal truths to our hearts and minds. It is a principle of power we need to develop in order to receive personal revelation that guides us along the pathways of righteousness.

> *"For it came to pass after I had desired to know the things that my father had seen, and believing that the Lord was able to make them known unto me, as I sat pondering in mine heart I was caught away in the Spirit of the Lord, yea, into an exceedingly high mountain, which I never had before seen, and upon which I never had before set my foot. And the Spirit said unto me: Behold, what desirest thou?" (1 Ne. 11:1–2)*

MOMENT OF TRUTH. The way Lehi's sons responded to their father's prophetic ministry is instructive by way of counsel and admonition. For the murmuring Laman and Lemuel, Lehi was acting on the basis of "the foolish imaginations of his heart" (1 Ne. 2:11). Nephi, on the other hand, acted with reverential respect and humble acceptance. He had a great desire to see the things his father had seen in vision. The process is noted as follows:

1. Cultivate a spiritual mode of inquiry.

Nephi had a great desire to know (see 1 Ne. 11:1).
He had faith in the principle that by seeking diligently one shall find (see 1 Ne. 10:19).
He knew that God is the same yesterday, today, and forever (see 1 Ne. 10:18).
He possessed the same mind-set of faithful inquiry that the Apostle James was to commend: "If any of you lack wisdom, let him ask of God, that giveth to all men liberally, and upbraideth not; and it shall be given him" (James 1:5–6).
Nephi had a conviction that the mysteries of God will be revealed by the power of the Holy Ghost (see 1 Ne. 10:19).

2. Inquire of the Lord following humble meditation and pondering.

The act of meditation and pondering means to contemplate, muse, or reflect upon things from the immediate and present to the infinite and universal. It is something we should all do more often. Meditation and pondering provide the opportunity to sort things out, to create new concepts and ideas, to receive pure inspiration—even revelation—for your needs and concerns. The prophets have always pondered that they might know the things of God (see 1 Ne. 11:1; D&C 138:1).

MODERN PROPHETS SPEAK

Gordon B. Hinckley:

> We need the Spirit of the Lord in our lives more. . . . But there is hardly time to reflect and think and pause and meditate. I daresay that most of those in this room today have not taken an hour in the last year to just sit down quietly, each man to himself, as a son of God, reflecting upon his place in this world, upon his destiny, upon his capacity to do good, upon his mission to make some changes for good. We need to. I recall so vividly President McKay in his old age in a meeting with his counselors and the Twelve saying, "Brethren, we need to take more time to meditate, to think quietly." (*Teachings of Gordon B. Hinckley* [Salt Lake City: Deseret Book, 1997], 334)

ILLUSTRATIONS FOR OUR TIME

Section 138 of the Doctrine and Covenants is a direct result of pondering over the scriptures and the Atonement of our Savior, Jesus Christ.

President Joseph F. Smith tells us that "on the third of October, in the year nineteen hundred and eighteen, I sat in my room *pondering* over the Scriptures. . . ." He had particular reference at this time to Peter's statement that Christ "went and preached unto the spirits in prison" (1 Pet. 3:19) while his body lay in the grave. "As I *pondered* over these things which are written," President Smith continued, "the eyes of my understanding were opened and the Spirit of the Lord rested upon me, and I saw the hosts of the dead, both small and great. . . ." He then gives us an account of his great vision concerning missionary work among the spirits of the dead.

Likening the Scriptures to Our Lives

1 Nephi 11:1—Nephi had a desire to know the things his father saw. He pondered and prayed and received revelation.

Application—We too can know and understand the things of God as we pay the price to pray and ponder over these precious truths—not just a cursory request, but rather a deep yearning of our very soul that requires the exercise of faith to the point of mental exertion (see *Lectures on Faith* 7:3).

SUMMARY

Joseph Smith, the Prophet of the Restoration, was the instrument through whom the Lord blessed mankind with the vast abundance of spiritual wealth contained in the Book of Mormon, the Doctrine and Covenants, the Pearl of Great Price, and the inspired translation of the Bible. The process of scriptural restoration was characterized by the Lord in this magnificent phrase: "And the scriptures shall be given, even as they are in mine own bosom, to the salvation of mine own elect" (D&C 35:20). Indeed, the sanctuary for the word of the Lord is no less than the bosom of the Lord Himself, and it is from this holy and perfect source that all scripture flows to mankind.

Think of the process of conversion and sanctification—what King Benjamin's followers were to experience as "a mighty change" (Mosiah 5:2). What is this process if it is not to take into one's own bosom that which has come directly from the Lord and then to allow this light to burn within as the power of faith unto repentance and righteous action? If we so endure to the end, we will increase in the light, "until the perfect day" (D&C 50:24). This mighty change will carry us forward toward the tree of life, where the love of God is granted in its fulness to the obedient and faithful travelers on the pathway of salvation. The Book of Mormon makes it clear that the only way to receive the love of God and gain eternal life is to get on the strait and narrow path, hold to the iron rod, and press forward with diligence. The Lord stands waiting to bless us if we but are obedient to his commandments and cleave to His words: "For they will hear my voice, and shall see me, and shall not be asleep, and shall abide the day of my coming; for they shall be purified, even as I am pure" (D&C 35:21).

CHAPTER FOUR

NEPHI'S VISION *of the* FUTURE

1 NEPHI 12–14

*"The Nephites were a blessed people, in that angels constantly
ministered unto them. They had revelations from Heaven to guide them.
They prospered in material things, and those who were zealous in keeping
God's commandments were benefitted and blessed. The mind and will of God
were made known to them by their holy prophets. Special reference is hereby
made to the account of Nephi's vision wherein an angel from the
Courts of Glory went with him in the journey of his dream,
and explained to him the meaning of all he saw."*
—GEORGE REYNOLDS AND JANNE M. SJODAHL, *COMMENTARY ON THE BOOK OF
MORMON*, ED. PHILIP C. REYNOLDS, 7 VOLS. (SALT LAKE CITY: DESERET BOOK,
1955–1961), 5:233.

THEMES *for* LIVING

The Savior's Life as a Beacon to Guide the Generations across Time
The New World and the Restoration of the Word of God
Winning the Battle of Good versus Evil in the Final Chapters of Human History

INTRODUCTION

Nephi had a great desire to experience the remarkable spiritual manifestations his father had seen. Because of Nephi's righteousness and divine calling he was given the privilege of receiving this vision wherein he was caught away by the Spirit and led by an angel. The angel instructs him and takes him through a series of inspired views regarding the future. Elder Bruce R. McConkie explains the function of angels as follows: "God's messengers, those individuals whom he sends (often from his personal presence in the eternal worlds), to deliver his messages (Luke 1:11–38); to minister to his children (Acts 10:1–8, 30–32); to teach them the doctrines of salvation (Mosiah 3); to call them to repentance (Moro. 7:31); to give them priesthood and keys (D&C 13; 128:20–21); to save them in perilous circumstances (1 Ne. 3:29–31; Dan. 6:22); to guide them in the performance of his work (Gen. 24:7); to gather his elect in the last days (Matt. 24:31); to perform all needful things relative to his work (Moro. 7:29–33)—such messengers are called angels" (*Mormon Doctrine,* 2d ed. [Salt Lake City: Bookcraft, 1966], 35).

Each of us, if we are worthy and if there is a need, according to the will of the Lord, can receive angelic messengers. Each of us, as well, can ponder the visions of the prophets and mingle our spiritual sensibility with theirs as we search and meditate upon the things of the Spirit. One of the great models for that process is Nephi, who sought and received the divine message proffered to his father, Lehi—thus providing a spiritual account of how two worthy and noble minds embraced the same message. They left a priceless guide for our own study and application.

Reading the account of Nephi's vision in Chapters 11 through 14 of 1 Nephi is akin to taking a grand spiritual tour through the centuries of time on the wings of divine inspiration. Through the eyes of Nephi, we are blessed with some two dozen different sequential scenes of human history that are opened up to us from a heavenly perspective. In most cases, each scene is ushered in when the angelic guide speaks the word "Look" or "Behold." We see played out on the mortal stage the key events forming a continuity of milestones leading from Nephi's time to the final scenes of the world's history. During the early scenes, the familiar images from Lehi's vision of the tree of life are replayed in all their glory for the young prophet Nephi and intermingled with the flow of history being portrayed in vision.

1. THE SAVIOR'S LIFE AS A BEACON TO GUIDE THE GENERATIONS ACROSS TIME

THEME. The mission and Atonement of the Savior, as communicated to mankind through holy writ and confirmed by the Spirit of God, serve as a beacon of hope and truth to guide the generations through mortality. When a nation, such as the Nephites, honored the covenant promises, they prospered and blossomed, but as they succumbed to pride and worldliness, they declined and ultimately perished. That is the witness and the warning of the Book of Mormon.

> *"And it came to pass that the angel said unto me: Look, and behold thy seed, and also the seed of thy brethren. And I looked and beheld the land of promise; and I beheld multitudes of people, yea, even as it were in number as many as the sand of the sea." (1 Ne. 12:1)*

MOMENT OF TRUTH. Nephi and his circle of loved ones constituted but a handful of God's children. Yet they were to transform themselves in time into mighty nations numbering in the millions. What a momentous view was given to Nephi to see how this branch of Israel would evolve and develop, ever unfolding or declining according to the willingness of the people to remain aligned with righteous principles. Early in his visionary experience, Nephi viewed the tree of life, the birth and ministry of the Savior, the land of promise, the generations of his people over time, the coming of the resurrected Lord to the land of promise, and the ultimate downfall of his people at the hands of the Lamanites (scenes 1 through 15 in the chart above).

When people ripen in iniquity, the result is inevitably contention and war. Nephi saw the wars that would occur before the coming of our Savior to the promised land. When the Savior came and taught the people, they had three generations of righteousness—nearly 200 years: "And it came to pass that there was no contention in the land, because of the love of God which did dwell in the hearts of the people. And there were no envyings, nor strifes, nor tumults, nor whoredoms, nor lyings, nor murders, nor any manner of lasciviousness; and surely there could not be a happier people among all the people who had been created by the hand of God" (4 Ne. 1:15–16). One can see through the eyes of Nephi and the later record of the Book of Mormon the results of the love of God in the hearts of those who embrace the gospel and live the teachings of the Savior.

As the people again turned to their vain imaginations and pride they were tempted. They were blinded by the devil and their hearts became hardened to such a point that eventually the Lamanites overpowered the Nephites and brought about their demise.

MODERN PROPHETS SPEAK

Spencer W. Kimball:

> This book [Book of Mormon] should convince of the futility of war and the haz-
> ards of unrighteousness. A few prophets swimming in a sea of barbarism find it dif-
> ficult to prevent the crumbling and final collapse of corrupt peoples. There is a great
> but conditional promise: "And this land shall be a land of liberty unto the Gentiles,
> and there shall be no kings upon the land. . . . And I will fortify this land against all
> other nations.
>
> ". . . I, the Lord, the king of heaven, will be their king, and I will be a light unto
> them forever, that hear my words" (2 Nephi 10:11–12, 14). (Spencer W. Kimball,
> *Faith Precedes the Miracle* [Salt Lake City: Deseret Book, 1972], 334)

ILLUSTRATIONS FOR OUR TIME

The War of Righteousness. One wonders why throughout the Book of Mormon there is so much
recorded concerning wars. We learn from the very beginning, "And there was war in heaven: Michael
and his angels fought against the dragon; and the dragon fought and his angels, And prevailed not; neither was their place found any more in heaven" (Rev. 12:7–8). Today, as in the past, we fight the war
against evil; this is part of life. Elder McConkie has taught us: "Our mortal probation is a war, a continuation of the war in heaven (Rev. 12:7–17), a war against the world, against evil, against Satan. And
there are no neutrals; all men are for the Lord or they are against him; they either serve under his banner or they live after the manner of the world and are in the bondage of sin. The only way for the
Christian soldiers to come off victorious is to put on the whole armor of God. Paul did, and as his life
drew to a close he was able to affirm, 'I have fought a good fight, . . . I have kept the faith' (2 Tim.
4:7). King Mosiah did likewise and after he had 'gone the way of all the earth,' Alma the younger was
able to say of him that he had 'warred a good warfare' because he had walked 'uprightly before God'
(Alma 1:1)." (*Doctrinal New Testament Commentary,* 3 vols. [Salt Lake City: Bookcraft, 1965–1973],
2:524).

Opposition in all things and temptations are part of the plan in order to prove ourselves worthy (see 2
Ne. 2:11; D&C 29:39), therefore in this sense we are at war continually against Satan and his hosts.
Every day as we arise, we must prepare for battle. We must arm ourselves in righteousness, with the
shield of faith (see D&C 27:17), conquering through prayer (see Alma 13:28; D&C 10:5; 3 Ne.
18:18). We must get off the road of temptation and put ourselves under the influence of the Spirit. We
must be about our Father's business of inviting all to come unto Christ. Each of us should seek to have
our own Sacred Grove in our lives. (Pinegar)

A Message for the Multimedia Age. Recently my wife and I had the privilege of offering a course on the Book of Mormon for young single adults in our stake institute program. These were bright, eager, well-read young people with a keen desire to learn and follow true principles. It occurred to us early on that these young minds were trained in a peculiarly modern way to align themselves with the extraordinary imagery that characterizes the account of the visions of Lehi and Nephi in the opening chapters of the Book of Mormon. Of all ages of mortality, our current generation—immersed as it is in an endless plethora of multimedia experiences arising from the technological marvels of the day—should most readily understand and relate to the extraordinary scenes that are so frequently projected onto our spiritual minds by the visionary prophets of God.

Yet the dizzying array of modern communications and media tools—satellite communications, Internet, CDs, DVDs, MP3s, handheld PDAs, streaming audio/video programming—all of this is but a weak surrogate of the power of the Spirit to teach and instruct minds that are open and hearts that are easily entreated. In the end, modern communications wizardry, for all its inventiveness and splash, has precious little truth to convey. When we are walking in the light of worldly glamour, we are "walking in darkness at noon-day" (D&C 95:6). But the word of God, conveyed through the Spirit, envelops one's whole being and opens up vistas of understanding that remind us who we really are, in the most vivid way imaginable—sons and daughters of God. "And the Spirit giveth light to every man that cometh into the world; and the Spirit enlighteneth every man through the world, that hearkeneth to the voice of the Spirit" (D&C 84:46). Further: "For by my Spirit will I enlighten them, and by my power will I make known unto them the secrets of my will—yea, even those things which eye has not seen, nor ear heard, nor yet entered into the heart of man" (D&C 76:10).

Thus a humble institute student, following in the footsteps of a Lehi or a Nephi as they reflected back to us the luminous visions of the Almighty, was able to report: "The Book of Mormon is a compass for the future. It teaches us how to have a broken heart and a contrite spirit. We are strengthened as we intertwine our testimonies with the strong testimonies of others (just as Nephi blended his vision with Lehi). . . . Above all things, we learn from the Book of Mormon to come unto Christ. I am so grateful when institute reminds me of this. We must not walk in our own light, but in the Savior's." What a magnificent message for a multimedia age. (Allen)

Likening the Scriptures to Our Lives

1 Nephi 12:19—Nephi saw the contention between his seed and the seed of his brothers. It was caused by the pride of his seed and the temptations of the devil.

Application—Let us avoid pride at all costs through humility and a willingness of our hearts to do the will of our Heavenly Father. As we cleave to the iron rod (see 1 Nephi 15:24), arm ourselves with the shield of faith (D&C 27:17), and pray (see Alma 13:28; 3 Nephi 18:18), we will be able to overcome temptation.

2. THE NEW WORLD AND
THE RESTORATION OF THE WORD OF GOD

THEME. The word of God, in purity and fulness, gives to mankind the essential compass for navigating the perilous landscape of mortality. In a sense, we are all bound for a promised land, moving through uncharted seas, endowed with the dependable and steady lodestar of the restored gospel of Jesus Christ to guide our journey.

"And the angel said unto me: Behold the formation of a church which is most abominable above all other churches, which slayeth the saints of God, yea, and tortureth them and bindeth them down, and yoketh them with a yoke of iron, and bringeth them down into captivity." (1 Ne. 13:5)

"And I looked and beheld a man among the Gentiles, who was separated from the seed of my brethren by the many waters; and I beheld the Spirit of God, that it came down and wrought upon the man; and he went forth upon the many waters, even unto the seed of my brethren, who were in the promised land." (1 Ne. 13:12)

"And after these plain and precious things were taken away it goeth forth unto all the nations of the Gentiles; and after it goeth forth unto all the nations of the Gentiles, yea, even across the many waters which thou hast seen with the Gentiles which have gone forth out of captivity, thou seest—because of the many plain and precious things which have been taken out of the book, which were plain unto the understanding of the children of men, according to the plainness which is in the Lamb of God—because of these things which are taken away out of the gospel of the Lamb, an exceedingly great many do stumble, yea, insomuch that Satan hath great power over them." (1 Ne. 13:29)

"For, behold, saith the Lamb: I will manifest myself unto thy seed, that they shall write many things which I shall minister unto them, which shall be plain and precious; and after thy seed shall be destroyed, and dwindle in unbelief, and also the seed of thy brethren, behold, these things shall be hid up, to come forth unto the Gentiles, by the gift and power of the Lamb. And in them shall be written my gospel, saith the Lamb, and my rock and my salvation. And blessed are they who shall seek to bring forth my Zion at that day, for they shall have the gift and the power of the Holy Ghost; and if they endure unto the end they shall be lifted up at the last day, and shall be saved in the everlasting kingdom of the Lamb; and whoso shall publish peace, yea, tidings of great joy, how beautiful upon the mountains shall they be." (1 Ne. 13:35–37)

MOMENT OF TRUTH. The angel continued to show Nephi the future. Nephi saw the rise of the church of the devil, witnessed the discovery of America in modern times, saw that plain and precious things were taken out of the Bible, viewed events related to the Apostasy, and rejoiced over the Restoration of the gospel in latter days, including the coming forth of the Book of Mormon and other scriptures and the building up of Zion (see items 16 through 21 in the chart above).

Among the gentile nations, Nephi saw the formation of the great and abominable church founded by the devil. The desires of this church were to have the things of the world and to bring the Saints down into captivity. It was this church that took the plain and precious things away from the Bible, causing so many to stumble, insomuch that Satan gained power over them. Nephi saw, however, that the Lord would remember the seed of his lineage and restore the plain and precious things, which shall come forth to all people.

The Spirit of God worked upon the Gentiles (Columbus and others) and brought them to the promised land, from which will flow the restored gospel. The Gentiles humbled themselves before the Lord and they were protected by the power of the Lord. We can surely see the importance of the coming forth of the Book of Mormon to restore the gospel (including the plain and precious things) that all might come to know and understand the true doctrine and the plan of redemption . . . that all might come unto Christ.

MODERN PROPHETS SPEAK

Ezra Taft Benson:

> Every member of the priesthood should understand the divine plan designed by the Lord to raise up the first free people in modern times. Here is how scripture says it was achieved:

> First: Prophecy is abundant that God deliberately kept the American continent hidden until after the Holy Roman Empire had been broken up and the various nations had established themselves as independent kingdoms. Keeping America hidden until this time was no accident (2 Nephi 1:6, 8).

> Second: At the proper time, God inspired Columbus to overcome almost insurmountable odds to discover America and bring this rich new land to the attention of the gentiles in Europe (1 Nephi 13:12).

Third: God revealed to his ancient American prophets that shortly after the discovery of America there would be peoples in Europe who would desire to escape the persecution and tyranny of the Old World and flee to America (1 Nephi 13:13–16).

Fourth: God told his prophets that the kingdoms in Europe would try to exercise dominion over the people who had fled to America, but that in the wars for independence the American settlers would win. (This is a remarkable prophecy in that 2,300 years before the Revolutionary War was fought, God through his prophets predicted who would win it.) (1 Nephi 13:16–19).

Fifth: The prophets were told that in the latter days when the Gentiles came to America, they would establish it as a land of liberty on which there would be no kings. The Lord declared that he would protect the land, and whosoever would try to establish kings either from within or without would perish (2 Nephi 10:8–14).

Sixth: Having declared America to be a land of liberty, God undertook to raise up a band of inspired and intelligent leaders who could write a constitution of liberty and establish the first free people in modern times. The hand of God in this undertaking is clearly indicated by the Lord himself in a revelation to the Prophet Joseph Smith in these words: ". . . I established the Constitution of this land, by the hands of wise men whom I raised up unto this very purpose . . ." (D&C 101:80).

Seventh: God declared that the United States Constitution was divinely inspired for the specific purpose of eliminating bondage and the violation of the rights and protection which belong to "all flesh" (See D&C 101:77–80).

Eighth: God placed a mandate upon his people to befriend and defend the constitutional laws of the land and see that the rights and privileges of all mankind are protected. He verified the declaration of the founding fathers, that God created all men free. He also warned against those who would enact laws encroaching upon the sacred rights and privileges of free men. He urged the election of honest and wise leaders and said that evil men and laws were of Satan (D&C 98:5–10).

Ninth: God predicted through his prophets that this great gentile nation, raised up on the American continent in the last days, would become the richest and most powerful nation on the face of the earth; even "above all other nations" (See 1 Nephi 13:15, 30; Ether 2:12).

Tenth: Concerning the United States, the Lord revealed to his prophets that its greatest threat would be a vast, worldwide "secret combination" which would not only threaten the United States but also seek to "overthrow the freedom of all lands, nations and countries" (Ether 8:25).

Eleventh: In connection with attack on the United States, the Lord told the Prophet Joseph Smith there would be an attempt to overthrow the country by destroying the Constitution. Joseph Smith predicted that the time would come when the Constitution would hang, as it were, by a thread, and at that time "this people will step forth and save it from the threatened destruction" (*Journal of Discourses*, 7:15). It is my conviction that the elders of Israel, widely spread over the nation, will at that crucial time successfully rally the righteous of our country and provide the necessary balance of strength to save the institutions of constitutional government.

Twelfth: The Lord revealed to the prophet Nephi that he established the gentiles on this land to be a free people forever, that if they were a righteous nation and overcame the wickedness and secret abominations that would rise in their midst, they would inherit the land forever (1 Nephi 14:1–2).

Thirteenth: On the other hand, if the Gentiles on this land reject the word of God and conspire to overthrow liberty and the Constitution, then their doom is fixed, and they "shall be cut off from among my people who are of the covenant" (1 Nephi 14:6; 3 Nephi 21:11, 14, 21; D&C 84: 114–115, 117).

Fourteenth: The great destructive force which was to be turned loose on the earth and which the prophets for centuries have been calling the "abomination of desolation" is vividly described by those who saw it in vision. Ours is the first generation to realize how literally these prophecies can be fulfilled now that God, through science, has unlocked the secret to thermonuclear reaction. (*God, Family, Country: Our Three Great Loyalties* [Salt Lake City: Deseret Book, 1974], 343–46)

ILLUSTRATIONS FOR OUR TIME

Nursing Fathers, Nursing Mothers. The Lord, in His infinite wisdom, knew that the gospel of liberty and truth could be restored to the earth only in an environment where the principles of liberty and truth were honored and constitutionally secured unto each individual (see D&C 134; 98:5–6; 101:77, 80). He therefore prepared the seedbed of the Restoration by empowering an emerging segment of the gentile flock "who did humble themselves before the Lord" (1 Ne. 13:16, as Nephi saw it in vision) and caused that they should be "lifted up by the power of God above all nations, upon the face of the land which is choice above all other lands" (v. 30). It was this new gentile nation that would be blessed to facilitate the coming forth of the restored word of God in all of its purity and fulness so that the covenant promises to Israel could be fulfilled.

Millennia earlier the prophet Isaiah had foreseen the nurturing role of the gentile nations as part of God's grand design for the Restoration in the latter days: "And kings shall be thy nursing fathers, and their queens thy nursing mothers: they shall bow down to thee with their face toward the earth, and lick up the dust of thy feet; and thou shalt know that I am the Lord: for they shall not be ashamed that wait for me" (Isa. 49:23). Is it any wonder that Nephi, who saw the unfolding of this very prophecy in his vision of the coming forth of the Book of Mormon and other latter-day scriptures, should cite this same passage for the edification of his readers (1 Ne. 21: 23) and that his brother Jacob should repeat it not just once but two times (2 Ne. 6:7; 10:9)? They rejoiced to perceive that the covenant promises would in the future be preserved unto their seed and extend blessings to all the world.

Because the enlightened Gentiles acted to serve the interests of the Almighty, they were blessed with the nurture of the gospel in all its fulness. Their service was rewarded with great blessings from God. Does this process continue even now? I heard an interesting answer to this question while serving a mission as a young elder in Germany many years ago. Apostle Ezra Taft Benson and his wife stopped by the mission home in Frankfurt for a visit around the Fourth of July, 1959, and (as my journal recorded) spoke with us informally about religious and political matters. At the time, he was completing his eight-year term as secretary of agriculture in the Eisenhower administration. Elder Benson told us, among other things, about his experiences with President Eisenhower and this man's spiritual power. He also said something that reminded me of the continuing role of the Gentiles (in particular the United States of America) in supporting God's design for the blessing of mankind. Elder Benson spoke to us about the government policy of providing foreign aid to many countries of the world and suggested that it was this policy, analogous to tithing, that was, in large measure, responsible for the prosperity of America. By blessing other nations, he said, America was being blessed by the Lord. This was a reminder to me that God's hand continues to be over this land, "which is choice above all other lands" (1 Ne. 13:30). Thus the nursing fathers should continue to be nurtured, and the nursing mothers should continue to be blessed from on high. (Allen)

Likening the Scriptures to Our Lives

1 Nephi 13:29—Due to the loss of many plain and precious things from the Bible, many stumble and Satan has power over them.
Application—We have the opportunity and duty to feast on the word of God from the Book of Mormon. The Book of Mormon and the other Restoration scriptures bring to light those things that were lost. The Prophet Joseph said that it was "the most correct of any book on earth, and the keystone of our religion, and a man would get nearer to God by abiding by its precepts, than by any other book" (*HC,* 4:461).

3. WINNING THE BATTLE OF GOOD VERSUS EVIL IN THE FINAL CHAPTERS OF HUMAN HISTORY

THEME. Our Father in Heaven controls the destinies of nations (see 1 Ne. 17:39–39) as the course of human events, under the design of the Almighty, moves inexorably forward toward the consummation of the preadvent period and the ushering in of the millennial reign. In all of God's laws there are consequences: blessings and cursings. The Gentiles who hearken to the Lord will be blessed through His manifestations both in word and power and will be numbered among the house of Israel. Those who seek to destroy (i.e., the adherents of the great and abominable church) shall fill the pit that they prepared for the destruction of others.

> *"And harden not their hearts against the Lamb of God, they shall be numbered among the seed of thy father; yea, they shall be numbered among the house of Israel; and they shall be a blessed people upon the promised land forever; they shall be no more brought down into captivity; and the house of Israel shall no more be confounded. And that great pit, which hath been digged for them by that great and abominable church, which was founded by the devil and his children, that he might lead away the souls of men down to hell—yea, that great pit which hath been digged for the destruction of men shall be filled by those who digged it, unto their utter destruction, saith the Lamb of God; not the destruction of the soul, save it be the casting of it into that hell which hath no end."* (1 Ne. 14:2–3)

> *"And it came to pass that I, Nephi, beheld the power of the Lamb of God, that it descended upon the saints of the church of the Lamb, and upon the covenant people of the Lord, who were scattered upon all the face of the earth; and they were armed with righteousness and with the power of God in great glory."* (1 Ne. 14:14)

MOMENT OF TRUTH. The vision of Nephi is concluded. Nephi sees the blessings and cursings concerning the Gentiles, the conflict between the great and abominable church and the Church of the Lamb of God, and the revelations given to the Apostle John. The angel explains to Nephi that there are only two churches: the Church of the Lamb of God and the church of the devil. Due to the wickedness of mankind, the wrath of the Lord is poured out upon the great and abominable church, and there will also be wars and rumors of war. John the Revelator has the commission to write concerning the last days and all the trials associated with them.

MODERN PROPHETS SPEAK

Bruce R. McConkie:
> The titles *church of the devil* and *great and abominable church* are used to identify all churches or organizations of whatever name or nature—whether political, philo-

sophical, educational, economic, social, fraternal, civic, or religious—which are designed to take men on a course that leads away from God and his laws and thus from salvation in the kingdom of God. . . . Any church or organization of any kind whatever which satisfies the innate religious longings of man and keeps him from coming to the saving truths of Christ and his gospel is therefore not of God. . . . Iniquitous conditions in the various branches of the great and abominable church in the last days are powerfully described in the Book of Mormon (2 Ne. 28; Morm. 8:28, 32–33, 36–38; D&C 10:56.) Nephi saw the "church which is most abominable above all other churches" in vision. He "saw the devil that he was the foundation of it"; and also the murders, wealth, harlotry, persecutions, and evil desires that are part of this organization (1 Ne. 13:1–10). (*Mormon Doctrine,* 2d ed. [Salt Lake City: Bookcraft, 1966], 137–39)

ILLUSTRATIONS FOR OUR TIME

The prophesied persecution will befall Saints, but they will also be "armed with righteousness and with the power of God in great glory" (1 Ne. 14:14), as related by Edward Partridge in the following account:

> I was taken from my house by the mob, George Simpson being their leader, who escorted me about half a mile, to the court house, on the public square in Independence; and then and there, a few rods from said court house, surrounded by hundreds of the mob, I was stripped of my hat, coat and vest and daubed with tar from head to foot, and then had a quantity of feathers put upon me; and all this because I would not agree to leave the county, and my home where I had lived two years.

> Before tarring and feathering me I was permitted to speak. I told them that the Saints had suffered persecution in all ages of the world; that I had done nothing which ought to offend anyone; that if they abused me, they would abuse an innocent person; that I was willing to suffer for the sake of Christ; but, to leave the country, I was not then willing to consent to it. By this time the multitude made so much noise that I could not be heard: some were cursing and swearing, saying, "call upon your Jesus," etc.; others were equally noisy in trying to still the rest, that they might be enabled to hear what I was saying.

> Until after I had spoken, I knew not what they intended to do with me, whether to kill me, to whip me, or what else I knew not. I bore my abuse with so much resignation and meekness, that it appeared to astound the multitude, who permitted me to retire in silence, many looking very solemn, their sympathies having been touched as I thought; and as to myself, I was so filled with the Spirit and love of God, that I had no hatred towards my persecutors or anyone else. (*HC,* 1:390–91)

Likening the Scriptures to Our Lives

1 Nephi 14:1—The Lord Himself will be manifest in word, power, and in very deed to take away the stumbling blocks.

Application—When we rely on the Lord—His words of eternal life, His priesthood with its lifesaving and exalting ordinances and covenants, and His infinite and eternal Atonement—the stumbling blocks are indeed removed and we shall be numbered with the house of Israel.

SUMMARY

Nephi, like his father, Lehi, before him, was privileged to view from a spiritual perspective the unfolding of the world's history from his day until the end of time. What these two prophets saw and communicated to us through the canon of scripture is a guide for our footsteps through these treacherous last days. Many of the things in the vision of Nephi have already occurred. We have witnessed some of the events in our own time. Nephi was a prophet and seer who clearly perceived that there would be a sore battle raging between the church of the devil and the Church of the Lamb, even The Church of Jesus Christ of Latter-day Saints. We have a responsibility to stand for truth and righteousness as witnesses (see Mosiah 18:8–9). We have a duty to warn our neighbor (see D&C 88:81). We have the sacred covenant privilege to build up the kingdom of God (see JST, Matt. 6:33). We have the obligation and commission to be a light to the world and saviors to mankind (see D&C 103:9–10; Obad. 1:21). We have a prophet today who is led by the Lord Jesus Christ. We are well counseled to give heed to his words, for they are as if the Lord Jesus Christ Himself gave them (see D&C 1:38; 3 Ne. 28:34–35). Should we fail to rise to this sacred duty of following the word, we would surely stand condemned. As the battle continues for the souls of men, we must do all in our power to bless and serve others that they might enjoy eternal life.

CHAPTER FIVE

"HEARKEN *to the* TRUTH, *and* GIVE HEED UNTO IT, THAT YE MIGHT WALK UPRIGHTLY BEFORE GOD"

1 NEPHI 16–22

*"I promise in the name of the Lord that all who give heed to our message,
and accept and live the gospel, will grow in faith and understanding.
They will have an added measure of peace in their lives and in their homes and by
the power of the Holy Ghost will speak similar words of testimony and truth. I do
this and leave my blessing upon you in the name of Jesus Christ. Amen."*
—SPENCER W. KIMBALL, *THE TEACHINGS OF SPENCER W. KIMBALL*, ED. EDWARD L.
KIMBALL (SALT LAKE CITY: BOOKCRAFT, 1982), 144.

THEMES *for* LIVING

Faith as a Daily Guiding Principle
Obedience as the Key to Perfection
Courage as the Basis for Transcending Adversity
The Scriptures as the Key to Wisdom
The Unbreakable Covenant

INTRODUCTION

We see played out in the lives of these ancient emigrant Saints a striving to measure up to the standards of faith, obedience, courage, and alignment with scriptural truth that were decreed by God to be the central characteristics of His covenant relationship with Israel. Those, like Lehi and Nephi, who became preeminent practitioners in righteous discipleship, stand as sentinels along the pathway to the tree of life; those, like Laman and Lemuel—ever murmuring—hover in the shadows as warning images of the effects of choosing the dead-end highways and byways of rebellion and transgression. Throughout the Book of Mormon we see demonstrated the rise and fall of the Nephite nation in accordance with their inclination either to "give heed" and obey or to set aside the principles embodied in the word of God and thus suffer the consequences of disobedience. Into a world where this grand dichotomy of lifestyle is so dramatically in evidence, the Lord, in His loving kindness, has introduced an infallible guidance system. Our Liahona is the word of God (see Alma 37:37–47). As we hearken to the Word and heed its divine message, we will walk uprightly before God. We will apply the scriptures to our lives (see 1 Ne. 19:23). The only sure way to return to the presence of our Heavenly Father is living by every word that proceedeth forth from the mouth of God (see D&C 84:43–46).

1. FAITH AS A DAILY GUIDING PRINCIPLE

THEME. Whether we are traversing the disorienting sands of the desert, navigating the perilous high seas on our way to the promised land, or simply trying to make it through the day, it is faith that constitutes the abiding principle of guidance from one moment to the next. Just as the Lord led and directed Lehi's family with the Liahona, even so will He guide and direct our course if we but open our understanding to the power of faith.

> *"And it came to pass that I, Nephi, beheld the pointers which were in the ball, that they did work according to the faith and diligence and heed which we did give unto them."*
> *(1 Ne. 16:28)*

MOMENT OF TRUTH. Imagine that you and your family are struggling to survive in the midst of an immense and hostile desert environment that appears ominously similar in all directions. You are heeding the directive of God to attain a promised land of safety, but how far away is it, and in which direction? Your provisions are strictly limited. Where do you turn, meanwhile, for nourishment and water? In His mercy and compassion, the Lord gave direction for His people by providing them with the Liahona: that "ball of curious workmanship" (1 Ne. 16:10). This miraculous device showed the way they should go according to the pointing of the spindles as well as instructions that would appear on the ball. Alma compared the Liahona to the word of God as the source of guidance for daily living (see Alma 37:37–48). This will always be a defining moment of truth in our own lives: Are we willing to live by the word of God provided through the scriptures, through the inspired pronouncements of our living prophets, and through personal inspiration given us by the power of the Holy Ghost?

MODERN PROPHETS SPEAK

Harold B. Lee:

> Now the only safety we have as members of this church is to do exactly what the Lord said to the Church in that day when the Church was organized. We must learn to give heed to the words and commandments that the Lord shall give through His prophet, "as he receiveth them, walking in all holiness before me; . . . as if from mine own mouth, in all patience and faith" (D&C 21:4–5). There will be some things that take patience and faith. You may not like what comes from the authority of the Church. It may contradict your political views. It may contradict your social views. It may interfere with some of your social life. But if you listen to these things, as if from the mouth of the Lord himself, with patience and faith, the promise is that "the gates of hell shall not prevail against you; yea, and the Lord God will disperse the powers of darkness from before you, and cause the heavens to shake for your good, and his name's glory" (D&C 21:6).(*The Teachings of Harold B. Lee*, ed. Clyde J. Williams [Salt Lake City: Bookcraft, 1996], 525–526)

ILLUSTRATIONS FOR OUR TIME

Living by the Word.

1. *The Word from Living Prophets.* I know that the only way back to the presence of the Father is by obeying His law and keeping His commandments; these are set forth by living prophets. As members of the Church, we are duty bound to sustain and follow the living prophets, and will be cast off if we do not (see 3 Ne. 28:34–35). I shall not forget 1 April 1989, when the prophet Ezra Taft Benson gave his landmark discourse on pride. Under the power of his words I sought forgiveness and still do. I took the time to compile 46 pages on pride and the steps one could take to overcome it with love and humility. As a family impacted by the prophet's warning, we studied this for two months in family home evening. I feel the same sort of love and devotion for our prophet today, President Gordon B. Hinckley.

2. *The Word from the Scriptures.* Every night my sweetheart and I search the scriptures together. When our children were at home, we had daily scripture time in the morning, and I could see how each day, little by little, the word would make a difference in their lives. Surely Alma was correct when he decided to preach the word of God because it had the greatest power to change lives (see Alma 31:5).

3. *The Word from the Holy Spirit.* Perhaps you can remember a recent occasion when the Spirit taught you (see D&C 36:2), gave you direction (see 1 Ne. 4:6), showed you the things to do (see 2 Ne. 32:5), brought something comforting to your remembrance (see John 14:26), or otherwise blessed your life. (Pinegar)

Guidance Systems. On 1 September 1983, just before dawn, a Boeing 747 bound for Seoul—Flight KE007 of the Korean Air Lines—was shot down over Sakhalin Island, northeast of Japan, by an SU-15 fighter of the Soviet Air Force, resulting in the loss of 269 passengers and crew, including a United States congressman. This tragedy set off an international firestorm of protest and launched a concerted inquiry into why an unarmed commercial airliner was brought down and why it was some 365 miles off track from the designated international air route at the time, flying over Soviet-controlled territory.

Such planes are equipped with highly sophisticated inertial navigation systems (INS), possessing three layers of redundancy to assure fail-safe operation. These systems ordinarily function independently to keep the plane on course with astonishing accuracy in reference to the stars and the earth itself. A simultaneous triple failure was unprecedented. The plane was also equipped with a so-called VOR guidance system that can follow beams emitted by radio beacons at way-stations. What's more, the plane also had a magnetic compass that could be used to steer the plane in relationship to the earth's magnetic field. With so many guidance systems on board, how could the plane have gone so far astray?

A widely accepted theory ultimately emerged that attributed the crash to technical errors as follows: Because the VOR at Anchorage, Alaska, the point of departure, was not operating that night, the pilots must have initially coupled the autopilot to the onboard magnetic compass with a heading, as it turns out, leading directly to the spot where the plane was later intercepted by the Soviet fighter jet. There were, as it turns out, no corrective VOR radio beacons in the area of the crash for the plane to pick up. The pilot had apparently neglected to follow the prescribed policy of shifting the autopilot from the magnetic compass to the fail-safe inertial guidance system—a step that would surely have enabled them to remain on course. As a result, the plane went off course directly to its doom.

By analogy, there are many guidance systems available to help individuals navigate the challenging routes of mortality. Some—such as the Spirit of Christ (Moro. 7:16), the scriptures, counsel from the Lord's prophets, and the promptings of the Holy Ghost—are God-centered and infallible. Others—such as aspiring to materialistic supremacy, yielding to sensual gratification, and selfish egotism—are world-centered and totally unreliable. To do anything less than "put your trust in that Spirit which leadeth to do good" (D&C 11:12) is to risk going off course to destruction.

If we will fix our attention on the Lord's guidance system—the spiritual lodestar of prophetic counsel and personal inspiration—we will not go astray. The Liahona that the Lord prepared for Lehi and his family in the wilderness is the perfect metaphor for this kind of INS, or "inspired navigation system." Such a system operates on the basis of faith and diligence, pointing toward life-sustaining resources and showing the way toward our ultimate destination. Alma saw in this a type of the Savior Himself: "For behold, it is as easy to give heed to the word of Christ, which will point to you a straight course to eternal bliss, as it was for our fathers to give heed to this compass, which would point unto them a straight course to the promised land" (Alma 37:44). (Allen)

Likening the Scriptures to Our Lives

1 Nephi 16:28—The Liahona worked according to their faith and diligence and the heed they gave unto the direction of the Lord.

Application—Our compasses for life—the living prophets (see D&C 21:4–5), the holy scriptures (see 2 Ne. 32:3), the Holy Spirit (see 2 Ne. 32:5), and the power of prayer (see James 1:5–6)—can and will direct us as we exercise our faith and diligence and give heed to the things we have been given (see Alma 37:37–47).

2. OBEDIENCE AS THE KEY TO PERFECTION

THEME. Obedience, based on faith, is the key to perfection. Nephi did whatsoever the Lord commanded him to do because he exercised his faith in all diligence. We can emulate his example.

> *"And it came to pass that the Lord spake unto me, saying: Thou shalt construct a ship, after the manner which I shall show thee, that I may carry thy people across these waters"*
> *(1 Ne. 17:8).*

MOMENT OF TRUTH. The voice of the Lord told Nephi to get into the mountain, where Nephi called upon the Lord. The Lord commanded Nephi to build a ship according to the directions that would be given him (see 1 Ne. 17). Laman and Lemuel doubted Nephi's ability and started to murmur. They complained about leaving Jerusalem, being unable to enjoy their wealth, and experiencing difficulties over the years in traveling. They doubted. They lacked faith. Throughout the Book of Mormon the prophets, and in this case Nephi, would attempt to show the doubting or wayward the goodness and mercy of God.

Nephi reminded his brothers about the following: The Lord had led the Israelites out of Egypt to safety, and the Egyptians had been drowned in the Red Sea; manna was provided for their food, water was given to them out of a rock, and the Lord led them day and night. The Israelites still hardened their hearts and reviled against Moses. The Israelites eventually became very wicked, and the Lord said that Jerusalem would be destroyed—this is when Lehi was commanded to leave Jerusalem. The Lord favors the righteous but will destroy the wicked. Nephi exhorted Laman and Lemuel in regard to their iniquity and failing to remember the Lord, but their hearts "were past feeling" (1 Ne. 17:45). Nephi had great anguish for his brothers and was fearful that they might be cast off forever. Laman and Lemuel became very angry and attempted to seize Nephi, that they might throw him into the ocean. Nephi, being full of the Spirit, commanded them not to touch him. He bore a fervent testimony of his faith and willingness to do all things the Lord commanded him to do. Nephi confounded Laman and Lemuel and then, in response to the Lord's command, he shocked them as a testimony that the Lord surely is their God. They recognized the power of the Lord, and Nephi encouraged them to worship the Lord and to honor their parents.

MODERN PROPHETS SPEAK

Spencer W. Kimball:

> Solitude is rich and profitable. When we pray alone with God, we shed all sham and pretense, all hypocrisy and arrogance. The Savior found his mountains and slipped away to pray. Paul, the great apostle, could not seem to get into the spirit of his new calling until he had found cleansing solitude down in Arabia. He went into solitude a worldly man and came out cleansed, prepared, regenerated. He was born of water in a Damascus river and of the spirit in an Arabian solitude. Enos found his solitary place in the forest. Moriancumer went to the mountain top to ask the Lord to touch the stones to light his people's way. And Nephi learned to build a ship through communication with his Lord on a mountain far from human ears. Joseph Smith found his solitude in the grove with only birds and trees and God to listen to his prayer. In solitude we, too, may pray with greater depth and fervor. (*Faith Precedes the Miracle* [Salt Lake City: Deseret Book, 1972], 209)

ILLUSTRATIONS FOR OUR TIME

"I Feel More Like a Subject for the Dissecting Room." Whatever the Lord asks us to do we *can* do, if we exercise our faith and choose to be obedient even as the Apostle Wilford Woodruff in the following account:

> The whole of that mission to England, from the beginning to the end, placed the apostles in such a position that they had to walk by faith from first to last. . . . As soon as we prepared ourselves to go on our mission to England . . . the devil undertook to kill us. I have myself been in Tennessee and Kentucky for two or three years, where, in the fall, there were not

enough well persons to take care of the sick during the ague months, and yet I never had the ague in my life until called to go upon that mission to England. There was not one solitary soul in the Quorum of the Twelve but what the devil undertook to destroy; and, as we said yesterday, when Brother Taylor and myself, the two first of the quorum ready for the trip, were on hand to start, I was shaking with the ague. And I had it every other day. And on my well day, when I did not have it, my wife had it. I got up and laid my hands upon her and blessed her, and blessed my child, having only one at the time, and I started across the river. And that man who sits behind me today, Brigham Young the President of the Church and kingdom of God upon the earth, paddled me across the Missouri river in a canoe, and that is the way I landed in Nauvoo. I lay down on a side of sole leather by the post office, and I did not know where to go. . . . I was not able to stand on my feet, and I lay down there. By and by the Prophet came along, and, said he: "Brother Woodruff, you are going on a mission?"

"Yes," I said, "but I feel more like a subject for the dissecting room than for a mission."

He reproved me for what I said and told me to get up and go. Brother Taylor, the only member of the Quorum of the Twelve who was well, and I traveled together, and on the way he fell to the ground. . . . Brother Taylor fell twice in that way, taken with the bilous fever, and no man in that quorum could boast that he went on that mission without feeling the hand of the destroyer, for it was laid upon us all. I had the shaking ague and lay on my back in a wagon, and was rolled over stumps and stones until it seemed as if my life would be shaken out of me. I left Brother Taylor behind, by his advice, for said he, "We are both sick, and if you stay you can't do anything here." . . . I got to Buffalo, New York.

From there I traveled along to Farmington, Connecticut, my native place, and I stayed there fifteen days at my father's house, coughing and shaking every day. My father never expected that I should leave my bed, and my stepmother did not expect that I should ever get better. A message came from an uncle of mine, who had just died, and his last words were: "I want you to send for friend Wilford. I want him to come and preach my funeral sermon."

My father said: "You can't go and preach that sermon, for you can't sit up in your bed."

Said I: "Never mind, get . . . your horse and wagon." And he did so, and I got into it, and rode over that morning in a chilly wind. And the hour that my ague was coming on I got before a big blazing fire and preached the funeral sermon of my friend. And the ague left me from that day, and I went back and went on my way rejoicing.

In process of time Brother Taylor came along, and he and I crossed the ocean together and arrived in England. And here I want to make a little statement of my experience in those days concerning circumstances that took place with me. When Brother Brigham left home he told me that all his family had was one barrel of rotten flour. Two hundred cents would have bought every pound of provision I left with my family when I left home. But we left our wives, for we had the commandment of God upon us; and we were either going to obey it, or die trying. That was the spirit of the elders of Israel; and I blessed my wife and child and left them in the hands of God, and to the tender mercies of our noble bishops. . . . We traveled without purse and scrip, and we preached without money and without price. Why? Because the God of heaven had called upon us to go forth and warn the world (Wilford Woodruff in Leon R. Hartshorn, comp., *Classic Stories from the Lives of Our Prophets* [Salt Lake City: Deseret Book, 1971], 118–120).

Likening the Scriptures to Our Lives

1 Nephi 17:45—Even though Laman and Lemuel had seen angels and heard his voice, the problem was that their hearts were past feeling.

Application—Let us willingly offer our hearts (broken hearts and contrite spirits) to the Lord. It is our sacrifice. When our hearts are hardened and past feelings, we are not only forgetful and apathetic toward the things of God, but we are no longer able to feel His Spirit (see D&C 8:2), which causes one to yield to His enticing.

3. COURAGE AS THE BASIS FOR TRANSCENDING ADVERSITY

THEME. In the portrait of Nephi we see tremendous courage in the face of relentless adversity. Though persecuted and beaten by his brothers, he praised the Lord and was diligent in exercising his faith prayerfully during the most trying circumstances.

> *"And I, Nephi, did go into the mount oft, and I did pray oft unto the Lord; wherefore the Lord showed unto me great things." (1 Ne. 18:3)*

> *"And it came to pass that Laman and Lemuel did take me and bind me with cords, and they did treat me with much harshness; nevertheless, the Lord did suffer it that he might show forth his power, unto the fulfilling of his word which he had spoken concerning the wicked. Nevertheless, I did look unto my God, and I did praise him all the day long; and I did not murmur against the Lord because of mine afflictions." (1 Ne. 18:11,16)*

MOMENT OF TRUTH. When Nephi had finished building the ship according to the instructions of the Lord, the word of the Lord came to Lehi that it was time to embark toward the promised land. Laman and Lemuel—having lapsed, like the sons of Ishmael and their wives, into an attitude of rudeness, light-mindedness, and overweening pride—bound and tormented Nephi for four days. "Nevertheless, the Lord did suffer it that he might show forth his power, unto the fulfilling of his word which he had spoken concerning the wicked" (1 Ne. 18:11). And power He did show. As the Liahona ceased to operate in the environment of rebellion and wickedness, a violent tempest arose, threatening to engulf the little party in a watery death. It was only the awful threat of destruction—more so than the entreaties of the faithful and humble in the family circle—that induced the older brothers to desist. Nephi was released. Based on his faithfulness, the compass was reactivated, and the emigrants from old Jerusalem soon reached the land of promise.

MODERN PROPHETS SPEAK

Gene R. Cook:

> Remember that the commandment is not just to have faith in a general sense. We are to have faith in a person, faith in Jesus Christ. When we seek to understand that better, we'll understand why we are to end all of our prayers "in the name of Jesus Christ." When we pray in that manner, we're asking for the grace of the Lord Jesus Christ to intervene on our behalf. If we can keep our faith centered in him it will help us to have much more power than if we pray without such faith. . . .
>
> It is faith in Christ that will deliver us from our own bonds; it is increasing our faith in Christ that will give us added power in prayer (*Receiving Answers to Our Prayers* [Salt Lake City: Deseret Book, 1996], 17–18).

ILLUSTRATIONS FOR OUR TIME

Responding to Adversity. Adversities are part of life. The righteous are not spared from them, for this life is a testing time, and the test is how we respond to adversity. Nephi did not murmur in his affliction—neither should we. He praised God—so should we. The Lord's most faithful servants exhibit a proper attitude in never charging God foolishly (see Job 1:22). (Pinegar)

"Short though Bitter Was Their Pain, Everlasting Is Their Joy." The Latter-day Saints have experienced few periods of adversity to surpass the torment and cruelty heaped upon their heads at the hands of the Missouri mobs during the formative years of the restored Church. The challenge for the faithful and devout in such circumstances has ever been to place adversity in an eternal context and remember the Lord's promise: "Blessed are they which are persecuted for righteousness' sake: for theirs is the kingdom of the heaven" (Matt. 5:10). As part of his journal entry for Monday, 22 April 1839, the Prophet Joseph Smith composes his moving and majestic account summarizing and memorializing the Saints' cruel persecution at the hands of the Missouri mobs, giving thanks for the Lord's steadying hand, and calling for civil redress: "The conduct of the Saints, under their accumulated wrongs and sufferings, has been praiseworthy; their courage in defending their brethren from the ravages of the mobs; their attachment to the cause of truth, under circumstances the most trying and distressing which humanity can possibly endure; their love to each other; their readiness to afford assistance to me and my brethren who were confined to a dungeon; their sacrifice in leaving Missouri, and assisting the poor widows and orphans, and securing them houses in a more hospitable land; all conspire to raise them in the estimation of all good and virtuous men, and has secured them the favor and approbation of Jehovah, and a name as imperishable as eternity . . . Marvel not, then, if you are persecuted. . . . Afflictions, persecutions, imprisonments, and death, we must expect, according to the scriptures. . . ." (*HC,* 3:329–331). As if to add a capstone to the monument of the Saints' endurance, the Prophet also quotes this verse as part of his narrative: "Short though bitter was their pain, everlasting is their joy" (330). (Allen)

Likening the Scriptures to Our Lives

1 Nephi 18:16—Nephi, with all his persecution and affliction from his brothers, never would murmur against the Lord, but rather praised Him.

Application—We should seek to show faith in the Lord and courage in our afflictions, recognizing that the hand of the Lord will be shown if we do all we can (see D&C 123:17). True faith in the Lord informs our souls that we are in His hands and He will do whatever is necessary to bring about His purposes, which will be for our good.

4. THE SCRIPTURES AS THE KEY TO WISDOM

THEME. The purpose of the scriptures is to reveal the word of God, teach the truth, and to testify of true principles so that people might be persuaded to believe in Christ. The Book of Mormon gives priceless insight into the lives of prophets of God, such as Nephi, who preserved for posterity the truths of salvation revealed to them through the Spirit.

> *"And after I had made these plates by way of commandment, I, Nephi, received a commandment that the ministry and the prophecies, the more plain and precious parts of them, should be written upon these plates; and that the things which were written should be kept for the instruction of my people, who should possess the land, and also for other wise purposes, which purposes are known unto the Lord." (1 Ne. 19:3)*

> *"And I did read many things unto them which were written in the books of Moses; but that I might more fully persuade them to believe in the Lord their Redeemer I did read unto them that which was written by the prophet Isaiah; for I did liken all scriptures unto us, that it might be for our profit and learning." (1 Ne. 19:23)*

MOMENT OF TRUTH. The new land was abundant in ore; therefore, the Lord commanded Nephi to prepare metal plates and make an additional record of his father's time for a wise purpose (see 1 Ne. 19:1–3). He did not know the reason. He simply knew that the Lord had a reason. So he recorded on the smaller plates that which he thought to be "sacred" (v. 6), things that would have a tendency to turn the hearts of the people toward the Savior: "And I, Nephi, have written these things unto my people, that perhaps I might persuade them that they would remember the Lord their Redeemer. Wherefore, I speak unto all the house of Israel, if it so be that they should obtain these things" (v. 18–19). Not only did Nephi record precious truths, he continually read to his brethren from the plates of brass, giving a record of the earlier prophets and dealings with divine matters: "Wherefore I spake unto them, saying: Hear ye the words of the prophet, ye who are a remnant of the house of Israel, a branch who have been broken off; hear ye the words of the prophet, which were written unto all the house of Israel, and liken them unto yourselves, that ye may have hope as well as your brethren from whom ye have been broken off; for after this manner has the prophet written" (v. 24).

MODERN PROPHETS SPEAK

Russell M. Nelson:

> Nephi said, "I did liken all scriptures unto us, that it might be for our profit and learning" (1 Nephi 19:23). He was advising us to weave the fiber of scriptural wisdom into the fabric of our own being. (*The Power within Us* [Salt Lake City: Deseret Book, 1988], 29)

ILLUSTRATIONS FOR OUR TIME

Daniel Ludlow:

> Nephi was like all of the great prophets when commanded to keep the records—they obeyed without question, because they trusted in the Lord and valued the principle and law of obedience (see D&C 130:19–21). The small plates of Nephi are of great value to us, as confirmed by the following statement: "These plates were started by Nephi about 570 B.C. and for approximately 440 years thereafter served as the religious record of the Nephite nation (2 Ne. 5:29–32; 1 Ne. 6:3, 5; 9:4; 1 Ne. 19:319:2–3, 5–6; Jacob 1:4.) Many of the religious writings from the brass plates of Laban were also copied onto these plates (2 Nephi 4:15; 24). Joseph Smith's translation of these plates occupies the first 133 pages of our present Book of Mormon. Thus, as Enos prophesied, the teachings of these records have been preserved (Enos, verse 16–17). (*A Companion to Your Study of the Book of Mormon* [Salt Lake City: Deseret Book, 1976], 57)

Likening the Scriptures to Our Lives

1 Nephi 19:3—Nephi, having now been commanded to make these small plates, was told to write the ministry, prophecies, and the plain and precious parts upon these plates for a wise purpose known only to the Lord.

Application—We should learn to obey without knowing why, because we love and have faith in God (see Moses 5:5–6). We now know that because of the loss of the 116 pages of the Book of Mormon manuscript, the small plates provided that necessary history.

5. THE UNBREAKABLE COVENANT

THEME. Israel is the Lord's people. He will not forget them, for He has them graven in the palms of His hands. In the last days, Israel will be scattered but will be nourished by the Gentiles and gathered once again because of their righteousness.

> *"For can a woman forget her sucking child, that she should not have compassion on the son of her womb? Yea, they may forget, yet will I not forget thee, O house of Israel. Behold, I have graven thee upon the palms of my hands; thy walls are continually before me." (1 Ne. 21:15–16)*

> *"Wherefore, the Lord God will proceed to make bare his arm in the eyes of all the nations, in bringing about his covenants and his gospel unto those who are of the house of Israel. Wherefore, he will bring them again out of captivity, and they shall be gathered together to the lands of their inheritance; and they shall be brought out of obscurity and out of darkness; and they shall know that the Lord is their Savior and their Redeemer, the Mighty One of Israel." (1 Ne. 22:11–12)*

> *"And he gathereth his children from the four quarters of the earth; and he numbereth his sheep, and they know him; and there shall be one fold and one shepherd; and he shall feed his sheep, and in him they shall find pasture. And because of the righteousness of his people, Satan has no power; wherefore, he cannot be loosed for the space of many years; for he hath no power over the hearts of the people, for they dwell in righteousness, and the Holy One of Israel reigneth." (1 Ne. 22:25–26)*

MOMENT OF TRUTH. Nephi's abiding commitment and desire was to teach his contemporaries and all future generations the principles of covenant righteousness so that they could enjoy the priceless blessings of the gospel of Jesus Christ. Thus he turned to the writings of Isaiah to bring greatest weight to his fervent testimony, beginning with what we know as Isaiah 48 and 49. These chapters are soaring pronouncements concerning the Lord's chosen people of Israel and how they would be liberated by the Messiah, who would gather them in once more from their scattered and chastened state with the help of the Gentile nations, "for the Lord hath comforted his people, and will have mercy upon his afflicted" (1 Ne. 21:13). Hope and loving kindness are the themes of Nephi's message to the repentant, and he presents to his brothers a masterful explanation of Isaiah's solemn witness (see 1 Ne. 22).

MODERN PROPHETS SPEAK

Jeffrey R. Holland:

> This poetic passage provides yet another reminder of Christ's saving role, that of protective, redeeming parent to Zion's children. He comforts his people and shows mercy when they are afflicted, as any loving father or mother would toward a child, but, as Nephi here reminds us through Isaiah, much more than any mortal father and mother could do. Although a mother may forget her sucking child (as unlikely as any parent might think that could be), Christ will not forget the children he has redeemed or the covenant he has made with them for salvation in Zion. The painful reminders of that watch care and covenant are the marks of the Roman nails graven upon the palms of his hands, a sign to his disciples in the Old World, his Nephite congregation in the New World, and to us in latter-day Zion that he is the Savior of the world and was wounded in the house of his friends. (*Christ and the New Covenant: The Messianic Message of the Book of Mormon* [Salt Lake City: Deseret Book, 1997], 84)

ILLUSTRATIONS FOR OUR TIME

The Gathering of Israel. Elder Bruce C. Hafen has given for us a great example of the caring Savior in comparison with the relationship of a loving mother and her child:

> Eve's experience as a mother opens our understanding of the Atonement's developmental nature. She found that the Lord heals our separation to make us "at one" with him, not by returning us magically to Eden but by leading us through a process of learning and growing day by day toward spiritual maturity. The Lord also draws on our understanding of a woman's perspective when he teaches us that he feels toward us the way a mother feels for her child: "For can a woman forget her sucking child, that she should not have compassion on the son of her womb?" Just as a mother could never forget her child, he said, "Yet will I not forget thee." And just as a mother's body may be permanently marked with the signs of pregnancy and childbirth, he said, "I have graven thee upon the palms of my hands." (1 Nephi 21:15–16.) For both a mother and the Savior, those marks memorialize a wrenching sacrifice, the sacrifice of begetting life—for her, physical birth; for him, spiritual rebirth. (*Women in the*

Covenant of Grace: Talks Selected from the 1993 Women's Conference, ed. Dawn Hall Anderson and Susette Fletcher Green [Salt Lake City: Deseret Book, 1994], 28–29) (Pinegar)

Isaiah and the Arches of Time. Many come upon the frequent passages from Isaiah in the Book of Mormon as if encountering a daunting cliff. These passages are clearly there for a divine purpose—not to serve as perplexing obstacles, but rather to be the means of ascending to a loftier perspective of gospel insight. Many of us remember being glued to our television screens on 20 July 1969, watching spellbound as Neil Armstrong stepped from the *Eagle* lunar module and onto the surface of the moon, uttering the now historic phrase: "That's one small step for man, one giant leap for mankind." The spectacular color imagery of the earth's orb taken on that *Apollo 11* mission, and on other space flights, allowed earthlings their first recorded glimpses of their magnificent blue-green, cloud-shrouded home from a heavenly perspective. But these views of earth were not the first to be discerned by mortals. As Moses was being instructed of the Lord millennia before, he "cast his eyes and beheld the earth, yea, even all of it; and there was not a particle of it which he did not behold, discerning it by the spirit of God" (Moses 1:27). Similarly, with a spiritual eye, Moroni saw his future readership, one and all: "Behold, I speak unto you as if ye were present, and yet ye are not. But behold, Jesus Christ hath shown you unto me, and I know your doing" (Morm. 8:35). It is reasonable to conclude that all of the Lord's prophets are blessed with this kind of visionary gift that enables them to lift us from the confines of our mortal landscape "with wings as eagles" (Isa. 40:31) and teach us saving truths from the Lord's heights.

Once you have seen the extraordinary images of the earth as perceived from the moon, you will never again ponder the earth in the same way. Once you have read Isaiah with the guidance of the Spirit, you will never again ponder God's plan of salvation and Israel's covenant calling in the same way, for you will have been lifted to a higher level of understanding by one of the greatest of God's anointed. The Savior commanded the Nephites to "search these things diligently, for great are the words of Isaiah" (3 Ne. 23:1). (Allen)

Likening the Scriptures to Our Lives

1 Nephi 21:15–16—The Lord, through His atoning sacrifice, has paid the price if we but repent. The marks of the nails are the reminders of the terrible price He paid for our sins.

Application—We must never forget the suffering in Gethsemane and the cruel cross at Calvary. If we remember, we will be drawn unto our Savior and lifted up at the last day (see 3 Ne. 27: 13–14).

1 Nephi 22:8—Israel, having been scattered, will be nourished in the gospel by the mighty nation among the Gentiles.

Application—This is the marvelous work that we are about—to help all mankind to come unto Christ by preaching His gospel and performing the saving ordinances of the gospel in this, the kingdom of God upon the earth. This is the mission of The Church of Jesus Christ of Latter-day Saints.

SUMMARY

The principles of faith, obedience, courage, and following the counsel of the prophets are continually reiterated in the Book of Mormon as basic tenets of the Lord's covenant with His chosen people and the blessings associated with it. Nephi chose to conclude his first book by expounding in summary fashion on the first law of heaven, even faith, with its companion, obedience, in these words: "Wherefore, my brethren, I would that ye should consider that the things which have been written upon the plates of brass are true; and they testify that a man must be obedient to the commandments of God. Wherefore, ye need not suppose that I and my father are the only ones that have testified, and also taught them. Wherefore, if ye shall be obedient to the commandments, and endure to the end, ye shall be saved at the last day. And thus it is. Amen" (1 Ne. 22:30–31).

CHAPTER SIX

"FREE *to* CHOOSE
LIBERTY AND ETERNAL LIFE"

2 NEPHI 2:1–2

*"'Look to the great Mediator,' Lehi said, 'and hearken unto his great commandments;
and be faithful unto his words, and choose eternal life, according to the will of his
Holy Spirit' (2 Ne. 2:28). Our Lord's mission was to bring to pass
'the great mediation of all men,' meaning that in his capacity as Mediator he had
power to intervene between God and man and effect a reconciliation.
This mediation or reconciliation was affected through his atoning sacrifice, a sacrifice
by means of which sinful men—by the proper use of agency—can wash away their
guilt and place themselves in harmony with God. Men 'are free to choose liberty and
eternal life, through the great mediation of all men, or to choose captivity and death,
according to the captivity and power of the devil' (2 Ne. 2:27).
Those choosing obedience receive the Holy Ghost, are reconciled to God in this world,
and continue in his presence in the world to come"*
—BRUCE R. MCCONKIE, *DOCTRINAL NEW TESTAMENT COMMENTARY*, 3 VOLS. (SALT
LAKE CITY: BOOKCRAFT, 1965–1973), 3:79.

THEMES *for* LIVING

A Legacy of Love and Truth: The Greatest Parental Gift
The Gift of the Atonement
Opposition in All Things
Free to Choose: The Doctrine of Agency

INTRODUCTION

Lehi, as a loving parent, taught his sons the plan of redemption—the goodness of God and His grace toward His children—in the hope that they might choose liberty and eternal life. We, as loving parents, should teach our children likewise. We must similarly testify that redemption comes through the Atonement of our Savior Jesus Christ, and we must seek righteousness in order to partake of the Atonement. Opposition is part of the plan and is necessary for our growth. Without trials and tribulation we cannot become perfected. As we come to recognize the law of opposition in all things we see that our choices—the use of our agency—determine our course and our blessings here on earth as well as in the eternities to come.

1. A LEGACY OF LOVE AND TRUTH: THE GREATEST PARENTAL GIFT

THEME. The greatest legacy that parents can leave for their children is to teach them the truths of salvation in clear and loving ways and to model these truths in the form of a righteous and exemplary lifestyle. What Lehi did for his children is a pattern that all of us can follow.

> *"Wherefore, my sons, I would that ye would remember; yea, I would that ye would hearken unto my words." (2 Ne. 1:12)*

MOMENT OF TRUTH. Lehi has come to the end of a long and productive life. He gathers his children and their families around him to give parting counsel (see 2 Ne. 1 and 2). Just as Jacob of old did with his sons, Lehi offers up patriarchal exhortations to his family circle. He pleads with Laman and Lemuel to remember the goodness of God, repent and keep the commandments, put on the armor of righteousness, and rebel no more against their brother Nephi. He reminds them pointedly that only righteous behavior will preserve liberty in the land for those who occupy it: "There shall be none to molest them, nor to take away the land of their inheritance; and they shall dwell safely forever" (2 Ne. 1:9). He blesses his other sons to follow the example of Nephi and enjoy the fruits of righteous living.

MODERN PROPHETS SPEAK

Joseph F. Smith:

> And if parents fail to do this and the children go astray and turn from the truth, then the Lord has said the sin shall be upon the heads of the parents. The loss of the children will be charged to the parents and they will be responsible for their apostasy

and darkness. I came to the conclusion, after reflection upon this subject, . . . I do not believe that it would be possible for me to be admitted into exaltation and glory in the Kingdom of God, if through my neglect of duty my children should become the children of darkness in this regard. . . . My children must not and will not turn away with my consent. I will plead with my children; I will endeavor with all the power I possess to have them as true and faithful to this gospel as it is possible for me to be; because, without all of them in the Kingdom of God I would feel that my household was not perfect (*Ye Are the Light of the World: Selected Sermons and Writings of Harold B. Lee* [Salt Lake City: Deseret Book, 1974], 274).

ILLUSTRATIONS FOR OUR TIME

"Just be Good . . . Just be Good." A wayward child is not the sign of a failing parent. A failing parent is one who has not taught his or her children. We are not perfect, and the Lord is surely aware of that, but we are required to try with all our heart, might, mind, and strength to teach our children the gospel of Jesus Christ (see D&C 68:25–28). As parents we must never give in, never give out, and never give up.

My father passed away on Mother's Day in 1947. I was the youngest in our family, a twelve-year-old deacon. I tried to be a good boy. I remember that when I would ask my angel mother what she wanted for her birthday, Mother's Day, and Christmas, the answer was always the same, "Oh, Ed, I have everything one would need. I don't need anything." I would implore her, "Mom, I want to give you a present." Her answer for many years was the same, "Ed, just be good . . . just be good." All she ever wanted for her children was for them to be good. Nothing else really mattered to her. I understand now that our joy and rejoicing is in our family, even as is our Heavenly Father's joy (see Moses 1:39).

Having said all this, there are times when, after we have done all, our children may choose for a time to turn away from the truth. What do we do? We pray unceasingly (see Mosiah 27:14), plead, and exhort when moved upon by the Spirit (see D&C 100:5–6; 121:41–44), or we may seek help from others. We certainly exercise patience in longsuffering. The goodness of God will then give us a sense of peace that we have done all in our power. Heavenly Father has done all in perfectness and infinite wisdom, yet some of His children chose to disobey and follow Lucifer. We simply must "cheerfully do all things that lie in our power; and then may we stand still, with the utmost assurance, to see the salvation of God, and for his arm to be revealed" (D&C 123:17). (Pinegar)

A Father's Love. What special message would you have for your children and other family members if you knew or suspected that your time was drawing nigh? There are in the scriptures detailed accounts of several occasions where prophets have offered farewell advice to their children: the blessings that Jacob (Israel) gave to his sons (Gen. 49), the blessings of Lehi for his sons and their families (2 Ne. 1–4); and the counsel of Alma for his sons Helaman, Shiblon, and Corianton (Alma 36–42). Under similar circumstances, during the stressful Liberty Jail episode, the Prophet Joseph Smith provided his family with tender communications.

After the Prophet Joseph had been confined to the squalor of Liberty Jail in Missouri at the hands of unrighteous lawmen for nearly four months, he penned a letter dated 21 March 1839 to Emma, with the salutation "Affectionate Wife."

The Prophet shows tender concern—even asking about the family dog—within the letter: "I want to be with you very much but the powers of mobocracy are too many for me at present. . . . My dear Emma, I very well know your toils and sympathize with you. If God will spare my life once more to have the privilege of taking care of you, I will ease your care and endeavor to comfort your heart. I want you to take the best care of the family you can, which I believe you will do all you can. I was sorry to learn that Frederick was sick but I trust he is well again and that you are all well. I want you to try to gain time and write to me a long letter and tell me all you can and even if Old Major is alive yet and what those little prattlers say that cling around your neck. Do you tell them I am in prison that their lives might be saved?" (*The Personal Writings of Joseph Smith,* rev. ed., comp. Dean C. Jessee [Salt Lake City: Deseret Book, 2002], 449–49; text modernized).

A few days later, on 4 April 1839, he sent another letter to Emma with similar tender expressions: "Dear Emma, I think of you and the children continually. If I could tell you my tale, I think you would say it was altogether enough for once, to gratify the malice of hell that I have suffered. I want to see little Frederick, Joseph, Julia, and Alexander, Joanna, and Old Major. And as to yourself, if you want to know how much I want to see you, examine your feelings, how much you want to see me, and judge for yourself. I would gladly walk from here to you barefoot, and bareheaded, and half naked, to see you and think it great pleasure, and never count it toil, but do not think I am babyish, for I do not feel so. I bear with fortitude all my oppression, so do those that are with me. Not one of us have flinched yet. I want you should not let those little fellows forget me. Tell them Father loves them with a perfect love, and he is doing all he can to get away from the mob to come to them. Do teach them all you can, that they may have good minds. Be tender and kind to them. Don't be fractious to them, but listen to their wants. Tell them Father says they must be good children and mind their mother. My dear Emma, there is great responsibility resting upon you, in preserving yourself in honor, and sobriety, before them, and teaching them right things, to form their young and tender minds, that they begin in right paths, and not get contaminated when young, by seeing ungodly examples" (Ibid., 464).

Thus we see the quality and depth of the Prophet Joseph's love for his wife and children and the manner in which he offered guidance and counsel at a time of great uncertainty. As it turned out, he was able to escape his confinement several days later and spend a few more years with Emma and his family before sealing his testimony with his martyrdom. The Prophet's example is a sobering lesson to all of us to cultivate the warmest relationships with our loved ones every day of our lives, for we are never fully certain but what it might be our last. (Allen)

Likening the Scriptures to Our Lives

2 Nephi 1:20–21—The Lord has promised "as ye shall keep my commandments ye shall prosper in the land" (2 Ne. 1:20). Lehi's soul yearned for joy in his children. He exhorted his sons to be men and be determined in mind and heart that they not be brought down into captivity. He told them: "And I have none other object save it be the everlasting welfare of your souls" (2 Ne. 2:30).

Application—Let us truly understand that there are consequences for our actions in all things. We should help our children realize that our joy is in their righteousness, just as Heavenly Father's joy is in all of His children. We, like Heavenly Father, seek only the happiness of our children. When they fully internalize this transcending truth, they often will listen with a softened heart because they understand our true purpose.

2. THE GIFT OF THE ATONEMENT

THEME. Redemption comes through our Savior, Jesus Christ. Those who believe in Him and who come forth with a broken heart and contrite spirit and repent, enduring to the end, will be saved.

"Wherefore, redemption cometh in and through the Holy Messiah; for he is full of grace and truth." (2 Ne. 2:6)

MOMENT OF TRUTH. As Lehi gathers his family members to his side during his final days of life, he directs a special message to his son Jacob, and, by extension, expressly to all his sons (2 Ne. 2:30), concerning the Atonement. It is instructive that he focuses on this subject as his final discourse and exhortation to his posterity. Clearly the Atonement occupied a central place in his heart, as it should in the hearts of all followers of Christ.

MODERN PROPHETS SPEAK

Jeffrey R. Holland:

> The literal meaning of the word *atonement* is self-evident: at-one-ment, the act of unifying or bringing together what has been separated or estranged. The atonement of Christ was indispensable because of the separating transgression, or fall, of Adam, which brought death into the world. In the words of Moroni, "By Adam came the fall of man. And because of the fall of man came Jesus Christ . . . ; and because of Jesus Christ came the redemption of man. And because of the redemption of man, . . . they are brought back into the presence of the Lord" (Mormon 9:12–13). (*Christ and the New Covenant: The Messianic Message of the Book of Mormon* [Salt Lake City: Deseret Book, 1997], 197–198)

ILLUSTRATIONS FOR OUR TIME

The Gap. In Lehi's discourse to his son Jacob concerning the Atonement, there is a statement of colossal import: "And men are instructed sufficiently that they know good from evil. And the law is given unto men. And by the law no flesh is justified" (2 Ne. 2:5). The implication is inescapable: no mortal can ever live the law of God perfectly. Hence no mortal can ever be justified to return to God's presence on the basis of a perfect record in abiding by the law. Some may be more faithful than others in keeping the commandments, but none can do it perfectly. There will always be a gap in performance that must be bridged.

Sometimes as a teacher I will draw two horizontal lines on the chalkboard, labeling the lower one "mortality" and the upper one "perfection." Then I will ask the students to locate themselves on the continuum stretching from the bottom line to the top. The dots will land at various points in the space defined by the two lines, but never will a dot be placed as high as the top line—perfection. There is always a gap between the highest dot and the top line. "So it appears that none of us can return to the presence of the Lord purely on the basis of being justified by the law, that is, through total obedience to the law. Correct?" My students always agree.

Then we read together the stirring testimony of Lehi concerning the Atonement: "Wherefore, redemption cometh in and through the Holy Messiah; for he is full of grace and truth. Behold, he offereth himself a sacrifice for sin, to answer the ends of the law, unto all those who have a broken heart and a contrite spirit; and unto none else can the ends of the law be answered. Wherefore, how great the importance to make these things known unto the inhabitants of the earth, that they may know that there is no flesh that can dwell in the presence of God, save it be through the merits, and mercy, and grace of the Holy Messiah, who layeth down his life according to the flesh, and taketh it again by the power of the Spirit, that he may bring to pass the resurrection of the dead, being the first that should rise. Wherefore, he is the firstfruits unto God, inasmuch as he shall make intercession for all the children of men; and they that believe in him shall be saved" (2 Ne. 2:6–9).

How magnificent are Lehi's words in defining how to bridge the "gap"—or gulf—through the "merits, and mercy, and grace of the Holy Messiah." How plain and simple is the logic. How persuasive is the doctrine. How beautiful is the message of hope and salvation. How exquisite is the text as a means of defining "grace." As Nephi was to say not many years hence: "For we labor diligently to write, to persuade our children, and also our brethren, to believe in Christ, and to be reconciled to God; for we know that it is by grace that we are saved, after all we can do" (2 Ne. 25:23). We are beneficiaries of the grace of the Savior, who closes the gap for each individual, after all he or she can do through faith, repentance, and righteous compliance with the principles and ordinances of the gospel. Resurrection is a gift to all, just as closing the gap can be for all who are obedient.

Lehi's deepest wish for his posterity is, therefore, "And now, my sons, I would that ye should look to the great Mediator, and hearken unto his great commandments; and be faithful unto his words, and choose eternal life, according to the will of his Holy Spirit; And not choose eternal death, according to the will of the flesh and the evil which is therein" (2 Ne. 2:28–29). Few thoughtful people would not be moved to a greater sense of reverence and commitment by Lehi's masterful presentation on the Atonement. (Allen)

The Greatest Knowledge We Can Have. Understanding the Atonement of Christ and its relationship to our eternal existence is the greatest knowledge we can have in order to return to God our Eternal Father. The Atonement is the center of the gospel of Jesus Christ. We become free through Christ by obedience. Yet it is by the grace of God that we are saved, after all we can do (see 2 Ne. 25:23). This is the knowledge that motivates change and genuine acceptance of Christ. The Book of Mormon was given as another witness and testament that Jesus is the Christ. It bears that witness with power and clarity.

The gift of the Atonement becomes the key to creating a difference in men's and women's lives. When we understand this doctrine—when we appreciate it and apply it—we change. We become converted. Converted people are truly different people, who act differently. Their hearts swell with gratitude. They feel (and are) indebted to the Lord their God for their very lives. (Pinegar)

Likening the Scriptures to Our Lives

2 Nephi 2:6–10—Lehi explains the Atonement and the requirements for us to make it efficacious in our lives.

Application—Let us seek to understand and appreciate the Atonement. If we do, we will be filled with gratitude. Gratitude will draw us to the Lord because of His most generous gift to us. This acts as a catalyst that brings about a change of attitude as well as behavior: we will want to follow our Savior and keep the commandments.

3. OPPOSITION IN ALL THINGS

THEME. We must face opposition in all things in order to grow and progress, for thereby we can exercise our God-given agency and be "free to choose liberty and eternal life, through the great Mediator of all men, or to choose captivity and death, according to the captivity and power of the devil; for he seeketh that all men might be miserable like unto himself" (2 Ne. 2:27).

> *"For it must needs be, that there is an opposition in all things. If not so, my first-born in the wilderness, righteousness could not be brought to pass, neither wickedness, neither*

holiness nor misery, neither good nor bad. Wherefore, all things must needs be a compound in one; wherefore, if it should be one body it must needs remain as dead, having no life neither death, nor corruption nor incorruption, happiness nor misery, neither sense nor insensibility." (2 Ne. 2:11)

MOMENT OF TRUTH. Lehi was no stranger to adversity and life-threatening challenges. He understood firsthand the goodness of God and the evils of Satan—and how these two forces constitute polar opposites that beckon for commitments from mortals placed here to be tested in their allegiance to their Creator. Within Lehi's own family, as within God's vast premortal realm, there were great differences in evidence: humility versus pride, spirituality versus selfishness, obedience versus rebellion. It is no wonder that the aging patriarch, in his parting discourse to his sons, sounded the eternal theme: "For it must needs be, that there is an opposition in all things" (2 Ne. 2:11). He could see clearly that Laman and Lemuel, and all who were with them, barring a change in their lifestyle, would harvest a miserable destiny of darkness and death. Conversely, Nephi and his circle would enjoy untold blessings of the Lord based on their faithfulness and obedience. For Nephi, and all like him, there would be welcome meaning to the maxim uttered by Lehi: "Adam fell that men might be; and men are, that they might have joy" (2 Ne. 2:25).

MODERN PROPHETS SPEAK

Jeffrey R. Holland:

> A related principle Lehi introduced as another backdrop to the eternal drama of the Fall and the Atonement is that of opposition, of contending enticements, a concept closely linked with choice and agency. If choice is to exist and agency is to have any meaning, alternatives must be presented. As Lehi phrased it, "It must needs be, that there is an opposition in all things" (2 Nephi 2:11). His reasoning and his vocabulary are clear and to the point. Righteousness has no meaning without the possibility of wickedness. Holiness would hold no delight unless we realized the pain of misery. Good could have no moral meaning if nothing could be considered bad. Even life—the nature and eternal possibilities of which are the subject of the plan of salvation and Lehi's discourse about it—would have no meaning if we knew nothing of the nature and limitations of death. (*Christ and the New Covenant: The Messianic Message of the Book of Mormon* [Salt Lake City: Deseret Book, 1997], 202)

ILLUSTRATIONS FOR OUR TIME

When Stumbling Blocks Are Stepping Stones. I was in my friend John's office for a little visit. We talked about our families and our joint callings in the Brigham Young University Fourth Stake. I asked how things were going and he gave me an interesting response: "Ed, I have this big problem I'm facing but I'm really excited, because when I achieve my goal I will have grown so much." That day my friend taught me a wonderful lesson: stumbling blocks are not really problems—they are stepping-stones for growth. (Pinegar)

A Staircase of Tribulation. Several years ago it was my privilege to serve in a branch presidency at the Missionary Training Center. As part of this calling I frequently attended the general devotional services along with members of the branch. On one occasion, Elder Richard G. Scott was the scheduled speaker. He invited questions from the audience, which consisted of several thousand aspiring missionaries. One young elder seated not far from me rose to the nearest microphone and asked the Apostle what to do when one came upon walls in life that seemed to act as barriers to progress. I shall never forget Elder Scott's thoughtful response. He said, in effect, that walls, when viewed from the right perspective, are not walls at all, but the vertical part of a step upward. Thus what might at first glance seem to be a barrier can turn out to be an opportunity for advancement. What positive and inspiring counsel! (Allen)

Likening the Scriptures to Our Lives

2 Nephi 2:11—Lehi teaches the doctrine of opposition in all things. This is an eternal verity, the law upon which man is allowed to fulfill his destiny. There must be consequences and blessings in all things.

Application—We must come to understand that there can be no growth or progress without trials, tribulations, affliction, and adversity. This is mortality. When we realize this fact, we stand forewarned and forearmed to better overcome the trials and vicissitudes of life.

4. FREE TO CHOOSE: THE DOCTRINE OF AGENCY

THEME. The gift of agency leaves us free to choose spiritual life or death here upon the earth.

> *"Wherefore, men are free according to the flesh; and all things are given them which are expedient unto man. And they are free to choose liberty and eternal life, through the great Mediator of all men, or to choose captivity and death, according to the captivity and power of the devil; for he seeketh that all men might be miserable like unto himself." (2 Ne. 2:27)*

MOMENT OF TRUTH. Lehi closes his mortal ministry with a plea to his children to use their agency in choosing the right. He was well aware of the pattern of rebellion and self-centered worldliness that Laman and Lemuel were wont to choose. He was also well aware that Nephi had a pleasing propensity to choose that which is righteous and edifying before God. For the aged patriarch, these two opposing lifestyles were the source of deep concern on the one hand, and deep joy and confidence on the other. He lays out with the tender feelings of a parent the choices and consequences, having no other object "save it be the everlasting welfare" of their souls (2 Ne. 2:30).

MODERN PROPHETS SPEAK

Brigham Young:

> All rational beings have an agency of their own; and according to their own choice they will be saved or damned.
>
> The volition of the creature is free; this is a law of their existence and the Lord cannot violate his own law; were he to do that, he would cease to be God. He has placed life and death before his children, and it is for them to choose. If they choose life, they receive the blessing of life; if they choose death, they must abide the penalty. This is a law which has always existed from all eternity, and will continue to exist throughout all the eternities to come. Every intelligent being must have the power of choice, and God brings forth the results of the acts of his creatures to promote his Kingdom and subserve his purposes in the salvation and exaltation of his children. . . . (*Discourses of Brigham Young*, sel. John A. Widtsoe [Salt Lake City: Deseret Book, 1925], 62)

ILLUSTRATIONS FOR OUR TIME

Marion D. Hanks:

> The trail to earthly and eternal happiness always leads back to the individual and the way each uses her agency. The prophet Lehi taught that God's children are "free according to the flesh; and all things are given them which are expedient unto man. And they are free to choose liberty and eternal life [through Christ], or to choose captivity and death" (2 Ne. 2:27). (*LDS Women's Treasury: Insights and Inspiration for Today's Woman* [Salt Lake City: Deseret Book, 1997], 450)

Likening the Scriptures to Our Lives

2 Nephi 2:27—We have been given agency, even moral agency, to act for ourselves as a free gift from our Heavenly Father. We can choose liberty and eternal life or captivity and death. We are free to choose.

Application—Let us truly understand that we are responsible and accountable for every thought we have and every action we do. As sons and daughters of God, we chose the plan of our Heavenly Father as presented by our elder Brother, Jesus Christ. This included the gift of agency. We can cherish this most precious personal freedom to choose for ourselves. We can choose life eternal or captivity and death. It is up to us.

SUMMARY

Lehi left his children a legacy of love and truth—the greatest parental gift of all. His example of righteous living, in the face of overwhelming adversity, was a message of courage and fortitude that he bequeathed to his posterity. He bore a moving and per-suasive testimony that mankind was lost except for the redeeming intercession of Jesus Christ, who brought about the resurrection for all and the hope of salvation for the obedient. The grand design of heaven provided for mortals an environment where opposition in all things was the operant condition of life and the only pathway to joy, happiness, and eternal progress. His final loving exhortation to his children was the same counsel that we should convey to our own families: "Look to the great Mediator, and hearken unto his great commandments: and be faithful unto his words, and choose eternal life, according to the will of his Holy Spirit; And not choose eternal death, according to the will of the flesh and the evil which is therein, which giveth the spirit of the devil power to captivate" (2 Ne. 2:28–29).

CHAPTER SEVEN

"I KNOW *in* WHOM I HAVE TRUSTED"

2 NEPHI 3–5

"When we are meek and 'settled' in our hearts (Luke 21:14), we know that the Lord watches over His church, filled as it is with imperfect leaders and people. To be sure, instructive feedback is needed at all levels, just as it is needed in healthy marriages and families. Information and inspiration are likewise needed at all levels. Having so said, it is the Lord's church, and those who are too eager to steady it and too quick to focus upon a single issue or concern will fail to comprehend the important undergirding function of meekness that includes trust in the Lord."
—NEAL A. MAXWELL, *MEEK AND LOWLY* (SALT LAKE CITY: DESERET BOOK, 1987), 14.

THEMES *for* LIVING

Joseph Smith—the Prophet of the Restoration
Testimony from the Heart—the Psalm of Nephi
Separation: the Ultimate Consequence of Sin

INTRODUCTION

From the very beginning, the Lord in His infinite goodness has provided living prophets to lead His Church and kingdom here upon the earth. In this dispensation, the Lord raised up the Prophet Joseph Smith to restore the gospel. The calling of Joseph was ordained of God from before the foundations of the earth and was heralded long before the time of the Restoration by other prophets, including Joseph in Egypt and Lehi in the promised land. This continuing heritage of covenant leadership was borne by Nephi, who trusted in the Lord and acknowledged his own personal weakness and total dependence upon the Lord. He was supported and strengthened by the Lord—and so are we, as we submit our will to that of the Father and cultivate "a broken heart and a contrite spirit" (2 Ne. 2:7; cf. 2 Ne. 4:32; 3 Ne. 9:20; 12:19; Ether 4:15; D&C 20:37; 59:8; 97:8). When we rebel against the prophets, we fail to trust in the Lord and subject ourselves to the ultimate consequence of sin—separation from God. Laman and Lemuel and their followers rejected truth, causing the separation from Nephi and his followers, which formed two separate nations: the Lamanites, who sought to be a law unto themselves, and the Nephites, who followed the teachings of the prophets.

1. JOSEPH SMITH—
THE PROPHET OF THE RESTORATION

THEME. Joseph Smith, the prophet of the dispensation of the fulness of times, "has done more, save Jesus only, for the salvation of men in this world, than any other man that ever lived in it" (D&C 135:3).

> *"But a seer will I raise up out of the fruit of thy loins; and unto him will I give power to bring forth my word unto the seed of thy loins—and not to the bringing forth my word only, saith the Lord, but to the convincing them of my word, which shall have already gone forth among them." (2 Ne. 3:11; cf. JST, Gen. 50:30)*

MOMENT OF TRUTH. Lehi, the prophet of separation from his unrighteous compatriots in Jerusalem, had a special kinship with Joseph, also a prophet of separation in the days of his father, Jacob, known as Israel. Lehi gives a patriarchal blessing to his youngest son, namesake of the ancient Joseph. As part of this touching blessing, Lehi cites a number of passages from Joseph of Egypt, his direct ancestor, concerning a coming prophet, like unto Moses, who would do a great work, "establishing peace among the fruit of thy loins, and bringing them to the knowledge of their fathers in the latter days, and also to the knowledge of my covenants, saith the Lord" (2 Ne. 3:12). The reference is to Joseph Smith, the great prophet of the Restoration.

MODERN PROPHETS SPEAK

Boyd K. Packer:

> For this is the one true Church, and hence its faithful members are entitled to that guidance; Jesus Christ is at its head, directing its course; Joseph Smith was the great prophet called to lead this final gospel dispensation; and we have a living prophet leading us today. These things I have come to know. Of them I bear witness in the name of Jesus Christ, amen. (*Let Not Your Heart Be Troubled* [Salt Lake City: Bookcraft, 1991], 240)

ILLUSTRATIONS FOR OUR TIME

A Prophet's Testimony of Joseph. Many years ago we lived next door to Ernie Wilkins and his wonderful family. Ernie's wife, Maurine, was the daughter of President Harold B. Lee. President Lee often visited. One day when I was going out to get the mail, I noticed President Lee standing in the front yard of their home. I had met him before but still lacked courage to go over and strike up conversation. That day, however, fear fled and I greeted him. I asked him some questions and then said that I sustained him with all my heart. As I started to leave he said, "Wait, Brother Pinegar. I want to tell you something about the Prophet Joseph." He added, "You mentioned that you sustain me as a prophet today and I am grateful for your faith and prayers. I want you to know how I love and sustain the prophet of the dispensation of the fulness of times . . . the Prophet Joseph. Yes, I am a prophet today, but Joseph—he was the Prophet of the Restoration. I love and revere the Prophet Joseph." I felt the depth of his love for the Prophet Joseph and the sincerity of his heart. I shall never forget the testimony of a prophet of God of the Prophet Joseph Smith. (Pinegar)

Likening the Scriptures to Our Lives

2 Nephi 3:24—There will be one raised up to do mighty wonders and great things in the sight of the Lord.

Application—The Prophet Joseph Smith was indeed this great one who would bring about a restoration to the house of Israel. How we should all thank God for the Prophet Joseph through which the dispensation of the fulness of times was ushered in.

> Joseph Smith, the Prophet and Seer of the Lord, has done more, save Jesus only, for the salvation of men in this world, than any other man that ever lived in it. In the short space of twenty years, he has brought forth the Book of Mormon, which he translated by the gift and power of God, and has been the means of publishing it on two continents; has sent the fulness of the everlasting gospel, which it contained, to the four quarters of the earth; has brought forth the revelations and commandments which compose this book of Doctrine and Covenants, and many other wise documents and instructions for the benefit of the children of men; gathered many thousands of Latter-day Saints, founded a great

city, and left a fame and name that cannot be slain. He lived great, and he died great in
the eyes of God and his people; and like most of the Lord's anointed in ancient times, has
sealed his mission and his work with his own blood; and so has his brother Hyrum. In life
they were not divided, and in death they were not separated! (D&C 135:3)

2. TESTIMONY FROM THE HEART—
THE PSALM OF NEPHI

THEME. It is natural that every follower of Christ should seek in his or her own sincere manner to express love for the Savior in the most humble and yet eloquent terms
possible. The Psalm of Nephi, as one model of this kind of spiritual utterance, gives
hope for eternal life on the basis of always seeking the Lord and trusting in Him.

> *"And when I desire to rejoice, my heart groaneth because of my sins; nevertheless, I know
> in whom I have trusted." (2 Ne. 4:19)*

MOMENT OF TRUTH. Consider what Nephi has gone through: As a young man he
was uprooted with little warning from his native environment to spend eight years in the
desert, enduring adversity of all kinds, including life-threatening torment at the hands of
his elder brothers. Then he completed a perilous sea journey halfway around the world
to a strange new land. His father, the spiritual anchor of the family, has just passed away,
and thus the elder brothers again take up their aggressive assault against him, forcing him
and his immediate circle, upon divine warning, to flee into the wilderness and start anew.
Where does he now center his thoughts? On his love for the scriptures, on his own perceived weaknesses, on being grateful for divine guidance, and on his abiding and unshakable faith in the Lord. His heartfelt expression of love for the Lord—despite all the tribulation he has been called upon to endure—is the pinnacle of spiritual witness.

MODERN PROPHETS SPEAK

Neal A. Maxwell:
> The prophet Nephi, who had progressed and advanced spiritually to a remarkable
> degree, still lamented about "sins which do easily beset me" (2 Nephi 4:18). Obviously,
> Nephi's sins were not major. But just as God cannot look upon sin with the lease degree
> of allowance (D&C 1:31), *as we become more like Him, neither can we.* The best people
> have a heightened awareness of what little of the worst is still in them! Indeed, the divine
> discontent, the justifiable spiritual restlessness that we feel, is a natural follow-on feel-
> ing in the disciple who has taken the Lord's counsel to "make you a new heart and a
> new spirit" (Ezek. 18:31). The "new" in us is bound to notice the "old" that remains.

However, it is vital for us to realize that if we are keeping the commandments and doing our basic duties, we are to that extent succeeding in that thing. Our sincere striving and seeking to keep the commandments counts for more than we know." (*Notwithstanding My Weakness* [Salt Lake City: Deseret Book, 1981] 16–17)

ILLUSTRATIONS FOR OUR TIME

A Psalm for All of Us. Nephi, in his humble and self-effacing way, relates to all of us in our trials here upon the earth.

1. He recognizes the goodness of God . . . and so should we.
2. He laments and has sorrow for sin . . . and so should we.
3. He struggles with temptation and sin . . . and so do we.
4. He acknowledges the support of the Lord . . . and so should we.
6. He was filled with the love of the Lord . . . and we can be too.
7. His enemies were confounded . . . and ours can be too.
8. His prayers are answered . . . and ours can be too.
9. He was filled with the Spirit . . . and we can be too.
10. He was blessed by the condescension of the Lord . . . and so are we.
11. He recognized that with all these blessings there is a choice to make: why does he linger in sorrow, slacken because of his afflictions, yield to sin, give way to temptations, and become angry because of his enemies? "Stop!" he says, and start anew: awaken your soul (be up and doing with a positive attitude)—he rejoiced in the Lord and praised Him forever because He is the rock of our salvation . . . and so should we.
12. He pleads with the Lord to redeem his soul . . . and so should we.
13. He seeks help to overcome his enemies . . . and so should we.
14. He seeks help to shake at the very appearance of sin (to abhor sin) . . . and so should we.
15. He seeks that the gates of hell will be closed because of his broken heart and contrite spirit . . . and we can qualify too.
16. He wants to walk in the low valley (walk with the Lord, in obedience) . . . and so should we.
17. He pleads with the Lord for the robe of righteousness, a way to escape, a straight path, and help against his enemies . . . and so can we.
18. He trusted in the Lord in all things, not in the arm of flesh . . . and so must we.
19. He had faith that the Lord would give to him what he asked for so long as he did not ask amiss . . . and so must we.
20. He would continue to pray and depend upon the rock of his righteousness . . . and so must we. (Pinegar)

Where Is the Poetry? Many years ago, while serving as a young missionary in Germany, I spoke with an older woman concerning the Book of Mormon. She was highly educated and very articulate, being familiar with a wide variety of subjects. It was encouraging when she agreed to read the Book of Mormon, especially since we had testified of its divine source (something that not infrequently dissuaded others). Upon one of our return visits, I asked her to give us her impressions of the book. Her response was instructive. She said that she was very conversant with the Bible, especially with the poetic sections of the Old Testament, such as the Psalms, which she read regularly with much benefit. The Book of Mormon was interesting, she reported, but it contained no uplifting poetry such as she admired in the Bible. To this we could only respond by drawing her attention to the plain and precious gospel truths contained in the Book of Mormon, often expressed with directness and clarity so that they could not be misunderstood. We encouraged her to continue with her reading, but we could discern in her attitude about the Book of Mormon that she was not looking at this material in the context of scripture, but rather out of an aesthetic interest. She wanted to be lifted poetically rather than spiritually. We eventually moved on to others more open to the message of the restored gospel.

In the final analysis, it is not the words, but rather the Word, that makes the difference. It is not the beauty of language, per se, but the confirmation of the Spirit of God that can change lives for the better and draw people closer to the Master. One hopes that all those with an eye for poetic expression, like the German lady, might, in their ponderings and meditations, come to accept the simple truth that God's greatest gift of joy is the gospel of Jesus Christ and its blessings to the obedient and faithful. (Allen)

Likening the Scriptures to Our Lives

2 Nephi 4:17–35—The Psalm of Nephi creates a bond between Nephi and all of us in our sojourn here upon the earth.

Application—We all struggle with our sins and temptations. We, like Nephi, must trust in the Lord, receive His love with gratitude, and recognize His gifts to us in all things. Then we can rejoice in the Lord and know He will help us in all situations as we ask not amiss.

3. SEPARATION:
THE ULTIMATE CONSEQUENCE OF SIN

THEME. We separate ourselves from God when we reject His word and fail to follow our living prophets.

> *"Wherefore, the word of the Lord was fulfilled which he spake unto me, saying that: Inasmuch as they will not hearken unto thy words they shall be cut off from the presence of the Lord. And behold, they were cut off from his presence. And he had caused the cursing to come upon them, yea, even a sore cursing, because of their iniquity. For behold, they had hardened their hearts against him, that they had become like unto a flint." (2 Ne. 5:20–21)*

MOMENT OF TRUTH. Following the death of Lehi, the older sons, Laman and Lemuel, lose no time in taking up their rebellious antics. When their murmuring turns to murderous design, Nephi is warned of the Lord to flee, and he and his righteous circle of associates separate themselves so that they might live "after the manner of happiness" (2 Ne. 5:27). The Nephites and the Lamanites become separate nations. The latter embrace an idle and uncivilized lifestyle; the former establish a Christ-centered lifestyle based on industry, self-reliance, and temple worship. Thus these peoples become a parable, as it were, for the doctrine of free agency and the consequences of choices in life—the obedient harvesting rich blessings of enduring joy, and the rebellious harvesting the dire and empty outcomes of a self-centered and anchorless existence, devoid of the fruits of the gospel of Christ and separated from the blissful fold.

MODERN PROPHETS SPEAK

Bruce R. McConkie:

> As with Adam, so with his seed. "By one man sin entered into the world, and death by sin; and so death passed upon all men, for that all have sinned" (Romans 5:12). In this mortal probation men have agency; they can choose for themselves. While here they are subject to laws—the laws of God, the laws of nature, the laws of men. And every law carries its own penalty. All men commit sin. "All have sinned, and come short of the glory of God" (Romans 3:23). "If we say that we have no sin, we deceive ourselves, and the truth is not in us. . . . If we say that we have not sinned, we make him [God] a liar, and his word is not in us" (1 John 1:8, 10). And as with Adam, so with all men; the justice of God requires that they pay the penalty for their disobedience. That penalty is to die spiritually, to die as to things of righteousness, to be cast out of the presence of God. (*A New Witness for the Articles of Faith* [Salt Lake City: Deseret Book, 1985], 93–94)

ILLUSTRATIONS FOR OUR TIME

The Choice. The gospel of Jesus Christ is based on choice and free agency. Joshua said it well to ancient Israel: "Choose you this day whom ye will serve; whether the gods which your fathers served that were on the other side of the flood, or the gods of the Amorites, in whose land ye dwell: but as for me and my house, we will serve the Lord" (Josh. 24:15). The consequences of choice are very clear: the faithful and obedient remain within the fold of the Lord; the rebellious and wicked suffer separation from the fold and relinquish the blessings that come from being close to the Lord. A stark and ominous illustration of this pattern was the separation that occurred between the Lamanites and the Nephites shortly after the death of Lehi. Because of the persistent, murderous designs of the older brothers, Nephi was commanded by the Lord to flee, thus leaving the rebellious band outside the circle of divine blessings.

In the larger gospel context, the doctrine of separation is the ultimate punishment for unrepentant sin. The Book of Mormon is a veritable handbook on the process of separation and a cogent reminder about the need to make choices that will allow us to stand in holy places and remain within the loving circle of the Lord's fold. There can be no more devastating verdict than this: "but where God and Christ dwell they cannot come, worlds without end" (D&C 76:112). By contrast, there can be no more welcome greeting than this: "Well done, thou good and faithful servant: thou hast been faithful over a few things, I will make thee ruler over many things: enter thou into the joy of thy lord" (Matt. 25:21). (Allen)

Believing the Words of the Prophets. In the Book of Mormon, there is a scripture concerning the consequences of not following the prophets that strikes to the very center of my soul: "And wo be unto him that will not hearken unto the words of Jesus, and also to them whom he hath chosen and sent among them; for whoso receiveth not the words of Jesus and the words of those whom he hath sent receiveth not him; and therefore he will not receive them at the last day; And it would be better for them if they had not been born. For do ye suppose that ye can get rid of the justice of an offended God, who hath been trampled under feet of men, that thereby salvation might come?" (3 Ne. 28:34–35). We offend God when we reject His prophets. We trample under our feet the very Savior of the world when we set aside the words of our living prophets. Elder Marion G. Romney gives us a simple example in this excerpt:

> It is an easy thing to believe in the dead prophets, but it is a greater thing to believe in the living prophets. I will give you an illustration.
>
> One day when President Grant was living, I sat in my office across the street following a general conference. A man came over to see me, an elderly man. He was very upset about what had been said in this conference by some of the Brethren, including myself. I could tell from his speech that he came from a foreign land. After I had quieted him enough so he would listen I said, "Why did you come to America?"
> "I came here because a prophet of God told me to come."
> "Who was the prophet?" I continued.
> "Wilford Woodruff."
> "Do you believe Wilford Woodruff was a prophet of God?"
> "Yes," said he.
> "Do you believe that his successor, President Lorenzo Snow, was a prophet of God?"
> "Yes, I do."
> "Do you believe that President Joseph F. Smith was a prophet of God?"
> "Yes, sir."
> Then came the sixty-four dollar question. "Do you believe that Heber J. Grant is a prophet of God?"

His answer: "I think he ought to keep his mouth shut about old age assistance."
Now I tell you that a man in his position is on the way to apostasy. He is forfeiting his chances for eternal life. So is everyone who cannot follow the living prophet of God. (*CR*, Apr. 1953, 125) (Pinegar)

Likening the Scriptures to Our Lives

2 Nephi 5:20—The Lamanites, because they wouldn't hearken to the words of Nephi, were cut off from the presence of the Lord.

Application—Let us hearken to our living prophets as they speak the word of the Lord, else we separate ourselves from the Lord (see 3 Nephi 28:34–35).

SUMMARY

We can truly relate to the Psalm of Nephi. We too know of the goodness of God. We too sorrow for sin. We are tempted and we often succumb. We look to God for our support in all things. Christ is the rock of our salvation. We seek our Heavenly Father in prayer and know He will bless us. Never let us forget the goodness of God in giving us living prophets to guide and direct us here upon the earth. Our task is to follow them as if the words they speak were given by our Savior Himself. And thus we can have the hope of always remaining within the circle of joy reserved for those who are obedient in living the commandments and who cultivate "a broken heart and a contrite spirit" (2 Ne. 2:7).

CHAPTER EIGHT

"O HOW GREAT *the* GOODNESS *of* OUR GOD"

2 Nephi 6–10

"How can you and I remember, always, the goodness of God, that we can retain a remission of our sins? The Apostle John recorded what the Savior taught us of a gift of remembrance which comes through the gift of the Holy Ghost: 'But the Comforter, which is the Holy Ghost, whom the Father will send in my name, he shall teach you all things, and bring all things to your remembrance, whatsoever I have said unto you' (John 14:26)."
—Henry B. Eyring, *To Draw Closer to God* (Salt Lake City: Deseret Book, 1997), 77–78.

THEMES *for* LIVING

Israel: the Lord's Covenant People
The Atonement: Redemption through the Lord Jesus Christ
Receiving the Blessings of the Atonement

INTRODUCTION

We are in a lost and fallen state. We are subject to death. There is no hope without the goodness of God and His plan of redemption. The Savior's infinite and eternal Atonement and resurrection provide for us hope of immortality and eternal life if we but come unto Him. The Atonement is the core of the gospel of Jesus Christ. When we appreciate the doctrine of the Atonement, we will be filled with gratitude as we exercise faith unto repentance, make and keep the ordinance of baptism, and live worthy of the gift of the Holy Ghost. We will become Saints of the Most High God by applying the Atonement to our lives.

1. ISRAEL: THE LORD'S COVENANT PEOPLE

THEME. Isaiah spoke concerning the house of Israel and of God's covenants with His people. He prophesied of the coming of the Messiah and the gathering of the last days:

> *"I will read you the words of Isaiah. And they are the words which my brother has desired that I should speak unto you. And I speak unto you for your sakes, that ye may learn and glorify the name of your God." (2 Ne. 6.4)*

MOMENT OF TRUTH. As a disciple of the Redeemer yet to come, Jacob was following in the footsteps of his father and his older brother Nephi. Like Lehi and Nephi, Jacob was shown by the Lord visions of the unfolding covenant history of Israel (see 2 Ne. 6:8–9). Also like Lehi and Nephi, he enjoined the people to live in righteousness and humility. And as his faithful brother, he turned to the writings of Isaiah to confirm the witness of his heart concerning his people.

Consider the context of Jacob's words and quotations in chapters 6 through 8: In his earlier years he had endured the harsh conditions of life in the wilderness; he suffered abuse at the hands of Laman and Lemuel; he had to flee with Nephi and others to a new location; he has seen in vision the destruction of his family's ancestral city of Jerusalem (which he had never known firsthand) and the captivity of the Israelites; and he now reaches out to his people to protect them from further dislocation and impart to them a sense of hope that the Lord will preserve them and their future seed as He had promised through the mouth of the prophet Isaiah. In Jacob's words: "I am desirous for the welfare of your souls. Yea, mine anxiety is great for you; and ye yourselves know that it ever has been. For I have exhorted you with all diligence; and I have taught you the words of my father; and I have spoken unto you concerning all things which are written, from the creation of the world" (2 Ne. 6:3).

MODERN PROPHETS SPEAK

Melvin J. Ballard:

> The primary purpose for which the Book of Mormon was originally prepared is set forth in Mormon's preface to the book, in which he says that the purpose of writing the book "is to show unto the remnant of the House of Israel what great things the Lord hath done for their fathers: and that they may know the covenants of the Lord, that they are not cast off forever—and also to the convincing of the Jew and Gentile that JESUS is the CHRIST, the ETERNAL GOD, manifesting himself unto all nations."

> In the third section of the book of Doctrine and Covenants the Lord said to the Prophet Joseph Smith that the chief purpose for which the Book of Mormon was written was that the testimony shall go to the knowledge of the Lamanites and other branched of the House of Israel concerning their forefathers (19th [and 20th] verse) "and for this very purpose are these plates preserved[,] which contain these records—that the promises of the Lord might be fulfilled which he made to his people; And that the Lamanites might know the promises of the Lord, and that they may come to the knowledge of their fathers, and that they might know the promises of the Lord, and that they may believe the gospel and rely upon the merits of Jesus Christ, and be glorified through faith in his name." (Editorial, *Improvement Era,* 1934, vol xxxvii, Mar. 1934, no. 3)

ILLUSTRATIONS FOR OUR TIME

How Far Can You See? In my youth, my father would often take us fishing in the high Canadian Rockies where, from the tops of the ridges, we had an astonishing view across the entire mountain range in all directions. Similarly, air travelers are continually delighted in rising above the land and into the higher reaches of the atmosphere, where they are presented with a captivating view of the earth below. Moreover, now that space travel is a reality, we can even see the entire earth hanging in space as an exquisite jewel of vitality. Reading the words of Isaiah, for me, is not unlike those experiences of flight and high altitude. Isaiah seemed to have an especially keen gift of transporting us with eloquent wisdom to higher planes from which to view the panorama of God's creation and the vista of His magnificent plan of redemption in action. The same kind of perspective is found in latter-day scripture: "The earth rolls upon her wings, and the sun giveth his light by day, and the moon giveth her light by night, and the stars also give their light, as they roll upon their wings in their glory, in the midst of the power of God. Unto what shall I liken these kingdoms, that ye may understand? Behold, all these are kingdoms, and any man who hath seen any or the least of these hath seen God moving in his majesty and power. I say unto you, he hath seen him; nevertheless, he who came unto his own was not comprehended" (D&C 88:45–48). Isaiah and the prophets of God help us comprehend the divine influence at work on our behalf to discern the Lord's hand in the forward movement of mortal history toward the consummation of God's grand design for His children.

With Isaiah, we can, in like measure, "mount up with wings as eagles" (Isa. 40:31) to the upper reaches of spiritual insight, and then return with greater confidence in our Savior and His plan for us. (Allen)

Likening the Scriptures to Our Lives

2 Nephi 10:7–8—The Lord will remember His covenant people and will gather them in.

Application—We are covenant people. Will we remember our covenant in regard to the seed of Abraham, that we may assist in the gathering of Israel and that through us and our seed all mankind may be blessed? (see D&C 110:11–16).

2. THE ATONEMENT: REDEMPTION THROUGH THE LORD JESUS CHRIST

THEME. Redemption from temporal and spiritual death comes through the Atonement of the Lord Jesus Christ. There is no other way.

> *"Wherefore, redemption cometh in and through the Holy Messiah; for he is full of grace and truth." (2 Ne. 2:6)*

> *"Remember, to be carnally-minded is death, and to be spiritually-minded is life eternal."* *(2 Ne. 9:39)*

MOMENT OF TRUTH. Jacob delivers a masterful discourse on the subject of the Atonement (see 2 Ne. 2:9–10). Together with the teachings of his father, Lehi, on this subject (2 Ne. 2:2), this statement about the redeeming mission of the Savior is one of the most comprehensive and lucid treatments of the subject in holy writ. Jacob covers each step of our existence in just a few pages: the premortal realm, the Creation and Garden of Eden, the Fall, birth into mortality, the mortal experience itself, death, the spirit world, the Resurrection (available to all), the Judgment, and the ultimate state (depending on one's obedience and faithfulness). He shows the interacting pathways traced on this landscape by the Savior, by Lucifer, and by different types of mortals (depending on their circumstances and actions). It is a remarkable treatise delivered in such a way as to stir up the listener (and the reader) to a sense of urgency to strengthen one's commitment unto righteousness in order to enjoy the matchless benefits of the Atonement. He concludes: "Therefore, cheer up your hearts, and remember that ye are free to act for yourselves—to choose the way of everlasting death or the way of eternal life" (2 Ne. 10:23).

MODERN PROPHETS SPEAK

Bruce R. McConkie:

The Law of Propitiation.

And so, according to the law of propitiation, Christ came to appease the demands of divine justice and effect a reconciliation between God and man. Thus John taught: "Jesus Christ the righteous is the propitiation for our sins: and not for ours only, but also [on conditions of repentance] for the sins of the whole world" (1 John 2:1–2). Our theological friend Paul expounds this doctrine by saying, "All have sinned, and come short of the glory of God." Indeed, the natural man is an enemy to God and has been cast out of his presence. But the saints, Paul continues, are "justified freely by [God's] grace through the redemption that is in Christ Jesus." How is it that the saints are justified? It is because "God hath set forth [his Son] to be a propitiation through faith in his blood, to declare his righteousness for the remission of sins that are past, through the forbearance of God; to declare . . . his righteousness: that he might be just, and the justifier of him which believeth in Jesus." (Romans 3:23–26) (*A New Witness for the Articles of Faith* [Salt Lake City: Deseret Book, 1985], 122–125)

ILLUSTRATIONS FOR OUR TIME

"How Can I Know the Lord Has Forgiven Me?" The following is an account told by President Harold B. Lee:

> Some years ago, President Romney and I were sitting in my office. The door opened and a fine young man came in with a troubled look on his face, and he said, "Brethren, I am going to the temple for the first time tomorrow. I have made some mistakes in the past, and I have gone to my bishop and my stake president, and I have made a clean disclosure of it all; and after a period of repentance and assurance that I have not returned again to those mistakes, they have now adjudged me ready to go to the temple. But, brethren, that is not enough. I want to know, and how can I know, that the Lord has forgiven me also."

> What would you answer one who might come to you asking that question? As we pondered for a moment, we remembered King Benjamin's address contained in the book of Mosiah. Here was a group of people asking for baptism, and they said they

viewed themselves in their carnal state: "And they all cried aloud with one voice, saying: O have mercy, and apply the atoning blood of Christ that we may receive forgiveness of our sins, and our hearts may be purified. . . . After they had spoken these
words the Spirit of the Lord came upon them, and they were filled with joy, having
received a remission of their sins, and having peace of conscience" (Mosiah 4:2, 3). There
was the answer. . . . In your soul-searching, if you seek for and you find that peace of conscience, by that token you may know that the Lord has accepted of your repentance. (*The
Teachings of Harold B. Lee,* ed. Clyde J. Williams [Salt Lake City: Bookcraft, 1996], 119)

Likening the Scriptures to Our Lives

2 Nephi 9:5–22—In these supernal verses, Jacob describes and expounds on the doctrine of the Atonement.

Application—When we begin to understand and start to appreciate the Atonement and its power in our
lives, we will change. The power in the Atonement causes one to want to repent and be drawn unto
Christ. The Atonement is love expressed. When we feel this love, it will motivate us to righteousness.

3. RECEIVING THE BLESSINGS
OF THE ATONEMENT

THEME. Receiving the blessings of the Atonement in our lives requires faith unto
repentance, receiving the life-saving ordinances, and continually pressing forward
with steadfastness in Christ.

> *"And he cometh into the world that he may save all men if they will hearken unto his
> voice; for behold, he suffereth the pains of all men, yea, the pains of every living creature,
> both men, women, and children, who belong to the family of Adam. And he suffereth this
> that the resurrection might pass upon all men, that all might stand before him at the great
> and judgment day. And he commandeth all men that they must repent, and be baptized
> in his name, having perfect faith in the Holy One of Israel, or they cannot be saved in
> the kingdom of God." (2 Ne. 9:21–23)*

MOMENT OF TRUTH. Jacob's remarkable sermon on the Atonement (2 Ne.
9–10) is more than a concept piece. It is an action piece, which calls for a pattern of
behavior that will bring one closer to the Savior and generate an improved condition
in one's life. The Book of Mormon contains some of the plainest statements about the
Atonement—its doctrine and its application—in all of the scriptures. No wonder the
Lord reserved this scriptural chronicle for our age, an age of complexity, sophistica-

tion, and rationalization. We needed clarity. We needed simplicity. We needed unfettered truth. What Jacob, Alma, Amulek, and others taught about the Atonement is crystal clear, as Nephi was to state shortly thereafter: "And now behold, my people, ye are a stiffnecked people; wherefore, I have spoken plainly unto you, that ye cannot misunderstand. And the words which I have spoken shall stand as a testimony against you; for they are sufficient to teach any man the right way; for the right way is to believe in Christ and deny him not; for by denying him ye also deny the prophets and the law" (2 Ne. 25:28).

MODERN PROPHETS SPEAK

Howard W. Hunter:

> What does the Atonement have to do with missionary work? Any time we experience the blessings of the Atonement in our lives, we cannot help but have a concern for the welfare of our brethren.
>
> Examples abound in the Book of Mormon that illustrate this principle. When Lehi partook of the fruit of the tree, symbolic of partaking of the Atonement, he said, "I began to be desirous that my family should partake" (1 Nephi 8:12). When Enos experienced his conversion and received a forgiveness of his sins, because of his faith in Jesus Christ he said, "I began to feel a desire for the welfare of my brethren, the Nephites" (Enos 1:9). Then he prayed for the Lamanites, the implacable enemies to the Nephites. Then there is the example of the four sons of Mosiah—Ammon, Aaron, Omner, and Himni—who received a forgiveness of sins through the Atonement and then labored for years among the Lamanites to bring them to Christ. The record states that they could not bear the thought that any soul should perish (see Mosiah 28:3).
>
> This supernal example of the covenanted one desiring to share the gospel with others is best illustrated by the example of Alma the Younger [quotes Alma 36:12–24]. . . .
>
> A great indicator of one's personal conversion is the desire to share the gospel with others. For this reason the Lord gave an obligation to every member of the Church to be missionaries. (*The Teachings of Howard W. Hunter,* ed. Clyde J. Williams [Salt Lake City: Bookcraft, 1997], 248–49)

ILLUSTRATIONS FOR OUR TIME

"Ye Would Not." I believe the way is clearly marked as to how we may apply the Atonement to our lives. Jacob offered counsel on things to be aware of that would impede our reception of the blessings of the Atonement. Though King Benjamin said there are many ways to sin (see Mosiah 4:29), here are a few examples of that which bars us from experiencing the full joy of Christ's embrace in our lives:

1. Transgressing the laws and failing to repent (see 2 Ne. 9:27). Unrepented sins separate us from the Lord, and we are exposed to the whole law (see D&C 19:15–19).

2. Wasting away our lives through idleness (see 2 Ne. 9:27). Every time one of my missionaries, for example, broke a rule or transgressed the commandments, it usually began with idleness.

3. Relying on one's own learning and not taking the counsel of God (see 2 Ne. 9:28–29). Some of God's children become enamored by their secular learning, thinking they know so much. The so-called learning of man changes with the passage of time. God's knowledge concerns verities . . . eternal and absolute truth. God is all-knowing, which, combined with His love for us, certainly qualifies Him to be the one offering counsel. Jacob said it best, "But to be learned is good if they hearken unto the counsels of God." (2 Ne. 9:29).

4. Allowing riches to become our treasure (see 2 Ne. 9:30). If our hearts are set upon our treasures we often forget the poor and the needy. Nevertheless, if we seek to do good with it, wealth is wonderful (see Jacob 2:19). There are people who can handle wealth. They are humble, remember their God, and are not lifted up in pride (see Alma 62:49).

5. Unwilling to hear the word of God . . . for they shall perish (see 2 Ne. 9:31). We should live by every word that proceedeth forth from the mouth of God (see D&C 84:43–46). In the vision of the tree of life, those who did not hold to the iron rod wandered off in strange paths and ended up in the spacious building or else perished in the depths of the river (hell).

6. Those who will not see . . . for they shall perish also (see 2 Ne. 9:32). If we fail to have an eye single to the glory of God we will be full of darkness; by way of contrast, we can be filled with light and comprehend all things (see D&C 88:67). (Pinegar)

Likening the Scriptures to Our Lives

2 Nephi 9:23–27—The Lord commands us to repent, be baptized, and endure to the end, else be damned. The law has been given, and we are subject to it.

Application—Let us realize that to make the Atonement totally efficacious in our lives we must apply the doctrine of Christ to our lives by obedience to the principles and ordinances of the gospel.

SUMMARY

The plan of happiness is wholly dependent upon the Atonement. The Atonement is the centerpiece of the gospel, for our very lives hang upon this magnificent, infinite, and eternal sacrifice of our Lord and Savior, Jesus Christ. President Hinckley said it best: "I cannot be grateful enough for the Atonement wrought by my Savior and my Redeemer. Through His sacrifice at the culmination of a life of perfection—that sacrifice offered in pain unspeakable—the bonds of death were broken, and the resurrection of all became assured. Beyond this, the doors of celestial glory have been opened to all who will accept divine truth and obey its precepts." And further: "I sense in a measure the meaning of His atonement. I cannot comprehend it all. It is so vast in its reach and yet so intimate in its effect that it defies comprehension. When all is said and done, when all of history is examined, when the deepest depths of the human mind have been explored, there is nothing so wonderful, so majestic, so tremendous as this act of grace when the Son of the Almighty, the prince of His Father's royal household, . . . gave His life in ignominy and pain so that all of the sons and daughters of God, of all generations of time, every one of whom must die, might walk again and live eternally" (*Teachings of Gordon B. Hinckley* [Salt Lake City: Deseret Book, 1997], 27–28).

CHAPTER NINE

"MY SOUL DELIGHTETH
in the WORDS *of* ISAIAH"

2 Nephi 11–25

*"Did not Isaiah abundantly testify of Christ? . . . When it is realized that
salvation comes alone through Jesus, and Isaiah was so vocal in declaring
this fact, it becomes essential that all people understand and believe him."*
—Mark E. Petersen, *Isaiah for Today* (Salt Lake City: Deseret Book, 1981), 43.

THEMES *for* LIVING

Keys to Understanding Isaiah's Magnificent Writings
Latter-day Temples and the Gathering of Israel
An Ensign to the Nations
By the Grace of God We Are Saved, After All We Can Do

INTRODUCTION

Is it any wonder that Nephi stated, "And now, I, Nephi, write more of the words of Isaiah, for my soul delighteth in his words. For I will liken his words unto my people, and I will send them forth unto all my children, for he verily saw my Redeemer, even as I have seen him" (2 Ne. 11:2)? Isaiah captured with uncommon excellence the dramatic contrast between the godly walk of the Saints in Zion and the uncertain meanderings of the misguided souls in Babylon. Isaiah saw the latter-day temple and the raising of an ensign to the nations. Isaiah's words are sustained by a vision of the sublime mission of the Redeemer and the atoning power of the Father's plan of salvation. We hear the repeated expressions of joy as Israel's faithful are gathered once again to the protecting care of Zion's resorts. We see in our mind's eye the unfolding of the earthly ministry of the Savior and His condescension in coming among the children of men with saving grace. We listen as Isaiah continually reminds us of our covenant obligations. Great are the words of Isaiah!

1. KEYS TO UNDERSTANDING ISAIAH'S MAGNIFICENT WRITINGS

THEME. Isaiah is without equal in his prophetic utterances regarding the Messiah, the Son of God and Savior of the world. Great blessings come when we do all we can to understand and apply his words to our lives. The Savior Himself has said:

> *"And now, behold, I say unto you, that ye ought to search these things. Yea, a commandment I give unto you that ye search these things diligently; for great are the words of Isaiah." (3 Ne. 23:1)*

MOMENT OF TRUTH. Nephi was moved by the spirit of prophecy to bear witness to the truthfulness of the gospel before his people (2 Ne. 11). He poured out his soul in the expression of joy over the things that delighted him most—the testimony of Isaiah, the opportunity of proving to his people "the truth of the coming of Christ" (v. 4), the covenants of the Lord, His grace, justice, power, and mercy. In all of this, Nephi chose to blend his witness with that of his brother Jacob and, especially, with the prophet Isaiah, declaring that "by the words of three, God hath said, I will establish my word. Nevertheless, God sendeth more witnesses, and he proveth all his words" (v. 3). With that, Nephi then wrote on the plates a great many chapters from the works of Isaiah, "that whoso of my people shall see these words may lift up their hearts and rejoice for all men" (v. 8).

Amid the suffocating darkness that comes of man's wickedness and rejection of the covenant blessings we see, here and there, evidence of penetrating light and glory: the rise of the exalted temple—"the mountain of the Lord's house" (2 Ne. 12:2)—to which many flock for instruction and truth; the glory of the Lord upon the dwelling places of Zion as a defense and a covert from storm and rain (2 Ne. 14:5–6); the ensign of the Restoration lifted up as a beckoning call to the scattered remnants of Israel (2 Ne. 15:26; 21:12); the rebirth of Light into the world—"For unto us a child is born, unto us a son is given" (2 Ne. 19:6); and the fulfillment of the promise of God to remember His people with forgiveness—"his hand is stretched out still" (2 Ne. 15:25; 19:12, 17, 21; 20:4).

Small wonder Nephi chose to include the rich and fulsome offering of Isaiah for his people and his readership "in the last days" (2 Ne. 25:8). He knew this witness would be of inestimable value in guiding the faithful and preparing them for the return of the Redeemer. Let us thank the Lord for the Book of Mormon as a new testament of Jesus Christ in these latter days.

MODERN PROPHETS SPEAK

Mark E. Petersen:

> "Great are the words of Isaiah," the Savior declared. (3 Nephi 23:1.) And great is his message to the Latter-day Saints.
>
> He gazed on our day and prophesied concerning it. He saw the restoration of the gospel and the work of the Prophet Joseph Smith.
>
> He foresaw the coming forth of the Book of Mormon as a marvelous work and a wonder, and observed its miraculous effect upon an unbelieving world. Even the blind would read its inspired pages, the deaf would hear its words, and "the poor among men shall rejoice in the Holy One of Israel." (Isaiah 29:19.) . . .
>
> Great destruction is projected for the wicked in these last days, but for the righteous there will be a joyful reward. In their midst the Lord of hosts "shall reign in Mount Zion and in Jerusalem" (both in America and Palestine), and his reign shall be glorious (Isaiah 24:23). (*Isaiah for Today* [Salt Lake City: Deseret Book, 1981], 1–4)

ILLUSTRATIONS FOR OUR TIME

Who Is Least Shall Be Great. When the mortal Savior discerned a reasoning among His disciples as to who was the greatest, He drew a small child to His side and said, "Whosoever shall receive this child in my name receiveth me: and whosoever shall receive me receiveth him that sent me: for he that is least among you all, the same shall be great" (Luke 9:48). Childlike humility is one of the essential qual-ities of great and noble people. Not long after this incident, the resurrected Savior again used the term "great" in reference to Isaiah as He instructed the American Israelites to ponder and study the words of the prophets.

When we encounter the words of Isaiah, we surely have a sense of the greatness of his prophetic office, the majestic scope of his vision, and the mastery of his discourse in pointing to the mission and divini-ty of the Savior. It is instructive that Isaiah, among all of the ancient prophets unsurpassed in the supremacy and mastery of his prophetic language, responded with contrition and meekness to his calling: "Then said I, Woe is me! For I am undone [i.e., overwhelmed by a sense of inadequacy]; because I am a man of unclean lips, and I dwell in the midst of a people of unclean lips: for mine eyes have seen the King, the LORD of hosts" (Isa. 6:5). Then the Lord dispatches one of his angels to reassure the newly called Prophet: "thine iniquity is taken away, and thy sin purged" (v. 7), whereupon Isaiah responds with humble words rem-iniscent of the Savior's own response in the premortal realm: "Here am I; send me" (verse 8; cf. Abr. 3:27).

This pattern of meekness in the face of a divine calling is not unlike the attitude of Moses on the mount: "Who am I, that I should go unto Pharaoh, and that I should bring forth the children of Israel out of Egypt?" (Ex. 3:11). The Lord responds with reassurance, "Certainly I will be with thee" (v. 12). But Moses persists: "O my Lord, I am not eloquent, neither heretofore, nor since thou has spoken unto thy ser-vant: but I am slow of speech, and of a slow tongue" (Ex. 4:10). Now the Lord comes back with this unas-sailable logic: "Who hath made man's mouth? Or who maketh the dumb, or deaf, or the seeing, or the blind? Have not I the LORD? Now therefore go, and I will be with thy mouth, and teach thee what thou shalt say" (v. 11–12). Moses, who rightly deserved to be called "very meek, above all the men which were upon the face of the earth" (Num. 12:3), mirrors Enoch's experience. The young lad Enoch complained that he was slow of speech, and the Lord countered that He would fill Enoch's mouth if he opened it (Moses 6:31—34; see D&C 33:8–11).

In a similar way, Jeremiah had to overcome deep feelings of inadequacy when he was called as prophet: "Then said I, Ah, Lord GOD! Behold, I cannot speak: for I am a child" (Jer. 1:6). Then the reassuring words of the Lord came to him: "Say not, I am a child; for thou shalt go to all that I shall send thee, and whatsoever I command thee thou shalt speak. Be not afraid of their faces: for I am with thee to deliver thee, saith the LORD. Then the LORD put forth his hand, and touched my mouth. And the LORD said unto me, Behold, I have put my words in thy mouth" (v. 7–8). In this manner, the Lord elevated the meek and lowly and turned perceived weakness into strength: "I give unto men weakness that they may be made humble; and my grace is sufficient for all men that humble themselves before me; for it the humble themselves before me, and have faith in me, them will I make weak things become strong unto them" (Ether 12:27).

The ancient records lay in plain view the key to service and the answer to feelings of inadequacy on the part of anyone called on the Lord's errand: His grace is sufficient to lift us above our weakness and infuse our souls with the strength and the vision to succeed. It matters not that a person fearful of teaching be called to teach, or a person fearful of speaking be called to speak, or a person fearful of leading be called to lead—when the Lord extends a calling, He provides the grace, the power, and the ability in the face of meekness. Indeed, one could almost say that their meekness qualified them to have the stretching office extended to them. (Allen)

Likening the Scriptures to Our Lives

2 Nephi 25:4—Isaiah's words are understood with the spirit of prophecy.

Application—The sons of Mosiah through prayer and fasting had the spirit of prophecy (see Alma 17:3). In order to enjoy this spirit of prophecy, we too have to give ourselves to much prayer and fasting.

2. LATTER-DAY TEMPLES AND THE GATHERING OF ISRAEL

THEME. Isaiah saw our day: the temple, the gathering of Israel, and the establishment of Zion. Nephi was also favored to view the latter days in prophetic vision, as were most certainly all the prophets before our time.

> *"And it shall come to pass in the last days, when the mountain of the Lord's house shall be established in the top of the mountains, and shall be exalted above the hills, and all nations shall flow unto it. And many people shall go and say, Come ye, and let us go up to the mountain of the Lord, to the house of the God of Jacob; and he will teach us of his ways, and we will walk in his paths; for out of Zion shall go forth the law, and the word of the Lord from Jerusalem" (2 Ne. 12:2–3).*

MOMENT OF TRUTH. Among the first initiatives undertaken by the Nephites upon separating themselves from the Lamanites was construction of a temple patterned after the great temple of Solomon. Clearly Nephi had a keen sense of covenant history and a commitment to align his growing branch of Israel with the practices of a Zion people (2 Ne. 5:16). One can imagine Nephi reading to his people on the steps of their newly constructed temple (or within its walls) Isaiah's pronouncements about "the mountain of the Lord's house" and about the future gathering of the scattered remnants of Israel.

MODERN PROPHETS SPEAK

Bruce R. McConkie:
> Why is the Lord gathering Israel in these last days? It is to fulfil the covenant made with Abraham and renewed with Isaac and Jacob and others. What is that covenant? It is not the gathering of Israel *per se*, but something far more important than the

mere assembling of a people in Jerusalem or on Mount Zion or at any designated place. It is not the allocation of Palestine for the seed of Abraham, or the designation of the Americas as the inheritance of Joseph, though each of these arrangements has a bearing on the fulfillment of the covenant. The gathering of Israel, at whatever place Deity specifies, is a necessary condition precedent, something that makes possible the fulfilling of the ancient covenant. What, then, is the covenant itself?

Jehovah promised—covenanted with—his friend Abraham that in him and in his seed, meaning the literal seed of his body, should "all the families of the earth be blessed, even with the blessings of the Gospel, which are the blessings of salvation, even of life eternal" (Abr. 2:8–11). (*The Mortal Messiah: From Bethlehem to Calvary*, 4 vols. [Salt Lake City: Deseret Book, 1979–1981], 4: 337–338)

ILLUSTRATIONS FOR OUR TIME

The Gathering of Israel. All can be partakers of the gospel of Jesus Christ. The Lord wants all of His children who are willing and obedient to come back into His presence (see 2 Ne. 26:33). His tender mercy is extended to all humankind.

Some of my Book of Mormon students at Brigham Young University and the Orem, Utah Institute of Religion were nonmembers. They often said after their conversion and baptism, "I didn't know why I came here at the beginning, but now I do. It was to receive the gospel." Surely the Lord leads all of His children who are willing to follow His light, diligently walking up to that which they have received and obeying the invitation to receive more. (Pinegar)

Likening the Scriptures to Our Lives

Bruce R. McConkie had the following to say about 2 Nephi 2 Nephi 12:2–3:
> This great prophecy, as is often the case, is subject to the law of multiple fulfillment. 1. In Salt Lake City and other mountain locations, temples, in the full and true sense of the word, have been erected, and representatives of all nations are flowing unto them to learn of God and His ways. In this connection and as part of the general fulfillment of Isaiah's prophecy is the fact that one of the world's greatest genealogical societies has been established in Salt Lake City—a society to which people of all nations come to do the ancestral research which must precede the performance of vicarious temple ordinances. 2. But the day is yet future when the Lord's house is to be built on that "Mount Zion" which is "the city of New Jerusalem" in Jackson County, Missouri (see D&C 84:2–4). Mount Zion, itself, will be the mountain of the Lord's house in the day when that glorious temple is erected. 3. When the Jews flee unto Jerusalem, it will be "unto the mountains of the Lord's house (D&C

133:13), for a holy temple is to be built there also as part of the work of the great era of restoration (Ezek. 37: 24–28). (Bruce R. McConkie, *Mormon Doctrine*, 2d. ed. [Salt Lake City: Bookcraft, 1966], 518).

Application—As the seed of Abraham, we have a great responsibility in these last days as has been described by Elder McConkie. We are responsible and accountable (see Jacob 5:70–76; D&C 138:53, 57).

3. AN ENSIGN TO THE NATIONS

THEME. The Lord will raise an ensign to the nations in the latter days, and many people will flow unto it to be fed spiritual truth. We are participating in that process today.

> *"And he will lift up an ensign to the nations from far, and will hiss unto them from the end of the earth; and behold, they shall come with speed swiftly; none shall be weary nor stumble among them." (2 Ne. 15:26)*

MOMENT OF TRUTH. Nephi, in his fledgling, but prospering, circle of Saints in the promised land, must have had a feeling of being scattered considering how far he was from his native Jerusalem and how separated he was from his older brethren due to their rejection of righteous ways. Is it any wonder that he was attracted to the writings of Isaiah, one of whose major themes was the scattering and eventual gathering of Israel? How much Nephi must have yearned for the security of his people, for their adherence to the principles of covenant integrity so that they might be gathered and preserved as a community of faithful servants unto the Lord. How much must he have anguished over the views given him of his people's future apostasy and decline. How much must he have rejoiced to view the latter-day Restoration and gathering in of the remnants of his lineage in a future age as confirmed by Isaiah: "The remnant shall return, yea, even the remnant of Jacob, unto the mighty God" (2 Ne. 20:21). Nephi clearly perceived, like Isaiah, the coming "times of refreshing" (Acts 3:19) when the Lord would raise up an ensign to signal the ushering in of the last days: "And the Lord will set his hand again the second time to restore his people from their lost and fallen state. Wherefore, he will proceed to do a marvelous work and a wonder among the children of men" (2 Ne. 25:17; cf. Isa. 29:14). Thus Nephi lays out plainly the design of the Lord in preserving these very records for the blessing of coming generations: "Wherefore, he shall bring forth his words unto them, which words shall judge them at the last day, for they shall be given them for the purpose of convincing them of the true Messiah" (2 Ne. 25:18).

MODERN PROPHETS SPEAK

Joseph Fielding Smith:

> [Isa. 11:11–16]
>
> We claim that this is being fulfilled in the gathering of the Latter-day Saints, and with them the Lord has set up the ensign to the nations. This chapter was quoted by Moroni to the Prophet Joseph Smith who said it was about to be fulfilled.
>
> Again the Lord said to Isaiah:
>
> "Fear not: for I am with thee: I will bring thy seed from the east, and gather them from the west;
>
> "I will say to the north, Give up; and to the south, Keep not back: bring my sons from far, and my daughters from the ends of the earth;
>
> "Even every one that is called by my name: for I have created him for my glory, I have formed him; yea, I have made him" (Isaiah 43: 5–7). (*Answers to Gospel Questions,* 5 vols. [Salt Lake City: Deseret Book, 1957–1966], 2: 181–82)

ILLUSTRATIONS FOR OUR TIME

High on the Mountain Top. The hymn "High on the Mountain Top" beautifully illustrates the ensign (a banner) that all nations will flow unto. This hymn memorializes the faith of the Latter-day Saints in the universal blessing of the restored gospel. The strong, ringing melody captures the enthusiasm of the words. "High on the Mountain Top" is a wholehearted assertion of the glory of Zion and a fervent restatement of scriptural prophecy. As is true of many of our finest hymn texts, this one is based closely on scripture. Joel H. Johnson's inspiration was Isaiah 2:2–3:

> And it shall come to pass in the last days, that the mountain of the Lord's house shall be established in the top of the mountains, and shall be exalted above the hills; and all nations shall flow unto it. And many people shall go and say, Come ye, and let us go up to the mountain of the Lord, to the house of the God of Jacob; and he will teach us of his ways, and we will walk in his paths: for out of Zion shall go forth the law, and the word of the Lord from Jerusalem.

In his brief autobiography, which he appended to his journal, Joel H. Johnson noted the following:

> After being baptized in 1831 I never lived but a short time in any one place on account of mob violence. And since I have been in Utah I have made eleven new places. Was never called on a mission without responding to the call and never asked to speak in

public on the principles of religion when I excused myself. I have written nearly or quite one thousand spiritual hymns and sacred songs, now in a manuscript entitled, "Zion's Songster, or the Songs of Joel" (Karen Lynn Davidson, *Our Latter-day Hymns: The Stories and the Messages* [Salt Lake City: Deseret Book, 1988], 34). (Pinegar)

The Keeper of the Gate. Several years ago a colleague in my high priests group recounted a story about an event that had recently taken place in the local temple where he was serving as a temple worker. Two young women had come to the recommend desk at the front of the temple to be admitted. They were greeted warmly by the official stationed there, who requested to see their recommends. As he described it, for some reason a feeling of uneasiness came over him. As he examined the first recommend he glanced at the authorizing signatures, then back into the eyes of the young woman. He felt impressed to say, "This is not the signature of your stake president, is it?" Chagrined, the young woman confessed that it was not. The official then counseled the two, in a kindly but firm way, to leave and return again when they were worthy to do so, and they would be welcome in the House of the Lord.

The event is a reminder to us all that the temples of the Most High are sacred precincts reserved for those who are sincerely striving to keep all of the commandments and abide by the standards of temple-worthy Saints. The temple experience is in many respects a type pointing to our eventual return to the home from whence we have come. Jacob made it clear that the process of admittance into our Heavenly Father's presence is by way of a very special gate keeper: "O then, my beloved brethren, come unto the Lord, the Holy One. Remember that his paths are righteous. Behold, the way for man is narrow, but it lieth in a straight course before him, and the keeper of the gate is the Holy One of Israel; and he employeth no servant there; and there is none other way save it be by the gate; for he cannot be deceived, for the Lord God is his name" (2 Ne. 9:41).

Nephi, Jacob's older brother, was inspired to include in his record on the small plates words concerning "the mountain of the Lord's house," "the house of the God of Jacob." Truly the temples of God are beacons of light that attract the interest and amazement of inquiring minds; they are instruments of gathering that stir up in the hearts of truth-seekers a faint echo of the mansions of heaven of which they were once tenants, and to which they are drawn. But the process of tenancy is to be accomplished in the Lord's way and according to the Lord's commandments: "And I give unto you, who are the first laborers in this last kingdom, a commandment that you assemble yourselves together, and organize yourselves, and sanctify yourselves; yea, purify your hearts, and cleanse your hands and your feet before me, that I may make you clean" (D&C 88:74). (Allen)

Likening the Scriptures to Our Lives

2 Nephi 21:12—An ensign shall be established to help gather Israel.

Application—We are part of the ensign—the Church, the temples. It is our duty to do temple work and spread the gospel (see D&C 138: 53–57; Jacob 5: 70–77).

4. BY THE GRACE OF GOD
WE ARE SAVED, AFTER ALL WE CAN DO

THEME. We are saved by the grace of God after we have done all in our power to demonstrate our faithful obedience to His commandments and enduring commitment to live as He would have us live. We cannot be saved without the help of our Savior Jesus Christ.

> *"For we labor diligently to write, to persuade our children, and also our brethren, to believe in Christ, and to be reconciled to God; for we know that it is by grace that we are saved, after all we can do." (2 Ne. 25:23)*

MOMENT OF TRUTH. After having recorded many chapters of Isaiah onto the small plates for the benefit of his people and posterity, Nephi makes a commentary on the selected quotations (2 Ne. 25). This commentary is among the most useful explications of the message of Isaiah available from any source, ancient or modern. As an introduction to his commentary, Nephi recaptures the essence of his Isaiah citations in one phrase: "Wherefore, I write unto my people, unto all those that shall receive hereafter these things which I write, that they may know the judgments of God, that they come upon all nations, according to the word which he hath spoken" (2 Ne. 25:3). Having through the grace of God escaped with his family from the predicted destruction of Jerusalem, Nephi knew firsthand the sureness of God's word with respect to the impending judgments that must in due course come upon the wicked should they reject the warnings of the prophets. As he further wrote, "And as one generation hath been destroyed among the Jews because of iniquity, even so have they been destroyed from generation to generation according to their iniquities; and never hath any of them been destroyed save it were foretold them by the prophets of the Lord" (2 Ne. 25:9). Thus Nephi issues his confirmation of God's design with respect to the geopolitical flow of history: no nation, no people, no generation can escape the judgments of God.

The scattering and gathering will proceed on the basis of God's purposes for mankind, according to their responsiveness to the word of truth as proclaimed by God's emissaries. Nephi had seen through prophetic vision the ultimate destiny of Israel's remnants throughout history, even down to the ushering in of the millennial reign. He yearned for the well-being of his people and their posterity. He agonized over their spiritual welfare. That is the context for his famous statement: "For we labor diligently to write, to persuade our children, and also our brethren, to believe in Christ, and to be reconciled to God; for we know that it is by grace that we are saved, after all we can do" (2 Ne. 25:23). And furthermore: "And we talk of Christ, we rejoice in Christ, we preach of Christ, we prophesy of Christ, and we write according to our prophecies, that our children may know to what source they may look for a remission of their sins" (2 Ne. 25:26).

All of these convictions were at work in Nephi's soul as he laid out his commentary on Isaiah and foresaw clearly the events of the latter days when these writings would be fulfilled—both unto the destruction of the wicked as well as the blessing of the faithful. Thus he declared, concerning the words he was recording, "Wherefore, they are of worth unto the children of men, and he that supposeth that they are not, unto them will I speak particularly, and confine the words unto mine own people: for I know that they shall be of great worth unto them in the last days; for in that day shall they understand them; wherefore, for their good have I written them" (2 Ne. 25:8).

MODERN PROPHETS SPEAK

Joseph Fielding Smith:

> As it was pointed out by Isaiah and others of the prophets many hundreds of years before his birth, Christ took upon himself the transgressions of all men and suffered for them, that they might escape, on conditions of their repentance, and acceptance of his gospel, and their faithfulness to the end (Isa. 53:1–12; 2 Ne. 9:17–27; 31:11–21). So we are saved by grace and that not of ourselves. It is the gift of God. (2 Ne. 9:81; 10:24–25; 25:23; Moro. 10:32–33).

> If Jesus Christ had not died for us, there would have come to us no salvation, and we would have remained absolutely in our sins, without redemption, and would have become subject to Satan and his emissaries forever and ever [2 Ne. 9:6–9]. But through the mercies of God, Christ came into the world and his blood was shed for the redemption of men, so that all who will believe and will acknowledge him and take upon them his commandments, enduring to the end, shall receive eternal life.

> So far as redemption from death is concerned, since we were not responsible for it, we will be redeemed from it, Therefore, *through the blood of Christ, every man shall come forth from the dead in the resurrection,* and the spirit and body shall be inseparably connected. Then man, if he has been righteous, shall receive a fulness of joy, and if unrighteous, he shall suffer, of course, for his transgressions, but every man has been given immortality, which means that he shall die again no more.

These are the doctrines that were taught by the Lord Jesus Christ. This is the burden of the message which we declare unto the world—Christ and him crucified for the redemption of men. (*Doctrines of Salvation,* 3 vols., ed. Bruce R. McConkie [Salt Lake City: Bookcraft, 1954–1956], 2:309–310)

ILLUSTRATIONS FOR OUR TIME

Two Blades of the Scissors.

Stephen E. Robinson:

The two major hazards of pitting faith against works as though they were competitors are (1) antinomianism and (2) do-it-yourself salvation. *Antinomianism* is the scholars' word for the talk without the walk—the belief that grace removes from us any obligation to do good works or that merely saying "Christ is Lord" will guarantee salvation even for wicked and unfaithful Christians. *Do-it-yourself salvation* is my term for the belief that we save ourselves, that we "work out our own salvation" without grace and without being justified through faith in Christ. Theologically we walk a tightrope between these two equally disagreeable extremes. The finished product of the covenant relationship, neither all grace nor all works, is a faithful Christian saved in the kingdom of God through the grace of Christ. Without the grace of Christ there is no salvation. But without our faithfulness there is no salvation either. Like two blades of the scissors, to borrow C. S. Lewis's analogy, both grace and works must be part of the process. That is why the relationship is described in the scriptures as a *covenant* rather than a gift of grace alone or a reward for works alone. The saved are involved in the salvation process and contribute to it because they are involved in the covenant and must "keep" it. Leave out grace or leave out our own efforts and desire, and you are left with only one half of the scissors—not enough to do the job. Latter-day Saints do not reject the proposition that we are saved by grace. We do, however, reject the proposition that grace can save us against our will or without our consent or while we rebel against Christ. (*Following Christ: The Parable of the Divers and More Good News* [Salt Lake City: Deseret Book, 1995], 91)

SUMMARY

The Book of Mormon illuminates the meaning of Isaiah's writings in ways that help us to better internalize and apply their message. We derive a great deal of insight into the importance of latter-day temples and the gathering of Israel. We see our own period of the Restoration as the lifting up of a great ensign to the nations, signaling the commencement of God's "marvellous work and a wonder" (Isa. 29:14; cf. 2 Ne. 25:17) in the latter days. We learn that it is by the grace of God we are saved, after all we can do.

Truly the Book of Mormon helps us understand Isaiah. Isaiah's purpose is to teach of the Lord Jesus Christ, the Messiah, of His coming and His Millennial reign. Isaiah speaks of Israel's trials and transgressions and her eventual return and gathering. He speaks of the coming forth of the Book of Mormon to restore the gospel in the latter days. In all of this, Isaiah exhorts the people to righteousness. Isaiah was a great prophet. His words are profound and we should delight in them, for they teach us of Christ, our Savior and King. Isaiah is a valuable part of why the Book of Mormon serves as another testament of Jesus Christ. Isaiah, Lehi, Nephi, Jacob—all of these mighty prophets combine their voices in a harmonious witness to the truthfulness of God's word and the efficacy of His plan of redemption on behalf of His children.

CHAPTER TEN

"HE INVITETH ALL
to COME UNTO HIM"

2 NEPHI 26–30

"The mission of the Church is glorious—to invite all of us to come unto Christ through proclaiming the gospel, perfecting our lives, and redeeming the dead. As we come unto Christ, we bless our own lives, those of our families, and our Father in Heaven's children, both living and dead."
—EZRA TAFT BENSON, *THE TEACHINGS OF EZRA TAFT BENSON* (SALT LAKE CITY: BOOKCRAFT, 1988), 179.

THEMES for LIVING

Looking Forward to the Coming of the Savior
The Lord's Design in Bringing Forth the Book of Mormon
Anticipating and Neutralizing the Strategies of Satan
The Importance and Power of the Book of Mormon
Covenant People and the Millennial Reign

INTRODUCTION

The plan of happiness is designed to bless Heavenly Father's children that they might gain immortality and eternal life. To bring this to pass, our Savior, like His disciples, invites all to come unto Christ and be perfected in Him. This is the purpose of the Church and Kingdom of God here upon the earth and will bring us glory and joy. In this dispensation of the fulness of times, the Restoration brought forth the Book of Mormon, the priesthood, and The Church of Jesus Christ of Latter-day Saints—with all of the saving ordinances—so that all mankind might have the opportunity of coming unto Christ.

1. LOOKING FORWARD
TO THE COMING OF THE SAVIOR

THEME. The gospel points us continually toward the coming of the Savior. It has been so from the beginning of time. Our spiritual eyes should be focused constantly on that moment, and our commitment should be to prepare ourselves diligently in all respects to be worthy to greet Him.

> *"For none of these iniquities come of the Lord; for he doeth that which is good among the children of men; and he doeth nothing save it be plain unto the children of men; and he inviteth them all to come unto him and partake of his goodness; and he denieth none that come unto him, black and white, bond and free, male and female; and he remembereth the heathen; and all are alike unto God, both Jew and Gentile." (2 Ne. 26:33)*

MOMENT OF TRUTH. With prophetic vision, Nephi sees the time when the Savior would visit the Nephites following His ministry in the Holy Land. The prelude to that visit was to be an unprecedented natural catastrophe that would leave much of the land in ruins and bring about the destruction of the wicked. Nephi is consumed with pain and grief over the loss of life: "O the pain, and the anguish of my soul for the loss of the slain of my people! For I, Nephi, have seen it, and it well nigh consumeth me before the presence of the Lord; but I must cry unto my God: Thy ways are just" (2 Ne. 26:7).

Nevertheless, Nephi takes comfort in seeing that the obedient are spared for the unspeakable experience of the coming of the resurrected Savior: "But behold, the righteous that hearken unto the words of the prophets, and destroy them not, but look forward unto Christ with steadfastness for the signs which are given, notwithstanding all persecution—behold, they are they which shall not perish. But the Son of righteousness shall appear unto them; and he shall heal them, and they shall have peace with him, until three generations shall have passed away, and many of the fourth generation shall have passed away in righteousness" (2 Ne. 26:8–9). Then Nephi looks forward in time and views the coming forth of the sacred record from the dust (the Book of Mormon) to prepare the people for the Second Coming of the Savior, thus confirming the eternal loving kindness of God: "He doeth not anything save it be for the benefit of the world; for he loveth the world, even that he layeth down his own life that he may draw all men unto him. Wherefore, he commandeth none that they shall not partake of his salvation" (2 Ne. 26:24).

MODERN PROPHETS SPEAK

Russell M. Nelson:

> The gospel of Jesus Christ provides hope for all in this wailing world. "Now, what do we hear in the gospel which we have received? A voice of gladness! A voice of mercy from heaven; and a voice of truth out of the earth; glad tidings for the dead; a voice of gladness for the living and the dead; glad tidings of great joy." (D&C 128:19.)

> Members of The Church of Jesus Christ of Latter-day Saints invite all to come unto Christ and be sanctified in him (*The Gateway We Call Death* [Salt Lake City: Deseret Book, 1995], 108–109).

ILLUSTRATIONS FOR OUR TIME

The Broken Heart of Charity. Within the magnificent six-spired Washington D.C. Temple there is a wall-sized mural depicting the Day of Judgment. The Savior stands majestically in the center, with concourses of His joyful followers to His right and the lost hordes of the shame-filled and wayward to His left. This is depicted in Matthew 25: "And before him shall be gathered all nations: and he shall separate them one from another, as a shepherd divideth *his* sheep from the goats: And he shall set the sheep on his right hand, but the goats on the left. Then shall the King say unto them on his right hand, Come, ye blessed of my Father, inherit the kingdom prepared for you from the foundation of the world" (Matt. 25:32–34).

My wife and I were living in that area of the country during the construction of the temple and thus had the opportunity to participate in the dedicatory session on 19 November 1974, conducted under the direction of Spencer W. Kimball. During our subsequent visits to the temple, I would take occasion to look intently at the mural of the "sheep and the goats" and ponder on the significance of the doctrine reflected in it. More often than not I found myself instinctively associating with those happy souls to the Savior's right-hand side (after all, was I not in the house of the Lord?) and sensing relief at not finding fellowship with those on his left. But was that the appropriate sentiment?

When Nephi was granted a vision of the unfolding of his people's destiny leading up to the time of the resurrected Savior's visit to America, he perceived the judgment that took place at that time, including the widespread destruction of the wicked. Was his mind-set one of relief at not having affinity with the wayward and prideful? Listen to his expression: "O the pain, and the anguish of my soul for the loss of the slain of my people! For I, Nephi, have seen it, and it well nigh consumeth me before the presence of the Lord; but I must cry unto my God: Thy ways are just" (2 Ne. 26:7). Further: "And when these things have passed away a speedy destruction cometh unto my people; for, notwithstanding the pains of my soul, I have seen it; wherefore, I know that it shall come to pass. . . . For the Spirit of the Lord will not always strive with man. And when the Spirit ceaseth to strive with man then cometh speedy destruction, and this grieveth my soul" (2 Ne. 26:10–11).

Pain and anguish of soul over the wicked? Being consumed with grief over the sinful? That is the perspective of a prophet and a man of charity. One of the grand themes of the Book of Mormon may be summarized in the essential quality of having a "broken heart and a contrite spirit" (see 2 Ne. 2:7; 4:32; 3 Ne. 9:20; 12:19; Morm. 2:14; Ether 4:15; Moro. 6:2). We are prone to think of this phrase as pertaining to inward humility and contrition of soul before our Father in Heaven—and so it does. Could the phrase not also refer to the quality of heart we bring to bear in our relationships with others—an ability to suspend judgment and exercise service-minded forebearance when others seem to stray or fall short in some way? Could a broken heart not also mean broken over the loss of blessings that others seem to relinquish when they wander into forbidden pathways? Could a contrite spirit not also imply being consumed with grief over the suffering that others—in some cases our immediate loved ones— must go through based on their choices? Wouldn't a charitable disciple of Christ possess this compassionate equality of soul?

> "And he spake this parable unto certain which trusted in themselves that they were righteous, and despised others: Two men went up into the temple to pray; the one a Pharisee, and the other a publican. The Pharisee stood and prayed thus with himself, God, I thank thee, that I am not as other men *are*, extortioners, unjust, adulterers, or even as this publican. I fast twice in the week, I give tithes of all that I possess. And the publican, standing afar off, would not lift up so much as *his* eyes unto heaven, but smote upon his breast, saying, God be merciful to me a sinner. I tell you, this man went down to his house justified *rather* than the other: for every one that exalteth himself shall be abased; and he that humbleth himself shall be exalted" (Luke 18:9–14; cf. Alma 31:11–19).

Thus it seems that the broken heart of charity—as it reaches out to do all in its power to rescue the disenfranchised, to reclaim the transgressor, to give hope through the gospel to the lost—comes very close to resonating with the Savior's pattern of love, which seeks to reclaim even those who may find themselves shifting toward His left-hand side. (Allen)

Likening the Scriptures to Our Lives

2 Nephi 25:26—They spoke of, rejoiced in, preached of, and prophesied of Christ so that their children would know where to look for the remission of sins.

Application—The plan of happiness given to us by our Heavenly Father is explicit with respect to the doctrine of Christ and His role as the author of our salvation and exaltation (see Hebrews 5:8–9). There is no other way but in and through the Lord Jesus Christ, the Savior and Redeemer of the world. We must know Him (see John 17:3). We must acknowledge Him as our personal advocate with the Father (see D&C 29:4; 45:3).

2. THE LORD'S DESIGN IN BRINGING FORTH THE BOOK OF MORMON

THEME. The gospel will be restored with the coming forth of the Book of Mormon.

"And in that day shall the deaf hear the words of the book, and the eyes of the blind shall see out of obscurity and out of darkness." (2 Ne. 27:29)

MOMENT OF TRUTH. Nephi had learned from his father's visions about the course of Israel's history and future destiny. Nephi himself, after much prayer and fasting, was privileged to partake of the heavenly vision firsthand (see 1 Ne. 12–14). Thus he was schooled of the Lord in the prophecies of Isaiah—who saw in vision the unfolding of the very same covenant plan—and could speak with authority about the nature and implications of Isaiah's words. We are the beneficiaries of Nephi's inspired commentary (see 1 Ne. 15; 2 Ne. 26–27) and his own related prophetic utterances and counsel (2 Ne. 28–33). Nephi illuminates with clarity the presentation in Isaiah 29 concerning the mysterious sealed book, a reference that has seemed fairly cryptic to the world. Nephi makes clear that this sealed book is none other than the record that he himself had initiated at God's command. With prophetic eye he looks forward to a time when this very record, extended and completed by a series of inspired prophets and compilers over the ages, would be brought forth "by the power of God" (Morm. 8:16) to a latter-day world hungry for the fulness of the everlasting gospel of Jesus Christ.

It would appear that one of the principal reasons the Lord directed that so many of the words of Isaiah be recorded in the Book of Mormon is so Nephi's inspired commentary could stand along side the original text to shed additional light and truth on these important themes "according to my plainness; in the which I know that no man can err" (2 Ne. 25:7).

MODERN PROPHETS SPEAK

Ezra Taft Benson:

> A powerful testimony to the importance of the Book of Mormon is to note where the Lord placed its coming forth in the timetable of the unfolding Restoration. The only thing that preceded it was the First Vision. In that marvelous manifestation, the Prophet Joseph Smith learned the true nature of God and that God had a work for him to do. The coming forth of the Book of Mormon was the next thing to follow. Think of that in terms of what it implies. The coming forth of the Book of Mormon preceded the restoration of the priesthood. It was published just a few days before the Church was organized. The Saints were given the Book of Mormon to read before they were given the revelations outlining such great doctrines as the three degrees of glory, celestial marriage, or work for the dead. It came before priesthood quorums and Church organization. Doesn't this tell us something about how the Lord views this sacred work? (*The Teachings of Ezra Taft Benson* [Salt Lake City: Bookcraft, 1988], 49)

ILLUSTRATIONS FOR OUR TIME

"As the Words of a Book That Is Sealed." In 2 Nephi 27 the terms "words of a book" and "the words of them which have slumbered" found in verse 6 refer to the teachings and message of the full record of the Nephites. In the golden plates (referred to as "the book" in verse 7) there is a sealed portion that was not to be given to us at this time. Verse 9 refers to the Prophet Joseph and his bringing forth of the Book of Mormon (that portion of the record not held back by the Lord) and sending some of the words to Charles Anthon (see JS—H 1:64). These events are encompassed in Isaiah's prophecy concerning the coming forth of the Book of Mormon. (See Isa. 29:11–12; and 2 Ne. 27:15–20). The fulfillment of this prophecy is recorded in the Pearl of Great Price. We read:

> In the midst of our afflictions we found a friend in a gentleman by the name of Martin Harris, who came to us and gave me fifty dollars to assist us on our journey [to Harmony, Pennsylvania]. Mr. Harris was a resident of Palmyra township, Wayne county, in the State of New York, and a farmer of respectability.

> By this timely aid was I enabled to reach the place of my destination in Pennsylvania; and immediately after my arrival there I commenced copying the characters off the plates. I copied a considerable number of them, and by means of the Urim and Thummim I translated some of them, which I did between the time I arrived at the house of my wife's father, in the month of December, and the February following.

Sometime in this month of February [1828], the aforementioned Mr. Martin Harris came to our place, got the characters which I had drawn off the plates, and started with them to the city of New York. For what took place relative to him and the characters, I refer to his own account of the circumstances, as he related them to me after his return, which was as follows:

I went to the city of New York, and presented the characters which had been translated, with the translation thereof, to Professor Charles Anthon, a gentleman celebrated for his literary attainments. Professor Anthon stated that the translation was correct, more so than any he had before seen translated from the Egyptian. I then showed him those which were not yet translated, and he said that they were Egyptian, Chaldaic, Assyriac, and Arabic; and he said they were true characters. He gave me a certificate, certifying to the people of Palmyra that they were true characters, and that the translation of such of them as had been translated was also correct. I took the certificate and put it into my pocket, and was just leaving the house, when Mr. Anthon called me back, and asked me how the young man found out that there were gold plates in the place where he found them. I answered that an angel of God had revealed it unto him.

He then said to me, *"Let me* see that *certificate."* I accordingly took it out of my pocket and gave it to him, when he took it and tore it to pieces, saying that there was no such thing now as ministering of angels, and that if I would bring the plates to him he would translate them. I informed him that part of the plates were *sealed,* and that I was forbidden to bring them. He replied, "I cannot read a sealed book." I left him and went to Dr. Mitchell, who sanctioned what Professor Anthon had said respecting both the characters and the translation (JS—H 1:61–65).

Likening the Scriptures to Our Lives

2 Nephi 27: 25–26—The Lord will bring about a marvelous work among this people, but the learned and wise who work darkness shall perish.

Application—The Lord can work with His children only according to their faith (see 2 Ne. 27:23). Many learned, though unwise, set themselves up with their own wisdom and knowledge, and it profits them not for they set aside the things of the Lord (see 2 Ne. 9:28–29). Remember, the learning of man is of little consequence when compared to the things of God.

3. ANTICIPATING AND NEUTRALIZING THE STRATEGIES OF SATAN

THEME. Satan shall rage in the hearts of men in the last days. He seeks to destroy the souls of men with false doctrines, with pride, and by lulling them away into false security.

> *"For behold, at that day shall he rage in the hearts of the children of men, and stir them up to anger against that which is good." (2 Ne. 28:20)*

> *"Because of pride, and because of false teachers, and false doctrine, their churches have become corrupted, and their churches are lifted up; because of pride they are puffed up." (2 Ne. 28:12)*

> *"And others will he pacify, and lull them away into carnal security, that they will say: All is well in Zion; yea, Zion prospereth, all is well—and thus the devil cheateth their souls, and leadeth them away carefully down to hell." (2 Ne. 28:21)*

MOMENT OF TRUTH. If, like Nephi, you had witnessed in vision the enormous destruction caused by Satan when he was to "rage in the hearts of the children of men" in the latter days (see 2 Ne. 28:20), would you not have wanted to warn your posterity by revealing the secrets of his diabolical strategies? That is precisely what Nephi does (2 Ne. 28). This portion of his record is Lucifer's playbook exposed in plain view. Nephi's strategy makes eerie sense to all of us nowadays as our nation's leadership expends enormous amounts of time and resources to learn the plans of terrorist groups who constantly plot the destruction of our way of life. To know and understand the enemy is to be forewarned; to have insight into the enemy's tactics is the first step in overthrowing the enemy's design and creating security and protection for one's family. The Lord wants us to be on full alert against the incursions of evil, and Nephi is one of the Lord's prominent voices on the battlefield of daily life where our chief defense is "the truth of God," which is "the rock" upon which we can establish our stand and achieve our victory (see 2 Ne. 28:28).

MODERN PROPHETS SPEAK

George Albert Smith:

> If we can but implant a knowledge of the Gospel of our Lord and faith in His ministry, in the hearts of the rising generation, we have gone a long way towards neutralizing the temptations and power of the adversary in this world. (*CR*, Apr. 1916, 47)

ILLUSTRATIONS FOR OUR TIME

Satan's Plan. Andrew Skinner observes the following about Satan's plan:

> . . . Satan's aim is to promote excess, exaggeration, and extremes in all things. We see this again and again in *The Screwtape Letters*. As Screwtape so aptly puts it, "All extremes except extreme devotion to the Enemy are to be encouraged" (Lewis, *The Screwtape Letters*, p. 38). For Latter-day Saints the connection here with 2 Ne. 28:20–21 is immediate: "For behold, at that day shall he rage in the hearts of the children of men, and stir them up to anger against that which is good. And others will he pacify, and lull them away into carnal security, that they will say: All is well in Zion; yea, Zion prospereth, all is well—and thus the devil cheateth their souls, and leadeth them away carefully down to hell."
>
> Against this backdrop, we note Lewis's firm (and insightful) belief that the devil will never tempt humans to commit a major sin when a minor one will do the job. As Screwtape further instructs his nephew, "Murder is no better than cards if cards can do the trick. Indeed, the safest road to Hell is the gradual one—the gentle slope, soft underfoot, without sudden turnings, without milestones, without signposts" (Lewis, *The Screwtape Letters*, p. 54). (*C. S. Lewis, the Man and His Message: An LDS Perspective,* ed. Andrew C. Skinner and Robert L. Millet [Salt Lake City: Deseret Book, 1999], 49–54)

Likening the Scriptures to Our Lives

2 Nephi 28: 20–20—Satan rages in the hearts of the children of men as demonstrated by his several strategies: anger, being against that which is good, carnal security, "all is well . . . all is well," flattery, there is no hell, there is no devil.

Application—The Book of Mormon exposes the devil for what he is. Let us realize that when we participate in any of the foregoing, as well as succumb to many other temptations, we allow the devil to influence us. We can be subject to him as we choose to do those things that separate us from God and cause us to lose the Spirit.

4. THE IMPORTANCE AND POWER OF THE BOOK OF MORMON

THEME. Through the Book of Mormon we can receive inspiration and direction for our lives. Gordon B. Hinckley said, "Believe in the Book of Mormon as the word of God. Study the Book of Mormon. Pray over the Book of Mormon. Let its inspiration come into your lives." (*Teachings of Gordon B. Hinckley* [Salt Lake City: Deseret Book, 1997], 199)

"And also, that I may remember the promises which I have made unto thee, Nephi, and also unto thy father, that I would remember your seed; and that the words of your seed should proceed forth out of my mouth unto your seed; and my words shall hiss forth unto the ends of the earth, for a standard unto my people, which are of the house of Israel."
(2 Ne. 29:2)

MOMENT OF TRUTH. Nephi knew through prophetic insight that his record would be brought forth in the fulness of times as a light shining out of the darkness. He also discerned that the record would be received by many with disbelief because of the blindness of sectarian philosophy, whereby the canon of scripture was believed closed. It must have thrilled Nephi to impart the Lord's own response to such narrow-mindedness: "Know ye not that there are more nations than one? Know ye not that I, the Lord your God, have created all men, and that I remember those who are upon the isles of the sea; and that I rule in the heavens above and in the earth beneath; and I bring forth my word unto the children of men, yea, even upon all the nations of the earth?" (2 Ne. 29:7). Nephi pressed forward with fervor in his mission to provide an additional testament of Jesus Christ in preparation for the day when the Lord's people would be gathered together once again and His word also would be "gathered in one" (2 Ne. 29:14).

MODERN PROPHETS SPEAK

George Albert Smith:

> The Book of Mormon contains evidence of the importance that our Heavenly Father attaches to reading the scriptures. He sent the sons of Lehi back to Jerusalem to recover the Old Testament scriptures, in order that they might retain the teachings of the Prophets. The Lord would not take them into a new country without preserving to them the privilege of reading his teachings to their forefathers.

> The importance of having the advice of the prophets of God is emphasized in the bringing forth of the Book of Mormon. (*Sharing the Gospel with Others,* sel. and comp. Preston Nibley [Salt Lake City: Deseret News Press, 1948], 43–44)

ILLUSTRATIONS FOR OUR TIME

Sprouting Seeds. The Book of Mormon is the textbook of conversion. One of its principal figures and teachers, Alma the Younger, compares faith to a seed and inspires his listeners to undertake a most practical exercise in spiritual horticulture: "But behold, if ye will awake and arouse your faculties, even to an experiment upon my words, and exercise a particle of faith, yea, even if ye can no more than desire to believe, let this desire work in you, even until ye believe in a manner that ye can give place for a portion of my words" (Alma 32:27).

From the earliest days of the Restoration, the Book of Mormon has drawn noble truth seekers into the fold. Take the story of Joseph Smith's younger brother, Samuel Harrison Smith, who as a 22 year old returned from his mission somewhat discouraged with the results. Yet look at what came of his labors: on Saturday, 14 April 1832, Brigham Young, "the Lion of the Lord" (*HC*, 7:435), was baptized after two years of intensive study and prayer centered on the Book of Mormon, a copy of which his brother Phineas had given him. Phineas had purchased the copy from Samuel Harrison Smith in April 1830, during the latter's early missionary labors. Samuel also provided a copy to Reverend John P. Greene, husband of Phineas's sister, Rhoda. Both were subsequently converted. Brigham Young had given his copy of the Book of Mormon to his sister, Fanny Young Murray, the mother-in-law of Heber C. Kimball, who, along with his family, also became converted because of it (see *Church History in the Fulness of Times*, [Church Educational System manual, 2000], 74–75).

The sprouting seeds that come from a sincere study of the Book of Mormon lead to the growth and maturation of a tree of faith: "Behold, by and by ye shall pluck the fruit thereof, which is most precious, which is sweet above all that is sweet, and which is white above all that is white, yea, and pure above all that is pure; and ye shall feast upon this fruit even until ye are filled, that ye hunger not, neither shall ye thirst" (Alma 32:42).

Is it any wonder that the Lord has commanded us to share the Book of Mormon with others so that they, too, can learn divine truth through spiritual confirmation (see Moro. 10:4)? As Nephi testified, the coming forth of the Book of Mormon is undeniable evidence that the Lord will fulfill His solemn promise: "And it shall come to pass that my people, which are of the house of Israel, shall be gathered home unto the lands of their possessions; and my word also shall be gathered in one. And I will show unto them that fight against my word and against my people, who are of the house of Israel, that I am God, and that I covenanted with Abraham that I would remember his seed forever" (2 Ne. 29:14). (Allen)

Likening the Scriptures to Our Lives

2 Nephi 29:11—We are judged by our works according to the standard of the written word of God.

Application—Let us consistently and devotedly base our values and standards for living upon the word of God as given in the scriptures and through His living prophets.

5. COVENANT PEOPLE
AND THE MILLENNIAL REIGN

THEME. Covenant people are all those who repent and come unto Christ. Israel will eventually be restored, and the wicked will be destroyed.

> *"For behold, I say unto you that as many of the Gentiles as will repent are the covenant people of the Lord; and as many of the Jews as will not repent shall be cast off; for the Lord covenanteth with none save it be with them that repent and believe in his Son, who is the Holy One of Israel." (2 Ne. 30:2)*

MOMENT OF TRUTH. The Lord had favored Nephi with a vision of His dealings with mankind from the beginning of time even unto the end thereof when He would institute His millennial reign. Nephi was able to experience vicariously the anguish of those who relinquished their covenant blessing through apostasy and rebellion; he was able to savor the unspeakable joy of those who purified themselves and participated in the blessings of covenant obedience. As Nephi came to the close of his portion of the sacred chronicle, he focused on the good news on the fruits of the Restoration in the latter days, and on the effects of a revived spirituality among the gathering remnants of Israel and the responsive Gentile nations: "And then shall they rejoice; for they shall know that it is a blessing unto them from the hand of God; and their scales of darkness shall begin to fall from their eyes; and many generations shall not pass away among them, save they shall be a pure and a delightsome people" (2 Ne. 30:6). Through Nephi's eyes we can look at ourselves in the mirror of divine light and see what we must do to become and remain a covenant people.

MODERN PROPHETS SPEAK

Joseph Fielding Smith:

> The promise now follows. If you, a rebellious nation, will repent and turn again unto the Lord, your sins, "though as scarlet, they shall be as white as snow; though they be red like crimson, they shall be as wool" (Isaiah 1:18). So, we see, this is not an individual promise, but one to a rebellious nation. No matter how many prophets the Lord sent to Israel and Judah, and how many times he pleaded with them, all through their history they were rebellious.

> Here we find a promise that if they would return to the Lord, their past sins would be forgotten, and he would again receive them as his people and bless them abundantly, and they should continue to be his covenant people. So we see that this pas-

sage does not apply to individuals and individual sins." (*Answers to Gospel Questions*, 5 vols. [Salt Lake City: Deseret Book, 1957–1966], 2:180)

There is also another consideration of vast importance to all the rulers and people of the world in regard to this matter. It is this: As this work progresses in its onward course, and becomes more and more an object of political and religious interest and excitement, no king, ruler, or subject, no community or individual, will stand *neutral*. All will at length be influenced by one spirit or the other, and will take sides either for or against the kingdom of God, and the fulfillment of the prophets, in the great restoration and return of his long-dispersed covenant people. . . . ("A Proclamation of the Twelve Apostles of the Church of Jesus Christ of Latter-day Saints," in *Messages of the First Presidency*, comp. James R. Clark, 6 vols [Salt Lake City: Bookcraft, 1965–1975], 1:257).

ILLUSTRATIONS FOR OUR TIME

Primordial Fear, Primordial Joy. A number of years ago I was introduced to the writings of the celebrated psychologist John Bowlby, who developed a series of pioneering studies about the causes of fear in children. Investigations of the experiences of children during the blitz of London in the Second World War and subsequent research caused him to conclude that the source of primordial fear in children goes back, in general, to a condition of their being alone, in dark places, suddenly separated from the support of loved ones, surrounded by strange noises, and accompanied by disorienting and unfamiliar figures and shapes. If that is the source of primordial fear, then it is reasonable to conclude that the source of primordial joy would be the opposite: being in familiar and comforting circumstances with loved ones in an atmosphere of light and pleasant sounds.

I think of that dichotomy of feelings while reading Isaiah. In the one instance, he speaks of the anguish of the unrighteous who are so ashamed of themselves on the Day of Judgment that they would seek total darkness and isolation rather than face the Lord of light: "And they shall go into the holes of the rocks, and into the caves of the earth, for the fear of the Lord shall come upon them and the glory of his majesty shall smite them, when he ariseth to shake terribly the earth" (2 Ne. 12:19). This horrific scene is amplified in Alma's counsel to his wayward son Corianton concerning the fate of those who die in their sins: "and these shall be cast out into outer darkness; there shall be weeping, and wailing, and gnashing of teeth, and this because of their own iniquity, being led captive by the will of the devil. Now this is the state of the souls of the wicked, yea, in darkness, and a state of awful, fearful looking for the fiery indignation of the wrath of God upon them; thus they remain in this state, as well as the righteous in paradise, until the time of their resurrection" (Alma 40:13–14).

By contrast, Isaiah describes also the mind-set of the righteous who will be transported with unfathomable joy when gathering to holy places during the millennial reign, singing: "Behold, God is my salvation; I will trust, and not be afraid; for the Lord Jehovah is my strength and my song; he also has become my salvation. Therefore, with joy shall ye draw water out of the wells of salvation. And in that day shall ye say: Praise the Lord, call upon his name, declare his doings among the people, make mention that his name is exalted. Sing unto the Lord; for he hath done excellent things; this is known in all the earth. Cry out and shout, thou inhabitant of Zion; for great is the Holy One of Israel in the midst of thee" (2 Ne. 22:2–6). Similarly: "Break forth into joy, sing together, ye waste places of Jerusalem: for the Lord hath comforted his people, he hath redeemed Jerusalem" (Isa. 52:9—a verse quoted not once but four times in the Book of Mormon: Mosiah 12:23; 15:30; 3 Ne. 16:19; 20:34).

Individuals who respond to the gathering call and follow the promptings of the Spirit by entering the fold of the Lord go from feelings of being alone in darkness to feelings of being enveloped in light where the sounds of the word of God can be heard. As Isaiah put it concerning the coming forth of the Book of Mormon, "And in that day shall the deaf hear the words of the book, and the eyes of the blind shall see out of obscurity and out of darkness. And the meek also shall increase, and their joy shall be in the Lord, and the poor among men shall rejoice in the Holy One of Israel" (2 Ne. 27:29–30). Thus the humble and the obedient cross into the realm of light, while those who would reject the invitation to receive salvation "without money and without price" (2 Ne. 26:25)—a free offering to which "all men are privileged the one like unto the other, and none are forbidden" (v. 28)—must of necessity remain alone, outside the circle of covenant blessings. "Wherefore, ye are not brought into the light, but must perish in the dark" (2 Ne. 32:4). The Lord, through his prophets, speaks plainly of the choice between primordial fear and loneliness, on the one hand, and primordial joy and togetherness, on the other. (Allen)

Likening the Scriptures to Our Lives

2 Nephi 30:2—Everyone can have a place among the covenant people of the Lord through faith in Christ, repentance, baptism, and receiving the gift of the Holy Ghost.

Application—When we choose to repent and follow the steps of spiritual rebirth, we make a covenant with the Lord. He will honor this covenant. Through obedience, we can have the blessings of eternal life by enduring to the end.

SUMMARY

What a great debt of gratitude we owe to the diligence and faithfulness of the prophet Nephi! Sharing his inspired vision, we can look forward to the Second Coming of the Savior and rejoice. We may deepen our understanding of the Lord's design in bringing forth the Book of Mormon in our day. We can become more skillful in anticipating and neutralizing the strategies of Satan. We can appreciate with greater insight and gratitude the power of the Book of Mormon. We can live more righteously as a covenant people, preparing ourselves and our posterity for the millennial reign.

The Lord restored His gospel by bringing forth the Book of Mormon. By living the word of God we will have power to resist temptation and avoid the deceptions of the devil. This gospel contained in the Book of Mormon is to be preached to every nation, kindred, tongue, and people. The remnant of the seed of Joseph shall know of their beginnings and many will be restored to the truth. Those who repent will become the covenant people of the Lord.

CHAPTER ELEVEN

"PRESS FORWARD WITH A STEADFASTNESS *in* CHRIST"

2 NEPHI 31–33

"Following these invitations to faith in the Lord Jesus Christ, repentance, baptism, and receiving the gift of the Holy Ghost, Nephi again eloquently asked for endurance, persistence, and perseverance. Every reader of the Book of Mormon thrills at this summary of the first principles of the gospel, one of the many truly majestic passages in the Book of Mormon! 'And now, my beloved brethren, after ye have gotten into this strait and narrow path, I would ask if all is done? Behold, I say unto you, Nay; for ye have not come thus far save it were by the word of Christ with unshaken faith in him, relying wholly upon the merits of him who is mighty to save' (2 Ne. 31:19)."
—JEFFREY R. HOLLAND, *CHRIST AND THE NEW COVENANT: THE MESSIANIC MESSAGE OF THE BOOK OF MORMON* [SALT LAKE CITY: DESERET BOOK, 1997], 54.

THEMES *for* LIVING

The Doctrine of Christ
Press Forward with Steadfastness and Endure to the End
Feast upon the Words of Christ and Enjoy the Blessings of the Spirit
The Divine Word as the Standard for Judgment

INTRODUCTION

We partake of the blessings of the Atonement by embracing the doctrine of Christ and enduring to the end. We are admonished to feast upon the words of Christ, for they will tell us all things to do. As we gain the Spirit it will show us all things to do. Through the power of the Word and the Spirit we are able to "press forward with a steadfastness in Christ" (2 Ne. 31:20).

1. THE DOCTRINE OF CHRIST

THEME. The doctrine of Christ contains within it the first four principles and ordinances of the gospel: faith in Jesus Christ, repentance through Jesus Christ, baptism for the remission of sins and taking the name of Jesus Christ upon you, and receiving the gift of the Holy Ghost from the Father because of Jesus Christ (see 3 Ne. 19:20–22; 21:3).

> *"Wherefore, the things which I have written sufficeth me, save it be a few words which I must speak concerning the doctrine of Christ; wherefore, I shall speak unto you plainly, according to the plainness of my prophesying." (2 Ne. 31:2)*

> *"And the Father said: Repent ye, repent ye, and be baptized in the name of my Beloved Son. And also, the voice of the Son came unto me, saying: He that is baptized in my name, to him will the Father give the Holy Ghost, like unto me; wherefore, follow me, and do the things which ye have seen me do." (2 Ne. 31:11–12)*

MOMENT OF TRUTH. Nephi now comes to the moment in his ministry where he must bring his sacred account on the small plates to a close. He has beheld many grand and extraordinary things pertaining to the design of heaven for humankind. He has viewed the generations of time, witnessed the coming and going of nations, perceived the flow of history from the beginning even until the end, and has watched the inevitable decline of the rebellious and the inexorable prosperity of the covenant faithful. Of all these grand episodes and supernal revelations, what does he, in his final remarks, choose to emphasize in his closing witness for future readers? It is the simple and pure doctrine of Christ. It is a solemn reminder of the efficacy of the principles of faith, repentance, baptism, and the gift of the Holy Ghost. It is an earnest plea to his readers to take upon themselves the name of Christ and endure to the end. All of this constitutes the key to joy and exaltation, and Nephi places his seal of testimony upon these final words of counsel as central to the gospel of Jesus Christ.

MODERN PROPHETS SPEAK

Bruce R. McConkie:

> What message do the Lord's ministers bear? What should they preach? The gospel of Jesus Christ! The word! The truths of salvation as recorded in the revelations! How sobering is Paul's charge! In God's holy name the command is to preach doctrine, sound doctrine, saving doctrine, the doctrine of Christ! (*Doctrinal New Testament Commentary,* 3 vols. [Salt Lake City: Bookcraft, 1965–1973], 3:114)

ILLUSTRATIONS FOR OUR TIME

Being Happy with What God Gives to Us. Elder Matthew Cowley has described for us the beauty and importance of living the doctrine of Christ, the principles of the gospel of Jesus Christ:

> The simple life is the good life. And we can have that simple life, all of us, if we will obey the simple principles of the gospel. I am not one to get up and try to grind out these profound principles, these mysteries. I do not understand them. But I try to understand the simple things: faith, repentance." (*Matthew Cowley Speaks* [Salt Lake City: Deseret Book, 1954], 269)

> My parents, I am thankful to say, always wanted us to feel good about the gospel, about obeying the principles of it, getting joy and happiness from it. It's supposed to lift us up, not depress us. I have in my office every day good and faithful members of this Church who are depressed, who are frustrated, who think they are not being saved, and most of those people whom I see are just as worthy as I and some more worthy. Why they are frustrated, I don't know, unless someone is trying to scare them into the celestial glory. I like to get fun out of this business—good, wholesome, righteous fun—get a kick out of it. When I obey the principles of this gospel, I am the happiest man on earth. When I don't, then I am depressed, then I have a right to worry about myself; but, when I am trying to do the best I know, then I tell you, I am having the time of my life." (*Ibid.,* 133)

Likening the Scriptures to Our Lives

2 Nephi 31:11–13—Repent (through faith on the Lord Jesus Christ), be baptized, and receive the gift of the Holy Ghost.

Application—To apply the Atonement of Christ fully in our lives, let us accept the principles and ordinances of the gospel (the doctrine of Christ). This will in turn allow us to take His name upon us and by obedience, we can partake of the blessings of God.

2. PRESS FORWARD WITH STEADFASTNESS AND ENDURE TO THE END

THEME. To press forward with steadfastness, with a firm and constant effort in Christ, and to endure to the end with unrelenting determination—these are the crowning attributes of discipleship.

> *"Wherefore, ye must press forward with a steadfastness in Christ, having a perfect brightness of hope, and a love of God and of all men. Wherefore, if ye shall press forward, feasting upon the word of Christ, and endure to the end, behold, thus saith the Father: Ye shall have eternal life." (2 Ne. 31:20)*

MOMENT OF TRUTH. Nephi was the Lord's witness of the fact that entering into a covenant relationship with God, though indispensable for salvation and exaltation, was, in and of itself, not enough. One must extend the covenant fidelity into eternity. One must endure to the end with an unyielding steadfastness in Christ, just as Nephi had exemplified through his ministry, and just as the prophets of the Lord have demonstrated in all dispensations of time.

MODERN PROPHETS SPEAK.

Neal A. Maxwell:

> "They are without principle," Moroni wrote. Without fixed principles and a clear destination, Nephi's metaphor of pressing forward amid "all these things" would give way to plodding persistence or mindless survival. But with gospel certitude his metaphor denotes a determined, zestful stride, even in those moments when there may seem to be nothing to be zestful about. Furthermore, in our day the striding forward "with a steadfastness in Christ" is to be accomplished amid the various expressions of how all things shall be in "commotion" in the world (see D&C 88:91; 2 Nephi 28:20). (*If Thou Endure It Well* [Salt Lake City: Bookcraft, 1996], 11)

> Consecration involves pressing forward "with a steadfastness in Christ" with a "brightness of hope, and a love of God and of all men . . . [while] feasting on the word of Christ" (2 Nephi 31:20). Jesus pressed forward sublimely. He did not shrink, such as by going only 60 percent of the distance toward the full atonement. Instead, He "finished [His] preparations" for all mankind, bringing a universal resurrection—not one in which 40 percent of us would have been left out (see D&C 19:18–19). (*If Thou Endure It Well* [Salt Lake City: Bookcraft, 1996], 52)

ILLUSTRATIONS FOR OUR TIME

The Parable of the Divers.

Stephen E. Robinson:

Many years ago, when I was somewhere between nine and eleven, I participated in a community summer recreation program in the town where I grew up. I remember in particular a diving competition for the different age groups held at the community swimming pool. Some of the wealthier kids in our area had their own pools with diving boards, and they were pretty good amateur divers. But there was one kid my age from the less affluent part of town who didn't have his own pool. What he had was raw courage. While the rest of us did our crisp little swan dives, back dives, and jackknives, being ever so careful to arch our backs and point our toes, this young man attempted back flips, one-and-a-halfs, doubles, and so on. But, oh, he was sloppy. He seldom kept his feet together, he never pointed his toes, and he usually missed his vertical entry. The rest of us observed with smug satisfaction as the judges held up their scorecards that he consistently got lower marks than we did with our safe and simple dives, and we congratulated ourselves that we were actually the better divers. "He is all heart and no finesse," we told ourselves. "After all, *we* keep *our* feet together and point *our* toes."

The announcement of the winners was a great shock to us, for the brave young lad with the flips had apparently beaten us all. However, I had kept rough track of the scores in my head, and I knew with the arrogance of limited information that the math didn't add up. I had consistently outscored the boy with the flips. And so, certain that an injustice was being perpetrated, I stormed the scorer's table and demanded an explanation. "Degree of difficulty," the scorer replied matter-of-factly as he looked me in the eye. "Sure, you had better form, but he did harder dives. When you factor in the degree of difficulty, he beat you hands down, kid." Until that moment I hadn't known that some dives were awarded "extra credit" because of their greater difficulty. . . .

Whenever I am tempted to feel superior to other Saints, the parable of the divers comes to my mind, and I repent. At least at a swim meet, we can usually tell which dives are the most difficult. But here in mortality, we cannot always tell who is carrying what burdens: limited intelligence, chemical depression, compulsive behaviors, learning disabilities, dysfunctional or abusive family background, poor health, physical or psychological handicaps—no one chooses these things. So I must not judge my brothers and sisters. I am thankful for my blessings but not smug about them, for

I *never* want to hear the Scorer say to me, "Sure, you had better form, but she had a harder life. When you factor in degree of difficulty, she beat you hands down."

So, enduring to the end doesn't have much to do with suffering in silence, overcoming all life's obstacles, or even achieving the LDS ideal ("pointing our toes" and "keeping our feet together"). It just means not giving up. It means keeping—to the best of our abilities—the commitments we made to Christ when we entered into the marriage of the gospel. It means not divorcing the Savior or cheating on him by letting some other love become more important in our lives. It means not rejecting the blessings of the atonement that he showered upon us when we entered his church and kingdom. (*Following Christ: The Parable of the Divers and More Good News* [Salt Lake City: Deseret Book, 1995], 34–38)

Likening the Scriptures to Our Lives

2 Nephi 31:20—Enduring to the end is sometimes called the fifth principle of the gospel.

Application—Nephi says, "Wherefore, ye must press forward with a steadfastness in Christ, having a perfect brightness of hope, and a love of God and of all men. Wherefore, if ye shall press forward, feasting upon the word of Christ, and endure to the end, behold, thus saith the Father: Ye shall have eternal life" (2 Ne. 31:20).

3. FEAST UPON THE WORDS OF CHRIST AND ENJOY THE BLESSINGS OF THE SPIRIT

THEME. The words of Christ are delicious. They will instruct us in all of our dealings. If we live worthy, the Holy Spirit will show us all things to do.

> *"Angels speak by the power of the Holy Ghost; wherefore, they speak the words of Christ. Wherefore, I said unto you, feast upon the words of Christ; for behold, the words of Christ will tell you all things what ye should do. . . . For behold, again I say unto you that if ye will enter in by the way, and receive the Holy Ghost, it will show unto you all things what ye should do." (2 Ne. 32:3, 5)*

MOMENT OF TRUTH. Nephi, being both a visionary servant of the Lord and a practical guide for his people, leaves a legacy of inspired advice. Follow divine counsel. Follow the Spirit. Pray always in the name of the Christ "that thy performance may be for the welfare of thy soul" (2 Ne. 32:9).

MODERN PROPHETS SPEAK

Ezra Taft Benson:

> His gospel is the perfect prescription for all human problems and social ills. But His gospel is effective only as it is applied in our lives. Therefore, we must "feast upon the words of Christ; for behold, the words of Christ will tell [us] all things what [we] should do" (Book of Mormon, 2 Nephi 32:3). (*Come unto Christ* [Salt Lake City: Deseret Book, 1983], 132)

ILLUSTRATIONS FOR OUR TIME

Feasting on the Word Will Inspire Us to Action. I was traveling to the Salt Lake City airport with my friend Robert Matthews on our way to a Know Your Religion lecture. At the time, he was in the midst of working on the topical guide, footnotes, and cross references for the new edition of the scriptures. I inquired as to the progress. He mentioned things were going well and added, "Last week I had an interesting experience. I was reading all the scriptures concerning prayer. It took several days and at the end of the project I had an overwhelming desire to pray." I have thought about that statement a lot over the years. Surely when we truly feast upon the words of Christ—I mean truly feast—we will be inspired to action. The word tells us all things to do. It is the food for our spirit, and our spirits direct our bodies. If we are not diligent in keeping the commandments, we sap our spiritual strength. The solution is to increase our faith. Faith comes by hearing the word of God (see Rom. 10:17). (Pinegar)

Likening the Scriptures to Our Lives

2 Nephi 32:3–5—The word will tell us all things to do. The Spirit will show us all things to do.

Application—If ever there was a panacea for life, it is the word of God and the Holy Spirit. Feasting upon the word should be a daily happening. It will keep us on the strait and narrow path and help us overcome temptation (see 1 Ne. 15:24) as we continually nurture it through faith, diligence, and patience (see Alma 32:40–43). When we keep the commandments we will be blessed to have His Spirit to be with us always (see D&C 20:77).

4. THE DIVINE WORD AS THE STANDARD FOR JUDGMENT

THEME. The purpose of the word of God is to persuade us to do good, to believe in Christ, and to endure to the end. We will be judged by the word of God given unto us.

"And I know that the Lord God will consecrate my prayers for the gain of my people. And the words which I have written in weakness will be made strong unto them; for it persuadeth them to do good; it maketh known unto them of their fathers; and it speaketh of Jesus, and persuadeth them to believe in him, and to endure to the end, which is life eternal." (2 Ne. 33:4)

MOMENT OF TRUTH. Nephi closes his record with a prophecy that he would one day meet many faithful and valiant souls at the judgment seat of God. He makes an impassioned plea that all who should receive his words would believe in them, "for they are the words of Christ, and he hath given them unto me; and they teach all men that they should do good" (2 Ne. 33:10). Then Nephi places the matter in a very personal context: "and you and I shall stand face to face before his bar; and ye shall know that I have been commanded of him to write these things, notwithstanding my weakness" (2 Ne. 33:11). To those of the house of Israel and mankind in general he says, "Farewell until that great day shall come" (v. 13), and to those who refuse to show respect for the word of God—whether from his own record (i.e., Nephi's), or from the record of the Jews (i.e., the Bible)—he says: "I bid you an *everlasting* farewell, for these words shall condemn you at the last day" (v. 14, italics added).

MODERN PROPHETS SPEAK

Neal A. Maxwell:

> The Lord can compensate for our communication weaknesses. Nephi wrote: "And the words which I have written in weakness will be made strong unto them." What key things did he convey? "For it *persuadeth them to do good;* it *maketh known unto them of their fathers;* and it *speaketh of Jesus,* and *persuadeth them to believe in him,* and to *endure to the end*" (2 Ne. 33:42; Nephi 33:4, italics added). (*Men and Women of Christ* [Salt Lake City: Bookcraft, 1991], 80–81)

ILLUSTRATIONS FOR OUR TIME

He's Talking About Me. An acquaintance of mine, John Condry, a business consultant by profession, once expressed to me what he considered to be the heart and soul of leadership: "The real-world lesson in leadership is brought home every day: Nothing happens until someone takes personal responsibility." Nephi gives an extraordinary lesson on personal responsibility at the end of his second book, focusing the light of individual responsibility and accountability upon the reader in a unique way. Nephi adduces a personal relationship between himself and that reader, saying, in effect, that there would be a future reunion, before the judgment seat of God, where the verity of the words he had written in his record would be confirmed (see 2 Ne. 33:11). Face-to-face is a rather personal posture for two people to assume, especially before the court of God. Nephi summarizes his entire Book of Mormon account by placing his witness and his message squarely at the feet of—or, better still—upon the shoulders of, the reader, with the injunction to take action based on the essence and spirit of his words. Thus the reader is encouraged to exercise leadership by taking personal responsibility for his or her behavior relative to the prophetic word.

For the reader, the fundamentally important transition is from casual observer to self-observed, from abstract persona to an involved individual who exclaims: "He is talking about me! I am the one being addressed. It is my salvation and immortality that is at stake!" (Allen).

Likening the Scriptures to Our Lives

2 Nephi 33:4—Nephi's continual concern for the welfare of God's children is again exemplified as he prayed for his people, wrote the things that could persuade them to do good and believe in Christ, and encouraged them to endure to the end.

Application—Let us follow the prophets and search the scriptures and by so doing receive the strength of the Lord to endure to the end.

SUMMARY

The central theme of the Book of Mormon is the Savior—His Atonement and the loving bestowal of His grace, mercy, and merits toward bringing about the immortality and eternal life of man. The central doctrine of the Book of Mormon is the Doctrine of Christ, which draws us onward with steadfastness as we strive to honor our covenant promises and endure to the end. When we feast upon the words of Christ, we enjoy the blessings of the Spirit. When we respect and embrace the divine word as given through the prophets of God, we prepare ourselves in righteousness for the Day of Judgment.

CHAPTER TWELVE

"SEEK YE *for the* KINGDOM *of* GOD"

JACOB 1–4

"The Kingdom of God is all that is real worth.
All else is not worth possessing, either here or hereafter."
—BRIGHAM YOUNG. *DISCOURSES OF BRIGHAM YOUNG,* ED. JOHN A. WIDTSOE
[SALT LAKE CITY: BOOKCRAFT, 1925], 444.

THEMES *for* LIVING

Magnifying Your Calling
Avoiding the Sins of Destruction: Pride, Greed, Immorality
Being Reconciled to God through the Atonement of Christ

INTRODUCTION

Each of us has eternal roles, church callings, and personal responsibilities. We should seek to improve and magnify our callings—this is our mission. We are responsible and accountable for our actions. Our actions are the eventual result of our thoughts, which, when dwelt upon, become the desires that move us. Surely the scripture is true, "For as he thinketh in his heart, so is he" (Prov. 23:7). This was the problem with so many of the Nephites—the wickedness of their hearts. When our hearts are not right, we seek after worldly things and the lusts of the flesh. Jacob's love for the people and awareness of his duty led him to teach and write vigorous admonitions.

1. MAGNIFYING YOUR CALLING

THEME. We receive great blessings when we accept callings with gratitude and then perform to our utmost ability while on the Lord's errand.

> *"And we did magnify our office unto the Lord, taking upon us the responsibility, answering the sins of the people upon our own heads if we did not teach them the word of God with all diligence; wherefore, by laboring with our might their blood might not come upon our garments, otherwise their blood would come upon our garments, and we would not be found spotless at the last day" (Jacob 1:19).*

MOMENT OF TRUTH. Jacob and his brother Joseph "had been consecrated priests and teachers of this people, by the hand of Nephi" (Jacob 1:18). Upon the passing of Nephi (see Jacob 1:12), Jacob succeeded his older brother and assumed the prophetic guidance of the people. One can only imagine his feelings to have to follow in such noble footsteps. Thus his words at this juncture provide a telling lesson in how to receive a calling from the Lord in all humility and diligence. This teaches the true definition of "magnifying a calling" with accountability and devotion.

MODERN PROPHETS SPEAK

Thomas S. Monson:

> I promise to be diligent. I will magnify my calling. What does it mean to magnify a calling? It means to build it up in dignity and importance, to make it honorable and commendable in the eyes of all mankind, to enlarge and strengthen it, to let the light of heaven shine through it to the view of other men. And how does one magnify a calling? Simply by performing the service that pertains to it. In short, we magnify our callings by learning what our duties are and then by performing them.

I pause when I think of the words of President John Taylor: "If you do not magnify your calling, God will hold you responsible for those whom you might have saved had you done your duty." (*Be Your Best Self* [Salt Lake City: Deseret Book, 1979], 147)

ILLUSTRATIONS FOR OUR TIME

Wilford Woodruff Magnified His Calling:

I was still holding the office of a Teacher, and knowing for myself that the fulness of the Gospel of Christ, which God had revealed to Joseph Smith, was true, I had a great desire to preach it to the inhabitants of the earth, but as a Teacher I had no authority to preach the gospel to the world. I went into the forest near Lyman Wight's [in Daviess county, Missouri] one Sunday morning, aside from the abodes of men, and made my desire known unto the Lord. I prayed that the Lord would open my way and give me the privilege of preaching the gospel. I did not make my request expecting any honor from man, for I knew that the preaching of the gospel was attended with hard labor and persecution. While I was praying, the Spirit of the Lord rested upon me, and testified to me that my prayer was heard, and that my request would be granted. I arose to my feet and walked some three hundred yards into a broad road, rejoicing. As I came into the road I saw Judge Elias Higbee standing before me. As I walked up to him he said, "Wilford, the Lord has revealed to me that it is your duty to go into the vineyard of the Lord and preach the gospel." I told him if that was the will of the Lord I was ready to go. I did not tell him that I had been praying for that privilege. I had been boarding at Lyman Wight's with Judge Higbee for months, and it was the first time he had ever named such a thing to me. (B. H. Roberts, *New Witnesses for God,* 3 vols. [Salt Lake City: The Deseret News, 1951], 1:238–39)

Wilford Woodruff had a desire to serve and was subsequently called to the work (see D&C 4:3). (See *The Discourses of Wilford Woodruff,* ed. G. Homer Durham [Salt Lake City: Bookcraft, 1969], vi–vii) (Pinegar)

Likening the Scriptures to Our Lives

Jacob 1:19—Jacob was responsible and accountable for his stewardship. He would take the sins of the people upon his own head if he failed to teach them the word of God with all diligence. He magnified his calling.

Application—Let us take seriously our callings as well as our eternal roles in life. We are responsible and accountable to the Lord to perform our duties with love and devotion. How we magnify our callings affects the lives of those around us. Let us resolve to make a list of priorities of things we are responsible and accountable for and then ensure that we do these things with all faith, diligence, and patience.

2. AVOIDING THE SINS OF DESTRUCTION: PRIDE, GREED, IMMORALITY

THEME. Our thoughts and hearts are the gateway to our actions. Great blessings attend pure devotion to the Lord; great sorrow derives from practicing pride, greed, and unrighteousness.

"Yea, it grieveth my soul and causeth me to shrink with shame before the presence of my Maker, that I must testify unto you concerning the wickedness of your hearts" (Jacob 2:6).

"And now behold, my brethren, this is the word which I declare unto you, that many of you have begun to search for gold, and for silver, and for all manner of precious ores, in the which this land, which is a land of promise unto you and to your seed, doth abound most plentifully. And the hand of providence hath smiled upon you most pleasingly, that you have obtained many riches; and because some of you have obtained more abundantly than that of your brethren ye are lifted up in the pride of your hearts, and wear stiff necks and high heads because of the costliness of your apparel, and persecute your brethren because ye suppose that ye are better than they" (Jacob 2:12–13).

"And now I, Jacob, spake many more things unto the people of Nephi, warning them against fornication and lasciviousness, and every kind of sin, telling them the awful consequences of them" (Jacob 3:12).

MOMENT OF TRUTH. Having assumed the role of spiritual leader of the people and curator of the sacred records following the ministry of Nephi, Jacob is mindful of the responsibility to cultivate and foster among the people an uncompromisingly obedient walk in life. Some 55 years have passed since Lehi and his family left Jerusalem (Jacob 1:1), and the little colony in the New World is now beginning to grow "numerous" (Jacob 3:13). With that growth, some "began to grow hard in their hearts" (Jacob 1:15)—the perfect seedbed for the creeping malignancy of pride, materialism, and immorality. Blessed with the spirit of prophecy and revelation, Jacob could perceive with utter clarity what lay ahead for his people, based on the consequences of their choices in life: "For because of faith and great anxiety, it truly had been made manifest unto us concerning our people, what things should happen unto them" (Jacob 1:5). He feared that the great "provocation" (Jacob 1:7) committed by the Israelites at the time of Moses and the giving of the Ten Commandments was about to be replayed in his day, and thus he prayed unto the Lord for guidance and was commanded to assemble the people at the temple and call them to repentance (Jacob 2:11). This he did with frankness, exposing the sins of pride and immorality that were threatening to tear families apart and causing the "fair daughters of this people" (Jacob 2:32) to cry unto the Lord in anguish. Jacob's sermon on overcoming wickedness is one of the masterpieces of spiritual discourse in the scriptures.

MODERN PROPHETS SPEAK

Dallin H. Oaks:

> In the Book of Mormon accounts, the pride of comparison resulted most frequently from the acquisition and use of riches, such as by wearing fine apparel. Thus, Alma the Younger gave this description of the Nephites in the land of Zarahemla, who "began to wax proud" because of their possessions, including their flocks, their gold, and their fine apparel: "The people of the church began to be lifted up in the pride of their eyes, and to set their hearts upon riches and upon the vain things of the world, that they began to be scornful, one towards another" (Alma 4:8). (*Pure in Heart* [Salt Lake City: Bookcraft, 1988], 97–98)

ILLUSTRATIONS FOR OUR TIME

If Only I Had Known. This story, as told by my friend Jaynann Payne to a BYU assembly, portrays the sorrow of sexual transgression:

> We will never forget that sweet young girl of sixteen who came to live with us one summer for the remaining months of her unwed pregnancy. My husband is an attorney and was handling the adoption of her baby. She hadn't wanted to marry the boy who was the father of her unborn child. She had been beguiled and had partaken of the bitter fruit.
>
> In September she gave birth to a beautiful little boy, and the day she was to leave the hospital, Dean and I had to go to Salt Lake City. We stopped at the hospital long enough to meet the couple who were adopting the baby. Under hospital rules, this young mother, sixteen years old, had to take her beautiful nine-pound boy from the arms of the nurse and hand him over to my husband, who then stepped outside the room and gave the baby to the adopting parents. It tore me apart to watch her and to see that young couple leave with her baby.
>
> She said to me, "Sister Payne, he lied to me when he said nobody would get hurt, and that because we loved each other, anything we did was alright. He didn't really love me. That is why I didn't marry him, because he wasn't worthy to be the father of my little boy. It's all a great big lie, and I don't want to live a lie!"
>
> "Oh, if only I had known five minutes before I was immoral how I would feel five minutes after I gave my baby away!"

For this girl not to have thought ahead about the consequences of her actions and not to have realized that lust is the mere image of love is indeed heartbreaking. It is so important to keep in tune, keep in touch, to receive the Spirit each and every day. We never know what is going to happen; and if we make the commitment in our private rooms, by the side of our beds, to our Father in heaven, of what we want to be in life—what we will do and what we won't do—and then ask for his help in keeping our commitments, he will help us in public and private (*BYU Speeches of the Year*, 10 February 1970). (Pinegar)

Likening the Scriptures to Our Lives

Jacob 2:16—Pride can destroy your very soul.

Application—Let us come to understand the devastating effect upon our very being when we allow pride to enter in—a "my will" rather than a "thy will" approach to life (see Ezra Taft Benson, *The Teachings of Ezra Taft Benson* [Salt Lake City: Bookcraft, 1988], 435). The Lord teaches us to be submissive, teachable, and humble in all things.

3. BEING RECONCILED TO GOD THROUGH THE ATONEMENT OF CHRIST

THEME. By receiving with gladness and thanksgiving all of the witnesses of the prophets concerning the Savior and His Atonement, we can cultivate "a hope, and our faith becometh unshaken" (Jacob 4:6).

> *"Now in this thing we do rejoice; and we labor diligently to engraven these words upon plates, hoping that our beloved brethren and our children will receive them with thankful hearts, and look upon them that they may learn with joy and not with sorrow, neither with contempt, concerning their first parents. For, for this intent have we written these things, that they may know that we knew of Christ, and we had a hope of his glory many hundred years before his coming; and not only we ourselves had a hope of his glory, but also all the holy prophets which were before us" (Jacob 4:3–4).*

MOMENT OF TRUTH. Having warned the people boldly concerning the insidious effects of their emerging pride and immorality, Jacob now brings forward the glorious case for embracing with full devotion the Lord's plan of salvation, with all of its attendant blessings of hope and joy. Thus he labored diligently to record on his plates the Lord's antidote to the darkness of sin: to accept the word of prophecy and revelation, that we might know of Christ's atoning sacrifice, and align ourselves with the principles of happiness and redemption. With fervor, Jacob declares the beautiful counsel:

"O all ye that are pure in heart, lift up your heads and receive the pleasing word of God, and feast upon his love; for ye may, if your minds are firm, forever" (Jacob 3:2).

MODERN PROPHETS SPEAK

Gordon B. Hinckley:

> I wish to remind everyone within my hearing that the comforts we have, the peace we have, and, most important, the faith and knowledge of the things of God that we have, were bought with a terrible price by those who have gone before us. Sacrifice has always been a part of the gospel of Jesus Christ. The crowning element of our faith is our conviction of our living God, the Father of us all, and of His Beloved Son, the Redeemer of the world. It is because of our Redeemer's life and sacrifice that we are here. It is because of His sacrificial atonement that we and all of the sons and daughters of God will partake of the salvation of the Lord. "For as in Adam all die, even so in Christ shall all be made alive" (1 Cor. 15:22). It is because of the sacrificial redemption wrought by the Savior of the world that the great plan of the eternal gospel is made available to us under which those who die in the Lord shall not taste of death but shall have the opportunity of going on to a celestial and eternal glory.
>
> In our own helplessness, He becomes our rescuer, saving us from damnation and bringing us to eternal life. (*Teachings of Gordon B. Hinckley* [Salt Lake City: Deseret Book, 1997], 27)

ILLUSTRATIONS FOR OUR TIME

Jacob preached the "pleasing" word and recorded it according to the will of God.

Mark L. McConkie:

> One of the great evidences that people have the spirit of the gospel is that they desire to share with others what they have. Father Smith, even before the Lord began to give revelations commanding men to share the gospel, felt the spirit of what was to come and desired to share what he knew with others. The Prophet Joseph Smith, of course, was the first missionary in this dispensation. The moment he returned from the grove and told his mother (or was it his parents?) that he had learned for himself "that Presbyterianism is not true"—and presumably he would soon relate to her and other family members the experience of his vision—at that moment he was involved in missionary service, first to his family and then to others. Father and Mother Smith were but a step behind him, and our records show that they were soon out speaking of their son's experiences to their neighbors. This was the pattern that characterized their entire

lives: the Prophet Joseph called the cadence, and his humble parents nobly marched the distance. (Mark L. McConkie, *The Father of the Prophet: Stories and Insights from the Life of Joseph Smith, Sr.* [Salt Lake City: Bookcraft, 1993], 107–108) (Pinegar)

What Is the Will of the Lord in Our Lives? Thoughts of Christ and His atoning sacrifice ought to influence all that we do. Our lives should reflect our taking counsel from the Lord. What is His will for our lives? Many sources, such as the words of living prophets, scriptures, and patriarchal blessings, can provide personal application when studied intensely and prayed upon. Our concern is not so much about material things when our hearts are right. We should always "seek not the things of this world but seek ye first to build up the kingdom of God, and to establish his righteousness; and all these things shall be added unto you" (JST Matt. 6:38). (Pinegar)

Likening the Scriptures to Our Lives

Jacob 4:11—We become reconciled to God through the Atonement of the Savior, who mediates, intercedes, and reunites. Through His redeeming love we receive the free gift of the resurrection and the hope of immortality and eternal life through His grace and merits "after all we can do" (2 Ne. 25:23).

Application—Let us never forget our debt to our Savior, recognizing our plight without the Atonement . . . thus we will feel gratitude and be inspired to change and seek to become like Christ.

SUMMARY

Jacob magnified his calling to preach the word and to engrave upon the plates sacred things pertaining to the revelations of God. He was a worthy successor in Nephi's place. He preached and testified of Christ and His atoning sacrifice. He condemned sin and exhorted the people to seek for the Kingdom of God and not the things of the world. He implored his people to avoid pride and, above all, to be pure and clean. He pleaded with his brethren to be true to their covenants of marriage. We should heed Jacob's words and repent of those things that are keeping us from the blessings of the gospel. These words, like all of the Book of Mormon, were written for our day. They were written for our sake that—learning from those who have gone before—we might be reconciled to God through the Atonement of Christ.

CHAPTER THIRTEEN

THE ALLEGORY *of the* OLIVE TREE

JACOB 5–7

"In Zenos' allegory as retold by Jacob, the Lord of the vineyard works almost desperately (certainly with frequent frustration and tears) to cultivate, protect, preserve, reclaim, and restore the trees of his vineyard. As with most symbols, there are multiple levels of meaning in this parable, with the vineyard representing at least (1) the individual child of God, (2) the House of Israel, and (3) the entire family of man. But the essential element in this story is Christ and his redemptive atonement, just as it was in Lehi's dream of the Tree of Life and the discourse Nephi gave his brothers on the meaning of that dream."
—JEFFREY R. HOLLAND, *CHRIST AND THE NEW COVENANT: THE MESSIANIC MESSAGE OF THE BOOK OF MORMON* [SALT LAKE CITY: DESERET BOOK, 1997], 164.

THEMES *for* LIVING

Zenos's Allegory of the Olive Tree
Be Wise and Honor Covenant Principles
Prevailing over the Anti-Christ

INTRODUCTION

We quote from Joseph Fielding Smith:

> The parable of Zenos, recorded by Jacob in chapter five of his book, is one of the greatest parables ever recorded. This parable in and of itself stamps the Book of Mormon with convincing truth. No mortal man, without the inspiration of the Lord, could have written such a parable. It is a pity that too many of those who read the Book of Mormon pass over and slight the truths which it conveys in relation to the history, scattering, and final gathering of Israel. Such members of the Church unto whom attention has been called to the great significance of this parable have said they fail to comprehend it. It is simple and very clear to the minds of those who earnestly seek to know the truth. No man without divine inspiration could have written such a parable as this.

> In brief, it records the history of Israel down through the ages, the scattering of the tribes to all parts of the earth; their mingling with, or being grafted in, the wild olive trees, or in other words the mixing of the blood of Israel among the Gentiles by which the great blessings and promises of the Lord to Abraham are fulfilled. After Abraham had been proved even to the extent of being willing to offer Isaac as a sacrifice, the Lord blessed him with the greatest of blessings, and said to him:

> > . . . By myself have I sworn, saith the Lord, for because thou hast done this thing, and hast not withheld thy son, thine only son:

> > That in blessing I will bless thee, and in multiplying I will multiply thy seed as the stars of the heaven, and as the sand which is upon the sea shore; and thy seed shall possess the gate of his enemies;

> > And in thy seed shall all the nations of the earth be blessed; because thou hast obeyed my voice. . . . (Genesis 22:16–18.)

> This remarkable parable portrays how, as branches of the olive tree (Israelites) were carried to all parts of the earth (the Lord's vineyard) and grafted into the wild olive trees (the Gentile nations). Thus they are fulfilling the promise that the Lord had made.

> Today Latter-day Saints are going to all parts of the world as servants in the vineyard to gather this fruit and lay it in store for the time of the coming of the Master. This parable is one of the most enlightening and interesting in the Book of

Mormon. How can any person read it without feeling the inspiration of this ancient prophet? (*Answers to Gospel Questions,* 5 vols. [Salt Lake City: Deseret Book, 1957–1966], 4:141–42)

1. ZENOS'S ALLEGORY OF THE OLIVE TREE

THEME. The allegory of the olive tree is about us and how we can participate in the glorious unfolding of the Lord's plan for the redemption of Israel and all those of the Gentiles who, through faith and obedience, confess His hand and are adopted into the fold. The allegory is a symbolic history of the Lord's dealings with His sons and daughters of the Second Estate—this mortal probationary phase of existence that gives us the opportunity to magnify our place in the covenant circle.

> *"For behold, thus saith the Lord, I will liken thee, O house of Israel, like unto a tame olive-tree, which a man took and nourished in his vineyard; and it grew, and waxed old, and began to decay" (Jacob 5:3).*

MOMENT OF TRUTH. Among Jacob's inventory of gospel resources was the record of his family's experiences, including the prophecies of Lehi and Nephi, and the brass plates of Laban, containing the sacred writings from the beginning of prophetic history. It was among the latter records that he found the words of Zenos, a prophet of ancient times about whom we know very little (see Hel. 8:19) and whose elegant and powerful witness has been lost from our current Old Testament compilation. Like his predecessors, Jacob was consumed by a desire to ensure that his posterity and future readers would have a clear understanding of their place in the Lord's plan of covenant redemption. Thus he turned to Zenos to convey the meticulous design of the Lord in guiding His people with longsuffering and charity. The allegory of Zenos and Jacob's inspired commentary confirm that the mighty promises made by the Lord to Abraham and the seed of Israel would be fulfilled—on behalf of the whole world—concerning the establishment of His gospel and Kingdom here upon the earth.

MODERN PROPHETS SPEAK

Jeffrey R. Holland:
> Throughout the Book of Mormon, the olive tree is the central figure for Israelite history, including the Lord's effort to redeem Israel, both individually and collectively. Here, very early in the Book of Mormon, it is noted that Israel's natural branches would be broken off and scattered, then later grafted back into their own true heritage. At its most important level of interpretation this meant, as Lehi taught, that

all of the house of Israel would come "to the knowledge of the true Messiah, their Lord and their Redeemer," (1 Nephi 10:14) truly a foundational teaching of the Book of Mormon. (*Christ and the New Covenant: The Messianic Message of the Book of Mormon* [Salt Lake City: Deseret Book, 1997], 162–63)

ILLUSTRATIONS FOR OUR TIME

The Drama of the Lord of the Vineyard. Over the years I have enjoyed discussing the allegory of Zenos (Jacob 5) with various priesthood, gospel doctrine, and institute classes. It has often proven helpful, with such a long discourse—the longest chapter in the Book of Mormon—to view the events of the allegory as a grand dramatic presentation reflecting the principles and milestones of vitality, including conflict, early harvest, tragedy and faith, and final labors and harvest. By experiencing the allegory of Zenos as an epic play in this way, one can more readily associate in fuller measure with the roles of the principal actors—including the servant advocate ("Spare it a little longer"—[v. 50]) and Lord of the vineyard himself ("What could I have done more for my vineyard?"—[v. 41]; "For it grieveth me that I should lose the trees of my vineyard"—[v. 66]; "And blessed art thou; for because ye have been diligent in laboring with me in my vineyard; and have kept my commandments . . . behold ye shall have joy with me because of the fruit of my vineyard"—[v. 75]).

This is more than history—it is inspired history that can be likened unto ourselves. We can gain perspective on how to magnify our offices and callings in the vineyard of the Lord, trimming away the moribund, nonproductive growth from our lives, and cultivating vitality of spirit and fruitfulness of service. The allegory of Zenos is a kind of covenant handbook of horticulture for spiritual gardening.

The vineyard of the Lord is the venue of miracles. The transformation that comes from living the gospel as part of the vineyard service is a miracle. The unfolding and inexorable prospering of the Kingdom of God on the earth is a miracle. We should be humbly grateful that the Lord, through the Book of Mormon and other scriptures, has provided us with a clear and unmistakable guidebook and script of the miraculous harvest process in these latter days. (Allen)

Likening the Scriptures to Our Lives

Jacob 5:70–77—The servant (prophet) brought other servants (you and me) to go into the vineyard (the earth) for the last time (dispensation of the fulness of times) to labor (do missionary work) that we might have joy in our fruit (bringing souls unto Christ—convert baptisms), and finally the season for preaching ends and the earth is burned. It is our duty to preach the gospel to every creature (see Morm. 9:22).

Application—The Prophet Joseph Smith declared, "After all that has been said, [our] greatest and most important duty is to preach the Gospel" (*Teachings of the Prophet Joseph Smith,* sel. Joseph Fielding Smith [Salt Lake City: Deseret Book, 1976], 113).

2. BE WISE AND HONOR COVENANT PRINCIPLES

THEME. The essence of the Restoration is a final gathering by the Lord of His faithful stewards. Those who eschew righteousness and refuse to repent are consigned to endless torment, as Jacob makes abundantly clear in his commentary on Zenos's allegory and its implications for understanding and following covenant principles.

> *"And the day that he shall set his hand again the second time to recover his people, is the day, yea, even the last time, that the servants of the Lord shall go forth in his power, to nourish and prune his vineyard; and after that the end soon cometh. Know ye not that if ye will do these things, that the power of the redemption and the resurrection, which is in Christ, will bring you to stand with shame and awful guilt before the bar of God? And according to the power of justice, for justice cannot be denied, ye must go away into that lake of fire and brimstone, whose flames are unquenchable, and whose smoke ascendeth up forever and ever, which lake of fire and brimstone is endless torment" (Jacob 6:2, 9–10).*

MOMENT OF TRUTH. Jacob had already experienced a major social distress when the Nephites were constrained to separate themselves from the murderous and vengeful followers of Laman and Lemuel. Now he looks out over the growing branch of Israel under his stewardship and senses a foment of forces that threaten, once again, to polarize the population into two camps: the chaste and obedient on the one hand, and the prideful and corrupt on the other. Thus his fervent appeal to his people is to repent or be "hewn down and cast into the fire" (Jacob 6:7) in like manner as with the unproductive branches of the olive trees in Zenos's allegory. "O then, my beloved brethren," he declares, "repent ye, and enter in at the strait gate, and continue in the way which is narrow, until ye shall obtain eternal life. O be wise; what can I say more?" (Jacob 6:11–12).

MODERN PROPHETS SPEAK

James E. Talmage:
Latter-day Revelation Concerning the Gathering of Israel

The Church commissioned to bring about the gathering of the elect into one place upon the face of the land—D&C 29:7, 8.

The covenant people to be gathered in one—D&C 42:36.

The restoration of the scattered Israel to be shown—D&C 45:17; see also verses 25, 43, 69.

The land of Missouri appointed and consecrated for the gathering of the saints—D&C 57:1, 2.

And they that have been scattered shall be gathered—D&C 101:13.

Moses appeared in the Kirtland Temple and committed unto Joseph Smith and Oliver Cowdery the keys of the gathering of Israel from the four parts of the earth—D&C 110:11.

This is Elias which was to come to gather together the tribes of Israel and restore all things—D&C 77:9; see also verse 14.

Let them who are among the Gentiles flee unto Zion, and those of Judah flee unto Jerusalem—D&C 133:12, 13. (*The Articles of Faith* [Salt Lake City: Deseret Book, 1981], 342–44)

ILLUSTRATIONS FOR OUR TIME

Leadership Principles for the Gathering. Since all of us are stewards in the gathering, much like the servants portrayed in Zenos's incomparable allegory of the olive trees, we would do well to understand the principles and procedures followed by the "Lord of the vineyard" so that we might, as He says, "have joy with me because of the fruit of my vineyard" (Jacob 5:75).

Many years ago I decided to examine the allegory of the olive trees from the standpoint of leadership. Each of the questions in the following checklist reflects a leadership principle embodied in the narrative of the allegory. You might wish to score yourself and then go back through Jacob 5 to determine how the Lord acted in order to maximize the harvest. What better leadership model is there than the Lord Himself?

General Principles
  1. Do you have a governing sense of purpose and mission in what you do? (See vv. 9, 49, 54, 61.)
  2. Do you maintain focus, without ever losing sight of the objective? (vv. 13, 35, 61)
  3. Do you understand and remain aligned with the "root" values of your enterprise? (v. 59)
  4. Are you firm in your commitment to action? (vv. 14, 75; cf. Abraham 3:17; 2 Ne. 24:24.)
  5. Is your engagement total and "impassioned"? (See throughout the entire allegory; cf. Mark 12:30; 2 Ne. 25:29; D&C 4:2.)
  6. Do you maintain an attitude of faith and hope? (vv. 53–54, 60, 77)

Every servant and steward in the Lord's vineyard is enjoined to "learn his duty, and to act in the office in which he is appointed, in all diligence" (D&C 107:99). Jacob's inclusion of Zenos's magnificent allegory allows future viewers to discern the breadth of the grand campaign in which they are called to service in preparation for the final harvest. (Allen)

Likening the Scriptures to Our Lives

Jacob 6:5–11—Jacob encourages us to repent and come with full purpose of heart unto God. If we reject the word of God we will be cast out to an endless torment.

Application—Now is the time for us as individuals to repent and align ourselves with the word of God. We cannot set it aside because we will stand accountable for everything we have done.

3. PREVAILING OVER THE ANTI-CHRIST

THEME. In the strength of God we can prevail against those who scheme to overthrow the doctrine of Christ.

> *"And it came to pass that he began to preach among the people, and to declare unto them that there should be no Christ. And he preached many things which were flattering unto the people; and this he did that he might overthrow the doctrine of Christ" (Jacob 7:2).*

MOMENT OF TRUTH. Jacob's concise record ends with an account of his dealings with the anti-Christ Sherem, whose brief ascendancy and sudden defeat represent the first of several such episodes reported in the Book of Mormon concerning those who would flatter the people away into spiritual detours. Against every anti-Christ, there is the ultimate antidote: the indisputable testimony of Christ as evidenced in the scriptures and confirmed through the Holy Ghost (see Jacob 7:11–12). Through the power of God, Sherem's misguided campaign came to naught: "And it came to pass that peace and the love of God was restored again among the people; and they searched the scriptures, and hearkened no more to the words of this wicked man" (Jacob 7:23).

MODERN PROPHETS SPEAK

Neal A. Maxwell:
> Just how crucial access is to time-transcending truth may be pondered in the setting in which Sherem, an agnostic, berated a prophet for preaching a Christ to come "many hundred years hence." Sherem declared that "there should be no Christ." Indeed, he said,

it was even blasphemous for prophets to teach of things to come, for "no man knoweth of such things; for he cannot tell of things to come" (Jacob 7:1–7). The anti-Christ was a "here and now" person who, ironically, put himself forward as if he were the judge of what constituted orthodoxy. So, alas, today—like Sherem, who ostensibly wished to uphold the law of Moses—some denounce modern prophets for telling of plain and precious things yet to come. Provincialism wears many blinders, and each is designed to deflect those fundamental truths which transcend time. How relentlessly the adversary seeks to grind mortals down to a single plane, knowing, as he does, that if mortals can be confined to now, then it is so easy to declare present appetite, instead of Jesus, as king. (*Plain and Precious Things* [Salt Lake City: Deseret Book, 1983], 58–59)

ILLUSTRATIONS FOR OUR TIME

The Devil's Deception. Anti-Christs are always deceived by the devil. Note both Sherem's and Korihor's confession as to why they spoke against Christ:

> And he spake plainly unto them, that he had been deceived by the power of the devil. And he spake of hell, and of eternity, and of eternal punishment. And he said: I fear lest I have committed the unpardonable sin, for I have lied unto God; for I denied the Christ, and said that I believed the scriptures; and they truly testify of him. And because I have thus lied unto God I greatly fear lest my case shall be awful; but I confess unto God. (Jacob 7:18–19)

> And Korihor put forth his hand and wrote, saying: I know that I am dumb, for I cannot speak; and I know that nothing save it were the power of God could bring this upon me; yea, and I always knew that there was a God. But behold, the devil hath deceived me; for he appeared unto me in the form of an angel, and said unto me: Go and reclaim this people, for they have all gone astray after an unknown God. And he said unto me: There is no God; yea, and he taught me that which I should say. And I have taught his words; and I taught them because they were pleasing unto the carnal mind; and I taught them, even until I had much success, insomuch that I verily believed that they were true; and for this cause I withstood the truth, even until I have brought this great curse upon me. (Alma 30:52–53)

In our day the devil seeks to deceive people by multiple means. Some are captured and chained in subtle ways by the devil. Some instances are more dramatic, as described by Newel Knight in this account:

> After the close of the meeting Brother Hyrum [Smith] and myself intended going to spend the night with one of the brethren who lived a short distance from my uncle's, but as we were ready to start, the Spirit whispered to me that I should tarry there at

my uncle's all night. I did so, and retired to bed, where I rested till midnight when my uncle came to my room and desired me to get up, saying he feared his wife [Electa Peck] was about to die. This surprised me, as she was quite well when I went to bed.

I dressed myself, and having asked my Heavenly Father to give me wisdom and power to rebuke the destroyer from the habitation, I went to the room where my aunt lay. She was in a most fearful condition; her eyes were closed, and she appeared to be in the last agonies of death. Presently she opened her eyes, and bade her husband and children farewell, telling them she must die for the redemption of this generation, as Jesus Christ had died for the generation in His day. Her whole frame shook, and she appeared to be racked with the most exquisite pain and torment; her hands and feet were cold, and the blood settled in her fingers; while her husband and children stood weeping around her bed.

This was a scene new to me, and I felt she was suffering under the power of Satan— that was the same spirit that had bound and overpowered me at the time Joseph cast him out. I now cried unto the Lord for strength and wisdom that we might prevail over this wicked and delusive power. Just at this time my uncle cried aloud to me saying: "O, Brother Newel, cannot something be done?"

I felt the Holy Spirit of the Lord rest upon me as he said this, and I immediately stepped forward, took her by the hand, and commanded Satan, in the name of the Lord Jesus Christ, to depart. I told my aunt she would not die, but that she should live to see her children grown up; that Satan had deceived her, and put a lying spirit in her mouth; that Christ had made the only and last atonement for all who would believe on His name; and that there should be no more shedding of blood for sin. She believed and stretched forth her hand, and cried unto me, and Satan departed from her. (As told in *Best-Loved Stories of the LDS People*, ed. Jack M. Lyon, Linda Ririe Gundry, and Jay A. Parry [Salt Lake City: Deseret Book, 1999] 3:155–56) (Pinegar)

Likening the Scriptures to Our Lives

Jacob 7:17–18—Sherem, who was deceived by the devil, soon comes to deny all of his false teachings.

Application—Why are people deceived by the devil? Because they are enticed by the things that are pleasing to the carnal mind (see Alma 30:53). We are counseled to do all in our power to be spiritually minded (see 2 Ne. 9:39). The carnal mind has been described as follows: "Unconverted men are so called (1 Cor. 3:3). They are represented as of a 'carnal mind, which is enmity against God' (Rom. 8:6, 7). Enjoyments that minister to the wants and desires of man's animal nature are so called (Rom. 15:27; 1 Cor. 9:11)" (M. G. Easton, *Illustrated Bible Dictionary*, rev. ed. [Grand Rapids, Michigan: Baker Book House, 1978]).

SUMMARY

The Lord has a great work for us to do in this the dispensation of the fulness of times. We are to take the gospel to every nation, kindred, tongue, and people. This is the last time He will set His hand to recover and gather His people. Let us watch and be ready and prepare ourselves against the power of Satan, for he seeks to bring us down to hell. Let us not be deceived by the sophistries of men, the lusts of the flesh, or anything that takes us away from the gospel of Jesus Christ. These are anti-Christs. The gospel message sounds with clarion echoes: Hold to the iron rod, pray with faith, listen to the Spirit, and follow our living prophets.

We are not involved in a work of the hour, nor in a work of the month or year. We are involved in a work that stretches from the foundations of the earth even until the ushering in of Christ's imminent return and beyond. The scriptures impart to us the divine perspective of how God's plan spans the eternities for the good of mankind. We are the servants in the Lord's vineyard who have the charge to help cultivate, nurture, and harvest the covenant crop. Through faith and diligence we can be wise and honor covenant principles. We can prevail over the pernicious forces of evil that would undermine and discredit the Doctrine of Christ. We can rise valiant and victorious to hear one day the blessed words in the Savior's parable: "Well done, thou good and faithful servant: thou hast been faithful over a few things, I will make thee ruler over many things: enter thou into the joy of thy lord" (Matt. 25:21; cf. Jacob 5:75; D&C 18:16).

CHAPTER FOURTEEN

"FOR a WISE PURPOSE"

ENOS, JAROM, OMNI, WORDS OF MORMON

*"Sometimes when we are asked to be obedient, we do not know why, except that the
Lord has commanded. From 1 Ne. 9:5 we read, 'Wherefore, the Lord hath
commanded me to make these plates for a wise purpose in him, which purpose
I know not.' Nephi followed instructions even though he didn't fully understand
the wise purpose. His obedience resulted in blessings to mankind all over
the world. By not obeying our present-day leaders, we plant our seeds in stony
places and may forfeit the harvest."*
—MARVIN J. ASHTON, *YE ARE MY FRIENDS* [SALT LAKE CITY: DESERET BOOK, 1982], 71.

THEMES *for* LIVING

The Power of Fervent Prayer
Following the Promptings of the Spirit
The Scriptures Point Unerringly toward Christ
Exercising Faith in the Wisdom of the Lord

INTRODUCTION

These four short books contain great teachings about our Savior Jesus Christ. When these teachings are applied in our lives, they will bring us great joy. In Enos, the principles of prayer as a manifestation of faith unto repentance and forgiveness are exemplified. Enos is converted and has an overwhelming concern for his fellowman. In Jarom, we learn that those who are not stiffnecked and exercise faith have the blessings of the Holy Ghost in their lives. In Omni, we hear Amaleki's great admonition to come unto Christ and partake of His salvation through the power of the redemption. In the Words of Mormon, Mormon inserts the small plates of Nephi into his abridgement for a wise purpose . . . which he does not know.

1. THE POWER OF FERVENT PRAYER

THEME. Prayer is the gateway to the "mighty change" (Mosiah 5:2) that will sweep away the guilt from our lives and align us with the patterns of divine truth.

> *"And my soul hungered; and I kneeled down before my Maker, and I cried unto him in mighty prayer and supplication for mine own soul; and all the day long did I cry unto him; yea, and when the night came I did still raise my voice high that it reached the heavens" (Enos 1:4).*

MOMENT OF TRUTH. Enos, the son of Jacob, continued in the righteous pathways commended to him by his father. However, he felt driven to seek a spiritual confirmation of his spiritual worthiness—in what he called "the wrestle which I had before God" (Enos 1:2)—and the means whereby his guilt could be "swept away" (v. 6). The contribution of Enos to the ongoing sacred record of the people was limited, in the main, to this one experience and its impact on his compassionate but futile mission to restore the Lamanites to the covenant. Nevertheless, this short case study in prayer is among the most celebrated of its kind in all of holy writ, and the name of Enos is eternally linked to the principle of righteous prayer as an indispensable element in the process of forgiveness and the dispensing of divine blessings.

MODERN PROPHETS SPEAK

Spencer W. Kimball:

> If you have not, I sincerely hope that the time will soon come when, as others before you have, you will struggle in the spirit and cry mightily and covenant sincerely, so that the voice of the Lord God will come into your mind, as it did to Enos, saying:

. . . thy sins are forgiven thee, and thou shalt be blessed.

Because of thy faith in Christ . . . I will grant unto thee according to thy desires. . . .
(Enos 5, 8, 12.)

For this is the ultimate object of all prayer, to bring men closer to God, to give them
a new birth, to make them heirs of his kingdom. (*Faith Precedes the Miracle* [Salt
Lake City: Deseret Book, 1972], 211–12)

ILLUSTRATIONS FOR OUR TIME

In the Due Time of the Lord. The scriptures make frequent reference to the phrase "in the own due
time of the Lord" or variants thereof (e.g., 1 Ne. 10:3), especially when it comes to such milestone
events as the coming forth of the word of the Lord, the gathering of Israel, the redemption of Zion,
and the inauguration of the millennial reign. "Zion shall be redeemed in mine own due time" (D&C
136:18), declared the Lord concerning the culmination of the latter-day Restoration.

How long is the "due time of the Lord"? We mortals, to whom it is not given to understand the thoughts of
God, nor perceive the details of His immortal agenda (Isa. 55:8–9), often yearn to know the Lord's timetable
when it comes to our individual circumstances. In some cases, the timing is explicit: "Yea, I would that ye
would come forth and harden not your hearts any longer; for behold, now is the time and the day of your salvation; and therefore, if ye will repent and harden not your hearts, *immediately* shall the great plan of redemption be brought about unto you" (Alma 34:31, italics added). At other times, for our own blessing and instruction, the Lord wisely leaves the timing open-ended: "Humble yourselves therefore under the mighty hand of
God, that he may exalt you in due time" (1 Pet. 5:6).

In our prayers do we not sometimes couch our words in terms of personal urgency and express our
desire for the prompt flow of blessings? I have previously written the recollection of my first lesson in
the efficacy of prayer, which was offered up at the scene of an accident (see Ed J. Pinegar and Richard J.
Allen, *Latter-Day Commentary on the Old Testament* [American Fork: Covenant Communications, 2001]
126). In that case, "the own due time of the Lord" was, miraculously, a matter of only several minutes. In
other cases, we are instead left to cultivate patience, strengthen faith, practice longsuffering, and wait upon
the Lord until, in His infinite wisdom, the time is right—which, in earth terms, may seem very long. The
Psalmist counseled: "Wait on the Lord: be of good courage, and he shall strengthen thine heart: wait, I say,
on the Lord" (Ps. 27:14).

When Enos had his "wrestle" before God concerning forgiveness of his sins, the "due time of the Lord"
was a full day: "and all the day long did I cry unto him; yea, and when the night came I did still raise
my voice high that it reached the heavens" (Enos 1:4). It was then that the answer to his prayer came,
and the "due time of the Lord" was fulfilled. For the Prophet Joseph Smith, the trials and tribulations,
the prayers and supplications, extended across many seasons before his mission was completed: "Thy

days are known, and thy years shall not be numbered less; therefore, fear not what man can do, for God shall be with you forever and ever" (D&C 122:9).

How much patience do we show in our prayers? How much faith do we bring to bear when pleading with the Lord on behalf of our families and our own personal lives? When it comes to the "due time of the Lord," do we have the courage to imbue our prayers, in all humility, with the essence of these words from the dedicatory prayer of the Kirtland Temple: "Help thy servants to say, with thy grace assisting them: Thy will be done, O Lord, and not ours" (D&C 109:44). If we can move forward in that same spirit, we will then be in tune with the principle of "grace for grace" taught in the ninety-third section of the Doctrine and Covenants: "I give unto you these sayings that you may understand and know how to worship, and know what you worship, that you may come unto the Father in my name, and in due time receive of his fulness" (D&C 93:19). (Allen)

Likening the Scriptures to Our Lives

Enos 1:3–8—Enos, having a concern for the welfare of his own soul, prayed mightily for forgiveness. His guilt was swept away through faith in Jesus Christ.

Application—The Lord has provided a way for us to repent: come forward with a broken heart and contrite spirit, confessing and forsaking our sins through faith in Jesus Christ (see Alma 34:15–17). The way to perfection is to repent perfectly.

2. FOLLOWING THE PROMPTINGS OF THE SPIRIT

THEME. The prophet leaders of the Nephites continually taught them the ways of the Lord . . . to repent and keep the commandments.

> *"Wherefore, the prophets, and the priests, and the teachers, did labor diligently, exhorting with all long-suffering the people to diligence; teaching the law of Moses, and the intent for which it was given; persuading them to look forward unto the Messiah, and believe in him to come as though he already was. And after this manner did they teach them. And it came to pass that by so doing they kept them from being destroyed upon the face of the land; for they did prick their hearts with the word, continually stirring them up unto repentance" (Jarom 1:11–12).*

MOMENT OF TRUTH. Jarom, the son of Enos, followed in the footsteps of his predecessors by keeping the sacred records of the covenant to preserve the chronicles of the Lord's dealings with His people. We know that Jarom was a spiritual person, for he referred to his own "prophesying" and "revelations" (Jarom 1:2). However, he was also humble and self-effacing in that he declined to provide much detail of his own ministry, preferring instead to confirm the witness of those who went before him: "For what could I write more than my fathers have written? For have they not revealed the plan of salvation? I say unto you, Yea; and this sufficeth me" (Jarom 1:2). Through the eyes of Jarom we see that the people had "multiplied exceedingly, and spread upon the face of the land" (Jarom 1:8), building mighty cities and a prosperous culture (in the case of the Nephites), or following a bellicose and wild existence (in the case of the more numerous Lamanites). In all of this we see the interplay of major tendencies among the people: on the one hand a strict adherence to righteous gospel principles according to the teachings of the prophets, and on the other the manifestation of "the hardness of their hearts, and the deafness of their ears, and the blindness of their minds, and the stiffness of their necks" (Jarom 1:3). This latter tendency could be kept in check only by the valiant, proactive ministry of the prophets, priests, and teachers: "for they did prick their hearts with the word, continually stirring them up unto repentance" (Jarom 1:12). Thus Jarom confirms that the promptings of the Spirit can prevail above the allure of worldly pride and materialism, if the people will only give heed and obey. His simple but fervent testimony has come down to us as an added witness of the truth of gospel principles.

MODERN PROPHETS SPEAK

Gordon B. Hinckley:

> We are becoming a great global society. But our interest and concern must always be with the individual. Every member of this church is an individual man or woman, boy or girl. Our great responsibility is to see that each is "remembered and nourished by the good word of God" (Moro. 6:4), that each has opportunity for growth and expression and training in the work and ways of the Lord, that none lacks the necessities of life, that the needs of the poor are met, that each member shall have encouragement, training, and opportunity to move forward on the road of immortality and eternal life. This, I submit, is the inspired genius of this the Lord's work. (*Teachings of Gordon B. Hinckley* [Salt Lake City: Deseret Book, 1997], 92)

ILLUSTRATIONS FOR OUR TIME

Be Something. Our prophets since Old Testament times have admonished us to "walk in all the ways which the Lord your God hath commanded you" (Deut 5:33). Jarom, along with the other Book of Mormon prophets, recorded that the leaders taught the people the ways of the Lord. Our prophets today continue to teach us the ways of the Lord. (Pinegar)

Likening the Scriptures to Our Lives

Jarom 1:12—The prophets and teachers preached concerning the coming of the Messiah and did "prick their hearts" continually with the word of God to stir them up unto repentance.

Application—Let us always hearken to the word of God, as it is taught to us by His servants. That which is right stirs to repentance.

3. THE SCRIPTURES POINT
UNERRINGLY TOWARD CHRIST

THEME. The scriptures provide a continuous flow of light illuminating the pathway to Christ. By following the word of God, we may come unto Christ and partake of gospel blessings.

> *"And now, my beloved brethren, I would that ye should come unto Christ, who is the Holy One of Israel, and partake of his salvation, and the power of his redemption. Yea, come unto him, and offer your whole souls as an offering unto him, and continue in fasting and praying, and endure to the end; and as the Lord liveth ye will be saved" (Omni 1:26).*

MOMENT OF TRUTH. Jarom conveyed the engraved record to his son, Omni, around 361 B.C. The period of time covered by the ministry of Omni, Omni's son Amaron, Amaron's brother Chemish, Chemish's son Abinadom, and Abinadom's son Amaleki, was approximately 200 years (down to 130 B.C.). The entire transitional period is covered in merely two-and-half pages of modern text, of which the majority was written by Amaleki. Amaleki was a personal witness to the events surrounding the life of the first Mosiah and his faithful group, who were led to safety by the Lord and discovered the parallel civilization founded by immigrants who had fled Jerusalem through divine intervention at the time of the Babylonian conquest. The theme of Amaleki's testimony is reflected in the joy of the benighted citizens of the newly discovered city and their leader Zarahemla to have access once again to the brass plates and a record of their covenant forefathers (Omni 1:14). We also learn that the last vestige of a third civilization, the Jaredites, including their records, had come to the attention of the people of Zarahemla shortly before Mosiah arrived.

Thus we see unfolding before our eyes the Lord's design in bringing together His word for the blessing of mankind. Though short, Amaleki's account contains a priceless witness concerning "Christ, who is the Holy One of Israel" (Omni 1: 26) and a memorable exhortation to his readership to honor the covenant principles "and endure to the end; and as the Lord liveth ye will be saved" (v. 26). Thereafter, Amaleki turns over the sacred chronicle to King Benjamin, the son of Mosiah, whom he knows "to be a just man before the Lord" (v. 25). Thus the continuity of testimony pointing to Christ remains uninterrupted.

MODERN PROPHETS SPEAK

Jeffrey R. Holland:

> Jacob's son Enos had a memorable spiritual experience because of his faith in Christ, a being, the heavenly voice told him, "whom thou hast never before heard nor seen" (Enos 1:8). Likewise Enos's son Jarom noted that the prophets (plural) of the Lord labored at "persuading them to look forward unto the Messiah, and believe in him to come as though he already was" (Jarom 1:11). Jarom's great-great nephew Amaleki delivered his record to King Benjamin, "exhorting all men to come unto . . . Christ, who is the Holy One of Israel, and partake of his salvation, and the power of his redemption. Yea, come unto him, and offer your whole souls as an offering unto him" (Omni 1:26). (*Christ and the New Covenant: The Messianic Message of the Book of Mormon* [Salt Lake City: Deseret Book, 1997], 98)

ILLUSTRATIONS FOR OUR TIME

A Missionary Example. Missionary work, family work, Church work, and life's work are about inviting all to come unto Christ. This is the purpose of the Church and kingdom of God. This is what the prophets do. This is the main thrust of the Book of Mormon. Moroni ends with the plea "come unto Christ, and be perfected in him" (see Moro. 10:32).

> How do you come unto Christ? Faith in Jesus Christ, taking upon us the name of Jesus Christ, repentance and baptism through Jesus Christ, and the gift of the Holy Ghost from God—these are the principles of the gospel that allow us to come unto Christ. We apply the Atonement to our lives and to the lives of our investigators as we teach them. This is the most incredible thing you will ever see in conversion. When the power of God is placed in an anointed servant of God, and that servant gives it by the power and authority of God to someone who is honest in heart, you can watch that person change before your very eyes. All of a sudden, their eyes will start to light up. They'll say, "Oh yes, I see, tell me more!" And in this process of enlightenment, guess what they receive? The Spirit.

> They know who they are. They recognize where they came from—"I am a child of God and I now understand his plan for me, and I need it in my life. I want to be baptized." (Ed J. Pinegar, adapted from *Especially for Missionaries,* 4 vols. [American Fork, UT: Covenant Communications, 1997], 3:18) (Pinegar)

Likening the Scriptures to Our Lives

Omni 1:26—Amaleki encouraged us to come unto Christ, to partake of His salvation and the power of His redemption, offering our whole souls (dedicating our lives to the Lord and His service), continuing in fasting and prayer, and enduring to the end—and we shall be saved.

Application—Let us be willing to offer a broken heart and contrite spirit and literally sacrifice all things to build up the kingdom of God. The Prophet Joseph has said, "Let us here observe, that a religion that does not require the sacrifice of all things never has power sufficient to produce the faith necessary unto life and salvation" (*Lectures on Faith*, 6:7).

4. EXERCISING FAITH IN THE WISDOM OF THE LORD

THEME. It is an attribute of Christ-centered living to follow the promptings of the Spirit with full faith in the Lord's divine will and wisdom, just as Mormon did in compiling his record.

> *"And I do this for a wise purpose; for thus it whispereth me, according to the workings of the Spirit of the Lord which is in me. And now, I do not know all things; but the Lord knoweth all things which are to come; wherefore, he worketh in me to do according to his will" (Words of Mormon 1:7).*

MOMENT OF TRUTH. When Mormon, the principal compiler and abridger of the sacred records, discovered the small plates of Nephi among the engraved annals of his people, he felt inspired to include these remarkable testimonies with his abridgement "for a wise purpose." He was pleased with the character of the added records "because of the prophecies of the coming of Christ" (v. 4) contained therein. Mormon's successor, his son Moroni, carried this same theme into his overview of the purposes of the completed work: "And also to the convincing of the Jew and Gentile that Jesus is the Christ, the Eternal God, manifesting himself unto all nations" (Book of Mormon title page).

MODERN PROPHETS SPEAK

Jeffrey R. Holland:
> At least six times in the Book of Mormon, the phrase *for a wise purpose* is used in reference to the making, writing, and preserving of the small plates. One such wise purpose—the most obvious one—was to compensate for the future loss of 116 pages of manuscript translated by the Prophet Joseph Smith from the first part of Mormon's abridgment of the large plates of Nephi (See D&C 3, 10). . . .

Obviously it would be exciting if someone were one day to find the lost 116 pages of the original manuscript of the Book of Mormon. But whatever those pages contain, it could not be more important or more fundamental to the purpose of the Book of Mormon than the teachings of these three prophets recorded on the small plates. Standing like sentinels at the gate of the book, Nephi, Jacob, and Isaiah admit us into the scriptural presence of the Lord. (*Christ and the New Covenant: The Messianic Message of the Book of Mormon* [Salt Lake City: Deseret Book, 1997], 34–36)

ILLUSTRATIONS FOR OUR TIME

Lucy Mack Smith:

Martin Harris, having written some one hundred and sixteen pages for Joseph, asked permission of my son to carry the manuscript home with him, in order to let his wife read it, as he hoped it might have a salutary effect upon her feelings.

Joseph was willing to gratify his friend as far as he could consistently, and he inquired of the Lord to know if he might do as Martin Harris had requested, but was refused. With this, Mr. Harris was not altogether satisfied, and, at his urgent request, Joseph inquired again, but received a second refusal. Still, Martin Harris persisted as before, and Joseph applied again, but the last answer was not like the two former ones. In this, the Lord permitted Martin Harris to take the manuscript home with him, on condition that he would exhibit it to none, save five individuals whom he had mentioned, and who belonged to his own family.

Mr. Harris was delighted with this, and bound himself in a written covenant of the most solemn nature, that he would strictly comply with the injunctions which he had received. Which being done, he took the manuscript and went home.

Joseph did not suspect but that his friend would keep his faith, consequently, he gave himself no uneasiness with regard to the matter. . . .

Mr. Harris had been absent nearly three weeks, and Joseph had received no intelligence whatever from him, which was altogether aside of the arrangement when they separated. . . . He set out in the first stage that passed for Palmyra, and, when he was left to himself, he began to contemplate the course which Martin had taken, and the risk which he (Joseph) had run in letting the manuscript go out of his hands—for it could not be obtained again, in case Martin had lost it through transgression, except by the power of God, which was something Joseph could hardly hope for—and that, by persisting in his entreaties to the Lord, he had perhaps fallen into transgression, and thereby lost the manuscript. When, I say, he began to contemplate these things, they troubled his spirit, and his soul was moved with fearful apprehensions. And, although he was now nearly worn out, sleep fled from his eyes, neither had he any desire for food, for he felt that he had done wrong, and how great his condemnation was he did not know.

Only one passenger was in the stage besides himself: this man observing Joseph's gloomy appearance, inquired the cause of his affliction, and offered to assist him if his services would be acceptable. Joseph thanked him for his kindness, and mentioned that he had been watching some time with a sick wife and child, that the child had died, and that his wife was still very low; but refrained from giving any further explanation. Nothing more passed between them upon this subject, until Joseph was about leaving the stage; at which time he remarked, that he still had twenty miles further to travel on foot that night, it being then about ten o'clock. To this the stranger objected, saying, "I have watched you since you first entered the stage, and I know that you have neither slept nor eaten since that time, and you shall not go on foot twenty miles alone this night; for, if you must go, I will be your company. Now tell me what can be the trouble that makes you thus dispirited?" . . .

The stranger then observed, "I feel to sympathize with you, and I fear that your constitution, which is evidently not strong, will be inadequate to support you. You will be in danger of falling asleep in the forrest [sic], and of meeting with some awful disaster."

Joseph again thanked the gentleman for his kindness, and, leaving the stage, they proceeded together. . . . On entering our house, the stranger remarked that he had brought our son through the forest, because he had insisted on coming, that he was sick, and needed rest, as well as refreshment, and that he ought to have some pepper tea to warm his stomach. After thus directing us, relative to our son, he said, that when we had attended to Joseph he would thank us for a little breakfast for himself, as he was in a haste to be on his journey again.

When Joseph had taken a little nourishment, according to the directions of the stranger, he requested us to send immediately for Mr. Harris. This we did without delay. And when we had given the stranger his breakfast, we commenced preparing breakfast for the family; and we supposed that Mr. Harris would be there, as soon as it was ready, to eat with us, for he generally came in such haste when he was sent for. At eight o'clock we set the victuals on the table, as we were expecting him every moment. We waited till nine, and he came not—till ten, and he was not there—till eleven, still he did not make his appearance. But at half past twelve we saw him walking with a slow and measured tread towards the house, his eyes fixed thoughtfully upon the ground. On coming to the gate, he stopped, instead of passing through, and got upon the fence, and sat there some time with his hat drawn over his eyes. At length he entered the house. Soon after which we sat down to the table, Mr. Harris with the rest. He took up his knife and fork as if he were going to use them, but immediately dropped them. Hyrum, observing this, said "Martin, why do you not eat; are you sick?" Upon which Mr. Harris pressed his hands upon his temples, and cried out in a tone of deep anguish, "Oh, I have lost my soul! I have lost my soul!"

Joseph who had not expressed his fears till now, sprang from the table, exclaiming, "Martin, have you lost that manuscript? Have you broken your oath, and brought down condemnation upon my head as well as your own?"

"Yes; it is gone," replied Martin, "and I know not where."

"Oh, my God!" said Joseph, clinching his hands. "All is lost! all is lost! What shall I do? I have sinned—it is I who tempted the wrath of God. I should have been satisfied with the first answer which I received from the Lord; for he told me that it was not safe to let the writing go out of my possession." He wept and groaned, and walked the floor continually.

At length he told Martin to go back and search again.

"No"; said Martin, "it is all in vain; for I have ripped open beds and pillows; and I know it is not there."

"Then must I," said Joseph, "return with such a tale as this? I dare not do it. And how shall I appear before the Lord? Of what rebuke am I not worthy from the angel of the Most High?"

I besought him not to mourn so, for perhaps the Lord would forgive him, after a short season of humiliation and repentance. But what could I do to comfort him, when he saw all the family in the same situation of mind as himself; for sobs and groans, and the most bitter lamentations filled the house. However, Joseph was more distressed than the rest, as he better understood the consequences of disobedience. And he continued pacing back and forth, meantime weeping and grieving, until about sunset, when, by persuasion, he took a little nourishment.

The next morning, he set out for home. We parted with heavy hearts, for it now appeared that all which we had so fondly anticipated, and which had been the source of so much secret gratification, had in a moment fled, and fled forever. (*History of*

Joseph Smith by His Mother [Salt Lake City: Stevens & Wallis, Inc., 1945], 124–29)
Likening the Scriptures to Our Lives

Words of Mormon 1:7—Mormon puts the small plates into his record for a wise purpose as inspired by the Spirit. He did not know why but sought to do the will of the Lord.

Application—We, like Nephi (see 1 Ne. 9:5) and Adam (see Moses 5:6), should exercise our faith and do the will of the Lord, even when we do not fully understand the reason for the commandment. We please the Lord when we act with faith (see Heb. 11:6).

SUMMARY

There is power in fervent prayer. There is guidance in the scriptures, which point unerringly toward Christ. Great blessings come from exercising faith in the wisdom of the Lord.

We all can learn from the "Enos experience." We need to plead for forgiveness, and when our guilt is swept away, our conversion will deepen. We will have a change of heart. We will care for our fellowmen. The record-keepers of the Book of Mormon, like our living prophets, speak of the goodness of God and admonish us to come unto Christ and partake of His salvation. To do so we must be willing to offer our whole souls.

The foreknowledge of God was demonstrated in His preparation of the small plates. Our Heavenly Father and our Savior have this central purpose—"to bring to pass the immortality and eternal life of man" (Moses 1:39). We have received the word of God, that we might be able to know and live His commandments and prove ourselves worthy of His grace. Oh how we ought to praise our Heavenly Father for His infinite goodness, His marvelous plan, the gift of His Beloved Son . . . all that we might partake of exaltation.

CHAPTER FIFTEEN

"ETERNALLY INDEBTED to OUR HEAVENLY FATHER"

MOSIAH 1–3

*"I am inclined to acknowledge the hand of God in all things. If I see a man inspired
with intelligence, with extraordinary ability and wisdom, I say to myself he is indebted
to God for that wisdom and ability; and that, without the providence or interposition
of the Almighty, he would not have been what he is. He is indebted to the Lord
Almighty for his intelligence, and for all that he has; for the earth is the Lord's and the
fulness thereof. God originated and designed all things, and all are his children. . . .
The children of men have sprung from the Almighty, whether the world is willing to
acknowledge it or not. . . . We live and move and have our being in God our heavenly
Father. And having sprung from him with our talents, our ability, our wisdom, we
should at least be willing to acknowledge his hand in all the prosperity that may attend
us in life, and give to him the honor and glory of all we accomplish in the flesh."*
—JOSEPH F. SMITH, *GOSPEL DOCTRINE: SELECTIONS FROM THE SERMONS AND WRITINGS OF
JOSEPH F. SMITH*, COMP. JOHN A. WIDTSOE [SALT LAKE CITY: DESERET BOOK, 191], 62.

THEMES for LIVING

The Word of God as the Central Parental Legacy
The Goodness of God and our Eternal Indebtedness to Him
Ponder the Prophecies Concerning the Coming of the Savior

INTRODUCTION

King Benjamin's teachings to his sons and his magnificent sermon comprise the first five chapters of the book of Mosiah. Much of his sermon consists of the divine message imparted to him by an angel of the Lord. His teachings embrace a variety of key gospel themes: the value of the scriptures in our lives, obedience to the commandments, cultivating universal love of God and all mankind, the goodness of God and His blessings to His children, the infinite indebtedness of mankind to God (i.e., that we are all unprofitable servants), the importance of continually praising God for all things, avoiding contention, the dire consequences of transgression (loss of the Spirit), rebellion as the essence of enmity toward God, the happy state of those who keep the commandments, the coming of Christ and His atoning sacrifice, the role and function of prophets in declaring the word of the Lord, the singularity of the name of Jesus Christ as the only source of salvation, the indispensable need to yield to the enticings of the Holy Spirit, and many other important doctrines. King Benjamin taught only the things that the Lord commanded him to teach. He gave great emphasis to the principle that we will be judged according to our works.

1. THE WORD OF GOD AS THE CENTRAL PARENTAL LEGACY

THEME. There is no more valuable legacy for parents to leave to their children than to teach them to value, search, understand, and heed the word of God as embodied in the holy scriptures and reflected in the spoken word of God's chosen servants.

> *"And it came to pass that he had three sons; and he called their names Mosiah, and Helorum, and Helaman. And he caused that they should be taught in all the language of his fathers, that thereby they might become men of understanding; and that they might know concerning the prophecies which had been spoken by the mouths of their fathers, which were delivered them by the hand of the Lord. And he also taught them concerning the records which were engraven on the plates of brass, saying: My sons, I would that ye should remember that were it not for these plates, which contain these records and these commandments, we must have suffered in ignorance, even at this present time, not knowing the mysteries of God" (Mosiah 1:2–3).*

MOMENT OF TRUTH. King Benjamin, being a man of great spirituality as well as a consummate political leader, created an environment for his people where they could enjoy "continual peace" (Mosiah 1:1). As he reaches the point in time where he knows that his mortal sojourn is about to come to an end, he calls his three sons to his side and instructs them in many important matters, most of which "are not written in this book" (Mosiah 1:8). What Mormon does single out from among King Benjamin's instructions to his sons is his impressive statement concerning the central place of the word of God in the plan of salvation. King Benjamin had caused his sons to be taught in the language of their forefathers, that they might become men of a sound understanding and come to know of the prophecies of their fathers and the indispensable value of the records (see Mosiah 1:2).

MODERN PROPHETS SPEAK

David O. McKay:

> Homes are made permanent through love. Oh, then, let love abound. If you feel that you have not the love of those little boys and girls, study to get it. Though you neglect some of the cattle, though you fail to produce good crops, even, study to hold your children's love. Loyalty is another element of the permanent home. The loyalty you afterwards want them to show to the Priesthood of God should be manifest in the home—love, loyalty, virtue. Cherish these principles, as you cherish and treasure your life. Set children the proper example. It is folly to tell a boy not to smoke, when you take your pipe out of your own mouth to tell him. Latter-day Saints, let us keep the commandments of God. Let us try to teach the children those commandments. . . . The Church in all its organizations is putting forth an effort to make ideal men in ideal communities; but after all, the responsibility of making those ideal men, those ideal boys and girls, rests with the parents, and next with the older brothers and sisters. The responsibility is with the family, God's unit in the social fabric of humanity. We shall never get away from it. (*CR*, Oct. 1917, 56–58)

ILLUSTRATIONS FOR OUR TIME

The Precious Student. The final writing of this current chapter of the book coincided with a blessed event—the birth of a little granddaughter. What a precious and beautiful soul she was, and how pleased and honored were her parents. I selected a verse of scripture to share with them on the occasion of the doting grandparents' initial visit to the hospital to celebrate this new arrival. Quite by coincidence, I was pondering at the time one of my favorite passages from the Doctrine and Covenants, concerning the transition of God's children from the first estate to the mortal world: "Even before they were born, they, with many others, received their first lessons in the world of spirits and were prepared to come forth in the due time of the Lord to labor in his vineyard for the salvation of the souls of men" (D&C 138:56). Looking down upon the newborn babe, only a few hours old, I wondered at the wisdom already invested in her heart and mind by virtue of the preparation and instruction she had received in the premortal realm. What she would later find arrayed in the scriptures, and what her parents would soon be teaching her about the gospel of Jesus Christ, would be a harmonizing echo of distant lessons already learned, a comforting reminder of former doctrines already mastered, and a wondrous review of divine instruction gleaned firsthand from the Creator Himself.

It is the nature of scripture study to be an adventure in remembrance. Those who read and ponder the word of God through the Spirit will experience that remarkable sensation of seeming to recover, line upon line, what was known long ago before the veil of forgetfulness was placed upon our understanding at birth. Thus the messengers of the holy scriptures will speak to us, "and their voice shall be as one that hath a familiar spirit" (2 Ne. 26:16; cf. Isaiah 29:4). According to this perspective, our learning is essentially an "unforgetting," as the ancient Greeks expressed it, not knowing how close upon the heels of the truth they really were. A wonderful and stimulating experience awaits this newest grandchild to be able to relearn in life, by a process of unforgetting through the blessings of the Spirit, what the Father and the Son have already taught her in her previous home on high. (Allen)

Likening the Scriptures to Our Lives

Mosiah 1:5–7—King Benjamin taught his sons concerning the value of the scriptures, without which they would have dwindled in unbelief. He testified of the truthfulness of the word of God and encouraged them to search diligently the sacred records.

Application—Let us come to realize that the prophets continually exhort us to search, hearken, and to live by the word of God. There is no other way to live (see D&C 84:43–48). It is our opportunity and solemn obligation to make a plan to search the scriptures regularly and feast upon the word of God.

2. THE GOODNESS OF GOD AND OUR ETERNAL INDEBTEDNESS TO HIM

THEME. King Benjamin continually taught of the goodness of God. It is a central tenet of the Christian faith that we come to this appreciation of our dependence on Him, for, in view of the infinite Atonement, we are indeed all unprofitable servants.

"I say unto you, my brethren, that if you should render all the thanks and praise which your whole soul has power to possess, to that God who has created you, and has kept and preserved you, and has caused that ye should rejoice, and has granted that ye should live in peace one with another—I say unto you that if ye should serve him who has created you from the beginning, and is preserving you from day to day, by lending you breath, that ye may live and move and do according to your own will, and even supporting you from one moment to another—I say, if ye should

serve him with all your whole souls yet ye would be unprofitable servants" (Mosiah 2:20–21).

MOMENT OF TRUTH. Many precious testimonies in the Book of Mormon take the form of benedictory statements from revered leaders. Messages of this type include Lehi's remarkable discourse on the Atonement and on the destiny of Israel delivered before his family, Nephi's superb final discourse on the doctrine of Christ, Jacob's memorable treatment of the allegory of the olive trees, and King Benjamin's masterful sermon before the people of Zarahemla prior to his death. The King's son and heir apparent, Mosiah, had sent a proclamation throughout the realm for the people to gather themselves together at the temple to hear the speech. In a singularly significant manner, each family was united with the doorway to their tent positioned toward the temple. One can imagine row upon row of concentric family circles radiating outward from the temple grounds as far as the eye could see, with all hearts tuned to receive the sacred instruction—"that they might rejoice and be filled with love toward God and all men" (Mosiah 2:4). So great was the multitude that King Benjamin caused his words to be written and disseminated among the people. This speech continues to be worthy of distribution to all people.

MODERN PROPHETS SPEAK

Joseph Fielding Smith:

> Then again, we do not pray or conduct exercises for his sake, but for our own. Our Redeemer has done everything that is essential for our salvation, and he has taught us that if we serve him with all our soul, and all our days, yet we are unprofitable servants and have done only that which it was our duty to do. Paul says we were bought with a price, and we are not our own (1 Cor. 6:20; 7:23). Our Redeemer has a perfect right to command us, and all that we do is for our own sakes. He can do without us, but we cannot do without him. We are told that we are unprofitable servants, (Mosiah 2:21–25; Luke 17:5–10) and so we are, if we think of trying to pay our Savior back for what he has done for us, for that we never can do; and we cannot by any number of acts, or a full life of faithful service, place our Savior in our debt. (*Doctrines of Salvation*, 3 vols., ed. Bruce R. McConkie [Salt Lake City: Bookcraft, 1954–1956], 1:15)

ILLUSTRATIONS FOR OUR TIME

Last words. "The tongues of dying men enforce attention like deep harmony." Thus spake William Shakespeare in *Richard II* (II.1.5–6). According to historical accounts, the following are the final words spoken by some individuals of note. On his deathbed, George Washington said "'Tis well." Thomas Beckett declared, "For the name of Jesus and the protection of the church I am ready to embrace death." Julius Caesar asked, "You, too, Brutus?" Dwight Eisenhower said, "I've always loved my children. I've always loved my wife. I've always loved my grandchildren. I've always loved my country."

Emily Dickinson declared, "the fog is rising." Thomas Edison said, "It's very beautiful over there." Nathan Hale stated, "I only regret that I have but one life to lose for my country." Joan of Arc requested, "Hold the cross high so I may see it through the flames!"

In a special way, we accord lasting significance to the final recorded pronouncements of the great prophets such as Jacob (Israel) in the Old Testament and Lehi, Nephi, Jacob, King Benjamin, Abinadi, Samuel, Mormon, Moroni, and others from the Book of Mormon. King Benjamin, in his last days, at a time when he declared "my whole frame doth tremble exceedingly" (Mosiah 2:30), exhorted his people in a final, masterful sermon, to obey the commandments of God: "And again, believe that ye must repent of your sins and forsake them, and humble yourselves before God; and ask in sincerity of heart that he would forgive you; and now, if you believe all these things see that ye do them" (Mosiah 4:10).

I can recall the last words said to me by my father, in his senior years. He had been experiencing a condition of increasing feebleness, so, to assist him in his personal care, I gave him a new electric razor. He looked at it, smiled gratefully, and then, much to my surprise, returned it to me, saying in a weak voice, "Do this for me." He was at the time too weak to do it on his own. I bent over and carefully shaved away his whiskers. That was the last sentence I remember him expressing to me. He passed away not long thereafter. "Do this for me." The symbolic meaning of that phrase still echoes in my mind, for it bears comparison to the righteousness he had exemplified throughout his life. What better way for children to honor the name of their parents than to follow their example and emulate the "godly walk and conversation" (D&C 20:69) they had cultivated as a legacy of faith and courage?

According to the gospels, the Savior's last words include the following: "It is finished" (John 19:30); "My God, my God, why hast thou forsaken me!" (Matt. 27:46; Mark 15:34); and "Father, into thy hands I commend my spirit" (Luke 23:46). His entire life can be summarized in the phrase "Come, follow me" (Luke 18:22), which is a glorious variant of the humble words, said in so many ways and under so many circumstances by parents everywhere as a last request to their children: "Do this for me." (Allen)

Likening the Scriptures to Our Lives

Mosiah 2:21–24—King Benjamin teaches us concerning the blessings of God in our lives and how He preserves us day to day, even lending us our very breath . . . and all the Lord requires of us is to keep His commandments, and then He doth immediately bless us.

Application—Let us take the opportunity to see, feel, and appreciate all the blessings of God in our lives every day. When we realize the goodness of God in our lives, we will be filled with gratitude, knowing full well that we can never repay Him for our abundant blessings. This gratitude will motivate us to keep the commandments.

3. PONDER THE PROPHECIES CONCERNING THE COMING OF THE SAVIOR

THEME. Without exception, the prophets of God have focused their message on the mission and Atonement of the Savior. Jesus Christ is the central theme of all prophetic discourse. All of us must adopt this as our guiding premise for spiritual prosperity.

> *"And he shall be called Jesus Christ, the Son of God, the Father of heaven and earth, the Creator of all things from the beginning; and his mother shall be called Mary" (Mosiah 3:8).*

> *"And moreover, I say unto you, that there shall be no other name given nor any other way nor means whereby salvation can come unto the children of men, only in and through the name of Christ, the Lord Omnipotent. For behold he judgeth, and his judgment is just; and the infant perisheth not that dieth in his infancy; but men drink damnation to their own souls except they humble themselves and become as little children, and believe that salvation was, and is, and is to come, in and through the atoning blood of Christ, the Lord Omnipotent. For the natural man is an enemy to God, and has been from the fall of Adam, and will be, forever and ever, unless he yields to the enticings of the Holy Spirit, and putteth off the natural man and becometh a saint through the atonement of Christ the Lord, and becometh as a child, submissive, meek, humble, patient, full of love, willing to submit to all things which the Lord seeth fit to inflict upon him, even as a child doth submit to his father" (Mosiah 3:17–19).*

MOMENT OF TRUTH. King Benjamin, like all the prophets before him, prophesied and taught concerning the coming of the Savior Jesus Christ and His Atonement. The crowning testimony of King Benjamin's final discourse to his people was a report given him by an angel of God about the mission of the Redeemer: "For the Lord hath heard thy prayers, and hath judged of thy righteousness, and hath sent me to declare unto thee that thou mayest rejoice; and that thou mayest declare unto thy people, that they may also be filled with joy" (Mosiah 3:4). Then King Benjamin conveys to his listeners (and by extension to his modern-day readers) a compelling witness of what the angel instructed him to say about the need to repent, overcome the natural man, and become as a saint through the Atonement of Christ.

MODERN PROPHETS SPEAK

Bruce R. McConkie:

> An angel from heaven recited to King Benjamin what well may be the greatest sermon ever delivered on the atonement of Christ the Lord. (Mosiah 3.) Abinadi made it clear

that God himself would redeem his people (Mosiah 13:32–33), that were it not for this redemption all mankind must have perished, and that the Lord redeemeth none of those who rebel against him and die in their sins (Mosiah 15). (*The Promised Messiah: The First Coming of Christ* [Salt Lake City: Deseret Book, 1978], 232)

ILLUSTRATIONS FOR OUR TIME

Obtaining and Keeping the Guidance of the Holy Spirit. Marion G. Romney taught four principles for obtaining and keeping the guidance of the Holy Spirit (adapted from "Guidance of the Holy Spirit," *Ensign,* Jan. 1980, 5).

1. Mighty Prayer
• Pray and fast for the blessing of the Holy Ghost (see 3 Ne. 19:9).

2. Search the Scriptures (see 2 Ne. 32:3)
• Faith comes by hearing the word of God (see Rom. 10:17) and the Holy Ghost is a blessing due to one's faith (see 1 Ne. 10:17).
• We live by the word of God (see D&C 84:44–46), and the word is understood by the power of the Holy Ghost (see D&C 68:4).

3. Live Righteously
• When we keep the commandments we are blessed always to have the Spirit (see D&C 20:77, 79).
• Through purity and by showing love we are blessed by the Spirit (see D&C 76:116).
• The fruit of the Spirit is goodness, righteousness, and truth (see Eph. 5:9)

4. Church Service
• We can only teach by the Spirit (see D&C 42:14).
• Our meetings are directed by the Spirit (see Moro. 6:9).
• We rely on the Spirit in every facet of the work, whether it is to testify (see 3 Nephi 28:11) or do the work of the ministry (see Acts 13:2–4; 16:6), and as disciples we have the joy of the Spirit (see Acts 13:52). (Pinegar)

Likening the Scriptures to Our Lives

Mosiah 3:19—King Benjamin, having been instructed by an angel to do so, taught us that the natural man is an enemy to God (one who is unrepentant—see Mosiah 2:38). The natural man will continue to be an enemy unless he yields to the enticings of the Holy Spirit, becoming a saint through the Atonement of our Savior Jesus Christ, becoming as a child . . . submissive, meek, humble, patient, full of love, and willing to submit to all things according to the will of the Lord.

Application—The application of this scripture to our lives has an exalting power. It is incumbent upon us, according to the principles of salvation, to repent, thus being forgiven of our sins. Let us therefore accept our Savior Jesus Christ and apply His Atonement to our lives in all things. Let us submit to the will of our Heavenly Father in all things. Let us exercise humility, for it is the beginning virtue of exaltation.

SUMMARY

We see reflected in these extraordinary passages of scripture the lesson that the word of God—as confirmed by the Holy Spirit—is the central legacy that parents can impart to their children, for the scriptures testify of the goodness of God and our eternal indebtedness to Him. The scriptures are informed by the spirit of prophecy concerning the mission and Atonement of the Savior. These are the themes that resonate in King Benjamin's speech. He loved and served his people. They were willing to listen to their prophet king. He taught them great truths that they understood and appreciated—truths that brought about a "mighty change" in their hearts (see Mosiah 5:2–4). If we choose to hearken to the words from the scriptures and our living prophets, we too can have this mighty change of heart. Our indebtedness to the Lord induces us to do our best in keeping His commandments, for He has promised us never-ending happiness if we do.

CHAPTER SIXTEEN

"YE ARE CALLED *the* CHILDREN *of* CHRIST"

Mosiah 4–6

*"King Benjamin and Alma both speak of 'a mighty change of heart.'
King Benjamin's congregation described that mighty change by saying that they had
'no more disposition to do evil, but to do good continually.' (Mosiah 5:2.)
Alma illustrated that change of heart when he described a people who 'awoke unto
God,' 'put their trust in' him, and were 'faithful until the end.' He challenged others
to 'look forward with an eye of faith' to the time when we will 'stand before God to
be judged' according to our deeds. Alma 5:7, 13, 15.) Persons who have
had that change in their hearts have attained the strength and stature
to dwell with God. That is what we call being saved."*
—Dallin H. Oaks, *The Lord's Way* [Salt Lake City: Deseret Book, 1991], 226.

THEMES *for* LIVING

Receiving a Remission of Our Sins
Living a Christlike Life
The Mighty Change of Heart: A Covenant Commitment

INTRODUCTION

King Benjamin continues and completes his sermon before the people of Zarahemla. He integrates into his discourse many gospel themes: salvation through Christ, the goodness of God, our own nothingness and fallen state, trust in the Lord, the need to repent and humble ourselves before the Lord, the need to remember and retain our dependence before God, standing steadfast in the faith, and much more. His message conveys the promise that if we will follow the covenant principles, we can then be filled with the love of God and retain a remission of our sins. He admonishes us to teach our children to honor the laws of God by walking in truth and soberness. Above all, we are to help those in need.

1. RECEIVING A REMISSION OF OUR SINS

THEME. The pathway leading to peace and relief from the burden of sin is always the same: to recognize our need to repent, exercise faith, and seek mercy through the Atonement of Jesus Christ.

> *"And it came to pass that after they had spoken these words the Spirit of the Lord came upon them, and they were filled with joy, having received a remission of their sins, and having peace of conscience, because of the exceeding faith which they had in Jesus Christ who should come, according to the words which king Benjamin had spoken unto them" (Mosiah 4:3).*

MOMENT OF TRUTH. As King Benjamin finishes delivering the message to his people that the angel of the Lord had imparted unto him, he becomes witness to a singularly remarkable event—the members of his audience have all fallen to the earth, "for the fear of the Lord had come upon them. And they had viewed themselves in their own carnal state, even less than the dust of the earth" (Mosiah 4:1–2). He sees that the Spirit of the Lord has succeeded in transforming their perception, enabling them to view themselves from a higher perspective, where mortal weaknesses are placed into sharp focus in contrast with saintly patterns of living, and consequently the process of repentance can proceed unimpeded. This leads to the remission of sins and the ushering in of a fulness of joy, "because of the exceeding faith which they had in Jesus Christ" (Mosiah 4:3).

MODERN PROPHETS SPEAK

Ezra Taft Benson:

> The Book of Mormon tells us of the Messiah's great atoning sacrifice. It describes how Jesus willingly suffered the pains of all men and specifies the conditions by which His atonement may bring us to a remission of our sins, a peace of conscience,

and great joy. (*The Teachings of Ezra Taft Benson,* ed. Sheri Dew [Salt Lake City: Bookcraft, 1988], 55)

ILLUSTRATIONS FOR OUR TIME

A New Way of Looking at Things. It was a beautiful spring day in a distant location where several colleagues and I were participating in a business retreat. Two of us were walking along the streets of the city preparing to rejoin our wives and other family members when we came upon a teenaged boy who seemed to be disoriented and in distress. As we passed, he gave us a look that suggested a combination of fear and longing. His arms reached out in a beckoning way to the pedestrians around him. He seemed to be challenged in multiple ways. Without stopping, we instinctively circumvented the spot where he was standing and continued on our way, silently. Then our pace slackened. Suddenly, my friend stopped and turned around. He walked the few steps back toward the young man and spoke with him. "What can we do to help?" was the question. The young man seemed somewhat relieved but was uncommunicative. My friend attempted for some time to communicate but could not seem to find any resolution. Finally, we concluded that nothing could be done, and we continued down the street.

I have often thought with admiration about the charity of my friend. Why was this simple event so memorable for me? Because my friend had a son who was similarly challenged—and so do I. Any family who is blessed to harbor and care for a challenged child will never again look upon an individual in that situation with the same eyes. There will always be more compassion than before. There will always be a greater level of understanding, because life will have imparted a new kind of perspective, a new way of looking at things.

The gospel of Jesus Christ also provides a new way of looking at things, one that has enduring consequences. King Benjamin warned us not to avoid the beggar, not to withhold our assistance and compassion under any circumstances. "For behold, are we not all beggars? Do we not all depend upon the same Being, even God, for all the substance which we have . . . ?" (Mosiah 4:19). So powerful was the king's discourse—based on angelic instruction—that his listeners collapsed under the burden of their own nothingness, perceiving themselves as "even less than the dust of the earth" (Mosiah 4:2; cf. Hel. 12:7–23). It was only in this state of perception—this new way of looking at things—that they could admit utter dependence upon the Lord, through whose redeeming merits and mercy alone the joy of redemption can come into one's life. (Allen)

Likening the Scriptures to Our Lives

Mosiah 4:11–12—King Benjamin reminds us, as part of our gratitude for having received a remission of our sins, to ponder always the goodness of God and retain in remembrance the following: God's greatness, our nothingness (without the help of the Lord), His long-suffering towards us, the need for humility and daily prayer, and the need to stand steadfastly in the faith. By doing so, we will be filled with His love, retain a remission of our sins, and grow in the knowledge of His glory.

Application—We can see the blessings that flow from remembering the goodness of God in our lives. Let us never forget His goodness lest we fall away (see Hel. 12:1–3).

2. LIVING A CHRISTLIKE LIFE

THEME. Living a Christlike life requires that we attempt to become like Him (see 3 Ne. 27:27) and begin to take upon ourselves His divine nature.

"And behold, I say unto you that if ye do this ye shall always rejoice, and be filled with the love of God, and always retain a remission of your sins; and ye shall grow in the knowledge of the glory of him that created you, or in the knowledge of that which is just and true. And ye will not have a mind to injure one another, but to live peaceably, and to render to every man according to that which is his due. And ye will not suffer your children that they go hungry, or naked; neither will ye suffer that they transgress the laws of God, and fight and quarrel one with another, and serve the devil, who is the master of sin, or who is the evil spirit which hath been spoken of by our fathers, he being an enemy to all righteousness. But ye will teach them to walk in the ways of truth and soberness; ye will teach them to love one another, and to serve one another. And also, ye yourselves will succor those that stand in need of your succor; ye will administer of your substance unto him that standeth in need; and ye will not suffer that the beggar putteth up his petition to you in vain, and turn him out to perish" (Mosiah 4:12–16).

"According as his divine power hath given unto us all things that pertain unto life and godliness, through the knowledge of him that hath called us to glory and virtue: Whereby are given unto us exceeding great and precious promises: that by these ye might be partakers of the divine nature, having escaped the corruption that is in the world through lust. And beside this, giving all diligence, add to your faith virtue; and to virtue knowledge; And to knowledge temperance; and to temperance patience; and to patience godliness; And to godliness brotherly kindness; and to brotherly kindness charity. For if these things be in you, and abound, they make you that ye shall neither be barren nor unfruitful in the knowledge of our Lord Jesus Christ. But he that lacketh these things is blind, and cannot see afar off, and hath forgotten that he was purged from his old sins. Wherefore the rather, brethren, give diligence to make your calling and election sure: for if ye do these things, ye shall never fall: for so an entrance shall be ministered unto you abundantly into the everlasting kingdom of our Lord and Saviour Jesus Christ" (2 Pet. 1:3–10; see D&C 4:6).

"Wherefore, my beloved brethren, pray unto the Father with all the energy of heart, that ye may be filled with this love, which he hath bestowed upon all who are true followers

of his Son, Jesus Christ; that ye may become the sons of God; that when he shall appear we shall be like him, for we shall see him as he is; that we may have this hope; that we may be purified even as he is pure. Amen" (Moro. 7:48).

MOMENT OF TRUTH. King Benjamin brings his people to the point where they have repented in full faith, being "filled with joy, having received a remission of their sins, and having peace of conscience" (Mosiah 4:3). He then continues his speech by guiding the people step by step toward a firm understanding of how they, having once tasted the love of God, might assure the continuation of this divine blessing in their lives forever, and "always retain a remission of your sins" (Mosiah 4:12). It is an inspiring exercise in transitions: from an inception to an unfolding, from a desirable moment of achievement to an enduring pattern of righteousness, from the sprouting of a seed (as Alma would later explain) to the maturing of "a tree springing up unto everlasting life" (Alma 32:41).

MODERN PROPHETS SPEAK

Harold B. Lee:

> What must I do to be saved? As I pondered these words, I thought of three essentials that are necessary to inspire one to live a Christlike life—or, speaking more accurately in the language of the scriptures, to live more perfectly as the Master lived. The first essential I would name in order to qualify is: There must be awakened in the individual who would be taught or who would live perfectly an awareness of his needs. . . . The second essential for perfection that I would name is found in the conversation the Master had with Nicodemus. . . . A man must be "born again" if he would reach perfection, in order to see or enter into the kingdom of God. . . . And then finally the third essential: to help the learner to know the gospel by living the gospel. Spiritual certainty that is necessary to salvation must be preceded by a maximum of individual effort. Grace, or the free gift of the Lord's atoning power, must be preceded by personal striving. Repeating again what Nephi said, "By grace . . . we are saved, after all we can do." (*Stand Ye in Holy Places* [Salt Lake City: Deseret Book, 1974], 208–213)

ILLUSTRATIONS FOR OUR TIME

The Yellow Pansies. Some people seem to be blessed with a "green thumb." My wife is like that, always cultivating a touch of natural color in the flower beds around our home. I recall fondly the winter when she managed to coax persistent growth from a small bed of yellow pansies around the base of a tree in the front yard—throughout the entire winter. Where the neighboring yards had been dutifully purged of all vestiges of floral expression from the expired seasons of growth, here was this radiant bed of yellow pansies that greeted me every day when I would return home from work.

Gospel flower beds are like that. We plant and cultivate the seeds of repentance and faith in our lives, and we receive joy in verdant beginnings and early blossoms. But it takes commitment and valor to maintain a lasting unfolding of the fruits of righteousness. When the winters of life come, and the winds of adversity and temptation whistle through the shadows of our mortal landscape, it is only through our enduring faith, anchored in the "merits, and mercy, and grace of the Holy Messiah" (2 Ne. 2:8), that we can hope to keep our spiritual garden alive and prospering.

King Benjamin described this kind of divine horticulture when he taught the people how to endure to the end: "And behold, I say unto you that if ye do this ye shall always rejoice, and be filled with the love of God, and always retain a remission of yours sins; and ye shall grow in the knowledge of the glory of him that created you, or in the knowledge of that which is just and true" (Mosiah 4:12). He then gave the key for all those who seek to maintain growth throughout winters on end: "And now, O man, remember and perish not" (Mosiah 4:50). (Allen)

Likening the Scriptures to Our Lives

Mosiah 4:13–16—King Benjamin reminds us that when we remember these things we will have a desire to live a Christlike life. We will have a desire to live peaceably with one another. We will bless our children so that they will not go hungry, transgress the laws of God, or quarrel one with another. We will teach our children to walk in truth and soberness (i.e., being serious-minded as to the things of the Lord) and to serve and love one another. We will seek to succor those in need.

Application—We have the grand opportunity to emulate our Savior Jesus Christ in our daily lives by striving to acquire His attributes and grow in the Spirit.

3. THE MIGHTY CHANGE OF HEART: A COVENANT COMMITMENT

THEME. The Spirit of the Lord can, if we are submissive and easily entreated, bring about a mighty change of heart.

> *"And they all cried with one voice, saying: Yea, we believe all the words which thou hast spoken unto us; and also, we know of their surety and truth, because of the Spirit of the Lord Omnipotent, which has wrought a mighty change in us, or in our hearts, that we have no more disposition to do evil, but to do good continually" (Mosiah 5:2).*

MOMENT OF TRUTH. When King Benjamin was giving his son Mosiah instructions to gather the people of Zarahemla together to hear his final counsel, he made this promise and commitment: "And moreover, I shall give this people a name, that thereby they may be distinguished above all the people which the Lord God hath brought out of the land of Jerusalem; and this I do because they have been a diligent people in keeping the commandments of the Lord. And I give unto them a name that never shall be blotted out, except it be through transgression" (Mosiah 1:11–12). True to his promise, the king declared to his people at the conclusion of his discourse the new name by which they would become known in all eternity: "And under this head ye are made free, and there is no other head whereby ye can be made free. There is no other name given whereby salvation cometh; therefore, I would that ye should take upon you the name of Christ, all you that have entered into the covenant with God that ye should be obedient unto the end of your lives. And it shall come to pass that whosoever doeth this shall be found at the right hand of God, for he shall know the name by which he is called; for he shall be called by the name of Christ" (Mosiah 5:8–9). The king then exhorts the people to "remember to retain the name written always in your hearts" (Mosiah 5:12) and to "be steadfast and immovable, always abounding in good works, that Christ, the Lord God Omnipotent, may seal you his" (Mosiah 5:15).

MODERN PROPHETS SPEAK

Henry B. Eyring:

> A choice to be good—even with the trials that come—will allow the Atonement to change your heart. In time and after persistence, your wants and even your needs will change. You remember that the people who believed King Benjamin's talk found such a change had come to them: "And they all cried with one voice, saying: Yea, we believe all the words which thou hast spoken unto us; and also, we know of their surety and truth, because of the Spirit of the Lord Omnipotent, which has wrought a mighty change in us, or in our hearts, that we have no more disposition to do evil, but to do good continually" (Mosiah 5:2).

> If we stay at it long enough, perhaps for a lifetime, we will have for so long felt what the Savior feels, wanted what he wants, and done what he would have us do that we will have, through the Atonement, a new heart filled with charity. And we will have become like him. (*To Draw Closer to God: A Collection of Discourses* [Salt Lake City: Deseret Book, 1997], 70–71)

ILLUSTRATIONS FOR OUR TIME

The "**Mighty Change.**" Stephen Robinson illustrates beautifully the process and challenges entailed in the "mighty change":

Surely someone, perhaps one of the spiritual masochists among us (or spiritual sadists—we have both in the Church), is going to object, "But what about 'the mighty change'? Did not the Spirit work a mighty change within the people of Benjamin so that they had *no more disposition to do evil, but to do good continually*?" (Mosiah 5:2). That is true, but what is being described there is a change in disposition, a change of desire, a change in our compass headings. From the moment of their conversion (or reconversion), the people of Benjamin changed their orientation and wanted righteousness rather than wickedness. It became their one goal. But that does *not* mean they achieved their goal instantaneously! It does *not* mean they never had another carnal thought or that they never subsequently lost any struggle against their carnal natures. At that moment, filled with the Spirit and clearly seeing the two paths before them, the people of Benjamin lost all desire to follow the path of evil. I feel the same way when I feel the Spirit, but I do not always feel the Spirit. And as with Moses, when the epiphany (divine appearance) is over, Satan sometimes takes his best shot (Moses 1:9–12). Therefore we must recharge our spiritual batteries regularly.

Great spiritual damage can be done by teaching the Saints that "the mighty change" means once truly converted we are never again tempted to sin. For if the Saints believe that the *truly* converted are never subsequently tempted, then when they are tempted—and they will be—they will conclude they are not really converted. However, being truly converted does not end the tests of mortality, for we will continue to be tested and tempted as long as we are in the flesh. Even as covenant members of the church of Jesus Christ, we will continue to be subject to the carnal impulses and other weaknesses that are a consequence of the Fall (*Following Christ: The Parable of the Divers and More Good News* [Salt Lake City: Deseret Book, 1995], 41–43).

Likening the Scriptures to Our Lives

Mosiah 5:2—The people of King Benjamin believed his words because the Holy Spirit manifested the truth unto them and simultaneously caused a mighty change in their hearts. Thus they had no desire to do evil but to do good continually.

Application—Let us seek to know the truth by the power of the Holy Spirit. The Spirit will show us all things to do (see 2 Ne. 32:5) and testify of the truth of all things (see Moro. 10:5), and thus the Holy Spirit will bless us in all things, certainly not just insisting on bringing to our remembrance past misdeeds (see John 14:26) that God chooses to "remember . . . no more" (D&C 58:42).

SUMMARY

King Benjamin has given us a magnificent training course not only in coming unto Christ, but in becoming like Christ. He, through the direction of an instructing angel, has given us a sure path upon which, through obedience, we might achieve a mighty change of heart. A change of heart brings a change of attitude and behavior, aligning our desires with God's, and because of our love we will obey. We may become like King Benjamin's people, who could truthfully say, following a mighty change in heart:

> And we, ourselves, also, through the infinite goodness of God, and the manifestations of his Spirit, have great views of that which is to come; and were it expedient, we could prophesy of all things. And it is the faith which we have had on the things which our king has spoken unto us that has brought us to this great knowledge, whereby we do rejoice with such exceedingly great joy. And we are willing to enter into a covenant with our God to do his will, and to be obedient to his commandments in all things that he shall command us, all the remainder of our days, that we may not bring upon ourselves a never-ending torment, as has been spoken by the angel, that we may not drink out of the cup of the wrath of God. (Mosiah 5:3–5)

The doctrines, principles, and covenants that King Benjamin presented, when personally applied, will fill our hearts with gratitude as we make the mighty change and keep our covenants faithfully, enduring to the end.

CHAPTER SEVENTEEN

"A SEER . . . BECOMETH A GREAT BENEFIT *to* HIS FELLOW BEINGS"

MOSIAH 7–11

"If we follow the advice, counsel, and teachings of the leaders of the Church in their instruction to us, we will not go amiss in that which is important for our own personal salvation and exaltation."
—HOWARD W. HUNTER, *THE TEACHINGS OF HOWARD W. HUNTER*, ED. CLYDE J. WILLIAMS [SALT LAKE CITY: BOOKCRAFT, 1997], 223.

THEMES *for* LIVING

The Light of Hope in the Darkness of Bondage
Vision of the Seer: The Lord's Blessing for Mankind
Listen to the Prophet's Voice

1. THE LIGHT OF HOPE
IN THE DARKNESS OF BONDAGE

THEME. The lesson of history resounds again and again: sin leads to bondage; hope and faith lead to deliverance.

> *"And again, that same God has brought our fathers out of the land of Jerusalem, and has kept and preserved his people even until now; and behold, it is because of our iniquities and abominations that he has brought us into bondage" (Mosiah 7:20).*

> *"But if ye will turn to the Lord with full purpose of heart, and put your trust in him, and serve him with all diligence of mind, if ye do this, he will, according to his own will and pleasure, deliver you out of bondage" (Mosiah 7:33).*

> *"And he also rehearsed unto them the last words which king Benjamin had taught them, and explained them to the people of king Limhi, so that they might understand all the words which he spake" (Mosiah 8:3).*

MOMENT OF TRUTH. A consistent pattern emerges from the Lord's dealings with His people over the generations: He moves and scatters both the righteous and the wicked according to His far-reaching plan to maximize the blessings of redemption for the greatest number of souls. Thus we have seen His tender influence in removing Lehi and his family from the dangers of impending bondage in Jerusalem (where the wicked were to be scattered by the Babylonians). Only a generation later, Nephi and his faithful few are again removed from the peril of unrighteous fraternity to the safety of a refuge where they could live in peace "after the manner of happiness" (2 Ne. 5:27). Not many generations hence we see the first Mosiah and his people again warned of the Lord to flee from the wrath of their enemies (Omni 1:12). He and his righteous group are led from the land of Nephi northward to Zarahemla, where they come upon yet another group—the Mulekites—who have likewise been divinely guided to a place of safety. In turn, this new group had come upon the last survivor of yet an earlier nation—the Jaredites—who had followed the Lord's counsel in removing themselves from the dislocations associated with the Tower of Babel (see Omni 1:20–22).

The principle of scattering is part of the Lord's agenda for His people, just as the principle of gathering is an instrument of strategic restoration for building, strengthening, and enlarging the tent of Zion. Thus it should not surprise us to see this divine process of diaspora (dispersion) and recovery played out multiple times in the

Book of Mormon. This demonstrates the Lord's watchful and compassionate intervention into the affairs of His sons and daughters, for all of whom He has infinite love and concern. Only three years into the reign of the second Mosiah (son of King Benjamin), the persistent "teasings" of the people (see Mosiah 7:1) resulted in the organization of an expeditionary force to locate the missing group of explorers who had traveled southward to investigate the land of their inheritance, Nephi-Lehi, from whence the first Mosiah had immigrated. As a result, Ammon and his courageous group wander some forty days in the wilderness before coming upon the residue of that group, now led by Limhi, who is the son of the notorious King Noah, who in turn was the son of Zeniff, the original outreach explorer from Zarahemla (see Mosiah 7:9).

It is through the Limhi/Noah/Zeniff chronicle (Mosiah 9–22) that we experience an amazing resonance of the scattering/gathering theme, which is a leitmotif throughout the Book of Mormon. Limhi and his people, as it turns out, are in bondage to the Lamanites because of the festering iniquity that has crept in among them through the materialistic and lascivious living of the previous King Noah and his minions. We witness the joy of Limhi and his people upon the arrival of Ammon, in whom they see the answer to their prayers for deliverance and the opportunity to return to the safety of Zarahemla. It is a chronic pattern captured once again by the ancient prophet-historians for the benefit of modern readers: sin and depravity lead to bondage—because they "were slow to remember the Lord our God"—(Mosiah 9:3); repentance and righteousness lead to liberty. God's people are scattered and gathered according to His design for the immortality and eternal life of man.

MODERN PROPHETS SPEAK

Joseph F. Smith:

> Every man and every woman should feel a deep and abiding interest in the work of the Lord, in the growth and development of the great latter-day cause, which cause is intended for the redemption of all men from the powers of sin, from all its contaminating effects, for the redemption of man from his own weakness and ignorance, and from the grasp that Satan holds upon the world, that men may be made free; for no man is or can be made free without possessing a knowledge of the truth and obeying the same. It is only the possession and observance of the truth that can make men free, and all those who do not possess and obey it are slaves and not free men. (*Gospel Doctrines: Selections from the Sermons and Writings of Joseph F. Smith*, comp. John A. Widtsoe [Salt Lake City: Bookcraft, 1919], 211)

ILLUSTRATIONS FOR OUR TIME

"I Will Go Where You Want Me to Go." Life presents for all of us a series of never-ending choices, some of small scope and some of large, but none without consequences. Agency, after all, was to be part of the Lord's plan of salvation "to see if they will do all things whatsoever the Lord their God shall command them" (Abr. 3:25). Many years ago I faced the challenging decision of which graduate school to attend in furthering my professional education. It was my great fortune and honor to be accepted by several reputable universities, any one of which could have provided a desirable environment for learning. I knelt in fervent prayer, after much discussion with my wife, and following a period of fasting and pondering, to ask the Lord's guidance on this matter concerning our future. The answer was clear and unmistakable. The decision was made. The move was accomplished. A new phase of life began and, as it turned out, there were many unexpected opportunities for service in the Church in the new geographical location, including a calling as a bishop, followed thereafter by a number of stake leadership positions. Was this a part of the equation? Through the eyes of faith, one concludes that it must have been. The call to serve can come in any environment, and through a multitude of opportunities, but one has to think that the Lord is above all coincidence and beyond all chance when it comes to moving us hither and yon in the interests of building the kingdom. "Help thy servants to say, with thy grace assisting them: Thy will be done, O Lord, and not ours" (D&C 109:44). (Allen)

When the Prophet Speaks, the Debate is Over. I suppose one of the greatest challenges in life is taking counsel and direction—especially when it goes against our own ideas and wishes. Pride may interfere. Sometimes we pick and choose the commandments of the Lord we want to fully embrace. Such a prideful course, after our own desires, separates us from the word and will of God. The breaking of any law or specific counsel from God or His servants has devastating effects. President Hinckley had the following to say regarding following our leaders' counsel:

> As we observe these . . . standards taught by the Church, many in the world will respect us and find strength to follow that which they too know is right. And, in the words of Isaiah, "Many people shall go and say, Come ye, and let us go up to the mountain of the Lord, to the house of the God of Jacob; and he will teach us of his ways, and we will walk in his paths" (Isaiah 2:3).

> We have no selfish desire in any of this, other than the wish that our brethren and sisters will be happy, that peace and love will be found in their homes, that they will be blessed by the power of the Almighty in their various undertakings in righteousness. (*Teachings of Gordon B. Hinckley* [Salt Lake City: Deseret Book, 1997], 83)

Elaine Cannon perhaps phrased it best when she said, "When the prophet speaks . . . the debate is over" ("If We Want to Go Up, We Have to Get On," *Ensign*, Nov. 1978, 108). Let us be easily entreated and believe with faith, since the prophets speak for God our Father and our Savior Jesus Christ (see D&C 1:38; 21:4–6). Let us seek understanding, but be believing. We are blessed when we follow our leaders, but we separate ourselves from God when we do not, in which case we suffer the devastating consequences (see 3 Ne. 28:34–35; D&C 20:15). (Pinegar)

Likening the Scriptures to Our Lives

Mosiah 8:18—Heavenly Father has provided the way whereby a man of God can do miracles through faith in the Lord Jesus Christ . . . thus blessing His fellowmen.

Application—We have the choice opportunity to exercise our faith to do the work of the Lord (see Ether 12:12–18). The power of the priesthood is in faith. "Faith and priesthood go hand in hand. Faith is power and power is priesthood. After we gain faith, we receive the priesthood. Then, through the priesthood, we grow in faith until, having all power, we become like our Lord. Our time here in mortality is set apart as a time of probation and of testing. It is our privilege while here to perfect our faith and to grow in priesthood power" (Bruce R. McConkie, "The Doctrine of the Priesthood," *Ensign*, May 1982, 32).

2. VISION OF THE SEER: THE LORD'S BLESSING FOR MANKIND

THEME. The Lord has not left us to wander blindly but has illuminated the pathway through the light imparted by his chosen servants: prophets, seers, and revelators.

> *"Now Ammon said unto him: I can assuredly tell thee, O king, of a man that can translate the records; for he has wherewith that he can look, and translate all records that are of ancient date; and it is a gift from God. And the things are called interpreters, and no man can look in them except he be commanded, lest he should look for that he ought not and he should perish. And whosoever is commanded to look in them, the same is called seer" (Mosiah 8:13).*

> *"And yet, I being over-zealous to inherit the land of our fathers, collected as many as were desirous to go up to possess the land, and started again on our journey into the wilderness to go up to the land; but we were smitten with famine and sore afflictions; for we were slow to remember the Lord our God" (Mosiah 9:3).*

MOMENT OF TRUTH. Ammon and his brethren brought to the people of Limhi renewed hope and the prospect of deliverance from their bondage. They also brought gospel tidings. And he also rehearsed unto them the last words which king Benjamin had taught them, and explained them to the people of Limhi" (Mosiah 8:3). In turn, Limhi shared with Ammon and his people the history of the three-generation excursion, including the failed attempt for an advance party to find the return route to Zarahemla. However, that party had accidentally discovered another land, one of desolation, and brought back artifacts, including a collection of 24 gold plates that held the promise of shedding light on the history of the fallen people. Limhi asked Ammon if he could interpret the plates, and it was this event that provided the framework for the significant dialogue about the role of seer. While Ammon could not read the plates, he reported to Limhi that he knew of a man (Mosiah) who had the gift of seership from God, which gift was the "means that man, through faith, might work mighty miracles; therefore he becometh a great benefit to his fellow beings" (Mosiah 8:18).

Thus we see the process unfolding whereby the Lord would preserve for the benefit of countless generations, including our modern age, the truths and principles reflected in the book of Ether—as well as in the record of Zeniff and his branch of Israel. Again, from a higher perspective, we see God's benevolent guidance as He moves his peoples in the pursuit of the redemptive process. The Book of Mormon is a dynamic framework for the amazingly intricate subsets of migration and movement. Various branches of the covenant people, who kept records while on the go, offer a spiritual syllabus for the enlightenment of all truth seekers.

MODERN PROPHETS SPEAK

Orson F. Whitney:

> "Seer" and "Prophet" are interchangeable terms, supposed by many to signify one and the same thing. Strictly speaking, however, this is not correct. A seer is greater than a prophet. One may be a prophet without being a seer; but a seer is essentially a prophet—if by "prophet" is meant not only a spokesman, but likewise a foreteller. Joseph Smith was both prophet and seer." (*Saturday Night Thoughts* [Salt Lake City: *Deseret News*, 1921], 39)

> To prepare God's people, and through them the world at large, for changes that must come in the carrying out of the divine program, is the function of the prophet, who foretells the future; of the seer, who looks through time into eternity; of the revelator, who delivers the word and will of the Universal Father to his children. The aims of the prophets are high and noble. They desire the happiness and progress of the race; yet almost invariably they are misunderstood, ridiculed, opposed and persecuted. (*CR*, Oct. 1917, 49)

ILLUSTRATIONS FOR OUR TIME

A Story of Beauty to Help Us Remember the Lord Always.

Elray L. Christiansen:

>Some time ago I read a story that had a profound influence upon me. I cannot recall its source. . . . Anyway, a young man had committed a serious crime and was languishing in jail, awaiting execution in payment for the crime (if that will pay it). During his last night on earth, of course, he did not sleep. Dawn found him standing at the window of his cell, holding the bars, looking out. He could see over the prison walls and behold the countryside and the sky.

>As the sky brightened with the dawning of the day, a change seemed to come over him—a change of values, a change of appreciation for what he had hitherto considered commonplace and unworthy of his notice. He observed the rich, brown earth, the leaves on the trees, the bright, green fields, and the sky. He gripped the bars of his cell and stared intently at the scene which lay before him, but which had gone unnoticed during his lifetime. Tears came to his eyes, and he realized for the first time the glory and magnificence of the world about him. As the muffled footsteps of the jailors approached the cell, he still stood at his window, transfixed by the unspeakable beauty of the dawning of the day and the rising sun.

>Of course, the beauty and the wonder of it had been there all during his twenty-three years. He had simply let *time* run out on him until now it was too late to fully enjoy it. I doubt if he is the only one who has failed to make the most of his opportunities and appreciate while there is still time to do so.

>"Time is so fleeting," said Hans Christian Andersen, "that if we do not remember God and learn of him in our youth, age may find us incapable of thinking of him" (Elray L. Christiansen, "The Endowment Time," *BYU Speeches of the Year,* March 14, 1962, 3–4).

Likening the Scriptures to Our Lives

Mosiah 10:11–17—The Lamanites depended upon their own strength, were ferocious, and believed in the false traditions of their fathers, in that they felt they had been wronged by Nephi. They were angry because they knew not the dealings of the Lord. They taught their children to hate the Nephites.

Application—We learn that when people separate themselves from the Lord they are left to themselves. They know not the dealings of the Lord, and thus they often feel hurt, become angry, and then rebel, just as did the Lamanites. As we ponder these events, we can learn from them and realize that when we find ourselves inclined to complain about something in the Church or find fault with our leaders, we are in sore need of repentance. Tolerance and understanding are central to the saintly walk of life, as is being humble, easily entreated, and obedient. Let us therefore seek the Lord and depend upon His strength in all things.

3. LISTEN TO THE PROPHET'S VOICE

THEME. Upon the prideful and impenitent the word of God falls as the sword of justice, but upon the humble and obedient it distills as the comforting dews from heaven.

> *"And it shall come to pass that except this people repent and turn unto the Lord their God, they shall be brought into bondage; and none shall deliver them, except it be the Lord the Almighty God" (Mosiah 11:23).*

> *"Now the eyes of the people were blinded; therefore they hardened their hearts against the words of Abinadi, and they sought from that time forward to take him. And king Noah hardened his heart against the word of the Lord, and he did not repent of his evil doings" (Mosiah 11:29).*

MOMENT OF TRUTH. King Noah, sunken in abject evil, wanton greed, and unfettered promiscuity, was the diametric opposite of his faithful namesake from the Old Testament. When Israel descends to the depths of depravity displayed by King Noah's generation—in what the Lord had decreed would be a land of promise for the faithful—there is always a response from heaven: prophetic intervention. In this case, King Noah was to have an encounter with one of the giants of prophetic candor and power, Abinadi. It is an encounter that begins with a majestic call to repentance (Mosiah 11:20–25) and continues with the predictable rejection of that call, culminating in an eventual second encounter of heightened forcefulness. This, in turn, led to the martyrdom of the Lord's anointed and the ultimate demise of the forces of evil. The entire episode is a case study in the condition of the heart, for Noah and his people displayed hearts of adamantine hardness and incorrigible recalcitrance. From them we can take a lesson for our own day, (i.e., that the Lord has commanded that we should bring before Him an acceptable offering of a broken heart and a contrite spirit).

MODERN PROPHETS SPEAK

M. Russell Ballard:

> And what a blessing this is in the lives of those who believe in and follow these living prophets and apostles! Knowing that there is a prophet of God on earth today doesn't relieve Latter-day Saints from the burden of thinking and acting for themselves. We all have the responsibility to respond to the whisperings of the Holy Spirit in our own lives. But the inspired counsel of God's chosen servants provides those who pay attention with an extra source of spiritual strength and insight. The principles of the gospel are clarified and the plan of salvation is explained so that all may know how to live in accordance with the Lord's teachings.
>
> Those who have access to latter-day revelation through living prophets and apostles face life's most demanding tests more confidently, because they know to whom they can turn to find the truth. (*Our Search for Happiness: An Invitation to Understand The Church of Jesus Christ of Latter-day Saints* [Salt Lake City: Deseret Book, 1993], 93)

ILLUSTRATIONS FOR OUR TIME

Howard W. Hunter:

> As the prophets from the beginning to the present day pass in review before our memory, we become aware of the great blessing which comes to us from the influence of a living prophet. History should teach us that unless we are willing to heed the warnings and follow the teachings of a prophet of the Lord, we will be subject to the judgments of God. (Howard W. Hunter, *The Teachings of Howard W. Hunter*, ed. Clyde J. Williams [Salt Lake City: Bookcraft, 1997], 226)

Many more examples could be cited. The key to our spiritual success and happiness is to hearken to our prophet's voice and those who lead us. (Pinegar)

Likening the Scriptures to Our Lives

Mosiah 11:20–23—Abinadi exhorts the people to repent, or else the Lord will deliver them into the hands of their enemies.

Application—Our choice in life is to repent in all sincerity or receive the condemnation of the Lord. He will have His people be humbled in order that they might repent (see Hel.11:4–11).

SUMMARY

From these episodes in the Book of Mormon, we are renewed in our conviction that the gospel of Jesus Christ brings us the light of hope in the darkness of bondage, whether that is the bondage of discouragement, the shackles of uncorrected sinfulness, or the confinement of rebelliousness and pride. Through modern-day scriptures, we are confirmed in our joy that the Lord has again restored to the earth the blessings of the vision of prophets, seers, and revelators, just as in ages past. When we ponder the written word of God and listen to the inspired pronouncements of His chosen servants, rich blessings wait in store.

We are blessed to have living prophets, seers, and revelators to guide the Church and teach us how to conduct our lives. As we live by every word that proceeds forth from the mouth of God, we will live by the words of our living prophet, who is in fact His mouthpiece. This shows our love and commitment, while keeping us on the straight and narrow path that leads to eternal life.

CHAPTER EIGHTEEN

"GOD HIMSELF . . . SHALL REDEEM HIS PEOPLE"

MOSIAH 12–17

"The only thing the Savior expects from us in return for his suffering is that we repent of our sins and keep his commandments. Although his sufferings were so intense that he the Son of God was caused 'to tremble because of pain and to bleed at every pore, and to suffer both body and spirit, and would that (he) might not drink the bitter cup, and shrink,' (Doc. and Cov. 19:18.) yet he, as would a true mother, counts it all worthwhile if, at the end of the earth, mankind, for whom he died, might gain eternal life and become his sons and daughters eternally through the acceptance of his gospel, which is God's plan for man's salvation."
—HAROLD B. LEE, *DECISIONS FOR SUCCESSFUL LIVING* [SALT LAKE CITY: DESERET BOOK, 1973], 115.

THEMES *for* LIVING

The Universal Message of the Prophets: Repent or Be Destroyed
The Fatherhood of Jesus Christ
"Every Sacrifice Which I, the Lord, Shall Command" (D&C 97:8)

1. THE UNIVERSAL MESSAGE OF THE PROPHETS: REPENT OR BE DESTROYED

THEME. Salvation comes solely through the redemptive mission of Jesus Christ. The message of the Savior, through His prophets, is that the faithful and obedient may come and freely partake of the eternal joys of the gospel, while the rebellious and impenitent will suffer the consequences of damnation.

> *"And it shall come to pass that except they repent I will utterly destroy them from off the face of the earth; yet they shall leave a record behind them, and I will preserve them for other nations which shall possess the land; yea, even this will I do that I may discover the abominations of this people to other nations" (Mosiah 12:8).*

> *"But now Abinadi said unto them: I know if ye keep the commandments of God ye shall be saved; yea, if ye keep the commandments which the Lord delivered unto Moses in the mount of Sinai" (Mosiah 12:33).*

> *"And moreover, I say unto you, that salvation doth not come by the law alone; and were it not for the atonement, which God himself shall make for the sins and iniquities of his people, that they must unavoidably perish, notwithstanding the law of Moses" (Mosiah 13:28).*

MOMENT OF TRUTH. Two years after Abinadi had delivered his initial call to repentance before the people of King Noah, he returned in disguise (Mosiah 12:1) to deliver anew the declaration that God's judgments would be poured out upon this rebellious generation. Quoting many familiar writings from his predecessor prophets, Abinadi tries, and convicts, his detractors in the court of God's justice. They are incapable of countering his irrefutable evidence of their wickedness in wantonly violating the Ten Commandments. His extraordinary pronouncements about the Atonement and the redeeming mission of the Savior constitute another beautiful witness of Christ's divinity. Like Nephi and Jacob before him, he offers commentary on Isaiah that clarifies many of the cited passages, and makes them more vibrantly instructive. Without fear for his life, Abinadi brings King Noah and his priests face to face with the unassailable truth that Christ is the author of their salvation.

MODERN PROPHETS SPEAK

Marion G. Romney:

"Repent or perish." There is, in my judgment, no more important message for the people of our day.

From the days of Adam "repent or perish" has been repeatedly and solemnly declared by the Father himself, his Son Jesus Christ, and their authorized representative, the prophets.

The truth of the message has been demonstrated as regularly as it has been declared. . . .

Although . . . scriptures . . . clearly and forcefully emphasize the message "repent or perish," they are not unkind, harsh, nor flippant. Neither are they arbitrary. They express the logical and inevitable consequences of the violation of natural law—that law which was "decreed in heaven defore the foundations of the world, upon which all blessings are predicated" (D&C 130:20).

These warnings have been declared to the world now for more that 140 years. The world is without excuse. ("Repent or Perish," *Ensign,* Apr. 1975, 3–5).

ILLUSTRATIONS FOR OUR TIME

Hope in the Lord Jesus Christ. Of all the doctrines found in the scriptures and preached from the pulpit, without doubt the most repeated principle is to repent with godly sorrow and turn back to God, begging for forgiveness. M. G. Easton, author of the *Illustrated Bible Dictionary,* describes the elements well:

> (1) a true sense of one's own guilt and sinfulness; (2) an apprehension of God's mercy in Christ; (3) an actual hatred of sin (Ps. 119:128; Job 42:5, 6; 2 Cor. 7:10) and turning from it to God; and (4) a persistent endeavour after a holy life in a walking with God in the way of his commandments. The true penitent is conscious of guilt (Ps. 51:4, 9), of pollution (51:5, 7, 10), and of helplessness (51:11; 109:21, 22). Thus he apprehends himself to be just what God has always seen him to be and declares him to be. But repentance comprehends not only such a sense of sin, but also an apprehension of mercy, without which there can be no true repentance (Ps. 51:1; 130:4). (M. G. Easton, *Illustrated Bible Dictionary,* rev. ed. [Grand Rapids, Michigan: Baker Book House, 1978], 595).

The Book of Mormon teaches to preach nothing save it be faith and repentance (see Mosiah 18:20; 25:15, 22; Alma 37:33; Hel. 6:4). Missionaries' primary message in teaching investigators is to have faith to accept, and courage to repent and live according to, the teaching. Every lesson taught, every principle or doctrine expounded upon, should embrace the principles of faith and repentance. Faith is the foundation of all righteousness, and it is through repentance that we can become righteous. How do we become perfect? Repent perfectly.

I will never forget a talk that Cecil B. DeMille gave at BYU in 1957. *The Ten Commandments* had recently been released, and everyone was viewing this epic film. He mentioned that the commandments of God could not be broken. As I sat there wondering, he then said, "We cannot break the Ten Commandments. We can only break ourselves against them." We are the ones who lose when separating ourselves from God. We lose His Holy Spirit. There is only one hope in this life and that is in the Lord Jesus Christ. He has redeemed our souls if we but repent. Repenting of our sins is the greatest thing we will do for our lives. Helping others repent will be of great worth to us (see Alma 29:9–10; James 5:20; D&C 15:6; D&C 31:5). We will feel and find joy in so doing (see Alma 36:24; D&C 18:10–16). (Pinegar)

Likening the Scriptures to Our Lives

Mosiah 11:20–23—Abinadi exhorts the people to repent, otherwise, the Lord will deliver them into the hands of their enemies.

Application—Let us learn that repentance is required if we would be found acceptable before the Lord.

2. THE FATHERHOOD OF JESUS CHRIST

THEME. Jesus Christ, the Son of God, is also the purest and most complete embodiment of the qualities and powers of the Father and is destined, moreover, to be the Head and Father of those faithful and obedient Saints who, as foretold by Isaiah and confirmed by Abinadi, become his declared generation, or "seed."

> *"But he was wounded for our transgressions, he was bruised for our iniquities; the chastisement of our peace was upon him; and with his stripes we are healed" (Mosiah 14:5).*

> *"And now Abinadi said unto them: I would that ye should understand that God himself shall come down among the children of men, and shall redeem his people" (Mosiah 15:1).*

MOMENT OF TRUTH. Abinadi is assailed by his third-degree interrogators because his message does not seem to them in conformity with the tenor of Isaiah's pronouncements about "good tidings of good" (Mosiah 12:21) and the comforts that accompany the salvation of Zion. What they fail to perceive in their hearts of stone is that "there could not any man be saved except it were through the redemption of God" (Mosiah 13:32) and that the Redeemer, for all His compassion and mercy, "cannot deny justice when it has its claim" (Mosiah 15:27). Thus King Noah and his priests—except for Alma—condemn Abinadi to death for telling them the truth "with power and authority from God" (Mosiah 13:6). He taught that transcending truth: Christ is our only hope unto salvation and eternal life.

MODERN PROPHETS SPEAK

John Taylor:

> From the facts in the case and the testimony presented in the scriptures it becomes evident that through the great atonement, the expiratory sacrifice of the Son of God, it is made possible that man can be redeemed, restored, resurrected, and exalted to the elevated position designed for him in the creation as a Son of God. . . .

> The Savior thus becomes master of the situation—the debt is paid, the redemption made, the covenant fulfilled, justice satisfied, the will of God done, and all power is now given into the hands of the Son of God—the power of the resurrection, the power of the redemption, the power of salvation, the power to enact laws for the carrying out and accomplishment of this design. Hence life and immortality are brought to light, the gospel is introduced, and he becomes the author of eternal life and exaltation. He is the Redeemer, the Resurrector, the Savior of man and the world; and he has appointed the law of the gospel as the medium which must be complied with in this world or the next, as he complied with his Father's law; hence "He that believeth and is baptized shall be saved; but he that believeth not shall be damned" (Mark 16:16).

> The plan, the arrangement, the agreement, the covenant was made, entered into, and accepted before the foundation of the world; it was prefigured by sacrifices, and was carried out and consummated on the cross.

> Hence being the mediator between God and man, he becomes by right the dictator and director on earth and in heaven for the living and for the dead, for the past, the present, and the future, pertaining to man as associated with this earth or the heavens, in time or eternity, the captain of our salvation, the apostle and high priest of our profession, the Lord and giver of life. (*The Gospel Kingdom: Selections from the Writings and Discourses of John Taylor,* ed. G. Homer Durham [Salt Lake City: Improvement Era, 1941], 114)

ILLUSTRATIONS FOR OUR TIME

The Royal Adoption. Elder Theodore M. Burton served as mission president in the West German Mission during my time there as a young missionary. I spent the last part of my service in the mission home in Frankfurt, where it was my great honor to get to know President Burton and his wife very well. One of the choice blessings that came with that opportunity was to spend the first part of each morning in gospel study with all of the mission home staff, learning from President Burton, a consummate student of the scriptures. I shall never forget the day he offered his insightful commentary on Abinadi, in particular on those passages that dealt with Isaiah's compelling question concerning the Savior: "And who shall declare his generation?" (Mosiah 14:8). President and Sister Burton had an adopted son who accompanied them on their mission. Because they were familiar with the complex legal process by means of which an adoption is completed, it was natural for President Burton to relate his personal experiences to the doctrine of adoption into the kingdom of God, whereby we become part of the family of Christ, as King Benjamin explained: "And now, because of the covenant which ye have made ye shall be called the children of Christ, his sons, and his daughters; for behold, this day he hath spiritually begotten you; for ye say that your hearts are changed through faith on his name; therefore, ye are born of him and have become his sons and his daughters" (Mosiah 5:7).

During our scripture study sessions and in a celebrated speech delivered to various congregations in our mission, President Burton explained this doctrine by describing the exceptional transition through which adults go in adopting a child. They must appear before the court and answer the sobering question: "Are you willing to take upon yourself all responsibility for the welfare and well-being of this child, to nurture and care for the child under all circumstances just as if the child were your natural-born child?" To answer yes to this question, and complete the legally binding covenants relative to the adoption, brings about an extraordinary change in the status of the adopting adults: the man becomes a father, and the woman becomes a mother, to the adopted child. Later, as a general authority, Elder Burton expressed it this way: "When we are baptized, we actually make a new covenant with God the Eternal Father to take upon us the name of his Only Begotten Son. Jesus Christ thus becomes by adoption our covenant Father. Thus, though he was, and is, our Elder *Brother,* he is also *now* our covenant *Father,* and we have become his covenant sons and daughters. We desire to be respectful and show our gratitude to him for the opportunity we have to become members of his royal family" ("To Be Born Again," *Ensign,* Sept. 1985, 69). (Allen)

Likening the Scriptures to Our Lives

Mosiah 16:2–5—Abinadi teaches the people that the wicked who will not repent are not redeemed by the Lord. They are carnal-minded, and hence are subject to the devil, thus remaining in a fallen state an enemy to God.

Application—Let us be firm in our conviction that redemption is in and through the Lord Jesus Christ. To take full advantage of His atoning sacrifice requires that we repent and follow His commandments. There is no other way.

3. "EVERY SACRIFICE WHICH I, THE LORD, SHALL COMMAND" (D&C 97:8)

THEME: Sacrifice is at the heart of the gospel of Jesus Christ. In comparison with the infinite atoning sacrifice of the Savior, there is nothing that man can do by way of a quid pro quo. Thus the sacrifice of all things in devotion to the cause of immortality and eternal life is never too high a price to pay, and even the sacrifice of all things leaves man a debtor before God (see Mosiah 2:21).

> *"And now, when Abinadi had said these words, he fell, having suffered death by fire; yea, having been put to death because he would not deny the commandments of God, having sealed the truth of his words by his death" (Mosiah 17:20).*

MOMENT OF TRUTH. After refuting the evil position of King Noah and his priests through the exquisite word of God, Abinadi dies as a martyr, "having sealed the truth of his words by his death" (Mosiah 17:20). He had but one purpose—to do the will of the Father, and through his extraordinary display of courage, he left a legacy of what it means to be spiritually committed to the sacrifice of all things while on the Lord's errand. Alma, a priest in Noah's court, was converted by Abinadi's teachings and conveyed the gospel message thereafter to a flourishing new branch of Israel.

MODERN PROPHETS SPEAK

Joseph B. Wirthlin:

> Another example of far-reaching effects of an inspired testimony is that of the prophet Abinadi. The testimony he bore as he called an apostate king, Noah, and his priests to repentance is one of the most significant doctrinal discourses in the Book of Mormon. The king and his priests, except one, rejected Abinadi's teachings and had him put to death. That one was Alma.

> Abinadi may have felt that he failed as a missionary because he had only one convert, so far as the record shows. However, that one convert, Alma, and his descendants were spiritual leaders among the Nephites and Lamanites for about three hundred years. His son Alma became the first chief judge of the Nephite people and the high priest over the Church. Alma's other descendants who became prominent religious leaders include his grandson Helaman; his great-grandson Nephi; and his great-great-great-grandson Nephi, who was the chief disciple of the resurrected Jesus Christ. All of this resulted from Abinadi's lone convert. (*Finding Peace in Our Lives* [Salt Lake City: Deseret Book, 1995], 220–21)

ILLUSTRATIONS FOR OUR TIME

Martyrdom of Joseph and Hyrum Smith, by Willard Richards.

Possibly the following events occupied near three minutes, but I think only about two, and have penned them for the gratification of many friends.

CARTHAGE, June 27, 1844.

A shower of musket balls were thrown up the stairway against the door of the prison in the second story, followed by many rapid footsteps.

While Generals Joseph and Hyrum Smith, Mr. Taylor, and myself, who were in the front chamber, closed the door of our room against the entry at the head of the stairs, and placed ourselves against it, there being no lock on the door, and no catch that was usable.

The door is a common panel, and as soon as we heard the feet at the stairs head, a ball was sent through the door, which passed between us, and showed that our enemies were desperadoes, and we must change our position.

General Joseph Smith, Mr. Taylor and myself sprang back to the front part of the room, and General Hyrum Smith retreated two-thirds across the chamber directly in front of and facing the door.

A ball was sent through the door which hit Hyrum on the side of his nose, when he fell backwards, extended at length, without moving his feet.

From the holes in his vest (the day was warm, and no one had his coat on but myself), pantaloons, drawers, and shirt, it appears evident that a ball must have been thrown from without, through the window, which entered his back on the right side, and passing through, lodged against his watch, which was in his right vest pocket, completely pulverizing the crystal and face, tearing off the hands and mashing the whole body of the watch. At the same instant the ball from the door entered his nose.

As he struck the floor he exclaimed emphatically, "I am a dead man." Joseph looked towards him and responded, "Oh, dear brother Hyrum!" and opening the door two or three inches with his left hand, discharged one barrel of a six shooter (pistol) at random in the entry, from whence a ball grazed Hyrum's breast, and entering his throat passed into his head, while other muskets were aimed at him and some balls hit him.

Joseph continued snapping his revolver round the casing of the door into the space as before, three barrels of which missed fire, while Mr. Taylor with a walking stick stood by his side and knocked down the bayonets and muskets which were constantly discharging through the doorway, while I stood by him, ready to lend any assistance, with another stick, but could not come within striking distance without going directly before the muzzle of the guns.

When the revolver failed, we had no more firearms, and expected an immediate rush of the mob, and the doorway full of muskets, half way in the room, and no hope but instant death from within.

Mr. Taylor rushed into the window, which is some fifteen or twenty feet from the ground. When his body was nearly on a balance, a ball from the door within entered his leg, and a ball from without struck his watch, a patent lever, in his vest pocket near the left breast, and smashed it into "pie," leaving the hands standing at 5 o'clock, 16 minutes, and 26 seconds, the force of which ball threw him back on the floor, and he rolled under the bed which stood by his side, where he lay motionless, the mob from the door continuing to fire upon him, cutting away a piece of flesh from his left hip as large as a man's hand, and were hindered only by my knocking down their muzzles with a stick; while they continued to reach their guns into the room, probably left handed, and aimed their discharge so far round as almost to reach us in the corner of the room to where we retreated and dodged, and then I recommenced the attack with my stick.

Joseph attempted, as the last resort, to leap the same window from whence Mr. Taylor fell, when two balls pierced him from the door, and one entered his right breast from without, and he fell outward, exclaiming, "Oh Lord, my God!" As his feet went out of the window my head went in, the balls whistling all around. He fell on his left side a dead man.

At this instant the cry was raised, "He's leaped the window!" and the mob on the stairs and in the entry ran out.

I withdrew from the window, thinking it of no use to leap out on a hundred bayonets, then around General Joseph Smith's body.

Not satisfied with this I again reached my head out of the window, and watched some seconds to see if there were any signs of life, regardless of my own, determined to see the end of him I loved. Being fully satisfied that he was dead, with a hundred men near the body and more coming round the corner of the jail, and expecting a return to our room, I rushed towards the prison door, at the head of the stairs, and through the entry from whence the firing had proceeded, to learn if the doors into the prison were open.

When near the entry, Mr. Taylor called out, "Take me." I pressed my way until I found all doors unbarred, returning instantly, caught Mr. Taylor under my arm and rushed by the stairs into the dungeon, or inner prison, stretched him on the floor and covered him with a bed in such a manner as not likely to be perceived, expecting an immediate return of the mob.

I said to Mr. Taylor, "This is a hard case to lay you on the floor, but if your wounds are not fatal, I want you to live to tell the story."

I expected to be shot the next moment, and stood before the door awaiting the onset. *(HC,* 6:619–21)

Likening the Scriptures to Our Lives

Mosiah 17:10, 20—Abinadi would not retract his testimony against his unrighteous detractors. He suffered death by fire because he would not deny the commandments of God—thus becoming a martyr by sealing his testimony of truth by his death. As was said of the Carthage massacre, "The testators are now dead, and their testament is in force" (D&C 135:5).

Application—We may not be asked to die for our beliefs, but we have certainly been asked to live for our beliefs. Let us realize that standing, living, and testifying for the truth is our duty (see Mosiah 18:8–9).

SUMMARY

In Abinadi's teachings we come to know the goodness of God and His plan of redemption that comes only through His beloved Son, Jesus Christ. To take full advantage of His atoning sacrifice, it is incumbent upon us to repent and come unto Him. The plea of Abinadi, like that of all the holy prophets, past and present, resonates through the generations of time: Repent and come unto Christ. That is the universal message of the prophets. By sincere repentance and adherence to gospel covenants, we can become the sons and daughters of God and thus, through spiritual adoption into the family of Christ, come to understand that "redemption cometh through Christ the Lord, who is the very Eternal Father" (Mosiah 16:15). If repentant, we will submit to the will of the Father in all things, as did Abinadi: "Verily I say unto you, all among them who know their hearts are honest, and are broken, and their spirits contrite, and are willing to observe their covenants by sacrifice—yea, every sacrifice which I, the Lord, shall command—they are accepted of me" (D&C 97:8).

CHAPTER NINETEEN

"NONE COULD DELIVER THEM *but* THE LORD"

MOSIAH 18–24

"The converted King Limhi promised his people that the Lord would deliver them from bondage if they would 'turn to the Lord with full purpose of heart' (Mosiah 7:33)."
—DALLIN H. OAKS, *PURE IN HEART* [SALT LAKE CITY: BOOKCRAFT, 1988], 21.

THEMES *for* LIVING

The Baptismal Covenant
The Inexorable Justice of God
The Deliverance of the Chastened and Humble
The Lord Will Gather the Faithful out of Bondage

INTRODUCTION

Alma gathers the faithful around him in seclusion to teach faith, repentance, and redemption through the Lord Jesus Christ. He explains to the eager congregants the commitment required in one's life to the baptismal covenant, and the people believe with joy and desire to be baptized. Being a true converted disciple requires that we genuinely love our brothers and sisters as we bear one another's burdens, mourn with those that mourn, comfort those who stand in need of comfort, and seek their welfare by standing as a willing witness of the truth in all places and circumstances (see Mosiah 18:9; 28:3; Alma 36:24). The Lord fulfills Abinadi's prophecy as wicked King Noah dies by fire, and demonstrates His love and power as He delivers Limhi's colony out of bondage. Similarly, He guides Alma's colony from the clutches of Amulon's sinister leadership back to Zarahemla. The message for our day and age is clear: He will deliver us from our enemies as we trust in Him and keep His commandments.

1. THE BAPTISMAL COVENANT

THEME. The ordinance of baptism is the sacred ceremonial declaration that one is willing to take upon himself or herself the name of Christ and live by solemn covenant in accordance with His laws. Such an ordinance, bestowing renewal, rebirth, cleansing, liberation, and spiritual adoption into the family of Christ, is a thing of transcendent beauty and joy.

> *"And it came to pass after many days there were a goodly number gathered together at the place of Mormon, to hear the words of Alma. Yea, all were gathered together that believed on his word, to hear him. And he did teach them, and did preach unto them repentance, and redemption, and faith on the Lord. And it came to pass that he said unto them: Behold, here are the waters of Mormon (for thus were they called) and now, as ye are desirous to come into the fold of God, and to be called his people, and are willing to bear one another's burdens, that they may be light; Yea, and are willing to mourn with those that mourn; yea, and comfort those that stand in need of comfort, and to stand as witnesses of God at all times and in all things, and in all places that ye may be in, even until death, that ye may be redeemed of God, and be numbered with those of the first resurrection, that ye may have eternal life—Now I say unto you, if this be the desire of your hearts, what have you against being baptized in the name of the Lord, as a witness before him that ye have entered into a covenant with him, that ye will serve him and keep his commandments, that he may pour out his Spirit more abundantly upon you?" (Mosiah 18:7–11).*

MOMENT OF TRUTH. Alma, having been touched by the Spirit as he listened to Abinadi's inspired words, had importuned King Noah to spare the life of this holy man. In so doing, he placed himself in mortal peril and had to flee and take refuge in the wilderness. The description of his secret convocations at the waters of Mormon with a small group of enthusiastic and receptive followers is one of the most celebrated accounts of conversion and baptism in all of scripture. Like the ordinance described in this passage (including the actual words used by Alma to baptize the converts), the landscape itself was one of great beauty and provided "a fountain of pure water" (Mosiah 18:5) to carry out the ordinance of baptism for "about two hundred and four souls" (Mosiah 18:16): "Yea, the place of Mormon, the waters of Mormon, the forest of Mormon, how beautiful are they to the eyes of them who there came to the knowledge of their Redeemer; yea, and how blessed are they, for they shall sing to his praises forever" (Mosiah 18:30).

MODERN PROPHETS SPEAK

Spencer W. Kimball:

> All members have been baptized by immersion in water and have received the Holy Ghost by the laying on of hands by properly authorized men who hold the holy priesthood. We all have been received by baptism into The Church of Jesus Christ when we have humbled ourselves before God, have desired to be baptized, have come forth with broken hearts and contrite spirits, and when we have witnessed before the Church that we are truly repentant of our sins and are willing to take upon us the name of Jesus Christ, having a determination to serve him to the end and thus manifest by our works that we have received the Spirit of Christ unto the remission of our sins. (*The Teachings of Spencer W. Kimball*, ed. Edward L. Kimball [Salt Lake City: Bookcraft, 1982], 112)

ILLUSTRATIONS FOR OUR TIME

Sacred Precincts. For every person whose life has been touched by the spirit of the gospel of Jesus Christ there is at least one place on earth to which a particularly fond spiritual memory is attached. For some that might be the scene where the Holy Ghost first whispered the comforting truth of redemption. For others that might be a room within one of the holy temples of God, or a place where communion with loved ones has rendered sacred the walls of a home or dwelling place.

I can still recall as if it were yesterday the pleasant surroundings of a certain secluded grove and a beautiful summer day many years ago when I had retired there, following an extended fast, to pour out my heart in prayer. I desired confirmation of the decision I had made to propose to a certain noble and fair daughter of Zion. It was there that the Spirit proffered a blessing of truth and comfort in unmistakable terms, and I cannot drive past that spot without thinking of the words "Did I not speak peace to your mind concerning the matter? What greater witness can you have than from God?" (D&C 6:23). That scene, together with the sealing room where she and I soon thereafter knelt across an alter together, remain fixed in my mind as unforgettable sacred precincts. Alma's ministry was rewarded with an out-pouring of the Spirit to a small group of enthusiastic converts at the edge of the secluded waters of Mormon: "And now it came to pass that all this was done in Mormon, yea, by the waters of Mormon, in the forest that was near the waters of Mormon; yea, the place of Mormon, the waters of Mormon, the forest of Mormon, how beautiful are they to the eyes of them who there came to the knowledge of their Redeemer; yea, and how blessed are they, for they shall sing to his praise forever" (Mosiah 18:30).

Revisiting such places of spiritual resort (either in reality or within our active memory), and reliving the ennobling events that transpired there, can renew one's strength, and provide inducement to remember with gratitude the Lord's compassion in walking with us, as it were, along the pathway of life. (Allen)

Likening the Scriptures to Our Lives

Mosiah 18:8–9—Alma taught that when we come into the Church we should be willing to bear one another's burdens, mourn with those that mourn, comfort those who stand in need of comfort, and stand as a witness at all times, in all things, and in all places.

Application—As members of the Church we have solemn responsibilities toward our fellowmen. These are not merely suggestions, but commandments. Let us remember our covenants at baptism as taught in D&C 20:37 and Moro. 6:1–4.

2. THE INEXORABLE JUSTICE OF GOD

THEME. Just as God will fulfill His promised blessings to the righteous without fail, He will also execute judgment upon those who reject His word and turn back His servants.

> *"And the king commanded them [his priests] that they should not return; and they were angry with the king, and caused that he should suffer, even unto death by fire" (Mosiah 19:20).*

> *"And also that king Noah and his priests had caused the people to commit so many sins and iniquities against God; and they also did mourn for the death of Abinadi; and also for the departure of Alma and the people that went with him, who had formed a church of God through the strength and power of God, and faith on the words which had been spoken by Abinadi" (Mosiah 21:30).*

MOMENT OF TRUTH. Abinadi had warned prideful King Noah and his courtiers that the same fate they inflicted upon him would, in turn, be inflicted upon them and their followers. Abinadi's last words amidst the blistering torture of a fiery grave, were: "Thus God executeth vengeance upon those that destroy his people. O God, receive my soul" (Mosiah 17:19). It was not long thereafter that the Lamanites invaded the colony, causing Noah and his priests to flee for their lives. When a search party came after Noah to deliver him up to the Lamanites as one of the conditions of forbearance on the part of the invading hosts, Noah refused to let his companions return, and they therefore pronounced summary judgment upon him, "and caused that he should suffer, even unto death by fire" (Mosiah 19:20). Thus we see that the Lord's word, delivered through the voice of His servants to the incorrigible and hardhearted, is sure of fulfillment.

MODERN PROPHETS SPEAK

Spencer W. Kimball:

> Remember, God is in his heavens. He knew what he was doing when he organized the earth. He knows what he is doing now. Those of us who break his commandments will regret and suffer in remorse and pain. God will not be mocked. Man has his free agency, it is sure, but remember, GOD WILL NOT BE MOCKED (See D&C 63:58).

> Our counsel then to you is to live strictly the laws of your Heavenly Father ("God Will Not Be Mocked," *Ensign*, Nov. 1974, 9)

ILLUSTRATIONS FOR OUR TIME

"A Natural-born Liar." Parents are accountable for teaching their children by word and deed. If we lead our children astray, even as King Noah led his people astray, we will be held accountable. Consider Elder LeGrand Richards's remarks—with a wry twist—about the impact of parents on behavior:

> Brother Ezra Taft Benson, in his beautiful address on the home, told us of the charge the Lord has laid upon the parents in Israel to teach their children faith in the living God, repentance and baptism, and the laying on of hands, and teach them to pray and to walk uprightly before the Lord in all things, with the statement that if they failed in so doing the sin would be upon the heads of the parents. I wish every father and mother in Israel realized what that meant and what it will mean when they give a reckoning for the stewardship that has been theirs to be privileged to be the parents of these chosen spirits who are permitted to come upon the earth in this day and time.

> A short time ago one of the leaders in the Aaronic Priesthood in one of our stakes handed me a copy of an article that appeared in a magazine that was published by the Kiwanis Club. I want to read a few excerpts from it:

There is a general opinion that the children are bright. In my opinion there is no greater fallacy. They are so dumb that it is a wonder we ever make really useful citizens out of them.

To illustrate, the article says:

I know a fellow, a Kiwanian by the way, who has two small boys. He is a well-educated, cultured gentleman, with a lovely wife and a nice home. Those two boys have been reared with every advantage. This man takes his golf clubs and hikes out to the golf course every Sunday morning of his life, and can you imagine it, those two boys are so dumb that they can't understand why they should be made to go to Sunday School? They think they should be permitted to go fishing or swimming Sunday morning instead of going to church! Nothing their father says to them seems to convince the dumb little creatures that they should spend two hours in church on Sunday morning.

To save time, I will relate one or two more of these comments. The next one is about the father and mother who always preface their meal with a cocktail. They have a son and a daughter in high school who went to a dinner-dance, and the father found out that the children each had a cocktail before dinner. Those two kids were so dumb that when they were called on the carpet by their dad, they couldn't understand why they shouldn't drink cocktails! I tell you, kids are dumb.

A man who occupied a prominent position in his community, when he was out in the yard and would hit his finger with a hammer or run against a wire clothesline, would make the sky blue with his profanity, and yet when his six-year-old boy called the cat a "damned cat" because it ran across the table, the father promptly spanked him and washed his mouth out with soap, but he was never able to make that dumb kid understand that it was wrong to swear.

And there was a mother who did not like to entertain company when she wasn't in the mood, and if someone would call and want to come over to visit her, she would immediately say she had house guests and couldn't receive them, or if they wanted to speak to her on the phone and she wasn't in the mood, she would turn to her little girl and say, "Tell them I am not home." Do you know that dumb little girl lies like Ananias. The mother has done all she can to break her of it, but the child is just a natural-born liar. (LeGrand Richards, *Outstanding Stories by General Authorities,* comp. Leon R. Hartshorn, 3 vols. [Salt Lake City: Deseret Book, 1970–73], 3: 212–13)

Likening the Scriptures to Our Lives

Mosiah 19:20—King Noah suffers death by fire as was prophesied by Abinadi (see Mosiah 17:18).

Application—Let us realize that when the prophets speak it is the same as the Lord speaking. When we come to understand and appreciate this eternal verity we will be more obedient to our prophets both living and dead. The words of our prophets will be fulfilled.

3. THE DELIVERANCE OF THE CHASTENED AND HUMBLE

THEME. There is a principle in the heavens according to which blessings are predicated upon obedience to divine law (see D&C 130:20). The scriptures provide ample evidence that the degree of liberty enjoyed by the Saints of God is a function of their humility, valor, and willingness to be instructed of the Spirit.

> *"And they did humble themselves even in the depths of humility; and they did cry mightily to God; yea, even all the day long did they cry unto their God that he would deliver them out of their afflictions. And now the Lord was slow to hear their cry because of their iniquities; nevertheless the Lord did hear their cries, and began to soften the hearts of the Lamanites that they began to ease their burdens; yet the Lord did not see fit to deliver them out of bondage"* (Mosiah 21:14–15).

MOMENT OF TRUTH. Limhi's people were in bondage to the Lamanites, which fulfilled Abinadi's prophetic warning. Thus Limhi's people were chastened of the Lord that they might learn obedience and humility. They finally humbled themselves and were delivered by the Lord out of the hands of their enemies so that they could return with their records to Zarahemla (see Mosiah 7:33; 20:21; 21:4; 22:13).

MODERN PROPHETS SPEAK

Marion G. Romney:
> With respect to the loss of personal liberty through the misuse of free agency, our daily lives are filled with tragic evidence. We see the alcoholic with his craving for drink, the dope fiend in his frenzy, and worse, the pervert with his irretrievable loss of manhood. Who will say that such persons enjoy liberty?

> Notwithstanding the fact that through its misuse, political, economic, and personal liberty are lost, free agency will always endure because it is an eternal principle.

However, the free agency possessed by any one person is increased or diminished by the use to which he puts it. Every wrong decision one makes restricts the area in which he can thereafter exercise his agency. The further one goes in the making of wrong decisions in the exercise of free agency, the more difficult it is for him to recover the lost ground. One can, by persisting long enough, reach the point of no return. He then becomes an abject slave. By the exercise of his free agency, he has decreased the area in which he can act, almost to the vanishing point ("The Perfect Law of Liberty," *Ensign*, Nov. 1981, 45).

ILLUSTRATIONS FOR OUR TIME

We can be in bondage to many things, as this story by Elder Hartman Rector, Jr. illustrates:

Our Heavenly Father wants us to be free; he doesn't want us to be in bondage to our appetites and passions. Therefore, he has given us commandments that are only calculated to make us free. And he tells us that all of his commandments are spiritual. [See D&C 29:34.] Never at any time has he given a commandment that is not spiritual. Even the Word of Wisdom is a spiritual commandment in that it primarily affects our spirits, and certainly it does.

To illustrate, I knew a man who was a member of the Church but had returned to his habit of smoking cigarettes. He said he didn't want to smoke but just couldn't help it. Of course, he could have overcome the habit if he had really wanted to while he had his body to help him. If the spirit tells the body not to pick up the cigarette, the body won't pick it up, and abstinence over time allows the spirit to overcome the desire.

This man finally suffered a stroke. His body was paralyzed with the exception of his right arm and his eyes. As his son-in-law picked him up from the porch of his house, where he'd fallen, with the only arm this man could move, he reached for the cigarette in his son-in-law's mouth. But he could not hold onto it. His son-in-law held the lighted cigarette to the stricken man's lips, but in his condition he could not hold it in his mouth.

For nine months this man lay on his bed. He actually wore out the pocket of his pajamas reaching into it for a cigarette that was not there. Then he died and went into the spirit world. Do you suppose he still wants a cigarette? On the basis of Amulek's statement, he does. But there is just one catch—there are no cigarettes in the spirit world. Would you suppose he is in paradise or in spirit prison? The answer seems only too obvious. (*Outstanding Stories by General Authorities*, Leon R. Hartshorn, comp., 3 vols. [Salt Lake City: Deseret Book, 1970–73], 2:195–96)

Likening the Scriptures to Our Lives

Mosiah 21:15—The Lord was slow to hear the prayers of the people of Limhi because of their wickedness.

Application—Let us learn to exercise our faith, even though we are not perfect, in order to receive answers to our prayers (see Mosiah 27:14). We sometimes take no thought save it is to ask (see D&C 9:7) and wonder why our prayers are not answered. "We give our hopes, our time, our talent, our thoughts, our words, our actions, to the temporalities of life, and, once in a while, we think of God. We come before Him in that pitiful form of unworthiness to crave His blessings and His favors. Do you wonder that we are often denied that which we ask for, and fail to receive that which we desire?" (Joseph F. Smith, *CR*, Oct. 1913, 7). Our prayers are answered according to our faith (see Mormon 9:37).

4. THE LORD WILL GATHER THE FAITHFUL OUT OF BONDAGE

THEME. The Lord answers the prayer of the humble and faithful by granting courage to face adversity and resilience to endure the burdens of mortality.

> "And it came to pass that the voice of the Lord came to them in their afflictions, saying: Lift up your heads and be of good comfort, for I know of the covenant which ye have made unto me; and I will covenant with my people and deliver them out of bondage. And I will also ease the burdens which are put upon your shoulders, that even you cannot feel them upon your backs, even while you are in bondage; and this will I do that ye may stand as witnesses for me hereafter, and that ye may know of a surety that I, the Lord God, do visit my people in their afflictions. And now it came to pass that the burdens which were laid upon Alma and his brethren were made light; yea, the Lord did strengthen them that they could bear up their burdens with ease, and they did submit cheerfully and with patience to all the will of the Lord. And it came to pass that so great was their faith and their patience that the voice of the Lord came unto them again, saying: Be of good comfort, for on the morrow I will deliver you out of bondage. . . . And in the morning the Lord caused a deep sleep to come upon the Lamanites, yea, and all their task-masters were in a profound sleep. And Alma and his people departed into the wilderness; and when they had traveled all day they pitched their tents in a valley, and they called the valley Alma, because he led their way in the wilderness" (Mosiah 24:13–16, 19–20).

MOMENT OF TRUTH. Alma, who has led a community of the righteous out of King Noah's iniquitous colony, establishes a prosperous city of Helam founded on the principles of charitable service and obedience to God's laws. Before long, the Lamanites discover the enticing new community and take it captive under the leadership of

Amulon, the ruler of the renegade priests from Noah's court. The citizens of Helam are placed under grievous burdens by the spiteful Amulon, and it is only through their humble prayers and dependence on the Lord that they are miraculously freed from bondage and are able to find their way to the Nephite leadership at Zarahemla.

MODERN PROPHETS SPEAK

Joseph Smith, Jr.:

> It is also of equal importance that men should have the idea of the existence of the attribute judgment in God, in order that they may exercise faith in him for life and salvation; for without the idea of the existence of this attribute in the Deity, it would be impossible for men to exercise faith in him for life and salvation, seeing that it is through the exercise of this attribute that the faithful in Christ Jesus are delivered out of the hands of those who seek their destruction; for if God were not to come out in swift judgment against the workers of iniquity and the powers of darkness, his saints could not be saved; for it is by judgment that the Lord delivers his saints out of the hands of all their enemies, and those who reject the gospel of our Lord Jesus Christ. But no sooner is the idea of the existence of this attribute planted in the minds of men, than it gives power to the mind for the exercise of faith and confidence in God, and they are enabled by faith to lay hold on the promises which are set before them, and wade through all the tribulations and afflictions to which they are subjected by reason of the persecution from those who know not God, and obey not the gospel of our Lord Jesus Christ, believing that in due time the Lord will come out in swift judgment against their enemies, and they shall be cut off from before him, and that in his own due time he will bear them off conquerors, and more than conquerors, in all things (*Lectures on Faith,* [Salt Lake City: Deseret Book] 1985, 4:14).

ILLUSTRATIONS FOR OUR TIME

The Bondage of Not Following Counsel. One form of bondage results from failure in the home. Note what J. Golden Kimball had to say:

> I have labored for the past six weeks in company with Apostle Lyman through the southern part of the state, largely in the interests of the Young Men's Mutual Improvement Associations, and I discover in associating among the people that there is a great missionary work to be performed here at home. There are something over twenty-five thousand young men, from fourteen up to my age, and only a very small percentage of that number are laboring earnestly and ardently to gain infor-

mation and knowledge pertaining to this great work. Talk about your missionary fields of labor, talk about the nations of the earth; I comprehend that the angel came with its message that the Gospel is to be preached to every nation, to every kindred, to every tongue and people; but I want to testify to you, my brethren and sisters, that the rising generation at home are being neglected. They are not being reached by the Priesthood of God; and if there is any place on the great earth where there needs an awakening and an uplifting, it is right here in Zion. And, I want to say to you, the fathers and the mothers are helpless, and they know not what to do.

I know the cause, too, and the sin will rest upon the parents. They have not followed this counsel, to instruct their children when they are young. President George Q. Cannon said we were in bondage, to a certain extent, because we had not followed counsel, and I want to testify that it is true. And I want to say there is a great sin resting upon some of the fathers and mothers, because they have not taught their children faith, repentance, baptism, and the reception of the Holy Ghost when they were eight years old. And they are now reaping the sorrow of their neglect. We need missionaries. I take the position that we need one hundred to start out with, to commence this mission here at home; and I don't know, before they get through with it, but they will have to preach on the street corners like the elders do in the states and in Europe (In Claude Richards, *J. Golden Kimball: The Story of a Unique Personality* [Salt Lake City: Deseret News Press, 1934], 143–145). (Pinegar)

Likening the Scriptures to Our Lives

Mosiah 23:14—The people, having had a wicked king, suffered painful consequences because of his unrighteousness. In a sense, they allowed this to happen because they did not stand up for truth and righteousness. Alma taught a great truth to the people: that they should trust no one to be a teacher or minister unto them save he be a man of God, walking in His ways and keeping His commandments.

Application—Let us always stand for truth and righteousness. Let us expect integrity from our government leaders and from those we choose to heed. It is our duty to follow our living prophets. There are erroneous philosophies and misguided secular teachings of men that can lead people away from our Savior Jesus Christ. By following the Spirit, we can discern such detractions and avoid them, doing all we can to redirect or combat those who teach against eternal truths.

SUMMARY

In the space of not many chapters we can discover a treasure of spiritual wisdom and memorable stories concerning important themes: the sacred baptismal covenant, the inexorable justice of God, the means whereby the chastened can look forward to deliverance, and the compassion of the Lord in gathering the faithful out of bondage.

There are many great lessons that can be learned from these passages. Here are just a few that we might consider for evaluation and as a compass to change our own lives: Do we remember our baptismal covenants and the obligation of renewing them week-ly? Review them carefully in Mosiah 18:8–9; Moro. 6:1–4; D&C 20:37; as well as scriptures concerning discipleship: 3 Ne. 5:13; John 13:34–35; Matt. 25:40; D&C 88:81, to name a few.

What does it mean to stand as a witness? (Mosiah 18:9.) How do we put ourselves in bondage? (Compare the stories of Limhi and Alma.) To be a leader we must be wor-thy of people's trust. (See Mosiah 23:14.) We should evaluate and rededicate our lives every day to our Heavenly Father, that we might build up the Kingdom of God.

CHAPTER TWENTY

TRUE CONVERSION
INSPIRES ONE *to* SHARE THE GOSPEL

MOSIAH 25–28; ALMA 36

"As a member of the Church, do you realize that, as a member-missionary, you have a sacred responsibility to share the gospel with friends and family? The Lord needs every member of the Church having the faith and courage to set a date to have someone prepared to be taught by the missionaries. Would each member of the Church prayerfully consider this sacred challenge?"
—EZRA TAFT BENSON, *THE TEACHINGS OF EZRA TAFT BENSON* [SALT LAKE CITY: BOOKCRAFT, 1988], 178.

THEMES *for* LIVING

Building up the Kingdom of God
Making Our Influence a Lighthouse Rather than a Shadow
When Angels Intervene
Singular Devotion to the Cause of Missionary Work

INTRODUCTION

Through the Book of Mormon record we relive the formal organization of the Church among the Israelites gathered in Zarahemla. We see through the prism of holy scripture the nuances in the commitment of these early standard-bearers—some of them peerless pillars of righteous leadership and others of misguided persuasion who are in dire need of the Lord's most dramatic intervention. We see the patience and love of a father—himself reformed—for his bright but misdirected son, who then (along with his colleagues of the rising generation) acquires a single-minded devotion to missionary work and the service to God that has become a beacon for the blessing of countless generations.

1. BUILDING UP THE KINGDOM OF GOD

THEME. Where there is covenant leadership on earth, with authorized representatives of the Lord's priesthood power, the Church will emerge in its divinely appointed structure to administer the ordinances and blessings of the gospel to the sons and daughters of God. The Book of Mormon provides an extraordinary portrait of this dynamic process among the ancient Israelite peoples of the New World, and especially in regard to the ministry of Alma and his successor son, both of whom were redoubtable spiritual pioneers in building the Kingdom of God.

> *"And it came to pass that the people of king Limhi did depart by night into the wilderness with their flocks and their herds, and they went round about the land of Shilom in the wilderness, and bent their course towards the land of Zarahemla, being led by Ammon and his brethren" (Mosiah 22:11).*

> *"And after they had been in the wilderness twelve days they arrived in the land of Zarahemla; and king Mosiah did also receive them with joy" (Mosiah 24:25).*

> *"And it came to pass that king Mosiah granted unto Alma that he might establish churches throughout all the land of Zarahemla; and gave him power to ordain priests and teachers over every church" (Mosiah 25:19).*

MOMENT OF TRUTH. The two colonies of Limhi and Alma the Elder, having been separately delivered from bondage through the blessings of God, unite with King Mosiah's people in the land of Zarahemla. Their records, together with the Jaredite chronicle—which is translated through the divine seership of King Mosiah—are made available to the people. Mosiah and Alma teach the gospel, and many believe and are baptized. Because the circle of adherents exceeds the maximum number of people who could "hear the word of God in one assembly" (Mosiah 25:20), Alma is authorized to establish the Church in seven different congregations throughout the land of Zarahemla. They are unified in purpose and doctrine: "And thus, notwithstanding there being many churches they were all one church, yea, even the church of God; for there was nothing preached in all the churches except it were repentance and faith in God" (Mosiah 25:22).

MODERN PROPHETS SPEAK

Gordon B. Hinckley:

> In Kirtland, a school of the prophets was established to teach those young in the faith. In our homes and Church activities, we now teach in the schools of the future prophets. In all these settings, let us teach with power and conviction and faith. Let there always be an affirmation of testimony in the work of which we are a part. And let us not forget these words of revelation, also given at Hiram, Ohio: "The keys of the kingdom of God are committed unto man on the earth, and from thence shall the gospel roll forth unto the ends of the earth, as the stone which is cut out of the mountain without hands shall roll forth, until it has filled the whole earth" (D&C 65:2).
>
> May the Lord bless us as builders of faith. May our testimonies strengthen and become as anchors to which others may secure their faith in hours of doubt and concern. May the candle of learning ever burn in our minds. Above all, may testimony grow in our hearts that this is in reality the church of the living God and that it will continue to move forward to fulfill its divine destiny. May we each do our part faithfully and with thanksgiving to the Lord for all the blessings he so wondrously bestows upon us as we follow his teachings and draw near to him. (*Faith: The Essence of True Religion* [Salt Lake City: Deseret Book, 1989], 122–23)

ILLUSTRATIONS FOR OUR TIME

The Bulldozer of Faith. On the bookshelf of my study is a miniature working model of a bulldozer, unusual in that its metal surfaces have been bronzed so that they catch and reflect light for all to see. There is a story behind this tiny replica of a mighty construction machine. Many years ago it was my honor to preside at a ground-breaking ceremony for a new chapel that would house a congregation of Saints one of the stakes of the Church in the eastern part of the United States. Such an event, which is repeated countless times throughout the far reaches of the Church in many lands each year, is especially joyful in that it celebrates the diligence of so many members who put their shoulder to the wheel and "push along"—as the well-known hymn describes the process of building the kingdom of God. In connection with this ground-breaking mentioned above, I was later joking with the local priesthood leaders that it might be appropriate to gild the nearby bulldozer as a memorial to the historic event. Imagine my surprise and delight when these same brethren, some time later, following the completion of the chapel, presented me with a miniature replica of that bulldozer—meticulously bronzed.

Faith is like that bulldozer. It is faith that clears the ground of our spiritual construction site and makes room for the Lord to build up a new man or new woman in place of the old. Faith lays the foundation of good works and erects the framework of service and hope upon which a life of goodness can be constructed. Faith is the finisher of our lives, the refiner of our testament to the divinity of the work. Faith builds a temple of God, which temple each son or daughter of God is, edified by the Spirit. To "edify," in its very root meaning, is to build a temple.

And in the collective community of Saints, thus edified, the building goes on. The tent of Zion is enlarged without interruption. The stakes are placed. The cords are extended. The kingdom is expanded "without hands" (as Daniel interpreted it), for it is not a mortal work, nor a work of any earthly institution, but a work of God that will roll on, empowered by faith, unified by a common destiny and doctrine (see Mosiah 25:22), until it has "filled the whole earth" (see Daniel 2:35; D&C 65:2). (Allen)

Likening the Scriptures to Our Lives

Mosiah 25:22—Nothing was preached in the Church but repentance and faith in God.

Application—To live the gospel, enjoy the blessings of the Spirit, and endure to the end, we are entreated to exercise our faith in Jesus Christ and become perfect by applying the Atonement to our lives through repentance (see 3 Ne. 27:20). We sometimes fail to realize that coming unto Christ and proving ourselves worthy requires faith unto repentance (see Alma 34:15–17). Repentance and faith are emphasized over and over in the Book of Mormon.

2. MAKING OUR INFLUENCE A LIGHTHOUSE RATHER THAN A SHADOW

THEME. The Book of Mormon often teaches by contrast, just as Lehi observed: "For it must needs be that there is an opposition in all things" (2 Ne. 2:11). Thus we see in the lives of Alma the Younger and the sons of Mosiah two sides of very resourceful minds—both the negative and destructive, as well as the positive and productive. In our own lives it behooves us to discern that our influence is felt for good far beyond the confines of our own personal space and time.

"For it came to pass that they did deceive many with their flattering words, who were in the church, and did cause them to commit many sins; therefore it became expedient that

those who committed sin, that were in the church, should be admonished by the church"
(Mosiah 26:6).

"Now the sons of Mosiah were numbered among the unbelievers; and also one of the sons
of Alma was numbered among them, he being called Alma, after his father; nevertheless,
he became a very wicked and an idolatrous man. And he was a man of many words, and
did speak much flattery to the people; therefore he led many of the people to do after the
manner of his iniquities. And he became a great hinderment to the prosperity of the church
of God; stealing away the hearts of the people; causing much dissension among the people;
giving a chance for the enemy of God to exercise his power over them" (Mosiah 27:8–9).

MOMENT OF TRUTH. Alma the Elder, a former member of King Noah's notorious court, had a personal understanding of the transition from a state of impiety to a state of penitent spirituality. He freely confessed his shadowed background to those who had gathered in self-imposed exile in the wilderness: "But remember the iniquity of king Noah and his priests; and I myself was caught in a snare, and did many things which were abominable in the sight of the Lord, which caused me sore repentance" (Mosiah 23:9). Then, in a remarkable foreshadowing of the life of his future son, Alma, he added: "Nevertheless, after much tribulation, the Lord did hear my cries, and did answer my prayers, and has made me an instrument in his hands in bringing so many of you to a knowledge of his truth" (v. 10).

Alma the Younger was a member of the rising, free-spirited generation of young people at Zarahemla who were not personal witnesses to the extraordinary teachings of King Benjamin and were not aligned with the spiritual traditions of the prophet-kings (Mosiah 26:1–4). He and his colleagues, the sons of Mosiah, were renegades toward the Church in the capital city and environs. Their injurious behavior drew many from the fountain of truth. Years later, the reformed Alma characterized his earlier behavior in rather strong terms before his son Helaman: "Yea, and I had murdered many of [God's] children, or rather led them away unto destruction; yea, and in fine so great had been my iniquities, that the very thought of coming into the presence of my God did rack my soul with inexpressible horror" (Alma 36:14). The two Almas provide persuasive testimony that an influence of darkness can be transformed into one of overwhelming light through repentance and faith in Jesus Christ.

MODERN PROPHETS SPEAK

Harold B. Lee:

The Apostle Paul impressed also the danger of false teachings by bad example.
Said he:

"But take heed lest by any means this liberty of yours become a stumbling block to them that are weak. . . .

"And through thy knowledge shall the weak . . . perish, for whom Christ died?

"But when ye sin so against the brethren, and would their weak conscience, ye sin against Christ" (1 Corinthians 8:9, 11–12) (*Stand Ye in Holy Places* [Salt Lake City: Deseret Book, 1974], 355).

ILLUSTRATIONS FOR OUR TIME

Joseph F. Smith:

> Don't do anything yourselves that you would have to say to your boy, "Don't do it." Live so that you can say, "My son, do as I do, follow me, emulate my example." That is the way fathers should live, every one of us; and it is a shame, a weakening, shameful thing for any member of the Church to pursue a course that he knows is not right, and that he would rather his children should not follow. (*Gospel Doctrine: Selections from the Sermons and Writing of Joseph F. Smith,* comp. John A. Widtsoe, [Salt Lake City: Deseret Book] 285).

Likening the Scriptures to Our Lives

Mosiah 26:3—Because of unbelief, people could not understand the things of God and thus their hearts were hardened.

Application—Let us be believing (see D&C 90:24). Adam exemplified this faith (see Moses 5:5–6). Exercising faith to believe and then seeking understanding is pleasing to God (see Heb. 11:6). Unbelief precipitates apathy, which is the antithesis of love . . . hence, obedience wanes, the heart is hardened, the Spirit is lost, and sin is the result.

3. WHEN ANGELS INTERVENE

THEME. Among other things, the Book of Mormon offers to modern readers an inventory of the Lord's manifold means of communicating with mortals. Nephi reminded his older brothers of their chronic insensitivity to the Lord's attempts to signal them the truth: "Ye are swift to do iniquity but slow to remember the Lord your God. Ye have seen an angel, and he spake unto you; yea, ye have heard his voice from time to time; and he hath spoken unto you in a still small voice, but ye were past feeling, that ye could not feel his words; wherefore, he has spoken unto you like unto the voice of thunder, which did cause the earth to shake as if it were to divide asunder" (1 Ne. 17:45). Similarly, in our day, there is wisdom in staying tuned to the Lord's Spirit, through the voices of the prophets, and through the scriptures, so that He is not constrained, as with Alma the Younger, to resort to more dramatic means: "How oft have I called upon you by the mouth of my servants, and by the ministering of angels, and by mine own voice, and by the voice of thunderings, and by the voice of lightnings, and by the voice of tempests, and by the voice of earthquakes, and great hailstorms, and by the voice of famines and pestilences of every kind, and by the great sound of a trump, and by the voice of judgment, and by the voice of mercy all the day long, and by the voice of glory and honor and the riches of eternal life, and would have saved you with an everlasting salvation, but ye would not!" (D&C 43:25).

> *"And again, the angel said: Behold, the Lord hath heard the prayers of his people, and also the prayers of his servant, Alma, who is thy father; for he has prayed with much faith concerning thee that thou mightest be brought to the knowledge of the truth; therefore, for this purpose have I come to convince thee of the power and authority of God, that the prayers of his servants might be answered according to their faith" (Mosiah 27:14).*

> *"Nevertheless, after wading through much tribulation, repenting nigh unto death, the Lord in mercy hath seen fit to snatch me out of an everlasting burning, and I am born of God" (Mosiah 27:28).*

MOMENT OF TRUTH. Alma the Younger and his royal colleagues are confronted by an angel of God who commands them to desist and repent of their errors. Years later, Alma bore his testimony to his son Helaman and recalled the traumatic but productive angelic visitation: "For I went about with the sons of Mosiah, seeking to destroy the church of God; but behold, God sent his holy angel to stop us by the way. And behold, he spake unto us, as it were the voice of thunder, and the whole earth did tremble beneath our feet; and we all fell to the earth, for the fear of the Lord came upon us" (Alma 36:6–7). Alma used similar language in bearing his testimony forthrightly to his son Shiblon: "But behold, the Lord in his great mercy sent his angel to declare unto me that I must stop the work of destruction among his people; yea, and I have seen an angel face to face, and he spake with me, and his voice was as thunder, and it shook the whole earth" (Alma 38:7).

It was on the basis of this angelic intervention, occasioned by the sincere and fervent prayer of their fathers, that these young men were redirected into righteous channels. Alma the Younger suffers great pains of remorse and shame but obtains forgivness. The conversion of these young men to the Savior and His gospel is deep and complete. They have an overwhelming desire to redress the evils they have perpetrated and preach the gospel—especially to the Lamanites. Alma and King Mosiah grant permission and receive the assurance of the Lord that these stalwart missionaries will be preserved through their faith. Surely the purpose of this last dispensation is to share the gospel with all the world. It is the spirit of the gospel, and our duty.

MODERN PROPHETS SPEAK

Prayers of faith bring down the powers of heaven in all things as described by the example below:

Gordon B. Hinckley:

> Your uplifted hands in the solemn assembly this morning became an expression of your willingness and desire to uphold us, your brethren and your servants, with your confidence, faith, and prayer. I am deeply grateful for that expression. . . . This office is not one to be sought after. The right to select rests with the Lord. He is the master of life and death. His is the power to call. His is the power to take away. His is the power to retain. It is all in His hands.
>
> I do not know why in His grand scheme one such as I would find a place. But having this mantle come upon me, I now rededicate whatever I have of strength or time or talent or life to the work of my Master in the service of my brethren and sisters. (*Teachings of Gordon B. Hinckley* [Salt Lake City: Deseret Book, 1997], 75)

ILLUSTRATIONS FOR OUR TIME

The Lost Pocket Knife. A prayer to God with faith can send angels, heal the sick, and in all things bless Heavenly Father's children. Here is a tender story of Orson F. Whitney when as a little boy he lost his pocketknife:

> Love of God, the very essence of religion, was always with me. I never doubted the Lord's existence, his goodness or his power. When in trouble my first thought was to pray to Him. I did not share the notion, expressed by some of my fellows, that "the Lord doesn't want us to bother him about every little thing." I have never believed that we trouble our Heavenly Father by craving blessings at his hand. Prayer is an expression of faith, and the exercise of faith, whereby comes spiritual development, is one of the great objects and privileges of this earthly existence, our "second estate," where we "walk by faith," as before we "walked by sight." I believed then and believe now, that God's ear is as open to the pleadings of a little child, as to the prayers of a congregation. . . .

A rather remarkable experience befell me when a child. I had lost my pocket knife—the first I ever owned. Grieving bitterly over the misfortune, I almost questioned Providence for permitting it to happen. Yes, I was just that unreasonable, not knowing any better, and being so constituted that it nearly tore my heart out to lose anything upon which I had set my affections. While sorrowing over my loss, I suddenly felt an influence of peace, and as I looked up to heaven through my tears, a ray of light seemed resting down upon me. All at once those splendid lines of Cowper's flashed into my mind:

> Judge not the Lord by feeble sense,
> But trust Him for His grace;
> Behind a frowning Providence
> He hides a smiling face.

Never to my knowledge had I seen or heard that verse before. But be that as it may, it had the effect of drying my tears and giving me the assurance that I should find my lost knife. A few minutes later I walked down the path to my mother's gate, and there, half hidden in the dust, lay my precious treasure. How eagerly I pounced upon it, and how grateful I was for its recovery, I need not say.

To some this incident may appear trivial. To me, it is anything but that. (*Through Memory's Halls* [Independence, Missouri: Press of Zion's Printing and Publishing Company, 1930], 70–71) (Pinegar)

Likening the Scriptures to Our Lives

Mosiah 27:14—The Lord answers the prayers of the people according to their faith. Therefore an Angel came to convince Alma of the power and authority of God.

Application—We can have the blessings of God in our lives as we exercise our faith through prayer. Alma changed after this experience; Laman and Lemuel did not change after their angelic visitations. Let us realize that angels—messengers of God—can be in the form of mortals (see D&C 42:6) as well as those from the other side of the veil. Thomas S. Monson has taught us that in our eternal roles and duties within the Church, we can be inspired to be an answer to someone's prayer. He said, "As we love the Lord, as we love our neighbor, we discover that our Heavenly Father will answer the prayers of others through our ministry" (*Live the Good Life* [Salt Lake City: Deseret Book, 1988], 114).

4. SINGULAR DEVOTION TO THE CAUSE OF MISSIONARY WORK

THEME. One may know that conversion is complete if the convert is spiritually moved by an overwhelming desire to share the good news with others, even as Alma and the sons of Mosiah were motivated to do missionary work.

> *"And now it came to pass that Alma began from this time forward to teach the people, and those who were with Alma at the time the angel appeared unto them, traveling round about through all the land, publishing to all the people the things which they had heard and seen, and preaching the word of God in much tribulation, being greatly persecuted by those who were unbelievers, being smitten by many of them. But notwithstanding all this, they did impart much consolation to the church, confirming their faith, and exhorting them with long-suffering and much travail to keep the commandments of God. And four of them were the sons of Mosiah; and their names were Ammon, and Aaron, and Omner, and Himni; these were the names of the sons of Mosiah. And they traveled throughout all the land of Zarahemla, and among all the people who were under the reign of king Mosiah, zealously striving to repair all the injuries which they had done to the church, confessing all their sins, and publishing all the things which they had seen, and explaining the prophecies and the scriptures to all who desired to hear them. And thus they were instruments in the hands of God in bringing many to the knowledge of the truth, yea, to the knowledge of their Redeemer. And how blessed are they! For they did publish peace; they did publish good tidings of good; and they did declare unto the people that the Lord reigneth"* (Mosiah 27:32–37).

> *"Now it came to pass that after the sons of Mosiah had done all these things, they took a small number with them and returned to their father, the king, and desired of him that he would grant unto them that they might, with these whom they had selected, go up to the land of Nephi that they might preach the things which they had heard, and that they might impart the word of God to their brethren, the Lamanites—That perhaps they might bring them to the knowledge of the Lord their God, and convince them of the iniquity of their fathers; and that perhaps they might cure them of their hatred towards the Nephites, that they might also be brought to rejoice in the Lord their God, that they might become friendly to one another, and that there should be no more contentions in all the land which the Lord their God had given them. Now they were desirous that salvation should be declared to every creature, for they could not bear that any human soul should perish; yea, even the very thoughts that any soul should endure endless torment did cause them to quake and tremble"* (Mosiah 28:1–3).

MOMENT OF TRUTH. Alma and the sons of Mosiah, following their conversion, have a great desire to share the gospel with all people—especially the Lamanites. As a result, they dedicate their lives to preaching the gospel, and their example continues, even today, to radiate an influence for good in the ongoing process of building up the kingdom of God.

MODERN PROPHETS SPEAK

Ezra Taft Benson:

Early in this dispensation the Savior placed on the Church the responsibility to share the gospel. On November 1, 1831, He said: "The voice of warning shall be unto all people, by the mouths of my disciples, whom I have chosen in these last days. And they shall go forth and none shall stay them, for I the Lord have commanded them" (Doctrine and Covenants 1:4–5).

Again, on December 27, 1832, He commanded: "Behold, I sent you out to testify and warn the people, and it becometh every man who hath been warned to warn his neighbor. Therefore, they are left without excuse, and their sins are upon their own heads" (Doctrine and Covenants 88:81–82).

When the Saints came West, President Brigham Young declared: "We wish the brethren to understand the facts just as they are; that is, there is neither man or woman in this Church who is not on a mission. That mission will last as long as they live, and it is to do good, to promote righteousness, to teach the principles of truth, and to prevail upon themselves and everybody around them to live those principles that they may obtain eternal life. This is the mission of every Latter-day Saint" (*Journal of Discourses* 12:19).

ILLUSTRATIONS FOR OUR TIME

Sharing the Gospel Is for Everyone.

M. Russell Ballard:

I had an experience some time ago in Idaho when I attended a stake conference there. The stake president mentioned he had a surprise for me and asked, "Will you trust me?" I responded, "Well, we trust all of our stake presidents; I trust you if you are right." He said, "Well, I think you will enjoy what is going to happen tomorrow in the general session of the conference."

Here is what happened. In the Sunday morning session, he called upon a little girl who was about ten years of age to come up to the pulpit and bear her testimony about being a "Primary missionary." What had happened was that the stake president had authorized the high council adviser to the Primary to implement an idea that children can also be missionaries. This high councilor went to the ward Primaries to teach the little children that they were missionaries too. This sweet little girl, whom we shall call Katie, learned from the high councilor that she could be a missionary. She came home to her father, who was the bishop of one of the wards, and said, "Daddy, I'm a Primary missionary, and I want to share the gospel with somebody." The bishop said, "Well, sweetheart, that's a wonderful thing, but we have only one or two nonmember families in our whole ward, so it might be a little difficult." But this little girl asked, "Who are they?" The bishop named the nonmember families, and his daughter promptly responded, "Let's you and me go visit them, and we'll invite them to come to our home for family home evening." Those of you who are fathers of little girls know how easily you succumb when a sweet daughter looks at you imploringly out of innocent, trusting eyes. And that's what happened to the bishop. So he and Katie went and knocked on the door of one nonmember family. When the mother of the family answered the door, little Katie said, "I am a Primary missionary, and we want you to come to our house for family home evening." This wonderful mother, I guess, had the same problem with those big, innocent eyes, and she agreed to bring her family to home evening. They came; they had a nice evening; they were not converted.

About two weeks later, Katie came home just as her mother was taking some banana bread out of the oven. Katie asked, "Can I have a loaf of that bread?" Her mother said, "Yes sweetheart, but what do you want it for?"

"I want to take it to Mrs. Johnson," she replied.

When Mrs. Johnson came to the door, Katie said, "I have something for you that I would like to give you, but I can only give it to you on one condition." When Mrs. Johnson asked what the condition was, Katie responded, "That you let the missionaries teach you the gospel." Mrs. Johnson smiled and said, "If that's the only condition for us to have the banana bread, then I'll agree that we will let the missionaries teach us the gospel."

The missionaries taught the gospel to the Johnsons, and they were baptized.

After Katie finished her testimony at the conference, Sister Johnson was the next to speak. I shall never forget what I felt when she thanked a little ten-year-old Primary missionary who had had the courage to invite her family to learn about the gospel.

When it was my turn to speak, I invited the bishop and his family, including Katie, to come up and stand by me, and then I invited the Johnson family to come up—mother, father, and three children. I said to them, "You have had a wonderful experience together. Bishop, you and Katie have shared with your neighbor the most precious thing in life, the gospel of Jesus Christ. But I want to tell you that if you think your heart is filled with joy today, wait till that day one year from now when the Johnson family kneels at the altar in the Idaho Falls Temple to be sealed for time and all eternity. That will be a moment in mortality that you will never, ever forget."

One year later, I performed their sealing. When I walked into the temple, there in the waiting room was Katie, now age eleven, the Primary missionary. She was not able to go to the sealing room because she wasn't old enough, but she was there waiting for her convert family to be sealed. The sealing room was filled with members of the ward. When the three Johnson children knelt around that altar and I sealed them to their parents, it was a bit of heaven on earth—all made possible because a little girl took seriously an assignment from an inspired and motivated high councilor who had the idea that children could be missionaries too and who taught little Katie that she could share the gospel with others (*Counseling with Our Councils: Learning to Minister Together in the Church and in the Family* [Salt Lake City: Deseret Book, 1997], 86–88)

Likening the Scriptures to Our Lives

Mosiah 28:3—The sons of Mosiah were converted to the Lord. They were filled with charity. They could not bear that any human soul should perish and endure endless torment. This thought caused them to quake and tremble.

Application—When we are truly converted, we will feel like the sons of Mosiah. We will have an overwhelming concern for the welfare of others. We will seek to serve and bless their lives (see Mosiah 18:8–9; D&C 108:7; Matt. 25:40). The question we need to answer is how much do we love God and our fellow brothers and sisters . . . for on this commandment—love—hangs all the law and the prophets (see Matt. 22:36–40).

SUMMARY

Fervent convictions can be cultivated as we study these stirring Book of Mormon stories about building up the Kingdom of God, assuring that our influence is positive and inspiring, tuning our hearts and minds to the messages from the Lord, and developing a sincere and singular devotion to the cause of missionary work.

Through the inspired teachings of Mosiah and Alma the Elder, many were brought into the fold. The power of the word and the Spirit was manifested in their preaching. The power of example—and in this case a very bad example—caused many people to fall away from, or not even accept, the teachings of the Church leaders. Alma the Younger and King Mosiah's sons were among the unbelievers and caused great problems in the Church. Through the faith and prayers of Alma and the people an angel appeared and convinced them to repent. The conversion of young Alma and the sons of Mosiah gives hope to all and verifies the principle of repentance, for they experienced a "mighty change." The results are legendary, as manifested in their love of their fellow brothers and sisters, their missionary labors, and their dedication to the Lord. All these teachings can be applied to our lives in a very real sense. We need not sink low before rising to the heights of true conversion.

CHAPTER TWENTY-ONE

"ALMA . . . DID JUDGE RIGHTEOUS JUDGMENTS"

Mosiah 29; Alma 1–4

"Even in the seemingly miscellaneous gospel gems there is plainness and preciousness. If, for instance, we assume there is only ancient relevance concerning the practice and purposes of priestcraft, we need to be braced by how germane that definition is for our time. 'He commandeth that there shall be no priestcrafts; for, behold, priestcrafts are that men preach and set themselves up for a light unto the world, that they may get gain and praise of the world; but they seek not the welfare of Zion.' (2 Nephi 26:29.) Do we not see such people working today (minus the label, of course) among the children of men? Alas, such match the criteria set forth not only as some lead out in the realm of religion but in the realm of irreligion."
—Neal A. Maxwell, *Plain and Precious Things* [Salt Lake City: Deseret Book, 1983], 86–87.

THEMES *for* LIVING

Principles of Righteous Government
Protecting the Kingdom of God against Priestcraft
Preserving a Framework of Liberty and Freedom of Conscience
Gaining Perspective on the Cycle of Prosperity and Pride

INTRODUCTION

Good government is essential for ruling the people. The Nephites establish the reign of the judges with Alma as the first chief judge. Contention arises as Amlici seeks to become king. He is rejected by the people, yet he persists and the result is war between the Amlicites and Nephites. Prosperity begins, and with it comes the cycle of prosperity and pride. Alma leaves the chief judgeship and seeks to pull down the pride of the people by preaching the word with pure testimony.

1. PRINCIPLES OF RIGHTEOUS GOVERNMENT

THEME. There is wisdom in elevating wise and righteous people to positions of leadership according to the voice of the people, for "it is not common that the voice of the people desireth anything contrary to that which is right; but it is common for the lesser part of the people to desire that which is not right; therefore this shall ye observe and make it your law—to do your business by the voice of the people" (Mosiah 29:26).

> *"Therefore, if it were possible that you could have just men to be your kings, who would establish the laws of God, and judge this people according to his commandments, yea, if ye could have men for your kings who would do even as my father Benjamin did for this people—I say unto you, if this could always be the case then it would be expedient that ye should always have kings to rule over you. Now I say unto you, that because all men are not just it is not expedient that ye should have a king or kings to rule over you"* (Mosiah 29:13,16).

> *"Therefore I will be your king the remainder of my days; nevertheless, let us appoint judges, to judge this people according to our law; and we will newly arrange the affairs of this people, for we will appoint wise men to be judges, that will judge this people according to the commandments of God"* (Mosiah 29:11).

MOMENT OF TRUTH. King Mosiah sends a written treatise among his people setting forth the dangers of royal government since kings so often become tyrannical despots who undermine the rule of law and violate righteous principles. He recommends a system of judges elected by the people in keeping with the highest standards of morality and civic order. The people are persuaded by Mosiah's logic and establish a series of judgeships, with Alma the Younger as the first chief judge. "And thus ended the reign of the kings over the people of Nephi" (Mosiah 29:47).

MODERN PROPHETS SPEAK

Brigham Young:

> I like a good government, and then I like to have it wisely and justly administered. The government of heaven, if wickedly administered, would become one of the worst governments upon the face of the earth. No matter how good a government is, unless it is administered by righteous men, an evil government will be made of it. (*Discourses of Brigham Young,* sel. John A. Widtsoe [Salt Lake City: Deseret Book, 1925], 147)

ILLUSTRATIONS FOR OUR TIME

Alvin Dyer:

> From Karl Marx has come the communistic form of government that menaces our present-day world with the doctrines of force and elimination of the gospel of Jesus Christ with faith in a personal God, instilling a hatred for all men that do not subscribe to the doctrines of Marxism. It is a question as to how long it will be until mankind will feel the full impact of this evil-inspired ideology, which opposes all that is righteous and good. The kingdom of evil continues its efforts in this manner to frustrate the plan of God through governments which deal with principles of force to achieve its ends.(*The Meaning of Truth,* rev. ed. [Salt Lake City: Deseret Book, 1961], 102–103)

Likening the Scriptures to Our Lives

Mosiah 29:26–27—King Mosiah taught that laws should be enacted by the voice of the people, and when people chose wickedness rather than righteousness the judgments of God would come upon them.

Application—As members of society, we are duty-bound to become involved in the process of encouraging and enacting laws and policies that will be for the good of all.

2. PROTECTING THE KINGDOM OF GOD AGAINST PRIESTCRAFT

THEME. It is the duty of the servants of God to be vigilant against any incursion by interlopers who undermine spiritual institutions by offering their own false imitation of the gospel for commercial gain and power. "Beware of false prophets, which come to you in sheep's clothing, but inwardly they are ravening wolves" (Matt. 7:15), is how the Savior expressed it.

"And it came to pass that in the first year of the reign of Alma in the judgment-seat, there was a man brought before him to be judged, a man who was large, and was noted for his much strength. And he had gone about among the people, preaching to them that which he termed to be the word of God, bearing down against the church; declaring unto the people that every priest and teacher ought to become popular; and they ought not to labor with their hands, but that they ought to be supported by the people. But Alma said unto him: Behold, this is the first time that priestcraft has been introduced among this people. And behold, thou art not only guilty of priestcraft, but hast endeavored to enforce it by the sword; and were priestcraft to be enforced among this people it would prove their entire destruction" (Alma 1:2–3, 12).

MOMENT OF TRUTH. During his first year as chief judge, Alma the Younger encounters the first instance of priestcraft to be introduced among the people. A large and articulate figure by the name of Nehor comes on the scene, luring many members of the Church away through his flattering discourse and attempting to professionalize the clergy. When he is confronted by Gideon, one of the aging heroes who assisted in the liberation of the people of Limhi, Nehor responds by slaying this revered man. As a result, Alma passes a sentence of execution upon Nehor for his acts of malice and murder, thus purging his wicked influence from among the people. But the seeds of priestcraft are sown, and Amlici, of the order of Nehor, will soon launch a revolution to challenge not only the Church, but the very institutions of civil liberty established by Mosiah.

MODERN PROPHETS SPEAK

Dallin H. Oaks:

> Priestcraft is the sin committed by the combination of a good act—such as preaching or teaching the gospel—and a bad motive. The act may be good and visible, but the sin is in the motive. On earth, the wrong motive may be known only to the actor, but in heaven it is always known to God. . . . The sin of priestcraft is a grievous one. Time after time the Lord has condemned those who appear to men to be his servants, but who, though they draw near to him with their lips, have removed their hearts far from him. This description of those who have no true motive to serve the Lord appears in Isaiah (29:13), in Matthew (15:8), in 2 Nephi (27:25), and in Joseph Smith's History (JSH 1:19). In modern as in ancient times, those who appear to be servants of the Lord and present themselves to labor in his vineyard are subject to the prophetic principle: "The laborer in Zion shall labor for Zion; for if they labor for money they shall perish" (2 Nephi 26:31). The prototype of those who appear to serve God but actually have other motives is King Amaziah, who "did that which was right in the sight of the Lord, but not with a perfect heart" (2 Chronicles 25:2).
> (*Pure in Heart* [Salt Lake City: Bookcraft, 1988], 16–18)

ILLUSTRATIONS FOR OUR TIME

Heber J. Grant:

> While Satan held the world in spiritual darkness, by means of priestcraft and idolatry, he shackled the masses with the chains of kingcraft, and thus held the world in both spiritual and civil bondage.
>
> As the time of the end drew nearer, God's Spirit descended upon men, impelling them to break the shackles of idolatry and priestcraft with which they were bound. (Heber J. Grant, *CR*, April 1930, 8)

Likening the Scriptures to Our Lives

Alma 1:26—Alma taught that the preacher teacher is no better than the learner, for they are equal, each according to his own strength.

Application—Let us never forget in the role of teaching or learning that each must labor according to his or her role in the learning process. Teachers usually use—although not exclusively so—the word spoken by the Spirit, while learners usually use their ears, mind, and hearts that they might understand and feel the Spirit to know that what is said is true. Thus both are edified, for it is done in the Spirit of truth (see D&C 50:17–22).

3. PRESERVING A FRAMEWORK OF LIBERTY AND FREEDOM OF CONSCIENCE

THEME. The Kingdom of God can best flourish in an environment where the inviolable agency of mankind is upheld through laws and institutions of liberty. It is incumbent upon free people to take every needful action for preserving freedom of conscience, including the freedom to worship Almighty God in peace.

> *"And it came to pass in the commencement of the fifth year of their reign there began to be a contention among the people; for a certain man, being called Amlici, he being a very cunning man, yea, a wise man as to the wisdom of the world, he being after the order of the man that slew Gideon by the sword, who was executed according to the law— Now this Amlici had, by his cunning, drawn away much people after him; even so much that they began to be very powerful; and they began to endeavor to establish Amlici to be a king over the people. . . . Therefore, if it were possible that Amlici should gain the voice of the people, he, being a wicked man, would deprive them of their rights and privileges of the church; for it was his intent to destroy the church of God. . . . And it came to pass that the voice of the people came against Amlici, that he was not made king over the peo-*

ple. Now this did cause much joy in the hearts of those who were against him; but Amlici did stir up those who were in his favor to anger against those who were not in his favor. And it came to pass that they gathered themselves together, and did consecrate Amlici to be their king. Now when Amlici was made king over them he commanded them that they should take up arms against their brethren; and this he did that he might subject them to him. Therefore the people of the Nephites were aware of the intent of the Amlicites, and therefore they did prepare to meet them; yea, they did arm themselves with swords, and with cimeters, and with bows, and with arrows, and with stones, and with slings, and with all manner of weapons of war, of every kind. . . . Nevertheless the Lord did strengthen the hand of the Nephites, that they slew the Amlicites with great slaughter, that they began to flee before them" (Alma 2:1–2, 4, 7, 8–10, 12, 18).

MOMENT OF TRUTH. Amlici seeks to become the king, thus promoting contention. He is defeated first by the voice of the people and in the resulting widespread conflict—despite his having secured an alliance with the Lamanite hordes.

MODERN PROPHETS SPEAK

Ezra Taft Benson:

> We all have a special citizenship responsibility. As the Prophet Joseph Smith said, "It is our duty to concentrate all our influence to make popular that which is sound and good, and unpopular that which is unsound." We must elect men to public office with a mandate higher than the ballot box. Yes, read what the Lord has said on this important subject in the ninety-eighth section of the Doctrine and Covenants and then read what He has said regarding our inspired Constitution in the one hundred first section. The days ahead are sobering and challenging and will demand the best within each of us if we are to preserve our freedom. (*The Teachings of Ezra Taft Benson* [Salt Lake City: Bookcraft, 1988], 674)

ILLUSTRATIONS FOR OUR TIME

Unrighteous Dominion. Wicked leaders and, in particular, all-powerful kings cause great hardship to come upon their people.

Mosiah taught at great length to show the disadvantages of a wicked king (see Mosiah 29:35–36). It is exceedingly difficult to depose of a wicked king (see Mosiah 29:21–23), and how they caused others to sin (see Mosiah 29:31). King Mosiah was right, as we see the results of kingship in the Book of Mormon: Noah (see Mosiah 13–20); Amlici, who sought to be king (see Alma 2:7–20); Amalickiah, who, like Amlici, sought to become king (see Alma 46:4–35); and the king-men who sought power over Pahoran (see Alma 61–62). As Mosiah attempted to convey (Mosiah 29:13, 16), "When the righteous are in authority, the people rejoice: but when the wicked beareth rule, the people mourn" (Prov. 29:2). (Pinegar)

Likening the Scriptures to Our Lives

Alma 3:26–27—Many people lost their lives as they contended over whether to be ruled by Amlici, who sought to be their king. In death they would be judged according to the spirit which they chose to obey.

Application—The Lord stands ready to reward us according to our faith, works, and the desires of our hearts (see Alma 41:3). The devil, on the other hand, will never support those who follow him but will speedily bring them down to hell (see Alma 30:60).

4. GAINING PERSPECTIVE ON THE CYCLE OF PROSPERITY AND PRIDE

THEME. So often individuals, communities, or entire nations allow abundance and prosperity to cloud spiritual vision and elevate pride as their primary motivator in life. It is a matter of ongoing urgency to follow prophetic counsel in avoiding pride and hard-heartedness, which inevitably lead to the collapse of moral values and the destruction of the spiritual aspect of life. There is no lesson from the Book of Mormon that is more pervasive than the admonition to avoid pride.

> *"And it came to pass in the eighth year of the reign of the judges, that the people of the church began to wax proud, because of their exceeding riches, and their fine silks, and their fine-twined linen, and because of their many flocks and herds, and their gold and their silver, and all manner of precious things, which they had obtained by their industry; and in all these things were they lifted up in the pride of their eyes, for they began to wear very costly apparel. . . . For they saw and beheld with great sorrow that the people of the church began to be lifted up in the pride of their eyes, and to set their hearts upon riches and upon the vain things of the world, that they began to be scornful, one towards another, and they began to persecute those that did not believe according to their own will and pleasure. And thus, in this eighth year of the reign of the judges, there began to be great contentions among the people of the church; yea, there were envyings, and strife, and malice, and persecutions, and pride, even to exceed the pride of those who did not belong to the church of God. And thus ended the eighth year of the reign of the judges; and the wickedness of the church was a great stumbling-block to those who did not belong to the church; and thus the church began to fail in its progress. And it came to pass in the commencement of the ninth year, Alma saw the wickedness of the church, and he saw also that the example of the*

church began to lead those who were unbelievers on from one piece of iniquity to another, thus bringing on the destruction of the people. Yea, he saw great inequality among the people, some lifting themselves up with their pride, despising others, turning their backs upon the needy and the naked and those who were hungry, and those who were athirst, and those who were sick and afflicted. . . . Now Alma . . . delivered the judgment-seat unto Nephihah. And this he did that he himself might go forth among his people, or among the people of Nephi, that he might preach the word of God unto them, to stir them up in remembrance of their duty, and that he might pull down, by the word of God, all the pride and craftiness and all the contentions which were among his people, seeing no way that he might reclaim them save it were in bearing down in pure testimony against them" (Alma 4:6, 8–12, 18–19).

MOMENT OF TRUTH. Following the defeat of Amlici and his revolutionary initiatives, many members of the Church become prosperous, forget God, and become prideful. Many become unkind and uncharitable, so much that their behavior impedes the growth of the Church. To counter this pernicious influence, Alma gives up the chief judgeship seat to preach the gospel, "bearing down in pure testimony against them" (Alma 4:19).

MODERN PROPHETS SPEAK

President Ezra Taft Benson:

> One of Satan's greatest tools is pride: to cause a man or a woman to center so much attention on self that he or she becomes insensitive to his Creator or fellow beings. It is a cause for discontent, divorce, teenage rebellion, family indebtedness, and most other problems we face. . . .
>
> In the scriptures there is no such thing as righteous pride. It is always considered as a sin. We are not speaking of a wholesome view of self-worth, which is best established by a close relationship with God. But we are speaking of pride as the universal sin, as someone has described it. Mormon writes that "the pride of this nation, or the people of the Nephites, hath proven their destruction" (Moroni 8:27). The Lord says in the Doctrine and Covenants, "Beware of pride, lest ye become as the Nephites of old" (D&C 38:39). Essentially, pride is a "my will" rather than "thy will" approach to life. The opposite of pride is humbleness, meekness, submissiveness, or teachableness (see Alma 13:28). . . .
>
> As we cleanse the inner vessel, there will have to be changes made in our own personal lives, in our families, and in the Church. The proud do not change to improve, but defend their position by rationalizing. Repentance means change, and it takes a humble person to change. But we can do it. (*The Teachings of Ezra Taft Benson* [Salt Lake City: Bookcraft, 1988], 435–36)

ILLUSTRATIONS FOR OUR TIME

The Milk of Kindness. My father was a generous man. I can recall with utter clarity the scene I saw through the front porch windows of my childhood home one blistering hot summer day. There was a gruff-looking stranger out there cutting down the weeds along the edge of the street. He paused to mop his brow from time to time. My father was also watching. Suddenly my father went to the kitchen and retrieved a new, unopened quart bottle of milk, walked past me, and went directly outside to speak with the stranger. They exchanged a few words, then my father handed the milk bottle to the man, who gratefully accepted it, opened it, and drank down the contents in nearly one draught.

There are two aspects to this memory for me. The one was seeing a total stranger drink down a quart of milk right from the jar—quite a feat in itself. The other was the grateful look on his face, which was matched only by the glow of satisfaction on my father's face after having done a kind deed for a total stranger. My father left a vivid reminder that I should offer what I have to those who need it.

In the eighth year of his tenure as chief judge and high priest among the people at Zarahemla, Alma the Younger perceived a destructive rift in the social fabric of his nation. A large segment of the population became dominated by self-consuming pride because of their abundant wealth and prosperity: "Yea, he saw great inequality among the people, some lifting themselves up with their pride, despising others, turning their backs upon the needy and the naked and those who were hungry, and those who were athirst, and those who were sick and afflicted" (Alma 4:12). He also saw others who remained compassionate and caring, "abasing themselves, succoring those who stood in need of their succor, such as imparting their substance to the poor and the needy, feeding the hungry, and suffering all manner of afflictions, for Christ's sake, who should come according to the spirit of prophecy" (Alma 4:13). Because of this dangerous rift, Alma transferred his chief judgeship to a worthy colleague and took upon himself the responsibility to go forth and preach the word of God to the people, "to stir them up in remembrance of their duty, and that he might pull down, by the word of God, all the pride and craftiness and all the contentions which were among his people, seeing no way that he might reclaim them save it were in bearing down in pure testimony against them" (Alma 4:19).

In effect, he was extending to them the promise that Isaiah, before him, had extended: "Ho, every one that thirsteth, come ye to the waters, and he that hath no money; come ye, buy, and eat; yea, come, buy wine and milk without money and without price" (Isa. 55:1; cf. 2 Ne. 9:50; 26:25). In his extraordinary discourse to the people, Alma asked them this penetrating question: "Have ye experienced this mighty change in your hearts?" (Alma 5:14)—this change that would cause them to keep all of the Lord's commandments, including repenting of the prideful denial of the petitions of the destitute and "turning your backs upon the poor and the needy, and in withholding your substance from them" (Alma 5:55). Charity to one's fellows is a reflection of the matchless charity of the Savior, who imparted the bread of life and the water of salvation freely to all of God's children. Similarly, the promised land, "flowing with milk and honey" (Ex. 33:3), is but a shadow anticipating the grandeur of the celestial realm where the faithful can feast at the table of everlasting happiness in the midst of heavenly glory. (Allen)

Likening the Scriptures to Our Lives

Alma 4:19—Alma sought to bring down the pride of the people by preaching the word of God and by bearing down in pure testimony against them so they would remember their duty.

Application—We should seek to bless others who are struggling through touching their hearts by the Spirit with the word of God. There is no greater power than the word of God to bring about change (see Alma 31:5).

SUMMARY

These chapters of the Book of Mormon remind us of deep and cherished values that the Lord would have us maintain and cultivate, including the principles of righteous government within a framework of liberty and freedom of conscience; honoring our priesthood covenants in the face of incursions by those operating with priestcraft motivation, and avoiding pride, selfishness, and hard-heartedness at all times, especially when the Lord has blessed us with prosperity and abundance.

There is only one way to happiness and peace—the Lord's way. When we go against the word of God or seek to have our will (pride) instead of the Lord's will we separate ourselves from the Lord and the Spirit. Pride surely is the destroyer of all mankind. Let us sincerely seek to overcome pride with humility and charity, as exemplified by our willingness to follow the Lord and His designated leaders, and with our selflessness in serving our fellow brothers and sisters.

CHAPTER TWENTY-TWO

"HAVE YE EXPERIENCED THIS MIGHTY CHANGE *in* YOUR HEARTS?"

Alma 5–7

*"And now behold, I ask of you, my brethren of the church, have ye spiritually been born of God?
. . . Have ye experienced this mighty change in your hearts?*

*"'Do ye exercise faith in the redemption of him who created you? Do you look forward with an
eye of faith, and view this mortal body raised in immortality, . . . to stand before God to be
judged according to the deeds which have been done in the mortal body?*

*"'I say unto you, can you imagine to yourselves that ye hear the voice of the Lord, saying unto
you, in that day: Come unto me ye blessed, for behold, your works have been the works of
righteousness upon the face of the earth?*

*"'Or . . . can ye imagine yourselves brought before the tribunal of God with your souls filled with guilt
and remorse, having . . . a remembrance that ye have set at defiance the commandments of God?*

"'I say unto you, can ye look up to God at that day with a pure heart and clean hands?'
(Alma 5:14–16, 18–19.)

*"Alma implies here that the 'exercise of faith in the redemption' of Christ sufficient to bring about
the mighty change in one's heart is prerequisite to obtaining a pure heart and clean hands. He
also implies that if on the great judgment day one can look up to God with a pure heart and
clean hands, he will hear the voice of the Lord saying unto him, 'Come unto me ye blessed'; if he
cannot do so, his soul will be filled with guilt and remorse."*
—Marion G. Romney, *Learning for the Eternities* [Salt Lake City: Deseret
Book, 1977], 127.

THEMES *for* LIVING

The Mighty Change
The Church Is a House of Order Governed by the Spirit of Prophecy and
Revelation
The Testimony of Jesus Christ

INTRODUCTION

Alma seeks to prompt repentance in the Saints of Zarahemla through a series of questions designed to prick their conscience. Question after question is asked imploringly, that their hearts might be touched. Many people repent, but some retain their pride. The order of the Church is established. Being full of charity, the members of the Church pray for all those who know not God. Alma goes to Gideon and testifies of Christ, encouraging the people to follow Him. These three chapters can help us evaluate our lives and bring us closer to our Savior.

1. THE MIGHTY CHANGE

THEME. Every individual who has a hope to one day inherit celestial glory must of necessity go through a mighty change of heart occasioned by faith, repentance, humility, and the transforming renewal of the Spirit. Only by strict obedience to all of the commandments of God can this mighty change of heart become a lasting essence of one's life.

> *"And now behold, I ask of you, my brethren of the church, have ye spiritually been born of God? Have ye received his image in your countenances? Have ye experienced this mighty change in your hearts?" (Alma 5:14).*

MOMENT OF TRUTH. Consider what has transpired in the years leading up to this singularly significant discourse of the prophet Alma. The Church has survived the onslaught of two highly articulate con artists, Nehor and Amlici—the one sectarian and the other political. Amlici, having failed to gain the voice of the people to make him king, has organized a revolutionary movement to seize power and undermine all civil liberties, even entering into an alliance with the invading Lamanites. Thousands on both sides of this conflict lose their lives, and it is only through their faith and diligence that the Nephites, led by Alma, come out victorious, but not without great cause to mourn. The Church, brought to a state of humility by these events, experiences a great expansion. Peace returns to the land. The people once again prosper. But with that prosperity comes the chronic malaise: pride. So great is the rift between the prideful and the humble in the land that Alma steps down from his judgeship and initiates a great reform movement launched by the word of God. His speech, faithfully recorded by the prophet/historian Mormon, is one of the greatest missives in all of holy writ and stands as a stark warning to our own generation to repent and experience the mighty change of heart that alone can lead to spiritual rebirth.

MODERN PROPHETS SPEAK

Neal A. Maxwell:

> In the divine developmental process we do not become saints in a season. We do not usually even fully finish putting off the natural man that quickly, given our weaknesses. The "mighty change" takes patience, but it is a grave error to postpone the putting off. . . . It is the putting off of the putting off that is our real problem (*Notwithstanding My Weakness* [Salt Lake City: Deseret Book, 1981], 68, 73).

ILLUSTRATIONS FOR OUR TIME

A doctrinal understanding of the mighty change (i.e., being born again or born of God) is critical, as this is our goal. The following treatment outlines the essential aspects of this process:

Ed Pinegar:

> Born of God or "born again" refers to the personal spiritual experience in which repentant individuals receive a forgiveness of sins and a witness from God that if they continue to live the commandments and endure to the end, they will inherit eternal life. The scriptures teach that just as each individual is "born into the world by water, and blood, and the spirit," so must one be "born again" of water and the Spirit and be cleansed by the blood of Christ (John 3:5; Moses 6:59). To be born of God implies a sanctifying process by which the old or natural man is supplanted by the new spiritual man who enjoys the companionship of the Holy Ghost and hence is no longer disposed to commit sin (Col. 3:9–10; Mosiah 3:19; *TPJS*, p. 51). When individuals are born again they are spiritually begotten sons and daughters of God and more specifically of Jesus Christ (Mosiah 5:7; 27:25). The Book of Mormon prophet Alma calls this inner transformation a "mighty change in your hearts" (Alma 5:14). . . .

> Persons who have experienced this mighty change manifest attitudinal and behavioral changes. Feeling their hearts riveted to the Lord, their obedience extends beyond performance of duty. President Harold B. Lee taught, "Conversion must mean more than just being a 'card-carrying' member of the Church with a tithing receipt, a membership card, a temple recommend, etc. It means to overcome the tendencies to criticize and to strive continually to improve inward weaknesses and not merely the outward appearances" (*Ensign*, June 1971, p. 8). Latter-day Saints believe that individuals who are truly born of God gladly give a life of service to their fellow beings—they share the gospel message, sacrifice their own time, energy, and resources for the benefit of others, and in general hold high the Light of Christ,

being faithful to all the commandments (*Encyclopedia of Mormonism,* 4 vols., ed. Daniel H. Ludlow [New York: Macmillan, 1992], 1:218)

Likening the Scriptures to Our Lives

Alma 5:11–14—Abinadi preached the word, and Alma the Elder believed with faith. A mighty change of heart took place in his soul. The questions are these: Have we been born of God? Have we received His image in our countenance? Have we experienced this mighty change of heart?

Application—Let us evaluate our lives, set goals, and make plans to become more like our Savior Jesus Christ. Too often we are so busy with the business of existing that we forget why we came to earth. We came to become "even as He is" (see 3 Ne. 27:27).

2. THE CHURCH IS A HOUSE OF ORDER GOVERNED BY THE SPIRIT OF PROPHECY AND REVELATION

THEME. God has ordained that prophets shall regulate the affairs of His Church and kingdom according to eternal principles.

> *"And now it came to pass that after Alma had made an end of speaking unto the people of the church, which was established in the city of Zarahemla, he ordained priests and elders, by laying on his hands according to the order of God, to preside and watch over the church. And it came to pass that whosoever did not belong to the church who repented of their sins were baptized unto repentance, and were received into the church. Nevertheless the children of God were commanded that they should gather themselves together oft, and join in fasting and mighty prayer in behalf of the welfare of the souls of those who knew not God" (Alma 6:1–2, 6).*

MOMENT OF TRUTH. Following Alma's extraordinary discourse to the people of Zarahemla, the people again have a clear vision of the covenant duties incumbent upon them. The order of the Church is established anew in Zarahemla. Many people repent and join the Church. They meet together often to fast and pray for those who know not God.

MODERN PROPHETS SPEAK

David O. McKay:

A careful analysis of the organization of the Church reveals the fact that it embodies all the strength of a strong central government and every virtue and necessary safeguard of a democracy. . . .

Truly, from the standpoint of enhancing efficiency and progress, the Church has that form of government which the nations today are seeking.

This is because it is patterned after the order which Christ himself established. On the sixth day of April 1830, the Prophet Joseph stated that the Church was organized after that order given in the New Testament. (*Gospel Ideals: Selections from the Discourses of David O. McKay* [Salt Lake City: Improvement Era, 1953], 95–96)

ILLUSTRATIONS FOR OUR TIME

The Order of the Church. Everything of God is done in order (see Mosiah 4:27; D&C 28:13; 109:8; 93:43, 50; 107:78–84). Orderliness in the Church sets the tone for the Spirit. How many times have you witnessed a moment when someone is late, is ill-prepared, or does something contrary to the normally accepted practice? Sadly, the Spirit of the meeting or event may be lost. Let us remember what President Joseph F. Smith said in regard to order:

> The house of God is a house of order, and not a house of confusion; and it could not be thus, if there were not those who had authority to preside, to direct, to counsel, to lead in the affairs of the Church. No house would be a house of order if it were not properly organized, as the Church of Jesus Christ of Latter-day Saints is organized. Take away the organization of the Church and its power would cease. Every part of its organization is necessary and essential to its perfect existence. Disregard, ignore, or omit any part, and you start imperfection in the Church; and if we should continue in that way we would find ourselves like those of old, being led by error, superstition, ignorance, and by the cunning and craftiness of men. We would soon leave out here a little and there a little, here a line and there a precept, until we would become like the rest of the world, divided, disorganized, confused and without knowledge; without revelation or inspiration, and without Divine authority or power. (*Gospel Doctrine: Selections from the Sermons and Writings of Joseph F. Smith,* comp. John A. Widtsoe [Salt Lake City: Deseret Book, 1919], 149)

Likening the Scriptures to Our Lives:

Alma 6:6—In the Church in Zarahemla, Church members were commanded to meet together oft. They were to fast and pray for all those who knew not God.

Application—Sometimes in our fasting we merely go without food, forgetting to fast with a purpose in mighty prayer to our Heavenly Father. We, in our concern for the well-being of all of Heavenly

Father's children, should pray for them to know God and come unto Christ. We should pray for world leaders to make choices that will bless lives. We should pray for the wicked to repent. In our personal lives, we should pray to increase our faith, to show more charity to our fellowmen, and to be more obedient to the commandments of God.

3. THE TESTIMONY OF JESUS CHRIST

THEME. Joy centers in our testimony of Jesus Christ and in the confirmation that others who are in our care and keeping are likewise motivated and inspired by their testimony of the Savior.

> *"For behold, I say unto you there be many things to come; and behold, there is one thing which is of more importance than they all—for behold, the time is not far distant that the Redeemer liveth and cometh among his people. . . . And behold, he shall be born of Mary, at Jerusalem which is the land of our forefathers, she being a virgin, a precious and chosen vessel, who shall be overshadowed and conceive by the power of the Holy Ghost, and bring forth a son, yea, even the Son of God. And he shall go forth, suffering pains and afflictions and temptations of every kind; and this that the word might be fulfilled which saith he will take upon him the pains and the sicknesses of his people. And he will take upon him death, that he may loose the bands of death which bind his people; and he will take upon him their infirmities, that his bowels may be filled with mercy, according to the flesh, that he may know according to the flesh how to succor his people according to their infirmities. Now the Spirit knoweth all things; nevertheless the Son of God suffereth according to the flesh that he might take upon him the sins of his people, that he might blot out their transgressions according to the power of his deliverance; and now behold, this is the testimony which is in me. Now I say unto you that ye must repent, and be born again; for the Spirit saith if ye are not born again ye cannot inherit the kingdom of heaven; therefore come and be baptized unto repentance, that ye may be washed from your sins, that ye may have faith on the Lamb of God, who taketh away the sins of the world, who is mighty to save and to cleanse from all unrighteousness" (Alma 7:7, 10–14).*

MOMENT OF TRUTH. Having set in order the affairs of the Church in the capital city of Zarahemla, Alma journeys to the east to preach in the city of Gideon. He testifies with prophetic words about the coming of Christ, His Atonement, and His goodness to us. He encourages the people to follow the Lord. Alma's joy in Gideon is to learn that the people are indeed humble and faithful followers of Christ, whereas his joy in Zarahemla was to have seen the people snatched from the "awful dilemma" (Alma 7:3) of graceless pride and destructive hard-heartedness.

MODERN PROPHETS SPEAK

Neal A. Maxwell:

> At the gate to heaven, Christ, the King of kings, waits for us with open arms. He awaits not only to certify us, but also to bestow a Shepherd's divine affection upon His sheep as we come Home. The reality that, if we are worthy, we should one day be so warmly received by the Lord of lords and King of kings is marvelous beyond comprehension!

> Yet He cannot fully receive us until we fully follow Him. His love for us is unconditional and perfect, but ours for Him is clearly not. Being just, He cannot deviate from His standards by giving us blessings without our obedience to the laws upon which such blessings are predicated. His devotion to truth is such that even in His mercy, He cannot lie, including to Himself, about our readiness. He knows our weaknesses, but, mercifully, He also knows how to succor us as we seek to cope with them. And whatever weaknesses remain in us, He will tutor us and train us to exculpate these, if we will but let Him. (*Even As I Am* [Salt Lake City: Deseret Book, 1982], 33–34)

ILLUSTRATIONS FOR OUR TIME

The Spirit of Repentance. President George Albert Smith declared, "When we possess the Spirit of the Lord we always have the spirit of repentance. Whenever our hearts are hard and we can't repent, we may know that we have not a proper spirit" (*The Teachings of George Albert Smith*, ed. Robert and Susan McIntosh [Salt Lake City: Bookcraft, 1996], 86). President Hinckley has reminded us: "There is room for improvement in every life" ("Each a Better Person," *Ensign*, Nov. 2002, 99). We may know that the Holy Ghost is with us when our sensitivity to sin, and fervency in doing something about it, increases. "A sensitive conscience is the evidence of a healthy spirit" (Keith B. McMullin, "Welcome Home," *Ensign*, May 1999, 80). Consider the following story by Monte J. Brough about a true convert's intense soul-searching:

> While serving my first mission, my companion and I were privileged to teach the Tony and Norma Johnson family of Ellesmere Port, England. As part of a missionary discussion, we taught that a truly repentant person would want to confess all his wrong-doings to the Lord in prayer, that a vague, blanket confession was inadequate because an individual should confess his sins in some clarity.

> When we returned three days later, Tony Johnson looked terrible. Upon inquiring, we learned he had not slept for three nights. He indicated he would finish one prayer, get into bed, then remember some other event or though that he felt should be part of his confession. He then would get out of bed and ask forgiveness for another wrongdoing.

While I realized Tony's depth of feeling was unusual, I left our meeting that evening knowing I had never spent three nights on my knees asking for forgiveness. I had never approached
that level of brokenheartedness and contriteness that repentance sometimes requires. I didn't
sleep well during the next few nights." ("Living the Law of Sacrifice," *Ensign,* Apr. 2000, 46)

Likening the Scriptures to Our Lives

Alma 7:11–12—Alma prophesies that our beloved Savior will go forth suffering pain and taking upon
Himself temptation and affliction, the pains and sicknesses of His people. He will take upon Himself
death that He may loose the bands of death. He will take upon Himself our infirmities that He may
know how to succor us in the flesh according to our infirmities.

Application—We should come to understand the goodness of our Savior and His overwhelming concern for us. He not only suffered in Gethsemane, died on the cross at Calvary, opened the gates through
the power of the resurrection, and provided all things for us to gain eternal life; He also lends us breath
(see Mosiah 2:21). He goes before our face (see D&C 84:85–88). He lends us strength (see Alma 26:12;
Mosiah 24:15) and He succors us according to our infirmities. Now, are we not filled with gratitude? Oh
how we ought to show our love and appreciation by keeping His commandments and serving our fellow
human beings!

SUMMARY

These passages from the Book of Mormon outline in detail the process of transformation known as "the mighty change of heart." They likewise remind us that the
Church is a house of order governed by the spirit of prophecy and revelation, and that
the central tenet of gospel living is our testimony of Jesus Christ.

The questions issued in Alma 5 by the prophet Alma are intended to be taken personally. Each of us must experience a change of heart in order to become more like
the Lord Jesus Christ. When we become as He is we will give our hearts to the Lord—
and then His will becomes our will, His joy is our joy, and His work is our work. What
could be more wonderful? We are indebted to our Savior for all things, and He loves
us unconditionally. He seeks to bless us at all times that we might fill the measure of
our creation. We should follow His teachings and invite all to come unto Christ.

CHAPTER TWENTY-THREE

"MORE *than* ONE WITNESS"

ALMA 8–12

"The Lord's manner of teaching and affirming, especially when it involves a covenant, has always provided more than one testimony. His admonition has always been that 'in the mouth of two or three witnesses shall every word be established.' (2 Corinthians 13:1)

"Indeed, when the Book of Mormon was to come forth through the inspired hand of the Prophet Joseph Smith, it was prophesied that 'three shall . . . be shown [the plates] by the power of God. . . . And in the mouth of three witnesses shall these things be established; and the testimony of three, and this work, in the which shall be shown forth the power of God . . . also his word, of which the Father, and the Son, and the Holy Ghost bear record—and all this shall stand as a testimony against the world at the last day' (Ether 5:3–4)."
—JEFFREY R. HOLLAND, *CHRIST AND THE NEW COVENANT: THE MESSIANIC MESSAGE OF THE BOOK OF MORMON* [SALT LAKE CITY: DESERET BOOK, 1997], 33.

THEMES *for* LIVING

The Lord's Universal Message to all Mankind: Repent and Come unto Christ
The Power of a Second Witness in Teaching Truth
The Key for Dealing with Unbelievers: Follow the Spirit
Quality of Heart as the Key to Spiritual Knowledge

INTRODUCTION

In the ministry of Alma and Amulek among the wicked inhabitants of Ammonihah we see demonstrated the valor and indomitable will of holy men who were sustained by the power of God. Like the missionary companionships of today, these two prophetic messengers of the Lord embody in dramatic fashion the law of multiple witnesses according to which our Heavenly Father always establishes His truth among men. The central theme of the message imparted by Alma and Amulek is the same as with missionaries in all dispensations, for they preached faith unto repentance and called for the people to practice righteousness.

1. THE LORD'S UNIVERSAL MESSAGE TO ALL MANKIND: REPENT AND COME UNTO CHRIST

THEME. The clarion call of all prophets is to preach repentance.

> *"And it came to pass that when Alma had come to the city of Ammonihah he began to preach the word of God unto them. Now Satan had gotten great hold upon the hearts of the people of the city of Ammonihah; therefore they would not hearken unto the words of Alma" (Alma 8:8–9).*

MOMENT OF TRUTH. After Alma had enjoyed remarkable success in his ministry in Gideon and had rested for a season at his home in Zarahemla (see Alma 8:1), he continued his initiative in the city of Melek, whose inhabitants likewise welcomed him in the spirit of righteousness. When Alma went northward to the city of Ammonihah, however, he found himself in the haunts of the hard-hearted who resolutely defied his entreaties. Thus he was forced to abandon his service on their behalf, and it was only through the intervention of an angel that he "speedily" (Alma 8:18) returned to the city to deliver the declaration of the Lord that the city would be destroyed if its inhabitants did not repent. It was the same angel who had guided Alma himself from a state of impenetrable hard-heartedness to transformational repentance in the early years of his life (Alma 8:15), thus Alma was surely the most experienced and understanding spokesman for the Lord on this errand. His ultimatum to the people of Ammonihah was swift, sure, and powerful, for he taught with the Spirit of the Lord.

MODERN PROPHETS SPEAK

Joseph Fielding Smith:

> "I think it is high time," the Prophet [Joseph Smith] wrote, "for a Christian world to awake out of sleep, and cry mightily to that God, day and night, whose anger we have

justly incurred." The condition of the world should be, he wrote, as a stimulant "to arouse the faculties, and call forth the energies of every man, woman or child that possesses feelings of sympathy for their fellows, or that is in any degree endeared to the budding cause of our glorious Lord." The Prophet was inspired to call upon the inhabitants to turn from their sins, and the Lord has called the weak to call upon the great to repent. This epistle was much like the calls to repentance by the prophets in ancient Israel, and without any questions was necessary to be given to the world shortly after the restoration of the Gospel and the Priesthood. (*Church History and Modern Revelation*, 4 vols. [Salt Lake City: The Church of Jesus Christ of Latter-day Saints, 1946–1949], 2:139)

ILLUSTRATIONS FOR OUR TIME

Alma's Persistence. Missionaries encounter rejection and persecution as they seek to take the message of our Savior, Jesus Christ, to all the world. Such was the case with Elder Simpson, a wonderful missionary with whom I had the pleasure of serving in the England London South Mission. He, like Alma, had not been successful in a certain area, but he had the persistence of Alma. He reviewed the area control book (containing vital information about the area, including the names of former investigators). He found a family that had been taught the discussions two or three times previously. The Spirit worked upon him so that he and his companion were inspired to return again. This time the family was ready to make the commitment to be baptized. I will never forget his jubilant phone call: "Remember that family in Southampton that had been taught several times? They are going to be baptized! Isn't that great, President?" The elders' obedience and persistence had been rewarded . . . as had Alma and Amulek's. (Pinegar)

Likening the Scriptures to Our Lives

Alma 9:30–33—Alma chastened the people to bring forth works meet for repentance. Their hearts were hardened against the word of God. They had become a lost and fallen people. They responded angrily and sought to cast him into prison.

Application—We should always realize that prophets have our welfare and possibility of eternal life in mind—and the greatest we can do for our personal welfare is to repent. Chastening helps us return to righteousness. Chastening is a form of God's love towards us (see D&C 95:1–2), as also with His prophets. We often are hurt, become angry, and then rebel.

2. THE POWER OF A
SECOND WITNESS IN TEACHING TRUTH

THEME. The Lord has proclaimed that His doctrine shall be established through the testimony of multiple witnesses: "In the mouth of two or three witnesses shall every word be established" (2 Cor. 13:1; comp. Matt. 18:16; D&C 6:28; 128:3).

"And now, when Amulek had spoken these words the people began to be astonished, seeing there was more than one witness who testified of the things whereof they were accused, and also of the things which were to come, according to the spirit of prophecy which was in them" (Alma 10:12).

MOMENT OF TRUTH. The angel of the Lord prepared the way for Amulek to receive Alma into his care as the fasting prophet returns to Ammonihah to deliver the Lord's ultimatum. Alma tarries many days with Amulek, blessing all members of his family (Alma 8:27; 10:11). Then finally the word of the Lord "came to Alma, saying, Go; and also say unto my servant Amulek, go forth and prophesy unto this people, saying—Repent ye, for thus saith the Lord, except ye repent I will visit this people in mine anger; yea, and I will not turn my fierce anger away" (Alma 8:29). Thus Amulek receives his official calling as Alma's companion, a calling that will shortly prove highly effective in establishing the truth of the Lord's word in the mouth of more than one witness.

MODERN PROPHETS SPEAK

Bruce R. McConkie:

Whenever the Lord has established a dispensation by revealing his gospel and by conferring priesthood and keys upon men, he has acted in accordance with the *law of witnesses* which he himself ordained. This law is: "In the mouth of two or three witnesses shall every word be established." (2 Cor. 13:1; Deut. 17:6; 19:15; Matt. 18:15–16; John 8:12–29.)

Never does one man stand alone in establishing a new dispensation of revealed truth, or in carrying the burden of such a message and warning to the world. In every dispensation from Adam to the present, two or more witnesses have always joined their testimonies, thus leaving their hearers without excuse in the day of judgment should the testimony be rejected. (*Mormon Doctrine,* 2d ed. [Salt Lake City: Bookcraft, 1966], 436–37)

ILLUSTRATIONS FOR OUR TIME

"My Sheep Hear My Voice." When Alvin R. Dyer arrived in Frankfurt, Germany, on 28 January 1960 to begin his tenure as European Mission president, he brought with him an inspiring and powerful testimony of missionary work. At the time, I was serving in the mission home in Frankfurt and thus was on hand to record in my journal these comments about Elder Dyer: "Our first impression was that he was a big rancher. He had long David O. McKay–type hair. . . . His powerful jaw gave him a certain force and one saw that he was a great personality. Like most general authorities, he could look right through you." The day after his arrival, Elder Dyer called the mission staff together to instruct them in the particulars of his strategy for missionary work. At the heart of his plan was the universal principle that one must teach by the Spirit (D&C 50) and never engage in debate: "Again I say, hearken ye elders of my church, whom I have appointed: Ye are not sent forth to be taught, but to teach the children of men the things which I have put into your hands by the power of my Spirit" (D&C 43:15). Like Alma and Amulek before the lawyers of Ammonihah, Elder Dyer declined descent into unproductive dialogue on worldly terms and instead espoused the high road of bold testimony-bearing as guided by the Spirit of the Lord.

When he served as president of the Central States Mission he conducted a mission-wide research poll among all of the converts of the mission, asking them to declare when they first knew that the gospel was true. Several thousand participated in the project. Elder Dyer learned that 82% of the converts knew the gospel was true *the first time they heard the missionaries bear witness of it*. Thus in most cases the transforming witness came not after a period of experience with the Church but *immediately* upon hearing the message for the first time as the missionaries spoke with the power of the Spirit. Elder Dyer testified that this phenomenon was a substantiation of the Savior's statement: "My sheep hear my voice, and I know them, and they follow me" (John 10:27). What a lesson that is for all of us as we accept the Lord's errand to convey the good news of the gospel to the peoples of the world. (Allen)

Likening the Scriptures to Our Lives

Alma 10:12—The people were astonished that there was more than one witness.

Application—We are to stand as witnesses for God at all times (see Mosiah 18:9). There is power in testifying as a witness for the Lord. Everything is established by two or three witnesses (see Matt. 18:16; 2 Cor. 13:1).

3. THE KEY FOR DEALING WITH UNBELIEVERS: FOLLOW THE SPIRIT

THEME. All those who embark in the service of God will from time to time encounter contrary spirits who vilify divine truth and disparage the good news of the Gospel of Christ. The Lord has made it clear that the most powerful strategy to use in all such cases is teaching by the Spirit.

> *"And this Zeezrom began to question Amulek, saying: Will ye answer me a few questions which I shall ask you? Now Zeezrom was a man who was expert in the devices of the devil, that he might destroy that which was good; therefore, he said unto Amulek: Will*

ye answer the questions which I shall put unto you? And Amulek said unto him: Yea, if it be according to the Spirit of the Lord, which is in me; for I shall say nothing which is contrary to the Spirit of the Lord. And Zeezrom said unto him: Behold, here are six onties of silver, and all these will I give thee if thou wilt deny the existence of a Supreme Being" (Alma 11:21–22).

"Now, when Amulek had finished these words the people began again to be astonished, and also Zeezrom began to tremble. And thus ended the words of Amulek, or this is all that I have written" (Alma 11:46).

"Now Alma, seeing that the words of Amulek had silenced Zeezrom . . . he opened his mouth and began to speak unto him, and to establish the words of Amulek" (Alma 12:1).

MOMENT OF TRUTH. The lawyers of Ammonihah were skilled in the cunning of rhetoric and the opportunism of generating diversionary reasons why people should retain their services. Among these was Zeezrom, he "being one of the most expert among them, having much business to do among the people" (Alma 10:31). In the case of Alma and Amulek, he saw an opportunity to stir up business for himself and his colleagues. But he had no idea what kind of power he was taking on, for these men of God could discern his thoughts through the Spirit (see Alma 12:3), and thus lay his pernicious plans open to view. What Zeezrom intended to be a tour de force of vainglorious legal manipulation turns out to be a turning point in his own spiritual life, for he soon comes to realize that his opponents, these troublemakers with a proclaimed divine agenda, were in fact speaking the truth. Far from shaming them with his legal manipulations, he is himself induced to take up their cause, so powerful and persuasive is their witness of the Savior and His plan of redemption. Thus the prophets of God, once again, display the only effective strategy for dealing with detractors and naysayers: teach by the Spirit.

MODERN PROPHETS SPEAK

Gordon B. Hinckley:

> As surely as this is the work of the Lord, there will be opposition. There will be those, perhaps not a few, who with the sophistry of beguiling words and clever design will spread doubt and seek to undermine the foundation on which this cause is established. They will have their brief day in the sun. They may have for a brief season the plaudits of the doubters and the skeptics and critics. But they will fade and be forgotten as have their kind in the past. (*Teachings of Gordon B. Hinckley* [Salt Lake City: Deseret Book, 1997], 124–25)

ILLUSTRATIONS FOR OUR TIME

"Pen Pal Convert." Here is a delightful story that teaches the need for preparation in order to teach doctrine to unbelievers:

> Helen Patten was in the fifth grade when she began writing to a pen pal by the name of Charlotte Alvoet in Dundee, Scotland.

> Helen told her what she did in Primary, later Mutual, and sent pictures of our temples, Church buildings, and places of interest in Utah.

> Last year an elder from Helen's ward, Bruce Draper, was called on a mission to Scotland. Since Helen secretly wished that he might teach the gospel to Charlotte, she wrote a letter to Elder Draper, telling him about Charlotte and giving her address in case he should be assigned to work in Dundee.

> About a week later Charlotte wrote to Helen telling her of the visit of two "Yanks." It so happened that Charlotte had gone to a concert so was not home when they first called. The elders waited about two hours for her return, but finally had to leave. They left word with her grandmother that they would call again the following Saturday. Charlotte returned home about fifteen minutes after they left. When she heard of the visit, she was so anxious to see these young men, that she wrote to Helen that she could hardly wait for the next Saturday to come.

> The next letter Helen received began, "Guess who was baptized yesterday! Guess who will be confirmed tomorrow! Guess who is the happiest girl in the world! ME ME ME!" She went on to write that both she and her mother had been converted in only two weeks!

> Subsequent letters told of her interest in church activities, her new friends, and her part in the MIA roadshow.

> On August 21, she wrote the following:

> > I just had to write this to you. I absolutely had to. I guess if I did not I would burst. Oh, the marvelous happening all because of being a Mormon. I must tell you from the beginning or I'll get too mixed up.

> > You see in Scotland we have no LDS schools, so when I was baptized I stayed at the school I had been attending previously, the Harris Academy. This is a Presbyterian school, where pupils of all Protestant faiths attend

(Methodist, Episcopalian, and all that). In school we have one period each week of instruction in religion, and this is in the Presbyterian faith. Well, when I was baptized, there was little change since all we did was read the Bible. But this year our teacher decided that an RI period should be informal and should be a period for debate, so he said he would ask us to write one question which he would try to answer and that the class would discuss.

I didn't ask one question, I asked six! I knew all the answers, but I wanted to explain our teachings and true doctrine to him.

I asked: (1) the interpretation of Revelation 14:6; (2) 1st Cor. 15:29, (baptism for the dead); (3) which is the true church of Jesus Christ; (4) the being of the Godhead (if they were three in one or three separate); (5) correct method of baptism; (6) reason for baptism.

None of my friends had questions, so mine were all copied. Ha! Ha! Well, a fortnight later (yesterday) the teacher decided that we would discuss the personality of our Father in heaven and the questions concerning that. Anyway, he blithered on for a wee while about heathens and atheists. Then we got down to business. I brought up the subject of our Father, Jesus Christ, and the Holy Ghost being three in one. We don't believe that, and I told him so. He asked me for proof, and joy, was he surprised when I rattled off a list of scriptures. You see, I sat up the night before reading the books I was given when the elders were teaching me. I had scriptures concerning our Father being separate from Jesus Christ and the Holy Ghost and our Father not being a spirit, I mean without a body. Anyway, after I had proved my point that they were not three in one, my master went on to another subject saying, "Of course, we all know God is a Spirit." Here little Charlotte broke in saying, "Excuse me, sir, but I beg to differ," and I got stuck into more scriptures about our Father in heaven having a body, hair, eyes, and back parts. It was marvelous. One thing led to another, and soon I was deep in telling the class the Joseph Smith story. I was inspired, and I know I had the Holy Ghost and the Spirit of the Lord within me as I talked. At the end I took over the class and was answering questions. Now twenty-one people know about Joseph Smith and heard my testimony as I bore it to them. They also saw the Book of Mormon.

May God bless you always,
and love,
Charlotte
(*Improvement Era,* Apr. 1962, 235, 281). (Pinegar)

Likening the Scriptures to Our Lives

Alma 11:37—Amulek taught Zeezrom that one cannot be saved in one's sins, for no unclean thing can enter the kingdom of heaven.

Application—There is only one way to gain exaltation—through the grace of God and repentance (see 2 Ne. 25:23). We must repent. Allowance is made for the sinner who repents, not for the sin (see D&C 1:31–33). Joseph Smith expressed it thus: "God does not look on sin with allowance, but when men have sinned, there must be allowance made for them" (*TPJS*, 240–41).

4. QUALITY OF HEART AS THE KEY TO SPIRITUAL KNOWLEDGE

THEME. The learning objective for the children of God is for them to know in full His "mysteries"—the fundamental truths of salvation (Alma 12:9). The degree to which they may know His truth is dependent upon how open their hearts are to receive such truth, and the heed and diligence they give to it. Thus the quality of one's heart—how receptive and soft it is, or how rejecting and hard it is—will determine how much of His word is "found in us" in the last day (Alma 12:13). And how much of His word is found in us will determine our ultimate future state of glory.

> *"Now Alma, seeing that the words of Amulek had silenced Zeezrom, for he beheld that Amulek had caught him in his lying and deceiving to destroy him, and seeing that he began to tremble under a consciousness of his guilt, he opened his mouth and began to speak unto him, and to establish the words of Amulek, and to explain things beyond, or to unfold the scriptures beyond that which Amulek had done" (Alma 12:1).*

> *"And they that will harden their hearts, to them is given the lesser portion of the word until they know nothing concerning his mysteries; and then they are taken captive by the devil, and led by his will down to destruction. Now this is what is meant by the chains of hell" (Alma 12:11).*

> *"And now, my brethren, behold I say unto you, that if ye will harden your hearts ye shall not enter into the rest of the Lord; therefore your iniquity provoketh him that he sendeth down his wrath upon you as in the first provocation, yea, according to his word in the last provocation as well as the first, to the everlasting destruction of your souls; therefore, according to his word, unto the last death, as well as the first" (Alma 12:36).*

MOMENT OF TRUTH. Once Zeezrom has seen the error of his ways, he becomes open to the witness of Amulek and Alma as they present the Lord's plan of salvation by the power of the Holy Ghost. Alma seconds and expands upon Amulek's teachings. He teaches the word of God, warns his listeners against being hard-hearted, and sets forth in clarity the consequences of persisting in the neglect of God's commandments. To persist in rejecting the invitation to come unto the Lord will provoke Him, just as the early Israelites had done at Sinai ("the first provocation"—Alma 12:36) when they relinquished the invitation to enter His rest.

MODERN PROPHETS SPEAK

Dallin H. Oaks:

> We teach and learn the mysteries of God by revelation from His Holy Spirit. If we harden our hearts to revelation and limit our understanding to what we can obtain by study and reason, we are limited to what Alma called "the lesser portion of the word." ("Nourishing the Spirit," *Ensign,* Dec. 1998, 10)

ILLUSTRATIONS FOR OUR TIME

The Gift of a Receptive Heart. A hardened heart is destructive to the soul. The Lord will not remove the agency of man, so he is left unto himself if hard of heart. If we would know God and His Beloved Son, we must present ourselves with a broken heart and a contrite spirit (see 3 Ne. 9:20; D&C 64:34). The seed (word of God) cannot grow in our hearts unless they are softened. Laman and Lemuel—in sharp contrast—hardened their hearts past feeling (see 1 Ne. 17:45). So many in Ammonihah suffered from the same spiritual disease. The natural man is very weak in his lost and fallen state. An excerpt from a story about Jacob Hamblin and the Indians demonstrates this so sadly:

> The following day Titse-gavats, the chief, came to me and said, "The band have all come on to the Clara except Ag-ara-poots, and he came on to the bluff in sight of it, and his heart hardened. You cannot soften his heart again. He has gone off alone. You had better pray for him to die, then there will be no bloodshed. Do not tell him what I have said to you."

> I did ask the Lord that, if it would be for the glory of His name, Ag-ara-poots might not have strength to shed the blood of any of us. In a few days the Piutes told me that he was not able to walk nor help himself to a drink of water. He lingered until spring and died (*Pioneer Stories,* comp. Preston Nibley [Salt Lake City: Deseret Book, 1965], 62–63).

Truly, our spiritual selves cannot walk without faith in God. We need Him, and He wants us. The greatest—and only true—gift we can offer God is our heart. We do not need to die in our sins, if we can only humble ourselves sufficiently. (Pinegar)

Likening the Scriptures to Our Lives

Alma 12:9–11—Alma taught that we are given a portion of the word according to the heed and diligence we give to the prophets. If we harden our hearts, we are given a lesser portion so that eventually we know nothing of the mysteries of the kingdom, and we are taken captive by the devil.

Application—We should learn that as we soften our hearts and are easily entreated we give heed to our prophets. We will be diligent in keeping the commandments, thus qualifying ourselves to receive a greater portion of the word of God.

SUMMARY

Among the important lessons reviewed in these passages of the Book of Mormon is that the Lord's universal message to all mankind is simply to repent and come unto Christ. This message, delivered with unmistakable clarity by the Lord's chosen servants is always confirmed through the power of a second witness or even multiple witnesses. Not all will receive these witnesses willingly, but the Lord has ordained that the most effective strategy is to teach by the Holy Spirit. The quality of the listeners' hearts will determine how much of the word of God they will accept: hardened hearts are not a fertile seedbed for truth; but hearts that are broken and spirits that are contrite will be open to the blessings of spiritual knowledge. One of the most compelling instances of the divine use of multiple witnesses is the Book of Mormon itself, which is, together with the Bible and other scripture, a powerful added witness for Jesus Christ. When we teach by the Spirit, we join the most effective and important witness as an additional witness. The law of witnesses has majesty. It is another way the Lord has of bringing credibility to His work. It has the power to establish truth. In our desire to follow the Savior, we should always remember to examine the "state of our heart." Is it broken, easily entreated, and yielding to the Lord? If we have experienced the mighty change, our attitudes and behavior will be according to the will of God.

CHAPTER TWENTY-FOUR

"GIVE US STRENGTH ACCORDING *to* OUR FAITH . . . *in* CHRIST"

ALMA 13–16

"Faith in God—faith in Jesus Christ as the Savior of the world; faith in His Gospel as a guide through life; a faith that springs from the heart and is therefore genuine; a faith that moves to noble and God-like action; such a faith is an anchor to the soul, immovable—infinite!

"Such is the faith that inspired the Apostles of our Lord. Such, the faith that gave strength and peace even in martyrdom to the despised and persecuted early Christians! Such is the faith that opened the heavens to the boy prophet Joseph Smith. Such is the faith that is the uplifting power among the leaders of the Church of Jesus Christ today!

"All who have such faith, though they may be tossed about in a sin-torn, tempestuous world, have nevertheless the safest and most steadfast anchor of the soul. Pray for it; strive for it; there is no salvation without it."
—DAVID O. MCKAY, *PATHWAYS TO HAPPINESS* [SALT LAKE CITY: BOOKCRAFT, 1957], 79.

THEMES *for* LIVING

The Priesthood and Foreordination
Persecution for Righteousness's Sake
The Agony of Guilt and the Ecstasy of Deliverance
Prophecy Is Always Fulfilled

INTRODUCTION

The Book of Mormon has preserved for our comfort and instruction many grand truths pertaining to salvation. In the experiences of Alma and Amulek as ministers among the people we see precious reminders of God's compassionate guidance and forebearance on behalf of His children. We learn that our sonship and daughtership with God is rooted in the premortal existence, where the purposes of life were unfolded for our future blessing, and callings were imparted to us on the premise of future faithfulness to covenant promises. We come to understand better through these remarkable pages that persecution is not foreign to our mortal journey, and that we can be freed of the agony of guilt and the consequences of sin by bringing ourselves into alignment with the patterns of faith and repentance upon which the plan of redemption is based. We come to appreciate more fully that the Lord's word will always be fulfilled.

1. THE PRIESTHOOD AND FOREORDINATION

THEME. We were prepared for our callings here upon the earth long before our birth. In the premortal courts of heaven we received our "first lessons in the world of spirits and were prepared to come forth in the due time of the Lord to labor in his vineyard for the salvation of the souls of men" (D&C 138:56).

> "And this is the manner after which they were ordained—being called and prepared from the foundation of the world according to the foreknowledge of God, on account of their exceeding faith and good works; in the first place being left to choose good or evil; therefore they having chosen good, and exercising exceedingly great faith, are called with a holy calling, yea, with that holy calling which was prepared with, and according to, a preparatory redemption for such" (Alma 13:3).

> "But that ye would humble yourselves before the Lord, and call on his holy name, and watch and pray continually, that ye may not be tempted above that which ye can bear, and thus be led by the Holy Spirit, becoming humble, meek, submissive, patient, full of love and all long-suffering; Having faith on the Lord; having a hope that ye shall receive eternal life; having the love of God always in your hearts, that ye may be lifted up at the last day and enter into his rest" (Alma 13:28–29).

MOMENT OF TRUTH. Alma, having explained to the people of Ammonihah that "it was expedient that man should know concerning the things whereof [God] had appointed unto them" (Alma 12:28), laid out details of the plan of salvation as proclaimed by angels and administered by those called and authorized "after the order of the Son, the Only Begotten of the Father" (Alma 13:9). In a remarkable discourse concerning the priesthood, Alma teaches the people to view their circumstances through the lens of a divine perspective—spanning the time from before the foundation of the earth until the great judgment and beyond. Priesthood callings, he taught, were antecedent callings in the premortal existence, where, in harmony with the principle of free agency, the faithful were foreordained "according to the foreknowledge of God, on account of their exceeding faith and good works" (Alma 13:3). Alma impressed upon his mostly rebellious listeners the startling truth about who they really were: sons and daughters of God with a marvelous opportunity to choose the right and honor their divine heritage. He reminds them of Melchizedek, who likewise had to issue the supreme call for repentance among his people before they could rise to the level of their potential and become a nation of peace. By honoring their relationship with God and fulfilling their covenant obligations, the people of Ammonihah could participate in the glorious plan of redemption and look forward with hope to the imminent coming of the Son of God to the earth. This was Alma's impassioned and inspired appeal to the people—one that, with but few exceptions, was rejected.

MODERN PROPHETS SPEAK

Spencer W. Kimball:

> Remember, in the world before we came here, faithful women were given certain assignments while faithful men were foreordained to certain priesthood tasks. While we do not now remember the particulars, this does not alter the glorious reality of what we once agreed to. We are accountable for those things which long ago were expected of us just as are those whom we sustain as prophets and apostles. (*My Beloved Sisters* [Salt Lake City: Deseret Book, 1979], 37)

ILLUSTRATIONS FOR OUR TIME

Looking Forward. Every Sunday members of the Church have the privilege to participate in the sacrament. As I watch those young men each week bear the vessels of the Lord with such humility and care, I am constantly reminded of the compassion of the Lord in allowing His young sons the sacred privilege of becoming His service representatives on earth, valiant future leaders in training. Alma taught that priesthood callings unto the Saints were of very ancient date, being initiated in the premortal existence "according to the foreknowledge of God, on account of their exceeding faith and good works" (Alma 13:3). That being the case, we can view these stalwart young Aaronic Priesthood brethren as fulfilling a destiny of the most extraordinary kind, being part of the elite corps of priesthood servants called "after the order of the Son, the Only Begotten of the Father" (Alma 13:9).

Alma explained that being called after the order of the Son imparts to the recipients a unique perspective, (i.e., one that is forward-looking and future-centered): "Now these ordinances were given after this manner, that thereby the people might look forward on the Son of God, it being a type of his order, or it being his order, and this that they might look forward to him for a remission of their sins, that they might enter into the rest of the Lord" (Alma 13:16). The priesthood that has been conferred upon these young men allows them, by its very nature (being named after the order of the Son), to look forward with hope to a continual remission of their sins according to the laws of faith and repentance. Through this ordination they can anticipate with the eye of faith their ultimate state of becoming verily the sons of God who will one day receive a reward of glory and immortality in keeping with Alma's admonition: "Having faith on the Lord; having a hope that ye shall receive eternal life; having the love of God always in your hearts, that ye may be lifted up at the last day and enter into his rest" (Alma 13:29). By the same token, the Lord allows all of us—men, women, and children—to look forward with hope to the blessings of a future domicile in the mansions of heaven as part of the eternal family of God. (Allen)

Likening the Scriptures to Our Lives

Alma 13:27–30—This is Alma's exhortation to be repentant and faithful.

Application—Alma's overwhelming concern for his people is demonstrated by his anxiety for us that we might hearken to his words and take action now and not procrastinate. The prophets and true Saints have these feelings for their fellow brothers and sisters (see 2 Ne. 33:3; Enos 1:9,11; Mosiah 28:3; Alma 6:6; 29:9–10; 34:33–35). Alma exhorts us to be humble, to watch and pray continually, so that we will not be tempted above that which we can bear.

2. PERSECUTION FOR RIGHTEOUSNESS'S SAKE

THEME. The righteous are not always, by virtue of their goodness, protected from harm.

> *"And they brought their wives and children together, and whosoever believed or had been taught to believe in the word of God they caused that they should be cast into the fire; and they also brought forth their records which contained the holy scriptures, and cast them into the fire also, that they might be burned and destroyed by fire" (Alma 14:8).*

> *"And Alma cried, saying: How long shall we suffer these great afflictions, O Lord? O Lord, give us strength according to our faith which is in Christ, even unto deliverance. And they broke the cords with which they were bound; and when the people saw this, they began to flee, for the fear of destruction had come upon them" (Alma 14:26).*

MOMENT OF TRUTH. The harvest of the season of preaching by Alma and Amulek in the city of Ammonihah is only modest, for the more part of the people refuse to believe in the words they had heard, instead reviling against the men of God and condemning the circle of believers to a fiery martyrdom. The Spirit constrains Alma from intervening to stop this persecution of the innocent, "for behold the Lord receiveth them up unto himself, in glory; and he doth suffer that the people may do this thing unto them, according to the hardness of their hearts, that the judgments which he shall exercise upon them in his wrath may be just" (Alma 14:11). After many days of silent suffering and abuse in prison, Alma and Amulek are empowered by the Spirit, "according to their faith which was in Christ" (Alma 14:28), to invoke judgment upon the Nehorian priests of the city, and the prison is destroyed by an earthquake, killing many and allowing the two prophets of God to emerge unscathed. As the prophet/abridger Mormon aptly describes it, the people of the city flee in panic, "even as a goat fleeth with her young from two lions" (Alma 14:29).

MODERN PROPHETS SPEAK

Harold B. Lee:

> To be persecuted for righteousness sake in a great cause where truth and virtue and honor are at stake is god-like. Always there have been martyrs to every great cause. The great harm that may come from persecution is not from the persecution itself but from the possible effect it may have upon the persecuted who may thereby be deterred in their zeal for the righteousness of their cause. Much of that persecution comes from lack of understanding, for men are prone to oppose that which they do not comprehend. Some of it comes from men intent upon evil. But from whatever cause, persecution seems to be so universal against those engaged in a righteous cause that the Master warns us, "Woe unto you when all men shall speak well of you! For so did their fathers to the false prophets." (Luke 6:26.) (*Decisions for Successful Living* [Salt Lake City: Deseret Book, 1973], 61–62)

ILLUSTRATIONS FOR OUR TIME

Why the Righteous Suffer.

Joseph Fielding McConkie and Robert Millett:

> God is not the author of evil, yet within limits and bounds he allows it to exist. This is done so that the righteous might merit the fulness of his glory and that the

wicked, the workers of evil, might in like fashion merit the fulness of his wrath. Suffering sanctifies the souls of the faithful. The inflicting of that suffering soils all that is decent and makes the perpetrator a fit companion to the devil, to merit as he has merited and to be rewarded as he will be rewarded. Mocking and scourging, bonds and imprisonment, flight and refuge, destitution and torment have been the common lot of Saints in all ages. Yet that God who is not unmindful of the sparrow that falls has witnessed it all—he "having provided some better things for them through their sufferings, for without sufferings they could not be made perfect" (JST, Hebrews 11:40). (*Doctrinal Commentary on the Book of Mormon*, 4 vols. [Salt Lake City: Bookcraft, 1987–1992], 3:109)

Likening the Scriptures to Our Lives

Alma 14:25–29—There is a great principle demonstrated in trials. Recall that when Nephi was bound by his brothers he prayed for strength to burst the bands (see 1 Ne. 7:17). Likewise did Alma pray for strength; also like Nephi, Alma and Amulek were freed according to their faith.

Application—This is a great lesson in life: pray for strength to overcome, not necessarily for the challenges and problems to go away. Remember: in the strength of the Lord we can do all things (see Alma 26:11–12).

3. THE AGONY OF GUILT AND THE ECSTASY OF DELIVERANCE

THEME. The Spirit can transform the travail of guilt in an anguished soul into the joy of redemption through penitence and obedience.

> *"And also Zeezrom lay sick at Sidom, with a burning fever, which was caused by the great tribulations of his mind on account of his wickedness, for he supposed that Alma and Amulek were no more; and he supposed that they had been slain because of his iniquity. And this great sin, and his many other sins, did harrow up his mind until it did become exceedingly sore, having no deliverance; therefore he began to be scorched with a burning heat. Now, when he heard that Alma and Amulek were in the land of Sidom, his heart began to take courage; and he sent a message immediately unto them, desiring them to come unto him. . . . And Alma baptized Zeezrom unto the Lord; and he began from that time forth to preach unto the people" (Alma 15:3–4,12).*

MOMENT OF TRUTH. Alma and Amulek are commanded by the Lord to leave the city of Ammonihah. They go to a neighboring area called Sidom, where the fleeing refugees from Ammonihah have gone, including the reformed persecutor, Zeezrom. The latter is languishing in the feverish agony of burdened conscience, believing that his lifestyle of wrongdoing has been responsible for the deaths of the two prophets and many others. When he learns that Alma and Amulek have been preserved, he calls the two to his sickbed, where, according to his faith, Alma is able to heal him. He is baptized and begins to preach the gospel. Amulek has relinquished all his wealth and been abandoned by his own family because of his faith, so his companion Alma "took him to his own house [in Zarahemla], and did administer unto him in his tribulations, and strengthened him in the Lord" (Alma 15:18). Thus ended the tenth year of the reign of the judges.

MODERN PROPHETS SPEAK

Orson F. Whitney:

> Though some of the sheep may wander, the eye of the Shepherd is upon them and sooner or later they will feel the tentacles of Divine Providence reaching out after them, and drawing them back to the fold. Either in this life or in the life to come, they will return. They will have to pay their debt to justice; they will suffer for their sins; and may tread a thorny path, but if it leads them at last, like the penitent prodigal, to a loving and forgiving Father's heart and home, the painful experience will not have been in vain. (cited in Russell M. Nelson, *The Gateway We Call Death* [Salt Lake City: Deseret Book, 1995], 53)

ILLUSTRATIONS FOR OUR TIME

Blessings and healings through the priesthood are always accomplished through faith in Jesus Christ. The following story is related by Wilford Woodruff:

> Mary Pitt . . . was something like the lame man who lay at the gate of the Temple called "Beautiful" at Jerusalem—she had not been able to walk a step for fourteen years, and confined to her bed nearly half that time. She had no strength in her feet and ankles and could only move about a little with a crutch or holding on to a chair. She wished to be baptized. Brother Pitt [Mary's brother] and myself took her in our arms, and carried her into the water and I baptized her. When she came out of the water I confirmed her. She said she wanted to be healed and she believed she had faith enough to be healed. I had had experience enough in this Church to know that it required a good deal of faith to heal a person who had not walked a step for fourteen years. I told her that according to her faith it should be unto her. It so happened that on the day after she was baptized, Brother Richards and President Brigham Young came down to see me. We met at Brother Kington's. Sister Mary Pitt was there also. I told President Young what Sister Pitt wished, and that she believed she

had faith enough to be healed. We prayed for her and laid hands upon her. Brother Young was mouth, and commanded her to be made whole. She laid down her crutch and never used it after, and the next day she walked three miles. (*Journal of Discourses*, 26 vols. [London: Latter-day Saints' Book Depot, 1854–86], 15:344)

Likening the Scriptures to Our Lives

Alma 15:16—Consider Amulek's price of discipleship. Amulek, even though he would not hear the Lord earlier, truly repented and gave his all to the building up of the kingdom of God. Consider what he did: forsook all his temporal wealth for the word of God, and he was even rejected by his friends and family.

Application—Now let us ponder on the sacrifice of our own discipleship.

4. PROPHECY IS ALWAYS FULFILLED

THEME. Prophecy, accurately termed "history reversed," cannot be refuted. If woe is prophesied contingent upon repentance, woe will come in the absence of repentance.

> *"For behold, the armies of the Lamanites had come in upon the wilderness side, into the borders of the land, even into the city of Ammonihah, and began to slay the people and destroy the city" (Alma 16:2).*

MOMENT OF TRUTH. Only some four years after Alma and Amulek had proclaimed the Lord's ultimatum to the people of Ammonihah (spoken around 82 B.C.; see Alma 8:16; 9:24), the great city of wickedness is destroyed by the invading Lamanite hordes: "But behold, in one day it was left desolate; and the carcasses were mangled by dogs and wild beasts of the wilderness" (Alma 16:10). So great was the stench of death in that vicinity that it was left desolate for many years, being referred to as "Desolation of Nehors; for they were of the profession of Nehor" (Alma 16:11). Alma and Amulek continue with their ministry, making the establishment of the Church general throughout all the land, bringing many souls unto Christ, and preparing them for the prophesied coming of the Lord to their land following His resurrection.

MODERN PROPHETS SPEAK

John Taylor:
> This nation and other nations will be overthrown, not because of their virtue, but

because of their corruption and iniquity. The time will come, for the prophecies will be fulfilled, when kingdoms will be destroyed, thrones cast down, and the powers of the earth shaken, and God's wrath will be kindled against the nations of the earth, and it is for us to maintain correct principles, political, religious, and social, and to feel towards all men as God feels. (*The Gospel Kingdom: Selections from the Writings and Discourses of John Taylor*, ed. G. Homer Durham [Salt Lake City: Improvement Era, 1941], 298)

ILLUSTRATIONS FOR OUR TIME

Preparing for the Second Coming. Alma's prophecy of the destruction of the city of Ammonihah was utterly fulfilled. The prophets have declared throughout time: repent or perish. If not destroyed in mortality, then we will pay for our sins in the hereafter (see D&C 19:15–19). Where do we stand in regard to our own personal repentance? Where does our country stand as to its reverence toward God? Ponder the following:

Ammonihah, a city pretending religion, a religion perfectly tolerant of any action save it be the preaching of the gospel of repentance! To preach repentance, to testify of Christ, to speak of the necessity of good works—these were sins too grievous to be borne. Their effect was to unite in wrath and bitterness the diversified factions within the congregations of this ever-tolerant religion. These missionaries of righteousness must be mocked, ridiculed, beaten, and imprisoned. Their adherents must be stoned, driven from the community, or burned at the stake. Such were the seeds they planted and such was the harvest they reaped in the desolation of Nehors. We are left to wonder to what extent Ammonihah is a prophetic foreshadowing of that which the scriptures denominate as the "desolation of abomination" (D&C 84:114, 117; D&C 88:85), events that will precede and attend the coming of our Lord and Master that will bring again that peace once known to the faithful of the Nephite nation. (Joseph Fielding McConkie and Robert L. Millet, *Doctrinal Commentary on the Book of Mormon*, 4 vols. [Salt Lake City: Bookcraft, 1987–1992], 3:119).

Likening the Scriptures to Our Lives

Alma 16:16—Because there was no inequality among the people, the Lord poured out His Spirit in rich abundance to prepare them for His coming.

Application—We learn from modern scripture the following: "Nevertheless, in your temporal things you shall be equal, and this not grudgingly, otherwise the abundance of the manifestations of the Spirit shall be withheld" (D&C 70:14).

SUMMARY

Great confidence is instilled in our hearts when we realize the knowledge and power of God. He knows the end from the beginning. He knows our hearts. He blesses us with His Holy Priesthood according to our faithfulness. Some may be required to pay the price of persecution in their lives. The fate of Ammonihah verifies the truth of prophetic warnings. When our prophet asks us to obey the commandments and especially do certain things, we should realize that it is always for our own good.

Finally, let us consider that our mission upon the earth commenced in the premortal existence, where we were called to service (as Alma reminded us) based on the principle of foreordination. When we came here on our mortal journey we knew beforehand that we would experience both the agony of guilt and the ecstasy of deliverance. We were present "when the morning stars sang together, and all the sons of God shouted for joy" (Job 38:7) over the great plan of salvation. We knew before the foundations of the earth were laid that God's word would always be fulfilled, then as now, and we rejoiced in the coming opportunity to complete our mortal probation with dignity, loyalty, and virtue—no matter what adversity might pour into our lives, no matter what sacrifice we might be called upon to make on behalf of the kingdom of God. Let us therefore press forward with courage to honor our covenant promises and look forward to the blessings of joy and glory that await the faithful in the courts of the Almighty.

CHAPTER TWENTY-FIVE

"THEY TAUGHT WITH THE POWER *and* AUTHORITY *of* GOD"

ALMA 17–22

"I believe . . . with all my heart that the field is white ready to harvest. . . . I think the answer to an increased number of converts does not lie particularly in our methods—effective as those methods are. . . .

"I think every member of the Church has the capacity to teach the gospel to nonmembers. . . . We need an awareness, an everyday awareness of the great power that we have to do this thing.

"Second, a desire. I think many of us realize that we could do it, but we lack the desire. Let every man single out another, a friend. Let him get on his knees and pray to the Lord to help him bring that man into the Church. I am as satisfied as I am of anything that with that kind of prayerful, conscientious, directed effort, there isn't a man in this Church who could not convert another. . . .

"Third, the faith to try. It is so simple. . . .

"Let us prepare ourselves more diligently for the great assignment which God has laid upon us to carry this work to the children of the earth wherever we may be permitted to go."
—GORDON B. HINCKLEY, *TEACHINGS OF GORDON B. HINCKLEY* [SALT LAKE CITY: DESERET BOOK, 1997], 365–367.

THEMES *for* LIVING

The Essence of Missionary Work: Teaching with the Spirit of Prophecy and Revelation
First a Servant, and Then a Teacher
When You Teach the One, You Teach the Many

INTRODUCTION

The sons of Mosiah demonstrate the attitude and behavior of truly converted souls. They are dedicated missionaries for the Lord Jesus Christ. They teach with the power and authority of God. They are led by the Spirit in all that they do.

1. THE ESSENCE OF MISSIONARY WORK: TEACHING WITH THE SPIRIT OF PROPHECY AND REVELATION

THEME. Dedication, scripture study, fasting, and prayer serve as the gateway for gaining the spirit of prophecy and revelation, and thereby teaching with the power and authority of God.

> *"Now these sons of Mosiah were with Alma at the time the angel first appeared unto him; therefore Alma did rejoice exceedingly to see his brethren; and what added more to his joy, they were still his brethren in the Lord; yea, and they had waxed strong in the knowledge of the truth; for they were men of a sound understanding and they had searched the scriptures diligently, that they might know the word of God. But this is not all; they had given themselves to much prayer, and fasting; therefore they had the spirit of prophecy, and the spirit of revelation, and when they taught, they taught with power and authority of God. And they had been teaching the word of God for the space of fourteen years among the Lamanites, having had much success in bringing many to the knowledge of the truth; yea, by the power of their words many were brought before the altar of God, to call on his name and confess their sins before him" (Alma 17:2–4).*

MOMENT OF TRUTH. As Alma is journeying toward the land of Manti one day, he is astonished to encounter his beloved colleagues, the sons of King Mosiah, who are now on their way back to Zarahemla after having labored some fourteen years in a highly successful missionary campaign among the Lamanites. The Book of Mormon record at this point turns to a recounting of the extraordinary experiences of the sons of Mosiah—one of the truly choice chronicles of missionary labors in all of the scriptures. We learn the secret of their success: from the beginning they practiced the godly regimen of feasting upon the word of God, praying diligently in the attitude of fasting, and thus cultivating within themselves the spirit of missionary work. This is, in essence, the spirit of prophecy and revelation, for, as Paul taught: "Wherefore I give you to understand . . . that no man can say that Jesus is the Lord, but by the Holy Ghost" (1 Cor. 12:3). The missionary report of the sons of Mosiah begins with the experiences of Ammon, he "being the chief among them" (Alma 17:18), who won the heart of King Lamoni and his court through the influence of the Spirit.

MODERN PROPHETS SPEAK

Gordon B. Hinckley:

> Our young people have an obligation to prepare themselves for missionary service . . .

> Live for the opportunity when you may go out as a servant of the Lord and an ambassador of eternal truth to the people of the world. "And this gospel of the kingdom shall be preached in all the world for a witness unto all nations; and then shall the end come." (Matt. 24:14.) This is our commission, and this is our obligation spoken anciently and reaffirmed in modern revelation. (*Teachings of Gordon B. Hinckley* [Salt Lake City: Deseret Book, 1997], 344–45)

ILLUSTRATIONS FOR OUR TIME

Preparation to Teach by the Spirit. Alma 17:2–3 is the basic formula for preparing to serve as a successful missionary.

1. Be "in the Lord" by following our Savior and keeping His commandments.
2. Wax strong in the knowledge of the truth.
3. Be of a sound understanding.
4. Search the scriptures diligently to know the word of God.
5. Pray and fast.

The reward is to have the Spirit of prophecy and revelation so that you will teach with the power and authority of God. Missionaries who are willing to work hard, being exactly, immediately, and courageously obedient will always enjoy the Spirit on their missions and have greater success in working with the people.

Pure motive helps bring souls to repentance: "Therefore, this was the cause for which the sons of Mosiah had undertaken the work, that perhaps they might bring them unto repentance; that perhaps they might bring them to know of the plan of redemption" (Alma 17:16). They cared deeply about the people (see Mosiah 28:3). (Pinegar)

Likening the Scriptures to Our Lives

Alma 17:2–3—The formula for teaching with the power and authority of God is explained.

Application—Let us seek the truth so as to be of a sound understanding as we search the scriptures diligently to know the word of God. Let us fast and pray so as to enjoy the spirit of prophecy and revelation, then we can teach with the power and authority of God.

2. FIRST A SERVANT, AND THEN A TEACHER

THEME. Missionary work is a "labour of love" (Heb. 6:10) anchored in a Christlike attitude of service toward those we teach.

> *"But Ammon said unto him: Nay, but I will be thy servant. Therefore Ammon became a servant to king Lamoni. And it came to pass that he was set among other servants to watch the flocks of Lamoni, according to the custom of the Lamanites" (Alma 17:25).*

MOMENT OF TRUTH. How do you approach a king with any hope to influence his thinking and behavior? "Being wise, yet harmless" (Alma 18:22; see D&C 111:11), Ammon first becomes a servant to the king and then seeks opportunities for awakening within him an awareness of the power of God. The famous incident in which Ammon displays his amazing strength in protecting the king's flocks from poachers serves as the tipping point for his missionary debut. Thereafter he is able to win over the confidence of King Lamoni and guide him over the threshold of honest curiosity and into the realm of spiritual enlightenment: "Now, this was what Ammon desired, for he knew that king Lamoni was under the power of God; he knew that the dark veil of unbelief was being cast away from his mind, and the light which did light up his mind, which was the light of the glory of God, which was a marvelous light of his goodness—yea, this light had infused such joy into his soul, the cloud of darkness having been dispelled, and that the light of everlasting life was lit up in his soul, yea, he knew that this had overcome his natural frame, and he was carried away in God" (Alma 19:6). On the basis of this life-changing event, Ammon is then able to enlarge the circle of conversion to include the queen and "many that did believe in their words . . . And thus the work of the Lord did commence among the Lamanites; thus the Lord did begin to pour out his Spirit upon them; and we see that his arm is extended to all people who will repent and believe on his name" (Alma 19:35–36).

MODERN PROPHETS SPEAK

Ezra Taft Benson:

> It was while I was on my first mission that I discovered the constant need for dependence on the Lord. I learned through experience that I could not convince another soul to come unto Christ. I learned that one cannot convert another by just quoting scrip-

ture. Conversion comes when another is touched by the Spirit of the Lord and receives a witness, independent of the missionary, that what he or she is being taught is true.

I learned that a missionary is only a vessel through whom the Lord can transmit His Spirit. To acquire that Spirit, a missionary must humble himself in prayer and ask our Heavenly Father to use him to touch the hearts of investigators.

The first lesson of missionary work is to be dependent on the Lord for our success. We must develop an attitude that it doesn't matter where we serve, but how. (*Come unto Christ* [Salt Lake City: Deseret Book, 1983], 95)

ILLUSTRATIONS FOR OUR TIME

How Much You Care. Ammon won the hearts of his Lamanite guards by showing forth the power of God in preserving the flocks of the king (see Alma 17:29–39). In missionary work, people must know you care before they will listen to your teachings. The old saying is true: "People don't care how much you know until they know how much you care." This was exemplified in the letters new converts wrote me. I would ask them to tell me of their conversion. They'd reply, "I felt the love of the missionaries so much I had to listen to what they were teaching . . . while listening I felt the Spirit and I knew the gospel was true and I wanted to be baptized." (Pinegar)

Likening the Scriptures to Our Lives

Alma 17:29—Ammon was grateful for the opportunity to show forth the power of God when the King's flocks were scattered. It gave him a chance to hold their attention and teach the word.

Application—If we are willing, the Lord will provide the opportunity and give us the strength—as well as the words—to bless people's lives. Elder Maxwell taught this beautiful principle: "God does not begin by asking us about our ability, but only about our availability, and if we then prove our dependability, he will increase our capability!" (*The Neal A. Maxwell Quote Book,* ed. Cory H. Maxwell [Salt Lake City: Bookcraft, 1997], 1).

3. WHEN YOU TEACH THE ONE, YOU TEACH THE MANY

THEME. Missionary work can be a wonderfully expanding enterprise: when you bless the life of one person by bringing him or her into the fold of the Savior, that person, in turn, might bring many more into the fold over time. Your efforts can be magnified in an endless spiritual ripple effect.

"And now, if your joy will be great with one soul that you have brought unto me into the kingdom of my Father, how great will be your joy if you should bring many souls unto me!" (D&C 18:16).

"And the voice of the Lord came to Ammon, saying: Thou shalt not go up to the land of Nephi, for behold, the king will seek thy life; but thou shalt go to the land of Middoni; for behold, thy brother Aaron, and also Muloki and Ammah are in prison" (Alma 20:2).

"And thus they might go forth and preach the word according to their desires, for the king had been converted unto the Lord, and all his household; therefore he sent his proclamation throughout the land unto his people, that the word of God might have no obstruction, but that it might go forth throughout all the land, that his people might be convinced concerning the wicked traditions of their fathers, and that they might be convinced that they were all brethren, and that they ought not to murder, nor to plunder, nor to steal, nor to commit adultery, nor to commit any manner of wickedness" (Alma 23:3).

MOMENT OF TRUTH. After his conversion, King Lamoni desires that Ammon should accompany him to the land of Nephi to meet his father, king over the entire realm. However, the Lord intervenes and directs Ammon to go to the land of Middoni, where Aaron and his colleagues are imprisoned. En route, Ammon and Lamoni encounter the older king, who chides his son for failure to attend the regal feast that has just taken place and orders him not to help the Nephite prisoners. In fact, he commands him to slay his Nephite companion. But Lamoni refuses to do so, declaring: "I know that they are just men and holy prophets of the true God" (Alma 20:15). In the struggle that ensues, the older king is humbled into submission by the powerful Ammon, confesses that he is moved by "the great love [Ammon] had for his son Lamoni" (Alma 20:26), and wishes now to learn more about the message of redemption being spread by the missionaries. As a result of this development, Aaron and his companions are freed and enjoy widespread success with their ministry. Aaron then goes to the land of Nephi, where he is instrumental in converting the older king, who is brought to the point of praying: "O God, Aaron hath told me that there is a God; and if there is a God, and if thou art God, wilt thou make thyself known unto me, and I will give away all my sins to know thee, and that I may be raised from the dead, and be saved at the last day" (Alma 22:18). He is then reborn spiritually and proclaims a state of religious freedom in the land, allowing the Nephite missionaries to preach the gospel freely.

MODERN PROPHETS SPEAK

Brigham Young:

> Let one go forth who is careful to prove logically all he says by numerous quotations from the revelations, and let another travel with him who can say, by the power of the Holy Ghost, Thus saith the Lord, and tell what the people should believe—what they should do—how they should live, and teach them to yield to the principles of salvation,—though he may not be capable of producing a single logical argument, though he may tremble under a sense of his weakness, cleaving to the Lord for strength, as such men generally do, you will invariably find that the man who testifies by the power of the Holy Ghost will convince and gather many more of the honest and upright than will the merely logical reasoner. (*Discourses of Brigham Young,* sel. John A. Widtsoe [Salt Lake City: Deseret Book, 1954], 330)

ILLUSTRATIONS FOR OUR TIME

An Inspired Missionary Motto. Cyril Figuerres, former president of the Japan Fukuoka Mission, created this as the mission motto:

Obedience Is the Price.
Faith Is the Power.
Love Is the Motive.
The Spirit Is the Key.
Christ Is the Reason.

What a beautiful motivating motto! Our missionary force is composed of true disciples of the Lord Jesus Christ, intent on building up the kingdom of God. It is noteworthy that the Spirit is the key; they know they do not labor by their own power, though they do labor with all their might.

President Benson has said the following:

> There are several areas that a missionary needs to be concerned with in order to be successful. First, he must develop a real deep spirituality. The Spirit is the most important matter in this glorious work. The Lord gives us a great law about teaching His gospel. He said, "And the Spirit shall be given you by the prayer of faith; and if ye receive not the Spirit ye shall not teach" (D&C 42:14).

> To be a successful missionary one must have the Spirit of the Lord. We are also taught that the Spirit will not dwell in unclean tabernacles. Therefore, one of the

first things a missionary must do to gain spirituality is to make sure his own personal life is in order (*The Teachings of Ezra Taft Benson* [Salt Lake City: Bookcraft, 1988], 198–99). (Pinegar)

Likening the Scriptures to Our Lives

Alma 20:26—The heart of King Lamoni's father is touched by the demonstration of Ammon's love for his son.

Application—Let us seek this pure love of Christ. It is the motivating power in every righteous act and calls forth the blessings of the Spirit upon our efforts.

SUMMARY

Effective missionaries prepare themselves to be instruments in the hands of the Lord. This takes a strong desire, devoted gleaning of gospel knowledge, cultivating a testimony of the gospel, exhibiting faith in the Lord Jesus Christ, and living worthy of the Spirit. Above all, missionary service requires that we have charity for all. This is our role as disciples of Christ in this the dispensation of the fulness of times. We are all missionaries.

These principles of missionary work are illustrated powerfully in the account of the campaign of the sons of Mosiah among the Lamanites. In the space of just a few chapters, we are reminded that the essence of missionary work is to teach with the spirit of prophecy and revelation. We learn that effective missionaries are first servants, then teachers, and that by teaching the one, we can teach the many. The Book of Mormon is our divine companion to missionary work in the latter days.

CHAPTER TWENTY-SIX

"CONVERTED UNTO *the* LORD"

ALMA 23–29

*"I hope you are all converts. I was in a meeting not long ago and I asked
how many were converts. Probably 50 per cent raised their hands. I said,
'I advise the rest of you to get converted.'"*
—HUGH B. BROWN, "FATHER, ARE YOU THERE?" BYU Stakes Fireside Address,
OCT. 8, 1967, 12.

THEMES *for* LIVING

Conversion to the Lord
Covenant of Peace
Rejoicing in the Blessings of the Lord
Seeking Refuge among the Saints
The Joy and Glory in Being an Instrument in the Hands of God

INTRODUCTION

These passages of scripture bring to life the joy of helping people come unto Christ. The sons of Mosiah and Alma were magnificent instruments in the hands of God to bring about the conversion of thousands of Lamanites. Surely they felt the depth of feeling described in a passage of the Doctrine and Covenants: "Remember the worth of souls is great in the sight of God; Wherefore, you are called to cry repentance unto this people. And if it so be that you should labor all your days in crying repentance unto this people, and bring, save it be one soul unto me, how great shall be your joy with him in the kingdom of my Father! And now, if your joy will be great with one soul that you have brought unto me into the kingdom of my Father, how great will be your joy if you should bring many souls unto me!" (D&C 18:10, 14–16).

1. CONVERSION TO THE LORD

THEME. Conversion to the Lord is a transforming experience, resulting in inner peace and a commitment to follow the commandments.

> *"And thousands were brought to the knowledge of the Lord, yea, thousands were brought to believe in the traditions of the Nephites; and they were taught the records and prophecies which were handed down even to the present time. And as sure as the Lord liveth, so sure as many as believed, or as many as were brought to the knowledge of the truth, through the preaching of Ammon and his brethren, according to the spirit of revelation and of prophecy, and the power of God working miracles in them—yea, I say unto you, as the Lord liveth, as many of the Lamanites as believed in their preaching, and were converted unto the Lord, never did fall away" (Alma 23:5–6).*

> *"And it came to pass that they called their names Anti-Nephi-Lehies; and they were called by this name and were no more called Lamanites" (Alma 23:17).*

MOMENT OF TRUTH. As a result of the adoption of a policy of religious freedom by the reigning king of the realm, many thousands of Lamanites in seven cities are converted through the efforts of the sons of Mosiah. They become a righteous, God-fearing, and industrious people. From that time forth they call themselves the Anti-Nephi-Lehies. Still, the rebellious Nephite apostate faction among the Lamanites (the Amalekites and Amulonites) reject the message of salvation—"save only one" (Alma 23:14)—and harden their hearts against the newly established Church. As so often happens in the Book of Mormon, there is joy for those who join covenant ranks, and tragedy for those who turn away.

MODERN PROPHETS SPEAK

Richard G. Scott:

> Sometimes the word converted is used to describe when a sincere individual decides to be baptized. However, when properly used, conversion means far more than that, for a new convert as well as the long-term member. . . .
>
> Stated simply, true conversion is the fruit of faith, repentance, and consistent obedience. . . . True conversion will strengthen your capacity to do what you know you should do, when you should do it, regardless of the circumstances. ("Full Conversion Brings Happiness," *Ensign,* May 2002, 24–26)

ILLUSTRATIONS FOR OUR TIME

"You Always Have Five Minutes."

Eika Olsen:

> "Do you have five minutes?" The question struck a responsive chord. And although I didn't have time to talk to those missionaries, I remembered that a friend once said that "if you have any time for your fellowmen, you must have time to listen to those who tell others of their beliefs. You always have five minutes." So I invited them in.
>
> Their message was interesting, and after their second visit a feeling began to grow inside me that maybe their words were true. However, my husband would have none of it. After I had visited with them four or five times, my husband became so angry that he threatened to leave me and the children if I didn't put an end to their visits.
>
> We vacationed in Austria that summer, and I tried to forget about religion, but I had such mixed feelings that after we came home to Denmark I told my husband that I must earnestly pray to know whether or not the message of the missionaries was true. He replied, "That's a good idea, and when you have done that, we won't talk about it any more."
>
> For three days I kept the Word of Wisdom and sought the Lord in prayer, but my prayers seemed empty words to me. Still, I persisted, and finally I found myself offering a sincere prayer with faith in Christ. I knew when I arose from my knees that if I didn't get an answer, I wouldn't pray any more. An hour later the doorbell rang. It was the missionaries.

When they walked into our living room, a strange feeling came over me. It started in my head and went completely through me, and I knew that my prayers had been answered. I went into the bedroom to thank the Lord and I laughed and cried and prayed, all at the same time.

When I returned to the living room, the elders told me they had been teaching a lady that day when they suddenly had nothing more to say to her. This had never happened to them before, but they made another appointment with her and left. On their way to the next appointment, they found themselves outside our apartment building, and our little boy ran up to them and asked if they were going to visit his mother. Since they had been rejected there before, they debated the matter, but one of them said the Spirit strongly impressed him to call. Ten days later, I was baptized.

There is a lovely conclusion to my story. At this time one of the General Authorities of the Church was visiting in Denmark and the missionaries took me to see him. He told me that if I would follow the counsel of Church leaders, it wouldn't be long before my husband was baptized. Surely he has made a mistake, I thought. My husband will never join the Church. That same evening my branch president asked me what I thought of the Church and I answered, "I have found so much love here." Then he said to me, "That same love you feel here you must take home to your husband."

I was a little angry. I loved my husband and thought such counsel unnecessary. But on the long drive home, I realized that I must speak kindly to my husband about the Church. My change of attitude made him curious, and when the children came home from church with sparkling eyes, he really began to investigate. Three months later my husband and our eight-year-old boy were baptized. It was truly one of the happiest days of my life. (*Remarkable Stories from the Lives of Latter-day Saint Women*, comp. Leon R. Hartshorn, 2 vols. [Salt Lake City: Deseret Book, 1973–75], 2:194–95)

Likening the Scriptures to Our Lives

Alma 24:10—King Lamoni expresses his gratitude to God for the opportunity to repent. Guilt had been taken away through the Savior, Jesus Christ.

Application—We should never forget the blessing of the principle of repentance. This is a gift from God through our Savior, Jesus Christ. When we repent, we bring joy to the Lord (see D&C 18:13).

2. COVENANT OF PEACE

THEME. "By this ye may know if a man repenteth of his sins—behold, he will confess them and forsake them" (D&C 58:43). As with the converted Lamanites who entered into a covenant of peace—eschewing the murderous practices they had hitherto embraced—all followers of Christ should repent of their sinful ways and forever abandon those practices that are contrary to the teachings of the Savior.

> *"And now it came to pass that when the king had made an end of these sayings, and all the people were assembled together, they took their swords, and all the weapons which were used for the shedding of man's blood, and they did bury them up deep in the earth. And this they did, it being in their view a testimony to God, and also to men, that they never would use weapons again for the shedding of man's blood; and this they did, vouching and covenanting with God, that rather than shed the blood of their brethren they would give up their own lives; and rather than take away from a brother they would give unto him; and rather than spend their days in idleness they would labor abundantly with their hands" (Alma 24:17–18).*

> *"Now when the Lamanites saw that their brethren would not flee from the sword, neither would they turn aside to the right hand or to the left, but that they would lie down and perish, and praised God even in the very act of perishing under the sword—" (Alma 24:22–23).*

MOMENT OF TRUTH. The Anti-Nephi-Lehies were so grateful for having received from God a forgiveness of sins—"through the merits of his Son" (Alma 24:10)—that they entered into a covenant beyond the baptismal covenant: They pledged to bury their weapons of war and never again shed the blood of their fellows. Many experienced death at the hands of their attacking Lamanite brothers, since they would not break their covenant. The result was that more joined the flock that day than were sent to their reward (see Alma 24:22, 26).

MODERN PROPHETS SPEAK

Howard W. Hunter:

> May you let the meaning and beauty and peace of the temple come into your everyday life more directly in order that the millennial day may come, that promised time when "they shall beat their swords into plowshares, and their spears into pruninghooks: nation shall not lift up sword against nation, neither shall they learn war any more . . . [but shall] walk in the light of the Lord" (Isa. 2:4–5). ("Follow the Son of God," *Ensign,* Nov. 1994, 88)

ILLUSTRATIONS FOR OUR TIME

Commitment to Our Covenants. As missionaries, and as future parents in Zion, we must remember that we don't change any faster than we make and keep commitments. The Lord calls them covenants. Our exaltation is determined by how well we have kept our baptismal, our priesthood, and our temple covenants. And when we keep those covenants, the promises and blessings are ours. I have learned that when covenants are deepened because our commitment is strong, our lives are different. If in your lives you find yourselves vacillating, look deep into your souls and check your level of commitment to your covenants. And when your level of commitment to your covenants has deepened to where you feel that it is life eternal to keep them, you will be a missionary for life. You will help many souls come unto Christ. When you make covenants with the Lord at that altar in the temple, and you become a mother or father, and find yourselves missionaries of a whole different sort, you will find that you'll never be totally converted until you learn to make and keep covenants by committing yourselves to the Lord.

Our blessings here and hereafter are dependent upon keeping the covenants we make with God. We recovenant each week. This is how Heavenly Father helps us—by continually reminding us of our commitments to His law and His covenants. The Spirit will help us keep those covenants, and keeping those covenants will exalt us. (Pinegar)

Likening the Scriptures to Our Lives

Alma 24:19—The Anti-Nephi-Lehies would not break their covenant of taking up arms. They would rather die than break their covenant.

Application—We learn from these magnificent repentant people the kind of devotion one must have to keep one's covenants. Do we honor our covenants: baptismal, priesthood, and temple? If not, we stand guilty before the Lord.

3. REJOICING IN THE BLESSINGS OF THE LORD

THEME. We cannot praise the Lord enough or thank Him too profusely for His bounteous blessings to us.

> *"My brothers and my brethren, behold I say unto you, how great reason have we to rejoice; for could we have supposed when we started from the land of Zarahemla that God would have granted unto us such great blessings?" (Alma 26:1).*

"Yea, I know that I am nothing; as to my strength I am weak; therefore I will not boast of myself, but I will boast of my God, for in his strength I can do all things; yea, behold, many mighty miracles we have wrought in this land, for which we will praise his name forever. . . . Therefore, let us glory, yea, we will glory in the Lord; yea, we will rejoice, for our joy is full; yea, we will praise our God forever. Behold, who can glory too much in the Lord? Yea, who can say too much of his great power, and of his mercy, and of his long-suffering towards the children of men? Behold, I say unto you, I cannot say the smallest part which I feel" (Alma 26:12, 16).

"And we have suffered all manner of afflictions, and all this, that perhaps we might be the means of saving some soul; and we supposed that our joy would be full if perhaps we could be the means of saving some" (Alma 26:30).

MOMENT OF TRUTH. In an expressive outpouring of emotion, Ammon recounts before his brethren the trials and blessings of their missionary labors and rejoices in the triumphs of conversion presided over by "the Lord of the harvest" (Alma 26:7). Aaron suspects that Ammon is carried away "unto boasting" (Alma 26:10), but Ammon assures him that he is fully aware of his nothingness, and only wishes to glorify God, "for in his strength I can do all things" (v. 12).

MODERN PROPHETS SPEAK

Ezra Taft Benson:

> The Lord has said that no one can assist with this work unless he is humble and full of love. (See Doctrine and Covenants 12:8.) But humility does not mean weakness. It does not mean timidity; it does not mean fear. A man can be humble and also fearless. A man can be humble and also courageous. Humility is the recognition of our dependence upon a higher power, a constant need for the Lord's support in His work. . . .

> We are engaged in missionary service to testify of the greatest event that has transpired in this world since the resurrection of the Master: the coming of God the Father and His Son, Jesus Christ, to the boy-prophet, Joseph Smith. We are sent out to testify of a new volume of scripture, a new witness for Christ.

> Missionary work provides us the happiest years of our lives. I know whereof I speak. I have tasted the joy of missionary work. There is no work in all the world that can bring an individual greater joy and happiness. (*Come unto Christ* [Salt Lake City: Deseret Book, 1983], 94–95, 97–98)

ILLUSTRATIONS FOR OUR TIME

The Joy in a Converted Soul. It was about 1969 when a young woman named Susan Gerszewski came to see me. "Bishop, you've got to take my name off the records of the Church."

I said, "Oh Susan, what's wrong?"

"My brothers think I'm a dork for being here at BYU, and I can't stand the pressure when I go home and my parents are wondering what's gone wrong with me."

All of a sudden, the Lord stepped in and words came out of my mouth like this: "Susan, I promise you that if you stay faithful, your brothers will join the Church and your parents' hearts will soften." Now how could I say that? I couldn't. Only the Lord could.

She said, "Oh I just don't know, Bishop, I just don't know." I said, "Well, Susan, is the Book of Mormon true?"

"Well, of course it is, Bishop."

"Do you love the Savior and do you believe in Heavenly Father?"

"Yes I do."

"Is the Prophet the head of the Church today?"

"Of course."

"Is this the true Church?"

"Of course it is. But I just can't stand the pressure."

I said, "Susan, will you be willing to try, because the Lord just gave you a promise." She said, "Well I guess I can try." That year she moved out of the ward, and I lost track of her.

In 1972 I volunteered to teach another religion class at BYU, besides Book of Mormon, before going to my dental office. There were about sixty students in this Gospel Principles class, and life was going merrily along. Then, on the last day to drop the class, this student came up to me and he said, "I've got to drop your class."

I asked, "How come?"

He said, "I'm on scholarship, and if I don't get a B or a B+ I could lose my scholarship; and I got a C+ on the test and, besides I'm not a Mormon." I looked at the information sheet I had students fill out before class, and I'd missed it. He'd checked "nonmember" so close to the "member" box that I'd missed it.

I said, "Well, Jim, you mean you're just afraid you won't get a B?"

He said, "Well, how can I? I'm not a member, and I just can't risk it."

I said, "Jim, I've got an idea. Do you normally study once a week for this class?"

He answered, "Yes."

I said, "Jim, I've got it. Would you mind studying with me Tuesday nights before class on Wednesday, for an hour?"

He said, "Yes, but what will that do?"

I continued, "Well, Jim, you want a B, right? Do you know who makes out the grade?"

He answered, "Well, you do."

I smiled. "That's right Jim, I'm guaranteeing you a B or a B+."

"You mean you'll guaran . . ."

"I guarantee it. Look, I'm going to teach you extra Tuesday nights. If you're in my house for an hour, I'll make up the test too. I'll even help you prepare for the test. Jim, I'm guaranteeing you this."

Jim replied, "That's a deal. I'm going to study with you."

So Jim came up to my house, and this went on for a couple of weeks. One day he asked, "Hey Brother Ed, could I bring my brother and my roommate up? We have banana splits and root beer floats and doughnuts every study night; we might as well have parties when you teach." And so I said, "You bet, you bring them up." So we went along for four more weeks, and then one night they came up and they were kind of kidding around a lot, so I said, "You guys are sure having a hoot tonight. What's up around here?"

They looked at each other as if to say, "OK, who's going to tell him?" and then Jim finally said, "Brother Ed, we've been thinking, and we talked to our bishop, and we all want to be baptized, and will you baptize us and confirm us members of the Church next week?"

As I floated down from the ceiling I said, "Yes, Jim. I will, I will, I will." Well, it turned out his name was Jim Gerszewski, but I had mispronounced his name. Jim was Susan's brother; Susan was at the baptism, and joy was felt by all.

You tell me that God our Father and Jesus Christ are not in charge of everything on this earth. How could those words come out of my mouth: "Your brothers will join the Church"? How, two years later, could one of those brothers be in my class? There were 20,000 students at BYU. Don't tell me that the Lord's hand isn't in all things that are good. All three boys served missions. All three were married in the temple.

So as I learned that year, the Spirit "will show unto you all things what ye should do" (2 Ne. 32:5). The vision in missionary work is to prepare people to feel the Spirit. Their needs are individual—you've got to be in tune to what they need. Once they feel the Spirit, you can invite them to make a commitment, and then you must follow up to help them keep that commitment. (Pinegar)

Likening the Scriptures to Our Lives

Alma 26:11–12, 16—Ammon is full of joy from the blessings of the Lord in bringing many souls unto Christ. He recognized that it was in the strength of the Lord that he could do these things. Therefore, he gloried in the Lord whom he praised continually.

Application—Let us always give the credit to the Lord in all that we do. He is our strength and our support. In and through the Lord Jesus Christ all things may be done.

4. SEEKING REFUGE AMONG THE SAINTS

THEME. The Lord has instructed the Saints to "stand in holy places." (See D&C 45:32; 101:22.) There is refuge and safety in gathering together in circles of Zion where strength comes through affinity with like-minded groups and congregations.

"And it came to pass that Ammon went and inquired of the Lord, and the Lord said unto him: Get this people out of this land, that they perish not; for Satan has great hold on the hearts of the Amalekites, who do stir up the Lamanites to anger against their brethren to slay them; therefore get thee out of this land; and blessed are this people in this generation, for I will preserve them" (Alma 27:11–12).

"And it came to pass that the voice of the people came, saying: Behold, we will give up the land of Jershon, which is on the east by the sea, which joins the land Bountiful, which is on the south of the land Bountiful; and this land Jershon is the land which we will give unto our brethren for an inheritance" (Alma 27:22).

MOMENT OF TRUTH. The Lord instructs Ammon to take the Anti-Nephi-Lehies out of the region of their origin and closer to the center place of the Nephite realm, where they can be granted safety and protection. They meet Alma on the journey to Zarahemla (Alma 27:16; cf. 17:1–4) and then continue to the capital city. The Saints there welcome them in full fellowship and give them the land of Jershon as their inheritance.

MODERN PROPHETS SPEAK

James E. Faust:
> "Who shall stand in his holy place?" May there be extended a helping hand to those who have wavered in their faith or who have transgressed, to bring them back. After fully repenting, they will have a special need for the redemptive portion of the endowment. May they know that their sins will no more be remembered. ("Who Shall Ascend into the Hill of the Lord?" *Ensign*, Aug. 2001, 5)

ILLUSTRATIONS FOR OUR TIME

The Hand of Fellowship. Fellowshipping thousands of new Saints may not be an opportunity in every stake, but every ward is filled with those who could use our love and fellowship. This story by Kathleen Pederson Whitworth teaches that principle beautifully:

> It was a lovely Sunday morning, but clouds of despair and discouragement had gathered within me. For weeks, I had felt increasingly unable to cope with numerous personal commitments and still give my family the quality time they needed. The harder I tried to foster a spirit of love and harmony, the more contention increased.
>
> My challenges seemed insurmountably great, and it was with a heavy heart that I sat

through the opening exercises of Relief Society. The lesson was on fellowshipping members—the new sister, the inactive sister, the active sister. "Remember," read the manual, "the worth of souls is great in the sight of God." (D&C 18:10.) I thought of the few sisters in our small community, many of them inactive. Once I had felt close to all of them, but after recent rebuffs by two or three sisters, I felt estranged from all of them—even those who were once close friends. I felt drained, empty. Why should I press my friendship on those who didn't want it?

"Right now," I thought bleakly, "I'm one of those active sisters who needs fellowship. I can't even cope with my own family. What makes me think I have anything to offer anybody else?"

When the teacher challenged us to fellowship one sister during the week, I dutifully wrote down a name. "How can I expect the Lord to help me," I thought, "if I'm not doing my share?" But a wave of hopelessness and guilt washed over me as I stuffed the name into my purse. "I know I'm not going to do anything with this. I have nothing to give. Who would want anything from me, anyway?"

Then the lesson was over. Before I could slip silently out the door, a sister from a neighboring community walked back and sat beside me. "Hey, I know this may sound crazy," she smiled, "but I've had the strongest feeling lately that I need to get better acquainted with you. How about getting together one day this week?"

Before I could answer, a second sister, one from my own community, was at my side. "Are you feeling okay, Kathy?"

I looked at her through rapidly brimming eyes. She put her hand on mine. The tears I had fought back all morning now began to fall, but my spirit soared, and I nodded in answer to her question.

I had not felt able to cope, nor worthy to ask the Lord for help. Yet he had known my anguish, and these sisters had answered his call. How could I not cope, I realized, with him on my side! ("He Knew My Need," *Ensign*, Mar. 1985, 14).

Likening the Scriptures to Our Lives

Alma 27:18—The joy of bringing souls unto Christ is truly the joy of this life (see Alma 29:9–10; Alma 36:24).

Application—As we help people come unto Christ, we will find joy.

5. THE JOY AND GLORY OF BEING AN INSTRUMENT IN THE HANDS OF GOD

THEME. Great satisfaction comes from investing our talents in full measure to the building up of the kingdom of God.

> *"I know that which the Lord hath commanded me, and I glory in it. I do not glory of myself, but I glory in that which the Lord hath commanded me; yea, and this is my glory, that perhaps I may be an instrument in the hands of God to bring some soul to repentance; and this is my joy. And behold, when I see many of my brethren truly penitent, and coming to the Lord their God, then is my soul filled with joy; then do I remember what the Lord has done for me, yea, even that he hath heard my prayer; yea, then do I remember his merciful arm which he extended towards me" (Alma 29:9–10).*

> *"But I do not joy in my own success alone, but my joy is more full because of the success of my brethren, who have been up to the land of Nephi. Behold, they have labored exceedingly, and have brought forth much fruit; and how great shall be their reward! Now, when I think of the success of these my brethren my soul is carried away, even to the separation of it from the body, as it were, so great is my joy" (Alma 29:14–16).*

MOMENT OF TRUTH. Mormon preserves for us the intimate and confessional expressions of Alma as he describes the rich feelings of being a committed missionary servant of the Lord. Alma had a great desire to preach the gospel to the whole world, and thus allows himself for a moment to wish for extramortal powers to reach the many: "O that I were an angel" (Alma 29:1). But then he repents of his zeal and glories in being just a mortal (albeit one of great prophetic gifts!) and confirms his gratitude before the Lord just to be able to do his job to the best of his ability. Missionary work was his joy and glory, and he also felt joy in the success of others.

MODERN PROPHETS SPEAK

Henry B. Eyring:

> Pray for the chance to encounter people who sense there could be something better in their lives. Pray to know what you should do to help them. Your prayers will be answered. You will meet people prepared by the Lord. You will find yourself feeling and saying things beyond your past experience. And then in time you will feel yourself drawing closer to your Heavenly Father, and you will feel the cleansing and the forgiveness the Savior promises His faithful witnesses. And you will feel His approval, knowing you have done what he asked of you, because He loves you and trusts you. ("A Child and a Disciple," *Ensign*, May 2003, 32)

ILLUSTRATIONS FOR OUR TIME

President Hugh B. Brown tells a wonderful story of his mission days in England:

> When I think of missionary work—and incidentally it is my first love—I remember the words of Alma, "I know that which the Lord hath commanded me, and I glory in it. I do not glory of myself, but I glory in that which the Lord hath commanded me; yea, and this is my glory, that perhaps I might be an instrument in the hands of God to bring some soul to repentance; and this is my joy."(Alma 29:9.)
>
> When I think back on early missionary experiences, there comes to mind one incident which I shall never forget. Fifty-six years ago I was in Norwich, England, on a mission. I had been tracting, and in those days we went three times to every door regardless of the reception. On this occasion I came to a door where I remembered the woman had been particularly antagonistic, and I knocked on the door with the big brass knocker. I knocked as a mature missionary knocks, for I had been there nearly two years. New missionaries, as you know, sometimes knock rather carefully hoping they won't be heard, but I knocked vigorously and had no response. I looked through the window and saw a woman sitting in the front room knitting. I recognized her, for she had given me a tongue lashing before, and I knew she wasn't deaf nor dumb. She wouldn't respond so I went around to the back door. . . . I took my walking stick and knocked on the door so hard that she came out like a setting hen comes off the nest in response to a troublesome boy. I think for several minutes she gave me the worst Scotch blessing I have ever had. But she had an impediment of speech; she had to stop every fifteen minutes to draw her breath, and when she did stop I said, "My dear lady, I apologize for having annoyed you, but our Heavenly Father sent me 6,000 miles to bring you a message and inasmuch as he sent me I can't go home until I give you that message." She said,

"Do you mean the Lord sent a message to me?" I said, "I mean just that. He sent it because he loves you." She said, "Tell me the message." And I told her as best I could the Joseph Smith story. She listened intently, apparently impressed. And then I again apologized for having been rude enough to insist on her coming out and then I added, "Sister, when you and I meet again, and we will meet again, you are going to say 'thank you, and thank God that you came to my back door and insisted on speaking to me.'"

That was in 1906. Ten years later, in 1916, I was in England again, this time in uniform. President George F. Richards was the president of the mission. He had the flu, and he called me at the military camp and asked if it was possible to get a leave and go down to Norwich and hold a conference for him. I, of course, was very glad to visit my old mission field. At the close of the morning session a woman and four grown daughters came down the aisle.

I was shaking hands with old friends, and as I took her by the hand she bowed her head and kissed my hand and wet it with her tears. She said, "I do thank God that you came to my door ten years ago. When you left that day I thought about what you had said, I couldn't get it out of my mind. I was fighting it, but I couldn't sleep that night. I kept thinking, 'God has sent a message to me.' But," she said, "I fought it for three days. I tried to find the missionaries from the address on the tract, and when I found them, you had returned to Canada. We continued to investigate until my daughters and I joined the Church, and next month we are leaving for Utah." I cite that as a word of encouragement to you, my brothers and sisters. The joy that comes into the heart of a man or woman who has been instrumental in the hands of God in carrying the message of life and salvation to some soul, be it only one, is a joy beyond anything that men in the world can know. I am sure I need not emphasize that to you for you know it from experience. (*Continuing the Quest* [Salt Lake City: Deseret Book, 1961], 61–63).

Likening the Scriptures to Our Lives

Alma 29:9–10—Alma's glory and joy was being an instrument in the hands of the Lord that he might bring some souls to repentance.

Application—Our glory and joy is helping people come unto Christ. This is the thing of most worth unto us (see D&C 15:6). Let us feel the value of doing good for others.

SUMMARY

This portion of the Book of Mormon portrays unfolding scenes of conversion to the Lord, of making a covenant of peace, of rejoicing in the blessings of the gospel, of seeking and finding refuge among the Saints, and of experiencing the profound joy and enduring glory in being an instrument in the hands of God. What lessons there are in these few pages!

Alma and the sons of Mosiah stand as beacons of light to show us the blessings of missionary work. They were truly instruments in the hands of God. They were ready to be used, they had a strong desire to serve, they were clean and pure, they knew their purpose, and they trusted in the Lord. They worked with all their heart, might, mind, and strength. They thrust in their sickles, and many souls were saved. We too can be instruments in the hands of God—in our homes as we bless each family member, at school, and at work, we can seek out others who need a friend or just a kind word to lift their spirits. In everything we do, every day of our lives, we should ask the question, "Whom can I bless? How can I serve?"

CHAPTER TWENTY-SEVEN

"ALL THINGS DENOTE THERE *is* A GOD"

ALMA 30–31

"Without acknowledgment of Deity, without recognition of the Almighty as the ruling power of the universe, the all-important element of personal and national accountability shrinks and dies. I am satisfied that this is one of the reasons for the great host of social problems with which we deal these days. Teen pregnancy, abandoned families, failure to recognize the property and rights of others, and many other problems, have resulted, in substantial part at least, from failure to recognize that there is a God to whom someday each of us must give an accounting."
—GORDON B. HINCKLEY, *TEACHINGS OF GORDON B. HINCKLEY* [SALT LAKE CITY: DESERET BOOK, 1997], 57–58.

THEMES *for* LIVING

The Ephemeral Word of the Anti-Christ Versus the Eternal Word of God
Irrefutable Testimonies for the Existence of God
The Virtue of the Word of God in Reclaiming Lost Souls

INTRODUCTION

Anti-Christs have been present and active from the beginning of time. They are inspired by the devil, Lucifer, he who was cast out of the Father's presence. Korihor exemplifies all of the false teachings of the devil in the form of misguided philosophies and sophistries of man. Anything that takes us away from our Savior is anti-Christ, whether it is found in magazines, newspapers, books, movies, television, videos, the Internet, or in sinister and alluring relationships. Anti-Christ temptations abound everywhere, for the devil is busy. The Lord has instructed us to fortify ourselves with the armor of Christ to withstand the temptations and every form of anti-Christian teaching. By studying the inspired strategies of Alma for vanquishing the onslaught of pernicious minds such as that of Korihor, we can learn how to take a stand for truth in the world and deflect "all the fiery darts of the wicked" (D&C 27:17).

1. THE EPHEMERAL WORD OF THE ANTI-CHRIST VERSUS THE ETERNAL WORD OF GOD

THEME. Along life's pathways we will not infrequently encounter travelers who actively campaign against the truths of the gospel. But the prideful cunning of the professed atheist wilts before the consuming fire of truth dispensed by the Holy Spirit.

> *"But it came to pass in the latter end of the seventeenth year, there came a man into the land of Zarahemla, and he was Anti-Christ, for he began to preach unto the people against the prophecies which had been spoken by the prophets, concerning the coming of Christ" (Alma 30:6).*

> *"And thus he did preach unto them, leading away the hearts of many, causing them to lift up their heads in their wickedness, yea, leading away many women, and also men, to commit whoredoms—telling them that when a man was dead, that was the end thereof" (Alma 30:18).*

MOMENT OF TRUTH. In the tradition of the naysayers Sherem, Nehor, and Amlici, Korihor intrudes upon the otherwise peaceful landscape of Zarahemla and actively spreads his anti-Christian teachings, causing many to fall away. He repudiates the prophecies concerning the coming of Christ, characterizing them as false traditions sustained by greedy priests as a means of yoking the people with the burden of ignorant servitude. Korihor is the consummate anti-Christ whose primary motivation is to elevate himself by undermining the joy of those in whose hearts the hope of eternal salvation and redemption burns. In a masterful display of inspired leadership, Alma dispels the momentary flicker of Korihor's worldly prowess through the overwhelming power of truth and spiritual light.

MODERN PROPHETS SPEAK

Spencer W. Kimball:

It is a real travesty today when we hear the voices of the atheist, the godless, and the anti-Christ who would deny us the right of public expression of our worship of the Master. First they moved against the long-established institution of prayer in our public schools. They would remove any vestige of Christianity or worship of the Savior of mankind in our public gatherings; they would remove the long-established tradition of prayer in our Congress, remove the "In God We Trust" insignia from our nation's emblems and seals and from our national coins.

The latest move of these anti-Christs would prohibit our own children from singing the beautiful and inspiring Christmas carols, relating to the Savior's birth or divinity, or "the heavenly angels singing" from our public schools. (*The Teachings of Spencer W. Kimball,* edited by Edward L. Kimball [Salt Lake City: Bookcraft, 1982], 411–12)

ILLUSTRATIONS FOR OUR TIME

Understanding Anti-Christs. King Benjamin mentioned that he could not name all the ways to sin (Mosiah 4:29–30); likewise, we cannot list all the forms anti-Christs take. The philosophies and sophistries of man are high on the list, of which Korihor was typical.

Bruce R. McConkie:

An antichrist is an opponent of Christ; he is one who is in opposition to the true gospel, the true Church, and the true plan of salvation. (1 John 2:19; 4:4–6.) He is one who offers salvation to men on some other terms than those laid down by Christ. Sherem (Jac. 7:1–23), Nehor (Alma 1:2–16), and Korihor (Alma 30:6–60) were antichrists who spread their delusions among the Nephites.

"Many deceivers are entered into the world, who confess not that Jesus Christ is come in the flesh. This is a deceiver and an antichrist." (2 John 7.) "Who is a liar but he that denieth that Jesus is the Christ?" John asked. "He is an antichrist, that denieth the Father and the Son." (1 John 2:22.) Though many modern day religionists profess to believe in Christ, the fact is they do not accept him as the literal Son of God and have not turned to him with the full knowledge and devotion necessary to gain salvation. "Whosoever receiveth my word receiveth me," he said, "and whosoever receiveth me, receiveth those, the First Presidency, whom I have sent, whom I have made counselors for my name's sake unto you." (D&C 112:20.)

The saints in the meridian of time, knowing there would be a great apostasy between their day and the Second Coming of our Lord, referred to the great apostate church as the anti-christ. "Little children, it is the last time," John said, "and as ye have heard that antichrist shall come, even now are there many antichrists; whereby we know that it is the last time." (1 John 2:18.) "And every spirit that confesseth not that Jesus Christ is come in the flesh is not of God: and this is that spirit of antichrist, whereof ye have heard that it should come; and even now already is it in the world." (1 John 4:3.) This great antichrist which is to stand as the antagonist of Christ in the last days, and which is to be overthrown when he comes to cleanse the earth and usher in millennial righteousness, is the church of the devil (Rev. 13; 17), with the man of sin at its head. (2 Thess. 2:1–12.). (Mormon Doctrine, 2d ed. [Salt Lake City: Bookcraft, 1966], 39–40)

Likening the Scriptures to Our Lives

Alma 30:12–18—Anti-Christs (like Korihor) taught deluded doctrines such as these: that there should be no Christ, hope is in vain, there can be no prophecy, righteous traditions are foolishness, you cannot know things that you cannot see, there could be no Atonement, everyone fares according to his own strength, whatever one does is not a crime, and when one dies that is the end of his or her existence.

Application—Through inspiration and sound reasoning we can recognize anti-Christs for what they are: servants of the devil, seeking to make us miserable like unto the devil. They seek to destroy our faith in Christ by placing doubt in our hearts. Let us quickly discern conflict between man's teachings and God's teachings, thereby cleaving to the word of God from our living prophets and the scriptures.

2. IRREFUTABLE TESTIMONIES FOR THE EXISTENCE OF GOD

THEME. By following the promptings of the Spirit, we can stand strong against the revilings of those who seek to discredit the truths of the Gospel of Jesus Christ.

"Now Alma said unto him: Will ye deny again that there is a God, and also deny the Christ? For behold, I say unto you, I know there is a God, and also that Christ shall come. And now what evidence have ye that there is no God, or that Christ cometh not? I say unto you that ye have none, save it be your word only. . . . But Alma said unto him: Thou hast had signs enough; will ye tempt your God? Will ye say, Show unto me a sign, when ye have the testimony of all these thy brethren, and also all the holy prophets? The scriptures are laid before thee, yea, and all things denote there is a God; yea, even the earth, and all things that

are upon the face of it, yea, and its motion, yea, and also all the planets which move in their
regular form do witness that there is a Supreme Creator" (Alma 30:39–40, 44).

"But behold, the devil hath deceived me; for he appeared unto me in the form of an angel,
and said unto me: Go and reclaim this people, for they have all gone astray after an
unknown God. And he said unto me: There is no God; yea, and he taught me that which
I should say. And I have taught his words; and I taught them because they were pleasing
unto the carnal mind; and I taught them, even until I had much success, insomuch that
I verily believed that they were true; and for this cause I withstood the truth, even until
I have brought this great curse upon me" (Alma 30:53).

MOMENT OF TRUTH. Korihor and Alma debate the existence of God. Korihor,
like all wicked people, seeks a sign. He is given his sign by being struck dumb. It is
only then that he confesses that he knew the truth all along, but was only deceived by
the devil. His end is a type of the ultimate fate of all anti-Christs, for he is "trodden
down, even until he was dead" (Alma 30:59). Mormon, looking back over the sad
chronicles of this and all similar anti-Christs, draws the unmistakable conclusion:
"And thus we see the end of him who perverteth the ways of the Lord" (Alma 30:60).

MODERN PROPHETS SPEAK

John A. Widtsoe:

> The evidences for the existence of God are so many and powerful that belief in a Supreme
> Being has always been well-nigh universal. Small groups, great in their own conceit, or
> blinded by false teachings, have at times declared themselves unbelievers in God's exis-
> tence; but such atheists, usually quibblers over words and definitions, have harbored in
> their hearts the realization of the existence of an intelligent overruling Power. . . .

> The existence of God is made evident to man because, first, all men have an inner con-
> sciousness of a higher power; second, nature is orderly, betokening the operation of an
> intelligent master mind; third, every experience in the effect of a cause, itself an effect of
> a higher cause, leading to a great first cause—God; fourth, men have received personal
> revelations of God; and fifth, every man by prayer may know that God lives. It is doubt-
> ful if the truth of any other fact of human experience is or can be so well attested.
> (Improvement Era, 38:287–88)

ILLUSTRATIONS FOR OUR TIME

Testimony Comes from Personal Revelation. Elder Boyd K. Packer teaches beautifully and clearly about
the testimony that there is a God:

Although a testimony of this plan is of crucial importance to us, we must not count on winning many debates on the plan of redemption versus the prevailing theories and philosophies of men.

I learned a long time ago that spiritual knowledge is described in a different language than is secular knowledge.

On this I had a valuable experience before I was a General Authority. It affected me profoundly. I sat on a plane next to a professed atheist who ridiculed my belief in God. I bore my testimony to him: "There is a God. I know He lives!"

He said: "You don't know. Nobody knows that. You can't know it." When I would not yield, the atheist posed perhaps the ultimate challenge to testimony. "All right," he said in a sneering, condescending way, "you say you know." Then, "Tell me how you know."

I could not do it. I was helpless to communicate. When I used the words spirit and witness, the atheist responded, "I don't know what you are talking about." The words prayer, discernment, and faith also were meaningless to him.

"You see," he said, "you don't really know. If you did, you would be able to tell me how you know."

Perhaps, I thought, I had borne my testimony to him unwisely, and I was at a loss as to what to do. Then came the experience. A thought, a revelation, came into my mind, and I said to the atheist: "Let me ask you a question. Do you know what salt tastes like?"

"Of course I do," was his reply.

"When did you taste salt last?"

"I just had dinner on the plane."

"You just think you know what salt tastes like," I said.

He insisted, "I know what salt tastes like as well as I know anything."

"If I gave you a cup of salt and a cup of sugar, could you tell the salt from the sugar if I let you taste them both?"

"Now you are getting juvenile," he said. "Of course I could tell the difference. I know what salt tastes like. I know it as well as I know anything."

"Then," I said, "assuming that I have never tasted salt, explain to me just what it tastes like."

After some thought, he ventured, "Well-I-uh, it is not sweet, and it is not sour."

"You've told me what it isn't, not what it is."

After several attempts, of course he could not do it. He could not convey, in words alone, so ordinary an experience as tasting salt.

I bore testimony to him once again and said: "I know there is a God. You ridiculed that testimony and said that if I did know, I would be able to tell you exactly how I know. My friend, spiritually speaking, I have tasted salt. I am no more able to convey to you in words alone how this knowledge has come than you are able to tell me what salt tastes like. But I say to you again, there is a God! He lives! And just because you don't know, don't try to tell me that I don't know, for I do!"

As we parted, I heard him mutter: "I don't need your religion for a crutch. I don't need it."

That to me was a great lesson on personal revelation. From it I learned about prompting and the truth of the scripture which says, "Treasure up in your minds continually the words of life, and it shall be given you in the very hour that portion that shall be meted unto every man" (D&C 84:85).

Since then I have never been embarrassed or ashamed that I could not explain in words alone everything I know spiritually, or tell just how I received it. From such experiences we will surely suffer some humiliation, but that is good for our faith. And we have an ever-present guide. We will be tested, but we will never be left without help. (*Memorable Stories and Parables of Boyd K. Packer* [Salt Lake City: Bookcraft, 1997], 57–60)

Likening the Scriptures to Our Lives

Alma 30:44—Alma testifies that there are many reasons one can know that there is a God. There is the testimony of those living, all the holy prophets, and the scriptures; all things denote there is a God: the earth, all things on the earth, the earth's motion, and the motion of the planets.

Application—We can know the truth of all things by the power of the Holy Ghost (see Moro. 10:3–5). We can see God in all things if we but have eyes to see and hearts that feel. Surely all these magnificent creations are not by happenstance, but by the hand of our God.

3. THE VIRTUE OF THE WORD OF GOD IN RECLAIMING LOST SOULS

THEME. The most potent force for instilling faith and turning hearts to righteousness is the word of God as presented by His inspired representatives. As Paul confirmed: "So then faith cometh by hearing, and hearing by the word of God" (Rom. 10:17).

> *"And now, as the preaching of the word had a great tendency to lead the people to do that which was just—yea, it had had more powerful effect upon the minds of the people than the sword, or anything else, which had happened unto them—therefore Alma thought it was expedient that they should try the virtue of the word of God" (Alma 31:5).*

"O Lord, wilt thou grant unto us that we may have success in bringing them again unto thee in Christ. Behold, O Lord, their souls are precious, and many of them are our brethren; therefore, give unto us, O Lord, power and wisdom that we may bring these, our brethren, again unto thee" (Alma 31:34–35).

MOMENT OF TRUTH. Alma and his sons Shiblon and Corianton; three of the sons of Mosiah (Ammon, Aaron, and Omer); Amulek, Alma's great companion; and their new convert Zeezrom seek to reclaim the apostate Zoramites by preaching the word of God to them. The Zoramites, idolatrous inhabitants of the city of Antionum, east of Zarahemla, had cultivated vain and empty sacraments centered around a Rameumptom, or "holy stand," from which they spouted rote formulas with precious little connection to spirituality (see Alma 31:21). Heartsick over this display of wickedness, Alma begins a masterful discourse concerning faith and the Atonement.

MODERN PROPHETS SPEAK

Brigham Young:

> Only a few men on the earth understand the charity that fills the bosom of our Savior. We should have charity; we should do all we can to reclaim the lost sons and daughters of Adam and Eve, and bring them back to be saved in the presence of our Father and God. If we do this, our charity will extend to the utmost extent that it is designed for the charity of God to extend in the midst of this people. (*Discourses of Brigham Young,* sel. John A. Widtsoe [Salt Lake City: Deseret Book, 1954], 273)

ILLUSTRATIONS FOR OUR TIME

Home Teaching and a German Dog. We all have an opportunity to help Saints who are struggling. It may not be an entire city or group of people—although many missionaries in the past and even today are asked to open new areas or countries. It could be with just one person, the person for whom we are home teacher or visiting teacher. President Monson tells a story of how one home teacher made the difference.

Thomas S. Monson:

> One Sunday afternoon I received a telephone call from Kaspar J. Fetzer, who served as a member of the high council of the Temple View Stake, with his specific assignment being home teaching. His voice was cheerful as he spoke with a thick German accent. He said, "Bishop Monson, I thank you for having your home teaching report in on time." Now, I knew this was simply an introduction; my report was always submitted on time. He continued, "Bishop, I don't understand the line on the report where you say you have twelve families that are inaccessible. What does that word mean?"

I explained that these were persons who rejected our home teachers, who wanted nothing to do with the Church.

"Vat?!" he countered. "They do not want the priesthood of God to visit them?"

"That's correct," I assured him.

Brother Fetzer then asked, "Bishop, could I please come to your home and obtain the names of these families and visit them as your helper?" I was overjoyed. I had been a bishop for five years and had met many high councilors, but this was the first time one of them had volunteered to do such personal work.

Brother Fetzer arrived within the hour, and I provided him a list of the names and addresses of those I had shown as being inaccessible. I had arranged the list with the most difficult family first, for I wanted my judgment to be vindicated.

Off he went with his special list, calling first on the Reinhold Doelle family, a family that lived in a spacious home, perhaps the loveliest in the ward. The home had a white picket fence that enclosed the large yard of grass and flowers, a yard carefully patrolled by a German shepherd guard dog, which barked or growled at any intruder a readily recognizable message: "Stay out!" Many years earlier, Brother Doelle had had a falling out with his home teacher, who was an Englishman. They had argued over World War I, and in that particular situation, the German side had emerged victorious. Home teachers had not been allowed in the home since that time.

Brother Fetzer checked his listing against the address that appeared on the house, left his car, and walked toward the gate. As he reached over the top of the gate to release the catch, he saw the big German shepherd dog charging at him. And the dog meant business! Instantly, Brother Fetzer exclaimed in his native German some message to the dog that caused it to come to a halt. He stroked the back of the dog and spoke softly in German, a language the dog's master used when speaking to it. The dog's tail began to wag, the gate was unlocked, and that home had a visit from a home teacher—the first such visit in many years.

Later that Sunday afternoon, Brother Fetzer returned to my home and, with a smile, reported, "Bishop, you can cross from your inaccessible list seven of these families, who will now welcome the home teachers."

A lesson had been taught. A lesson had been learned. A truth had been verified: Where there is a will, there is a way.

Long years after this incident, I was waiting in a wedding reception line to enter the home of a prominent family in Salt Lake City. A woman standing in line before me turned and greeted me. I recognized her as Sister Doelle from my old ward. She said the family lived now in California and that Brother Doelle had passed away. Then she said, "I wonder what ever became of that wonderful home teacher, Brother Fetzer, who called at our home when we lived in your ward. His visit changed our lives. We determined then and there to mend our ways and become active in the Church. Why, today I am in the presidency of our Relief Society in Palm Springs. We shall always be grateful for that special visit from a very special home teacher."

While Kaspar Fetzer had gone to his eternal reward, I am certain he would have been pleased with the result of that visit. (*Inspiring Experiences That Build Faith: From the Life and Ministry of Thomas S. Monson* [Salt Lake City: Deseret Book, 1994], 27–29)

Likening the Scriptures to Our Lives

Alma 31:5—Alma, seeking to reclaim the apostate Zoramites, taught them the word of God, which has the greatest power to cause one to do good. They tried the virtue of the word of God.

Application—The only real power for change is in the word, in Christ (see John 1; Rev. 19:13). By the word of God all things are done (see Jacob 4:9). We live by His word (see D&C 84:43–46). The word can lead us along the path to the tree of life so that we can avoid temptation (see 1 Ne. 15:24; Hel. 3:29). In His word is life eternal.

SUMMARY

The Book of Mormon verifies that the ephemeral word of anti-Christs cannot survive before the eternal word of God, given the many irrefutable testimonies for the existence of a supreme being. When valiant servants of the Lord disseminate the word of God through the Spirit, souls can be reclaimed and lives mended.

Life is full of trials and tribulations, challenges and catastrophes, and a whole host of tests to see if we will be true and faithful to our covenants. We are bombarded from every side with temptations to persuade us to follow Babylon, the world, the anti-Christs. When we hold on to the iron rod with pure intent, when we pray with faith, and when we attend to our duties in the kingdom loyally, we can come away victors, for Satan cannot then sift us as wheat. We come to know God through prayer and following His word. It is His word that will lead us to the tree of life, where we can partake of the love of God and eternal life. This is the word that Alma used to persuade the Zoramites to repent. This is the word we, too, must live by (see D&C 84:43–46).

CHAPTER TWENTY-EIGHT

"THE WORD *is* IN CHRIST UNTO SALVATION"

ALMA 32–35

"You can teach the word of God . . . in a way that is more likely to give them a desire to repent and to try to live it. They may think they have heard preaching enough. But they must do more than hear the word of God; they must plant it in their hearts by trying it. You can make that more likely if you talk with them about it in a way that helps them feel how much God loves them and how much they need God."
—HENRY B. EYRING, *TO DRAW CLOSER TO GOD: A COLLECTION OF DISCOURSES*
[SALT LAKE CITY: DESERET BOOK, 1997], 187.

THEMES *for* LIVING

Prophets Teach the Word of God
The Seed of Faith: "Springing up in You unto Everlasting Life"
How to Plant the Seed: Believe in Christ
The Atonement: Majestic Gateway of Grace Leading to Immortality and Eternal Life

INTRODUCTION

There can never be enough said about the word of God and its power in one's life. This is a frequent theme in the Book of Mormon. Alma, like the prophets before him, extolled the virtue of the word of God. Prophets have continued the encouragement to hold to, live by, and search always the word of God—the way back to our Heavenly Father. As we hearken to the words of Christ, we will nourish the word with faith, diligence, and patience.

1. PROPHETS TEACH THE WORD OF GOD

THEME. As the prophets of the Lord spread the word of God among the people, it attracts those whose hearts are accepting and humble. This process of gathering was likened by the Savior to the action of fishing: "Again, the kingdom of heaven is like unto a net, that was cast into the sea, and gathered of every kind: Which, when it was full, they drew to shore, and sat down, and gathered the good into vessels, but cast the bad away" (Matt. 13:47–48). We have the opportunity to respond to the word of God with gratitude and humility, planting it within our hearts, where it can grow through nourishment and charity.

> *"But behold, if ye will awake and arouse your faculties, even to an experiment upon my words, and exercise a particle of faith, yea, even if ye can no more than desire to believe, let this desire work in you, even until ye believe in a manner that ye can give place for a portion of my words" (Alma 32:27).*

MOMENT OF TRUTH. As Alma and Amulek preach the word of God in the land of Antionum, east of Zarahemla, where the apostate Zoramites had congregated, they find that their net of spiritual outreach has gathered in the poor and destitute who had been excluded from local houses of worship. On one special day, these people are assembled on a hill called Onidah to hear the Nephite prophets expound the gospel. Alma is overjoyed to discern "that their afflictions had truly humbled them, and that they were in a preparation to hear the word" (Alma 32:6). He then speaks to their humility and answers the heartfelt question, "What shall we do?" (Alma 32:9). He encourages them to exercise their faith and experiment upon the word.

MODERN PROPHETS SPEAK

Neal A. Maxwell:
> To supply what is lacking in our faith we must first make room for its conscious development—in our souls and in our schedules. . . .

In the process of building faith, wrote Alma, we must "experiment on the word" of the Master, giving "place" sufficient to experiment upon each essential "thing" the gospel requires of us. Out of such cumulative experience comes the real, cumulative evidence. (*Men and Women of Christ* [Salt Lake City: Bookcraft, 1991], 97–98).

ILLUSTRATIONS FOR OUR TIME

It All Begins with Humility. The capacity to learn and grow is dependent on one's humility. Humility is the beginning of change and growth in one's life. The Zoramites who listened were compelled to be humble, having been expelled from their synagogues. (Sometimes the word or some external force must humble us.) When we understand our dependence upon God, we will be humble. This is expressed through prayer—"Our Heavenly Father, we ask thee . . ." Humility brings with it many blessings and traits: submissiveness, the state of being easily entreated, a broken heart and contrite spirit, a willingness to change and to be teachable. This makes it possible for the seed or the word of God to be planted in our hearts. So begins the great experiment of faith.

I remember a missionary who was struggling in the MTC. He had an unresolved problem that needed attention, but he did not want to address it. Finally, the stake president compelled him to deal with it by sending him home. A very difficult situation occurred with the elder and me, for I was this bad news. He was extremely upset. I mentioned that upon his return to the MTC, he should come and see me. Upon his return, he visited with me, and I noticed he was more at peace. A week went by and he came to my office again and gave me a report. He said, "Oh, President, I have never been so happy here at the MTC. I love the Lord. I love my companions. I love you. I write down every word you say at the firesides. My faith is growing and I'm doing everything you asked me to do . . . and it works." As he was compelled to be humble, as he started to try by experimenting on the word, his faith was increased and he changed. He was a wonderful missionary—and it all began with humility. (Pinegar)

Likening the Scriptures to Our Lives

Alma 32:27–28—Alma taught that we should arouse our faculties and experiment upon the word. To begin to exercise our faith, we need only have a sincere desire and believe enough to give place for the word. Once placed in our hearts, the seed will begin to enlarge our soul and enlighten our understanding; thus we will begin to feel that it is a good seed as it becomes delicious to us.

Application—Let us take the word into our hearts and live it so that it can have an effect upon us. The Lord has taught clearly about doing His will to know of the truth. "If any man will do his will, he shall know of the doctrine, whether it be of God, or whether I speak of myself" (John 7:17).

2. THE SEED OF FAITH: "SPRINGING UP IN YOU UNTO EVERLASTING LIFE"

THEME. If we desire to try the word of God in faith, we will find that it enlarges and enlightens our souls. Then, if we will nourish the word with continuing faith and hope, and with charitable obedience, it will bring us everlasting blessings.

> *"Now, we will compare the word unto a seed. Now, if ye give place, that a seed may be planted in your heart, behold, if it be a true seed, or a good seed, if ye do not cast it out by your unbelief, that ye will resist the Spirit of the Lord, behold, it will begin to swell within your breasts; and when you feel these swelling motions, ye will begin to say within yourselves—It must needs be that this is a good seed, or that the word is good, for it beginneth to enlarge my soul; yea, it beginneth to enlighten my understanding, yea, it beginneth to be delicious to me" (Alma 32:28).*

> *"But if ye will nourish the word . . . by your faith with great diligence, and with patience, looking forward to the fruit thereof, it shall take root; and behold it shall be a tree springing up unto everlasting life. And because of your diligence and your faith and your patience with the word in nourishing it, that it may take root in you, behold, by and by ye shall pluck the fruit . . . and ye shall feast upon this fruit even until ye are filled, that ye hunger not, neither shall ye thirst. Then, my brethren, ye shall reap the rewards of your faith, and your diligence, and patience, and long-suffering, waiting for the tree to bring forth fruit unto you" (Alma 32:41–43).*

MOMENT OF TRUTH. Once Alma has provided the context for an experiment in faith, he guides the humbled Zoramites in a step-by-step program that will elevate them toward a fulfillment of their desire for liberation and enlightenment. Alma teaches the people this principle: "if ye have faith ye hope for things which are not seen, which are true" (Alma 32:21). His masterful discourse then enlarges on this theme by comparing the operation of faith with the germination of a seed within the soul. By careful observation of the unfolding of the seed (the vitality of the word of God as it opens up within the penitent and humble heart), the seeker after truth can know of the seed's goodness. He or she can then exercise ongoing faith by nourishing the seed with diligence and patience until it can take root and develop into a tree of life, bearing supernal blessings of spiritual fruit for the faithful.

MODERN PROPHETS SPEAK

Neal A. Maxwell:

> How vital it is to be rooted and grounded in order to take the scorching heat that
> will be a part of that special summer of circumstances which precedes the second
> coming of the Son of Man in power and glory and majesty. A brief, scorching sea-
> son, that summer will climax the centuries as the special moment among the mil-
> lennia of mortal time (*We Will Prove Them Herewith* [Salt Lake City: Deseret Book,
> 1982], 16–17).

ILLUSTRATIONS FOR OUR TIME

The Power of the Word. We nourish the word with faith—faith to accept it, faith to act upon it, faith
to utilize the power of it. We nourish the word with patience, calmly waiting for the fruit with perseverance and long-suffering even as one waits for the harvest of his crops. The word cannot take root
with passive reading or occasional study—it must be done as the Lord has prescribed for it to be effective in one's life.

One day while sitting in my institute office, I heard a tender knock on my door. I invited the person
in. The visitor requested a few minutes to visit. As we started our conversation, it wasn't long before
tears came to the eyes of my young friend, who said, "I don't understand it. I read the scriptures every
day. Why did I do what I did? And now I am not in full fellowship in the Church." I expressed sympathy and attempted to express my love and hope that things would be better. The person wanted to
know why the sin could have happened when all of us are taught if you hold to the iron rod you will
have power to overcome and deal with temptation. We discussed 1 Nephi 15:24. One must hearken
to the word of God (which means not only to listen, but to do) and hold fast (which means to own,
keep, retain, believe, embrace, and apply the word with a firm, lasting, permanent, and unwavering
commitment). Yes, the power of the word comes only to those who hearken and hold fast—which is
more than casual reading of the scriptures. Like all things, it must be done with real intent and exercising one's faith. Lessons had been taught. Hope had been restored. The future was brighter. (Pinegar)

Likening the Scriptures to Our Lives

Alma 32:40–43—Alma taught that if we nourish the word with faith, diligence, and patience we will
eventually partake of its precious fruit: happiness, the love of God, and eternal life (see 1 Ne. 8:10; 1
Ne. 11:25; 1 Ne. 15:36).

Application—Let us do all we can to exercise our faith in the word by believing, allowing our faith to
move us to action, and receiving the power of faith in our lives with all diligence (working with all our
heart, might, mind and strength), and then patiently waiting for the word to sprout with its precious
fruit according to the will of God.

3. HOW TO PLANT THE SEED: BELIEVE IN CHRIST

THEME. The essence of the Book of Mormon is "the convincing of the Jew and Gentile that JESUS is the CHRIST, the ETERNAL GOD, manifesting himself unto all nations" (from the Book of Mormon title page). The seed of faith will flourish in the soil of devotion to the Redeemer and continual humble prayer for His redemptive grace.

> *"And thou didst hear me because of mine afflictions and my sincerity; and it is because of thy Son that thou hast been thus merciful unto me, therefore I will cry unto thee in all mine afflictions, for in thee is my joy; for thou hast turned thy judgments away from me, because of thy Son" (Alma 33:11).*

> *"And now, my brethren, I desire that ye shall plant this word in your hearts, and as it beginneth to swell even so nourish it by your faith. And behold, it will become a tree, springing up in you unto everlasting life. And then may God grant unto you that your burdens may be light, through the joy of his Son. And even all this can ye do if ye will. Amen" (Alma 33:23).*

MOMENT OF TRUTH. Alma's inspired discourse on faith evokes in his Zoramite listeners the question about the next step, or "in what manner they should begin to exercise their faith" (Alma 33:1). Alma then proceeds to provide a framework for action by scriptural evidence that the object of faith must be the Son of God. He quotes Zenos and Zenock to that effect and evinces similar testimony from the history of Moses. He continues to encourage them to plant the word in their hearts.

MODERN PROPHETS SPEAK

David B. Haight:

> As members of The Church of Jesus Christ of Latter-day Saints, we testify of Christ. Our hope is in Christ. Our salvation is in Christ. Our efforts, hopes, and desires to build up the kingdom of God on earth are centered in and through his holy name. We proclaim, as did John the Baptist upon seeing Jesus approaching the river Jordan, "Behold the Lamb of God, which taketh away the sin of the world" (John 1:29). He taught the doctrines of his gospel, so that every soul may have the opportunity to gain the blessings of eternal life. (*A Light unto the World* [Salt Lake City: Deseret Book, 1997], 123)

ILLUSTRATIONS FOR OUR TIME

The Role of Prayer in Building Faith. We worship our Heavenly Father through prayer. These are our private and sacred moments with God, to be heard of Him and not man. This communion—built upon love, trust, respect, and reverence—is explained by the words of Alma as he quotes from the prophet Zenos. He tells how his prayers are heard in the wilderness, in his fields, in his home, in his closet, and in congregations—and how they are answered through the goodness and mercy of God because of His Beloved Son, Jesus Christ. The power of prayer is the key for knowing God and our Savior and drawing on the powers of heaven. (Amulek expanded upon this in Alma 34.)

I'll never forget a conversation I had with Truman Madsen as I was coming out of my Book of Mormon class; I looked at him and said, "Tru, what is the greatest need in the Church today?" He said, "Ed," paused for about one second, and concluded, "prayer."

Give serious thought to prayer. Without it we cannot have charity. "Pray unto the Father with all the energy of heart, that ye may be filled with [His] love" (Moro. 7:48). Prayer gives us our Savior's love while helping us learn to love like He does. (Pinegar)

Likening the Scriptures to Our Lives

Alma 33:2–3—Alma taught that we can worship God through prayer.

Application—As we pray, we truly worship in reverence, giving honor and adoration to our Heavenly Father in the name of Jesus Christ. We can worship in the wilderness, our fields, our offices, our homes, our private places, and our congregations. Prayer is the divine communication between God and all mankind.

4. THE ATONEMENT: MAJESTIC GATEWAY OF GRACE LEADING TO IMMORTALITY AND ETERNAL LIFE

THEME. It is the infinite Atonement of Christ that "brings about means unto men that they may have faith unto repentance" (Alma 34:15).

> *"And behold, this is the whole meaning of the law, every whit pointing to that great and last sacrifice; and that great and last sacrifice will be the Son of God, yea, infinite and eternal" (Alma 34:14).*

> *"Therefore may God grant unto you, my brethren, that ye may begin to exercise your faith unto repentance, that ye begin to call upon his holy name, that he would have mercy upon you" (Alma 34:17).*

"And now behold, my beloved brethren, I say unto you, do not suppose that this is all; for after ye have done all these things, if ye turn away the needy, and the naked, and visit not the sick and afflicted, and impart of your substance, if ye have, to those who stand in need—I say unto you, if ye do not any of these things, behold, your prayer is vain, and availeth you nothing, and ye are as hypocrites who do deny the faith" (Alma 34:28).

"And now, as I said unto you before, as ye have had so many witnesses, therefore, I beseech of you that ye do not procrastinate the day of your repentance until the end; for after this day of life, which is given us to prepare for eternity, behold, if we do not improve our time while in this life, then cometh the night of darkness wherein there can be no labor performed" (Alma 34:33).

MOMENT OF TRUTH. As Alma completes his moving and inspiring discourse on faith in Christ, Amulek stands to blend his testimony with that of his missionary companion. He testifies of Christ, defining the infinite Atonement of the Redeemer as the essential empowering act that ignites and sustains faith, infuses hope with eternal meaning and substance, and generates the reality that the great plan of redemption can be brought about "immediately" for the penitent, humble, and obedient (see Alma 34:31). Elder Jeffrey R. Holland characterizes Amulek's message as follows:

> Amulek, even though a new missionary, had a stunning grasp of theology, for he had been tutored by an angel, (see Alma 8:20, 27; 10:6–10) had the influence of the Holy Spirit, and had labored at the side of Alma. Taking his lead from Alma's marvelous sermon on "the word" being likened to a seed—a metaphor Alma continued through the staff (tree) Moses raised in the wilderness on to the "tree" springing up to everlasting life—Amulek asked the people of Zoram to have enough faith to "plant the word in [their] hearts, that [they might] try the experiment of its goodness." (Alma 34:4; see also 32:28–43; 33:19, 23.) (*Christ and the New Covenant: The Messianic Message of the Book of Mormon* [Salt Lake City: Deseret Book, 1997], 124-125)

MODERN PROPHETS SPEAK

Spencer W. Kimball:

> Because men are prone to postpone action and ignore directions, the Lord has repeatedly given strict injunctions and issued solemn warnings. Again and again in different phraseology and throughout the centuries the Lord has reminded man so that he could never have excuse. And the burden of the prophetic warning has been that *the time to act is now, in the mortal life.* One cannot with impunity delay his compliance with God's commandments.

Note Amulek's words, especially those forceful statements involving timing. . . .

Even if we leave aside the many scriptures which bear similar testimony, reading and prayerfully meditating upon this one [Alma 34:21–34] brings an awe-inspiring conviction of the need to repent—*now!*" (*The Miracle of Forgiveness* [Salt Lake City: Bookcraft, 1959], 9–10).

ILLUSTRATIONS FOR OUR TIME

Faith unto Repentance. Throughout the Book of Mormon there is emphasis on the goodness of God and the invitation to come unto Christ. To do this one must exercise faith unto repentance. All the prophets have preached the doctrine of repentance, from Father Adam to our present day, and the message will never change. Missionaries, as messengers of the Lord, help people exercise their faith unto repentance. Every discussion has the elements of faith to accept and to do through repentance, i.e., to change. Every bishop in the Church has a dynamic experience with the Atonement on a regular basis as he seeks to help people exercise their faith unto repentance. All have sinned. All need to repent. There are sins of commission and omission. What do we need to stop doing and what do we need to start doing?

Repentance is not so much an event as it is a process. True, there is the event of baptism, with guilt being swept away, and knowing one's forgiveness in regard to a particular sin in time—but there is also a continuing process of becoming better. We are not yet in a state of perfection, hence we are in the state of becoming through repentance. If we understand this, we acknowledge our unworthiness and dependence upon God, repenting earnestly and often. Repentance brings about sanctification and justification through our Savior, Jesus Christ, by the power of the Holy Ghost. We can progress. We can become "just." Those who are just will be made perfect "through Jesus" (D&C 76:69).

I have witnessed joy through repentance in my own life and vicariously through the lives of others as a bishop. I can still see the brightness of a smile or a tear-filled eye as they would say, "Oh, Bishop Ed, I'm so happy. Heavenly Father and my Savior love me. I feel clean again. I want to be good forever. I am so thankful for the Atonement of my Savior. How can I ever repay Him?" And of course they know how—by living a righteous life. Repentance is the companion of righteousness. (Pinegar)

Likening the Scriptures to Our Lives

Alma 34:9—Amulek taught that all mankind would perish were it not for the Atonement of the Lord Jesus Christ.

Application—It is incumbent upon us never to forget the blessings of the Atonement—this infinite and eternal sacrifice—in our lives. If we remember, this gratitude can move us to righteous action: we will repent and apply the Atonement to our lives. If we don't, we must suffer (see D&C 19:15–19). Heavenly Father has given us the choice.

SUMMARY

What a magnificent blessing to us in the latter days that the Lord has seen fit to preserve the resplendent words of Alma and Amulek concerning faith and the Atonement. We learn that faith is a seed "springing up in you unto everlasting life" (Alma 33:23). We learn how to plant the seed—by believing in Christ. We learn further that the Atonement is the majestic gateway of grace leading to immortality and eternal life for all who are prayerful, humble, obedient, and valiant.

The doctrines taught in these chapters can, if obeyed, lead us back to the presence of our Heavenly Father. The Word, whether Christ Himself or His spoken or printed word, is a power in our lives if planted in our hearts. It will yield the fruit of eternal life through our Savior, Jesus Christ, as we nurture it with faith, diligence, and patience. The word of our prophets will inspire us to pray and exercise faith unto repentance, thus preparing our heart's soil for bounteous harvest.

CHAPTER TWENTY-NINE

COUNSEL FROM A LOVING FATHER: "GIVE EAR to MY WORDS"

ALMA 36–39

"It is the duty of parents to teach their children the principles of the gospel and to be sober-minded and industrious in their youth. They should be impressed from the cradle to the time they leave the parental roof to make homes and assume the duties of life for themselves, that there is a seed time and harvest, and as man sows, so shall he reap. . . . And above all else, let us train our children in the principles of the gospel of our Savior, that they may become familiar with the truth and walk in the light which it sheds forth to all those who will receive it. 'He that seeketh me early,' the Lord has said, 'shall find me, and shall not be forsaken.' It behooves us, therefore, to commence in early life to travel in the straight and narrow path which leads to eternal salvation."
—JOSEPH F. SMITH, *GOSPEL DOCTRINE: SELECTIONS FROM THE SERMONS AND WRITINGS OF JOSEPH F. SMITH*, COMP. BY JOHN A. WIDTSOE [SALT LAKE CITY: DESERET BOOK, 1939], 295–96.

THEMES for LIVING

Teaching the Word of God as a Compass for Our Lives
The Joy of Edifying and Uplifting Our Children
Repentance: The Indispensable Lesson

INTRODUCTION

The Book of Mormon is one of the Lord's greatest tools for teaching parents how to counsel their children in righteousness. From the loving concern of Lehi and Sariah for their children at the outset of the chronicle to the intimate partnership of Mormon and his son Moroni at the end there is a continuous flow of inspiring examples of parent-child relationships. Consider the elder Alma's anxiety and ultimate joy in his son Alma. Consider further the latter's splendid legacy of instruction for his sons recorded in these current chapters.

The covenant bond is at its heart patriarchal: the word of truth flows from our Father in heaven to His sons and daughters. In resonance with this pattern, fathers and mothers are commissioned to reinforce the word of truth as they instruct their children in the operation of covenant principles. Jacob's legacy of blessings for his twelve sons (see Gen. 49) is no different in character from the blessings of truth that all fathers in Zion have the opportunity to bestow upon their children. Mothers in Zion have the same sacred commission to impart principles of righteousness to their children. There is no duty or obligation so great as for parents to teach their children. Parents are held strictly accountable. The Doctrine and Covenants makes this clear: "And again, inasmuch as parents have children in Zion, or in any of her stakes which are organized, that teach them not to understand the doctrine of repentance, faith in Christ the Son of the living God, and of baptism and the gift of the Holy Ghost by the laying on of the hands, when eight years old, the sin be upon the heads of the parents. And they shall also teach their children to pray, and to walk uprightly before the Lord" (D&C 68:25, 28). This is our primary purpose as parents—to teach our children. There is no greater guidebook for this purpose than the Book of Mormon.

1. TEACHING THE WORD OF GOD AS A COMPASS FOR OUR LIVES

THEME. The leading principle for parents to teach their children is to feast upon the word of Christ—"the bread life" (see John 6)—and make it the driving force of their mortal journey.

> "And now, O my son Helaman, behold, thou art in thy youth, and therefore, I beseech of thee that thou wilt hear my words and learn of me; for I do know that whosoever shall put their trust in God shall be supported in their trials, and their troubles, and their afflictions, and shall be lifted up at the last day" (Alma 36:3).

"Yea, I say unto you, my son, that there could be nothing so exquisite and so bitter as were my pains. Yea, and again I say unto you, my son, that on the other hand, there can be nothing so exquisite and sweet as was my joy" (Alma 36:21).

"For behold, it is as easy to give heed to the word of Christ, which will point to you a straight course to eternal bliss, as it was for our fathers to give heed to this compass, which would point unto them a straight course to the promised land" (Alma 37:44).

"And now, my son, see that ye take care of these sacred things, yea, see that ye look to God and live. Go unto this people and declare the word, and be sober. My son, farewell" (Alma 37:47).

MOMENT OF TRUTH. Alma imparts his fatherly counsel and blessing upon Helaman, telling him of his remarkable conversion, teaching and expounding on a variety of doctrines and principles, explaining how the word of God is a Liahona or compass for our lives, and sharing with him his testimony of the gospel. He commissions his son with the solemn record-keeping obligation and turns the engraved plates over to him, explaining their sacredness and admonishing him to declare the word and to remain true to his calling.

MODERN PROPHETS SPEAK

Thomas S. Monson:

> There are those who dismiss these responsibilities, feeling they can be deferred until the child grows up. Not so, the evidence reveals. Prime time for teaching is fleeting. . . . Children learn through gentle direction and persuasive teaching. They search for models to imitate, knowledge to acquire, things to do, and teachers to please.

> Parents and grandparents fill the role of teacher. So do siblings of the growing child. In this regard, I offer four simple suggestions for your consideration:

> 1. Teach prayer
> 2. Inspire faith
> 3. Live truth, and
> 4. Honor God
>
> ("Teach the Children," *Ensign*, Nov. 1997, 17).

ILLUSTRATIONS FOR OUR TIME

Who Will Teach the Children? A story told by my sweetheart, Patricia, in general conference, when she was serving as Primary general president, emphasizes the importance of teaching our children:

> One day as Ed and I were maneuvering the streets of England, he turned to me with tears in his eyes, and he said, "Look." I turned and saw a child on the side of the road. And then he said, "Who will teach the children?" That thought will not leave my mind or my heart. Who will teach the children? Who will teach the child who asks, "Will Heavenly Father really answer my prayer?" Who will teach Kate when at five years of age she asks, "Why do we need Jesus?" Who will teach the children? Please, will you? Will you? Will you help teach the children?
>
> Since my call I've knelt and asked, "Father, what do you want the children to be taught?"
>
> Teach and show the children that Heavenly Father loves them and has confidence in them because they are his children.
>
> Teach and show them that they do need Jesus, our Savior, our guide. Help them understand and accept his love and trust him and follow him. Teach them that our prophet, President Howard W. Hunter, has said, "We should at every opportunity ask ourselves, 'What would Jesus do?' and then be more courageous to act upon the answer." He also said, "We must know Christ better than we know him; we must remember him more often than we remember him; we must serve him more valiantly than we serve him" (*Ensign,* Sept. 1994, p. 5).
>
> Teach the children that at eight years of age, when they are baptized and receive the Holy Ghost, they will be responsible for their choices. Teach them that they will be tempted, but as they listen to the still, small voice of the Holy Ghost, he will help them with their choices.
>
> We can teach the children these gospel truths and all of the truths of the plan of happiness that Heavenly Father wants his children to understand and live. Family home evening can be one of those safe and loving places where the Spirit is felt. With eight children in our home, I also have vivid memories that family home evening wasn't always easy. Remember other opportunities for teaching: family prayer, family scripture study (don't give up!), in the classroom, in the hall, in the neighborhood. ("Teach the Children," *Ensign,* Nov. 1994, 78–79). (Pinegar)

Likening the Scriptures to Our Lives

Alma 36:2—Alma entreated Helaman to hear his words and to learn from him. He taught him to trust in the Lord, for the Lord would support him in all his trials and tribulations and lift him up at the last day. (This is in contrast to the observation concerning the devil's mode of "support" in Alma 30:60.)

Application—Too often we fail as parents in actually teaching our children the word of God. We do so many wonderful things, but we leave it to seminary and Church auxiliaries to teach the precious word of God to our children. We are responsible to teach our children.

Alma 37:32–37—Alma taught Helaman many wonderful things: teach the people to hate sin; preach repentance and faith in Jesus Christ; be humble, meek, and lowly of heart; withstand temptation through faith; and never be weary of good works. He admonished Helaman to do the following: learn wisdom in his youth; keep the commandments; pray for God's support; let all his doings be in the Lord, his thoughts be directed to the Lord, the affections of his heart be placed upon the Lord; counsel with the Lord in all things (so that the Lord would direct him to do good); lie down unto the Lord at night; and in the morning let his thanks be unto his Heavenly Father.

Application—We should take this advice to ourselves personally and instruct our children as well, consecrating our lives to God's service.

Alma 37:38–45—The Liahona directed the early emigrants to the promised land and gave them instructions from the Lord. It worked according to their faith and in keeping with the diligence and the heed—their obedience—that they gave unto it. The words of Christ constitute our Liahona for life. The words of Christ will lead us—if we are faithful, diligent, and receptive—to a place beyond this mortal sphere. The words of Christ are our Liahona for eternal life.

Application—Let us daily feast on, search in, and live by, the words of God. Let us liken them unto our lives so we can internalize the word of God and indeed become even as He is.

2. THE JOY OF EDIFYING AND UPLIFTING OUR CHILDREN

THEME. An important aspect of parental instruction is to recognize the good in young people and to encourage, energize, and motivate them to attain their divine potential.

"And now, my son, I trust that I shall have great joy in you, because of your steadiness and your faithfulness unto God; for as you have commenced in your youth to look to the Lord your God, even so I hope that you will continue in keeping his commandments; for

blessed is he that endureth to the end. I say unto you, my son, that I have had great joy in thee already, because of thy faithfulness and thy diligence, and thy patience and thy long-suffering among the people of the Zoramites" (Alma 38:2–3).

"And now, as ye have begun to teach the word even so I would that ye should continue to teach; and I would that ye would be diligent and temperate in all things" (Alma 38:10).

"Use boldness, but not overbearance; and also see that ye bridle all your passions, that ye may be filled with love; see that ye refrain from idleness" (Alma 38:12).

MOMENT OF TRUTH. Alma bestows his fatherly blessing and counsel on his son Shiblon. He praises him and encourages him to continue in his faithfulness. He outlines positive character traits, as well as their bounds.

MODERN PROPHETS SPEAK

Ezra Taft Benson:
> Praise your children more than you correct them. Praise them for even their smallest achievement. Encourage your children to come to you for counsel with their problems and questions by listening to them every day. Discuss with them such important matters as dating, sex, and other matters affecting their growth and development, and do it early enough so they will not obtain information from questionable sources. . . .
>
> Parents are directly responsible for the righteous rearing of their children, and this responsibility cannot be safely delegated to relatives, friends, neighbors, the school, the church, or the state. . . .
>
> Youth of the Church and of the nation need more than physical comforts. We will need to leave them more than lands and stacks. (*The Teachings of Ezra Taft Benson* [Salt Lake City: Bookcraft, 1988], 499–501)

ILLUSTRATIONS FOR OUR TIME

We Love, Therefore We Teach. Teaching children is tough work. I recall the time my wife, Pat, said to me, "Sweetheart, why don't you put a little more into teaching the lesson for family home evening?" We had good lessons and times together, but she wanted a little more effort, you know, kind of like the Relief Society's lessons . . . so I put more into it. I went to the bookstore and bought some masonite, flannel material, characters for the story, Velcro, and colored pencils. I got the whole works. I made the flannel board, colored in the characters and things for the presentation, and prepared a lesson. I was ready to go.

Monday night came. I was on fire. I started the lesson, and the children were in rapt attention for a minute; then a child said, "How long will this last?" "Just a few minutes," I responded, and on I went. Not more than a minute went by when another child said, "Did you get the donuts for treats?" I stopped and assured them that I had the donuts and continued the lesson. And then it happened—one of the older children, realizing the lesson was geared to the little ones, said, "Dad, I've got homework. How much longer?" That did it. I burst into tears and said, "I've worked for hours on this lesson and you don't even care. You can't even give me ten or fifteen minutes to help you." Silence prevailed, and then Pat said, "Look what you have done to Daddy." They all started to cry. They said they were sorry. I told them I was sorry, too. I added that I wanted to teach them because I loved them. Heavenly Father had asked me to help them grow up in light and truth and know the gospel of Jesus Christ. (Pinegar)

Likening the Scriptures to Our Lives

Alma 38:2–3—Alma had great joy in his son Shiblon. He praised him for his steadiness, faithfulness, diligence, and patience, and encouraged him to continue in keeping the commandments.

Application—We should at every opportunity give our children PIE: *praise* them honestly and genuinely; *instruct* them in the ways of the Lord; *encourage* them to be faithful to the end.

3. REPENTANCE: THE INDISPENSABLE LESSON

THEME: Parents have the solemn obligation to teach the principle of repentance to their children, so that they may participate in the divine blessings of the Atonement.

> *"For thou didst not give so much heed unto my words as did thy brother, among the people of the Zoramites. Now this is what I have against thee; thou didst go on unto boasting in thy strength and thy wisdom. And this is not all, my son. Thou didst do that which was grievous unto me; for thou didst forsake the ministry, and did go over into the land of Siron among the borders of the Lamanites, after the harlot Isabel"* (Alma 39:2–3).

> *"And now, my son, I would say somewhat unto you concerning the coming of Christ. Behold, I say unto you, that it is he that surely shall come to take away the sins of the world; yea, he cometh to declare glad tidings of salvation unto his people"* (Alma 39:15).

> *"Behold, he bringeth to pass the resurrection of the dead. But behold, my son, the resurrection is not yet. Now, I unfold unto you a mystery; nevertheless, there are many mysteries which are kept, that no one knoweth them save God himself. But I show unto you one thing which I have inquired diligently of God that I might know—that is concerning the resurrection"* (Alma 40:3).

"O, my son, this is not the case; but the meaning of the word restoration is to bring back again evil for evil, or carnal for carnal, or devilish for devilish—good for that which is good; righteous for that which is righteous; just for that which is just; merciful for that which is merciful" (Alma 41:13).

MOMENT OF TRUTH. Alma, with tenderness, yet correcting early on with clarity, admonishes his son Corianton to repent. He teaches him the key doctrines most relevant to the occasion: atonement, resurrection, and restoration according to one's righteousness. Presently he will declare the celebrated adage that "wickedness never was happiness" (Alma 41:10). Alma, himself an authority on repentance, is precisely the right person to counsel his son on this subject, and his patriarchal admonition serves to redirect this young man into the right channels (see Alma 42:31, where Corianton is again called to the ministry).

MODERN PROPHETS SPEAK

Spencer W. Kimball:

> Discipline is probably one of the most important elements in which a mother and father can lead and guide and direct their children. It certainly would be well for parents to understand the rule given to the priesthood in section 121. Setting limits to what a child can do means to that child that you love him and respect him. If you permit the child to do all the things he would like to do without any limits, that means to him that you do not care much about him. (*Teachings of Spencer W. Kimball*, ed. Edward L. Kimball [Salt Lake City: Bookcraft, 1982], 340–41)

ILLUSTRATIONS FOR OUR TIME

The Wooden Splinter. In a special location at home I keep a small reminder of a big lesson I learned one time as a young father. It is a sharp wooden splinter about an inch and a half in length that was retrieved from the tire of our family car many years ago, at a time when one of our daughters was learning to drive. One day, while she was driving that particular car, she rounded a corner and managed to bump up over the curb. Soon thereafter, the tire went flat, which occasioned the need for a fatherly rescue. Making the logical assumption that the impact had caused the problem, I took the occasion to advise her to be more careful. It was, I thought, the perfect teaching moment—and so it was, but for the father rather than the daughter. The repairman soon discovered the problem with the tire: it was not the bump, but rather an imbedded wooden splinter that was at fault. I apologized to my daughter for the misplaced blame—she was always very forgiving—and resolved to be less judgmental in the future when carrying out my fatherly teaching duties. Recently I was counseling with my son on some family matters and retrieved the wooden splinter to relive for his benefit the lesson I had learned so many years ago. We enjoyed a good chuckle at my expense.

As parents teach, they need to remember constantly that they, too, are imperfect and have need of continuing education and constant correction. When Alma exhorted his sons to live righteously, he did so in the context of his own grievous past. He taught repentance with authority, because he himself was an authority on repentance: "Yea, I say unto you, my son, that there could be nothing so exquisite and so bitter as were my pains. Yea, and again I say unto you, my son, that on the other hand, there can be nothing so exquisite and sweet as was my joy" (Alma 36:21). What a powerful testimony of the effects of repentance and the application of the principles of the Atonement! The Savior reminded us: "And why beholdest thou the mote that is in thy brother's eye, but considerest not the beam that is in thine own eye?" (Matt. 7:3). Parents as teachers would do well to clothe truth in humility, doctrine in compassion, and principles in charity. (Allen)

Likening the Scriptures to Our Lives

Alma 39:11–13—Alma was instructed by the Spirit to call Corianton to repentance because of his bad example. Alma commanded him to fear God and to refrain from his iniquities.

Application—We, as parents and leaders, when moved upon by the Holy Ghost, should lovingly call to repentance those in our care (see D&C 121:41–44).

SUMMARY

These chapters of the Book of Mormon summarize the essence of the parental syllabus for instruction. We need to teach the word of God as a compass for our lives. We need to savor the joy of edifying and uplifting our children as we admonish them to hold to the iron rod. We need to remember that repentance is the indispensable lesson, since it serves as the means for bringing about the Atonement in our lives.

Parents should love their children even as our Heavenly Father and Savior love us—unconditionally. We are duty bound to teach and train our children. We have been taught how to correct our children (see D&C 121:41–44). Our greatest joy is in our posterity. Their growth and accomplishments bring us joy and satisfaction. Recognizing these facts as eternal truths we must be about our work and our glory—loving and teaching our children the gospel of Jesus Christ, and encouraging them to walk uprightly before the Lord that they might enjoy the blessings of exaltation.

CHAPTER THIRTY

"THE GREAT PLAN *of* HAPPINESS"

ALMA 40–42

"Fundamental to a man's understanding about his identity and purpose upon this planet is to know that God has a plan of salvation also called a plan of happiness, a plan of mercy, etc. (Alma 24:14; 42:8; 42:15)."
—NEAL A. MAXWELL, *BUT FOR A SMALL MOMENT*
[SALT LAKE CITY: BOOKCRAFT, 1986], 62.

THEMES *for* LIVING

Understanding Death, the Spirit World, and the Resurrection
Understanding the Doctrine of Restoration
Understanding Justice and Mercy

INTRODUCTION

Alma, having chastened Corianton, seeks to help him understand precious doctrines that can help him reform. Alma realized that his son's mind was troubled as to the doctrines that give specific hope for the future as well as accountability for the present. The devil teaches the opposite of accountability and hope (see 2 Ne. 28:7–8; Alma 30:18). When we see that people believe the misguided philosophy of "Eat, drink, and be merry, for tomorrow we die—and that is the end of our existence," it is easier to understand their behavior, though we grieve over the resulting negative consequences that must surely befall them. Such was the case of Corianton. The good news was that Corianton listened to his father, and his life was apparently turned around for the better. He was called to return to the ministry (see Alma 42:31), he preached the word with his brothers and many people heeded their words (see Alma 49:30), and later he was involved in taking supplies to the people who had traveled by ship to the northern lands (see Alma 63:10). The Book of Mormon thus chronicles in specific terms the pattern of repentance and recovery that the wayward can follow.

1. UNDERSTANDING DEATH, THE SPIRIT WORLD, AND THE RESURRECTION

THEME. The scriptures teach us the answers to the grand queries of life: Where do we come from? Where do we go after death? What is our ultimate destiny? Alma's counsel to his son Corianton lifts us to a fuller understanding of the future stages of human life along the way to perfection.

> *"Now, concerning the state of the soul between death and the resurrection—Behold, it has been made known unto me by an angel, that the spirits of all men, as soon as they are departed from this mortal body, yea, the spirits of all men, whether they be good or evil, are taken home to that God who gave them life. And then shall it come to pass, that the spirits of those who are righteous are received into a state of happiness, which is called paradise, a state of rest, a state of peace, where they shall rest from all their troubles and from all care, and sorrow. And then shall it come to pass, that the spirits of the wicked, yea, who are evil—for behold, they have no part nor portion of the Spirit of the Lord; for behold, they chose evil works rather than good; therefore the spirit of the devil did enter into them, and take possession of their house—and these shall be cast out into outer darkness; there shall be weeping, and wailing, and gnashing of teeth, and this because of their own iniquity, being led captive by the will of the devil. Now this is the state of the souls of the wicked, yea, in darkness, and a state of awful, fearful looking for the fiery indignation of the wrath of God upon them; thus they remain in this state, as well as the righteous in paradise, until the time of their resurrection" (Alma 40:11–14).*

MOMENT OF TRUTH. How does one counsel a son (or daughter) who chooses to travel on byways rather than highways, who lapses into unrighteous behavior and misses the mark when it comes to understanding the plain and precious truths of the gospel? Alma's handling of this delicate situation in the case of his son Corianton is a model of both exactitude and compassion. He introduces the dialogue with this charitable understatement: "For thou didst not give so much heed unto my words as did thy brother" (Alma 39:2). He then teaches his son concerning righteousness, death, the spirit world, the resurrection, and the God-bestowed freedom that mortals have to choose the right. Understanding these doctrines is critical to covenant fidelity.

MODERN PROPHETS SPEAK

Bruce R. McConkie:

THE SPIRIT PRISON

> There are two distinct senses in which the expression spirit prison is used: 1. Since disembodied spirits cannot gain a fulness of joy until their resurrection (D&C 93:33–34), they consider their habitation in the spirit world as one of imprisonment, and so the whole spirit world (including both paradise and hell) is a *spirit prison.* It was to the *righteous spirits in prison,* those who were in paradise that our Lord preached while his body was in the tomb. (1 Pet. 3:18–21; 4:6; D&C 76:73–74.)

> In the vision of the redemption of the dead, President Joseph F. Smith saw that during his ministry to the spirits in prison, "the Lord went not in person among the wicked and disobedient who had rejected the truth," but that he went "declaring liberty to the *captives who had been faithful,*" to the vast assemblage of the righteous, for they *"had looked upon the long absence of their spirits from their bodies as a bondage." (Gospel Doctrine,* 5th ed., pp. 472–476.)

> 2. In a more particular sense, however, the *spirit prison* is hell, that portion of the spirit world where the wicked dwell. (Moses 7:37–39.) Before Christ bridged the gulf between paradise and hell—so that the righteous could mingle with the wicked and preach them the gospel—the wicked in hell were confined to locations which precluded them from contact with the righteous in paradise. Abraham told the rich man in hell that between him and Lazarus (who was in paradise) there was a great gulf fixed so that none could go from paradise to hell or from hell to paradise. . . . (Luke 16:19–31.)

THE RESURRECTION

The *resurrection* is the creation of an immortal soul; it consists in the uniting or reuniting of body and spirit in immortality. . . . Resurrected beings have bodies of flesh and bones, tangible, corporeal bodies, bodies that occupy space, digest food, and have power, outwardly, to appear as mortal bodies do. (Luke 24.) . . .

Two events of transcendent importance make possible the resurrection: 1. *The fall of Adam;* and 2. *The redemptive sacrifice of the Son of God.* Adam's fall brought temporal or natural death into the world; that is, as a result of Adam's fall mortality was introduced, and mortality is the forerunner of death. Christ's redeeming sacrifice ransomed men from the effects of Adam's fall in that mortality is replaced by immortality, or in other words in that the dead come forth in the resurrection . . . This doctrine of a universal resurrection was known and taught from the beginning. . . . (see D&C 29:42–50; Moses 5:6–15.)

Christ was the firstfruits of the resurrection (1 Cor. 15:23), and because of his resurrection, "by the power of God," all men shall come forth from the grave. (Morm. 9:13)

To those who lived before the resurrection of Christ, the day of his coming forth from the dead was known as the *first resurrection.* Abinadi and Alma, for instance, so considered it. (Mosiah 15:21–25; Alma 40.) To those who have lived since that day, the first resurrection is yet future and will take place at the time of the Second Coming. (D&C 88:96–102.) We have no knowledge that the resurrection is going on now or that any persons have been resurrected since the day in which Christ came forth excepting Peter, James, and Moroni, all of whom had special labors to perform in this day which necessitated tangible resurrected bodies. (*Mormon Doctrine,* 2d ed. [Salt Lake City: Bookcraft, 1966], 637–43)

ILLUSTRATIONS FOR OUR TIME

Hope for a Discouraged Missionary. Hope lends optimism to life. It helps us carry on when we are downhearted and discouraged. It helps us repent. Hope is the doctrine that is expressly connected to faith and charity. We cannot live without hope. If hope is gone, sin lies at the door. When we realize that there is life after death and that our reward is directly connected to our actions here on earth, we look to God and seek to keep His commandments. Our hope must extend beyond this life, or we would be "of all men most miserable" (1 Cor. 15:19). Hope is continually activated when one appreciates any doctrine or principle of the gospel. Understanding becomes a key to hope. If we understand, we can press on. President Monson tells a heartwarming story about a missionary who almost quit because he was without hope:

As a mission president, I was afforded the privilege of guiding the activities of precious young men and women, missionaries whom the Lord had called. Some had problems, others required motivation; but one came to me in utter despair. He had made his decision to leave the mission field when but at the halfway mark. His bags were packed, his return ticket purchased. He came by to bid me farewell. We talked; we listened; we prayed. There remained hidden the actual reason for his decision to quit.

As we arose from our knees in the quiet of my office, the missionary began to weep almost uncontrollably. Flexing the muscle of his strong right arm, he blurted out, "This is my problem. All through school my muscle power qualified me for honors in football and track, but my mental power was neglected. President Monson, I'm ashamed of my school record. It reveals that "with effort" I have the capacity to read at but the level of the fourth grade. I can't even read the Book of Mormon. How then can I understand its contents and teach others its truths?"

The silence of the room was broken by my nine-year-old son who, without knocking, opened the door and, with surprise, apologetically said, "Excuse me. I just wanted to put this book back on the shelf."

He handed me the book. Its title: *A Child's Story of the Book of Mormon,* by Deta Petersen Neeley. I turned to the preface and read that the book had been written with a carefully selected vocabulary on a fourth-grade level. A sincere prayer from an honest heart had been dramatically answered.

My missionary accepted the challenge to read the book. Half laughing, half crying, he declared: "It will be good to read something I can understand."

Clouds of despair were dispelled by the sunshine of hope. He completed an honorable mission, is now married for eternity to a choice companion, and has children of his own. His life is a testimony of the nearness of our Father and the availability of His help. (*Inspiring Experiences That Build Faith: From the Life and Ministry of Thomas S. Monson* [Salt Lake City: Deseret Book, 1994], 145–46) (Pinegar)

Likening the Scriptures to Our Lives

Alma 40:12–13—The spirits of the righteous are received into a state of rest, peace, and happiness, while the wicked are cast into outer darkness weeping and wailing until the resurrection.

Application—We need to realize that we are blessed or punished according to our works. Our happiness here and status hereafter depends on our efforts.

2. UNDERSTANDING
THE DOCTRINE OF RESTORATION

THEME. "Whatever principle of intelligence we attain unto in this life, it will rise with us in the resurrection" (D&C 130:18). This is how the Prophet Joseph Smith expressed an important dimension of the doctrine of restoration. There is no discontinuity in one's spiritual makeup in the transition from this world to the next. Goodness translates to goodness, evil to evil. If we align ourselves in this life with that which is evil, then this same disposition will continue with us into the next sphere of existence.

> *"And it is requisite with the justice of God that men should be judged according to their works; and if their works were good in this life, and the desires of their hearts were good, that they should also, at the last day, be restored unto that which is good. And if their works are evil they shall be restored unto them for evil. Therefore, all things shall be restored to their proper order, every thing to its natural frame—mortality raised to immortality, corruption to incorruption—raised to endless happiness to inherit the kingdom of God, or to endless misery to inherit the kingdom of the devil, the one on one hand, the other on the other—The one raised to happiness according to his desires of happiness, or good according to his desires of good; and the other to evil according to his desires of evil; for as he has desired to do evil all the day long even so shall he have his reward of evil when the night cometh" (Alma 41:3–5).*

MOMENT OF TRUTH. Alma's son Corianton has clearly misunderstood the doctrine of restoration, musing perhaps that the effects of his wayward behavior could be transformed magically into something good in the final analysis. With precision but tenderness, Alma disabuses his son of that false notion by declaring the now famous dictum: "Behold, I say unto you, wickedness never was happiness" (Alma 41:10). In truth we are restored to a state of happiness or misery when we are resurrected according to the degree of righteousness that we have obtained in this life.

MODERN PROPHETS SPEAK

Joseph Fielding Smith:
> When I was a small boy, too young to hold the Aaronic Priesthood, my father placed a copy of the Book of Mormon in my hands with the request that I read it. I received this Nephite record with thanksgiving and applied myself to the task which had been assigned to me. There are certain passages that have been stamped upon my mind, and I have never forgotten them. One of these is in the 27th chapter of 3rd

Nephi, verses 19 and 20. It is the word of our Redeemer to the Nephites as he taught them after his resurrection. It is as follows:

"And no unclean thing can enter into his kingdom; therefore nothing entereth into his rest save it be those who have washed their garments in my blood, because of their faith, and the repentance of all their sins, and their faithfulness unto the end.

"Now this is the commandment: Repent, all ye ends of the earth, and come unto me and be baptized in my name, that ye may be sanctified by the reception of the Holy Ghost, that ye may stand spotless before me at the last day."

The other passage is in the 10th verse of chapter 41 in the book of Alma and is as follows:

"Do not suppose, because it has been spoken concerning restoration, that ye shall be restored from sin to happiness. Behold, I say unto you, wickedness never was happiness."

These two passages I have tried to follow all the days of my life, and I have felt to thank the Lord for this counsel and guidance, and I have endeavored to stamp these sayings on the minds of many others. What a wonderful guide these teachings can be to us if we can get them firmly fixed in our minds!" (*CR,* Oct. 1964, 6)

ILLUSTRATIONS FOR OUR TIME

The Stamp of Truth. Alma has taught us that we are restored according to our works through the grace of God. It really becomes the law of the harvest: we reap as we sow. We are simply restored with good for good, righteousness to happiness, evil for evil, sin to misery. In mortality, this law is in effect. When we are righteous, we are happy. When we sin we are unhappy. Oh, we may try to gloss over our sins and attempt to have happiness, but it just fades as a moment of mortal pleasure—pleasure based on the wants of the flesh. In my own life I can testify without question that the happiest moments in life are when I know I am doing what the Lord wants me to do. Conversely, the unhappiest moments are when I wanted my will instead of the Lord's will. We must be clean and pure in order to be restored to the presence of our Heavenly Father.. (Pinegar)

Likening the Scriptures to Our Lives

Alma 41:1—Alma taught the doctrine of restoration, which is simply that you receive good for good and evil for evil.

Application—We reap what we sow. The law of the harvest is the principle by which we progress and are blessed (see D&C 130:20–21).

3. UNDERSTANDING JUSTICE AND MERCY

THEME. In a masterful process of divine balance, the fulcrum being the Atonement of Jesus Christ, justice and mercy are eternally harmonized for "the truly penitent" (Alma 42:24). It is through the balancing grace of our Lord that we are saved, "after all we can do" (2 Ne. 25:23).

> *"Therefore, according to justice, the plan of redemption could not be brought about, only on conditions of repentance of men in this probationary state, yea, this preparatory state; for except it were for these conditions, mercy could not take effect except it should destroy the work of justice. Now the work of justice could not be destroyed; if so, God would cease to be God. And thus we see that all mankind were fallen, and they were in the grasp of justice; yea, the justice of God, which consigned them forever to be cut off from his presence. And now, the plan of mercy could not be brought about except an atonement should be made; therefore God himself atoneth for the sins of the world, to bring about the plan of mercy, to appease the demands of justice, that God might be a perfect, just God, and a merciful God also. . . . But God ceaseth not to be God, and mercy claimeth the penitent, and mercy cometh because of the atonement; and the atonement bringeth to pass the resurrection of the dead; and the resurrection of the dead bringeth back men into the presence of God; and thus they are restored into his presence, to be judged according to their works, according to the law and justice" (Alma 42:13–15, 23).*

MOMENT OF TRUTH. Alma continues his counsel to Corianton by teaching him the great doctrines of justice and mercy and how they relate one to another. Alma instructs his son that it is through the Atonement of Christ that mercy is empowered on behalf of the obedient (see Alma 42:15). He counsels his son: "Do not endeavor to excuse yourself in the least point because of your sins, by denying the justice of God; but do you let the justice of God, and his mercy, and his long-suffering have full sway in your heart; and let it bring you down to the dust in humility" (Alma 42:30).

MODERN PROPHETS SPEAK

Bruce R. McConkie:
    JUSTICE

That which conforms to the mind and will of God and is righteous and proper before him is *just*. A just punishment, for instance, is one that is deserved because the recipient violated the law, thus meriting the particular penalty that always accompanies violation of that law. *Justice* deals with the unbending, invariable results that always and ever flow from the same causes. It carries a connotation of righteousness, fairness, impartiality. It embraces the principle and practice of just dealing, of conformity to a course of perfect rectitude, of adherence to a standard of complete integrity.

Justice is one of the attributes of God. "Publish the name of the Lord," Moses proclaimed, "ascribe ye greatness unto our God. He is the Rock, his work is perfect: for all his ways are judgment: a God of truth and without iniquity, *just* and right is he." (Deut. 32:3–4.) "*Justice* and judgment are the habitation of thy throne: mercy and truth shall go before thy face," the psalmist wrote. (Ps. 89:14.) "There is no God else beside me," the Lord says, "a *just* God and a Saviour." (Isa. 45:21; Zeph. 3:5; Zech. 9:9; Rev. 15:3–4.). . . .

MERCY

In the gospel sense, mercy consists in our Lord's forbearance, on certain specified conditions, from imposing punishments that, except for his grace and goodness, would be the just reward of man.

Because mercy is an attribute of Deity (Ex. 33:19; Rom. 9:15–18; 2 Cor. 1:3; Eph. 2:4; 1 Pet. 1:3), men are thereby enabled to have faith in him unto life and salvation. . . .

No cry of thanksgiving and relief seems to come more gratefully from the prophetic voice than the comforting exclamation, *"His mercy endureth for ever!"* (1 Chron. 16:34, 41; 2 Chron. 5:13; 7:3, 6; Ezra 3:11; Ps. 106:1; 107:1; 118:1–4; 136; Jer. 33:11.) Certainly his mercy is manifest in all his doings—his creative enterprises and his hand-dealings in all ages with all people. (Ps. 136.)

The atoning sacrifice of our Lord, upon which all things rest, came because of his infinite mercy. (D&C 29:1.) Through his condescension, grace, and mercy he has visited the children of men and given great promises to them. (2 Ne. 4:26; 9:53.) . . .(*Mormon Doctrine,* 2d ed. [Salt Lake City: Bookcraft, 1966], 483–86)

ILLUSTRATIONS FOR OUR TIME

Our Heavenly Father and Savior, Jesus Christ, mete out justice. They have made the laws upon which it operates. Mercy is ours to claim in repentance through the power of the Atonement. We must be willing to accept the goodness of God. Guilt can and will be swept away through repentance—we can and will be forgiven. Remember that guilt unto repentance is of the Lord but guilt beyond repentance is of the devil. The following story is related by Boyd K. Packer:

The Mediator

There once was a man who wanted something very much. It seemed more important than anything else in his life. In order for him to have his desire, he incurred a great debt.

He had been warned about going into that much debt, and particularly about his creditor. But it seemed so important for him to do what he wanted to do and to have what he wanted right now. He was sure he could pay for it later.

So he signed a contract. He would pay if off sometime along the way. He didn't worry too much about it, for the due date seemed such a long time away. He had what he wanted now, and that was what seemed important.

The creditor was always somewhere in the back of his mind, and he made token payments now and again, thinking somehow that the day of reckoning really would never come.

But as it always does, the day came, and the contract fell due. The debt had not been fully paid. His creditor appeared and demanded payment in full.

Only then did he realize that his creditor not only had the power to repossess all that he owned, but the power to cast him into prison as well.

"I cannot pay you, for I have not the power to do so," he confessed.

"Then," said the creditor, "we will exercise the contract, take your possessions, and you shall go to prison. You agreed to that. It was your choice. You signed the contract, and now it must be enforced."

"Can you not extend the time or forgive the debt?" the debtor begged. "Arrange some way for me to keep what I have and not go to prison. Surely you believe in mercy? Will you not show mercy?"

The creditor replied, "Mercy is always so one-sided. It would serve only you. If I show mercy to you, it will leave me unpaid. It is justice I demand. Do you believe in justice?"

"I believed in justice when I signed the contract," the debtor said. "It was on my side then, for I thought it would protect me. I did not need mercy then, nor think I should need it ever. Justice, I thought, would serve both of us equally as well."

"It is justice that demands that you pay the contract or suffer the penalty," the creditor replied. "That is the law. You have agreed to it and that is the way it must be. Mercy cannot rob justice."

There they were: One meting out justice, the other pleading for mercy. Neither could prevail except at the expense of the other.

"If you do not forgive the debt there will be no mercy," the debtor pleaded.

"If I do, there will be no justice," was the reply.

Both laws, it seemed, could not be served. They are two eternal ideals that appear to contradict one another. Is there no way for justice to be fully served, and mercy also?

There is a way! The law of justice can be fully satisfied and mercy can be fully extended-but it takes someone else. And so it happened this time.

The debtor had a friend. He came to help. He knew the debtor well. He knew him to be shortsighted. He thought him foolish to have gotten himself into such a predicament. Nevertheless, he wanted to help because he loved him. He stepped between them, faced the creditor, and made this offer.

"I will pay the debt if you will free the debtor from his contract so that he may keep his possessions and not go to prison."

As the creditor was pondering the offer, the mediator added, "You demanded justice. Though he cannot pay you, I will do so. You will have been justly dealt with and can ask no more. It would not be just."

And so the creditor agreed.

The mediator turned then to the debtor. "If I pay your debt, will you accept me as your creditor?"

"Oh yes, yes," cried the debtor. "You save me from prison and show mercy to me."

"Then," said the benefactor, "you will pay the debt to me and I will set the terms. It will not be easy, but it will be possible. I will provide a way. You need not go to prison."

And so it was that the creditor was paid in full. He had been justly dealt with. No contract had been broken.

The debtor, in turn, had been extended mercy. Both laws stood fulfilled. Because there was a mediator, justice had claimed its full share, and mercy was fully satisfied.

Each of us lives on a kind of spiritual credit. One day the account will be closed, a settlement demanded. However casually we may view it now, when that day comes and the foreclosure is imminent we will look around in restless agony for someone, anyone, to help us.

And, by eternal law, mercy cannot be extended save there be one who is both willing and able to assume our debt and pay the price and arrange the terms for our redemption.

Unless there is a mediator, unless we have a friend, the full weight of justice untempered, unsympathetic, must, positively must, fall on us. The full recompense for every transgression, however minor or however deep, will be exacted from us to the uttermost farthing.

But know this: Truth, glorious truth, proclaims there is such a mediator.

"For there is one God, and one mediator between God and men, the man Christ Jesus." (1 Timothy 2:5.)

Through Him mercy can be fully extended to each of us without offending the eternal law of justice. (Boyd K. Packer, *Memorable Stories and Parables of Boyd K. Packer* [Salt Lake City: Bookcraft, 1997], 9.)

Likening the Scriptures to Our Lives

Alma 42:15—Alma taught that the plan of justice and mercy could only operate upon the power of the Atonement of the Lord Jesus Christ. Mercy could not be brought about save there was an infinite Atonement to pay the demands of justice . . . thus God is merciful and just.

Application—We should feel gratitude for the goodness of God in giving His beloved Son to atone for our sins. When we realize His mercy for us we too should be more merciful. We obtain mercy no more than we are merciful (see 3 Ne. 12:7; 14:2).

SUMMARY

How much insight comes to mankind through a clear understanding of death, the spirit world, and the resurrection as revealed through the scriptures. How much wisdom comes from a correct understanding of the doctrine of restoration. How much happiness comes from a calm and purposeful understanding of the doctrines of justice and mercy.

So often in life people go astray because of their own wants and desires. They choose to sin. This cannot be an excuse, for we have the light of Christ and we can receive the gift of the Holy Ghost. Sometimes individuals sin due to the lack of understanding. Throughout the Book of Mormon, the prophets continually attempt to help the wayward by calling attention to God's loving kindness in past ages and exhorting the people to remember the goodness of God in preserving them. Alma taught this doctrine to his son Corianton. Remember that an appreciation of the doctrines, principles, and covenants associated with the blessings of God fills us with gratitude, and then our attitudes, desires, and behavior can change. The doctrines taught in these chapters can bring us into full accord with the plan of happiness, which gives one hope, the power to carry on, and the power to change.

CHAPTER THIRTY-ONE

"FIRM IN THE FAITH *of* CHRIST"

ALMA 43–52

"Great cultures stagnate in war shadows and cease to survive when continuous wars make people migrants and when fields are abandoned and livestock is appropriated for nonproducing soldiers; when in wartime forests are destroyed without replanting and farmers and builders become warriors. Men cannot plant, cultivate, and harvest when in camps, nor build when on the run. Long and bloody wars mean sacked, burned, ruined cities, confiscatory taxes, degenerated peoples, and decayed cultures.

"Victory and defeat alike leave countries devastated and the conqueror and the conquered reduced. Wickedness brings war and war vomits destruction and suffering, hate, and bloodshed upon the guilty and the innocent alike.

"This book [the Book of Mormon] should convince of the futility of war and the hazards of unrighteousness. A few prophets swimming in a sea of barbarism find it difficult to prevent the crumbling and final collapse of corrupt peoples. There is a great but conditional promise:
"And this land shall be a land of liberty unto the Gentiles, and there shall be no kings upon the land. . . .
"And I will fortify this land against all other nations.
". . . I, the Lord, the king of heaven, will be their king, and I will be a light unto them forever, that hear my words (2 Nephi 10:11–12, 14)."
—SPENCER W. KIMBALL, *FAITH PRECEDES THE MIRACLE* [SALT LAKE CITY: DESERET BOOK, 1972], 333–34.

THEMES *for* LIVING

In Defense of Our Families and Our Liberties
The Title of Liberty
A Contrast of Causes: Deception and Fraud Versus Devotion and Faith
Wickedness as the Seedbed of Turmoil

INTRODUCTION

There was war in heaven and it continues today. It was—and is—a war over the souls of mankind. In a portion of that conflict, the Lamanites and apostate Nephites combined to war against the Nephites. When people ripen in iniquity the result is always war. Those who are attacked have the right to defend themselves. The wars we see in the Book of Mormon and in the world today are a reflection of life as it unfolds in larger perspective. Life itself is a battle. We are at war individually with the wicked one—even the devil. We must defend ourselves. In the war with Satan and his servants, we must come off conqueror (see D&C 10:5). Those who are righteous and keep the commandments are blessed of the Lord and preserved. Moroni was such a man. This is his story as preserved and passed down by Mormon, who saw fit to name his son after the great and righteous warrior.

1. IN DEFENSE OF OUR FAMILIES AND OUR LIBERTIES

THEME. "For it must needs be, that there is an opposition in all things," Father Lehi proclaimed (2 Ne. 2:11). "But woe to that man by whom the offense cometh!" (Matt. 18:7). One perennial manifestation of this is the constant clash among humankind of the force of materialism and unrighteous dominion on the one hand and the force of liberty and justice for all on the other. In the end, freedom and the dignity of humankind as the offspring of Deity will prevail, but not without constant vigilance in upholding the standards of the gospel with courage and faithfulness. "Eternal vigilance is the price of the freedom of the soul as well as of the state" (Francis M. Lyman, *Improvement Era*, 7:176), and "Freedom can be killed by neglect as well as by direct attack" (Ezra Taft Benson, *God, Family, Country: Our Three Great Loyalties* [Salt Lake City: Deseret Book, 1974], 361).

> *"And he also knowing that it was the only desire of the Nephites to preserve their lands, and their liberty, and their church, therefore he thought it no sin that he should defend them by stratagem; therefore, he found by his spies which course the Lamanites were to take" (Alma 43:30).*

> *"Nevertheless, the Nephites were inspired by a better cause, for they were not fighting for monarchy nor power but they were fighting for their homes and their liberties, their wives and their children, and their all, yea, for their rites of worship and their church. And they were doing that which they felt was the duty which they owed to their God; for the Lord had said unto them, and also unto their fathers, that: Inasmuch as ye are not guilty of the first offense, neither the second, ye shall not suffer yourselves to be slain by the hands of your enemies" (Alma 43:45–46).*

"And now, Zerahemnah, I command you, in the name of that all-powerful God, who has strengthened our arms that we have gained power over you, by our faith, by our religion, and by our rites of worship, and by our church, and by the sacred support which we owe to our wives and our children, by that liberty which binds us to our lands and our country; yea, and also by the maintenance of the sacred word of God, to which we owe all our happiness; and by all that is most dear unto us." (Alma 44:5).

MOMENT OF TRUTH. The prophet-chronicler Mormon shifts his attention from the ecclesiastical ministry of Alma and his sons among the people to focus on the lessons that flow from a different arena: the consuming conflict between the invading Lamanites (led by apostate Nephite commanders) and the forces of Captain Moroni. This conflagration is the collision of two diametrically opposite forces: power-hungry pride and opportunism on the one hand and the cause of liberty for church and family on the other. The Lamanites, under king Zerahemnah, seek to bring the Nephites into bondage. Moroni, the great captain of the armies, leads the Nephites to victory on the basis of several factors: they were better prepared, their desires were pure, they were "inspired by a better cause" (Alma 43:45), they were not guilty of the first offense nor the second (see Alma 43:46), and they had a strong faith in Jesus Christ (Alma 44:5).

MODERN PROPHETS SPEAK

David O. McKay:

So fundamental in man's eternal progress is his inherent right to choose that the Lord would defend it even at the price of war. Without freedom of thought, freedom of choice, freedom of action within lawful bounds, man cannot progress. The Lord recognized this and also the fact that it would take man thousands of years to make the earth habitable for self-governing individuals. Throughout the ages advanced souls have yearned for a society in which liberty and justice prevail. Men have sought for it, fought for it, have died for it. Ancient freemen prized it; slaves longed for it; the Magna Charta demanded it; the Constitution of the United States declared it.

"This love of liberty which God has planted in us," said Abraham Lincoln, "constitutes the bulwark of our liberty and independence. It is not our frowning battlements, our bristling seacoasts, our army, and our navy. Our defense is in the spirit which prizes liberty as the heritage of all men, in all lands, everywhere. Destroy this spirit, and we have planted the seeds of despotism at our very doors." (*Gospel Ideals: Selections from the Discourses of David O. McKay*, comp. G. Homer Durham [Salt Lake City: Improvement Era, 1953], 288)

ILLUSTRATIONS FOR OUR TIME

Gordon B. Hinckley:

> When all is said and done, we of this Church are people of peace. . . .
>
> This places us in the position of those who long for peace, who teach peace, who work for peace, but who also are citizens of nations and are subject to the laws of our governments. Furthermore, we are a freedom-loving people, committed to the defense of liberty wherever it is in jeopardy. I believe that God will not hold men and women in uniform responsible as agents of their government in carrying forward that which they are legally obligated to do. It may even be that He will hold us responsible if we try to impede or hedge up the way of those who are involved in a contest with forces of evil and repression. ("War and Peace," *Ensign*, May 2003, 80)

Likening the Scriptures to Our Lives

Alma 43:9–10—The Nephites sought to preserve their homes, their families, their rights of liberty, and their freedom to worship God. They knew that the Lamanites, should they overpower the Nephites, would destroy those who worshipped God.

Application—We have the inalienable right to fight for freedom (see D&C 134:2–4). We are duty bound to seek and protect the rights and properties of individuals.

2. THE TITLE OF LIBERTY

THEME. Liberty in the pursuit of God's agenda "to bring to pass the immortality and eternal life of man" (Moses 1:39) is a cause that supersedes all mortal priorities and worldly interests. The security and well-being of our families, an environment of liberty in which the kingdom of God can flourish, and the right to practice our inalienable rights of conscience—all these are invaluable assets worth preserving and fighting for in order that spiritual progress can continue unimpeded.

> *"And now it came to pass that after Helaman and his brethren had appointed priests and teachers over the churches that there arose a dissension among them, and they would not give heed to the words of Helaman and his brethren; But they grew proud, being lifted up in their hearts, because of their exceedingly great riches; therefore they grew rich in their own eyes, and would not give heed to their words, to walk uprightly before God"* (Alma 45:23–24).

"Thus we see how quick the children of men do forget the Lord their God, yea, how quick to do iniquity, and to be led away by the evil one" (Alma 46:8).

"Yea, we see that Amalickiah, because he was a man of cunning device and a man of many flattering words, that he led away the hearts of many people to do wickedly; yea, and to seek to destroy the church of God, and to destroy the foundation of liberty which God had granted unto them, or which blessing God had sent upon the face of the land for the righteous' sake" (Alma 46:10).

"And it came to pass that he rent his coat; and he took a piece thereof, and wrote upon it—In memory of our God, our religion, and freedom, and our peace, our wives, and our children—and he fastened it upon the end of a pole. And he fastened on his head-plate, and his breastplate, and his shields, and girded on his armor about his loins; and he took the pole, which had on the end thereof his rent coat, (and he called it the title of liberty) and he bowed himself to the earth, and he prayed mightily unto his God for the blessings of liberty to rest upon his brethren, so long as there should a band of Christians remain to possess the land—" (Alma 46:12–13).

MOMENT OF TRUTH. Alma solicits a confirmation from his son Helaman ever to be valiant in the exercise of his sacred charge over the records of the people. Alma then shares with his son the essence of his most recent prophecy concerning the eventual downfall of the Nephite nation—because of pride and iniquity. Thereafter, Alma departs from the land, never to be seen again. Helaman and the brethren go throughout the cities declaring the word of God, yet the people grow in pride and worldly entanglements. They forget their God who had preserved them. With flattery, the cunning and ruthless Amalickiah leads many of the people away from the Church. Moroni, being inspired of God, raises the title of liberty as a rallying force to galvanize the people in remembering their ancient Israelite heritage (with reference to the rent coat of their forebear Joseph) and taking a stand in the cause of righteousness. The people respond with a solemn pledge to maintain their liberty and preserve their rights in the face of the onslaught of tyranny.

MODERN PROPHETS SPEAK

Ezra Taft Benson:

> Of course, the war in heaven over free agency is now being waged here on earth, and there are those today who are saying, "Look, don't get involved in the fight for freedom. Just live the gospel." That counsel is dangerous, self-contradictory, unsound. . .

Now, part of the reason we may not have sufficient priesthood bearers to save the Constitution, let alone to shake the powers of hell, is because unlike Moroni, I fear, our souls do not joy in keeping our country free, and we are not firm in the faith of Christ, nor have we sworn with an oath to defend our rights and the liberty of our country.

Moroni raised a title of liberty and wrote upon it these words: "In memory of our God, our religion, and freedom, and our peaces, our wives, and our children." Why didn't he write upon it "Just live your religion; there's no need to concern yourselves about your freedom, your peace, your wives, or your children"? The reason he didn't do this was because all these things were a part of his religion, as they are of our religion today.

Should we counsel people, "Just live your religion. There's no need to get involved in the fight for freedom"? No, we should not, because our stand for freedom is a most basic part of our religion; this stand helped get us to this earth, and our reaction to freedom in this life will have eternal consequences. Man has many duties, but he has no excuse that can compensate for his loss of liberty. (*CR,* Oct. 1966, 122)

ILLUSTRATIONS FOR OUR TIME

A Personal Credo. We see repeatedly the problem of forgetting our God and thus making ourselves more vulnerable to the evil one. We need an individual title of liberty, a mission statement of what we believe. We then need to set goals for carrying out our mission statement. Think of Abraham Lincoln's personal creed:

I believe in God, the Almighty Ruler of nations, our great and good merciful Maker, our Father in heaven, who notes the fall of a sparrow and numbers the hairs on our heads. I recognize the sublime truth announced in the Holy Scriptures and proved by all history that those nations are blessed whose God is the Lord. I believe that the will of God prevails. Without him, all human reliance is vain. With that assistance I cannot fall. I have a solemn vow registered in heaven to finish the work I am in, in full view of my responsibility to God, with malice toward none; with charity for all; with firmness in the right, as God gives me to see the right.

Mahatma Gandhi wrote his resolution for life:

Let then our first act every morning be to make the following resolve for the day:
I shall not fear anyone on earth.
I shall fear only God.
I shall not bear ill toward anyone.

I shall not submit to injustice from anyone.
I shall conquer untruth by truth.
And in resisting untruth I shall put up with all suffering.

These great leaders from the past lived what they believed and made a big difference in the lives of countless individuals. Take the time to write down your values and standards for your life. Look to the scriptures and counsel from prophets. Reflect upon these and your personal goals, and merge them together into a comprehensive statement so you will have a plan to follow our Savior and enjoy the blessings of exaltation. (Pinegar)

Likening the Scriptures to Our Lives

Alma 46:12—Moroni rent his coat and wrote on it, "In memory of our God, our religion, and freedom, and our peace, our wives, and our children." This was a title of liberty to which the people rallied.

Application—We can make an inviolable commitment to meet the challenges of life head-on with courage and in keeping with covenant principles of righteousness. To prepare ourselves for all eventualities and help translate our gospel values into action, we can write mission statements, creeds, and blueprints (our own title of liberty) to establish and clarify our goals in life. When goals and purposes are established and people agree to them, there is unity in the cause and it will be much easier to stay the course without veering to the right or left because of societal distractions.

3. A CONTRAST OF CAUSES: DECEPTION AND FRAUD VERSUS DEVOTION AND FAITH

THEME. Mormon reminds us in the midst of his account: "Yea, and we also see the great wickedness one very wicked man can cause to take place among the children of men" (Alma 5:9). We of the twentieth century are well aware of the truth of this statement, for we have lived through the horrendous consequences of tyrannical dominance imposed by evil men upon countless millions of human beings. But tyranny is not indomitable. The light of the gospel, illuminating the hearts and motivations of devoted sons and daughters of God, can cause tyranny to dissipate beneath the inexorable onward force of God's plan.

> *"Now these dissenters, having the same instruction and the same information of the Nephites, yea, having been instructed in the same knowledge of the Lord, nevertheless, it is strange to relate, not long after their dissensions they became more hardened and impenitent, and more wild, wicked and ferocious than the Lamanites—drinking in with the traditions of the Lamanites; giving way to indolence, and all manner of lasciviousness; yea, entirely forgetting the Lord their God" (Alma 47:36).*

MOMENT OF TRUTH. In a telling comparison, Mormon shows the contrast between the vile and fraudulent Amalickiah and the inspiring and noble Moroni—portraits of suffocating darkness versus dazzling light cast against the canvass of epic events. The apostate Nephites, those who had dissented from the Church, have now joined forces with the Lamanites. They are more hardened and wicked than even the Lamanites. Amalickiah conspires to become the king over all the Lamanites. He incites them to battle against the Nephites to bring about his wicked agenda. Like all hardened apostates, the contenders against the faith cannot leave the Church alone, for their leader is now the devil himself. For a time, the innovative Moroni is able to repulse the invaders through stratagem and impressive advance preparations. Even in the midst of contention and attacks, the people of God are able to preserve their safety and dignity: "there never was a happier time among the people of Nephi, since the days of Nephi, than in the days of Moroni" (Alma 50:23).

MODERN PROPHETS SPEAK

Joseph Smith:

> After a man has sinned against the Holy Ghost, there is no repentance for him. He has got to say that the sun does not shine while he sees it; he has got to deny Jesus Christ when the heavens have been opened unto him, and to deny the plan of salvation with his eyes open to the truth of it; and from that time he begins to be an enemy. This is the case with many apostates of The Church of Jesus Christ of Latter-day Saints.

> When a man begins to be an enemy to this work, he hunts me, he seeks to kill me, and never ceases to thirst for my blood. He gets the spirit of the devil—the same spirit that they had who crucified the Lord of life—the same spirit that sins against the Holy Ghost. You cannot save such persons; you cannot bring them to repentance; they make open war, like the devil, and awful is the consequence. (*Discourses of the Prophet Joseph Smith,* comp. Alma P. Burton [Salt Lake City: Deseret Book, 1977], 222)

ILLUSTRATIONS FOR OUR TIME

The Hearts of Men Are Tested during Trying Times. In the early days of the Church, there were trying times. The apostates seemed to be the ones who would continually persecute the Saints and in particular the Prophet Joseph. When something would go wrong, it was convenient for the apostates to blame the Prophet to the point of physical abuse and even martyrdom. Such was the case when the Kirtland Safety Society failed.

Joseph Fielding Smith:

> When the national crash came most of the brethren were swept into the financial vortex. Many of those who lost their means in this panic, and who had subscribed for stock in the Kirtland Society, laid the blame for their loss at the door of the Prophet Joseph Smith. The fact is that he had warned them of these dangers, but they had turned a deaf ear to all his pleadings. Now that the crash had come they became bitter in their souls and we find men who had stood in the councils of the Church, who had witnessed the visions of angels and had in apparent humility pledged themselves to give all to the building up of the kingdom of God, now turning away in bitterness and their love for the Prophet and those who loyally stood by him, turned to hate. The Prophet said it seemed "as though all the powers of earth and hell were combining their influence in an especial manner to overthrow the Church at once, and make a final end." Enemies not in the Church aided these apostates and united with them in various schemes to overthrow the Prophet looking upon him as the cause of all the evils that had come upon them. This apostasy found its way into all of the councils of the Church. (*Church History and Modern Revelation,* 4 vols. [Salt Lake City: The Church of Jesus Christ of Latter-day Saints, 1946–1949], 3:92)

Likening the Scriptures to Our Lives

Alma 48:11–13,17–19—Moroni was a mighty man. He had a perfect understanding, he rejoiced in liberty and freedom, his heart was full of thanksgiving to God, he labored for the welfare of his people, he had faith in Christ, and he had sworn with an oath to defend his people. If all men had been like unto him the powers of hell would have been shaken forever. He was like Ammon and his brothers, Alma and his sons, including Helaman and his brethren, who were all men of God.

Application—We have exemplary models we can follow. We have examples of righteousness from the scriptures and from our living prophets today. We too should be examples to all mankind (see 3 Ne. 12:16).

4. WICKEDNESS AS THE SEEDBED OF TURMOIL

THEME. Where there is internal division, the body politic cannot stand with enduring strength. Victory over the forces of evil requires unity of the faith and diligence in keeping the commandments of God.

> *"And now it came to pass that, as soon as Amalickiah had obtained the kingdom he began to inspire the hearts of the Lamanites against the people of Nephi; yea, he did appoint men to speak unto the Lamanites from their towers, against the Nephites" (Alma 48:1).*

"And thus we see how merciful and just are all the dealings of the Lord, to the fulfilling of all his words unto the children of men; yea, we can behold that his words are verified, even at this time, which he spake unto Lehi, saying: Blessed art thou and thy children; and they shall be blessed, inasmuch as they shall keep my commandments they shall prosper in the land. But remember, inasmuch as they will not keep my commandments they shall be cut off from the presence of the Lord" (Alma 50:19–20).

"But behold, this was a critical time for such contentions to be among the people of Nephi; for behold, Amalickiah had again stirred up the hearts of the people of the Lamanites against the people of the Nephites, and he was gathering together soldiers from all parts of his land, and arming them, and preparing for war with all diligence; for he had sworn to drink the blood of Moroni" (Alma 51:9).

"For it was his first care to put an end to such contentions and dissensions among the people; for behold, this had been hitherto a cause of all their destruction. And it came to pass that it was granted according to the voice of the people" (Alma 51:16).

MOMENT OF TRUTH. The relentless Lamanites and Amalickiahites continue their campaign against the Nephites. Moroni and the Nephites had prepared well for war. Because of their fidelity to the principles of righteousness, they prosper for a time, largely because Moroni's defensive strategy proved so effective. However, internal strife and wickedness brought about through the insurrection of the king-men weaken the Nephites, and they lose many cities to the enemy. Moroni and his armies regroup and recover some of their cities.

MODERN PROPHETS SPEAK

Russell M. Nelson:

> We must realize that we are at war. The war began before the world was, and it will continue. The forces of the adversary are extant upon the earth. All of our virtuous motives, if transmitted only by inertia and timidity, are no match for the resolute wickedness of those who oppose us. (*The Power within Us* [Salt Lake City: Deseret Book, 1988], 99)

ILLUSTRATIONS FOR OUR TIME

In Defense of Righteousness. We are at war as individuals with Satan and his hosts, who seek to make us miserable like unto themselves. This war began in premortal life and continues here upon the earth. We must defend ourselves against Satan's temptations. Here is a strategic plan that can help:

1. Put on the armor of Christ.

   "Wherefore, lift up your hearts and rejoice, and gird up your loins, and take upon you my whole armor, that ye may be able to withstand the evil day, having done all, that ye may be able to stand. Stand, therefore, having your loins girt about with truth, having on the breastplate of righteousness, and your feet shod with the preparation of the gospel of peace, which I have sent mine angels to commit unto you; Taking the shield of faith wherewith ye shall be able to quench all the fiery darts of the wicked; And take the helmet of salvation, and the sword of my Spirit, which I will pour out upon you, and my word which I reveal unto you, and be agreed as touching all things whatsoever ye ask of me, and be faithful until I come, and ye shall be caught up, that where I am ye shall be also. Amen" (D&C 27:15–18; see Eph. 6:11–18).

2. Exercise Righteousness.

   Keep the commandments and you will always have His Spirit to be with you (see Moro. 4:3). The Spirit will show you all things to do (see 2 Ne. 32:5), even to the point of anticipating where evil will attack (see Alma 43:24).

3. Keep your desires pure.

   Desire to serve God with all your heart, might, mind, and strength (see D&C 4:2) and with an eye single to His glory (see D&C 88:67).

4. Remain committed to a righteous cause (see Alma 43:45–46).

5. Search and feast upon the word.

   We can hold to the rod of iron, stay on the narrow path, and overcome temptation (see 1 Ne. 15:24; Hel. 3:29).

6. Pray to overcome and avoid temptation (see 3 Ne. 18:18).

   The Lord will help us and give us strength (see Ether 12:27) as we defend ourselves. (Pinegar)

Likening the Scriptures to Our Lives

Alma 50:1—Moroni did not stop making preparations to defend his people against the Lamanites.

Application—There is a war going on for the souls of all mankind. We must never let up in our righteous preparations and resistance of evil.

SUMMARY

For each of us there is the continual opportunity to raise our own title of liberty in defense of our families and our freedoms. At every turn we can discern a contrast of causes: deception and fraud on the one hand, and devotion and valor on the other. We can plant our seeds of faith firmly in covenant soil and nurture of a harvest of righteousness and peace. Or we can choose to invest our mortality in the soil of wickedness as the seedbed of turmoil and destruction. The Book of Mormon offers a clear choice, with endless variations on the ultimate consequences, whether spiritual liberty or spiritual death.

CHAPTER THIRTY-TWO

"THEY DID OBEY . . . EVERY WORD OF COMMAND WITH EXACTNESS"

ALMA 53–63

"Latter-day Saints are instructed by the Lord to bring up their children 'in light and truth.' (D&C 93:40.) This phrase is most significant. Truth embraces knowledge. The Prophet defined it as 'knowledge of things as they are, and as they were, and as they are to come. . . .' (D&C 93:24.) These are the great truths that the gospel teaches. Light connotes forsaking of evil. Therefore, to bring up children in light and truth we must teach them the word of God and inspire them to forsake evil.

"When children reach maturity they usually reflect in their lives what their parents taught them. This is illustrated in the tribute paid to their mothers by the 2,000 young men referred to in the Book of Mormon as the sons of Helaman. . . .

"Without a knowledge of the word of God, these noble mothers never could have built into their sons such an abiding conviction that 'if they did not doubt, God would deliver them'; and neither could they have inspired in their sons an unshakable faith that their mothers knew what they were talking about."
—MARION G. ROMNEY, LEARNING FOR THE ETERNITIES [SALT LAKE CITY: DESERET BOOK, 1977], 123–24.

THEMES *for* LIVING

Honoring our Covenants with the Lord
Faith in God: Doubt Not, Fear Not
Charity and Meekness Overcome Misunderstandings

INTRODUCTION

The story of the stripling warriors, the sons of Helaman, is legendary in the Church. These young men full of faith, having been taught by their mothers, were courageous and indomitable in battle. They would lay down their lives for the higher cause if necessary—but the Lord did preserve them. They became the rallying cry and energy that enabled Moroni and his generals to redeem the land eventually from the scourge of invading Lamanites and the cancerous influence of internal rebellion. We may be a strength to church and country if we similarly honor our covenants in faith.

1. HONORING OUR COVENANTS WITH THE LORD

THEME. The bonds between Heavenly Father and His children are always sealed and confirmed by covenants. Zion is a covenant society. Honor and dignity attend the covenant promises made in the name of Christ and perpetuated through obedience and integrity. There is no greater legacy than an uninterrupted chain of honored covenants that illuminate the lives of God's people; there is no greater hope in life than the hope of covenants fulfilled and the bestowal of blessings from on high in answer to covenant valor.

> *"But behold, as they were about to take their weapons of war, they were overpowered by the persuasions of Helaman and his brethren, for they were about to break the oath which they had made. And Helaman feared lest by so doing they should lose their souls; therefore all those who had entered into this covenant were compelled to behold their brethren wade through their afflictions, in their dangerous circumstances at this time. But behold, it came to pass they had many sons, who had not entered into a covenant that they would not take their weapons of war to defend themselves against their enemies; therefore they did assemble themselves together at this time, as many as were able to take up arms, and they called themselves Nephites. And they entered into a covenant to fight for the liberty of the Nephites, yea, to protect the land unto the laying down of their lives; yea, even they covenanted that they never would give up their liberty, but they would fight in all cases to protect the Nephites and themselves from bondage" (Alma 53:11–17).*

MOMENT OF TRUTH. The converted Lamanites of Jershon, known as Ammonites, those who were the harvest of missionary labors by the sons of Mosiah, had made a solemn covenant never again to take up arms. However, because of the dire straits in which the Nephite nation found itself as a result of encroachments by the warring Lamanites, the Ammonites are about to relinquish their oath and join in the fray. Helaman encourages them to keep their covenant. The young Ammonites, who were not a party to the oath of nonaggression, desire to fight for the freedom of all the Nephites. They enter into a covenant to fight for liberty and right even unto laying down their lives if necessary. Their majestic and noble initiative proves to be the tipping point in the fight for justice.

MODERN PROPHETS SPEAK

Joseph Smith:

> And may God enable us to perform our vows and covenants with each other, in all fidelity and righteousness before Him, that our influence may be felt among the nations of the earth, in mighty power, even to rend the kingdoms of darkness asunder, and triumph over priestcraft and spiritual wickedness in high places, and break in pieces all kingdoms that are opposed to the kingdom of Christ, and spread the light and truth of the everlasting Gospel from the rivers to the ends of the earth. (*HC* 2:375)

ILLUSTRATIONS FOR OUR TIME

"Promises Fulfilled."

Stella Oaks:

> We were living in Twin Falls, Idaho, at the time of my husband's death. I had the serious concern of my ability to meet the needs of our three children, Dallin, aged seven, Merrill, three and a half, and Evelyn, fourteen months. I wondered how I would even be able to drive the car 250 miles in the move back to Utah County. How would I be able to earn enough to educate the children as Lloyd and I had planned? Then there was the problem of making the adjustment back to a career of teaching when all my dreams, expectations, and careful preparations were geared to the rearing of a large family and my role as a wife. I knew I could not perform my responsibilities alone, but my spirit was disciplined to covenant with the Lord. I would do all things he desired of me. This decision was also helped by the phrase my husband had uttered so many times during our family prayers: "We dedicate all our time, talents, and energies to Thy service." I felt sealed within this promise.
>
> But it takes great spiritual effort to walk constantly by faith, and I had much learning to do as I was trying to meet the demands of daily survival and decision making. The words of my blessing came vividly to my consciousness: "Cry unto the Lord and he will hear thee and what seemeth a mountain shall become a molehill because of thy faith and integrity."

Several distinct blessings came to me at that very time of communion with the Lord. I was able to drive the car back to Utah with great ease; previously I had not driven farther than Burley, some forty miles away. Contrary to my former needs, I was now able to feel completely invigorated after only five to six hours' sleep. My Father in Heaven had also blessed me with three choice spirits to raise, and I discovered in them a strong sense of our family mission. They were equally dedicated to the goal of a happy, cooperative home. Another great blessing was the arrival of an unexpected insurance policy, which enabled me to pay off my husband's medical school expenses.

Before leaving to take up my new life and doubled parental responsibility, I sought a blessing from our stake patriarch, L. G. Kirkman, who promised me specific blessings. I was promised, depending on my faith, that my children would be able to have all the education they would desire. I was promised the strength to maintain a strong united home. I was also told that I would be able to make a personal contribution in both my profession and in my community. Let me explain the fascinating ways these promises have been fulfilled to the letter.

In his senior year at Brigham Young University, Dallin came home one day to tell me that he had been awarded the first University of Chicago Law School scholarship ever to be awarded to a BYU student. I was overjoyed and thought back to the blessing I had received fourteen years before. On another occasion the blessing was brought back to my mind when late one afternoon I arrived home from the school board office and found a letter addressed to my son Merrill. He opened it later in the evening and we were thrilled to discover that he had been granted a scholarship from the National Health Foundation, providing his fees for a full medical school education. He was accepted at five medical schools. I later discovered that this was their only scholarship awarded in Utah. As Evelyn was beginning college, she received the highly competitive Elks scholarship, providing her with books and tuition fees for the duration of her undergraduate degree. Later she was awarded a scholarship from the BYU College of Family Living, which enabled her to attend the Merrill Palmer College of Family Living in Detroit. (*Remarkable Stories from the Lives of Latter-day Saint Women,* comp. Leon R. Hartshorn, 2 vols. [Salt Lake City: Deseret Book, 1973–75], 2:185–86)

Likening the Scriptures to Our Lives

Alma 53:20–21—The sons of Helaman were taught to keep the commandments and to walk uprightly before the Lord. They were serious minded (sober minded) and were courageous and kept their covenants.

Application—The greatest thing we can ever do is to teach the word so that others might increase in their faith in the Lord Jesus Christ. Teachers (parents, and all who teach), arise—the next generation is dependent upon you!

2. FAITH IN GOD: DOUBT NOT, FEAR NOT

THEME. The legacy of faith as taught by devoted parents—and especially through the nurturing guidance of mothers—yields a harvest of valor and courage in the lives of grateful and obedient children of Zion.

> *"Now they never had fought, yet they did not fear death; and they did think more upon the liberty of their fathers than they did upon their lives; yea, they had been taught by their mothers, that if they did not doubt, God would deliver them. And they rehearsed unto me the words of their mothers, saying: We do not doubt our mothers knew it" (Alma 56:47–48).*

MOMENT OF TRUTH. Two great theaters of military action are established to protect the Nephite nation from the invading hordes: one of them under the control of Captain Moroni and his troops, and the other one led by Helaman with the help of his little army of 2,000 (eventually 2,060) stripling warriors from the Ammonite colony. The strategic mastery and indomitable courage of these generals and their colleagues would eventually carry the day and reestablish peace in the land, but not before an enormous price is paid in casualties and societal upheavals. Amid clashing armies and internal insurrection is the inextinguishable glow of glory associated with the sons of Helaman, who exercise great faith as they rise to the challenge of securing the liberty and rights of their people. Because they had been taught so well by their mothers, they loved liberty and truth more than their own lives. Their faith, which had power to dispel doubt and fear, was so strong that they knew the Lord would deliver them. Even though all of them, to a man, are wounded in battle, some severely, not a single one succumbs to the blows of the enemy.

MODERN PROPHETS SPEAK

George Albert Smith:

> I wonder sometimes as I see mothers leaving their children to the care of somebody else, seeking the social privileges of life, how many of them have read the story of the 2,060 sons of Helaman. I want to say to the mothers of this Church, if they will do their duty, they hold in their hands a power for righteousness and an uplift for a race of people not yet born, that will have something more to do than we have yet done, and it will take giants all their time to do it. So, I say, along with love, along with ten-

derness, along with charity and kindness to your associates, teach your daughters that are soon to become the mothers of men, what a power is placed in their keeping, and how they may exercise it to bless the world. (*Millennial Star,* 95:173).

ILLUSTRATIONS FOR OUR TIME

The Faith of a Child. The great faith of children responds readily to their parents' open demonstration of faith. President James E. Faust cites the tender comfort he received from his grandmother one night—with her assurance that Jesus was watching over them—as the "first cornerstone" of a testimony "forged by a lifetime of experiences" ("A Growing Testimony," *Ensign,* Nov. 2000, 53). President Hinckley similarly looks back to a blessing his father gave him for an earache as "the earliest instance of which I have recollection of spiritual feelings" ("My Testimony," *Ensign,* May 2000, 70). How important it is for parents to worthily instill such depth of faith and testimony!

Prior to each school year I would give my children a blessing. When special problems or concerns arose they would ask for a blessing, especially if they were sick. Brett, our little kindergarten boy, wasn't feeling so well one day. He said, "Daddy, I need a prayer [a blessing]." He had watched the other children receive their blessings for school. That night I gave him a blessing before bed. He slept peacefully through the night and in the morning was up for scripture time with the family. Kristi remarked, "Brett, I thought you were sick." He replied, "Didn't you know Daddy gave me a blessing . . . I have to be well." Oh, the faith of a child! (Pinegar)

Likening the Scriptures to Our Lives

Alma 56:47–48—The sons of Helaman did not fear death. They doubted not because they were full of faith, just as their mothers had taught them.

Application—Let us do all we can to increase our faith and the faith of others (see Luke 17:5; 22:32). Faith overpowers doubt and fear. All things can be done in faith (see Ether 12).

3. CHARITY AND MEEKNESS OVERCOME MISUNDERSTANDINGS

THEME. In all great campaigns to advance the cause of liberty and righteousness, leaders motivated by nobility of purpose and grandness of heart overcome misunderstanding and dissension through openness, charity, meekness, and a willingness to follow the guidance of the Almighty. Inspired unity brings strength; keeping an eye single to the glory of God—rather than succumbing to egocentric interests—fosters fellowship in building the kingdom of God.

"And now behold, I say unto you, I fear exceedingly that the judgments of God will come upon this people, because of their exceeding slothfulness, yea, even the slothfulness of our government, and their exceedingly great neglect towards their brethren, yea, towards those who have been slain. . . . But why should I say much concerning this matter? For we know not but what ye yourselves are seeking for authority. We know not but what ye are also traitors to your country. Or is it that ye have neglected us because ye are in the heart of our country and ye are surrounded by security, that ye do not cause food to be sent unto us, and also men to strengthen our armies? Have ye forgotten the commandments of the Lord your God? Yea, have ye forgotten the captivity of our fathers? Have ye forgotten the many times we have been delivered out of the hands of our enemies? Or do ye suppose that the Lord will still deliver us, while we sit upon our thrones and do not make use of the means which the Lord has provided for us? Yea, will ye sit in idleness while ye are surrounded with thousands of those, yea, and tens of thousands, who do also sit in idleness, while there are thousands round about in the borders of the land who are falling by the sword, yea, wounded and bleeding? Do ye suppose that God will look upon you as guiltless while ye sit still and behold these things? Behold I say unto you, Nay. Now I would that ye should remember that God has said that the inward vessel shall be cleansed first, and then shall the outer vessel be cleansed also" (Alma 60:14, 18–23).

"I, Pahoran, who am the chief governor of this land, do send these words unto Moroni, the chief captain over the army. Behold, I say unto you, Moroni, that I do not joy in your great afflictions, yea, it grieves my soul. . . . And now, in your epistle you have censured me, but it mattereth not; I am not angry, but do rejoice in the greatness of your heart. I, Pahoran, do not seek for power, save only to retain my judgment-seat that I may preserve the rights and the liberty of my people. My soul standeth fast in that liberty in the which God hath made us free. . . . Gather together whatsoever force ye can upon your march hither, and we will go speedily against those dissenters, in the strength of our God according to the faith which is in us" (Alma 61:2, 9, 17).

"And now it came to pass that when Moroni had received this epistle his heart did take courage, and was filled with exceedingly great joy because of the faithfulness of Pahoran, that he was not also a traitor to the freedom and cause of his country" (Alma 62:1).

MOMENT OF TRUTH. With supplies dangerously low and troop strength being rapidly depleted, Moroni finds himself in a crisis of survival. Helaman, too, is finding that his margin of safety is dissipating, even though the stripling warriors have provided, for a time, the edge of victory. Why have reinforcements not come from the government in Zarahemla, Helaman asks in his report to Moroni. Moroni has his suspicions, since the Lord has informed him through the Spirit: "If those whom ye have appointed your governors do not repent of their sins and iniquities, ye shall go up to battle against them" (Alma 60:33). In an urgent and candidly direct epistle to Pahoran, governor of the land, Moroni demands immediate support for the armies, lest he return to the capital and compel action through military intervention. Pahoran responds with the startling news that an internal insurrection has deposed the administration and calls on Moroni for recourse against the king-men traitors. The tragic developments in Zarahemla constitute an altogether sad commentary on the consequences of iniquity in high places. Through bold and brilliant maneuvers, Moroni and Pahoran are able to restore the government and ultimately rid the land of enemy influence. We can learn a lifetime of boldness from Moroni's appeal to Pahoran for redress, just as we can learn a lifetime of nobility and pure-heartedness from Pahoran's charitable response.

MODERN PROPHETS SPEAK

Neal A. Maxwell:

> There was an exchange of correspondence between Moroni, the chief captain of the armies, and Pahoran, who was chief judge and governor of the land in a time of great turmoil. (Alma 60–61.) Anxious Moroni did not have all the facts, as is evident in his biting complaint to Pahoran. Pahoran's meek reply is a lesson to us all, as it certainly must have been to Moroni. . . .

> Where individuals have said too much with too little data, meekness plays a very crucial, correcting role in what follows. (*Meek and Lowly* [Salt Lake City: Deseret Book, 1987], 23–25)

ILLUSTRATIONS FOR OUR TIME

"Charity Never Faileth." Just as charity transformed the situation with Moroni and Pahoran into one of amity and cooperation, it is well to remember that the doctrine and principle of charity may defuse many contentious situations. Such was the case in the mission field, where contention, misunderstandings, lack of communication, backbiting, and gossiping probably ruin more days than anything else. We must learn to bridle our tongue, our passions, for contention is of the devil (see 3 Ne. 11:28–29).

It was 10:30 at night, a time when every missionary should be in bed. If the mission president's phone rings at 10:30 at night, something's wrong. The phone rang. I answered and heard the voice of a great zone leader. "Hello, President, I've got a problem. One of the couples is upset with two of the missionaries because something happened that didn't go right, and the bishop's upset now, and I'm the zone leader, and you told me to take care of it, and I don't know what to do. The couple's angry at me, and the elders didn't think they were at fault, and the bishop's ready to call you up. I just don't know what to do."

I said, "Elder, pray tonight, and you call me tomorrow morning at 6:30 and we will counsel together on the things that the Lord would have you do."

Later that night the couple called. "President Pinegar, we want to see you tomorrow morning." I said, "I have a commitment." "No, we have to see you." I asked, "What's the matter?" They responded "These two elders in our ward . . . and you know . . . well they deserve . . . and we want to make sure they understand it now." That was the basic tone of the conversation. Everyone was upset.

The next morning the zone leader called and reported that contention was still rampant. The zone leader asked, "President, what shall I do?"

I said, "Elder, first have a kneeling prayer, then read them Moroni 7:44–48; John 13:34–35, and Matthew 25:40. Then suggest in the spirit of love and charity, 'Let us solve our problem so we can be happy in the service of the Lord.'" Two hours later the phone rang. "President, I just had the greatest day of my life. President, you never grow until you have a challenge. I was just sick to my stomach, but the Spirit of the Lord was so strong. We all cried, we all hugged, we all loved each other. We're going to do it. We made up. Things are right, and, President, the Lord healed us. The Lord healed us." (Pinegar)

Likening the Scriptures to Our Lives

Alma 61:9—Pahoran did not react disapprovingly to Moroni's letter. He loved and trusted Moroni.

Application—Let us emulate the character and disposition of Pahoran. His example of being positive, proactive, and full of charity should remind us to act and do as the Savior would in all situations.

SUMMARY

Lives are stabilized and sanctified when we honor our covenants with the Lord. When we have faith in God, we do not doubt or fear. Moreover, charity and meekness overcome the inevitable misunderstandings that arise at times among family members and associates. What great, God-given patterns of living are put forward and confirmed in the Book of Mormon!

The sons of Helaman demonstrated a deep and abiding faith in the power of the Lord Jesus Christ. This faith came because they were taught by their mothers, and they did not doubt it was true. We, too, can do all things by faith. It is through faith, hope, and charity that we are qualified for the work (see D&C 4:5). Faith, hope, and charity are integrally connected—as we increase in faith by hearing the word (see Rom. 10:17), reinforcing it through prayer (see Hel. 3:35), so likewise we grow in our charity, the pure love of Christ. Pahoran demonstrated this, as it has been demonstrated on countless occasions in our day as well: witness the modern examples utilized for this chapter. All of these examples witness the effects of the balm of Gilead—the comforting influence of the Spirit of God at work in venues of pure and healing love. Surely, charity never faileth. If we truly love God, we will keep the commandments (see John 14:15).

CHAPTER THIRTY-THREE

"A SURE FOUNDATION"

HELAMAN 1–5

"Like the polar star in the heavens, regardless of what the future holds, there stands the Redeemer of the world, the Son of God, certain and sure as the anchor of our immortal lives. He is the rock of our salvation, our strength, our comfort, the very focus of our faith. In sunshine and in shadow we look to Him, and He is there to assure and smile upon us. He is the central focus of our worship."
—GORDON B. HINCKLEY, "WE LOOK TO CHRIST," *ENSIGN*, MAY 2002, 90.

THEMES *for* LIVING

Guarding against Internal Dissension, the Seedbed for Destruction
Zion Flourishes When Pride Is in Check
Pride as a Pitfall to Righteousness
The Doctrine of Remembering

INTRODUCTION

Through the wise and experienced perspective of the prophet-historian Mormon, we here encounter a panoramic vista of vast opposing forces: the inexorable forward thrust of divine power, as contrasted to the halting, corrupting, all-too enticing, and often irrepressible force of pride. There is no doubt about the final outcome, for "the works, and the designs, and the purposes of God cannot be frustrated, neither can they come to naught" (D&C 3:1). But what painful lessons we mortals have to learn before we can proclaim defeat over the seeds of pride and rebellion constantly germinating within our souls. "And thus we may see" is Mormon's frequent editorial signature statement introducing his readers to the obvious truth that only faith, repentance, and compliance with all of the Lord's commandments can make us as little children, eradicating pride from our lives and preparing us to receive the blessings of the Spirit.

The contention and internal strife over who should be the chief judge causes bloodshed and gives rise to the beginning of Kishkumen and his wicked band. They evolve into the notorious Gadianton band of robbers that prove the eventual destruction of the Nephite nation. Nevertheless, through the faithfulness of Helaman and his sons, many are brought into the Church, while others still cannot avoid the effects of pride. Helaman's wonderful teachings as recalled by his sons, Lehi and Nephi, teach us the power of the doctrine of remembering. In the contrasting portraits of pride and humility, rebellion and alignment with God's will, iniquity and righteousness, we see clearly in these pages the lessons we are to remember.

1. GUARDING AGAINST INTERNAL DISSENSION, THE SEEDBED FOR DESTRUCTION

THEME. Contention diverts from spiritual objectives and saps the energy needed for spiritual growth. By way of contrast, peace, unity, and the light of the gospel are the fruits of righteous endeavor and the sure foundation of covenant honor.

> *"Now these are not all the sons of Pahoran (for he had many), but these are they who did contend for the judgment-seat; therefore, they did cause three divisions among the people" (Hel. 1:4).*

> *"But behold, Paanchi, and that part of the people that were desirous that he should be their governor, was exceedingly wroth; therefore, he was about to flatter away those people to rise up in rebellion against their brethren" (Hel. 1:7).*

> *"Therefore, Kishkumen was not known among the people of Nephi, for he was in disguise at the time that he murdered Pahoran. And Kishkumen and his band, who had covenanted*

with him, did mingle themselves among the people, in a manner that they all could not be found; but as many as were found were condemned unto death" (Hel. 1:12).

"And behold, in the end of this book ye shall see that this Gadianton did prove the overthrow, yea, almost the entire destruction of the people of Nephi" (Hel. 2:13).

MOMENT OF TRUTH. The early chapters of Helaman represent a remarkable chronicle of what happens when a society is racked by disunity and political foment. The death of Pahoran, chief judge, opens the way for a heated contention in the land concerning a successor. Some of the sons of Pahoran contend for the judgment seat. Pahoran is elected by the voice of the people; however, his brother Paanchi inspires an insurrection that results in the murder of Pahoran by the secretive Kishkumen as part of an evil conspiracy. Meanwhile, the Lamanites are amassing at the borders of the land with the intent to seize the Nephite strongholds. Because of the political intrigue and rebellion among the Nephites, defenses are lax. The result is predictable: "And it came to pass that because of so much contention and so much difficulty in the government, that they had not kept sufficient guards in the land of Zarahemla; for they had supposed that the Lamanites durst not come into the heart of their lands to attack that great city Zarahemla" (Hel. 1:18). In fact, the city falls to the Lamanite invaders, but not for long. The precipitous enemy thrust into the heart of Zarahemla and the ensuing campaign to take over all of the Nephite cities is quickly thwarted by Moronihah (successor to, and son of, the celebrated Captain Moroni), who, with the preaching help of Nephi and Lehi, retakes the capital and other captured cities to restore peace.

However, the fragile peace is soon disrupted with the rise of Gadianton as leader of the ruthless band of Kishkumen. The conspiracy attempts to murder the newly elected chief judge, Helaman, son of Helaman, but is thwarted when a servant discovers the intruding Kishkumen and stabs him to death. Gadianton and his bloodthirsty band retreat into the wilderness to continue their evil plotting that will send shockwaves over the Nephite landscape for generations and prove to be the virtual undoing of the entire nation, as Mormon notes in his commentary.

MODERN PROPHETS SPEAK

Ezra Taft Benson:

> But, as so often happens, the people rejected the Lord. Pride became commonplace. Dishonesty and immorality were widespread. Secret combinations flourished because, as Helaman tells us, the Gadianton robbers "had seduced the more part of the righteous until they had come down to believe in their works and partake of their spoils." (Helaman

6:38.) "The people began to be distinguished by ranks, according to their riches and their chances for learning." (3 Nephi 6:12.) And "Satan had great power, unto the stirring up of the people to do all manner of iniquity, and to the puffing them up with pride, tempting them to seek for power, and authority, and riches, and the vain things of the world," even as today. (3 Nephi 6:15) (*A Witness and a Warning: A Modern-Day Prophet Testifies of the Book of Mormon* [Salt Lake City: Deseret Book, 1988], 38)

ILLUSTRATIONS FOR OUR TIME

True to Our Values. Lack of unity destroys individual souls, as well as families, wards, stakes, communities, and nations. The Lord reminds us that if we are not one we are not his (see D&C 38:27). If we live a self-deceptive life of hypocrisy, we will not be blessed with the Holy Spirit. We must be true to our values and standards. We must be true to the Lord. Families that have agreed-upon righteous values will be one. There will be no value collisions: "When should I be home? Whom can I date? Is sixteen really the acceptable year to date? Is the homework done? Do I go to seminary? Are family scripture time, family prayer, family council, and family home evening really that important? Is temple worthiness a goal? Should we be married in the temple? Is a mission for every young man?"—and the list of things that we value goes on and on.

My sweetheart and I have five beautiful daughters and three handsome sons (thanks to their mother). One day, while at the dinner table, we were having a lively discussion about life—especially about teenage social life. One lovely daughter who was about fifteen-and-a-half casually mentioned a party that was coming up and that she would be going with a boy. We'll call him John. I casually mentioned that that sounded like a date. She quickly said, "No, it's kinda like a group party." I suggested we talk for a moment, and I reminded her of the things we had taught in our family. The problem was that with five daughters I somehow had not reemphasized the value and standard of dating at sixteen. It was my fault for not being a better teacher. I told her that it would be inappropriate. She was upset and stormed out of the room. For several days it was as if I was invisible—she ignored me and I was praying for guidance on how to handle the disunity.

Finally, I invited her into my room and as she sat there I proceeded to explain to her how I wanted to be a good father and follow the prophet, and I began to cry. I pleaded for her help. The Spirit was magnificent. It brought "oneness." She felt my concern. She, too, began to cry. She blurted out, "Oh, Daddy, I don't want to go to that dumb party." We hugged, and I was so grateful for a righteous daughter. (Pinegar)

Likening the Scriptures to Our Lives

Helaman 1:2, 7, 9–11—Great contention arose over who should become the chief judge. Paanchi sought to overturn the voice of the people, and Kishkumen kills Pahoran.

Application—Let us remember always that contention is of the devil (see 3 Ne. 11:29) and seek for harmony. Unity is required of the Lord: if we are not one we are not His (see D&C 38:27). Agreed-upon values will bring unity to the cause as well as the family.

2. ZION FLOURISHES WHEN PRIDE IS IN CHECK

THEME. The harvest of good fruit is bounteous when the weeds of pride are eradicated. Beware of the seeds of pride concealed below the surface, waiting to germinate.

"Nevertheless Helaman did fill the judgment-seat with justice and equity; yea, he did observe to keep the statutes, and the judgments, and the commandments of God; and he did do that which was right in the sight of God continually; and he did walk after the ways of his father, insomuch that he did prosper in the land" (Hel. 3:20).

"Yea, we see that whosoever will may lay hold upon the word of God, which is quick and powerful, which shall divide asunder all the cunning and the snares and the wiles of the devil, and lead the man of Christ in a strait and narrow course across that everlasting gulf of misery which is prepared to engulf the wicked" (Hel. 3:29).

"And they were lifted up in pride, even to the persecution of many of their brethren. Now this was great evil, which did cause the more humble part of the people to suffer great persecutions, nd to wade through much affliction. Nevertheless they did fast and pray of Christ, unto the filling their souls with joy and consolation, yea even to the purifying and the sancification of their hearts, which sanctification comeh becuse of their yielding their hearts unto God." (Hel. 3:35).

MOMENT OF TRUTH. Helaman's righteous leadership brings about a change in many people and they unite themselves with the Church by the tens of thousands. While some are still lifted up in pride, many hold to the word of God, fast and pray, and are blessed. This period of time constitutes an oasis of reform and a flowering of righteousness across a landscape too often marred by the ugliness of rebellion and war. For a moment in history, the growth of an enlightened and industrious civilization, upheld by principles of liberty and abetted by the preservation of a just peace, extends itself to all parts of the land, even to the vast domain to the north. Mormon emphasizes that he cannot provide but "a hundredth part of the proceedings of this people" (Hel. 3:14), but he does record that Helaman fulfilled his office with honor and raised up his two sons, Nephi and Lehi, "unto the Lord" (Hel. 3:21). Mormon also concludes about this period of time: "Thus we see that the gate of heaven is open unto all, even to those who will believe on the name of Jesus Christ, who is the Son of God" (Hel. 3:28). All of this good news was possible only because the incipient seeds of pride, still quivering just below the surface in some quarters, were being held in check by the power of God and the receptiveness of the hearts of the righteous.

MODERN PROPHETS SPEAK

George Q. Cannon:

> I have learned in my life that when one man is blessed more than his fellows, temptation comes in, pride comes in, and the adversary is apt to suggest to him that he is so much better than his fellowmen. Therefore, if I wanted to have any gifts from the Lord, I never have felt—and I do not think I ever shall, I certainly will not with my present state of feeling—to have these myself, I would like somebody else to have them also. I would not want to be the richest man in the community; I would not want to be the most gifted, the most prominent or the most honored in any respect. I would want others to share in these blessings. Then I would have less fear concerning the effect of them upon myself. When I am blessed I want to see the Latter-day Saints blessed, I want to see the people of God receive the gifts of God, and enjoy them so that we shall all grow, increase and develop together. (*JD,* 22:104)

ILLUSTRATIONS FOR OUR TIME

The Universal Sin. Pride, the universal sin, was the downfall of the Jaredite and Nephite nations. It is our problem, too, as individuals. During the period of time where Helaman the Second was guiding the people, a great many responded in righteousness to the teachings of the gospel, and the Church prospered spiritually; nevertheless, many struggled to one degree or another with pride. This commentary would not be complete without a portion of the masterful discourse on pride by President Ezra Taft Benson, included below.

> Pride is a damning sin in the true sense of that word. It limits or stops progression. (See Alma 12:10–11.) The proud are not easily taught. (See 1 Ne. 15:3, 7–11.) They won't change their minds to accept truths, because to do so implies they have been wrong. Pride adversely affects all our relationships—our relationship with God and His servants, between husband and wife, parent and child, employer and employee, teacher and student, and all mankind. Our degree of pride determines how we treat our God and our brothers and sisters. Christ wants to lift us to where He is. Do we desire to do the same for others? ("Beware of Pride," *Ensign,* May 1989, 4).

Likening Scriptures to Our Lives

Hel.3:35—The humble Nephites fasted and prayed. They became strong in their humility and firm in their faith. They were full of joy. Their hearts were purified and sanctified because they yielded their hearts to God.

Application—We should realize the power of mighty prayer and fasting in our lives. When we pay the price of fasting and prayer the blessings of heaven follow (see Mosiah 27:22; Alma 5:46; Alma 17:3; 3 Nephi 18:18; Alma 13:28).

3. PRIDE AS A PITFALL TO RIGHTEOUSNESS

THEME. Overweening pride and penitent humility cannot exist in the heart at the same time. The Savior taught: "No man can serve two masters: for either he will hate the one, and love the other; or else he will hold to the one, and despise the other. Ye cannot serve God and mammon" (Matt. 6:24).

> *"And it came to pass in the fifty and fourth year there were many dissensions in the church, and there was also a contention among the people, insomuch that there was much bloodshed" (Hel. 4:1).*

> *"And in the fifty and seventh year they did come down against the Nephites to battle, and they did commence the work of death; yea, insomuch that in the fifty and eighth year of the reign of the judges they succeeded in obtaining possession of the land of Zarahemla; yea, and also all the lands, even unto the land which was near the land Bountiful" (Hel. 4:5).*

> *"And it was because of the pride of their hearts, because of their exceeding riches, yea, it was because of their oppression to the poor, withholding their food from the hungry, withholding their clothing from the naked, and smiting their humble brethren upon the cheek, making a mock of that which was sacred, denying the spirit of prophecy and of revelation, murdering, plundering, lying, stealing, committing adultery, rising up in great contentions, and deserting away into the land of Nephi, among the Lamanites" (Hel. 4:12).*

MOMENT OF TRUTH. After a period of spiritual enlightenment and commercial growth among the Nephites, a faction of the people again allow pride to take root in their hearts. Contention among the Nephites results in bloodshed. The dissenters unite with the Lamanites and take the land of Zarahemla once more. Mormon observes: "Now this great loss of the Nephites, and the great slaughter which was among them, would not have happened had it not been for their wickedness and their abomination which was among them; yea, and it was among those also who professed to belong to the church of God" (Hel. 4:11). The enormous destruction heaped upon the people evokes a humble realization of their spiritual eclipse, and thus repentance begins to soften the force of pride and rebellion that had overcome them. Once again, they see that their own iniquity has enervated them to the point of collapse "in the space of not many years" (Hel. 4:26). Hence they are able to regroup and regain a portion—but not all—of their lands and cities under the leadership of Moronihah.

MODERN PROPHETS SPEAK

Joseph Fielding Smith:

> As a result of Adam's children hearkening to the voice of Lucifer and following him, *governments were established in the earth which were not under the direction of revelation.* Nor did they hearken to the commandments of the Lord. Men arose and *usurped* the right to rule and reign. They ignored the mandates and the rights and privileges of him whose right it is to rule and reign, and as men spread upon the face of the earth they forgot God.
>
> The result has been wickedness, strife, unrest, and contention, with all their attendant evils. And so we find the world today. *The world is sick* and has been sick during its mortal history, but today we are living in very troublous times. The hearts of men are failing them. Selfishness, unrighteousness, the desire to possess, to take advantage, and withal the fear that accompanies evil are found in the hearts of men. (*Doctrines of Salvation*, 3 vols., ed. Bruce R. McConkie [Salt Lake City: Bookcraft, 1954–1956], 3:314).

ILLUSTRATIONS FOR OUR TIME

The Miracle of Sight. As a young boy I enjoyed astronomy, spending hours outdoors at night observing the stars and planets with my modest though effective 100-power telescope. What a thrill it was to admire the rings of Saturn and the moons of Jupiter with this tool that made the invisible miraculously visible to the eye. What an inspiration it was to explore the craters of the moon many decades before the advent of Apollo and the era of firsthand lunar discovery. To elevate one's sight above the distractions of daily routine and "see" God moving in His majesty is a gift from the Spirit. There is a spiritual telescope of infinitely higher magnification that brings the divine into focus. That inner process of seeing is activated through the Spirit when we respond prayerfully and submit humbly to the invitation to come unto Christ.

The Book of Mormon itself is such a spiritual telescope. In a series of telling statements, Mormon shows how the truth of God's immortal plan of salvation is made apparent through spiritual insight of the highest order: "Thus we may see that the Lord is merciful unto all who will, in the sincerity of their hearts, call upon his holy name. Yea, thus we see that the gate of heaven is open unto all, even to those who will believe on the name of Jesus Christ, who is the Son of God. Yea, we see that whosoever will may lay hold upon the word of God, which is quick and powerful, which shall divide asunder all the cunning and the snares and the wiles of the devil, and lead the man of Christ in a strait and narrow course across that everlasting gulf of misery which is prepared to engulf the wicked—And land their souls, yea, their immortal souls, at the right hand of God in the kingdom of heaven" (Hel. 3:27–30). Elder Henry B. Eyring has pointed out that with such passages Mormon is inviting us to look into his telescope, and to share his spiritually heightened view (see *To Draw Closer to God*, 147–148).

The memorable formula of "thus we see" is echoed a few passages later when Mormon summarizes the painful insights of the Nephites who were forced through extreme suffering to rekindle their spiritual light: "and they saw that they had been a stiffnecked people" (Hel. 4:21); "they saw that their laws had become corrupted" (Hel. 4:22); "they saw that they had become weak" (Hel. 4:24); "they saw that . . . except they should cleave unto the Lord their God they must unavoidably perish" (Hel. 4:25); "they saw that the strength of the Lamanites was as great as their strength, even man for man. And thus had they fallen into this great transgression; yea, thus had they become weak, because of their transgression, in the space of not many years" (Hel. 4:26).

What a profound insight is proffered to anyone enabled to see through the spiritual lens of truth. By studying the Book of Mormon prayerfully, with real intent, with a sincere desire to know the truth, any individual can receive the blessing of spiritual insight whereby the Lord "will manifest the truth of it unto you, by the power of the Holy Ghost. And by the power of the Holy Ghost ye may know the truth of all things" (Moro. 10:4–5). (Allen)

Likening the Scriptures to Our Lives

Hel. 4:12—The Nephites were destroyed because of their pride, exceeding riches, oppression of the poor, smiting their brethren, mocking sacred things, denying the Spirit, murdering, and all manner of wickedness.

Application—We can be destroyed temporally and spiritually through sin. We always place our eternal blessings in jeopardy when we sin; without sincere repentance and enduring obedience, we stand to receive eternal and endless punishment—God's punishment (see D&C 19:4–12).

4. THE DOCTRINE OF REMEMBERING

THEME. From the outset, the Book of Mormon presents itself as a guidebook for the process of "remembering." Moroni, through whose hands the plates last passed, imbued his summary title page with the spirit of remembering: "Which is to show unto the remnant of the House of Israel what great things the Lord hath done for their fathers; and that they may know the covenants of the Lord, that they are not cast off forever—And also to the convincing of the Jew and Gentile that JESUS is the CHRIST, the ETERNAL GOD, manifesting himself unto all nations." Alma taught his son Helaman the doctrine of remembering when he commissioned him to take over the responsibility to keep the plates: "And now, it has hitherto been wisdom in God that these things should be preserved; for behold, they have enlarged the memory of this people, yea, and convinced many of the error of their ways, and brought them to the knowledge of their God unto the salvation of their souls" (Alma 37:8). It is through remembering the mercy of the Lord and honoring our covenants with Him that we realize all spiritual blessings.

> *"For they remembered the words which their father Helaman spake unto them. And these are the words which he spake: Behold, my sons, I desire that ye should remember to keep the commandments of God; and I would that ye should declare unto the people these words. Behold, I have given unto you the names of our first parents who came out of the land of Jerusalem; and this I have done that when you remember your names ye may remember them; and when ye remember them ye may remember their works; and when ye remember their works ye may know how that it is said, and also written, that they were good" (Hel. 5:5–6).*

> *"O remember, remember, my sons, the words which king Benjamin spake unto his people; yea, remember that there is no other way nor means whereby man can be saved, only through the atoning blood of Jesus Christ, who shall come; yea, remember that he cometh to redeem the world" (Hel. 5:9).*

> *"And now, my sons, remember, remember that it is upon the rock of our Redeemer, who is Christ, the Son of God, that ye must build your foundation; that when the devil shall send forth his mighty winds, yea, his shafts in the whirlwind, yea, when all his hail and his mighty storm shall beat upon you, it shall have no power over you to drag you down to the gulf of misery and endless wo, because of the rock upon which ye are built, which is a sure foundation, a foundation whereon if men build they cannot fall" (Hel. 5:12).*

> *"And they did remember his words; and therefore they went forth, keeping the commandments of God, to teach the word of God among all the people of Nephi, beginning at the city Bountiful" (Hel. 5:14).*

MOMENT OF TRUTH. As a new reform movement sweeps the land in the wake of widespread destruction due to pride, arrogance, and material obsession, Helaman's righteous sons Nephi and Lehi remember their father's legacy of wise counsel. They recall that their own names symbolize their forefathers' devoted service and covenant valor. They focus continually on the central truth that Christ is the Rock, the sure foundation to build upon. Nephi and Lehi then go forth and preach the word with great power unto the convincing of thousands of Nephites and Lamanites to embrace the gospel. They even extend their ministry to the land of Nephi, where imprisonment cannot contain them nor restrain their inspired pronouncements. Thousands of Lamanites renounce aggression and join the fold of Saints as a result of the work of these two prophets of God and the outpouring of the Spirit of God.

MODERN PROPHETS SPEAK

Henry B. Eyring:

> How can you and I remember, always, the goodness of God, that we can retain a remission of our sins? The Apostle John recorded what the Savior taught us of a gift of remembrance which comes through the gift of the Holy Ghost: "But the Comforter, which is the Holy Ghost, whom the Father will send in my name, he shall teach you all things, and bring all things to your remembrance, whatsoever I have said unto you." (John 14:26.). . . .

> I pray that we may make the simple choices which will lead us there to dwell with Him. And I pray that we will remember and be grateful for the gift of the Atonement and the gift of the Holy Ghost, which make that journey possible. (*To Draw Closer to God: A Collection of Discourses* [Salt Lake City: Deseret Book, 1997], 76–80).

ILLUSTRATIONS FOR OUR TIME

A Penny in the Shoe. Our spiritual growth begins when we recognize and remember the goodness of God. Until we "confess . . . his hand in all things" (D&C 59:21), we will not progress toward becoming Christlike.

There are many ways to "remember." As a young bishop, I tried to remember to do the things that the Lord would have me do. It seemed like life was full, for I never had time to do everything I wanted to do. My mind would drift to the cares of the world, so to get away from such things, I put a little penny in my shoe. Six years wearing that penny in my shoe helped be ever mindful of the things of the Lord. I also put one word—yes, just one word—in places where I would read and recall: *Remember.* As soon as I viewed that word, I would think, "I must keep Heavenly Father's commandments. I must remember the goodness of God. I must stay on the straight and narrow path." If I but remember—the word, the process, the action. The scriptures use the word *remember* to tell us to get busy, to do what is right. In remembering we become mindful of the love of God: why He does what He does; and that love is the greatest source of all motivation in serving other people.

Those who have been endowed also wear a sacred garment to remember their covenants. The Lord has made covenants with us that we might remember. King Benjamin counseled his people to remember the name they took upon themselves, and to imprint it on their minds. Through baptism we too have taken upon ourselves the name of Jesus Christ. Every Sabbath day, as we partake of the sacrament of our Savior Jesus Christ, we should be in the process of remembering. Let us follow carefully the words we have heard so often, in order that we may do that which we have promised to do:

> O God, the Eternal Father, we ask thee in the name of thy Son, Jesus Christ, to bless and sanctify this bread to the souls of all those who partake of it, that they may eat in *remembrance* of the body of thy Son, and witness unto thee, O God, the Eternal Father, that they are willing to take upon them the name of thy Son and always *remember* him and keep his commandments which he has given them; that they may always have his Spirit to be with them. Amen. (D&C 20:77; italics added) (Pinegar)

Likening the Scriptures to Our Lives

Hel. 5:6, 9, 12, 14— Helaman counsels his sons Nephi and Lehi to remember to keep the commandments. They were to remember their names so that they would emulate the good works of their forebears. Moreover, they were to remember the words of King Benjamin and recall that they could be saved only through the Atonement of our Savior, Jesus Christ.

Application— Let us, too, remember, lest by forgetting we trample under our feet the God of Israel, the Lord Jesus Christ (see Hel. 6:31; 12:2). It is through remembering that we honor our covenants with the Lord every Sabbath day as we partake of the sacrament (see D&C 20:77, 79).

SUMMARY

We cannot be one with ourselves and our God if we are not united to the will of God. Our pride will be swallowed up in our willingness to do His will. Our Rock of salvation is Jesus Christ, our Lord and Savior. He is our sure foundation. These priceless chapters in the Book of Mormon help us to remember in gratitude our eternal debt to the Savior for His matchless Atonement. They help us remember to guard against internal dissension, which is always the seedbed for destruction. They help us remember that Zion flourishes when pride—that gaping pitfall to righteousness—is kept in check. By learning how to "grow up unto the Lord," as did Helaman's sons, Nephi and Lehi (see Hel. 3:21), we as children of our Father in Heaven can enjoy a fuller spiritual view of our pathway home.

CHAPTER THIRTY-FOUR

"HOW COULD YOU HAVE FORGOTTEN YOUR GOD?"

HELAMAN 6–12

"In this land, as well as in other lands, men have forgotten God. They are not worshiping him with all their might, mind, and strength. They are not worshiping him at all. I am speaking now of the general run of mankind. Instead of keeping his commandments they are violating them. More people disregard the commandments than keep them. . . . This rebellion against God—for that is what it is—is not confined to those who do not profess religion or even to belief in the Lord Jesus Christ, for the evil has crept within the borders of the Church itself, and there are many who call themselves Latter-day Saints who are guilty of these offenses."
—JOSEPH FIELDING SMITH, *DOCTRINES OF SALVATION*, 3 VOLS., ED. BRUCE R. MCCONKIE [SALT LAKE CITY: BOOKCRAFT, 1954–1956], 3:25.

THEMES *for* LIVING

Righteousness Brings Blessings of Peace and Prosperity
The Cycle of Pride: The Need for Enduring Vigilance and Repentance
Humility as the Gateway to Redemption and Inner Peace
Why We Sometimes Forget Our God

INTRODUCTION

The law of the harvest—we reap what we sow—is evidenced in these chapters of Helaman. If we are faithful, we receive blessings of peace and prosperity. If we forget our God and become prideful, we lose the Spirit and are left to the influence of Satan, ripening in iniquity. To overcome our pride, we must cultivate a broken heart and a contrite spirit.

1. RIGHTEOUSNESS BRINGS BLESSINGS OF PEACE AND PROSPERITY

THEME. When we learn "to be the humble followers of God and the Lamb" (Hel. 6:5), the Lord blesses us with peace of heart and "the fulness of the earth" (D&C 59:16). Righteousness brings both spiritual prosperity and temporal blessings, though not always in immediate conjunction.

> *"And it came to pass that when the sixty and second year of the reign of the judges had ended, all these things had happened and the Lamanites had become, the more part of them, a righteous people, insomuch that their righteousness did exceed that of the Nephites, because of their firmness and their steadiness in the faith" (Hel. 6:1).*

> *"And it came to pass that many of the Lamanites did come down into the land of Zarahemla, and did declare unto the people of the Nephites the manner of their conversion, and did exhort them to faith and repentance" (Hel. 6:4).*

> *"And behold, there was peace in all the land, insomuch that the Nephites did go into whatsoever part of the land they would, whether among the Nephites or the Lamanites.*

> *And it came to pass that the Lamanites did also go whithersoever they would, whether it were among the Lamanites or among the Nephites; and thus they did have free intercourse one with another, to buy and to sell, and to get gain, according to their desire" (Hel. 6:7–8).*

MOMENT OF TRUTH. As a result of the extraordinary ministry of Lehi and Nephi among the Lamanites, even in the strongholds of the land of Nephi to the south, "the more part of the Lamanites were convinced of them [the miraculous events attending the missionary campaign], because of the greatness of the evidences which they had received" (Hel. 5:50). This efflorescence of peace and righteousness among the Lamanites results in a widespread reformation of the spiritual life of the people: "And they did fellowship one with another, and did rejoice one with another, and did have great joy" (Hel. 6:3). The prosperity of reformed thought and practice extends to the commercial life of the entire land, including the land to the south, called Lehi, and the land to the north, called Mulek after the immigrant son of Zedekiah (Hel. 6:10). There is a tremendous upsurge in the wealth and well-being of the people because they remember the covenants of the Lord.

MODERN PROPHETS SPEAK

Spencer W. Kimball:

> Peace is the fruit of righteousness. It cannot be bought with money, and cannot be traded nor bartered. It must be earned. The wealthy often spend much of their gains in a bid for peace, only to find that it is not for sale. But the poorest as well as the richest may have it in abundance if the total price is paid. Those who abide the laws and live the Christ-like life may have peace and other kindred blessings, principal among which are exaltation and eternal life. They include also blessings for this life. (*The Miracle of Forgiveness* [Salt Lake City: Bookcraft, 1969], 363–64)

ILLUSTRATIONS FOR OUR TIME

The First Fruits of Redemption. "The windows of heaven," referenced in Malachi 3:10, must be very large indeed. Our experience over the years has been without exception that temporal matters can be managed with much greater success when one's tithes and offerings are attended to willingly and promptly. My wife and I rejoice every time we have the opportunity to pay our tithing. We have learned the principle of preparing the tithing check first, because the satisfaction of doing our part to help build the kingdom of God is the most motivating of themes. From the beginning the Lord has made known His respect for His children when we remember to sacrifice on behalf of our covenants: "And Abel, he also brought of the firstlings of his flock and of the fat thereof. And the Lord had respect unto Abel and to his offering" (Gen. 4:4; see also Moses 5:20).

I recall vividly a young schoolteacher who came into the bishop's office to talk with me about the principle of tithing. Having just joined the Church with his family, he was accommodating himself to a new kind of spiritual life with challenging obligations. He expressed a willingness to honor his covenants in every way, but readily confessed that every penny of his earnings was already committed to the demands of family support. I referred him to the famous passage from Malachi about putting the Lord to the test with tithes and offerings to see if He will not open the windows of heaven "and pour you out a blessing, that there shall not be room enough to receive it"; then I asked if he would be willing to follow the Lord's counsel. He paused for a moment, then courageously went ahead and paid his tithing. One week later, he returned to my office with unconcealed excitement to report that an unexpected raise in pay that week had made up the entire difference. He was overjoyed with gratitude to his Heavenly Father. Not many years later, he was called as bishop of that ward.

The principle of our paying to the Lord the firstfruits of our fields (see 2 Chr. 31:5) and the firstlings of our flocks (see Mosiah 2:3) has symbolic significance for our spiritual vitality. Moroni explained it this way: "And the first fruits of repentance is baptism; and baptism cometh by faith unto the fulfilling the commandments; and the fulfilling the commandments bringeth remission of sins" (Moro. 8:25). First things come first in the process of orderly progression and growth. Similarly, the Lord, when he gathers together His faithful, will remember, through grace and charity, first of all, those who willingly honored their covenants of sacrifice and obedience and remembered their promises: "They are Christ's, the first fruits, they who shall descend with him first, and they who are on the earth and in their graves, who are first caught up to meet him; and all this by the voice of the sounding of the trump of the angel of God" (D&C 88:98). What an infinite return on our sacrificial offerings, for our widow's mite yields a harvest of eternal glory in the first fruits of redemption. (Allen)

Likening the Scriptures to Our Lives

Helaman 6:3, 7, 9—The conversion of many Lamanites brought great joy to the members of the Church. They fellowshipped one with another and enjoyed peace throughout the land. They had free interchange of communications and commerce, and both the Lamanites and Nephites enjoyed prosperity.

Application—Agreement on a value system brings unity and peace. It can bring prosperity as an accompanying blessing. When we as a family or group become unified, the synergy produces gratifying results in all phases of life.

2. THE CYCLE OF PRIDE: THE NEED FOR ENDURING VIGILANCE AND REPENTANCE

THEME. Prosperity in worldly things can all too often cloud spiritual vision and cause the people to lapse, in their ease and pride, into disobedience and iniquity.

> *"For behold, the Lord had blessed them so long with the riches of the world that they had not been stirred up to anger, to wars, nor to bloodshed; therefore they began to set their hearts upon their riches; yea, they began to seek to get gain that they might be lifted up one above another; therefore they began to commit secret murders, and to rob and to plunder, that they might get gain" (Hel. 6:17).*

> *"But behold, Satan did stir up the hearts of the more part of the Nephites, insomuch that they did unite with those bands of robbers, and did enter into their covenants and their oaths, that they would protect and preserve one another in whatsoever difficult circumstances they should be placed, that they should not suffer for their murders, and their plunderings, and their stealings" (Hel. 6:21).*

"And thus we see that the Spirit of the Lord began to withdraw from the Nephites, because of the wickedness and the hardness of their hearts" (Hel. 6:35).

"Yea, how could you have given way to the enticing of him who is seeking to hurl away your souls down to everlasting misery and endless wo? O repent ye, repent ye! Why will ye die? Turn ye, turn ye unto the Lord your God. Why has he forsaken you? It is because you have hardened your hearts; yea, ye will not hearken unto the voice of the good shepherd; yea, ye have provoked him to anger against you. And behold, instead of gathering you, except ye will repent, behold, he shall scatter you forth that ye shall become meat for dogs and wild beasts. O, how could you have forgotten your God in the very day that he has delivered you? But behold, it is to get gain, to be praised of men, yea, and that ye might get gold and silver. And ye have set your hearts upon the riches and the vain things of this world, for the which ye do murder, and plunder, and steal, and bear false witness against your neighbor, and do all manner of iniquity" (Hel. 7:16–21).

MOMENT OF TRUTH. The brief period of near universal peace and prosperity in the land is ruptured with a takeover of government leadership by secret conspirators, unleashing a seething epidemic of iniquity, especially among the Nephite population. The evil covenant of Gadianton gains power. The cycle of wickedness and pride begins anew. Satan gets hold of the people's hearts. The Spirit of the Lord is withdrawn (Hel. 6:35). Despite the warnings of the prophets—including righteous Lamanite servants of the Lord—the Nephites largely turn a deaf ear to the word of God and permit the Gadianton plague to envelope the highest circles of government. By contrast, the Lamanites flourish in righteousness and extinguish the secret combinations from their ranks. Mormon invokes "And thus we see"—his rhetorical signature—multiple times in these verses to remind us of the destructive consequences of pride and iniquity. The cycle of human propensities is brought home again and again in the scriptures: humility leads to righteousness and prosperity; ease gives way to pride; the prophets warn and teach; the people suffer the consequences of disobedience (turmoil, wars, destruction, pestilence); they listen and repent; they do the will of God and prosper; then all too often they lapse again. Why can we not learn enduringly to take the high road of obedience?

MODERN PROPHETS SPEAK

Dallin Oaks:
> Pride must be a special challenge in this dispensation, because the Book of Mormon, which was written to the people of our day, contains the most intensive and repetitive teachings about the evils of pride. It identifies pride as the cause of the spiritual and temporal downfall of the people of God. (*Pure in Heart* [Salt Lake City: Bookcraft, 1988], 104)

ILLUSTRATIONS FOR OUR TIME

The Cost of Pride. Andrew C. Skinner outlines an example set forth by C. S. Lewis concerning the devastating effect of pride.

> Satan is the epitome of pride, and it is this fact that is at the core of what Lewis is trying to tell us: "it was through Pride that the devil became the devil" (Lewis, *Mere Christianity,* p. 110). Lewis has also pointed out that "the devil is a liar," just as the above passage in the book of Moses has stated. Thus the ugly truth is made plain: pride and dishonesty go together because those who possess pride are not being honest about their true standing before God and their fellowmen. As Terry Glaspey says in summarizing the views of Lewis: "Pride, at its root, is self-centeredness. It is the desire that everything and everyone revolve around our own perceived needs and wants, the refusal to see things through the eyes of others. Pride is . . . a purely spiritual sin, birthed in Hell itself. It is the sin that made Satan who he is, for he refused to bow to God's rightful authority as Creator. When we are proud, we cut ourselves off from God and from others" (Glaspey, *Not a Tame Lion,* pp. 210–11). (Andrew C. Skinner and Robert L. Millet, *C. S. Lewis, the Man and His Message: An LDS Perspective* [Salt Lake City: Deseret Book, 1999], 45–47)

Likening the Scriptures to Our Lives

Helaman 6:17, 21, 34–35—The Nephites became greedy and sought to be lifted up one above another. Satan stirred their hearts to wickedness, they began to dwindle in unbelief, and thus the Spirit of the Lord withdrew.

Application—The price of wickedness and hardness of heart is a horrible loss—that of the gift of the Holy Ghost. We need this gift for comfort in our trials, direction in our lives, and guidance in all things. When we separate ourselves from God due to our wickedness, we lose the Spirit. Let us live worthy of the Spirit, otherwise we are at the mercy of the devil and susceptible to his temptations.

3. HUMILITY AS THE GATEWAY TO REDEMPTION AND INNER PEACE

THEME. Through the tutorials of suffering and sorrow, we can be moved to humility. The Lord will have us learn eventually (either now or in the hereafter) that every knee shall bow and give glory to God (see D&C 88:104). We will learn that humility is the only way to receive the blessings of God.

"And it came to pass that the people saw that they were about to perish by famine, and they began to remember the Lord their God; and they began to remember the words of Nephi. . . . And it came to pass that the judges did say unto Nephi, according to the words which had been desired. And it came to pass that when Nephi saw that the people had repented and did humble themselves in sackcloth, he cried again unto the Lord, saying: O Lord, behold this people repenteth; and they have swept away the band of Gadianton from amongst them insomuch that they have become extinct, and they have concealed their secret plans in the earth. Now, O Lord, because of this their humility wilt thou turn away thine anger, and let thine anger be appeased in the destruction of those wicked men whom thou hast already destroyed. . . . O Lord, thou didst hearken unto my words when I said, Let there be a famine, that the pestilence of the sword might cease; and I know that thou wilt, even at this time, hearken unto my words, for thou saidst that: If this people repent I will spare them. Yea, O Lord, and thou seest that they have repented, because of the famine and the pestilence and destruction which has come unto them. And now, O Lord, wilt thou turn away thine anger, and try again if they will serve thee? And if so, O Lord, thou canst bless them according to thy words which thou hast said. And it came to pass that in the seventy and sixth year the Lord did turn away his anger from the people, and caused that rain should fall upon the earth, insomuch that it did bring forth her fruit in the season of her fruit. And it came to pass that it did bring forth her grain in the season of her grain. And behold, the people did rejoice and glorify God, and the whole face of the land was filled with rejoicing; and they did no more seek to destroy Nephi, but they did esteem him as a great prophet, and a man of God, having great power and authority given unto him from God" (Hel. 11:7–9, 14–18).

MOMENT OF TRUTH. Nephi, having demonstrated unfailing obedience and valor, is blessed of the Lord to hear words of singular comfort and confirmation: "Blessed art thou, Nephi, for those things which thou hast done; for I have beheld how thou hast with unwearyingness declared the word, which I have given unto thee, unto this people. And thou hast not feared them, and hast not sought thine own life, but hast sought my will, and to keep my commandments. And now, because thou hast done this with such unwearyingness, behold, I will bless thee forever; and I will make thee mighty in word and in deed, in faith and in works; yea, even that all things shall be done unto thee according to thy word, for thou shalt not ask that which is contrary to my will" (Hel. 10:4–5). Nephi is then commanded to give a spiritual ultimatum to the people: they should repent or be destroyed (Hel. 10:14). When the people fail to respond, Nephi invokes the Lord's intervention to inflict a sore famine upon the people. The ensuing suffering brings the people down into the depths of humility once again; therefore, Nephi prays that the Lord will bring rain to the landscape. This miraculous cycle of famine and relief has the desired effect, and the repentant people rejoice in the blessings from heaven. The people uphold

Nephi as a great prophet (Hel. 11:18). However, the stabilizing effect of spiritual rejuvenation is short lived, for the Gadianton influence soon waxes strong once again and suffocates a brief flickering of remembrance among the people.

MODERN PROPHETS SPEAK

Spencer W. Kimball:

> The recognition of guilt should give one a sense of humility, of a "broken heart and a contrite spirit," and bring him to the proverbial "sackcloth and ashes" attitude. This does not mean that one must be servile and self-effacing to the destructive point, but rather one must have an honest desire to right the wrong.

> Whatever our predispositions when influenced by the pride of our hearts, the person convinced of his sin and suffering godly sorrow for it in humility is reduced—or rather in this case elevated—to tears. Thus he expresses anguish for his folly and for the grief it has brought to the innocent. Those who have not been through the experience may not comprehend this reaction, but the spiritual writers with their deep insight understood that there is a healing balm in tears for the humble soul who is reaching toward God. Jeremiah wrote: "Oh that my head were waters, and mine eyes a fountain of tears, that I might weep day and night." (Jeremiah 9:1.) The Psalmist cried in his anguish: "I am weary with my groaning; all the night make I my bed to swim; I water my couch with my tears." (Psalm 6:6.) And again he pleaded: "Turn thee unto me, and have mercy upon me; for I am desolate and afflicted." (Psalm 25:16) (*The Teachings of Spencer W. Kimball*, ed. Edward L. Kimball [Salt Lake City: Bookcraft, 1982], 88–89)

ILLUSTRATIONS FOR OUR TIME

True Humility Brings Repentance and Change. The two following incidents, related by the principal of one of Utah's high schools, illustrate clearly the difference between a repentant and a self-justifying attitude. Two boys had been caught stealing—one had taken some money from another student's locker, and the other had stolen some tools from the manual training department. . . . The boys were called into the office and each one was interviewed separately. The boy who had taken the money was resentful. He said that he was not the only boy in the school who was stealing. Why did not the principal find the others and punish them too? Anyway, he felt that he had a right to take money if a fellow didn't know better than to leave it in a locker that wasn't locked.

The boy who had taken the tools felt altogether different. He was ashamed to think that he would lower himself to the level of a thief. He explained that he knew better than to steal but he had seen the tools lying around, they were just what he needed in doing some work at home, he couldn't afford to buy them, and thinking that perhaps they would never be missed, he took them. When he reached home, he could not make proper explanation to his parents and he was sent back to the school to be disciplined.

The principal was anxious to help both boys—he not only wanted them to finish their schooling—he wanted them to learn one of life's greatest lessons—that honesty is one of the grandest principles in the world. He explained to them that they would have to appear before the teachers of the school, make a statement of the whole affair, and give assurances that such actions would never be repeated.

The boy who had stolen the money flatly refused. He would rather quit school than, as he called it, "be disgraced." The law of the school was enforced and he was asked to withdraw. He left the school with defiance in his soul and with a sort of determination that he would get even with somebody—though he didn't seem to know just who it should be.

Out of the school he found that he had lost the respect of his old comrades, and the new ones who took their places were of a far inferior sort. He soon went from bad to worse until when last heard of he had been sent to the State Industrial School where he might be prevented from committing further crime.

The boy, on the other hand, who had taken the tools agreed to do as the principal required. It was a hard thing to do, of course. In fact, it was the hardest he had ever encountered. He not only was ashamed for what he had done, but how could he ever look those teachers in the face again? But feeling really sorry for the offense, he found courage to take the penalty. He was so manly and frank about it that every one of the teachers, who heard his confession, came to admire him more than ever before. They became his friends and took particular pains to help him find and develop his better self. When he was graduated from the school two years later he was an honor student—respected by every student who knew him. The humility of repentance had led him into a new life. Let us remind ourselves of that beautiful passage in the Doctrine and Covenants, Sec. 112, the tenth verse: "Be thou humble, and the Lord thy God shall lead thee by the hand, and give thee answer to thy prayers" (Adam S. Bennion, *Exceptional Stories from the Lives of Our Apostles,* comp. Leon R. Hartshorn [Salt Lake City: Deseret Book, 1972], 25–26).

Likening the Scriptures to Our Lives

Helaman 11:4, 7, 9—The Nephites were humbled because of the famine. (Oh, how much better it is to be humbled by the word! See Alma 32:14.) They begin to remember the Lord and humble themselves unto repentance.

Application—The virtue of humility brings about a willingness to change. We become easily entreated. We have a relationship with God and depend upon Him for all things. We have a broken heart and contrite spirit. Let us choose to be humbled by the word rather than by external pressures.

4. WHY WE SOMETIMES FORGET OUR GOD

THEME. The Nephites exhibited a trait common to so many of us from time to time: we forget the goodness of God and fail to honor our covenants with full devotion. In this we offend God most grievously (see D&C 59:21).

> *"Yea, and we may see at the very time when he doth prosper his people, yea, in the increase of their fields, their flocks and their herds, and in gold, and in silver, and in all manner of precious things of every kind and art; sparing their lives, and delivering them out of the hands of their enemies; softening the hearts of their enemies that they should not declare wars against them; yea, and in fine, doing all things for the welfare and happiness of his people; yea, then is the time that they do harden their hearts, and do forget the Lord their God, and do trample under their feet the Holy One—yea, and this because of their ease, and their exceedingly great prosperity. And thus we see that except the Lord doth chasten his people with many afflictions, yea, except he doth visit them with death and with terror, and with famine and with all manner of pestilence, they will not remember him" (Hel. 12:2–3).*

MOMENT OF TRUTH. After a brief resurgence of spirituality, the people again begin to fall prey to the culture and practices. The people continue on with their misguided decline in the process of "ripening again for destruction" (Hel. 11:37). It is at this point that Mormon, weary perhaps at the distressing cycle of pride that manifests itself repeatedly in the chronicle of the people, gives vent to the anguish of his soul. He declares: "O how great is the nothingness of the children of men; yea, even they are less than the dust of the earth" (Hel. 12:7). The great prophet-historian expresses in poetic cadence his unmitigated distress over the hard-heartedness of the people after so many witnesses had been proffered them and so many blessings bestowed. Even the dust of the earth moves under God's command, he points out—but mankind, in its iniquity, refuses to move according to the patterns of truth. That is the reason the plan of repentance was initiated: "for this cause, that men might be saved, hath repentance been declared. Therefore, blessed are they who will repent and hearken unto the voice of the Lord their God; for these are they that shall be saved" (Hel. 12:22–23).

MODERN PROPHETS SPEAK

Harold B. Lee:

> It is frightening to observe that in places where there is the greater prosperity, there is the unmistakable evidence that, like the peoples of other dispensations, when they

prosper they forget God. They are seemingly rich in things that money can buy, but they are devoid of most of the precious things money cannot buy. (*The Teachings of Harold B. Lee,* ed. Clyde J. Williams [Salt Lake City: Bookcraft, 1996], 327)

ILLUSTRATIONS FOR OUR TIME

The Winds of God. Mormon, in his stirring recapitulation of the vagrancy and unsteadiness of humankind (Hel. 12:4–26), echoes a theme that King Benjamin taught his people: "Ye cannot say that ye are even as much as the dust of the earth" (Mosiah 2:25). Similarly, Mormon concludes that man in his nothingness is even *less* than the dust of the earth: "For behold, the dust of the earth moveth hither and thither, to the dividing asunder, at the command of our great and everlasting God" (Helaman 12:8; see Mosiah 4:2). By contrast, man, who is made in the image of God, is moved by no such propensity to obedience. Without the warming winds of benign redemption, activated by the softening of hearts and the effects of godly sorrow (2 Cor. 7:10), mankind will be left alone in despair and isolation. Therefore, Mormon prays earnestly: "And may God grant, in his great fulness, that men might be brought unto repentance and good works, that they may be restored unto grace for grace, according to their works. And I would that all men might be saved" (Hel. 12:24–25). (Allen)

Likening the Scriptures to Our Lives

Hel. 12:1–3—The Nephites demonstrated the unsteadiness of the hearts of men. In prosperity they hardened their hearts and forgot their God due to the easiness of the way. Save the Lord chasten His people with all manner of afflictions, they will not remember Him.

Application—It is hard to remember the goodness of God when everything is going well, but at such times it is paramount for us to remember. Every day we must count our blessings and give credit to our Heavenly Father. There is an example wherein the people prospered and never forgot God and did remember His goodness towards them in all things (see Alma 62:49–50). We too should be humble and grateful for all things.

SUMMARY

Righteousness brings blessings of peace and prosperity, while pride, as it cycles through the human condition, unleashes the forces of destruction. Hence there is the need for enduring vigilance and repentance. Impenitence is the primary source of suffering, while humility is the gateway to redemption and inner peace. In the face of such manifest truths, there always remains the question why we sometimes forget our God and need to be reminded, often in forceful ways.

These lessons in Helaman give us direction as to what is expected of us to remember our God, to overcome pride, and to keep our hearts steady concerning the things pertaining to eternal life. We simply cannot allow ourselves to forget the goodness of God in our lives at any time. Let us always remember Him—just as we have covenanted to do—and keep His commandments.

CHAPTER THIRTY-FIVE

"REPENT *and* TURN TO THE LORD"

HELAMAN 13–16

"The great and dreadful day of the Lord is near at hand. In preparation for this great event and as a means of escaping the impending judgments, inspired messengers have gone forth to the nations of the earth carrying this testimony and warning.

"The nations of the earth continue in their sinful and unrighteous ways. The unbounded knowledge with which men have been blessed has been used to destroy mankind instead of to bless the children of men as the Lord intended. Two great world wars in the past twenty-five years, with fruitless efforts at lasting peace, are solemn evidence that peace has been taken from the earth because of the wickedness of the people. Nations cannot endure in sin. They will be broken up, but the kingdom of God will endure forever.

"Therefore, as a humble servant of the Lord, I call upon the leaders of nations to humble themselves before God, to seek his inspiration and guidance. I call upon rulers and people alike to repent of their evil ways. Turn unto the Lord, seek his forgiveness and unite yourselves in humility with his kingdom. There is no other way.

"If you will do this, your sins will be blotted out, peace will come and remain, and you will become a part of the kingdom of God in preparation for Christ's second coming, which is near at hand. But if you refuse to repent or to accept the testimony of his inspired messengers and unite yourselves with God's kingdom, then the terrible judgments and calamities promised the wicked will be yours."
—EZRA TAFT BENSON, *A LABOR OF LOVE: THE 1946 EUROPEAN MISSION OF EZRA TAFT BENSON* [SALT LAKE CITY: DESERET BOOK, 1989], 244.

THEMES *for* LIVING

The Prophets' Warning Voice: Repent or Be Destroyed
"Salvation Cometh"—Prophets Testify of Christ
The Solemn Choice: Prideful Defiance or Humble Obedience

INTRODUCTION

Like all prophets, Samuel the Lamanite called the people to repentance. They had sought for that which can never be, for they had sought happiness in iniquity (see Hel. 13:38). Samuel prophesied of Christ and His coming. Some believed his words and were baptized, while many were angry and sought his life. Satan had a great hold upon their hearts. Nevertheless, Samuel boldly proclaimed the truth, and when the message given him by an angel of God was fully delivered, he returned to his own Lamanite people to continue his ministry and was never heard of again among the Nephites. However, his intrepid and valiant prophecies still remind us of the continual need for repentance unto a remission of sins through the merits and grace of Jesus Christ.

1. THE PROPHETS' WARNING VOICE: REPENT OR BE DESTROYED

THEME. The Lord's word, bestowed upon the people, can be removed and His Spirit withdrawn if the people persist in iniquity and refuse to repent when warned by the prophets.

> *"Yea, heavy destruction awaiteth this people, and it surely cometh unto this people, and nothing can save this people save it be repentance and faith on the Lord Jesus Christ, who surely shall come into the world, and shall suffer many things and shall be slain for his people" (Hel. 13:6).*

MOMENT OF TRUTH. Despite the Lord's promises to the Nephites that He would bless the penitent and favor those who returned to His pathways, they turn a deaf ear and persist in their iniquities. At the same time, the Lamanites were strictly observing to keep the commandments of God (see Hel. 13:1). So Samuel, the great Lamanite prophet, was sent by the Lord to call the Nephites to repentance. He warns them from the walls of their great city of Zarahemla that if they do not repent they shall be destroyed. Speaking the words taught him by an angel of the Lord, he adjures his listeners to change their iniquitous patterns of living lest the Lord carry out His awesome promise: "Therefore, thus saith the Lord: Because of the hardness of the hearts of the people of the Nephites, except they repent I will take away my word from them, and I will withdraw my Spirit from them" (Hel. 13:8). Samuel attests that it is only for the sake of the remaining righteous that the nation is being spared. "But behold, your days of probation are past; ye have procrastinated the day of your salvation until it is everlastingly too late, and your destruction is made sure; yea, for ye have sought all the days of your lives for that which ye could not obtain; and ye have sought for happiness in doing iniquity, which thing is contrary to the nature of that righteousness which is in our great and Eternal Head" (Hel. 13:38; cf. Alma 41:10).

MODERN PROPHETS SPEAK

Spencer W. Kimball:

> Has the world ever seen a more classic example of indomitable will, of faith and courage than that displayed by Samuel the Prophet: "One of the Lamanites who did observe strictly to keep the commandments of God. . . ." Visualize, if you can, this despised Lamanite standing on the walls of Zarahemla and while arrows and stones were shot at him, crying out to his white accusers that the sword of justice hung over them. So righteous was he that God sent an angel to visit him. His predictions were fulfilled in due time relating to the early coming of Christ, his ministry, death and resurrection, and the eventual destruction of these Nephite people. So great faith had he that the multitudes could not harm him until his message was delivered and so important was his message that subsequently the Savior required a revision of the records to include his prophecies concerning the resurrection of the Saints. (*CR*, Apr.1949, 109).

ILLUSTRATIONS FOR OUR TIME

The Shadow of Iniquity. The theme of "repent or be destroyed" was preached and demonstrated throughout the Book of Mormon. The Jaredites and the Nephites fulfilled the Lord's prophecies given through His prophets in that they did not repent and they were destroyed. The acts of unrighteous individuals not only bring about self-destruction but also destroy the lives of the people they victimize and abuse. (Pinegar)

Likening the Scriptures to Our Lives

Hel. 13:5, 8, 10—The Lord gave Samuel, the Lamanite prophet, the words to speak. Samuel warned the Nephites that the Lord would take away His Spirit if they did not repent. He then prophesied that the Lord would visit them with utter destruction.

Application—All blessings are predicated upon obedience. The doctrine that has been most taught since the beginning of time is repentance. This still holds true today.

2. "SALVATION COMETH"— PROPHETS TESTIFY OF CHRIST

THEME. From the beginning of time, the message of the prophets has centered on

Christ and His redeeming mission. Isaiah proclaimed before Israel: "Behold, thy salvation cometh; behold, his reward is with him, and his work before him" (Isa. 62:11). King Benjamin confirmed, "There is no other name given whereby salvation cometh; therefore, I would that ye should take upon you the name of Christ, all you that have entered into the covenant with God that ye should be obedient unto the end of your lives" (Mosiah 5:8).

> *"And behold, he said unto them: Behold, I give unto you a sign; for five years more cometh, and behold, then cometh the Son of God to redeem all those who shall believe on his name" (Hel. 14:2).*

> *"And it shall come to pass that whosoever shall believe on the Son of God, the same shall have everlasting life" (Hel. 14:8).*

MOMENT OF TRUTH. Samuel makes clear his commission and his purpose: "for this intent have I come up upon the walls of this city, that ye might hear and know of the judgments of God which do await you because of your iniquities, and also that ye might know the conditions of repentance; And also that ye might know of the coming of Jesus Christ, the Son of God, the Father of heaven and of earth, the Creator of all things from the beginning; and that ye might know of the signs of his coming, to the intent that ye might believe on his name. And if ye believe on his name ye will repent of all your sins, that thereby ye may have a remission of them through his merits" (Hel. 14:11–13). Samuel identifies with dramatic clarity the signs that will attend the Savior's birth: a day and a night and a day with continual light, plus the appearance of a brilliant new star and other heavenly manifestations. The signs accompanying His death are also prophesied: three days without light plus great earthquakes and tempests. Upon His glorious resurrection at the end of the three-day period, many are to be resurrected and appear among the people (see Hel. 14:25; cf. Matt. 27:52–53). All of these signs are given, Samuel declares, "that whosoever will believe might be saved, and that whosoever will not believe, a righteous judgment might come upon them" (Hel. 14:29).

MODERN PROPHETS SPEAK

Joseph Fielding Smith:

> Without question we are rapidly approaching the great day of the Lord, that time of "refreshing," when he will come in the clouds of heaven to take vengeance upon the ungodly and prepare the earth for the reign of peace for all those who are willing to abide in his law. It is only just that the Lord would speak again from the heavens, before that great day shall come, and commission his servants and send them forth to

proclaim repentance and once again say to the people, "The kingdom of heaven is at hand." . . . True it is, that the warnings given of old are to be heeded, but near the approach of these great events, it is right, and reason compels us to believe, that the Lord would again raise his voice through his appointed servants in a warning that the people might know that this great and dreadful day is even now at our doors. It is to be a day of peace and joy to the righteous, but a dreadful day to the wicked. (*The Restoration of All Things* [Salt Lake City: Deseret Book, 1973], 302–303)

ILLUSTRATIONS FOR OUR TIME

"He May Be a Man of God."

B. H. Roberts (regarding Parley P. Pratt):

Mrs. Walton expressed her willingness to open her house for Elder Pratt to preach in and proposed to lodge and feed him. Here at last was an opening. He began holding meetings at Mrs. Walton's, and was soon afterwards introduced to the investigation meetings held by Mr. Taylor and his religious friends.

They were delighted with his preaching. He taught them faith in God, and in Jesus Christ; called upon them to repent of their sins and to be baptized in the likeness of Christ's burial, for the remission of them; and promised them the Holy Ghost through the laying on of hands, together with a full enjoyment of all its gifts and blessings. All this, and much more that he taught, was in strict harmony with what they themselves believed; but what he had to say about Joseph Smith and the Book of Mormon perplexed a great many, and some of their members even refused to investigate the Book of Mormon, or examine the claims of Apostle Pratt to having divine authority to preach the gospel and administer in the ordinances thereof.

It was at this juncture that the noble independence and boldness of spirit, so conspicuous in John Taylor throughout his life, asserted itself. He addressed the assembly to the following effect:

> We are here, ostensibly in search of truth. Hitherto we have fully investigated other creeds and doctrines and proven them false. Why should we fear to investigate Mormonism? This gentleman, Mr. Pratt, has brought to us many doctrines that correspond with our own views. We have endured a great deal and made many sacrifices for our religious convictions. We have prayed to God to send us a messenger, if he has a true church on earth. Mr. Pratt has come to us under circumstances that are peculiar; and there is one thing that commends him to our consideration; he has come amongst us without purse

or scrip, as the ancient apostles traveled; and none of us are able to refute his doctrine by scripture or logic. I desire to investigate his doctrines and claims to authority, and shall be very glad if some of my friends will unite with me in this investigation. But if no one will unite with me, be assured I shall make the investigation alone. If I find his religion true, I shall accept it, no matter what the consequences may be; and if false, then I shall expose it.

After this, John Taylor began the investigation of Mormonism in earnest. He wrote down eight sermons which Apostle Pratt preached and compared them with the scripture. He also investigated the evidences of the divine authenticity of the Book of Mormon and the Doctrine and Covenants. "I made a regular business of it for three weeks," he says, "and followed Brother Parley from place to place." The result of his thorough investigation was conviction; and on the 9th of May, 1836, he and his wife were baptized. (*Classic Stories From the Lives of Our Prophets,* comp. Leon R. Hartshorn [Salt Lake City: Deseret Book, 1971], 70–71)

Likening the Scriptures to Our Lives

Hel. 14:29–31—Samuel taught the people that they bring condemnation upon themselves through their own choices. We are free to act for ourselves. The Lord has given us a way to know good from evil (see Moro. 7:16).

Application—We are responsible and accountable for our actions. As we come to realize this, we will hopefully make righteous choices (see 2 Ne. 2:27).

3. THE SOLEMN CHOICE: PRIDEFUL DEFIANCE OR HUMBLE OBEDIENCE

THEME. Because the Lord loves us, He chastens us: "whom I love I also chasten that their sins may be forgiven, for with the chastisement I prepare a way for their deliverance in all things out of temptation, and I have loved you" (D&C 95:1).

"And now, it came to pass that there were many who heard the words of Samuel, the Lamanite, which he spake upon the walls of the city. And as many as believed on his word went forth and sought for Nephi; and when they had come forth and found him they confessed unto him their sins and denied not, desiring that they might be baptized unto the Lord. But as many as there were who did not believe in the words of Samuel were angry with him; and they cast stones at him upon the wall, and also many shot arrows at him as he stood upon the wall; but the Spirit of the Lord was with him, insomuch that they could not hit him with their stones neither with their arrows. Now when they saw that

they could not hit him, there were many more who did believe on his words, insomuch that they went away unto Nephi to be baptized" (Hel. 16:1–3).

MOMENT OF TRUTH. In summary, Samuel reiterates the love of the Lord for His covenant people: "for behold, they have been a chosen people of the Lord; yea, the people of Nephi hath he loved, and also hath he chastened them; yea, in the days of their iniquities hath he chastened them because he loveth them" (Hel. 15:3; cf. Prov. 3:12; Heb. 12:6). Samuel implores the people to emulate the far more righteous Lamanites and to remember the multiple witnesses they have received of the truth of the gospel. "And now behold, saith the Lord, concerning the people of the Nephites: If they will not repent, and observe to do my will, I will utterly destroy them, saith the Lord, because of their unbelief notwithstanding the many mighty works which I have done among them; and as surely as the Lord liveth shall these things be, saith the Lord" (Hel. 15:17). In the wake of these pronouncements some of the people believe Samuel and are baptized, while others harden their hearts even more and attempt to kill him.

MODERN PROPHETS SPEAK

Dallin H. Oaks:

> The prophets who chronicled the wickedest times in Nephite history usually referred to the hardness of the hearts of the people, and to Satan "get[ting] hold upon the hearts of the children of men" (Helaman 6:30; see also Helaman 6:35; 7:15; Mormon 3:12; 4:11). Similarly, the Lord told the Prophet Joseph Smith that Satan "hath put it into [the] hearts" of wicked men to attempt to frustrate the work of the Restoration, and "Satan has great hold upon their hearts; he stirreth them up to iniquity against that which is good" (D&C 10:10, 20). As we read in the Book of Mormon, "Behold, there are many that harden their hearts against the Holy Spirit, that it hath no place in them" (2 Nephi 33:2; see also Alma 12:9–11). (*Pure in Heart* [Salt Lake City: Bookcraft, 1988], 115)

ILLUSTRATIONS FOR OUR TIME

Wrong Way—Do Not Enter. Our next-door neighbor many years ago performed an act of inordinate courage to save the lives of some strangers. He and his wife were driving along a stretch of interstate highway one day when he glanced across the median strip to behold a terrifying sight. There was a car across the way driving parallel to his own car but moving directly into the line of traffic in the opposite lanes. My friend watched with utter horror as trucks and cars swerved to avoid collision with the intruding vehicle driving in the wrong direction along the innermost lane. What to do?

In a split second, my friend had made his decision. He accelerated and looked for the next opportunity to cross over the median. Soon he came to a connecting road and maneuvered quickly toward the opposite lanes of traffic, coming to a screeching halt on the inner shoulder of the opposite lanes. Despite significant dangers to himself, he then ran towards the errant vehicle and flagged it down amid the swerving and dodging vehicles.

Incredibly, the elderly couple whom he forced to stop off to the side of traffic were at first indignant. What business did this stranger have interrupting their trip? Soon they realized, however, that he had surely saved their lives, and they were grateful for the Christian act of charity and deliverance.

This true story is like a modern-day parable of the reactions of the world in nearly all ages to the ministry of the prophets of God. The eternal message is one of warning: the call to repentance, the admonition to heed the word of God and be saved. In modern terms, it is the alarm sounded when one foolishly travels down a one-way street in the wrong direction. So often this warning is met with hardness of heart and with stubborn and prideful rebellion. "What business do you have to tell me I cannot propel myself into the jaws of destruction?" However, the alarm of the prophets is powered by the spirit of charity.

Would we not all do well to choose our bearings in life based on eternal principles, and to observe with care the directions of our journey day-by-day? Should we not accept in the spirit of gratitude and humility the loving though firm entreaties of the prophets of God as they teach us to move faithfully and securely toward a destination of peace and redemption? (Allen)

Likening the Scriptures to Our Lives

Hel. 16:22–23—Satan did stir the people up to contend with one another and to do iniquity. Therefore, he had great hold upon their hearts—and this after they had witnessed all the signs and wonders that had been prophesied.

Application—Signs and wonders are not enough to give belief or cause one to repent. Our hearts must be right. We are to offer a broken heart and a contrite spirit in order to be able to change.

SUMMARY

The clarion words of Samuel surely ring true. If we do not repent we must suffer and even be destroyed. The governing principle is to recognize the Savior in our lives. He has taught us through His prophets to be believing and not harden our hearts. A hardened heart is the sure way to lose the blessings of the Lord in our lives, and Samuel's words are needed today just as they were thousands of years ago. Will we hearken to the words of the prophets of God? They speak His words, and they are the words that, when followed, can lead us to eternal life.

CHAPTER THIRTY-SIX

"ON *the* MORROW COME I INTO *the* WORLD"

3 NEPHI 1–7

"There was no excuse for any of the inhabitants of the New World not to know of the coming of their Messiah. Samuel the Lamanite had prophesied that there would be no darkness during the night of his birth, and the promised sign had now been seen by all. When else was there ever a night when the brightness of noonday prevailed over whole continents from the going down of the sun on one day to its rising on the next?"
—BRUCE R. MCCONKIE, *THE MORTAL MESSIAH: FROM BETHLEHEM TO CALVARY,* 4 VOLS. [SALT LAKE CITY: DESERET BOOK, 1979–1981], 1:347.

THEMES *for* LIVING

Signs of the Savior's Birth
Meeting the Enemy "In the Strength of the Lord"
Avoiding the Slippery Slope of Worldly Pride

INTRODUCTION

The book of Third Nephi begins with the prophesying of Jesus Christ's birth, life, atoning sacrifice, resurrection, and visitation to this the American continent. The signs are given and many believe, yet some hearts are hardened and they fall prey to the devil and his Gadianton robbers. The Nephites prosper in righteousness, but again the cycle of pride is evident from the record.

1. SIGNS OF THE SAVIOR'S BIRTH

THEME. The Lord blesses the world with heralding signs of His ministry and mission in order to help His children prepare for the momentous events of the kingdom.

> *"And it came to pass that the words which came unto Nephi were fulfilled, according as they had been spoken; for behold, at the going down of the sun there was no darkness; and the people began to be astonished because there was no darkness when the night came" (3 Ne. 1:15).*

> *"And it had come to pass, yea, all things, every whit, according to the words of the prophets. And it came to pass also that a new star did appear, according to the word"*
> *(3 Ne. 1:20–21; see Hel. 14:2–7).*

> *"And it came to pass that from this time forth there began to be lyings sent forth among the people, by Satan, to harden their hearts, to the intent that they might not believe in those signs and wonders which they had seen; but notwithstanding these lyings and deceivings the more part of the people did believe, and were converted unto the Lord. And it came to pass that Nephi went forth among the people, and also many others, baptizing unto repentance, in the which there was a great remission of sins. And thus the people began again to have peace in the land" (3 Ne. 1:22–23).*

MOMENT OF TRUTH. The faithful watch earnestly for the fulfillment of the prophecies concerning the birth of the Savior. Their detractors conspire to put the faithful to death in the event the signs are not forthcoming. It is a period of great anxiety. Nephi, son of Nephi, pours out his heart before the Lord "all that day" (3 Ne. 1:12) on behalf of his people. It is then that the extraordinary answer comes: "Lift up your head and be of good cheer; for behold, the time is at hand, and on this night shall the sign be given, and on the morrow come I into the world, to show unto the world that I will fulfil all that which I have caused to be spoken by the mouth of my holy prophets. Behold, I come unto my own, to fulfil all things which I have made known unto the children of men from the foundation of the world, and to do the will, both of the Father and of the

Son—of the Father because of me, and of the Son because of my flesh. And behold, the time is at hand, and this night shall the sign be given" (3 Ne. 1:13–14).

Then there unfolds the sequence of remarkable signs of the birth of the Lord Jesus Christ, including a night without darkness and the appearance of a brilliant new star in the heavens. The "more part of the people" (3 Ne. 1:22) are converted unto the Lord, yet Satan sends forth an undercurrent of lies to counteract the powerful effect of the signs given of the Savior's birth. The deceit of the evil one continues to have an influence on the people.

MODERN PROPHETS SPEAK

Boyd K. Packer:

> We live in troubled times—very troubled times. We hope, we pray, for better days. But that is not to be. The prophecies tell us that. We will not as a people, as families, or as individuals be exempt from the trials to come. No one will be spared the trials common to home and family, work, disappointment, grief, health, aging, ultimately death. ("The Cloven Tongues of Fire," *Ensign,* May 2000, 8).

ILLUSTRATIONS FOR OUR TIME

Imagine the joy of seeing the prophesied sign of the Lord Jesus Christ's birth. And yet some would still not believe, though they'd seen the signs of His birth (see 3 Ne. 1:22). In Moses' day, the Egyptians had the same problem after witnessing signs: "And it shall come to pass, if they will not believe thee, neither hearken to the voice of the first sign, that they will believe the voice of the latter sign. And it shall come to pass, if they will not believe also these two signs, neither hearken unto thy voice, that thou shalt take of the water of the river, and pour it upon the dry land: and the water which thou takest out of the river shall become blood upon the dry land" (Ex. 4:8–9).

Faith, not signs, brings true change. Change occurs within the heart and is not due to external signs. We should not seek signs to believe, for they will follow those with faith (see D&C 63:7–12). President Joseph F. Smith cautioned, "Show me Latter-day Saints who have to feed upon miracles, signs and visions in order to keep them steadfast in the Church, and I will show you members of the Church who are not in good standing before God, and who are walking in slippery paths. It is not by marvelous manifestations unto us that we shall be established in the truth, but it is by humility and faithful obedience to the commandments and laws of God" (*Gospel Doctrine: Selections from the Sermons and Writings of Joseph F. Smith,* comp. John A. Widstoe [Salt Lake City: Deseret Book, 1919], 7). As President Kimball's title teaches us, faith *precedes* the miracle. Faith adds meaning to the miracle. (Pinegar)

Likening the Scriptures to Our Lives

3 Nephi 1:12–13—Nephi, having prayed mightily, received an answer to his prayer. The Lord spoke to him and told him that on the morrow the sign would be given concerning His birth and that He would fulfill all the prophecies He had caused His prophets to give.

Application—Revelations are usually given because we ask with a sincere heart with faith in mighty prayer. The Lord is no respecter of persons and each of us has this right. Let us always remember that He speaks to us through His living prophets. Their words will be fulfilled as if spoken by the Lord Himself (see D&C 1:38; 21:4–6).

2. MEETING THE ENEMY "IN THE STRENGTH OF THE LORD"

THEME. When we forsake iniquity and rise up in majesty against the foe, supplicating the Lord for protection, the strength of the Lord will help us prevail.

> *"And in the fifteenth year they did come forth against the people of Nephi; and because of the wickedness of the people of Nephi, and their many contentions and dissensions, the Gadianton robbers did gain many advantages over them. And thus ended the fifteenth year, and thus were the people in a state of many afflictions; and the sword of destruction did hang over them, insomuch that they were about to be smitten down by it, and this because of their iniquity" (3 Ne. 2:18–19).*

> *"And now it came to pass when Lachoneus received this epistle he was exceedingly astonished, because of the boldness of Giddianhi demanding the possession of the land of the Nephites, and also of threatening the people and avenging the wrongs of those that had received no wrong, save it were they had wronged themselves by dissenting away unto those wicked and abominable robbers" (3 Ne. 3:11).*

MOMENT OF TRUTH. The people begin to number their years according to the time when the sign of the Savior's birth was given (see 3 Ne. 2:8). Because of the iniquity of the Nephites, the Gadianton robbers are able to gain much advantage in their quest to overpower the country. Giddianhi, the Gadianton leader, sends an audacious epistle to Lachoneus, governor of the land, demanding that the Nephites surrender all of their goods and properties and become "partners" with the robbers (3 Ne. 3:7). Lachoneus rebuffs the demand and pulls all of the people to a central location where their prayers and the strength of unity allow them to withstand the encroachments and attacks. Gidgiddoni, the Nephite prophet-general, is able to provide the needed leadership to prevail, despite the ferocious and terrifying appearance of the armies of the enemy. In fact, "the Nephites did not fear them; but they did fear their God and did supplicate him for protection" (3 Ne. 4:10). The people of God meet the enemy "in the strength of the Lord" and are victorious, offering mighty praises to the Lord. "And now behold, there was not a living soul among all the people of the Nephites who did doubt in the least the words of all the holy prophets who had spoken; for they knew that it must needs be that they must be fulfilled" (3 Ne. 5:1). In an aside, Mormon bears witness of the truth of his record and prophesies the eventual gathering of Zion. However, the righteousness of the people of Nephi is to be short-lived.

MODERN PROPHETS SPEAK

Thomas S. Monson:

> This is your world. Whether you like it or not, you are engaged in the race of your life. At stake is eternal life—yours. What shall be the outcome? Will you be a leader of men and a servant of God? Or will you be a servant of sin and a follower of Satan? Decisions determine destiny. In the quiet of your study, surrounded by books written by the finest minds of men, listen for and hearken to the Master's invitation: ". . . learn of me; for I am meek and lowly in heart: and ye shall find rest unto your souls." (Matthew 11:29–30.) Such learning transcends the classroom, it endures beyond graduation, it meets the test of experience. (*Pathways to Perfection* [Salt Lake City: Deseret Book, 1973], 253)

ILLUSTRATIONS FOR OUR TIME

When We Find Fault. When we sin we literally empower the devil to have greater influence upon us. We lose the light of the Lord, putting ourselves in jeopardy. Korihor is a good example from the past. Alma told him, "Behold, I know that thou believest, but thou art possessed with a lying spirit, and ye have put off the Spirit of God that it may have no place in you; but the devil has power over you, and he doth carry you about, working devices that he may destroy the children of God" (Alma 30:41–42). If we backbite, complain, and find fault with the Brethren, we plunge ourselves into this sort of darkness.

President John Taylor explained:

> Now, if we yield obedience to God and to the spirits that dwell within us, then will our light become like that of the just that shineth brighter and brighter unto the perfect day; but if we do not yield an obedience to the law and word and order of the Church and Kingdom of God upon the earth, the light that is within us will become darkness, and then, as it is said, how great is that darkness! We see sometimes men of that character. They are

occasionally referred to as cranks, or, as the Germans use that term, *sick*. They lose the light, spirit and power of God, and they do not comprehend the order of the Church and Kingdom of God, nor do they place themselves in the way to obtain a knowledge of these things. The first thing they begin to do is to try to pervert the order of God, and to find fault with their brethren in the Holy Priesthood—with their Bishops, with their Bishop's Counselors, with the High Council, perhaps with the Presidents of Stakes, as the case may be, or with the Apostles, or with the First Presidency; no matter which, or how, or when, or where. Now, if these men were walking in the light as God is in the light they would have fellowship one with another, and the blood of Christ would cleanse them from all sin; but when they begin to murmur and complain, to find fault and to give way to improper influences, they give place to the devil, and he takes possession just as fast and as far as he can, and forces upon them feelings, ideas and principles that are at variance with the law and order, and word and will of God. (*JD*, 26:130–31)

Sin separates us from God and allows the devil to lead us away captive. As we are—in an unrepentant condition—led "carefully down to hell" (2 Ne. 28:21), we tend to justify ourselves. The cycle begins. We delude ourselves even more. We rationalize our sins and find fault with our leaders. This is the beginning of individual apostasy. (Pinegar)

Likening the Scriptures to Our Lives

3 Ne. 4:33—The Nephites, because of their wickedness, were sorely afflicted by the Gadianton robbers but were finally delivered out of the hands of their enemies. Their hearts were filled with joy because of the goodness of God in preserving them. They knew it was because they had repented and had become stronger in their humility.

Application—Humility is the beginning of spiritual growth. Let us consider our ways and choose to receive the blessings of God as we humbly seek our Heavenly Father through repentance.

3. AVOIDING THE
SLIPPERY SLOPE OF WORLDLY PRIDE

THEME. Pride, as it clouds spiritual vision and filters out the promptings of the Lord, leads to inevitable destruction. Penitent humility and obedience to divine commandments are the only sure antidotes to pride.

> *"But it came to pass in the twenty and ninth year there began to be some disputings among the people; and some were lifted up unto pride and boastings because of their exceedingly great riches, yea, even unto great persecutions" (3 Ne. 6:10).*

"Now the cause of this iniquity of the people was this—Satan had great power, unto the stirring up of the people to do all manner of iniquity, and to the puffing them up with pride, tempting them to seek for power, and authority, and riches, and the vain things of the world" (3 Ne. 6:15).

MOMENT OF TRUTH. After the great victory over the forces of evil, the Nephites return to their own places of residence throughout the land and enjoy an abundance of prosperity. That is when they come face to face with their nemesis: "And now there was nothing in all the land to hinder the people from prospering continually, except they should fall into transgression" (3 Ne. 6:5). On the slippery slope of wealth and pride they quickly lapse into forgetfulness and neglect of their covenant obligations: "And the people began to be distinguished by ranks, according to their riches and their chances for learning; yea, some were ignorant because of their poverty, and others did receive great learning because of their riches" (3 Ne. 6:12). Save for a few righteous and stalwart Lamanites, the people degrade into gross inequality and begin to sin willfully against the light of the gospel. Prophets arise and are rejected. Civil justice collapses through the spread of secret and murderous combinations, and the government dissolves into tribal compacts. Mormon characterizes the dizzying dissolution of order and peace this way: "And thus six years had not passed away since the more part of the people had turned from their righteousness, like the dog to his vomit, or like the sow to her wallowing in the mire" (3 Ne. 7:8). With great power, Nephi, who has daily interaction with angels (see 3 Ne. 7:18), commands the people to repent, and performs astounding miracles among them. However, there are relatively few who are willing to be reclaimed from their iniquity on the eve of the great geophysical dislocations that are to attend the death and resurrection of the Lord.

MODERN PROPHETS SPEAK

Jeffrey R. Holland:

> That kind of faithfulness brought prosperity so great that "nothing in all the land [could] hinder the people from prospering continually, except they should fall into transgression." But fall into transgression they did, as a result of those two challenges that were forever the destruction of Nephite righteousness—pride and riches (3 Nephi 6:5; see also v.10.). In a short time, great inequality developed in the Nephite church, insomuch that it "began to be broken up; yea, insomuch that in the thirtieth year the church was broken up in all the land save it were among a few of the Lamanites who were converted unto the truth faith; and they would not depart from it." (3 Nephi 6:14) (*Christ and the New Covenant: The Messianic Message of the Book of Mormon* [Salt Lake City: Deseret Book, 1997], 254)

ILLUSTRATIONS FOR OUR TIME

The warning has been given by the prophets about single-hearted obsession with material wealth and riches at the expense of balance and valor in living the gospel. Let us become aware of the trial of prosperity and guard against an allegiance to worldly abundance without regard for covenant honor. Here are several warnings applicable to our day and challenge:

M. Russell Ballard:

> We would do well to remember the prosperity cycle found in the Book of Mormon when those persons blessed for their righteousness became wealthy and then forgot the Lord. Let us not forget the Lord in our day of prosperity. Let us maintain the spirit of the law of sacrifice and always thank Him for what we have, even if it is not as much as some others have. . . .
>
> If I have a fear, it is that the principle of sacrifice may be slipping away from us. This principle is a law of God. We are obliged to understand it and practice it. If being a member of this Church becomes too easy, testimonies will become shallow, and the roots of testimony will not go down into the soil of faith as they did with our pioneer forefathers. May God grant each of us an understanding of the law of sacrifice and a conviction that it is necessary today. It is vitally important that we understand this law and live it. ("The Law of Sacrifice," *Ensign,* Oct. 1998, 11, 13)

Likening the Scriptures to Our Lives

3 Ne. 6:15—The cause of the iniquity among the Nephites was the result of yielding to the temptations of Satan. They were puffed up with pride and sought for power, authority, riches, and the vain things of the world.

Application—Satan has the power to tempt us in many ways. We must fortify ourselves by remaining diligent in prayer with all our hearts (see 3 Ne. 18:18–19), seeking the kingdom of God before riches (see Jacob 2:18).

SUMMARY

On the eve of the Savior's entry to this world upon His mission of redeeming sacrifice, the American Israelites are witness to the extraordinary signs of His birth. Soon thereafter, they are beset with assault after assault from the forces of conspiracy and evil and learn to meet the enemy "in the strength of the Lord." Nevertheless, in the space of not many years they are carried down on the slippery slope of worldly pride and find themselves, with few exceptions, in a state of spiritual squalor, having rejected the prophets of God. From this we can learn great lessons.

We see that the words of the Lord's prophets shall all be fulfilled (see D&C 1:38). Those who are faithful will be vindicated in times to come. In addition, we learn again that iniquity will separate us from God and His light, and put us within the power of the devil if we do not repent. We are counseled to be wise and learn from those of the past (see Jacob 4:5; 6:12; Morm. 9:31). Moreover, the Lord once again teaches in these passages the evils of pride and its ruinous effects in the lives of individuals and families. How surely we are instructed to overcome all aspects of pride through humility and charity. Mormon sets the example for us to emulate as we aspire to understand and appreciate our discipleship: "Behold, I am a disciple of Jesus Christ, the Son of God. I have been called of him to declare his word among his people, that they might have everlasting life" (3 Ne. 5:13). In this way we too can become pure disciples of the Lord Jesus Christ.

CHAPTER THIRTY-SEVEN

"WHOSOEVER WILL COME, HIM WILL I RECEIVE"

3 NEPHI 8–11

"The clarion call of the Church is for all to come unto Christ, regardless of their particular circumstances."
—HOWARD W. HUNTER, THAT WE MIGHT HAVE JOY [SALT LAKE CITY: DESERET BOOK, 1994], 53.

THEMES *for* LIVING

The Fulfillment of Prophecy at the Time of the Savior's Death
The Lord Invites All to Come unto Him
The Testimony of the Father and the Son

INTRODUCTION

The Book of Mormon is a handbook for safety and refuge in the Lord by means of obedience and sanctification. The Lord's prophets, from the beginning of the world, have warned of the lethal consequences of ongoing, unrepentant sin. Such was the warning of Samuel the Lamanite to the Nephite people as they persisted in their downward spiral into the abyss of prideful worldliness and rebellious self-satisfaction. The people, blinded as to spiritual truth and deaf as to the clarion call to repentance, are consumed by the cataclysmic destruction that takes place at the time of the Savior's death. The word of the Lord is thereby fulfilled, as it always is, "whether by mine own voice, or by the voice of my servants, it is the same" (see D&C 1:38). The events covered by these chapters of Third Nephi demonstrate anew that the wicked will be punished and the more righteous will be preserved. The Savior is introduced to the surviving multitudes by the voice of Elohim, our Heavenly Father, and shows Himself unto the people in an overwhelming manifestation of majesty and love. He then teaches the doctrine of the kingdom and encourages all to come unto Him through faith, repentance, and the ordinance of baptism by water and by fire—so that He might receive them as His own.

1. THE FULFILLMENT OF PROPHECY AT THE TIME OF THE SAVIOR'S DEATH

THEME. Out of divine charity, the Lord reveals far in advance the consequences—always destructive and often catastrophic—for continued disobedience. Such was the case at the time of the Savior's death when widespread destruction occurred throughout the land as foretold by Samuel the Lamanite. The Lord always speaks with the "voice of warning" (D&C 1:4) when it is called for. This has been the case in the latter days. The Lord, "knowing the calamity which should come upon the inhabitants of the earth" (D&C 1:17), has continued to warn us in this dispensation to repent or face certain destruction.

> "... there arose a great storm ... tempest ... thunder ... shake the whole earth ... whole face of the land was changed ... cities were sunk ... inhabitants thereof were slain ... places were left desolate ... whirlwind ... earth became deformed ... rocks were rent in twain ... thick darkness ... not any light ... for the space of three days ..." (3 Ne. 8:5–23).

MOMENT OF TRUTH. Nephi, son of Nephi, continues his ministry of miracles among the people, but the harvest is small, and many harbor doubts about the fulfillment of the prophecies attendant with the Savior's death: "And there began to be great doubtings and disputations among the people, notwithstanding so many signs had been given" (3 Ne. 8:4). Then on the fourth day of the first month in the 34th year following the Savior's birth, catastrophe occurs. As a result of the wickedness of the people, the prophesied devastations on the American continent take place at the time of the Savior's death. Many great cities are destroyed and many of the people are slain. However, the "more righteous" (3 Ne. 9:13) are spared.

MODERN PROPHETS SPEAK

Spencer W. Kimball:

> Tidal waves swallowed entire communities, and fire consumed many cities and human bodies. The labors of centuries were embalmed in ashes to a greater degree than Pompeii and Herculaneum; and earth convulsions of such intensity and prolongation that "the face of the whole earth was deformed" (see 3 Ne. 8:17), these earth spasms being a revolt by the created earth against the crucifixion of its Creator. (*CR,* Apr. 1963, 64–65)

ILLUSTRATIONS FOR OUR TIME

Favor of the Lord. As far as I can recall, the only time my father displayed anger with me as a child was on one occasion where, through an insensitive oversight, I showed ingratitude following a day-long family outing. As I look back on it, my father's disciplinary response at that time was but a reflection of the essence of the famous passage from the 59th section of the Doctrine & Covenants: "And in nothing doth man offend God, or against none is his wrath kindled, save those who confess not his hand in all things, and obey not his commandments" (v. 21). When the remnants of Israel in America experienced the wrath of a just God through the foretold geophysical upheavals at the time of the Savior's death, they understood, though in many cases too late, the grave consequences of disobedience and ingratitude. In the Savior's pronouncements to the fallen people, He emphasized not once, but three times, His fatherly desire to gather the favored people and nourish them "as a hen gathereth her chickens under her wings" (3 Ne. 10:4–6). Clearly, He yearns to favor His children through divine charity and grace.

The Lord's favor toward His children is a theme that runs through the Book of Mormon, beginning with Nephi's opening words about "having been highly favored of the Lord" (1 Ne. 1:1). The word "favor," including its derivatives, is used in 37 verses in the standard works, fully 30 of them in the Book of Mormon. We learn from the Book of Mormon the simple steps for gaining the favor of the Lord: by not murmuring (1 Ne. 3:6), by being righteous (1 Ne. 17:35) and obedient (2 Ne. 1:19; Mosiah 1:13), through prayer (Mosiah 10:13), through faith (Alma 9:20), by being "zealous" in the spiritual sense (Alma 27:30), and through humility (Alma 48:20).

Mormon sounds the theme of favor once more in reference to the Savior's visit to America following His resurrection: "And it came to pass that in the ending of the thirty and fourth year, behold, I will show unto you that the people of Nephi who were spared, and also those who had been called Lamanites, who had been spared, did have great favors shown unto them, and great blessings poured out upon their heads, insomuch that soon after the ascension of Christ into heaven he did truly manifest himself unto them" (3 Ne. 10:18). The reason for such favor is made clear: "And it was the more righteous part of the people who were saved, and it was they who received the prophets and stoned them not; and it was they who had not shed the blood of the saints, who were spared" (3 Ne. 10:12). From this we can derive one of the principal lessons of the Book of Mormon concerning the favor of the Lord: *receive His prophets*. Just as Samuel of old warned the people in frank terms to repent and become a righteous people, we today have the extraordinary benefit of hearing the voice of God's prophets directly. Because of this opportunity, we can gain the favor of God through obedience and righteousness and thereby prepare ourselves for "the tribulation of those days" (Matt. 24:29) in the not too distant future when the Lord will return again "in he clouds of heaven with power and great glory" (Matt. 24:30). (Allen)

Likening the Scriptures to Our Lives

3 Ne. 8:1—Nephi kept the record. He was a just man. He performed many miracles in and through the Lord Jesus Christ, for he had been cleansed from all iniquity.

Application—The power of the priesthood is inseparably connected with the powers of heaven and operates on the principle of righteousness (see D&C 121:36). Our righteousness, cleanliness, and purity, are brought about through our repentance. This is the requirement to bring down the powers of heaven on our behalf. This power is faith. Let us do all in our power to be worthy instruments in the hands of the Lord to do His work here upon the earth.

2. THE LORD INVITES ALL TO COME UNTO HIM

THEME. The Lord encourages all people to repent and come unto Him. He will receive them "as a hen gathereth her chickens under her wings" (3 Ne. 10:6). This is one of the missions of The Church of Jesus Christ of Latter-day Saints, the kingdom of God: to invite all to come unto Christ that they might have life everlasting.

> *"O all ye that are spared because ye were more righteous than they, will ye not now return unto me, and repent of your sins, and be converted, that I may heal you? Yea, verily I say unto you, if ye will come unto me ye shall have eternal life. Behold, mine arm of mercy is extended towards you, and whosoever will come, him will I receive; and blessed are those who come unto me" (3 Ne. 9:13–14).*

MOMENT OF TRUTH. In the wake of the massive destruction that had occurred through seismic upheavals, the voice of the Lord is heard throughout the land declaring that iniquity was the root cause of the disaster, and that the "more righteous," having been spared, are to repent and return unto Him, "that I may heal you" (3 Ne. 9:13). His glorious promise is announced: "And as many as have received me, to them have I given to become the sons of God; and even so will I to as many as shall believe on my name, for behold, by me redemption cometh, and in me is the law of Moses fulfilled" (3 Ne. 9:17). He calls for a new kind of sacrifice from that moment on, even "a broken heart and a contrite spirit" (3 Ne. 9:20), leading to the baptism of fire and the Holy Ghost. After many hours of silence, the voice of the Savior is again heard by all of the people as He issues a universal invitation to repent and come unto Him. Thereafter the three-day period of darkness disperses and the pervasive lamentation is supplanted by rejoicing among the survivors.

MODERN PROPHETS SPEAK

Howard W. Hunter:

> We hope you can see that by emphasizing the mission of the Church in a three-fold manner, we are leading toward one objective for each individual member of the Church. That is for all to receive the ordinances of the gospel and make covenants with our Heavenly Father so they may return to his presence. That is our grand objective. The ordinances and covenants are the means to achieving that divine nature that will return us into his presence again. . . .

> Keep in mind the purpose: to invite all to come unto Christ. (*The Teachings of Howard W. Hunter,* ed. Clyde J. Williams [Salt Lake City: Bookcraft, 1997], 218)

ILLUSTRATIONS FOR OUR TIME

The Lord Wants Us to Be Missionaries. The mission of the Church and kingdom of God is to invite all to come unto Christ.

The Lord needs us as missionaries to help all mankind come unto Christ. This is the message of the Book of Mormon—this is our message to the world. President Kimball has taught us concerning the urgency of the work:

> Again I am impressed to ask anew the question—is each of us doing all we can to take the gospel to the inhabitants of the earth whom the Lord has placed within our circle of influence?

There is an urgency about this work that I feel some have not sensed, but it is an urgency that is real nonetheless. The Spirit will renew this sense of urgency in the soul of each person who asks God for help in these matters.

"Behold, the field is white already to harvest; therefore, whoso desireth to reap, let him thrust in his sickle with his might, and reap while the day lasts, that he may treasure up for his soul everlasting salvation in the kingdom of God." (D&C 6:3.)

The Lord has advised us, "For if you will that I give unto you a place in the celestial world, you must prepare yourselves by doing the things which I have commanded you and required of you." (D&C 78:7.)

Is there in the Church today anyone who knows not the call of the Lord for "every member to be a missionary"? Is there any family in the Church today that knows not the need for more missionaries? . . .

Our great need, and our great calling, is to bring to the people of this world the candle of understanding to light their way out of obscurity and darkness and into the joy, peace, and truths of the gospel.

I believe we must not weary in our well-doing. I believe it is time again to ask ourselves the question, what can I do to help take the gospel to others and to the inhabitants of this world? ("Are We Doing All We Can?" *Ensign,* Feb. 1983, 3) (Pinegar)

Likening the Scriptures to Our Lives

3 Ne. 11:37–38—The Lord is very specific as He invites people to come unto Him and partake of the blessings of Heaven through repentance, becoming as a little child, and receiving the ordinance of baptism. (There are thirteen references to a form of the word "baptize" in chapter 11.)

Application—The message of all dispensations is to repent and come unto Christ. To become as a child requires us to be "submissive, meek, humble, patient, full of love, willing to submit to all things which the Lord seeth fit to inflict upon him, even as a child doth submit to his father" (Mosiah 3:19). This is what the Lord requires of us, and He set the example, as the next theme shows.

3. THE TESTIMONY OF THE FATHER AND THE SON

THEME. It is a fundamental principle of truth that the Father, the Son, and the Holy Ghost testify of one another before the world. This act of divine witnessing is the pattern and model for all testimony bearing.

> *"Behold my Beloved Son, in whom I am well pleased, in whom I have glorified my name—hear ye him. And it came to pass, as they understood they cast their eyes up again towards heaven; and behold, they saw a Man descending out of heaven; and he was clothed in a white robe; and he came down and stood in the midst of them; and the eyes of the whole multitude were turned upon him, and they durst not open their mouths, even one to another, and wist not what it meant, for they thought it was an angel that had appeared unto them. And it came to pass that he stretched forth his hand and spake unto the people, saying: Behold, I am Jesus Christ, whom the prophets testified shall come into the world. And behold, I am the light and the life of the world; and I have drunk out of that bitter cup which the Father hath given me, and have glorified the Father in taking upon me the sins of the world, in the which I have suffered the will of the Father in all things from the beginning. And it came to pass that when Jesus had spoken these words the whole multitude fell to the earth; for they remembered that it had been prophesied among them that Christ should show himself unto them after his ascension into heaven" (3 Ne. 11:7–12).*

> *"Behold, verily, verily, I say unto you, I will declare unto you my doctrine. And this is my doctrine, and it is the doctrine which the Father hath given unto me; and I bear record of the Father, and the Father beareth record of me, and the Holy Ghost beareth record of the Father and me; and I bear record that the Father commandeth all men, everywhere, to repent and believe in me. And whoso believeth in me, and is baptized, the same shall be saved; and they are they who shall inherit the kingdom of God. And whoso believeth not in me, and is not baptized, shall be damned" (3 Ne. 11:31–34).*

MOMENT OF TRUTH. The people assemble themselves to ponder the extraordinary events they have experienced. Thrice they hear a small but piercing voice from the heavens, and upon the third occasion they are finally able to understand the thrilling message. God the Father, Elohim, introduces His Beloved Son, the Savior and Redeemer of the World, the Lord Jesus Christ. Christ descends from heaven in full view of the people, identifies Himself as the living Christ, and begins teaching the doctrine of the kingdom. His message is one of covenant: His will is that the people should exercise faith in Him, repent of their sins, and be baptized in water and through the Holy Ghost as a sacred covenant of obedience and righteousness.

MODERN PROPHETS SPEAK

Jeffrey R. Holland:

> To the Nephites gathered at the temple, He would say, "Behold, I am Jesus Christ, . . . the light and the life of the world; and I have drunk out of that bitter cup which the father hath given me, and . . . I have suffered the will of the Father in all things from the beginning" (3 Nephi 11:10–11). That is His own introduction of Himself, the declaration He feels best tells us who He is. (*Trusting Jesus* [Salt Lake City: Deseret Book, 2003] 41–42)

ILLUSTRATIONS FOR OUR TIME

A Prophet's Testimony. It was an unusual invitation. The leaders of some two dozen Utah stakes were asked to meet on a particular day at the Manti Temple for a solemn assembly with President David O. McKay and the other General Authorities. There was much conjecture about the nature and purpose of the meeting. What new policy or doctrinal innovation might be forthcoming that would require such a solemn gathering? I remember the sense of anticipation we felt as a bishopric while motoring down to the meeting. The assembly room of the temple was packed with many hundreds of priesthood leaders, all of whom were honored to have the sacrament blessed and passed to them by General Authorities. Then there was rapt silence as the prophet arose, a tall and stately figure of leadership with his silver hair and white suit, and announced to us the reason he had brought us all together—simply to confirm that Jesus is the Christ, that He lives, and that He is at the head of this work. It was a powerful reminder about what is of primary and preeminent importance in this world—the Atonement of Jesus Christ and the reality of His life and mission. All were edified to be thus filled with the word of inspiration. All rejoiced in the compassion of a just Father in Heaven and His Son to have opened the way for the faithful and valiant to return one day to Their holy presence. No one in attendance will ever forget the witness of the Spirit that day that God lives, that His Prophet speaks for Him, and that life is indeed full of joy and hope. (Allen)

Likening the Scriptures to Our Lives

3 Ne. 11:7—The Father introduces His Son and testifies of His sacred mission and holiness, just as He did at the time of the Savior's baptism (Matt. 3:17), upon the Mount of Transfiguration (Matt. 17:5), and in the Sacred Grove (JS—H 1:17).

Application—Let us remember with gratitude the testimony of the Father for the Son and, in turn, testify of the goodness of God and the truth of the gospel "at all times, and in all places" (Mosiah 18:9).

SUMMARY

The Book of Mormon testifies that the Lord's words, as conveyed through His prophets, will all be fulfilled. The destruction at the time of the Savior's death had been foretold when Samuel warned the people to relinquish sin and return to their covenant vows. "And now, whoso readeth, let him understand," counsels Mormon, "he that hath the scriptures, let him search them, and see and behold if all these deaths and destructions by fire, and by smoke, and by tempests, and by whirlwinds, and by the opening of the earth to receive them, and all these things are not unto the fulfilling of the prophecies of many of the holy prophets" (3 Ne. 10:14). The Lord made this clear in His announcement to the survivors: "And many great destructions have I caused to come upon this land, and upon this people, because of their wickedness and their abominations" (3 Ne. 9:12). At the same time, the longsuffering invitation of the Lord to the people, enjoining them to be valiant and faithful, is again reemphasized: "O all ye that are spared because ye were more righteous than they, will ye not now return unto me, and repent of your sins, and be converted, that I may heal you?" (3 Ne. 9:13). These passages then convey the wondrous testimony of the Father concerning His Beloved Son, the Redeemer of the world, to whom we must give ear. The Lord invites all to come unto Him and testifies, in turn, of the Father and Holy Ghost.

Heavenly Father and our Savior, Jesus Christ, stand waiting to bless us. There is only one way. We must come unto Christ with all our heart and soul. The prophecies and teachings are clear: we must learn to follow and obey, or we will lose the blessings of the Lord and be damned. The doctrine of Christ is to come unto Him and be perfected in Him.

CHAPTER THIRTY-EIGHT

THE SERMON *at* *the* TEMPLE . . . *the* HIGHER LAW

3 NEPHI 12–15

"In His Sermon on the Mount the Master has given us somewhat of a revelation of His own character, which was perfect, or what might be said to be 'an autobiography, every syllable of which He had written down in deeds,' and in so doing has given us a blueprint for our own lives. Anyone clearly understanding the true import of His words comes to the realization that an unworthy member of the Church, although he might be in the kingdom of God, yet would not be of the kingdom because of his unworthiness."
—HAROLD B. LEE, *THE TEACHINGS OF HAROLD B. LEE,* ED. CLYDE J. WILLIAMS
[SALT LAKE CITY: BOOKCRAFT, 1996], 13.

THEMES *for* LIVING

The Beatitudes: The Lord's Agenda for Blessing His People
The Salt of the Earth and the Light of This People
Living the Higher Law
The Nature of True Discipleship

INTRODUCTION

The Lord Jesus Christ, the Savior of the world, delivers the higher law to the people at the temple. This is the law of celestial living. This is the law which, when kept, leads to eternal life. It is the pattern of the life for the disciples of the Lord Jesus Christ—the law that will make us free. When we learn to love His law it will become our way of living, and we will become even as He is.

1. THE BEATITUDES:
THE LORD'S AGENDA FOR BLESSING HIS PEOPLE

THEME. The Savior teaches the doctrine of happiness through the magnificent beatitudes. The word "blessed" refers to "enjoying spiritual happiness and the favor of God; enjoying heavenly felicity" *(An American Dictionary of the English Language,* Noah Webster, 1828).

> *"Blessed are ye if ye shall give heed unto the words of these twelve whom I have chosen. . . . blessed are ye if ye shall believe in me and be baptized. . . . more blessed are they who shall believe in your words. . . . Yea, blessed are the poor in spirit who come unto me, for theirs is the kingdom of heaven. And again, blessed are all they that mourn, for they shall be comforted. And blessed are the meek, for they shall inherit the earth. And blessed are all they who do hunger and thirst after righteousness, for they shall be filled with the Holy Ghost. And blessed are the merciful, for they shall obtain mercy. And blessed are all the pure in heart, for they shall see God. And blessed are all the peacemakers, for they shall be called the children of God. And blessed are all they who are persecuted for my name's sake, for theirs is the kingdom of heaven. And blessed are ye when men shall revile you and persecute, and shall say all manner of evil against you falsely, for my sake; For ye shall have great joy and be exceedingly glad, for great shall be your reward in heaven; for so persecuted they the prophets who were before you" (3 Ne. 12:1–12).*

MOMENT OF TRUTH. After the Savior has empowered His disciples to baptize the people, He turns to the multitude and reveals the agenda by which He will bless the faithful. This sequence of illuminating sayings, very similar to the "Beatitudes" given in the Sermon on the Mount, is a wondrous endowment of truth and divine love that outlines the resplendent array of blessings held in store by the Lord to bless His followers.

MODERN PROPHETS SPEAK

Blessed are ye if ye shall give heed unto the words of these twelve whom I have chosen.

Boyd K. Packer:

> Follow the Brethren. Three words. There is nothing in your life that will destroy you if you will follow the Brethren. (*Things of the Soul* [Salt Lake City: Bookcraft, 1996], 79–80).

Yea, blessed are the poor in spirit who come unto me for theirs is the kingdom of heaven.

Bruce R. McConkie:

> The poor in spirit! If they come unto Christ, salvation is theirs; and it is so often easier for those who are not encumbered with the cares and burdens and riches of the world to cast off worldliness and set their hearts on the riches of eternity than it is for those who have an abundance of this world's goods. (Bruce R. McConkie, *The Mortal Messiah: From Bethlehem to Calvary*, 4 vols. [Salt Lake City: Deseret Book, 1979–1981], 2:121)

And again, blessed are all they that mourn, for they shall be comforted.

Harold B. Lee:

> We are here to help lift the eyes of those who mourn from the valley of despair to the light upon the mountain peaks of hope, to endeavor to answer questions about war, to bring peace to troubled souls, not as the world giveth, but only that which comes from the Prince of Peace. We are here to lift all of us out of the shadows into life and light. (*Ye Are the Light of the World: Selected Sermons and Writings of Harold B. Lee* [Salt Lake City: Deseret Book, 1974], 251–52)

And blessed are the meek, for they shall inherit the earth.

Gordon B. Hinckley:

> The Lord has said that the meek shall inherit the earth. (Matthew 5:5.) I cannot escape the interpretation that meekness implies a spirit of gratitude as opposed to an attitude of self-sufficiency, an acknowledgment of a greater power beyond oneself, a recognition of God, and an acceptance of his commandments. This is the beginning of wisdom. Walk with gratitude before him who is the giver of life and every good gift. (*Faith: The Essence of True Religion* [Salt Lake City: Deseret Book, 1989], 82)

And blessed are all they who do hunger and thirst after righteousness, for they shall be filled with the Holy Ghost.

Neal A. Maxwell:
> There is too the significant blessing of personal momentum that always comes when we practice decision making in which we both *reject wrong* and *choose the good.* We thus avoid what one prophet called the in-betweenness of the "sorrowing of the damned." (Mormon 2:13.) It is not enough to reach a bland behavioral point when we no longer take pleasure in sin; we must hunger and thirst for righteousness. (*Notwithstanding My Weakness* [Salt Lake City: Deseret Book, 1981], 104)

And blessed are the merciful, for they shall obtain mercy.

Bruce R. McConkie:
> Mercy is for the merciful; mercy is reserved for the righteous; mercy comes to those who keep the commandments. And the Old Testament prophets had similar insight. Hosea said: "Sow to yourselves in righteousness, reap in mercy; break up your fallow ground: for it is time to seek the Lord, till he come and rain righteousness upon you." (Hosea 10:12). (*The Promised Messiah: The First Coming of Christ* [Salt Lake City: Deseret Book, 1978], 246)

And blessed are all the pure in heart, for they shall see God.

Harold B. Lee:
> If you would see God, you must be pure. . . . Only the righteous saw him as the Son of God. Only if you are the pure in heart will you see God, and also in a lesser degree will you be able to see the "God" or good in man and love him because of the goodness you see in him. Mark well that person who criticizes and maligns the man of God or the Lord's anointed leaders in his Church. Such a one speaks from an impure heart. (*Decisions for Successful Living* [Salt Lake City: Deseret Book, 1973], 59)

ILLUSTRATIONS FOR OUR TIME

A Simple Lesson. He was the meekest of elders, a humble farm boy called as a servant of the Lord among a distant people. His speech was homey, his social skills basic, his only polish the weather-tanned skin of a man of the soil. But when he opened his mouth to bear fervent testimony of the truth of the gospel and the sacredness of the Book of Mormon, there was something special there, something that resonated with simple grandeur. He spoke the words that were in his heart as conveyed by the Holy Spirit. We, his missionary colleagues, noticed the radiance shining from his frontier countenance and learned from him. So did the families he taught. The lesson is simple: It is not the learning of the world or cultural sophistication that changes hearts; rather, it is the word of God, spoken by His humble servants, and confirmed by the Spirit, that touches lives and opens the soul for gospel illumination. "And blessed are the meek, for they shall inherit the earth" was the promise of the Savior to his listeners in Jerusalem (Matt. 5:5) as well as in America (3 Ne. 12:5). This young elder, by now of patriarchal age, is doubtless just the type of person who shall indeed inherit the earth. (Allen)

Likening the Scriptures to Our Lives

3 Ne. 12:1–11—The Lord teaches us the celestial way of living: how to live happily. How blessed (how happy) are those who do these things.

Application—The way to happiness is to give heed to the word, believe in Christ, and be baptized both by water and fire. In this way we come unto Him. Those who do so will be comforted in mourning. They will be meek, will hunger and thirst after righteousness, will be merciful, will be pure in heart, will be peacemakers, and will have the privilege of discipleship, even though they may be persecuted for His name's sake. We should seek to do these things in order to obtain happiness here and in the hereafter.

2. THE SALT OF THE EARTH AND THE LIGHT OF THIS PEOPLE

THEME. Being part of the fold of Christ brings great blessings but also great responsibilities to glorify God through righteous living.

> *"Verily, verily, I say unto you, I give unto you to be the salt of the earth; but if the salt shall lose its savor wherewith shall the earth be salted? The salt shall be thenceforth good for nothing, but to be cast out and to be trodden under foot of men. Verily, verily, I say unto you, I give unto you to be the light of this people. A city that is set on a hill cannot be hid. Behold, do men light a candle and put it under a bushel? Nay, but on a candlestick, and it giveth light to all that are in the house; Therefore let your light so shine before this people, that they may see your good works and glorify your Father who is in heaven" (3 Ne. 12:13–16).*

MOMENT OF TRUTH. The Savior, having outlined the blessings awaiting those who follow in His footsteps, now explains that His disciples are to be "the salt of the earth" and "the light of this people" (3 Ne. 12:13, 14). With that opportunity and privilege comes great responsibility, for participating in the Abrahamic covenant entails becoming servants of the Most High who carry the gospel message to the world.

MODERN PROPHETS SPEAK

Joseph F. Smith:

> Christ, teaching his disciples, called attention to the importance of their position and place in the world. Though poor and despised of men, yet he told them they were the salt of the earth, the light of the world.
>
> Then he encouraged them to effort and achievement by showing them that their exalted position would avail them little, unless they made proper use of their high callings.
>
> These conditions and instructions apply admirably to the Latter-day Saints, who are indeed the salt of the earth, and in whom is vested the gospel light of the world; who, as the apostle said of the Former-day Saints, are a chosen generation, a royal priesthood, an holy nation, a peculiar people; that they should show forth the praises of him who called them out of darkness into his marvelous light.
>
> But all this availeth little or nothing, unless the Saints consider themselves of some consequence, and let their light shine, collectively and individually; unless they are model in their behavior, honest, zealous in the spread of truth, tolerant of their neighbors, "having your conversation honest among the Gentiles; that whereas they speak against you as evil-doers, they may by your good works, which they shall behold, glorify God in the day of visitation."
>
> One fault to be avoided by the Saints, young and old, is the tendency to live on borrowed light, with their own hidden under a bushel; to permit the savor of their salt of knowledge to be lost; and the light within them to be reflected, rather than original.
>
> Every Saint should not only have the light within himself, through the inspiration of the Holy Spirit, but his light should so shine that it may be clearly perceived by others.
>
> Men and women should become settled in the truth, and founded in the knowledge of the gospel, depending upon no person for borrowed or reflected light, but trusting only upon the Holy Spirit, who is ever the same, shining forever and testifying to the individual and the priesthood, who live in harmony with the laws of the gospel, of the glory and the will of the Father. They will then have light everlasting which cannot be obscured. By its shining in their lives, they shall cause others to glorify God; and by their well-doing put to silence the ignorance of foolish men, and

show forth the praises of him who hath called them out of darkness into his marvelous light. (*Gospel Doctrine: Selections from the Sermons and Writings of Joseph F. Smith,* comp. by John A. Widtsoe [Salt Lake City: Deseret Book, 1919], 87–88)

ILLUSTRATIONS FOR OUR TIME

Some Questions and Answers. We are to be the salt of the earth. What does this mean?

Hoyt W. Brewster, Jr.

Those who are the true "salt of the earth" bring out the wholesome "savor of men" (D&C 101:39–40; 103:10; Matt. 5:13; 3 Ne. 12:13). Webster defines *savor* as a verb meaning "to have a specified taste or quality; a special flavor or quality." Faithful members of the Church, the true "salt of the earth," should provide a special quality in whatever social situation they find themselves. Their presence should be edifyingly *savory,* bringing out the best in others and adding to the righteous pleasure of all. (*Doctrine and Covenants Encyclopedia* [Salt Lake City: Bookcraft, 1988], 492–93).

We are to be the light of the world. To whom does this apply and what do we do in regard to this light?

As defined by the Lord, the "light to the world" is the everlasting covenant, or, in other words, the fulness of the gospel of Jesus Christ as revealed through his church (D&C 45:9, 28). Isaiah wrote of a "standard" that was to be set up to the people of this world (Isa. 49:22; 1 Ne. 21:22). Elder Marion G. Romney identified the Church as that standard of which Isaiah spoke (*CR,* Apr. 1961, p. 119).

To the Church the Lord declared: "Arise and shine forth, that thy light may be a standard for the nations" (D&C 115:5). The charge to the Saints in all ages has been to dispel darkness with the light of the gospel (Matt. 5:14–16; 3 Ne. 12:14–16; D&C 115:42–5). For example, Paul declared that his mission was to open the eyes of the people and "to turn them from darkness to light, and from the power of Satan unto God" (Acts 26:18). (*Doctrine and Covenants Encyclopedia* [Salt Lake City: Bookcraft, 1988], 325)

Likening the Scriptures to Our Lives

3 Ne.12:13–16—As members of the Church, we are reminded by the Lord to honor our covenants. We are the salt of the earth, and if we lose our savor, we are good for nothing. The Lord also indicates that we are to be a light unto the world and to do good works that we might glorify our Heavenly Father.

Application—We, as disciples of Christ, are duty bound because we have made covenants with the Lord. "When men are called unto mine everlasting gospel, and covenant with an everlasting covenant, they are accounted as the salt of the earth and the savor of men; They are called to be the savor of men; therefore, if that salt of the earth lose its savor, behold, it is thenceforth good for nothing only to be cast out and trodden under the feet of men" (D&C 101:39–40). We, as salt of the earth, as Elder McConkie indicates, "ha[ve] power, in other words, to be the seasoning, savoring, preserving influence in the world, the influence which would bring peace and blessings to all others" (*Mormon Doctrine,* 2d ed. [Salt Lake City: Bookcraft, 1966], 668).

As a light (see 3 Nephi 15:12), we are to show people the way to Christ for He is the light and life of the world (see 3 Nephi 18:24).

3. LIVING THE HIGHER LAW

THEME. The gospel is structured to help us progress to ever higher levels of spirituality in ever more perfect compliance with the patterns of heaven. The law of Moses was a schoolmaster that was intended to help the people look forward to Christ. The Lord—as Jehovah of the Old Testament—gave the law of Moses and now proceeds to give the higher law.

> *"Marvel not that I said unto you that old things had passed away, and that all things had become new. Behold, I say unto you that the law is fulfilled that was given unto Moses. Behold, I am he that gave the law, and I am he who covenanted with my people Israel; therefore, the law in me is fulfilled, for I have come to fulfil the law; therefore it hath an end" (3 Ne. 15:3–5).*

MOMENT OF TRUTH. The Lord had already announced a new and illuminating doctrine to the people during the three-day period of profound darkness: "And ye shall offer up unto me no more the shedding of blood; yea, your sacrifices and your burnt offerings shall be done away, for I will accept none of your sacrifices and your burnt offerings. And ye shall offer for a sacrifice unto me a broken heart and a contrite spirit. And whoso cometh unto me with a broken heart and a contrite spirit, him will I baptize with fire and with the Holy Ghost," (3 Ne. 9:19–20). Now, continuing His sermon at the temple in Bountiful, the Lord expounds on this remarkable new form of sacrifice by unfolding to the people the transition from the old patterns of external ordinances under the law of Moses to the new patterns of devotion and spirituality characteristic of the higher law. He makes it clear that the law of Moses was fulfilled in Him. At the same time, He declares that all prophetic utterance applying to a later date was still in force and valid, and that the sacred covenant between the

Lord and His people was still in effect. The old law was centered in codes and regulations of an outward nature, all pointing to Christ; the new law is centered in the Savior Himself: "Behold, I am the law, and the light. Look unto me, and endure to the end, and ye shall live; for unto him that endureth to the end will I give eternal life" (3 Ne. 15:9).

MODERN PROPHETS SPEAK

Jeffrey R. Holland:

> Thus it is crucial to understand that the law of Moses was overlaid upon, and thereby included, many basic parts of the gospel of Jesus Christ, which had existed before it. It was never intended to be something apart or separated from, and certainly not something antagonistic to, the gospel of Jesus Christ. It was more elementary than the full gospel—thus its schoolmaster's role in bringing people to the gospel—but its purpose was never to have been different from the higher law. Both were to bring people to Christ. (*Christ and the New Covenant: The Messianic Message of the Book of Mormon* [Salt Lake City: Deseret Book, 1997], 147)

ILLUSTRATIONS FOR OUR TIME

A Preparatory Gospel. The law of Moses was a preparatory gospel. It was a schoolmaster to help people not only look forward to Christ but prepare for Christ. In life there are many preparatory experiences that prepare us for greater blessings. It is line upon line, precept upon precept, here a little and there a little—such is the process of growth. Tithing is an example of a lesser law preparing for the law of consecration.

Joseph Fielding Smith:

> This was, in fact, the inauguration of the law of tithing, the lesser law, to be a schoolmaster for the members of the Church, like the Law of Moses was to Israel, to prepare them for the higher law which had been taken away because of disobedience (*Church History and Modern Revelation,* 4 vols. [Salt Lake City: The Church of Jesus Christ of Latter-day Saints, 1946–1949], 3:45).

There are other examples where the Lord uses principles of preparation to help us be more pure and live the celestial law.

Joseph F. Smith:

> Self-respect, deference for sacred things, and personal purity are the beginnings and the essence of wisdom. The doctrines of the gospel, the Church restraint, are like

school-masters to keep us in the line of duty. If it were not for these schoolmasters, we would perish and be overcome by the evil about us. We see men who have freed themselves from Church restraint and from the precious doctrines of the gospel, who perish about us every day! They boast of freedom, but are the slaves of sin.

Let me admonish you to permit the gospel schoolmaster to teach you self-respect and to keep you pure and free from secret sins that bring not only physical punishment, but sure spiritual death. You cannot bide the penalty which God has affixed to them—a penalty often worse than death. It is the loss of self-respect, it is physical debility, it is insanity, indifference to all powers that are good and noble—all these follow in the wake of the sinner in secret, and of the unchaste. Unchastity, furthermore, not only fixes its penalty on the one who transgresses, but reaches out unerring punishment to the third and fourth generation, making not only the transgressor a wreck, but mayhap involving scores of people in his direct line of relationship, disrupting family ties, breaking the hearts of parents, and causing a black stream of sorrow to overwhelm their lives.

Such a seeming simple thing, then, as proper conduct in a house of worship leads to good results in many respects. Good conduct leads to self-respect, which creates purity of thought and action. Pure thought and noble action lead to a desire to serve God in the strength of manhood and to become subservient to the schoolmasters, Church restraint, and the doctrines of the gospel of Christ. (Joseph F. Smith, *Improvement Era*, Vol. 9, 1905–6, pp. 337–339; see *Gospel Doctrine: Selections from the Sermons and Writings of Joseph F. Smith,* compiled by John A. Widtsoe [Salt Lake City: Deseret Book, 1939], 335)

The Lord will surely help us become perfected just as we help and school our children to grow and become better children of God here upon the earth.

Likening the Scriptures to Our Lives

3 Nephi 12:17–48—The Lord explains that the law of Moses is fulfilled in Him. The higher law is now given for us to live.

Application—The higher law is a law for celestial living. It is a law of the heart and soul. It is not a schoolmaster of specific behaviors, but a law of living a Christlike life that we might become perfect. This is the charge: to become as He is—and we can (see 3 Ne. 27:27; Moro. 7:48).

4. THE NATURE OF TRUE DISCIPLESHIP

THEME. We are to be perfect, even as the Father and the Son are perfect. This process of perfection comes by living the Lord's word—both inwardly through a broken heart and a contrite spirit, as well as outwardly through a godly walk and conversation.

MOMENT OF TRUTH. These are the teachings that the true disciples of our Savior embrace, internalize, and practice in order to become more like Him. The Savior fulfills the commandment of the Father by teaching the Saints in America words of truth very similar to those He taught to His followers in Jerusalem. In this way, the Book of Mormon is a confirming testimony of the universality of divine instruction. There is but one gospel, just as there is to be but "one fold, and one shepherd" (3 Ne. 15:21).

MODERN PROPHETS SPEAK

Ezra Taft Benson:

> To walk in the steps of Jesus is to emulate His life and to look unto Him as our source of truth and example. Each of us would do well to periodically review His teachings in the Sermon on the Mount so that we are totally familiar with His way. In that sermon, one of the greatest of all sermons, we are told to be a light to others, to control our anger, to reconcile bad feelings with others before bringing gifts to the Lord, to love our enemy, to refrain from unholy and unvirtuous practices, to not allow lust to conceive in our hearts. We are further instructed how to pray, how to fast, and how to regulate our priorities. When these teachings are applied, Jesus said, we are like the wise man who built his house on a firm, solid foundation.
>
> We, His disciples, must follow the way of the Master. He is our guide to happiness here and eternal life hereafter. Our success in life will be determined by how closely we learn to walk in His steps. (*Come unto Christ* [Salt Lake City: Deseret Book, 1983], 37)

ILLUSTRATIONS FOR OUR TIME

A disciple of Jesus Christ is one who believes, follows, and attempts to live as the Savior lived. One need not have a special title or calling but rather be converted to the gospel of Jesus Christ and truly attempt to be even as He is. Everyone can be a pure disciple of Jesus Christ if he or she chooses to follow and represent Him in righteousness. Such is an example of a sweet sister missionary as told by Elder Elray L. Christiansen:

Last spring I attended the quarterly conference in one of the stakes in southern Idaho. Among the missionaries who reported was Sister Santana, a young woman of Mexican nationality. She had come to that stake to report her mission to those who had sent her. One of the families there had provided the funds for her mission, and it was reported that this Mexican girl had been instrumental in bringing into the Church more than fifty people during her time in the mission field.

Among other things, she said through an interpreter: "My testimony is the brightest gem in my possession. It is of more worth to me than is my life. I hope to bear it in good deeds." And she added, to those who had helped her, *"Muchas gracias."* It touched our hearts to see her with this priceless combination of treasures—a testimony and a desire to bear it in good deeds.

Any individual who has a testimony that is borne in clean living and in good works can expect to feel in that testimony a tremendous motivating power. It will help to direct him in his life, to guide him, to prompt him, to warn him. It becomes a formidable weapon against evil itself.

Some have asked, "How may one receive a living, impelling, life-directing testimony such as you speak of? How is such knowledge obtained?" The question was answered by Jesus, when he said:

"My doctrine is not mine, but his that sent me.

"If any man will do his will, he shall know of the doctrine, whether it be of God, or whether I speak of myself." (John 7:16–17.)

So any individual who will qualify himself by doing the will of God may find this same assurance, and there is no other way that I know anything about. (*CR,,* October 1952, 54)

Likening the Scriptures to Our Lives

3 Ne. 14:21–23—The Lord teaches us that it requires more than just supposing we have done things in His name but that we do things according to the will of God (see Luke 6:46) with a motive of love (see Moro. 7:5–11). We must come to know Him in order to gain eternal life.

Application—We need to yield our hearts to our God (see Hel. 3:35). It is most appropriate to seek to please God and do His will because we love Him (see John 14:15). We need to be motivated by love. We will know of the truth of His doctrine as we live it (see John 7:17) with an eye single to His glory (see D&C 88:67). As we do these things, we will know God and Jesus Christ and they will know us.

SUMMARY

The message of the Savior to His listeners in America two millennia ago is universal and timeless. In the "Beatitudes" He revealed His agenda for blessing them and all covenant peoples of every generation. He taught them that they were "the salt of the earth" and "a light to this people" (3 Ne. 12:13–14). With the law of Moses fulfilled in Him, He taught them how to live the higher law of perfection, including the practices that characterize the nature of true discipleship.

In these marvelous chapters of 3 Nephi, the Lord Jesus Christ gives to us His law for living. No cursory lesson can possibly do justice to these celestial and transcendent truths. What He taught should serve as the basis for a lifetime of study and application. He instructs us later in His discourse that we need to ponder and meditate over these teachings. These are the words to live by. These are our standards and values for living. They become our strength in the hour of need. They come as principles with a promise, even happiness and eventual eternal life.

CHAPTER THIRTY-NINE

"BEHOLD, MY JOY *is* FULL"

3 Nephi 16–19

"I do not look upon the Savior of the world as a man of gloom, nor do I regard the Gospel he gave to the world as one of despair, or one which is intended to kill the joy in humanity. . . .

"Christ did not come to take the color out of life, and I attribute the large measure of indifference to his word, indeed the resistance which is set up against it, in no small part to the erroneous interpretation of his cause, of his life and his service under which the world has suffered for centuries of time.

"'Men are that they might have joy.' It is as natural to long for joy as it is to live, and it would be a perversion of the fundamental philosophy of things if religion were to be interpreted as an imposition upon life, to take out its joy and its gladness."
—STEPHEN L. RICHARDS, [*CR*, APR. 1928], 30.

THEMES *for* LIVING

Ponder, Pray, and Prepare Your Minds
The Sacrament of the Lord
The Doctrine and Power of Prayer
Teach the People and Minister to Them in Love

INTRODUCTION

The Lord, following His initial teachings, encourages the Saints to go and ponder the things they had been taught. But first, out of compassion, He prays for and blesses the people, including their infirm and their little children. The Lord institutes the sacrament and the order of prayer in and through His name. Before departing, He empowers the disciples to give the Holy Ghost unto them who believe. The disciples minister to the people the following day, and the Savior returns to continue His instructions about the need to pray to the Father continually.

1. PONDER, PRAY, AND PREPARE YOUR MINDS.

THEME. Spiritual blessings flow to those whose hearts and minds are open, who search diligently, and who are sincerely prayerful in their quest to know the truth and become worthy, obedient children of God.

> *"Therefore, go ye unto your homes, and ponder upon the things which I have said, and ask of the Father, in my name, that ye may understand, and prepare your minds for the morrow, and I come unto you again" (3 Ne. 17:3).*

MOMENT OF TRUTH. Jesus directs the people to go to their homes, where they are to ponder the things they have seen and heard and pray sincerely that they might understand His teachings. In this manner, they prepare themselves for the following day when He should return. Thus He gives a memorable lesson concerning the vital importance of pondering about, and praying concerning, the principles of righteousness. The Savior then tarries long enough to bless their infirm and their little children. Miracles take place and angels minister to the little children encircled by fire. The people are blessed with unforgettable images to take with them to their homes as the basis for pondering and praying.

MODERN PROPHETS SPEAK

Bruce R. McConkie:

> Faith is thus born of scriptural study. Those who study, ponder, and pray about the scriptures, seeking to understand their deep and hidden meanings, receive from time to time great outpourings of light and knowledge from the Holy Spirit. This is what happened to Joseph Smith and Sidney Rigdon when they received the vision of the degrees of glory (D&C 76, superscription).

However talented men may be in administrative matters; however eloquent they may be in expressing their views; however learned they may be in worldly things—they will be denied the sweet whisperings of the Spirit that might have been theirs unless they pay the price of studying, pondering, and praying about the scriptures. (*Sermons and Writings of Bruce R. McConkie,* ed. Mark L. McConkie [Salt Lake City: Bookcraft, 1998], 238)

ILLUSTRATIONS FOR OUR TIME

The Miracle of a Child. Recently, in a conversation with me and my wife, a friend related a personal experience illustrating how close young children can be to the Spirit. Our friend was watching over his young four-year-old son one day while his wife was away from the home. At one point, the father realized that his son had been gone from his presence for some time. Concerned, the father conducted a search of the home, looking in every nook and cranny where the boy might have gone. Finding no trace, he searched the yard. There was still no sign of the boy. Now genuinely alarmed, the father searched through the house and yard again, repeatedly. When the boy could still not be found, the father went to the neighbors on all sides, only to learn that they had not seen the boy. Presently the entire neighborhood took up the search, going through the home again and again, and looking everywhere in the community. Everyone was enlisted in the increasingly frantic quest to find the missing boy. The father called the police. They came and searched as well. No trace. The boy had vanished. Everyone became anxious.

Then a little girl from a neighboring house took action concerning her lost friend. She went back into her own home and prayed to the Lord for help. Immediately she crossed back over into the boy's home and went directly to the master bedroom, walking up to a storage bench equipped with a hinged lid. She opened the lid—and there was the boy, sound asleep. No one had thought to look in that precise place—not the father, not the neighbors, not the police. But the girl looked there because that is how the Lord directed her. Once more, the verity of Alma's statement about little children was confirmed: "little children do have words given unto them many times, which confound the wise and the learned" (Alma 32:23). Our friend had learned firsthand that little children can be very close to the Spirit. Jesus said, "Suffer little children, and forbid them not, to come unto me: for of such is the kingdom of heaven" (Matt. 19:14). When the Savior was with the Nephites following His resurrection, He blessed the little children "one by one" (3 Ne. 17:21) and prayed for them. "And he spake unto the multitude, and said unto them: Behold your little ones. And as they looked to behold they cast their eyes towards heaven, and they saw the heavens open, and they saw angels descending out of heaven as it were in the midst of fire; and they came down and encircled those little ones about, and they were encircled about with fire; and the angels did minister unto them" (3 Ne. 17:23–24). The angels minister to little children more often than we understand or realize. (Allen)

Likening the Scriptures to our Lives

3 Ne. 17:20—Because of faith, the Savior's joy was full.

Application—Let us remember that we bring the Father and the Son great joy when we exercise our faith. On the basis of faith, we are able to receive greater blessings. We truly please God by our faith (see Heb. 11:6). Faith is the foundation of righteousness and the first and primary principle of living the gospel of Jesus Christ. Our faith causes us to do what we do; it moves us to action. As we spiritually exert ourselves, our faith gives us the power to do all things.

2. THE SACRAMENT OF THE LORD

THEME. As "the living bread" (John 6:51) and "the fountain of living waters" (Jer. 17:13), the Savior is commemorated in the sacrament as all supplicants renew their covenants and commit to live lives worthy of His Spirit. The sacrament is a profoundly sacred ordinance instituted to help us remember.

> *"And this shall ye always observe to do, even as I have done, even as I have broken bread and blessed it and given it unto you. And this shall ye do in remembrance of my body, which I have shown unto you. And it shall be a testimony unto the Father that ye do always remember me. And if ye do always remember me ye shall have my Spirit to be with you. And it came to pass that when he said these words, he commanded his disciples that they should take of the wine of the cup and drink of it, and that they should also give unto the multitude that they might drink of it. . . . And when the disciples had done this, Jesus said unto them: Blessed are ye for this thing which ye have done, for this is fulfilling my commandments, and this doth witness unto the Father that ye are willing to do that which I have commanded you. And this shall ye always do to those who repent and are baptized in my name; and ye shall do it in remembrance of my blood, which I have shed for you, that ye may witness unto the Father that ye do always remember me. And if ye do always remember me ye shall have my Spirit to be with you. And I give unto you a commandment that ye shall do these things. And if ye shall always do these things blessed are ye, for ye are built upon my rock" (3 Ne. 18:6–8, 10–12).*

MOMENT OF TRUTH. The Lord institutes the sacrament among the Nephites. In an event of unimaginable poignancy and holiness, the disciples and the multitude are taught by the Redeemer Himself how to administer this ordinance, which commemorates the atoning sacrifice and grants unto the participants the sacred privilege of renewing their covenant vows before the Lord.

MODERN PROPHETS SPEAK

Gordon B. Hinckley:

> We are a covenant people. . . . The first of these is the covenant of the sacrament, in which we take upon ourselves the name of the Savior and agree to keep His commandments with the promise in His covenant that He will bless us with His spirit. If our people would go to sacrament meeting every week and reflect as they partake of the sacrament on the meaning of the prayers which are offered, . . . if they would listen to the language of those prayers, which were given by revelation, and live by them, we would be a better people, all of us would be. That is the importance of the sacrament meeting. (*Teachings of Gordon B. Hinckley* [Salt Lake City: Deseret Book, 1997], 146–147)

ILLUSTRATIONS FOR OUR TIME

The Renewing of Covenants. We renew our baptismal covenants with the symbolic representation of our Savior's body and blood. We recognize and remember His infinite and eternal sacrifice—the infinite Atonement. In partaking of the sacrament, we renew all our covenants, including those having to do with baptism, the priesthood, and the temple.

President Hinckley has said, "Each of us has made a covenant with the Lord and we renew that covenant as we partake of the sacrament. We take upon ourselves covenants in His holy house, and that covenant is in similitude of the covenant that Jehovah made with Abraham, that He would be our God and we would be His people" ("Pres. Hinckley Continues Rapid Pace," *LDS Church News, 1997*, 03/01/97).

Elder Delbert L. Stapley reviewed the covenants involved with membership in the Church:

> (1) The gospel of our Lord Jesus Christ is a covenant between God and his people. (2) When baptized by an authorized servant of God, we covenant to do God's will and to obey his commandments. (3) By partaking of the Sacrament we renew all covenants entered into with the Lord and pledge ourselves to take upon us the name of his Son, to always remember him and keep his commandments. (4) There is an oath and covenant which belongs to the priesthood wherein men receiving this holy power pledge themselves faithfully to keep all the commandments of God and to magnify their callings in the priesthood, which is God's gift of his power and authority unto them. (5) In connection with all ordinances pertaining to the temples of our God, men and women accept covenants and obligations which relate to the endowment and to the eternity of the marriage and family relationship. All these doctrines and more are necessary and vital to the salvation, exaltation and eternal happiness of God's children. (*CR,* Oct. 1965, 14)

When we appreciate the covenants that God has made with His children and the blessings associated with them, we will change. We will have a strong desire to keep our covenants and witness before God our willingness to do so by partaking of the sacrament.

Likening the Scriptures to Our Lives

3 Ne. 18:11—The Lord reminds us that those who repent and are baptized in His name shall do it in remembrance of His body and blood, which He sacrificed for us. If we always remember Him we will always have His Spirit to be with us.

Application—We have the glorious opportunity to renew our covenants as we partake of the sacrament. Let us remember that as we keep the commandments the blessing of the Spirit will be in our lives.

3. THE DOCTRINE AND POWER OF PRAYER

THEME. Prayer is intimate communication with God, the channel for inspiration, the most direct means for expressing gratitude, the posture and essence of humility, the witness of a broken heart, the voice of a contrite spirit, the start and the finish of the quest for forgiveness. All of these things and many more characterize the nobility and the sacredness of prayer to our Heavenly Father. The Lord taught the substance and manner of prayer on every occasion where He ministered to the people. Prayer is the soul of gospel living.

> *"Behold, verily, verily, I say unto you, ye must watch and pray always lest ye enter into temptation; for Satan desireth to have you, that he may sift you as wheat" (3 Ne. 18:18).*

> *"Pray in your families unto the Father, always in my name, that your wives and your children may be blessed" (3 Ne. 18:21).*

> *"Therefore ye must always pray unto the Father in my name" (3 Ne. 18:19).*

MOMENT OF TRUTH. The Savior encourages the people to pray always lest they be tempted by the devil. He demonstrates pointedly the manner of prayer: "And as I have prayed among you even so shall ye pray in my church, among my people who do repent and are baptized in my name. Behold I am the light; I have set an example for you" (3 Ne. 18:16). The people are to pray in their families—always in the Savior's name. Following His departure, the disciples pray for what they desire most: the Holy Ghost (see 3 Ne. 19:9).

MODERN PROPHETS SPEAK

Jeffrey R. Holland:

> I can hardly imagine what it might be like to have *heard* the Savior pray in that set-
> ting, but I cannot even comprehend what is meant when they say that "no tongue
> can speak, neither can there be written by any man, neither can the hearts of men
> conceive" what they *saw* the Savior pray. It's one thing to *hear* such a prayer. It's sure-
> ly something altogether more to *see* one. What *did* they see? Well, it can't be writ-
> ten. But suffice it to say that this is the great, consummate, concluding example the
> Savior sets for those people that day, the culminating jewel, the crowning, post-
> sacramental counsel given to the Twelve and all others who would take up the cross
> and follow him—they must pray always. ("'For a Wise Purpose'" *Ensign,* Jan. 1996,
> 18–19)

ILLUSTRATIONS FOR OUR TIME

The Wisdom of Prayer. The Lord has counseled us to pray lest we be tempted beyond that which we
can withstand (see Alma 13:27–28; 3 Ne. 18:15,18). Elder J. Golden Kimball reminds us: "Remember
this always: Temptation somewhere in the life of all finds us, as this life is a testing time. Therefore,
watch and pray and ask God to leave us not in temptation and deliver us from evil, as temptation is
ever lying in wait, and in a thousand forms is temptation repeated. There is divine wisdom in praying
always and avoiding the very appearance of evil" (from Claude Richards, *J. Golden Kimball: The Story
of a Unique Personality* [Salt Lake City: Deseret News Press, 1934], 329).

Remember that each person has a different level of temptation in different aspects of his or her life. The
Word of Wisdom is always a challenge to those who have allowed a habit to take hold of them.
Patriarch Eldred G. Smith tells this simple story of the power of prayer and how it helps us overcome
temptation:

> Humility is one of the qualities that help build faith. Would a missionary be suc-
> cessful if he were not humble? He has to be teachable with a receptive mind before
> he can teach others, and to be teachable, he must be humble. And we should all be
> missionaries.

> All the requirements of living the gospel become easier through humility.

> A young man told me his experience in becoming a member of the Church. . . .
> He said the missionaries came to the lesson on the Word of Wisdom. He and his
> wife were both users of tobacco. After the meeting was over and the missionaries

had left, they talked it over with each other and decided among themselves, "Well, if that is what the Lord wants and if this is the Lord's Church, we will try it." He said that he was not particularly concerned about himself, he thought he could do it easily. He was worried about his wife; she had never tried to quit before. On the other hand, he had quit several times. After proving to himself that he could quit, of course, he went back to the use of cigarettes again. But he said in this case it was just the reverse. His wife quit without any apparent difficulty, but he had tremendous difficulty. He became nervous and irritable. He could not rest. He was cranky among his fellow workers. He could not sleep at night. But inasmuch as his wife had quit, he was not going to be outdone by her. So, one night, he became so restless, so disturbed that he could not sleep, and his wife suggested to him that he pray about it. He thought that was a good joke. He ridiculed the idea of prayer; he said, "This is something I have to do. Nobody can help me with this. I can do this." But as the night passed, and he had done everything he could to stimulate sleep and rest without any success, finally in despair, he humbled himself enough to kneel at the side of the bed and pray vocally. According to his own testimony, he said that he got up from his prayer, got into bed, went to sleep, and has never been tempted by cigarettes since. He has absolutely lost the taste for tobacco. He said, "The Word of Wisdom was not a health program for me. It was a lesson in humility." He said, "I had to learn humility." That is what it meant to him. As it is with many of the requirements of the Church, we have to demonstrate humble obedience. (*CR,* Apr. 1955, 42)

Likening the Scriptures to Our Lives

3 Ne. 18:19–21—The Lord instructs us to pray in His name. We are to ask (as directed by the Spirit) the things that are right (see D&C 88:64–65), doing so with faith that it shall be given us. We are instructed to pray in our families that all might be blessed.

Application—We should always remember that our Savior, Jesus Christ, is our advocate. We pray in His name. We can only come to the Father in and through the Lord, Jesus Christ (see John 14:6). Let us seek in our prayers for wisdom and strength to do the will of the Father (see Hel. 10:5).

4. TEACH THE PEOPLE AND MINISTER TO THEM IN LOVE

THEME. Ministering to the people of the kingdom of God in accordance with the instructions of the Savior brings about miraculous spiritual blessings for the Saints.

The Spirit is bestowed, joy is spread, and unity assured. The essence of the ministry is to lift people up toward a more righteous mode of living so that the Lord might grant His choicest blessings to His humble and obedient children.

> *"And the twelve did teach the multitude; and behold, they did cause that the multitude should kneel down upon the face of the earth, and should pray unto the Father in the name of Jesus. And the disciples did pray unto the Father also in the name of Jesus. And it came to pass that they arose and ministered unto the people. And when they had ministered those same words which Jesus had spoken—nothing varying from the words which Jesus had spoken—behold, they knelt again and prayed to the Father in the name of Jesus. And they did pray for that which they most desired; and they desired that the Holy Ghost should be given unto them. And when they had thus prayed they went down unto the water's edge, and the multitude followed them. And it came to pass that Nephi went down into the water and was baptized. And he came up out of the water and began to baptize. And he baptized all those whom Jesus had chosen. And it came to pass when they were all baptized and had come up out of the water, the Holy Ghost did fall upon them, and they were filled with the Holy Ghost and with fire" (3 Ne. 19:6–13).*

MOMENT OF TRUTH. Following the ascension of the Lord, the Nephite disciples begin to teach and minister unto the people. So great is the multitude that the disciples divide the people into twelve groups, with a disciple conveying to each group the words of Christ. They pray for the Holy Ghost and then commence the work of baptism—beginning with the disciples. The Holy Ghost fills them, and they are encircled "as if it were by fire" (3 Ne. 19:14). The Savior again appears and instructs them to pray. He prays also, and their faces shine with glorious light. The Savior prays to the Father in words of unspeakable grandeur before the people. The Savior extols the people for their faith.

MODERN PROPHETS SPEAK

Merrill J. Bateman:

> The record indicates that the multitude went forth *"one by one* until they had all gone forth, and did see with their eyes and did feel with their hands, and did know of a surety" (3 Nephi 11:15; emphasis added). Although the multitude totaled 2,500 souls, the record states that "all of them did see and hear, every man for himself" (3 Nephi 17:25). If each person were given 15 seconds to approach the resurrected Lord, thrust their hand into his side, and feel the prints of the nails, more than 10 hours would be required to complete the process.

> The record indicates that later in the day the Savior "took their little children, *one by one,* and blessed them" (3 Nephi 17:21; emphasis added). The scriptures do not indicate how

many children were there, but one surmises that in a multitude of 2,500, there must have been a few hundred. Again, it would have taken hours to complete the blessings.

Why did Jesus take the time to invite each individual to feel the wounds in his hands and feet and put their hand into his side? Why did he bless each child rather than give a collective pronouncement? Would the personal touch of his hands and the power of his spirit be more efficacious in a "one by one" relationship? The answer is given by the Savior himself when he said:

And ye see that I have commanded that none of you should go away, but rather have commanded that ye should come unto me, that ye might feel and see; even so shall ye do unto the world [3 Nephi 18:25]. (*Brigham Young University 1997–98 Speeches* [Provo, Utah: Brigham Young University Publications and Graphics, 1998], 15).

ILLUSTRATIONS FOR OUR TIME

A Beloved Teacher. We are nurtured by the good word of God by inspirational teachers—men and women of God who care, who teach and minister by the Spirit. There is probably no role within the family or in any Church setting that is as powerful as that of being a teacher. We have all been blessed by our parents or that friend, coach, or special teacher who has made a difference in our lives. President Monson shares with us this special story that demonstrates "A Beloved Teacher":

It was my experience as a small boy to come under the influence of a great teacher, Lucy Gertsch. We met for the first time on a Sunday morning. She accompanied the Sunday School superintendent into the classroom and was presented to us as a teacher who actually requested the opportunity to teach us. We learned that she had been a missionary and loved young people.

Lucy Gertsch was beautiful, soft-spoken, and interested in us. She asked each class member to introduce himself or herself, and then she asked questions that gave her an understanding and insight into the background of each boy, each girl. She told us of her childhood in Midway, Utah; and as she described that beautiful valley, she made its beauty live, and we desired to visit the green fields and clear streams she loved so much. She never raised her voice. Somehow rudeness and boisterousness were incompatible with the beauty of her lessons. She taught us that the present is here and that we must live in it. She made the scriptures actually come to life. We became personally acquainted with Samuel, David, Jacob, Nephi, and the Lord Jesus Christ. Our gospel scholarship grew. Our deportment improved. Our love for Lucy knew no bounds.

In our Sunday School class, she taught us concerning the creation of the world, the fall of Adam, the atoning sacrifice of Jesus. She brought to her classroom as honored guests Moses, Joshua, Peter, Thomas, Paul, and even Christ. Though we did not see them, we learned to love, honor, and emulate them.

Never was her teaching so dynamic nor its impact more everlasting than one Sunday morning when she sadly announced to us the passing of a classmate's mother. We had missed Billy that morning but knew not the reason for his absence. The lesson featured the theme "It is more blessed to give than to receive." Midway through the lesson, our teacher closed the manual and opened our eyes and our ears and our hearts to the glory of God. She asked, "How much money do we have in our class party fund?" Depression days prompted a proud answer: "Four dollars and seventy-five cents." Then ever so gently she suggested: "Billy's family is hard-pressed and grief-stricken. What would you think of the possibility of visiting the family members this morning and giving them your fund?"

Ever shall I remember the tiny band walking those three city blocks, entering Billy's home, greeting him and his brother, sisters, and father. Noticeably absent was his mother. Always I shall treasure the tears that glistened in the eyes of all as the white envelope containing our precious party fund passed from the delicate hand of our teacher to the needy hand of a grief-stricken father. We fairly skipped back to the chapel. Our hearts were lighter than they had ever been, our joy more full, our understanding more profound. A God-inspired teacher had taught her boys and girls an eternal lesson of divine truth. "It is more blessed to give than to receive."

The years have flown. The old chapel is gone, a victim of industrialization. The boys and girls who learned, who laughed, who grew under the direction of that inspired teacher of truth have never forgotten her love or her lessons. (*Inspiring Experiences That Build Faith: From the Life and Ministry of Thomas S. Monson* [Salt Lake City: Deseret Book, 1994], 211)

Likening the Scriptures to Our Lives

3 Ne. 19:9—The people prayed for that which they most desired—that they might receive the Holy Ghost.

Application—The Holy Ghost is the greatest source for comfort, direction, inspiration, and guidance for a righteous life on earth. It is the gift from Heavenly Father because of His Beloved Son. We fundamentally need the gift and blessing of the Holy Ghost in our lives. We should do all in our power to be worthy of this blessing through increasing our faith (see 1 Nephi 10:17), cultivating love for God, purifying ourselves (see D&C 76:116), and being obedient (see D&C 20:77, 79).

SUMMARY

These chapters record the priceless instruction of the Savior on some gospel fundamentals: how to ponder, pray, and prepare our minds with regard to spiritual matters; being worthy of the blessings of the sacrament of the Lord; the doctrine and power of using prayer on a regular basis; and how to teach the people and minister to them in love. In all of these things the Lord is the ultimate model.

The Lord loves us. He wants us to be happy and partake of the blessings of eternal life. His joy is for us to grow and become even as He is. He wants us to understand the doctrines, principles, and covenants that will help us return to the presence of our Heavenly Father. This is why He takes time to commission others to teach us the same. We must do certain things through our own agency in order to partake of the blessings of His gospel teachings. If we draw on the powers of heaven through our prayers, we will be protected and blessed in all that we do.

CHAPTER FORTY

"THEN WILL I GATHER THEM IN"

3 Nephi 16, 20–21

"We are to build up and establish Zion, gather the House of Israel, and redeem the nations of the earth. This people have this work to do, whether we live to see it or not. This is all in our hands. . . .

"It is obligatory upon us to see that the House of Israel have the Gospel preached to them; to do all that is in our power to gather them to the land of their fathers, and to gather up the fulness of the Gentiles before the Gospel can go with success to the Jews. . . .

"We are now gathering the children of Abraham who have come through the loins of Joseph and his sons, more especially through Ephraim, whose children are mixed among all the nations of the earth."
—Brigham Young, *Discourses of Brigham Young,* sel. John A. Widtsoe [Salt Lake City: Deseret Book, 1954], 437.

THEMES *for* LIVING

Participating in the Promised Gathering of Israel

INTRODUCTION

When the risen Lord visited the remnants of Israel in America, He gave them divine standards for righteous living and the power and authority to minister in all things for the salvation of His children within the covenant framework of Zion. Moreover, He granted a higher perspective of how they fit into the grand design for the future gathering of Israel from the four quarters of the earth in fulfillment of sacred promises to their forefathers, Abraham, Isaac, and Jacob. Just as He had caused them to be gathered to the temple for instruction, in like manner would the Father, through the Son, gather His children from their long dispersal over time back to holy places of refuge and enlightenment as part of the gospel plan of redemption. The Savior's instruction to the ancient American Saints about the gathering—including His interpretive citation of the Old Testament prophets, especially Isaiah—is a magnificent reaffirmation for us today of the covenant patterns of Zion that would emerge as part of the restoration of all things leading up to the Second Coming.

1. PARTICIPATING IN THE PROMISED GATHERING OF ISRAEL

THEME. According to the dynamics of the grand covenant enterprise, the Lord scatters and gathers His people for the ultimate blessing of mankind. The scattering process may serve to protect (as with Lehi's emigrating colony), correct (because of iniquity or wickedness), or connect (as with the modern-day dispersal of missionaries throughout the world to spread the gospel message among the honest-at-heart). The gathering process is much the same: to protect the Saints by bringing them to holy places of refuge within the stakes of Zion where houses of the Lord abound (sacred temples, as well as chapels and righteous homes), to correct the Saints in an ongoing way through inspired instruction by the prophets of God, and to connect the Saints one with another and with the Holy Spirit.

> *"And I command you that ye shall write these sayings after I am gone, that if it so be that my people at Jerusalem, they who have seen me and been with me in my ministry, do not ask the Father in my name, that they may receive a knowledge of you by the Holy Ghost, and also of the other tribes whom they know not of, that these sayings which ye shall write shall be kept and shall be manifested unto the Gentiles, that through the fulness of the Gentiles, the remnant of their seed, who shall be scattered forth upon the face of the earth because of their unbelief, may be brought in, or may be brought to a knowledge of me, their Redeemer. And then will I gather them in from the four quarters of the earth; and then will I fulfil the covenant which the Father hath made unto all the people of the house of Israel" (3 Ne. 16:4–5).*

"And then shall the remnants, which shall be scattered abroad upon the face of the earth, be gathered in from the east and from the west, and from the south and from the north; and they shall be brought to the knowledge of the Lord their God, who hath redeemed them" (3 Ne. 20:13).

"And verily I say unto you, I give unto you a sign, that ye may know the time when these things shall be about to take place—that I shall gather in, from their long dispersion, my people, O house of Israel, and shall establish again among them my Zion" (3 Ne. 21:1).

MOMENT OF TRUTH. The Savior teaches the people about the scattering and gathering of Israel, prophesying of their spiritual and literal gathering in the latter days. There will be signs and events that show that the gathering of the house of Israel has started, and it is going on today. The coming forth of the Book of Mormon among the nations as part of "a great and a marvelous work" (3 Ne. 21:9) to restore the word of God and the fulness of the gospel is among the greatest signs that the Lord has commenced the gathering of His people.

MODERN PROPHETS SPEAK

Joseph Smith:

> One of the most important points in the faith of the Church of the Latter-day Saints, through the fullness of the everlasting Gospel, is the gathering of Israel (of whom the Lamanites constitute a part)—that happy time when Jacob shall go up to the house of the Lord, to worship Him in spirit and in truth, to live in holiness; when the Lord will restore His judges as at first, and His counselors as at the beginning; when every man may sit under his own vine and fig tree, and there will be none to molest or make afraid; when He will turn to them a pure language, and the earth will be filled with sacred knowledge, as the waters cover the great deep; when it shall no longer be said, the Lord lives that brought up the children of Israel out of the land of Egypt, but the Lord lives that brought up the children of Israel from the land of the north, and from all the lands whither He has driven them. That day is one, all important to all men. (*HC,* 2:357)

ILLUSTRATIONS FOR OUR TIME

Everyday Gatherings in Zion. The gathering of Israel proceeds at multiple levels in full spiritual vigor. While tens of thousands of stalwart missionaries seek to gather the remnants of Israel from around the world, families of the Church—"the children of the prophets" and "the children of the covenant" as Christ characterized them (3 Ne. 20:25, 26)—gather together continually. Elder L. Tom Perry assures us, "If we will build righteous traditions in our families, the light of the gospel can grow ever brighter in the lives of our children from generation to generation. We can look forward to that glorious day when we will all be united together as eternal family units to reap the everlasting joy promised by our Eternal Father for His righteous children. Our family activities and traditions can be a beacon to the rest of the world as an example of how we should live to merit His choice blessings and live in peace and harmony until the day that He returns to rule and reign over us" (*Ensign*, May 1990, 20). Through missionary work, temple work, worship services, and family activities (especially family home evening and family reunions), we can participate in the gathering of Zion foretold by prophets in every age and confirmed by the risen Lord: "And I will remember the covenant which I have made with my people; and I have covenanted with them that I would gather them together in mine own due time" (3 Ne. 20:29). (Allen and Pinegar)

Likening the Scriptures to Our Lives

3 Ne. 20:1—The multitude continued to pray until finally the Lord told them to cease their prayers but always to pray in their hearts.

Application—Our heart is the center of our soul; along with our mind, it is the decision- and affection-center of our very being. Consequently, when our hearts are drawn out in prayer, we truly have our minds centered on the things of the Lord and the welfare of others (see Mosiah 24:12; Alma 34:27; D&C 19:28). Such a focus of thought on God's will facilitates gathering our fellowmen unto Christ.

SUMMARY

When the Savior appeared to the Israelite remnants in America following the predicted upheavals that cleansed the land, the surviving multitudes were "gathered together . . . round about the temple which was in the land Bountiful" (3 Ne. 11:1). How fitting that they were thus assembled near a holy place in a state of "marveling and wondering" (3 Nephi 11:1), with open hearts and minds ready to receive the glorious Visitor into their midst. The Savior taught them how to live a celestial law and how to magnify their role as part of the design of the Father to gather His children to Zion and, eventually, to their eternal heavenly home.

Jesus counseled them to gather to their homes to ponder and internalize the light He had given them. When word was "noised abroad" concerning the Savior's visit and announced return, the multitudes flocked in from all regions of the land (3 Ne. 19:1–3). The disciples "gathered" them together into twelve major groups (not without analogy to the twelve tribes of Israel) to hear the words that the Savior had given them (3 Ne. 19:5–8). The Savior appeared again and taught them about the gathering—in the broadest sense of the term—that would characterize the work of Zion in the latter days among the Gentile nations and the remnants of Israel. This kindles within the hearts and souls of devout Saints everywhere the desire to become active participants in the gathering together of the Lord's sons and daughters and the gathering in one of His sacred word (2 Ne. 29:14). The sign given by the Savior that this ultimate gathering had commenced was the restoration of the gospel and priesthood in our time, including the coming forth of the Book of Mormon.

How privileged we are to take part in these consummating events and celebrate the glorious renewal of God's work: "And then shall they say: How beautiful upon the mountains are the feet of him that bringeth good tidings unto them, that publisheth peace; that bringeth good tidings unto them of good, that publisheth salvation; that saith unto Zion: Thy God reigneth!" (3 Ne. 20:40, cf. Isa. 52:7; Mosiah 15:18).

CHAPTER FORTY-ONE

"HE DID EXPOUND ALL THINGS UNTO THEM"

3 NEPHI 22–26

"Who has seen such marvelous things as Jesus did among the Nephites? And who has heard such wondrous words of divine wisdom as fell from his lips on the American continent? . . . Jesus 'did expound all things, even from the beginning until the time that he should come in his glory . . .' In the providences of the Lord, we have slivers and fragments of what Jesus gave the Nephites. Sections 29, 45, 63, 76, 77, 88, 93, 101, 107, 132, 133, and 138 in the Doctrine and Covenants, and the books of Moses and Abraham in the Pearl of Great Price, all contain truths of transcendent worth about the doings of Deity from the beginning to the end."
—BRUCE R. MCCONKIE, *THE MORTAL MESSIAH: FROM BETHLEHEM TO CALVARY*, 4 VOLS. [SALT LAKE CITY: DESERET BOOK, 1979–1981], 4: 369.

THEMES *for* LIVING

The Establishment of Zion in the Latter Days
Searching the Words of Isaiah and the Prophets
Keeping Vital Records of Truth
Understanding All Things from the Beginning to the End

INTRODUCTION

What greater revelation could there be than the manifestation of divine truth directly from the Savior Himself? He opened up unto them a fuller vision of the plan of salvation—from the beginning even until the end of time, when He would return in glory to the earth. He testified of the heavenly commission of the prophets ("great are the words of Isaiah"—3 Ne. 23:1), commanded that the canon of scripture be studied continually, directed that omissions be corrected, and supplemented what the people had already received by giving them the key prophecies from Malachi. Truly the words of the prophets from the past give insight and meaning to our lives. They teach us the precious doctrines that bring us closer to our spiritual objectives as we understand and apply them. All such prophecies point to the atoning mission of the Savior.

1. THE ESTABLISHMENT
OF ZION IN THE LATTER DAYS

THEME. One of the grand themes of the Book of Mormon is the "great mercies" and "everlasting kindness" of the Lord in watching over and lifting up Israel (see 3 Ne. 22:7–8). Emanating from the account of the Lord's dealings with His people over the millennia there is always the promise of the ultimate gathering together of the House of Israel in the latter days and the establishment of an enduring theocratic society of Zion with the Lord Himself as the Lawgiver and Head.

> *"Sing, O barren, thou that didst not bear; break forth into singing, and cry aloud, thou that didst not travail with child; for more are the children of the desolate than the children of the married wife, saith the Lord" (3 Ne. 22:1).*

> *"Enlarge the place of thy tent, and let them stretch forth the curtains of thy habitations; spare not, lengthen thy cords and strengthen thy stakes" (3 Ne. 22:2).*

> *"For a small moment have I forsaken thee, but with great mercies will I gather thee" (3 Ne. 22:7).*

MOMENT OF TRUTH. The Savior recites Isaiah concerning the house of Israel. The Lord's people will overcome their past iniquities and participate in the building up of Zion in the latter days. Scattered Israel, those without the gospel, are to be gathered into Zion and endowed with truth (see D&C 82:14; Isa. 33:20). The Savior emphasizes that He will forgive scattered Israel for her wickedness as she returns to Him in faithfulness. He reassures the people that He will not forget Israel and the covenant promises He has made.

MODERN PROPHETS SPEAK

Ezra Taft Benson:

> In the scriptures there are set forth three phases of the gathering of Israel. One, the gathering of Israel to the land of Zion which is America, this land. That is under way and has been under way since the Church was established and our missions abroad were inaugurated. Then two, the return of the lost tribes, the ten lost tribes, from the land of the north (see D&C 133). And the third phase is the reestablishment of the Jews in Palestine as one of the events to precede the second coming of the Master. (*The Teachings of Ezra Taft Benson* [Salt Lake City: Bookcraft, 1988], 91)

ILLUSTRATIONS FOR OUR TIME

Missionary Work Establishes Zion.

David B. Haight:

> What a privilege and a blessing to be a small part of this great work! With that heritage, however, comes a great responsibility. The Lord needs messengers to match His message. He needs those who are able to wield the mighty and eternal influence that He has placed in their hands. In section 88, where the Lord speaks of hastening His work, He gives to the laborers of His kingdom a commandment to "prepare yourselves, and sanctify yourselves; yea, purify your hearts, and cleanse your hands and your feet before me, that I may make you clean" (D&C 88:74)
> ("Missionary Work—Our Responsibility," *Ensign*, Nov. 1993, 62–63).

Likening the Scriptures to Our Lives

3 Ne. 22:2—The Lord quotes Isaiah (He having given Isaiah these words in the first place) and teaches the concept of establishing the kingdom, comparing it to a large tent. The tent is literally held up and strengthened by the individual stakes. These stakes are units of the kingdom throughout the earth.

Application—Each stake in the Church is part of the kingdom of God. As members of the Church grow in righteousness and numbers, the tent (the kingdom of God on earth) is enlarged and made stronger. Our duty is to prepare the people and gather the righteous into the Lord's fold that they might partake of eternal life.

2. SEARCHING THE WORDS OF ISAIAH AND THE PROPHETS

THEME. The prophets of God are the messengers of salvation who convey to mankind the words of Christ. For that reason, we are commanded to search the scriptures diligently because they lead us into the pathways of faith, repentance, and baptism, and enable us to endure to the end.

> *"And now, behold, I say unto you, that ye ought to search these things. Yea, a command-ment I give unto you that ye search these things diligently; for great are the words of Isaiah"* (3 Ne. 23:1).

> *"And whosoever will hearken unto my words and repenteth and is baptized, the same shall be saved. Search the prophets, for many there be that testify of these things"* (3 Ne. 23:5).

MOMENT OF TRUTH. The Lord testifies of the greatness of the words of Isaiah—"For surely he spake as touching all things concerning my people which are of the house of Israel" (3 Ne. 23:2)—and encourages the people to search the words of the prophets as the source of truth unto salvation. It is instructive that the Lord demonstrates for the people the actions He calls for, for He expounds the scriptures unto them, even "all things" (3 Ne. 26:1) from the beginning until the consummation of His work. What greater instruction concerning the word of God can one have than from the Word Himself (see Luke 24:27, 32)?

MODERN PROPHETS SPEAK

Joseph Smith:

> Search the scriptures—search the revelations which are published and ask your Heavenly Father, in the name of His Son Jesus Christ, to manifest the truth unto you, and if you do it with an eye single to His glory nothing doubting, He will answer you by the power of His Holy Spirit. You will then know for yourselves and not for another. You will not then be dependent on man for the knowledge of God; nor will there by any room for speculation. . . . For when men receive their instruction from Him that made them, they know how He will save them. . . . Again we say: Search the Scriptures, search the Prophets and learn what portion of them belongs to you. (*Teachings of the Prophet Joseph Smith,* comp. Joseph Fielding Smith [Salt Lake City: Deseret Book Co, 1976], 11–12)

ILLUSTRATIONS FOR OUR TIME

Why Are Isaiah's Words So Great and Important? Here are some interesting facts concerning the Prophet Isaiah and those quoting from his words:

Victor L. Ludlow:

The following list suggests some reasons why Isaiah's prophecies about the last days are so important:

1. Some fifty-three of the sixty-six chapters of the book of Isaiah, if they do not deal exclusively with the latter days, contain verses pointing to our time. (Those that do not are 7–9, 15–16, 20–21, 23, 36–39, and 46.) It would seem that the prophet spent more time envisioning our day than he did teaching in his own!

2. Nephi writes of Isaiah's prophecies, "I know that they shall be of great worth unto them *in the last days;* for *in that day* shall they understand them; wherefore, for their good I have written them." (2 Ne. 25:8; italics added.)

3. Nephi's brother Jacob writes, "And now, behold, I would speak unto you concerning things which are, and *which are to come:* wherefore, I will read you the words of Isaiah." (2 Ne. 6:4; italics added.)

4. As one scholar has described Isaiah, "Never perhaps has there been another prophet like Isaiah, who stood with his head in the clouds and his feet on the solid earth, *with his heart in the things of eternity* and with mouth and hand in the things of time, with his spirit in the eternal counsel of God and his body in a very definite moment of history." (Robinson, *The Book of Isaiah,* p. 22; italics added.)

5. A latter-day apostle, Bruce R. McConkie, has said, "Much of what Isaiah . . . has to say is yet to be fulfilled. If we are to truly comprehend the writings of Isaiah, we cannot overstate or overstress the plain, blunt reality that he is in fact the prophet of the restoration, the mighty seer of Jacob's seed who foresaw our day." *(Ensign,* Oct. 1973, p. 81.)

6. One clue to finding Isaiah's passages about the last days is to note his banner-phrase "in that day," for it occurs forty-two times throughout his work, almost always in conjunction with prophecies about our day.

7. Like the messianic prophecies, the prophecies of the last days in the writings of Isaiah are often written on many levels and find fulfillment in ages beyond those in which they were spoken or recorded. For this reason, some latter-day prophecies seem juxtaposed or out of place against fairly mundane historical background. But Isaiah is not alone in this prophetic style. In Revelation, John repeatedly moves backward and forward in time to make his point and strengthen his rhetoric, though in doing so he often confuses those who do not have the same prophetic insight as he does. For an

Isaianic example, Isaiah launches forth in a declaration of the restoration of the gospel in chapter 5, verses 26–30 in the midst of what could be a call to repentance for any age.

8. Jews reading Isaiah miss the messianic references, which apply to Jesus Christ, while the traditional Christian readers usually overlook the glorious message of the Restoration. Latter-day Saints stand apart in their perspective of Isaiah because, with their fuller understanding of the gospel, they should be able to see how Isaiah's prophecies can find a full range of fulfillment and application. (*Isaiah: Prophet, Seer, and Poet* [Salt Lake City: Deseret Book, 1982], 55–57)

Likening the Scriptures to Our Lives

3 Nephi 23:1—The Lord commands the people to search these things (the words of Isaiah), for Isaiah's words are great.

Application—When we come to understand Isaiah, we will truly understand the role of the house of Israel. "A major reason for searching Isaiah's prophecies, as declared by the Savior and confirmed by Nephi and Jacob, is that Isaiah spoke concerning all the house of Israel and the covenants unto them which were to be fulfilled in the latter days"(*Great Are the Words of Isaiah,* Monte S. Nyman [Salt Lake City: Bookcraft, 1980], 3).

3. KEEPING VITAL RECORDS OF TRUTH

THEME. It is wisdom in God that His word is promulgated in spoken form and preserved in written form to be handed down to His children, including all that is "expedient" for them to know (see 2 Ne. 3:19; 3 Ne. 26:9; D&C 75:10; 88:127). The reason is clear, as Alma explained to his son Helaman: "And now, it has hitherto been wisdom in God that these things should be preserved; for behold, they have enlarged the memory of this people, yea, and convinced many of the error of their ways, and brought them to the knowledge of their God unto the salvation of their souls. Yea, I say unto you, were it not for these things that these records do contain, which are on these plates, Ammon and his brethren could not have convinced so many thousands of the Lamanites of the incorrect tradition of their fathers; yea, these records and their words brought them unto repentance; that is, they brought them to the knowledge of the Lord their God, and to rejoice in Jesus Christ their Redeemer. And who knoweth but what they will be the means of bringing many thousands of them, yea, and also many thousands of our stiffnecked brethren, the Nephites, who are now hardening their hearts in sin and iniquities, to the knowledge of their Redeemer?" (Alma 37:8–10). It is ultimately from the written records that the people will be judged (see 2 Ne. 29:11; 3 Ne. 27:25–26; D&C 128:7–8; Moses 6:5; Rev. 20:12).

"And Jesus said unto them: How be it that ye have not written this thing, that many saints did arise and appear unto many and did minister unto them? And it came to pass that Nephi remembered that this thing had not been written. And it came to pass that Jesus commanded that it should be written; therefore it was written according as he commanded" (3 Ne. 23:11–13).

"And it came to pass that he commanded them that they should write the words which the Father had given unto Malachi, which he should tell unto them. And it came to pass that after they were written he expounded them" (3 Ne. 24:1).

MOMENT OF TRUTH. The Savior commands Nephi to add to the sacred record the confirmation of Samuel's prophecy concerning the resurrection of the dead that took place at the time of the Savior's resurrection. He then quotes the Prophet Malachi (chapters 3 and 4 of the Old Testament account), as commanded by the Father, so these words can be added to the record. Malachi's prophecies were spoken about 430 B.C., long after the departure of Lehi from Jerusalem; therefore, the New World colony of Israelites did not have these vital passages concerning the law of tithing as well as the mission of Elijah and the sealing powers of the priesthood. With the addition of the Elijah prophecy to the Book of Mormon account, this significant key prophecy is preserved in all four standard works of the Church (see also D&C 2:2; 27:9; 98:16; 110:15; JS–H 1:39).

MODERN PROPHETS SPEAK

Wilford Woodruff:

> I have never spent any of my time more profitably for the benefit of mankind than in my journal writing, for a great portion of the Church history has been compiled from my journals and some of the most glorious gospel sermons, truths, and revelations that were given from God to this people through the mouth of the Prophets Joseph and Brigham, Heber and the Twelve could not be found upon the earth on record only in my journals and they are compiled in the Church history and transmitted to the saints of God in all future generations. Does not this pay me for my troubles? It does. (Journal, Mar. 17, 1857)

ILLUSTRATIONS FOR OUR TIME

Wisdom—One Line at a Time. Fundamental to the gospel of Jesus Christ is the doctrine of incremental investiture of truth: "For behold, thus saith the Lord God: I will give unto the children of men line upon line, precept upon precept, here a little and there a little; and blessed are those who hearken unto my precepts, and lend an ear unto my counsel, for they shall learn wisdom; for unto him that receiveth I will give more; and from them that shall say, We have enough, from them shall be taken away even that which they have" (2 Ne. 28:30; cf. Isaiah 28:10, 13; D&C 98:12; 128:21). Alma indicated that the Lord endows us with truth to the extent we have the faith to receive it (see Alma 12:10). The Savior restrained Mormon from including His entire proceedings with the Saints in America as part of the future Book of Mormon, saying: "I will try the faith of my people" (3 Ne. 26:11). Faith opens the channels of truth; obedience in record keeping preserves the truth.

Years ago I came across a striking passage from the Prophet Joseph Smith that suggests this doctrine applies not only to our acquisition of scriptural truth but also to the inspiration that comes to us. The Prophet was explaining one of the key reasons for keeping careful records: "If you assemble from time to time, and proceed to discuss important questions, and pass decisions upon the same, and fail to note them down, by and by you will be driven to straits from which you will not be able to extricate yourselves, because you may be in a situation not to bring your faith to bear with sufficient perfection or power to obtain the desired information; or, perhaps, for neglecting to write these things when God had revealed them, not esteeming them of sufficient worth, the Spirit may withdraw and God may be angry; and there is, or was, a vast knowledge, of infinite importance, which is now lost" (*HC,* 2:199). (Allen)

Likening the Scriptures to Our Lives

3 Ne. 25:5–6—The Lord was commanded of the Father to put Malachi into the record (see 3 Nephi 24:1). The coming of Elijah was foretold, as well as his function to "turn the heart of the fathers to the children, and the heart of the children to their fathers, lest I come and smite the earth with a curse" (3 Ne. 25:6).

Application—The redemption of the dead was instituted with the power of Elijah to seal on earth for all eternity (see D&C 110:13–16). He turned the hearts of the people: they seek after their dead and do vicarious work for them. This is part of the three-fold mission of the Church. This is our work to do (see D&C 128:15, 24; D&C 138:53–54).

4. UNDERSTANDING ALL THINGS FROM THE BEGINNING TO THE END

THEME. The fulness of the Restoration is to result in "a time to come in the which nothing shall be withheld" (D&C 121:28). The Savior's visit to the ancient American Saints provided a foretaste of that glorious promise as He "did expound all things, even from the beginning until the time that he should come in his glory—yea, even all things which should come upon the face of the earth" (3 Ne. 20:3). One of the greatest blessings of God to mankind is the endowment of truth and knowledge He bestows to His faithful and devout followers.

"And now it came to pass that when Jesus had told these things he expounded them unto the multitude; and he did expound all things unto them, both great and small. And he saith: These scriptures, which ye had not with you, the Father commanded that I should give unto you; for it was wisdom in him that they should be given unto future generations. And he did expound all things, even from the beginning until the time that he should come in his glory—yea, even all things which should come upon the face of the earth, even until the elements should melt with fervent heat, and the earth should be wrapt together as a scroll, and the heavens and the earth should pass away" (3 Ne. 26:1–3).

MOMENT OF TRUTH. The Savior expounds all things from the beginning to the end. So glorious is His message of truth that Mormon is allowed to share scarcely "a hundredth part of the things which Jesus did truly teach unto the people" (3 Ne. 26:6). He is restrained from bringing more forward into view, since the Savior declared: "I will try the faith of my people" (3 Ne. 26:11). The "more part" (3 Ne. 26:7) of the repository of unspeakable truth from the Savior's visit was left sealed upon the plates of Nephi until a later time when the faith of the people would merit an expanded account.

MODERN PROPHETS SPEAK

Harold B. Lee:

Some people get impatient because the Lord hasn't revealed more than He has—unmindful of the fact that He already has revealed more than we are able to digest. (*The Teachings of Harold B. Lee,* ed. Clyde J. Williams [Salt Lake City: Bookcraft, 1996], 424)

ILLUSTRATIONS FOR OUR TIME

The Truth Shall Make You Free. I spent many years at The Johns Hopkins University on the faculty and in the administration. The motto of that great institution, the first American university founded as a purely graduate organization, is, interestingly enough, "Veritas Vos Liberabit"—"The Truth Shall Make You Free." Indeed, in a certain sense, the intellectual output of that institution in medicine, public health, science, applied physics, psychology, the arts, and so forth has contributed to the freeing of the human condition from ignorance and the shackles of temporal restriction. Such is the mission of all institutions of higher learning. The Lord Himself has commanded us to seek learning out of the best books (D&C 88:118; 109:7, 14). We are to "study and learn, and become acquainted with all good books, and with languages, tongues, and people" (D&C 90:15). We are to learn "of things both in heaven and in the earth, and under the earth; things which have been, things which are, things which must shortly come to pass; things which are at home, things which are abroad; the wars and the perplexities of the nations, and the judgments which are on the land; and a knowledge also of countries and of kingdoms" (D&C 88:79).

There is, however, a spiritual aegis under which such broad access to knowledge becomes an adjunct to higher truth, i.e., "That ye may be prepared in all things when I shall send you again to magnify the calling whereunto I have called you, and the mission with which I have commissioned you" (D&C 88:80). I recall several times when my mission president, Theodore M. Burton, who had a doctorate in chemistry, recited his rather extraordinary intellectual accomplishments before Church audiences, saying that he was doing so not to boast, but simply to state that if the Church were based on anything but true principles, he would have detected it, using his training and credentials, and rejected it out of hand. He was underscoring the fact that "Mormonism" is a rational theology based on logical truth and confirmed by faith through the witness of the Holy Spirit. When the Savior spoke the words "the truth shall make you free," He most certainly was centering His instruction on truth of a higher kind—the expedient principles of salvation and the fundamental doctrines of celestial liberation. Temporal truth and knowledge can prepare us for our missions in life; however, it is "pure knowledge" (D&C 121:42) that will ultimately free the spirit of mankind to rise in majesty to overcome the temporal and spiritual death through the Atonement of the Savior.

One day when I was going through the card file of The Johns Hopkins University Library, I came across a section of references to the writings by James Talmage, who had studied geology there many decades earlier. It was a pleasant surprise that underscored for me the partnership of both temporal as well as spiritual truth. Elder Talmage (who later served as president of the University of Utah and then as a member of the Quorum of the Twelve) had traversed the pathways of truth across its full spectrum—from the science of understanding the creation to the principles of understanding the Creator Himself, even "Jesus the Christ." We can do the same by seeking learning and wisdom from the best books in order to magnify our callings and prepare ourselves to be more enlightened servants of God and to interact more knowledgeably with the peoples of the earth, thus enabling us to spread the gospel of Jesus Christ under commission of the Abrahamic covenant. At the same time, we need to keep in mind the counsel of Jacob in the Book of Mormon concerning the educated of the world: "But to be learned is good if they hearken unto the counsels of God" (2 Ne. 9:29). The liberating truth on which we should center our most devoted attention is the gospel of Jesus Christ and its saving principles. (Allen)

Likening the Scriptures to Our Lives

3 Ne. 26:9–11—Mormon wrote those things that the Lord inspired him to write. He recorded that the things that had been written were to try our faith: if we believed these things greater things would be manifested to us; if not, the greater things would be withheld to our condemnation. Mormon tried to write more, but the Lord forbade it that our faith might be tested.

Application—We are here to be tested (see Abr. 3:25). We are free to choose (see 2 Nephi 2:27). We please God with our faith (see Heb.11:6). It is faith for which we plead (see Luke 17:5). Through searching and hearing the Word (see Rom. 10:17) and praying with all our heart (see Hel. 3:35) our faith will increase. Let us remember that faith is the foundation of all righteousness (see *Lectures on Faith* [Salt Lake City: Deseret Book, 1985], 1:1).

SUMMARY

The message of the Redeemer to the ancient Saints contains precious wisdom with universal application: the divinely decreed process of establishing Zion in the latter days, the importance of searching the words of Isaiah and all of the Lord's prophets, the indispensable duty to keep vital records of truth and inspiration, and the ongoing quest to understand all things from the beginning to the end. The prophets speak His words (see D&C 21:4–6). It behooves us to follow the prophets and their counsel; otherwise we put ourselves against our God (see 3 Ne. 28:34–35). Let us therefore allow these marvelous sayings of Jesus from the book of Third Nephi to lift us up, give us hope, and inspire us to live more Christlike lives.

CHAPTER FORTY-TWO

"THIS *is* MY GOSPEL"

3 Nephi 27–30; 4 Nephi

"It is the beginning of wisdom for us mortals to accept the simple but verifiable truths about eternal purpose as found in Jesus Christ. He has summed it all up, commencing with the words 'This is my gospel.' The straightforward explanation that follows each of these declarations gives to mankind the 'good news'—the glorious news—concerning Jesus' coming as our Rescuer and our Savior and our Atoner. His gospel gives to humankind the answers to the search for meaning and eternal purpose."
—Neal A. Maxwell, *Even As I Am* [Salt Lake City: Deseret Book, 1982], 4.

THEMES *for* LIVING

The Gospel of Jesus Christ
Bringing Souls unto Christ
Only the Love of God Brings Happiness

INTRODUCTION

The visit of the Savior to America following His resurrection provided the forum for imparting to His "other sheep" (John 10:16) the message of redemption. The Savior's instruction concerning the central core of the gospel is given in profound clarity: That He came to the earth to do the will of the Father, to be lifted up on the cross and die for all mankind, that He might draw all men unto Him through His atoning sacrifice. This is the gospel. Helping people come unto Christ should be our greatest desire, just as it was with the Three Nephites. Happiness comes through the love of God—by receiving His Beloved Son and living the principles of the gospel of Jesus Christ.

1. THE GOSPEL OF JESUS CHRIST

THEME. Simple and profound, all-encompassing in its heavenly majesty, the gospel of Jesus Christ is the gateway to be lifted up and enter the rest (i.e., the fulness of the glory), of God (D&C 84:24). The Savior's witness about His atoning mission gives the pattern of action that is required of all who will gain eternal life and exaltation.

"Therefore, whatsoever ye shall do, ye shall do it in my name; therefore ye shall call the church in my name; and ye shall call upon the Father in my name that he will bless the church for my sake. . . . If it be called in my name then it is my church, if it so be that they are built upon my gospel. Verily I say unto you, that ye are built upon my gospel; therefore ye shall call whatsoever things ye do call, in my name; therefore if ye call upon the Father, for the church, if it be in my name the Father will hear you; And if it so be that the church is built upon my gospel then will the Father show forth his own works in it" (3 Ne. 27:7–10).

"Behold I have given unto you my gospel, and this is the gospel which I have given unto you—that I came into the world to do the will of my Father, because my Father sent me. And my Father sent me that I might be lifted up upon the cross; and after that I had been lifted up upon the cross, that I might draw all men unto me, that as I have been lifted up by men even so should men be lifted up by the Father, to stand before me, to be judged of their works, whether they be good or whether they be evil" (3 Ne. 27:13–14).

"Now this is the commandment: Repent, all ye ends of the earth, and come unto me and be baptized in my name, that ye may be sanctified by the reception of the Holy Ghost, that ye may stand spotless before me at the last day. Verily, verily, I say unto you, this is my gospel; and ye know the things that ye must do in my church; for the works which ye have seen me do that shall ye also do; for that which ye have seen me do even that shall ye do; . . ." (3 Ne. 27:20–21).

MOMENT OF TRUTH. The Lord teaches the people that the Church should be called in His name and be founded upon His gospel, which is that He came to do the will of the Father, to be lifted up upon the cross and to atone for the sins of mankind. He then instructs the people how to live the gospel to the fullest.

MODERN PROPHETS SPEAK

Gordon B. Hinckley:

> This is The Church of Jesus Christ of Latter-day Saints, the only true and living church upon the face of the whole earth. A minister said to me one time, "It is egotistical to say that." I said, "I didn't say that. The Lord said it. I am only quoting." This is The Church of Jesus Christ of Latter-day Saints. We can and we must recognize the good in other churches and in other people. We can disagree without being disagreeable. We must be tolerant. We must work with others who are engaged in good causes to bring about good results. But we must never lose sight of the fact that the God of heaven brought forth this work in this the Dispensation of the Fulness of Times, that His true church might be upon the earth. (*Teachings of Gordon B. Hinckley* [Salt Lake City: Deseret Book, 1997], 549)

ILLUSTRATIONS FOR OUR TIME

The Gospel Is to Be Understood and Lived.

Bruce R. McConkie:

> In the broadest sense, all truth is part of the gospel; for all truth is known to, is ordained by, and comes from Deity; and all truth is aidful to progression and advancement. But in the high spiritual sense in which the term is used in the revelations, the gospel is concerned with those particular religious truths by conformity to which men can sanctify and cleanse their own souls, thus gaining for themselves salvation in the eternal worlds. . . .
>
> Our revelations say that the Book of Mormon contains the fulness of the gospel. (D&C 20:9; 27:5; 42:12; 135:3.) This is true in the sense that the Book of Mormon is a record of God's dealings with a people who had the fulness of the gospel, and therefore the laws and principles leading to the highest salvation are found recorded in that book. In the same sense the Bible and the Doctrine and Covenants contain the fulness of the gospel. (*Mormon Doctrine,* 2d ed. [Salt Lake City: Bookcraft, 1966], 331–34)

Likening the Scriptures to Our Lives

3 Nephi 27:13–21—Christ came to do the will of His Father. He was sent to be lifted up upon the cross that He might draw all mankind unto Him. Whoso repents and is baptized and endures to the end will be held guiltless. Only those who wash their garments in His blood will be clean and worthy to enter His kingdom. The commandment was given: repent, be baptized, be sanctified by the reception of the Holy Ghost that we may stand spotless before Him at the last day. This is the gospel.

Application—We need not think that the Lord has made it complicated to gain eternal life. We need to exercise our faith unto repentance, take upon ourselves the name of Jesus Christ through baptism, become sanctified by the reception of the Holy Ghost, and endure to the end. This is the doctrine of Christ (see 2 Ne. 31). As we live the gospel, access priesthood blessings, and participate in the ordinances of the temple, we can have the blessings of eternal lives.

2. BRINGING SOULS UNTO CHRIST

THEME. The Savior grants to each individual the opportunity to serve Him with full devotion by bringing souls unto Him and thus gain "fulness of joy" (3 Ne. 28:10).

> *"And again, ye shall not have pain while ye shall dwell in the flesh, neither sorrow save it be for the sins of the world; and all this will I do because of the thing which ye have desired of me, for ye have desired that ye might bring the souls of men unto me, while the world shall stand" (3 Ne. 28:9).*

> *"And whether they were in the body or out of the body, they could not tell; for it did seem unto them like a transfiguration of them, that they were changed from this body of flesh into an immortal state, that they could behold the things of God. But it came to pass that they did again minister upon the face of the earth; nevertheless they did not minister of the things which they had heard and seen, because of the commandment which was given them in heaven. And now, whether they were mortal or immortal, from the day of their transfiguration, I know not; But this much I know, according to the record which hath been given—they did go forth upon the face of the land, and did minister unto all the people, uniting as many to the church as would believe in their preaching; baptizing them, and as many as were baptized did receive the Holy Ghost" (3 Ne. 28:15–18).*

MOMENT OF TRUTH. In an act of divine munificence, the Savior grants to each of the disciples what they desire of Him. All choose to continue valiantly with their labors for the souls of men. However, three of the disciples express the desire to remain on the earth and bring souls unto Him until such time as the work of the Lord should be finished. Their wish is granted and their natures are transformed by Him so that they would not taste of death and would thereafter feel no sorrow "save it were for the sins of the world" (3 Ne. 28:38).

MODERN PROPHETS SPEAK

Joseph Fielding Smith:

> We know that John the Revelator and the three Nephites were granted the privilege of remaining on the earth in the translated state, to "bring souls unto Christ." We know that this was the request of John and likewise the desire of the three Nephites.
>
> It is reasonable to believe that they were engaged in this work as far as the Lord permitted them to go during these years of spiritual darkness. There are legends and stories which seem to be authentic, showing that these holy messengers were busy among the nations of the earth, and men have been entertained by them unawares. We may also well believe that these translated prophets have always been busy keeping constraint upon the acts of men and nations unbeknown to mortal man.
>
> Translated beings have not passed through death; that is, they have not had the separation of the spirit and the body. This must wait until the coming of the Savior. In the meantime they are busy fulfilling their glorious mission in preparing the way for the elders of Israel to go forth with the message of salvation in all parts of the world. (*Answers to Gospel Questions*, 5 vols. [Salt Lake City: Deseret Book, 1957–1966], 2:46)

ILLUSTRATIONS FOR OUR TIME

Teaching with Love. Did the sons of Mosiah have the love of God in their hearts? Did they have the love of Christ in their hearts? Even the very thought that any human soul would perish, caused them to tremble and quake. They wanted to help everyone come unto Christ because they knew that was the only way unto salvation.

Until we love others and have a desire for the welfare of their souls, we will never have sufficient power to bring them to Christ. . . . When we love our fellow brothers and sisters enough we will be able to teach them with the Spirit, that they might come unto Christ.

The Whitmer brothers asked the prophet Joseph what would be the most important thing they could do. The Lord replied, "And now, behold, I say unto you, that the thing which will be of the most worth unto you will be to declare repentance unto this people, that you may bring souls unto me, that you may rest with them in the kingdom of my Father. Amen" (D&C 15:6; 16:6).

This theme has not changed . . . John the Revelator, The Three Nephites, Alma, and the list goes on with modern missionaries today.

We pray for all those who know not God (see Alma 6:6). We thrust in our sickle (see D&C 31:5). The worth of souls is great in the sight of God; hence this is our joy as well. We seek to bring many unto Christ and we shall have joy (see D&C 18:10–16). This is our joy and glory (see Alma 29:9–10). This is the purpose of this last dispensation: Invite all to come unto Christ. (Pinegar)

Likening the Scriptures to Our Lives

3 Ne. 28:9–10—The three Nephites desire to stay on the earth to bring souls unto Christ. They would not taste of death, yet they would sorrow for the sins of the world. They would receive a fulness of joy in the kingdom of our Heavenly Father.

Application—There is great joy over a soul who repents (see D&C 18:13). We should seek this joy of bringing souls to Christ. This was Alma's joy and glory (see Alma 29:9–10). This is how we are forgiven (see D&C 31:5).

3. ONLY THE LOVE OF GOD BRINGS HAPPINESS

THEME. It is by cultivating the love of God in our hearts and actions that we can gain happiness in this life and eternal joy in the mansions of our Father. The love of God supplants worldly pride and iniquity.

"And it came to pass that there was no contention in the land, because of the love of God which did dwell in the hearts of the people. And there were no envyings, nor strifes, nor tumults, nor whoredoms, nor lyings, nor murders, nor any manner of lasciviousness; and surely there could not be a happier people among all the people who had been created by the hand of God" (4 Ne. 1:15–16).

"And now I, Mormon, would that ye should know that the people had multiplied, insomuch that they were spread upon all the face of the land, and that they had become exceedingly rich, because of their prosperity in Christ. And now, in this two hundred and first year there began to be among them those who were lifted up in pride, such as the wearing of costly apparel, and all manner of fine pearls, and of the fine things of the world. And from that time forth they did have their goods and their substance no more common among them. And they began to be divided into classes; and they began to build up churches unto themselves to get gain, and began to deny the true church of Christ" (4 Ne. 1:23–26).

MOMENT OF TRUTH. Following the Savior's visit, the disciples continue with their ministry in full devotion. The people become righteous. Even the detractors at the time of the Savior's American manifestations who persecuted the Lord's anointed were reclaimed. The record states that "the people were all converted unto the Lord" (4 Ne. 1:2). In this manner the Savior's prophecy about the universal influence of His intervention is fulfilled on behalf of all those living at the time: "and none of them are lost; and in them I have a fulness of joy" (3 Ne. 27:31). During the ensuing period there are no contentions or disputations for many years. The people have all things in common. Miracles are wrought. The people keep all of the commandments of the Lord. This extraordinary transformation came because of the love of God that dwelt in their hearts. It is only after the passing of the first generation from the time of the appearance of Christ that iniquity and disunity begin once again to creep into the ranks of the people. Because of prosperity they begin to forget their God and allow pride to fill their hearts and lead them to adopt wicked practices. The Gadianton conspiracy lifts its ugly head again. The disciples begin "to sorrow for the sins of the people" (4 Ne. 1:44). To protect the sacred records, Ammaron, the current curator, "being constrained by the Holy Ghost" (4 Ne. 1:48), buries them within the earth, until such time as they would once more come to the remnant of the house of Jacob "according to the prophecies and the promises of the Lord" (4 Ne. 1:49).

MODERN PROPHETS SPEAK

George Q. Cannon:

> Whence comes your enjoyment? Whence come the glorious feelings that you have when you feel the best? Do they come from the outside? Do external circumstances produce real happiness of the kind that I describe? Doubtless, they contribute to happiness; but the purest joy, the greatest happiness, that which is most heavenly proceeds from within. A man must carry the principles of happiness and the love of God in his own breast, or he will not be happy.

> It is not true enjoyment when it comes from any other source. Not from without, therefore, must we expect happiness and exaltation but from within. Deity is within us, and its development brings happiness and joy inexpressible. (*Gospel Truth: Discourses and Writings of President George Q. Cannon,* sel. by Jerreld L. Newquist [Salt Lake City: Deseret Book, 1987], 78)

ILLUSTRATIONS FOR OUR TIME

The Visit. We are a visiting church. Home teachers, visiting teachers, priesthood and Relief Society leaders—all are about the Lord's errand, continually visiting homes and circles of Saints to strengthen the Church and enlarge the kingdom of God. In all of this the model for the edifying visit is Jesus Christ. Consider the pattern that emerges from His visit to the Americas:

The Savior bore testimony. "Behold, I am Jesus Christ the Son of God. I created the heavens and the earth, and all things that in them are. I was with the Father from the beginning. I am in the Father, and the Father in me; and in me hath the Father glorified his name" (3 Ne. 9:15).

The Savior taught the fundamentals of the gospel. The Savior stressed that His mission is to teach the basic principles of the gospel to His people (faith, repentance, baptism, the gift of the Holy Ghost, enduring to the end) so that the Father will lift them up and redeem them (see 3 Ne. 11:31–41; 27:13–21). "Therefore, whoso remembereth these sayings of mine and doeth them, him will I raise up at the last day" (3 Ne. 15:1).

The Savior brought enduring gifts to the people. Peace, light, and love were all given in rich measure.

The Savior brought a life-changing influence. "Old things are done away, and all things have become new. Therefore, I would that ye should be perfect even as I, or your Father who is in heaven is perfect" (3 Ne. 12:47–48).

The Savior taught us who we are. "And as many as have received me, to them have I given to become the sons of God" (3 Ne 9:17); "that ye may be the children of your Father who is in heaven" (3 Ne. 12:45); "And behold, ye are the children of the prophets; and ye are of the house of Israel: and ye are of the covenant which the Father made with your fathers, saying unto Abraham: And in thy seed shall all the kindred of the earth be blessed. The Father having raised me up unto you first, and sent me to bless you in turning away every one of you from his iniquities; and this because ye are the children of the covenant" (3 Ne. 20:25–26).

The Savior taught us how to gain a fulness of truth. "Ponder upon the things which I have said, and ask of the Father, in my name, that ye may understand, and prepare your minds for the morrow, and I come unto you again" (3 Ne. 17:3).

The Savior taught us how to participate in the ultimate fulfilling of the Father's covenant with the house of Israel. "Through the fulness of the Gentiles, the remnant of their seed . . . may be brought in, or may be brought to a knowledge of me, their Redeemer. And then will I gather them in from the four quarters of the earth; and then will I fulfil the covenant which the Father hath made unto all the people of the house of Israel" (3 Ne. 16:4–5).

The Savior taught us how to endure to the end. Follow the appointed priesthood leaders (3 Ne. 12:1); carry out the ordinance of the sacrament (3 Ne. 18:1–14); watch and pray (3 Ne. 18:15, 18); pray in and for our families (3 Ne. 18:21); gather together in meetings (3 Ne. 18:22); strengthen the missionary effort (3 Ne. 18:24); studythe scriptures (3 Ne. 23:1, 5; 23:8–14); and pay tithing (3 Ne 24:10).

After studying the record of the Savior's visit in America so many times, it is impossible for me to look upon any visit—whether by individuals coming to my own home or by myself going to the homes of others—without envisioning the standards laid out so compellingly in Third Nephi. Questions are ever present in my mind: Is testimony borne? Are the fundamentals of the gospel given central emphasis? Are gifts of an enduring and spiritual nature dispensed? Is there a pervading sense of helping one another to be better people, more like the Savior? Is there an emphasis on our great potential as sons and daughters of God? Is there an impetus given to pondering and praying? Is there a strengthening of the commitment to honor our covenants? Is there practical reinforcement of the principle of enduring to the end? No visit could be as perfect as the visit of the Savior to His Saints. But we can strive to follow His pattern and improve day by day, that we too may bless the lives of those we contact. (Allen)

Likening the Scriptures to Our Lives

4 Ne. 1:15–16—Following the Savior's teaching that led the people to come unto Him, there was no contention in all the land because of the love of God which did dwell in their hearts: no envyings, strifes, tumults, whoredoms, lyings, murders, or any lasciviousness (lusting). They were a happy people.

Application—Our happiness is totally dependent upon partaking of the fruit of the tree of life—the love of God. This is what it means to come unto Christ. Happiness lies in accepting, following, and living the doctrines of the gospel. Happiness is righteousness (see Mosiah 2:41).

SUMMARY

The Savior, through His visit to America, gave us a resplendent portrait of what it means to live the gospel, to enjoy the blessings of bringing souls unto Him, and to know the happiness that can come only from the love of God and obedience to His commandments. Living the gospel of Jesus Christ entails not only coming unto Christ and applying the Atonement to our lives, but helping others to come to Christ as well. As we live the teachings of Christ and labor to assist in the work of saving souls, we can become a righteous people. In righteousness we will find happiness. There is no other way.

CHAPTER FORTY-THREE

"HOW COULD YE HAVE DEPARTED FROM *the* WAYS *of the* LORD!"

MORMON 1–6; MORONI 9

"How his heart must have pained and his whole being ached as Mormon would write: "It is by the wicked that the wicked are destroyed." (See Mormon 4:5.) Then as he saw both armies at Cumorah, in their last bloody struggles, too late to reform, too hardened to repent, too stubborn to change, observing with terror their destroyers marching to the final battlefield where their bodies, too numberous to ever be burried, would rot in the sun:

. . . with that awful fear of death which fills the breasts of all the wicked, did they await to receive them. (Mormon 6:7.)

"And now to see them hewn down like alfalfa before the mowing machine or as the grain before the combine, twenty-three times ten thousand of Mormon's army alone fell, and their flesh, and bones, and blood lay upon the face of the earth, . . . to molder upon the land, and to crumble and to return to their mother earth. (Mormon 6:15.)

"There was little else that the wounded general could do now but to weep and to write and to prophesy and warn."
—SPENCER W. KIMBALL, "THE LAMANITES: THEIR BURDEN—OUR BURDEN," *BYU SPEECHES OF THE YEAR*, 25 APR. 1967, 5–6.

THEMES *for* LIVING

The Voice from the Past: The Sacred Record of Truth
Hope amidst the Gloom of Iniquity

INTRODUCTION

The sacred records reach one of the final Nephite chroniclers, Mormon. He, like all the prophets before him, writes with the intent to persuade people to come unto Christ. In this case, he is constrained, by commandment, to show us the chaos and calumny that characterize the final state of a people "without Christ and God in the world" (Morm. 5:16)—to the end that we might all realize the awful consequences of iniquity. In their wickedness, the Nephites are eventually destroyed in the great battles with the Lamanites. However, in the midst of this bleak landscape, we may see the stalwart valor and love of Mormon and his son Moroni.

1. THE VOICE FROM THE PAST: THE SACRED RECORD OF TRUTH

THEME. During His personal ministry at Bountiful, the Savior made clear the original source of the written word of truth: "And behold, all things are written by the Father; therefore out of the books which shall be written shall the world be judged" (3 Ne. 27:26). The Book of Mormon, as prepared and preserved by the hand of God through His earthly servants, is the basis upon which its readers will be judged. We are well counseled to give heed to its message.

> "And behold, ye shall take the plates of Nephi unto yourself, and the remainder shall ye leave in the place where they are; and ye shall engrave on the plates of Nephi all the things that ye have observed concerning this people" (Morm. 1:4).

> "Therefore I write unto you, Gentiles, and also unto you, house of Israel, when the work shall commence, that ye shall be about to prepare to return to the land of your inheritance; Yea, behold, I write unto all the ends of the earth; yea, unto you, twelve tribes of Israel, who shall be judged according to your works by the twelve whom Jesus chose to be his disciples in the land of Jerusalem. And I write also unto the remnant of this people, who shall also be judged by the twelve whom Jesus chose in this land; and they shall be judged by the other twelve whom Jesus chose in the land of Jerusalem. And these things doth the Spirit manifest unto me; therefore I write unto you all. And for this cause I write unto you, that ye may know that ye must all stand before the judgment-seat of Christ, yea, every soul who belongs to the whole human family of Adam; and ye must stand to be judged of your works, whether they be good or evil; And also that ye may believe the gospel of Jesus Christ, which ye shall have among you; and also that the Jews, the covenant people of the Lord, shall have other witness besides him whom they saw and heard, that Jesus, whom they slew, was the very Christ and the very God. And I would that I could persuade all ye ends of the earth to repent and prepare to stand before the judgment-seat of Christ" (Morm. 3:17–22).

> *"And behold, they shall go unto the unbelieving of the Jews; and for this intent shall they go—that they may be persuaded that Jesus is the Christ, the Son of the living God; that the Father may bring about, through his most Beloved, his great and eternal purpose, in restoring the Jews, or all the house of Israel, to the land of their inheritance, which the Lord their God hath given them, unto the fulfilling of his covenant; And also that the seed of this people may more fully believe his gospel, which shall go forth unto them from the Gentiles; for this people shall be scattered, and shall become a dark, a filthy, and a loathsome people, beyond the description of that which ever hath been amongst us, yea, even that which hath been among the Lamanites, and this because of their unbelief and idolatry" (Morm. 5:14–15).*

MOMENT OF TRUTH. After nearly a millennium of painstaking record keeping by an uninterrupted series of inspired prophets, the sacred trust is passed on to Mormon. As a lad of around 10 years of age—"a sober child . . . quick to observe" (Morm. 1:2)—Mormon is visited by the archivist Ammaron, who gives him the charge to take over the writing commission at the age of 24. This occurs as planned, and Mormon is inspired to write the message of truth to the future Gentiles, to the future house of Israel, and "unto all the ends of the earth" (Morm. 3:18) so that the Lord's plan of salvation might go forward in the latter days according to the heavenly design, "unto the fulfilling of his covenant" (Morm. 5:14). Ultimately Mormon hides up all the records in the Hill Cumorah, "save it were these few plates which I gave unto my son Moroni" (Morm. 6:6). In this manner, the extraordinary chain of witnessing by chosen men of God continues until the final hours of the Nephite nation and is then suspended until the last of the archivists, as a resurrected messenger of God, appears to the Prophet Joseph Smith at the dawn of a new and glorious dispensation.

MODERN PROPHETS SPEAK

Jeffrey R. Holland:

> The Book of Mormon is the sacred expression of Christ's great last covenant with mankind. It is a new covenant, a new testament from the New World to the entire world. Reading it was the beginning of my light. It was the source of my first spiritual certainty that God lives, that he is my Heavenly Father, and that a plan of happiness was outlined in eternity for me. It led me to love the Holy Bible and the rest of the Standard Works of the Church. It taught me to love the Lord Jesus Christ, to glimpse his merciful compassion, and to consider the grace and grandeur of his atoning sacrifice for my sins and the sins of all men, women, and children from Adam to the end of time. The light I walk by is his light. His mercy and magnifi-

cence lead me in my witness of him to the world. (*Christ and the New Covenant: The Messianic Message of the Book of Mormon* [Salt Lake City: Deseret Book, 1997], 351)

ILLUSTRATIONS FOR OUR TIME

Let Us Never Forget. Over the years my wife and I have found that one question in particular seems to be a favorite for engendering discussion in teaching environments at church and at home: "What is your favorite scripture?" or "Which scripture has special meaning in your life?" Such a question invites the recollection of a cherished memory—one in which a nourishing connection with the Spirit has left a bright mile marker along the pathway of life.

Book of Mormon favorites that frequently come up include such universally valued passages as Nephi's famous pronouncement starting: "I will go and do the things which the Lord hath commanded" (1 Ne. 3:7) or Lehi's couplet: "Adam fell that men might be; and men are, that they might have joy" (2 Ne. 2:25). King Benjamin is often remembered with his inspired reminder: "when ye are in the service of your fellow beings ye are only in the service of your God" (Mosiah 2:17). Similarly, Alma's famous comparison of faith to a seed (Alma 32) is often cited, as is his fatherly counsel to his son Corianton: "Behold, I say unto you, wickedness never was happiness" (Alma 41:10). People often refer to favorite passages in 3 Nephi, particularly those in which the Savior blesses the little children: "and he took their little children, one by one, and blessed them, and prayed unto the Father for them" (3 Ne. 17:21). Frequently the celebrated passage from Ether is recalled where the Lord promises that His grace will compensate for our weaknesses: "for if they humble themselves before me, and have faith in me, then will I make weak things become strong unto them" (Ether 12:27). Understandably, Moroni's concluding statement—"And when ye shall receive these things. . . ." (Moro. 10:4)—is seldom overlooked. (Allen)

Likening the Scriptures to Our Lives

Mormon 5:9, 14—Mormon wrote these things for a remnant of the house of Israel, for the Gentiles, and for the Jews, that they might be persuaded that Jesus is the Christ.

Application—Truly the Book of Mormon is to persuade all mankind to come unto Christ and know of the goodness of God and the covenants He has made with us. Oh, that we might be persuaded to come unto Christ fully and forsake the world!

2. HOPE AMIDST THE GLOOM OF INIQUITY

THEME. When the people are ensconced with prideful self-satisfaction in iniquity and evil, they are "as a vessel is tossed about upon the waves, without sail or anchor, or without anything wherewith to steer her" (Morm. 5:18). Only through faith in

Jesus Christ, through humility and obedience, and through honoring the covenant promises can a people emerge from the mortal vale in a state of spiritual liberty and joy, having stayed on the course toward the destination of the heavenly home.

> *"But behold, the land was filled with robbers and with Lamanites; and notwithstanding the great destruction which hung over my people, they did not repent of their evil doings; therefore there was blood and carnage spread throughout all the face of the land, both on the part of the Nephites and also on the part of the Lamanites; and it was one complete revolution throughout all the face of the land" (Morm. 2:8).*

> *"But behold this my joy was vain, for their sorrowing was not unto repentance, because of the goodness of God; but it was rather the sorrowing of the damned, because the Lord would not always suffer them to take happiness in sin" (Morm. 2:13).*

> *"But behold, I was without hope, for I knew the judgments of the Lord which should come upon them; for they repented not of their iniquities, but did struggle for their lives without calling upon that Being who created them" (Morm. 5:2).*

> *"And now, my son, I dwell no longer upon this horrible scene. Behold, thou knowest the wickedness of this people; thou knowest that they are without principle, and past feeling; and their wickedness doth exceed that of the Lamanites" (Moro. 9:20).*

> *"My son, be faithful in Christ" (Moro. 9:25).*

MOMENT OF TRUTH. Mormon proceeds to compile his final record "concerning the destruction of my people, the Nephites" (Morm. 6:1). Mayhem and chaos had been no strangers to him, "for behold, a continual scene of wickedness and abominations has been before mine eyes ever since I have been sufficient to behold the ways of man" (Morm. 2:18). Yet in his exemplary mission as prophet, general, priesthood leader, historian, and father, this remarkable figure on the landscape of God's earthly footstool stands as an example of courage, faithfulness, hope, and unbounded charity—even toward a benighted people whose "day of grace was passed" (Morm. 2:15).

MODERN PROPHETS SPEAK

Bruce R. McConkie:
> Truly, wrath and vengeance are bedfellows. When the Lord pours out his wrath without measure, the wicked suffer the vengeance of a just God in exactly the same proportion. It is their day of reckoning; they are given measure for measure

as their deeds warrant; it is a day of retribution and avengement. It is "the day when the Lord shall come to recompense unto every man according to his work, and measure to every man according to the measure which he has measured to his fellow man" (D&C 1:10). (*The Millennial Messiah: The Second Coming of the Son of Man* [Salt Lake City: Deseret Book, 1982], 500)

ILLUSTRATIONS FOR OUR TIME

Wickedness Brings Suffering. When I was a bishop, I witnessed the sorrow of sin—the trials that resulted from yielding to temptation. Wickedness cannot bring happiness (see Mosiah 2:41; Alma 41:10). President Kimball explains that when the law is broken there are consequences:

> There are many causes for human suffering—including war, disease, and poverty—and the suffering that proceeds from each of these is very real, but I would not be true to my trust if I did not say that the most persistent cause of human suffering, that suffering which causes the deepest pain, is sin—the violation of the commandments given to us by God. There cannot be, for instance, a rich and full life unless we practice total chastity before marriage and total fidelity after. There cannot be a sense of wholeness and integrity if we lie, steal, or cheat. There cannot be sweetness in our lives if we are filled with envy or covetousness. Our lives cannot really be abundant if we do not honor our parents. If any of us wish to have more precise prescriptions for ourselves in terms of what we can do to have more abundant lives, all we usually need to do is to consult our conscience. . . . (*The Teachings of Spencer W. Kimball,* ed. Edward L. Kimball [Salt Lake City: Bookcraft, 1982], 155–56) (Pinegar)

Likening the Scriptures to Our Lives

Morm. 3:16; Moro. 9:6—Mormon did all in his power to help the Nephites because he had the love of God in his heart. The people were hard-hearted and without faith; therefore, the prayers were in vain.

Application—We must remember to have pure hearts and to act with faith that the Lord will assist us in our trials and tribulations. Let us do our best in our stewardships and duties to help people come unto Christ, regardless of their situation or the hardness of their hearts. Let us labor without ceasing. We must never give up.

SUMMARY

The Book of Mormon is a welcome voice from the past—the sacred record of truth preserved by the Lord as a compass for our day and age. It is a beacon of hope amidst the gloom of iniquity that all too frequently characterizes worldly conditions. The Lord has preserved His sacred record that all might be persuaded to come unto Christ. The Lord will not allow us to have happiness in wickedness. Faith, repentance, and obedience are the requisite gateways to the peace and joy that come as blessings from the Lord.

CHAPTER FORTY-FOUR

"I SPEAK UNTO YOU *as if* YE WERE PRESENT"

MORMON 7–9

"God the Father and his beloved Son did appear to Joseph Smith. This was the greatest event that has transpired in the world since the resurrection of the Master. This is our message and our warning to the world. It is a world message from a world organization—The Church of Jesus Christ of Latter-day Saints. These warnings of the prophets, ancient and modern, shall in very deed be fulfilled. The Lord is 'angry with the wicked.' He is 'holding his Spirit from the inhabitants of the earth.' The one hope for this wicked world is to accept and live the gospel, to keep the commandments, to heed the warnings of the prophets, ancient and modern."
—EZRA TAFT BENSON, *GOD, FAMILY, COUNTRY: OUR THREE GREAT LOYALTIES* [SALT LAKE CITY: DESERET BOOK, 1974], 95.

THEMES *for* LIVING

Repent, Believe in Christ, and Be Baptized
The Book of Mormon: A Light in a Day of Darkness

INTRODUCTION

Mormon and Moroni exhort us to repent, believe in Christ, be baptized, and prepare ourselves for the imminent return of the great Lawgiver and Judge of mankind in His glory. They graphically describe the conditions of wickedness that will prevail at the time of the coming forth of the Book of Mormon. This mighty word of Christ, preserved by the hand of God and brought forth miraculously in a day when miracles had ceased because the people "dwindle in unbelief, and depart from the right way, and know not the God in whom they should trust" (Morm. 9:20), confirms the truth of the Bible and proves that God is the same yesterday, today, and forever.

1. REPENT, BELIEVE IN CHRIST, AND BE BAPTIZED

THEME. The unchanging God of miracles has brought forth a latter-day miracle, even the restoration of the Gospel and the Book of Mormon, which supports the Bible and invites all mankind to repent, believe in Christ, and prepare for the Day of Judgment.

> *"Know ye that ye must come to the knowledge of your fathers, and repent of all your sins and iniquities, and believe in Jesus Christ, that he is the Son of God, and that he was slain by the Jews, and by the power of the Father he hath risen again, whereby he hath gained the victory over the grave; and also in him is the sting of death swallowed up. . . . Therefore repent, and be baptized in the name of Jesus, and lay hold upon the gospel of Christ, which shall be set before you, not only in this record but also in the record which shall come unto the Gentiles from the Jews, which record shall come from the Gentiles unto you" (Morm. 7:5, 8).*

> *"Behold, I say unto you that whoso believeth in Christ, doubting nothing, whatsoever he shall ask the Father in the name of Christ it shall be granted him; and this promise is unto all, even unto the ends of the earth. . . . And he that believeth and is baptized shall be saved, but he that believeth not shall be damned" (Morm. 9:21, 23).*

MOMENT OF TRUTH. Mormon offers up his final witness of the truth of the gospel and calls for all to repent and come unto Christ. His son Moroni then announces that his father has been killed in battle, leaving him alone to uphold the sacred trust of preserving the record. Their joint declarations encapsulate the essence of the gospel of Jesus Christ, constituting a prophetic summary of the covenant promises and a profoundly moving exhortation for all their modern readers to receive the message of truth and prepare for the Day of Judgment through faith and righteous obedience.

MODERN PROPHETS SPEAK

George Albert Smith:

> It is the gospel of Jesus Christ that we bear. It is the desire to save the souls of the children of men that burns in our hearts. It is not that we may build ourselves up and become a mighty people financially; it is not that we may have our names glorified in the earth for our accomplishments; but it is that the sons and daughters of God, wherever they may be, may hear this gospel, which is the power of God unto salvation to all those who believe and obey its precepts. And those who believe will follow the pattern given by the Savior when he said to his disciples, "He that believeth and is baptized shall be saved; but he that believeth not shall be damned" (Mark 16:16). (*The Teachings of George Albert Smith*, ed. Robert and Susan McIntosh [Salt Lake City: Bookcraft, 1996], 89)

ILLUSTRATIONS FOR OUR TIME

"Please, Sir, Will You Baptize Me?" There are many yet on the earth among all sects, parties, and denominations, who are blinded by the subtle craftiness of men, whereby they lie in wait to deceive, and who are only kept from the truth because they know not where to find it: (D&C 123:12). While some have the virtuous desire to bring such people to Christ, lacking His authority, they verify "that a man must be called of God, by prophecy, and by the laying on of hands by those who are in authority, to preach the Gospel and administer in the ordinances thereof" (the fifth Article of Faith). Elder L. Tom Perry recently commented upon the outlook of those who possess the fulness of the gospel: "We live in a world that is crying for righteous leadership based on trustworthy principles" ("Called of God," *Ensign*, Nov. 2002, 7). Elder John A. Widstoe, speaking upon the need for a living prophet, remarked, "Men are suffering, hungering for authoritative leadership. Men have been led by men so long, churches have been made by man so often, things have come through human agencies for so many years, that in this day of high intelligence, of the greatest knowledge of the world, men resent the thought that when they deal with the greatest of all realities, religion, and all that pertains to it, they must follow man-made leadership" (*CR*, Apr. 1931, 59). The following story about Heber C. Kimball's missionary labors demonstrates vividly the eagerness with which people come unto Christ in the appointed way:

> Having mentioned my intention of going to Downham and Chatburn, to several of the brethren, they endeavoured to dissuade me from going, informing me there could be no prospect of success whatever, as several ministers of different denominations had endeavored in vain to raise churches in these places, and had frequently preached to them, but to no effect, as they had resisted all the efforts and withstood the attempts of all sects and parties for the last thirty years, who, seeing all their attempts fail, had given them up to hardness of heart. I was also informed they

were very wicked places. However, this did not discourage me, believing that the Gospel of Jesus Christ could reach the heart, when the gospels of men proved abortive; I consequently told those brethren that these were the places I wanted to go to, for that it was my business not to call the righteous but sinners to repentance. . . .

In Chatburn I was cordially received by the inhabitants, who turned out in great numbers to hear me preach. They procured a large tithing barn, placing a barrel in the center, upon which I stood. I preached to them the first principles of the Gospel, spoke in simplicity upon the principles revealed by our Lord and Savior Jesus Christ, the conditions of pardon for a fallen world and the blessings and privileges of those who embraced the truth; I likewise said a little on the subject of the resurrection. My testimony was accompanied by the Spirit of the Lord, and was received with joy, and these people who had been represented as being hard and obdurate, were melted into tenderness and love. I told them that, being a servant of the Lord Jesus Christ, I stood ready at all times to administer the ordinances of the Gospel, and explained what was necessary to prepare them for baptism; that when they felt to repent of and forsake their sins, they were ready to be baptized for the remission of sins, like the jailor and his household, and Cornelius and his house. When I concluded I felt someone pulling at my coat. . . . I turned round and asked what was wanted. Mrs. Elizabeth Partington said, "Please sir, will you baptize me?" "And me?" "And me?" exclaimed more than a dozen voices. Accordingly I went down into the water and baptized twenty-five. I was engaged in this duty, and confirming them and conversing with the people until after midnight.

The next morning I returned to Downham, and baptized between twenty-five and thirty in the course of the day.

The next evening I returned to Chatburn. The congregation was so numerous that I had to preach in the open air, and took my stand on a stone wall, and afterwards baptized several. These villages seemed to be affected from one end to the other; parents called their children together, spoke to them on the subjects which I had preached about, and warned them against swearing and all other evil practices, and instructed them in their duty.

We were absent from Preston five days, during which time Brother Fielding and I baptized and confirmed about 110 persons; organized branches in Downham, Chatburn, Waddington and Clithero; and ordained several to the lesser Priesthood, to preside. This was the first time the people in those villages ever heard our voices, or saw an American.

I cannot refrain from relating an occurrence which took place while Brother Fielding and myself were passing through the village of Chatburn on our way to Downham: having been observed approaching the village, the news ran from house to house, and immediately the noise of their looms was hushed, and the people flocked to their doors to welcome us and see us pass. More than forty young people of the place ran to meet us; some took hold of our mantles and then of each others' hands; several having hold of hands went before us singing the songs of Zion, while their parents gazed upon the scene with delight, and poured their blessings upon our heads, and praised the God of heaven for sending us to unfold the principles of truth and the plan of salvation to them. The children continued with us to Downham, a mile distant. Such a scene, and such gratitude, I never witnessed before. "Surely," my heart exclaimed, "out of the mouths of babes and sucklings thou hast perfected praise." What could have been more pleasing and delightful than such a manifestation of gratitude to Almighty God; and from those whose hearts were deemed too hard to be penetrated by the Gospel, and who had been considered the most wicked and hardened people in that region of country. (*Exceptional Stories from the Lives of Our Apostles,* comp. Leon R. Hartshorn [Salt Lake City: Deseret Book, 1972], 119–121)

Likening the Scriptures to Our Lives

Mormon 9:20—Miracles have ceased because of unbelief, because people have departed from the right way and know not the God they should trust.

Application—When we believe and exercise our faith, we can receive divine help and be instruments in the hand of the Lord to do miracles (see 3 Ne. 8:1).

2. THE BOOK OF MORMON: A LIGHT IN A DAY OF DARKNESS

THEME. Let us be grateful for the great kindness of the Lord in illuminating the bleak landscape of our latter-day godless civilization with the brilliant light of truth and wisdom restored through the Book of Mormon.

". . . and it shall come in a day when it shall be said that miracles are done away; and it shall come even as if one should speak from the dead. And it shall come in a day when the blood of saints shall cry unto the Lord, because of secret combinations and the works of darkness. Yea, it shall come in a day when the power of God shall be denied, and churches become defiled and be lifted up in the pride of their hearts; yea, even in a day when leaders of churches and teachers shall rise in the pride of their hearts, even to the envying of them who belong

to their churches. . . . And there shall also be heard of wars, rumors of wars, and earthquakes in divers places. Yea, it shall come in a day when there shall be great pollutions upon the face of the earth; there shall be murders, and robbing, and lying, and deceivings, and whoredoms, and all manner of abominations; when there shall be many who will say, Do this, or do that, and it mattereth not, for the Lord will uphold such at the last day. . . . O ye wicked and perverse and stiffnecked people, why have ye built up churches unto yourselves to get gain?. . . Behold, the Lord hath shown unto me great and marvelous things concerning that which must shortly come, at that day when these things shall come forth among you. Behold, I speak unto you as if ye were present, and yet ye are not. But behold, Jesus Christ hath shown you unto me, and I know your doing. And I know that ye do walk in the pride of your hearts; and there are none save a few only who do not lift themselves up in the pride of their hearts, unto the wearing of very fine apparel, unto envying, and strifes, and malice, and persecutions, and all manner of iniquities; and your churches, yea, even every one, have become polluted because of the pride of your hearts" (Morm. 8:26–36).

MOMENT OF TRUTH. Moroni prophesies that the Book of Mormon will come forth in a day of wickedness as irrefutable proof that God is unchanging and continues His work of salvation for all those who come unto Him in faith and obedience.

MODERN PROPHETS SPEAK

Bruce R. McConkie:

> This is the great day of Satan's power. It is the day of false Christs, false prophets, false miracles, false religions, false doctrines, false philosophies. It is a day when fables take precedence over facts, when all but the very elect are deceived. Of this day our Lord said: "There shall also arise false Christs, and false prophets, and shall show great signs and wonders, insomuch, that, if possible, they shall deceive the very elect, who are the elect according to the covenant." (JS—M 1:22; Rev. 13:13–14.)

> Moroni, writing with fervor and in power, described conditions that would exist when the Book of Mormon should come forth. (*Mormon Doctrine,* 2d ed. [Salt Lake City: Bookcraft, 1966], 730)

ILLUSTRATIONS FOR OUR TIME

A Silent Sermon. He wasn't feeling too well, this silver-haired octogenarian, but he completed his temple sealing assignment that day (as he had done faithfully for so many years) and then the next afternoon, despite continuing weakness, he did his home teaching as so often before. The following day his infirmity had worsened to the extent that he was taken to the hospital, from whence he never returned. A week later his earthly mission was complete, and he was "taken home to that God" who gave him life (Alma 40:11). Such was the example of my wife's father, who preached a powerful, if silent, sermon on devotion and faithfulness during that last opportunity for service in the kingdom.

When Mormon and Moroni closed the book on their mortal ministry, grieving in their hearts over the travail and suffering of their wayward compatriots, they preached two sermons: one in glorious resounding language of conviction and testimony of the Savior, the other a silent sermon of service and indefatigable loyalty to the gospel cause—despite overwhelming adversity. In one of Moroni's last pronouncements, he bore fervent witness, declaring: "Behold, I say unto you that whoso believeth in Christ, doubting nothing, whatsoever he shall ask the Father in the name of Christ it shall be granted him; and this promise is unto all, even unto the ends of the earth. . . . Behold, I speak unto you as though I spake from the dead; for I know that ye shall have my words" (Morm. 9:21, 30). Similarly, countless Saints in numberless family circles of Zion have left behind and will yet leave behind a legacy of courage, speaking clearly to their descendants, as if in silent sermons from a different and better world, words of truth and encouragement—just by their example of service. (Allen)

Likening the Scriptures to Our Lives

Morm. 8:35–41—Moroni saw our day: pride, hearts set on the vain things of the world, love of money, all manner of iniquity abounding, adornment of churches rather than care for the poor, praise of the world, and secret combinations. The Lord said these were an abomination in His sight.

Application—Let us be sure that we seek the Lord and His commandments and are not found with pride in our hearts and improper attention to outward things.

SUMMARY

The message of the Book of Mormon is profoundly simple and universal: Repent, believe in Christ, be baptized, and endure to the end. The Book of Mormon, having come forth by the hand of God as a light in a day of darkness, is the handbook for spiritual survival and covenant prosperity.

We have the blessing of the Book of Mormon in our lives. Let us recognize the condition of the world in these last days and keep ourselves free from sin by searching these words of living truth.

CHAPTER FORTY-FIVE

"NEVER *has* MAN BELIEVED *in* ME AS THOU HAST"

ETHER 1–6

"'At that day ye shall know that I am in my Father, and ye in me, and I in you.' They will be one with him as he is one with his Father. 'He that hath my commandments, and keepeth them, he it is that loveth me: and he that loveth me shall be loved of my Father, and I will love him, and will manifest myself to him.' The promise is not theirs alone—the Twelve are but the pattern; all that they receive will come also to every faithful person who abides the law that entitles him to receive the same gifts and blessings. Jesus, after his death and resurrection, will manifest himself to all who have faith enough to rend the veil and see their Lord.

"Jesus was then asked: 'Lord, how is it that thou wilt manifest thyself unto us, and not unto the world?' His reply: 'If a man love me, he will keep my words: and my Father will love him, and we will come unto him, and make our abode with him.' (John 14:18–23.) Not only will the Lord Jesus appear to the faithful, but he, in his goodness and grace, will also manifest the Father. Mortal man will see the Father and the Son."
—BRUCE R. MCCONKIE, *THE MILLENNIAL MESSIAH: THE SECOND COMING OF THE SON OF MAN* [SALT LAKE CITY: DESERET BOOK, 1982], 678–79.

THEMES *for* LIVING

The Lord Will Answer Our Prayers
The Lord Will Lead Us
Seeing with the Vision of Faith
The Voice of Warning and Wisdom from the Past

INTRODUCTION

The record of the Jaredites, including many glorious and edifying passages about faith and the relationship between God and man, is abridged by Moroni as the Book of Ether. He also gives inspired commentary on the recorded events, and reports revelation from the Lord concerning the key role this record, as part of the entire Book of Mormon, is to play in the latter-day Restoration. The power of prayer is demonstrated through the account of the brother of Jared and his extraordinary experience of being admitted into the presence of the Lord by virtue of his exceedingly great faith. We see the emigrant history of a small colony being led from the Tower of Babel to the promised land. We see the rise of a mighty nation from small beginnings and begin to understand how events are shaped by the choices—both good and evil—that individuals make. Above all, we see the inescapable truth that joy and happiness are products of obedience to the Lord's commandments and that misery and destruction are the wages of sin. The Jaredite journey—from the seat of evil to the promised land—is analogous to the journey of every mortal. Consequently, record of the journey becomes a guiding parable for modern-day readers who wish to learn about the pathway toward immortality and eternal life, and the pitfalls to avoid while underway.

1. THE LORD WILL ANSWER OUR PRAYERS

THEME. The Lord has compassion upon those who cry unto Him for guidance.

"And it came to pass that the brother of Jared did cry unto the Lord, and the Lord had compassion upon Jared; therefore he did not confound the language of Jared; and Jared and his brother were not confounded. . . . And it came to pass that the brother of Jared did cry unto the Lord, and the Lord had compassion upon their friends and their families also, that they were not confounded. And it came to pass that Jared spake again unto his brother, saying: Go and inquire of the Lord whether he will drive us out of the land, and if he will drive us out of the land, cry unto him whither we shall go. . . . The brother of Jared did cry unto the Lord according to that which had been spoken by the mouth of Jared. And it came to pass that the Lord did hear the brother of Jared, and had compassion upon him, and said unto him: Go to and gather together thy flocks, both male and female, of every kind; and also of the seed of the earth of every kind; and thy families; and also Jared thy brother and his family; and also thy friends and their families, and the friends of Jared and their families. And when thou hast done this thou shalt go at the head of them down into the valley which is northward. And there will I meet thee, and I will go before thee into a land which is choice above all the lands of the earth. And there will I bless thee and thy seed, and raise up unto me of thy seed, and of the seed of

thy brother, and they who shall go with thee, a great nation. And there shall be none greater than the nation which I will raise up unto me of thy seed, upon all the face of the earth. And thus I will do unto thee because this long time ye have cried unto me" (Ether 1:35, 37–43).

MOMENT OF TRUTH. Moroni proceeds "to give an account of those ancient inhabitants who were destroyed by the hand of the Lord upon the face of this north country" (Ether 1:1). He follows the record of the Jaredites preserved on the 24 plates of gold found by the people of Limhi (Mosiah 8:8–9). We learn that one family circle at the time of the Lord's scattering of the people associated with the Tower of Babel is given divine guidance toward the promised land as a result of the earnest entreaties for help by the spiritual leader of the group, who is identified only as the brother of Jared. The opening passages of the account are a prime example of the power of prayer—both to open the floodgate of blessings from the Lord, as well as to invoke His wrath when it is neglected (see Ether 2:14–15).

MODERN PROPHETS SPEAK

Marion G. Romney:

> One of our greatest needs today is to turn to God in true prayer so that we may conquer Satan and escape the hands of the servants of Satan that uphold his work. I should like to call your attention to some of the essentials of effective prayer. One of them is belief in God, the Eternal Father, as taught by Joseph Smith.

> There is a world of difference in the attitude in which one prays understandingly to "our Father which art in heaven" and that of one whose prayer is addressed to some unknown god thought of as "cosmic energy," "universal consciousness," or as "the first great cause." No man prays to a theoretical god with the faith and expectation that his petition will receive sympathetic personal consideration. But one can understandingly pray to the true and living God with the assurance that his prayers will be heard and answered. When God is believed in as our Eternal Father, we can to a degree understand our relationship to him—that he is the Father of our spirits, a loving parent who is interested in his children individually and whom they can love with all their hearts, might, mind, and strength.

> Such a belief is essential to true prayer because intelligent beings will not pray fervently to a God they do not know. Such praying will be done only by people who believe their prayers can be heard and answered by an understanding, sympathetic parent. (*Look to God and Live* [Salt Lake City: Deseret Book, 1971], 200–201)

ILLUSTRATIONS FOR OUR TIME

Cords of Safety. Many years ago, on the occasion of my younger son's birthday, I decided to take him and several of his teenage friends on a boating trip to Lake Powell in southern Utah. The long journey to the lake passed quickly in anticipation of the excitement that lay ahead. In our enthusiasm we scarcely noticed the ominous clouds gathering on the horizon. When we reached the marina where the cabin cruiser was moored, we checked in with the harbormaster to get the latest weather report. What he said stunned us: a very unusual weather disturbance had come up, with 80-mile-per-hour winds threatening the area that evening.

Disappointed, we thought it best under the circumstances to remain in the harbor with the boat tied to the dock. "No," cautioned the harbormaster. "If those winds hit the marina, the boats moored here may be seriously damaged or destroyed. There is too much danger and exposure here. I would recommend that you take the boat down the main channel of the lake and find a deep side canyon with high cliffs and more shelter. You can tie up onto the shore and weather the storm." By then, the winds were starting to rise and the clouds were darkening, so we quickly loaded our gear onto the boat and made our way with some trepidation several miles downstream to the nearest side canyon with high, protective walls. There we ran the prow of the boat up onto the sandy shore at the head of the canyon and secured the boat with strong mooring cords and anchors on all sides. Then we waited. The sky blackened with threatening storm formations. The wind howled. We were concerned and offered many prayers. I spent the entire night watching over the nervously sleeping young men. It was one long prayer. But the cliffs gave protection from three sides and the anchor cords held. The massive storm must have passed nearby but it providentially spared us a direct assault. With morning came the calm. We offered a prayer of gratitude for the protection granted us, and the birthday outing continued with great enjoyment.

Given the raging forces of temptation and evil that surround us in these latter days, is there not wisdom in seeking the safety of a harbor with high protective cliffs? Are we not well counseled to secure our vessels—our family institutions—with many sturdy cords and anchors? Analogies abound: the cliffs are the covenant principles that provide shelter from temptation and worldly contamination—the armament of prayer, scripture study, support from the community of Saints, and communion with the Spirit. The sturdy cords and anchors are well described by Moroni in an upcoming passage: "Wherefore, whoso believeth in God might with surety hope for a better world, yea, even a place at the right hand of God, which hope cometh of faith, maketh an anchor to the souls of men, which would make them sure and steadfast, always abounding in good works, being led to glorify God" (Ether 12:4). The harbormasters of life are the prophets and watchmen in Zion who counsel us with inspired wisdom (see Isa. 52:8; Jer. 31:6; Mosiah 12:22; 15:29; 3 Ne. 16:18). The Lord commands us to "stand in holy places, and . . . not be moved" (D&C 45:32; 101:22) in order to participate in the blessings of His Church and priesthood.

We all face the journey of life, sometimes through uncharted waters. Noah knew something of survival on the high seas. It was through the direct guidance of the Lord that Lehi's stalwart band weathered the ocean storms to cross the deep successfully. The early Jaredite families followed divine counsel for some 344 days to reach the promised land despite the onslaught of "mountain waves" and "great and terrible tempests" (Ether 6:6). The key is to follow the guidance of the Spirit and heed the word of the heavenly Harbormaster. The journey begins with faith and ends with unceasing gratitude: "And they did sing praises unto the Lord; yea, the brother of Jared did sing praises unto the Lord, and he did thank and praise the Lord all the day long; and when the night came, they did not cease to praise the Lord" (Ether 6:9). We can do no less. (Allen)

Likening the Scriptures to Our Lives

Ether 1:43—The brother of Jared showed real intent—desire and faith—as he prayed, crying unto the Lord for a long while.

Application—Let us remember to pray with faith, fervently, with real intent, believing—and continually, not just as a cursory request, but with a longing heart and righteous reason. Our prayers will be answered. Let us have the faith to accept this principle and live it.

2. THE LORD WILL LEAD US

THEME. Moroni's title page to the Book of Mormon makes clear that this sacred volume will "show unto the remnant of the House of Israel what great things the Lord hath done for their fathers." In this tradition, Moroni provides through the Book of Ether yet another testament to the principle that the Lord will guide us toward the promised land.

> *"And it came to pass that the Lord commanded them that they should go forth into the wilderness, yea, into that quarter where there never had man been. And it came to pass that the Lord did go before them, and did talk with them as he stood in a cloud, and gave directions whither they should travel. And it came to pass that they did travel in the wilderness, and did build barges, in which they did cross many waters, being directed continually by the hand of the Lord. And the Lord would not suffer that they should stop beyond the sea in the wilderness, but he would that they should come forth even unto the land of promise, which was choice above all other lands, which the Lord God had preserved for a righteous people. And he had sworn in his wrath unto the brother of Jared, that whoso should possess this land of promise, from that time henceforth and forever, should serve him, the true and only God, or they should be swept off when the fulness of his wrath should come upon them" (Ether 2:5–8).*

MOMENT OF TRUTH. Through mighty prayer, the brother of Jared learns from the Lord that He would preserve them, based on His divine compassion, from the turmoil and dislocations of the day and lead them to a better place. Preparations for this journey to the promised land, centuries before Lehi and his family immigrated from Jerusalem, include gathering together all manner of horticulture and animal stock (among them "deseret," or honey bees—Ether 2:3), learning not to neglect prayerful duties, building watertight transoceanic barges, equipping the barges with light through stones illuminated by the finger of the Lord (Ether 3:6), and gathering together needed provisions for the journey. The Lord indicates that their destination is a "land of promise, which was choice above all other lands, which the Lord God had preserved for a righteous people" (Ether 2:7). At the outset of this short book, Moroni anticipates the exact woeful outcome of this grand tale: an entire nation emerged through faith from a small family circle, only to dwindle in unbelief and suffer extinction because its people turned their backs on the Lord.

MODERN PROPHETS SPEAK

Spencer W. Kimball:

> Let us hold fast to the iron rod. The Savior urged us to put our hand to the plow without looking back. In that spirit we are being asked to have humility and a deep and abiding faith in the Lord and to move forward—trusting in him, refusing to be diverted from our course, either by the *ways* of the world or the *praise* of the world. I see that quality of readiness and devotion in our people today. There is so much yet to be done! Let us, then, move forward; let us continue the journey with lengthened stride. The Lord will lead us along, and he will be in our midst and not forsake us. (*Ensign,* May 1980, 81)

ILLUSTRATIONS FOR OUR TIME

The Spirit Told Me to Stop. One of my professional and Church colleagues, Roy Moore, recently related to me a story about a near brush with death he had experienced a number of years ago. As he was returning home from work one evening, he reached a stop light at an intersection with a four-lane highway on the outskirts of Reno, Nevada. As the light turned green there was no traffic in view from either direction, so he moved across the first two lanes to the center of the intersection. Suddenly, unexpectedly, he had the distinct impression that he was to cease moving immediately. "The Spirit told me to stop," he said, "so I slammed on the brakes so hard I stalled the car just short of the next two lanes." For an instant he scanned the terrain and saw no other vehicle. Then seconds later a whoosh of yellow exploded out of nowhere and streaked by at high speed only a few feet in front of him. Soon thereafter a police car loomed into view, skidded and careened to a near stop at the red light, and then barreled onward in hot pursuit of the other vehicle. As my friend gained his composure and slowly made his way along the highway, he felt the most overpowering sense of peace and gratitude. "Such an experience makes you know there is a God and makes you feel deep gratitude for His guidance." He said a silent prayer of thanks. On the news that evening, a reporter recounted the outcomes of a high-speed chase involving a renegade youth in a yellow car who had run over and killed a pedestrian by speeding through an intersection in town. A policeman responded, and during the 90-mile-an-hour chase on a four-lane highway heading away from town, the runaway driver narrowly avoided a collision with another vehicle at one of the intersections. The news reporter had made reference to my friend, who had narrowly escaped death.

The Lord counseled: "But ye are commanded in all things to ask of God, who giveth liberally; and that which the Spirit testifies unto you even so I would that ye should do in all holiness of heart, walking uprightly before me, considering the end of your salvation, doing all things with prayer and thanksgiving" (D&C 46:7). (Allen.)

Likening the Scriptures to Our Lives

Ether 2:14—At the end of a four-year period, after the Lord had blessed the Jaredites, the brother of Jared forgot to pray and was chastened of the Lord.

Application—Let us never forget our God and cease to pray.

3. SEEING WITH THE VISION OF FAITH

THEME. "And blessed are all the pure in heart, for they shall see God" (3 Ne. 12:8). This promise of the Savior is the best summary of the principle that is illustrated in the account of how the brother of Jared was blessed by admittance into the presence of the Lord through his great faith. All of God's children are given the commandment to prepare for this grand experience through obedience to the principles and ordinances of the gospel.

> *"And it came to pass that when the brother of Jared had said these words, behold, the Lord stretched forth his hand and touched the stones one by one with his finger. And the veil was taken from off the eyes of the brother of Jared, and he saw the finger of the Lord; and it was as the finger of a man, like unto flesh and blood; and the brother of Jared fell down before the Lord, for he was struck with fear. . . . And the Lord said unto him: Because of thy faith thou hast seen that I shall take upon me flesh and blood; and never has man come before me with such exceeding faith as thou hast; for were it not so ye could not have seen my finger. Sawest thou more than this?" (Ether 3:6, 9).*

"Behold, the Lord showed himself unto him, and said: Because thou knowest these things ye are redeemed from the fall; therefore ye are brought back into my presence; therefore I show myself unto you. Behold, I am he who was prepared from the foundation of the world to redeem my people. Behold, I am Jesus Christ. I am the Father and the Son. In me shall all mankind have life, and that eternally, even they who shall believe on my name; and they shall become my sons and my daughters. And never have I showed myself unto man whom I have created, for never has man believed in me as thou hast. Seest thou that ye are created after mine own image? Yea, even all men were created in the beginning after mine own image. Behold, this body, which ye now behold, is the body of my spirit; and man have I created after the body of my spirit; and even as I appear unto thee to be in the spirit will I appear unto my people in the flesh" (Ether 3:13–16).

MOMENT OF TRUTH. The brother of Jared, while pleading with the Lord to give them light for the journey across the sea, beholds the finger of the Lord as He touches the stones to illuminate them. The perception of the divine presence causes the beholder to fall down in fear: "And he saith unto the Lord: I saw the finger of the Lord, and I feared lest he should smite me; for I knew not that the Lord had flesh and blood" (Ether 3:8). The Lord confirms that He would take upon Himself flesh and blood during His mortal ministry, commends the brother of Jared for his great faith, and proceeds to show Himself fully, bearing witness of His atoning mission. "Wherefore, having this perfect knowledge of God, he could not be kept from within the veil; therefore he saw Jesus; and he did minister unto him" (Ether 3:20).

MODERN PROPHETS SPEAK

Bruce R. McConkie:

And as with the prophets and seers of ancient and modern times, so with all the saints who will obey the same laws, all shall see the Lord, for God is no respecter of persons. "Verily, thus saith the Lord," he decrees: "It shall come to pass that every soul who forsaketh his sins and cometh unto me, and calleth on my name, and obeyeth my voice, and keepeth my commandments, shall see my face and know that I am." (D&C 93:1.) And again: "Sanctify yourselves that your minds become single to God, and the days will come that you shall see him; for he will unveil his face unto you, and it shall be in his own time, and in his own way, and according to his own will." (D&C 88:68.) See 2 Pet. 1:1–19. (*Doctrinal New Testament Commentary*, 3 vols. [Salt Lake City: Bookcraft, 1965–1973], 3:399)

ILLUSTRATIONS FOR OUR TIME

"The Most Glorious Being."

Melvin J. Ballard:

> Two years ago, about this time, I had been on the Fort Peck Reservation for several days with the brethren, solving the problems connected with our work among the Lamanites. . . . There was no precedent for us to follow, and we just had to go to the Lord and tell Him our troubles, and get inspiration and help from Him. On this occasion I had sought the Lord, under such circumstances, and that night I received a wonderful manifestation and impression which has never left me. I was carried to this place—into this room. I saw myself here with you. I was told there was another privilege that was to be mine; and I was led into a room where I was informed I was to meet someone. As I entered the room I saw, seated on a raised platform, the most glorious being I have ever conceived of, and was taken forward to be introduced to Him. As I approached He smiled, called my name, and stretched out His hands toward me. If I live to be a million years old I shall never forget that smile. He put His arms around me until my whole being was thrilled. As He finished I fell at His feet, and there saw the marks of the nails; and as I kissed them, with deep joy swelling through my whole being, I felt that I was in heaven indeed. The feeling that came to my heart then was: Oh! If I could live worthy, though it would required four-score years, so that in the end when I have finished I could go into His presence and receive the feeling that I *then* had in His presence, I would give everything that I am and ever hope to be! (*Best-Loved Stories of the LDS People,* 3 vols., ed. Jack M. Lyon, Linda Ririe Gundry, and Jay A. Parry, [Salt Lake City: Deseret Book, 1997], 1:275–276)

Likening the Scriptures to Our Lives

Ether 3:13—The Lord truly showed Himself unto the brother of Jared because of his faith. He saw the premortal Christ and learned that He would take upon Himself a body of flesh and blood.

Application—We too can know our God and our Savior. We can pray and put away our fears and jealousies and humble ourselves before God. The veil shall be rent and in the Spirit we can see God (see D&C 67:10). If we continue faithful and gain true charity, we can become the sons and daughters of God so that when the Savior appears we will be like Him and see Him as He is (1 Jn. 3:2).

4. THE VOICE OF WARNING AND WISDOM FROM THE PAST

THEME. The word of God comes by way of warning as well as wisdom. By learning lessons of life through the spiritual triumphs of some and the painful mistakes of others we can cultivate wisdom and bring ourselves closer to the Lord.

> *"And in that day that they shall exercise faith in me, saith the Lord, even as the brother of Jared did, that they may become sanctified in me, then will I manifest unto them the things which the brother of Jared saw, even to the unfolding unto them all my revelations, saith Jesus Christ, the Son of God, the Father of the heavens and of the earth, and all things that in them are" (Ether 4:7).*

> *"And he that believeth not my words believeth not my disciples; and if it so be that I do not speak, judge ye; for ye shall know that it is I that speaketh, at the last day. But he that believeth these things which I have spoken, him will I visit with the manifestations of my Spirit, and he shall know and bear record. For because of my Spirit he shall know that these things are true; for it persuadeth men to do good. And whatsoever thing persuadeth men to do good is of me; for good cometh of none save it be of me. I am the same that leadeth men to all good; he that will not believe my words will not believe me—that I am; and he that will not believe me will not believe the Father who sent me. For behold, I am the Father, I am the light, and the life, and the truth of the world. Come unto me, O ye Gentiles, and I will show unto you the greater things, the knowledge which is hid up because of unbelief. Come unto me, O ye house of Israel, and it shall be made manifest unto you how great things the Father hath laid up for you, from the foundation of the world; and it hath not come unto you, because of unbelief. Behold, when ye shall rend that veil of unbelief which doth cause you to remain in your awful state of wickedness, and hardness of heart, and blindness of mind, then shall the great and marvelous things which have been hid up from the foundation of the world from you—yea, when ye shall call upon the Father in my name, with a broken heart and a contrite spirit, then shall ye know that the Father hath remembered the covenant which he made unto your fathers, O house of Israel" (Ether 4:10–15).*

MOMENT OF TRUTH. Moroni is commanded to write and then seal up the record concerning the brother of Jared and his kinsmen. He proclaims the charge given him by the Lord pertaining to the future readership of the work: the Spirit is to confirm the truth of these things to those who receive them in faith (Ether 4:11) as long as they "rend that veil of unbelief which doth cause you to remain in your awful state of wickedness, and hardness of heart, and blindness of mind" (Ether 4:15). In this manner the analogy with the experience of the brother of Jared is extended to those who will believe the message of the Book of Mormon—for such the veil will be lifted to reveal "the great and marvelous things which have been hid up from the foundation of the world from you" (*Ibid.*). The sign for the ushering in of the era where this promise can be fulfilled is the coming forth of the record in the latter days, at a time when three witnesses will be called to confirm the truth of the origins of the work (see Ether 4:17). After Moroni has provided this prophetic preface to the history of the Jaredites, he continues with the story, recounting how the barges are driven by the winds to the promised land.

MODERN PROPHETS SPEAK

Bruce R. McConkie:

> How wondrous are the words of Christ! Their plainness, the reasoning and logic they set forth, the self-evident witness they bear of their divine origin—where else in all that is written are there words like these? Truly he that does not believe these words and others like them does not believe in Christ, and he that does believe shall receive the manifestations of the Holy Spirit and shall prepare himself for ever greater revelations. And so the cry goes forth among us:
>
> > *Come unto me, O ye Gentiles, and I will show unto you the greater things, the knowledge which is hid up because of unbelief.*
> >
> > *Come unto me, O ye house of Israel, and it shall be made manifest unto you how great things the Father hath laid up for you, from the foundation of the world; and it hath not come unto you, because of unbelief.*
>
> The call is unto us; the call is unto the Jews; the call is unto the Gentiles; the call is unto all men: Come, believe, obey, and prepare for the greater revelation that is promised!
>
> > *Behold, when ye shall rend that veil of unbelief which doth cause you to remain in your awful state of wickedness, and hardness of heart, and blindness of mind, then shall the great and marvelous things which have been hid up from the foundation of the world from you—yea, when ye shall call upon the Father in my name, with a broken heart and a contrite spirit, then shall ye know that the Father hath remembered the covenant which he made unto your fathers, O house of Israel.*
>
> O that we might rend the heavens and know all that the ancients knew! O that we might pierce the veil and see all that our forebears saw! O that we might see and know and feel what the elect among the Jaredites and among the Nephites saw and heard and

felt! He who is no respecter of persons calls us with his own voice; if we will but attune our ears we shall hear his words! (*The Mortal Messiah: From Bethlehem to Calvary,* 4 vols. [Salt Lake City: Deseret Book, 1979–1981], 4:371–372).

Belief in the various truths must be accepted if salvation is to be won, it cannot be parceled out in such a way as to accept one essential truth and reject another. All phases of the doctrines of salvation are so intertwined with each other that it is not possible to believe one part without also believing all parts of which knowledge has been gained. Thus no one can believe in Christ without believing in his Father also. (Matt. 11:27; John 5:23; 6:44; 12:44–46; 14:1, 6.) And no one can accept Christ without accepting the prophets who testify of him. "He that believeth not my words believeth not my disciples," the Lord said. "But he that believeth these things which I have spoken, him will I visit with the manifestations of my Spirit, and he shall know and bear record. . . . *He that will not believe my words will not believe me—that I am; and he that will not believe me will not believe the Father who sent me.*" (Ether 4:11, Ether 4:10–12). (*Mormon Doctrine,* 2d ed. [Salt Lake City: Bookcraft, 1966], 78–79)

ILLUSTRATIONS FOR OUR TIME

The Case against Kings. Jared and his brother, having convened a solemn assembly of sorts, were confronted with the dilemma of a heretofore free people calling for a king (Ether 6:19–22; see 2 Ne. 5:18; Sam. 8:5). In most such historical cases—bringing immense credit to the few exceptions, like Mosiah and George Washington—great men, even of prophetic stature, cannot dissuade the people, though the case against kings is a very strong one.

The transformation of this continent into a land of complete liberty awaited a future day. Nephi, himself roped into becoming a reluctant monarch, foresaw the time when Gentiles would come "out of captivity" (1 Ne. 13:13, 16, 19, 30) to this land. The Book of Mormon provides the most forceful case against kings, whatever may be said of monarchies in other lands (see Article of Faith 12), for America is proof against such an establishment. God has so declared. Nephi recorded: "And this land shall be a land of liberty unto the Gentiles, and there shall be no kings upon the land, who shall raise up unto the Gentiles. And I will fortify this land against all other nations. And he that fighteth against Zion shall perish, saith God. For he that raiseth up a king against me shall perish, for I, the Lord, the king of heaven, will be their king, and I will be a light unto them forever, that hear my words" (2 Ne. 10:11–14).

An overwhelming case may be presented against any king who obscures or assaults one's allegiance to the King of kings, Christ our Lord. He is the source of all power, using it only to overrule everything for our good. In God we may trust. Thomas Paine wrote—in *Common Sense*—at the height of the American Revolution: "But where, says some, is the King of America? I'll tell you. Friend, he reigns above." The Founding Fathers directly ascribed their success to this Source. Elder Melvin J. Ballard declared, "Other nations might boast of their kings, but the King of America, proclaimed by the patriotic fathers who founded it and established it, is the great God of heaven" (*CR,* Oct. 1928, 109). During World War I, President Heber J. Grant manifested absolute confidence in the outcome of the conflict: "Every Mormon believes in the Book of Mormon, and the Book of Mormon teaches that this is a land choice above all other lands, and that no king, or kaiser for that matter, will ever reign here" (*Gospel Standards: Selections from the Sermons and Writings of Heber J. Grant,* ed. G. Homer Durham [Salt Lake City: The Improvement Era, 1941], 242). Elder Whitney corroborated this: "He is the God of freedom, his gospel is 'the perfect law of liberty;' he is the God of this land, the land of liberty, and the only King who will ever rule over it. You need not fear that any German kaiser will ever set up his throne upon this land. Read the Book of Mormon and be convinced" (Orson F. Whitney, *CR,* Apr. 1918, 76).

Likening the Scriptures to Our Lives

Ether 4:12—We are persuaded to do good because of the Lord Jesus Christ. He leads us to do good, and is the source of all good. If we believe in His words we will believe in Him. He was sent by the Father and is the Light and Life of the world.

Application—Let us look to our Savior (see Moro. 7:15–17) and the influence of the Spirit, which will lead us to do good (see D&C 11:12). Let us remember that we are in a fallen state and need the help of our God in all things.

SUMMARY

Consider the priceless merit of the message contained in these few chapters of the Book of Mormon. We are instructed that the Lord will answer our prayers and guide us on our life's journey if we will but exercise faith and obey His commandments. We are promised, by analogy with the singularly remarkable experience of the brother of Jared, that we can see with the vision of faith and behold the mysteries of God reserved unto the valiant and obedient. We are taught to hear the voice of warning and discern the voice of wisdom as reflected in this extraordinary source of truth.

Specifically in regard to prayer, we learn that this principle is an indispensable part of the gospel of Jesus Christ. There is an application of action that one must invest to receive answers to prayers and to perceive and know God. We learn also that it is indeed a sin not to call upon our God in fervent and faithful prayer. Our prayers will be answered. As we seek to believe, we can receive manifestations of the Spirit and be led to that which is good: "I am the same that leadeth men to all good" (Ether 4:12). In addition, Moroni records that there shall be three witnesses to the Book of Mormon and that they, too, shall play a providential role in helping to establish these things and stand as a testimony for the truth.

CHAPTER FORTY-SIX

"BY FAITH ALL THINGS *are* FULFILLED"

ETHER 7–15

"It is only necessary for us to say that the whole visible creation, as it now exists, is the effect of faith. . . . So, then, faith is truly the first principle in the science of Theology, and, when understood, leads the mind back to the beginning, and carries it forward to the end; or, in other words, from eternity to eternity.

"As faith, then, is the principle by which the heavenly hosts perform their works, and by which they enjoy all their felicity, we might expect to find it set forth in a revelation from God as the principle upon which his creatures here below must act in order to obtain the felicities enjoyed by the saints in the eternal world; and that, when God would undertake to raise up men for the enjoyment of himself, he would teach them the necessity of living by faith, and the impossibility there was of their enjoying the blessedness of eternity without it, seeing that all the blessings of eternity are the effects of faith."
—JOSEPH SMITH, *LECTURES ON FAITH* [SALT LAKE CITY: DESERET BOOK, 1985], 7:5–6, 17, 19–20.

THEMES *for* LIVING

Faith as the Foundation of All Righteousness
The Humble Are Strengthened through the Grace of Christ
The Blessings of the New Jerusalem and the Renewed Jerusalem
Prophecy Confirmed: The End of a Fallen Nation

INTRODUCTION

Moroni describes the tragic demise of the mighty Jaredite nation in the final chapters of Ether. Why are modern readers exposed to these scenes of devastation and woe? Because, as Moroni's father, Mormon, taught Moroni in summarizing the similar chronicle of the Nephite extinction, "a knowledge of these things must come unto the remnant of these people, and also unto the Gentiles . . . therefore I write a small abridgment, daring not to give a full account of the things which I have seen, because of the commandment which I have received, and also that ye might not have too great sorrow because of the wickedness of this people" (Morm. 5:9). Such gripping annals convey both a warning to avoid the lethal choices of unremitting sinfulness—"and it is by the wicked that the wicked are punished" (Morm. 4:5)—as well as the promise of hope in the redeeming blessings reserved for the righteous. No matter what our weaknesses may be, the Lord's compensatory and elevating grace will transform mortal weakness into strength . . . if we will humble ourselves in full devotion and obedience. Rather than fall prey to the annihilating forces of evil that consumed the Jaredites, we can instead rise toward a state of spiritual purity reflected in the life of the brother of Jared, whose faith was such that he could not be withheld from the presence of the Lord. Pervasive throughout the Book of Mormon are stark contrasts of good and evil, pride and humility, hardness of heart and contrition of soul, showing us the way of punishment and death on the one hand, and of joy and immortality on the other. In this presentation of opposites, the Book of Ether follows the pattern of instruction ordained of the Lord.

1. FAITH AS THE FOUNDATION OF ALL RIGHTEOUSNESS

THEME. As Ether declared: "by faith all things are fulfilled" (Ether 12:3). Faith is "an anchor to the souls of men," making them "sure and steadfast, always abounding in good works, being led to glorify God" (Ether 12:4).

> *"I would show unto the world that faith is things which are hoped for and not seen; wherefore, dispute not because ye see not, for ye receive no witness until after the trial of your faith. For it was by faith that Christ showed himself unto our fathers, after he had risen from the dead; and he showed not himself unto them until after they had faith in him; wherefore, it must needs be that some had faith in him, for he showed himself not unto the world. But because of the faith of men he has shown himself unto the world, and glorified the name of the Father, and prepared a way that thereby others might be partakers of the heavenly gift, that they might hope for those things which they have not seen. Wherefore, ye may also have hope, and be partakers of the gift, if ye will but have faith" (Ether 12:6–9).*

MOMENT OF TRUTH. In making his abridgement of the 24 plates of gold, Moroni comes across the prophecies of Ether, who "could not be restrained because of the Spirit of the Lord which was in him" (Ether 12:2). Ether's inspired discourse on faith stimulates Moroni to provide his own commentary on this subject, declaring that "faith is things which are hoped for and not seen" (Ether 12:6; cf. Alma 32:21; Heb. 11:1). Moroni's exposition on the importance and power of faith in doing all things is among the most glorious statements on this subject in holy writ, for he saw Jesus and testified that He "hath talked with me face to face" (Ether 12:39).

MODERN PROPHETS SPEAK

Gordon B. Hinckley:
> As we reflect on those who have gone before us, and as we consider our present labors for the good of ourselves and others, would that we all might say each day, "I am doing my work faithfully and in good faith."

> Let us look again to the power of faith in ourselves, faith in our associates, and faith in God our Eternal Father. Let us prayerfully implement such faith in our lives. (*Faith: The Essence of True Religion* [Salt Lake City: Deseret Book, 1989], 108)

ILLUSTRATIONS FOR OUR TIME

The Tree House. My friends and I, when we were very young boys, constructed a makeshift tree house in a tall ash tree in the back of the yard. From that perch we could see in all directions and thus imagined to ourselves that we had conquered the world. One spring day, while we were idling away our time in the tree house, we happened to observe a neighbor planting potatoes in his garden immediately adjacent to the tree. When he was finished with the work, we sneaked down and, in a shameful boyish prank, removed the potato eyes from several mounds closest to the tree. As the season progressed, we observed the neighbor tending his garden with care as his crop of potatoes came up and flourished abundantly—all except for the few mounds close to our tree house. I can recall seeing him from the tree house one day as he stood and looked intently at the mystery mounds, no doubt wondering why those plants had not come up. At that point, our amusement turned to shame, for our unkindness had interrupted the flow of growth and interfered with what we would one day come to understand as the operation of faith.

When the Savior taught the people the parable of the sower, He referred to four possible scenarios: seeds falling by the wayside where fowls devoured them up, seeds falling on stony ground where they could not take root, seeds falling among thorns that choked up their growth, and—finally—seeds that fall on fertile ground and flourish. He was teaching a celebrated lesson on faith, as it pertains to the word of God planted in the hearts of individuals. Some with shallow understanding are susceptible to the incursions of the wicked one who "catcheth away that which was sown" (Matt. 13:19); some with hard hearts fail to allow the word to take root with sufficient strength for future tribulation; and some, subservient to pride and worldliness, allow the word to be stifled altogether. Only those who receive the word in faith and cultivate it with sincere devotion, as Alma taught (Alma 32), receive the abundance of the spiritual harvest.

As Moroni came to the end of his abridgment of the Book of Ether, he included a few magnificent passages from the words of the prophet Ether, who taught "that by faith all things are fulfilled. Wherefore, whoso believeth in God might with surety hope for a better world, yea, even a place at the right hand of God, which hope cometh of faith, maketh an anchor to the souls of men, which would make them sure and steadfast, always abounding in good works, being led to glorify God" (Ether 12:4). In his commentary on this statement, Moroni includes a reference to the Savior's commandment that these things are to come forth to the children of men in the latter days according to a certain principle: "And it is by faith that my fathers have obtained the promise that these things should come unto their brethren through the Gentiles" (Ether 12:22).

The commandment given to Moroni to preserve the word of God for future generations was in effect the commission of the sower. Under the principles of the Abrahamic covenant, this same commission is given to the faithful to extend the blessings of the gospel of Jesus Christ unto all the world, so that the word of God may be disseminated and take root in the hearts of believers everywhere. What a dishonor if we fall short in this sacred obligation and deprive our neighbors of the opportunity to receive the word of God in faith. On the other hand, what glorious blessings are reserved to those who share the gospel every day, planting the seeds of the word of God in charity, and helping others cultivate the garden of salvation in all its abundance. (Allen)

Likening the Scriptures to Our Lives

Ether 12:6–22—It is by faith that all things are done.

Application—Let us realize that faith is a principle of power to do all things in righteousness. We can increase our faith (see Luke 17:5) through prayer (see Hel. 3:35), scripture study (see Rom. 10:17), and by practicing the principles of the gospel in our lives.

2. THE HUMBLE ARE STRENGTHENED THROUGH THE GRACE OF CHRIST

THEME. The Lord gives us both strengths as well as weaknesses. If we will acknowledge our weaknesses in humility and importune the Lord for blessings, having faith, He will impart grace sufficient to make our weaknesses strong so that we might fulfill our stewardships in life.

> *"And if men come unto me I will show unto them their weakness. I give unto men weakness that they may be humble; and my grace is sufficient for all men that humble themselves before me; for if they humble themselves before me, and have faith in me, then will I make weak things become strong unto them. Behold, I will show unto the Gentiles their weakness, and I will show unto them that faith, hope and charity bringeth unto me—the fountain of all righteousness. And I, Moroni, having heard these words, was comforted, and said: O Lord, thy righteous will be done, for I know that thou workest unto the children of men according to their faith; . . . And it came to pass that the Lord said unto me . . . because thou hast seen thy weakness thou shalt be made strong, even unto the sitting down in the place which I have prepared in the mansions of my Father" (Ether 12:27–29, 37).*

MOMENT OF TRUTH. Moroni desires strongly to impart the lessons of truth that the Lord wants future generations to receive through the account of the Jaredite experience. However, Moroni also has a keen sense of inadequacy in writing and agonizes that future readers will mock his performance: "And thou hast made us that we could write but little, because of the awkwardness of our hands. Behold, thou hast not made us mighty in writing like unto the brother of Jared, for thou madest him that the things which he wrote were mighty even as thou art, unto the overpowering of man to read them" (Ether 12:24). It is at that point that the Lord teaches Moroni and—by extension—all of us, a powerfully comforting lesson about the operation of faith and the eternal gift of grace. The Lord gives men weakness that they may be humble, and if they are humble and apply faith to service, the Lord will provide, through grace, the compensatory gifts essential to elevate from weakness to strength.

MODERN PROPHETS SPEAK

Gene R. Cook:

> The Lord didn't give us *weaknesses* (impatience, laziness, anger, lust, and so forth). But he did give us *weakness*. That weakness has more to do with the state of mortality than with individual character flaws. When you were a spirit you didn't have your mortal weakness. But the Lord gave us bodies in a fallen state—which is a *state of weakness*—because that is the only way we could become as he is. (*Searching the Scriptures: Bringing Power to Your Personal and Family Study* [Salt Lake City: Deseret Book, 1997], 59–60)

ILLUSTRATIONS FOR OUR TIME

Humility and Spiritual Growth. As part of the perfection process, the Book of Mormon instructs us that we must be humble or we will not learn (see 2 Nephi 9:42). And in Ether 12:25–28, we are told that becoming humble is part of the process of learning, recognizing our weaknesses, and becoming strong and great in the Lord's hands. Humility is essential to that process:

> And if men come unto me I will show unto them their weakness. I give unto men weakness that they may be humble; and my grace is sufficient for all men that humble themselves before me; for if they humble themselves before me, and have faith in me, then will I make weak things become strong unto them. (Ether 12:27)

Certainly the people in the Book of Mormon had a hard time with humility, and we have a hard time, too. But we are told that when God loves a people, he chastens them (see Hebrews 12:6). Chastening often results in humility, and we cannot grow without humility.

Humility is the beginning virtue or the precursor of all spiritual growth. Until we are humble, we cannot grow. Elder Richard G. Scott describes this virtue in even greater detail:

> Humility is the precious, fertile soil of righteous character. It germinates the seeds of personal growth. When cultivated through the exercise of faith, pruned by repentance, and fortified by obedience and good works, such seeds produce the cherished fruit of spirituality. (See Alma 26:22.) Divine inspiration and power then result. Inspiration is to know the will of the Lord. Power is the capability to accomplish that inspired will. (See D&C 43:15–16.) Such power comes from God after we have done "all we can do" (2 Ne. 25:23). ("The Plan for Happiness and Exaltation," *Ensign*, Nov. 1981, 11) (Pinegar)

Likening the Scriptures to Our Lives

Ether 12:27—Men are given weakness that they might become humble. If they appeal with faith to the Lord, He will strengthen them in all things.

Application—Humility (understanding one's relationship to God and being totally dependent upon Him) empowers one to receive God's grace. Indeed, humility is the beginning virtue of exaltation.

3. THE BLESSINGS OF THE NEW JERUSALEM AND THE RENEWED JERUSALEM

THEME. The Lord has ordained that the seat of the millennial government will be in a glorious capital called the New Jerusalem, the inheritance of Joseph on the American continent, as well as in the rebuilt and renewed Jerusalem of old (the inheritance of the Jewish people and other Israelite tribes of the covenant), situated in the Holy Land. It is to these centers and associated regions that the faithful and righteous, "whose garments are white through the blood of the Lamb" (Ether 13:10), are to be gathered in the days of the Second Coming.

> *"Behold, Ether saw the days of Christ, and he spake concerning a New Jerusalem upon this land. And he spake also concerning the house of Israel, and the Jerusalem from whence Lehi should come—after it should be destroyed it should be built up again, a holy city unto the Lord; wherefore, it could not be a new Jerusalem for it had been in a time of old; but it should be built up again, and become a holy city of the Lord; and it should be built unto the house of Israel" (Ether 13:4–5).*

MOMENT OF TRUTH. Moroni records the prophecies of Ether concerning the promised land, the New Jerusalem, and the Jerusalem from which Lehi's colony came. Ether had been entirely rejected by his people and had to seek safe refuge in a cave by day so that he could venture forth regularly under the canopy of night "viewing the things which should come upon the people" (Ether 13:13). Did he perhaps sigh for respite as he maneuvered among the sleeping hordes of warriors who were waiting for the dawn to commence again their murderous campaigns of destruction? Surely he saw in his mind's eye the future glories of the New Jerusalem in his native land and the renewed Jerusalem in far off Palestine, and took comfort in the scene of a future day when people would read his record (which he was completing in the cave at night) and be inspired to do better than his Jaredite compatriots.

MODERN PROPHETS SPEAK

Joseph Smith:

> Now many will feel disposed to say, that this New Jerusalem spoken of, is the Jerusalem that was built by the Jews on the eastern continent. But you will see, from Revelation 21:2, there was a New Jerusalem coming down from God out of heaven, adorned as a bride for her husband; that after this, the Revelator was caught away in the Spirit, to a great and high mountain, and saw the great and holy city descending out of heaven from God. Now there are two cities spoken of here. As everything cannot be had in so narrow a compass as a letter, I shall say with brevity, that there is a New Jerusalem to be established on this continent, and also Jerusalem shall be rebuilt on the eastern continent. (See Book of Mormon, Ether 13:1–12) (*HC,* 2:262)

ILLUSTRATIONS FOR OUR TIME

Both Law and Truth. My wife and I were living in the eastern part of the country during the period of time when the Washington D.C. Temple was being constructed. Upon completion of that magnificent six-spired edifice, we went one day to the top of the Washington Monument to enjoy the panoramic view. From that high perspective, the great "temples of constitutional government" were resplendent in their architectural beauty—the Lincoln Memorial to the west, the Jefferson Monument to the south, and the U. S. Capitol to the east. However, we were thrilled to view another imposing edifice to the north. It was the noble Temple of the Lord rising against the horizon—an apt reminder that the Restoration was inaugurated soon after the Lord brought about the establishment of a system of laws in America that would foster the inalienable rights and agency of man: "And for this purpose have I established the Constitution of this land, by the hands of wise men whom I raised up unto this very purpose, and redeemed the land by the shedding of blood" (D&C 101: 80).

In the millennial government of the Messiah, there are to be two grand centers of gathering: the New Jerusalem on the American continent and the Old Jerusalem (renewed) in the Holy Land. Isaiah makes prophetic reference to this future establishment: "And many people shall go and say, Come ye, and let us go up to the mountain of the Lord, to the house of the God of Jacob; and he will teach us of his ways, and we will walk in his paths: for out of Zion shall go forth the law, and the word of the Lord from Jerusalem" (Isa. 2:3; cf. Micah 4:2). It is appropriate that this same passage is also quoted by Jacob (2 Ne. 12:3), for his ministry among the emigrant remnants of Israel, like that of his older brother Nephi, took place in the New World, which was ordained of God to be the gathering place for Joseph's seed (see Ether 13:8).

The famous phrase "for out of Zion shall go forth the law" was explained by President Harold B. Lee as follows:

> I have often wondered what the expression meant, that out of Zion shall go forth the law. Years ago I went with the brethren to the Idaho Falls Temple, and I heard in that inspired prayer of the First Presidency a definition of the meaning of that term "out of Zion shall go forth the law." Note what they said: "We thank thee that thou hast revealed to us that those who gave us our constitutional form of government were men wise in thy sight and that thou didst raise them up for the very purpose of putting forth that sacred document [as revealed in Doctrine and Covenants section 101]. . . .We pray that kings and rulers and the peoples of all nations under heaven may be persuaded of the blessings enjoyed by the people of this land by reason of their freedom and under thy guidance and be constrained to adopt similar governmental systems, thus to fulfill the ancient prophecy of Isaiah and Micah that . . . 'out of Zion shall go forth the law and the word of the Lord from Jerusalem.'"

(Donald W. Parry, Jay A. Parry, and Tina M. Peterson, *Understanding Isaiah* [Salt Lake City: Deseret Book, 1998], 27)

Isaiah must have foreseen the day when a great Gentile nation would arise based on laws that were consonant with celestial principles—a seedbed meet for the Restoration and the establishment of Zion and the New Jerusalem. Hence the phrase "out of Zion shall go forth the law." From Jerusalem, the birthplace of the Savior, the eternal influence of the word of God would flow forever. Such might be the implication of the phrase "and the word of the Lord from Jerusalem." In the confluence of the two—the everlasting principles of celestial law and the redeeming word of truth—are met all of the essential powers and precepts leading to immortality and eternal life. (Allen)

Likening the Scriptures to Our Lives

Ether 12:34—Charity is the love that the Lord has for the children of men. This charity is what we must possess in order to inherit the mansions of our Father.

Application—One can see that without charity we are nothing (see Moro. 7:44); therefore we must pray with all the energy of our hearts for this blessing so that when the Savior appears we will be like him (see Moro. 7:48).

4. PROPHECY CONFIRMED: THE END OF A FALLEN NATION

THEME. A theme of the Book of Mormon is that the promised land will remain a haven of peace and liberty for the righteous who keep the commandments of the Lord. On the other hand, those who turn their backs on the Lord, after all He has done to gather them to such a choice land, will be swept away if they fail to heed His call for repentance (see 1 Ne. 2:20; Jarom 1:9; Omni 1:6; Ether 2:8–10).

> *"And Akish did administer unto them the oaths which were given by them of old who also sought power, which had been handed down even from Cain, who was a murderer from the beginning. And they were kept up by the power of the devil to administer these oaths unto the people, to keep them in darkness, to help such as sought power to gain power, and to murder, and to plunder, and to lie, and to commit all manner of wickedness and whoredoms. . . . And it came to pass that they formed a secret combination, even as they of old; which combination is most abominable and wicked above all, in the sight of God; For the Lord worketh not in secret combinations, neither doth he will that man should shed blood, but in all things hath forbidden it, from the beginning of man. And*

they have caused the destruction of this people of whom I am now speaking, and also the destruction of the people of Nephi. And whatsoever nation shall uphold such secret combinations, to get power and gain, until they shall spread over the nation, behold, they shall be destroyed; for the Lord will not suffer that the blood of his saints, which shall be shed by them, shall always cry unto him from the ground for vengeance upon them and yet he avenge them not" (Ether 8:15–16, 18–19, 21–22).

"But behold, the Spirit of the Lord had ceased striving with them, and Satan had full power over the hearts of the people; for they were given up unto the hardness of their hearts, and the blindness of their minds that they might be destroyed; wherefore they went again to battle" (Ether 15:19).

MOMENT OF TRUTH. The Jaredites ripen in iniquity. As prophesied by Ether, they move relentlessly day by day toward utter destruction. The secret combinations (those who covenant with one another by the spirit of the devil like unto the Gadianton robbers) begin to flourish and overrun the land. Akish, by the power of the devil, administers the secret oaths to gain power, murder, and plunder. "And thus we see that the Lord did visit them in the fulness of his wrath, and their wickedness and abominations had prepared a way for their everlasting destruction" (Ether 14:25). The horrendous battles that ensue bring about the deaths of millions of people until only one soul remains, Coriantumr, the last king, repentant—but too late. The nation had perished in iniquity, leaving him to wander southward until he, the last surviving Jaredite, was discovered by the people at Zarahemla and reported concerning his nation that "the severity of the Lord fell upon them according to his judgments" (Omni 1:22).

MODERN PROPHETS SPEAK

Ezra Taft Benson:
> Now undoubtedly Moroni could have pointed out many factors that led to the destruction of the people, but notice how he singled out the secret combinations, just as the Church today could point out many threats to peace, prosperity, and the spread of God's work, but it has singled out as the greatest threat the Godless conspiracy. There is no conspiracy theory in the Book of Mormon—it is a conspiracy fact.

> Then Moroni speaks to us in this day and says, "Wherefore, the Lord commandeth you, when ye shall see these things come among you that ye shall awake to a sense of your awful situation, because of this secret combination which shall be among you. . . ." (Ether 8:24.)

The Book of Mormon further warns that "whatsoever nation shall uphold such secret combinations, to get power and gain, until they shall spread over the nation, behold they shall be destroyed. . . ." (Ether 8:22.)

This scripture should alert us to what is ahead unless we repent, because there is no question but that as people of the free world, we are increasingly upholding many of the evils of the adversary today. By court edict godless conspirators can run for government office, teach in our schools, hold office in labor unions, work in our defense plants, serve in our merchant marines, etc. As a nation, we are helping to underwrite many evil revolutionaries in our country.

Now we are assured that the Church will remain on the earth until the Lord comes again— but at what price? The Saints in the early days were assured that Zion would be established in Jackson County, but look at what their unfaithfulness cost them in bloodshed and delay. (*God, Family, Country: Our Three Great Loyalties* [Salt Lake City: Deseret Book, 1974], 322)

ILLUSTRATIONS FOR OUR TIME

Destruction of the Wicked. There can be no doubt that the Lord will destroy the wicked. The loss of life is one thing, for all must die. The loss of one's soul is everything. As confirmed by the following quotes, the Lord will keep His promises. We will be destroyed if we do not repent.

Moroni's writings reflect two dimensions of his own experience. First, having witnessed the destruction of his people, Moroni was vitally interested in identifying the personal attributes that must be nurtured to avoid the onset of social decay. Where individual faith flourishes, society is less likely to enter into the pathway of unbelief and wickedness that ultimately destroyed Jaredite and Nephite civilization. One of the great passages Moroni included in the book of Ether proclaims:

"Whoso believeth in God might with surety hope for a better world, yea, even a place at the right hand of God, which hope cometh of faith, maketh an anchor to the souls of men, which would make them sure and steadfast, always abounding in good works, being led to glorify God" (Ether 12:4).

W. Cole Durham, Jr.:

> Faith and hope for a better world are mutually supportive, and whether directed at improved conditions in this life or in the next, both inhibit the process of decadence. Both allay the despair and self-abandonment which lead to disintegration; both engender in their stead the abundance of good works that is the outer manifestation of charity. Moreover, men cannot possess faith, hope, and charity unless they are "meek, and lowly of heart" (Moro. 7:43); and accordingly, where these traits are found, the pride and envy and self-seeking that undermine social order cannot take root (see Moro. 7:45). Finally, to

the extent that men are engaged in the humble quest for Christ, they are involved in a process whereby they may "lay hold on every good thing" (Moro. 7:21), which is quite the reverse of courting tragedy through decadence ("Moroni," *Ensign*, June 1978, 56).

Likening the Scriptures to Our Lives
Ether 8:24—We are admonished never to allow secret combinations among us or we will become subject to all the iniquity associated with such evil alliances.

Application—Let us be assiduously active against sin. We cannot allow apathy to cause us to fail to act in the war against sin. We should let our voice be heard and not look the other way. Let it not be said of us that through tolerance and permissiveness we supported secret and destructive combinations.

SUMMARY

In the dark and ominous panorama of the history of nations in iniquitous decline, we still view the beacons of prophetic light that glow in the darkness, teaching that faith is the foundation of all righteousness, that the humble are strengthened through the grace of Christ, that the righteous can look forward to the resplendent glory of the New Jerusalem and the renewed Jerusalem, and that prophecy will ever be confirmed—both to the everlasting blessing of the faithful, as well as to the everlasting punishment of those who reject the Lord and rebel against His Spirit.

We watch in horror as the Jaredite nation, consumed by their recalcitrant wickedness, is swept off this continent as prophesied by the messengers of the Lord (see Ether 2:8), their downfall being anchored in a total commitment to evil combinations of conspiratorial malice and anger, which separated them from the Spirit of the Lord (Ether 15:19). Yet in all of this bleakness, we discover an opposite kind of anchor: the magnificent illumination of the fire of faith and the glow of hope as it prospers in the souls of those with an unceasing commitment to the Lord and eternal fidelity to covenant principles. "Wherefore, whoso believeth in God might with surety hope for a better world, yea, even a place at the right hand of God, which hope cometh of faith, maketh an anchor to the souls of men, which would make them sure and steadfast, always abounding in good works, being led to glorify God" (Ether 12:4). Once again, the Book of Mormon shows us "a more excellent hope," one that can lead us to "receive an inheritance in the place which thou hast prepared" (Ether 12:32).

CHAPTER FORTY-SEVEN

"TO KEEP THEM *in the* RIGHT WAY"

MORONI 1–6

"It was the Savior who left the ninety and nine to go out and find the one. Now we are obsessed with the ninety and nine, and we are not very much concerned with the one. But the ninety and nine will go along pretty well. They don't need a lot of attention. . . . Let's work at it. Let us do something about these people and those who are cold in their faith. They are worth saving and bringing back. Do you know who they are? Have you identified them? Start with that step. And then put them to work. No man or woman will grow in this Church unless he or she is busy and has something to do. . . .

"With the ever-increasing number of converts, we must make an increasingly substantial effort to assist them as they find their way. Every one of them needs three things: a friend, a responsibility, and nurturing with the "good word of God" (Moro. 6:4). It is our duty and opportunity to provide these things."
—GORDON B. HINCKLEY, *TEACHINGS OF GORDON B. HINCKLEY* [SALT LAKE CITY: DESERET BOOK, 1997], 539.

THEMES *for* LIVING

The Lord's Key for Helping Us Remember Our Covenants
The Church: Divine Institution for Nurture

INTRODUCTION

Moroni, at first not supposing he would write more, adds a few additional items of spiritual wisdom to his record. We can feel deep gratitude to the Lord for these precious truths concerning such gospel topics as the sacramental prayers, the requirements for baptism, our nurturing responsibility as members, the doctrine of fasting and praying, the commandment to meet together oft to partake of the sacrament, the constant need for repentance, and the need to conduct our meetings by the Spirit. These chapters are short, but they contain practical gems pertaining to the fulness of the gospel (see D&C 20:9; 3 Ne. 20:30).

1. THE LORD'S KEY FOR HELPING US REMEMBER OUR COVENANTS

THEME. The sacrament ordinance helps us focus on our covenant obligations to the Lord and reminds us regularly of how we can always have His Spirit to be with us.

> *"Wherefore, I write a few more things, contrary to that which I had supposed; for I had supposed not to have written any more; but I write a few more things, that perhaps they may be of worth unto my brethren, the Lamanites, in some future day, according to the will of the Lord" (Moro. 1:4).*

> *"O God, the Eternal Father, we ask thee in the name of thy Son, Jesus Christ, to bless and sanctify this bread to the souls of all those who partake of it; that they may eat in remembrance of the body of thy Son, and witness unto thee, O God, the Eternal Father, that they are willing to take upon them the name of thy Son, and always remember him, and keep his commandments which he hath given them, that they may always have his Spirit to be with them. Amen" (Moro. 4:3).*

> *"O God, the Eternal Father, we ask thee, in the name of thy Son, Jesus Christ, to bless and sanctify this wine to the souls of all those who drink of it, that they may do it in remembrance of the blood of thy Son, which was shed for them; that they may witness unto thee, O God, the Eternal Father, that they do always remember him, that they may have his Spirit to be with them. Amen" (Moro. 5:2).*

MOMENT OF TRUTH. Moroni, having completed the abridgment of the Book of Ether, continues with his perilous existence, moving about in secret solitude among contending Lamanite factions. He knows that he will be killed if he is captured—unless he openly denies the Christ. This he refuses to do; therefore, he must avoid being discovered at all costs. Within this framework of threatened existence, he still dwells on what he might do to add value to the lives of his Lamanite brethren. He determines to add to the record he has already made by including choice and uplifting instructions on how to conduct the affairs of the kingdom according to universal covenant principles such as fervent prayer, priesthood callings and ordinations, and partaking worthily of the sacrament. We are fortunate that Moroni added his special book to the Book of Mormon, because it contains priceless wisdom to strengthen testimonies and build faith, including the famous promise that begins "And when ye shall receive these things . . ." (Moro. 10:4). This verse has provided ready reference for thousands of missionaries to invite the reader to confirm the veracity of the record through prayer and the confirming witness of the Holy Spirit.

MODERN PROPHETS SPEAK

David B. Haight:

> The weekly opportunity of partaking of the sacrament of the Lord's Supper is one of the most sacred ordinances of The Church of Jesus Christ of Latter-day Saints and is further indication of His love for all of us. Associated with the partaking of the sacrament are principles that are fundamental to man's advancement and exaltation in the kingdom of God and the shaping of one's spiritual character. We should reflect in our own weekday conduct the spiritual renewal and commitments made on Sunday. We may fail to recognize the deep spiritual significance this ordinance offers to each of us personally. Is it possible that a casual attitude on our part of routine formality of this sacred occasion might deaden our opportunity for spiritual growth? (*Ensign*, May 1983, 14)

ILLUSTRATIONS FOR OUR TIME

With Pure Hands. While visiting a branch of the Church as a member of a stake presidency some time ago, I sat on the stand observing the young Aaronic Priesthood brethren as they prepared to administer the sacrament. They were impressive in their Sunday attire, doing their best to fulfill their duty in acting as ministers on the Lord's errand. The sacrament song that day was a well-known hymn whose text begins: "While of these emblems we partake, In Jesus' name and for his sake, Let us remember and be sure Our hearts and hands are clean and pure" ("While of These Emblems We Partake," *Hymns*, no. 174). Just as we were singing the words "Our hearts and hands are clean and pure," I happened to look down at one of the young deacons on the front row and caught him in a priceless pose. He was leaning forward, elbows on knees, with both hands outstretched in front of him, palms facing upward toward his countenance. He was staring intently at those two hands, with fixed gaze, as if to take stock of his spiritual worthiness and make sure his hands were, indeed, clean and pure. What a great lesson from a dedicated young man. What came to my mind immediately was the scriptural passage "Be ye clean that bear the vessels of the Lord" (Isa. 52:11; 3 Ne. 20:41; D&C 38:42; 133:5). This event was, for me, a vivid reminder that we should all be continually mindful of the Lord's commandment not "to partake of my flesh and blood unworthily" (3 Ne. 18:28)—or knowingly to allow others to do so— as we work together to achieve more Christlike patterns of living. (Allen)

Likening the Scriptures to Our Lives

Moroni 4:5—The Sacramental prayers remind us of our covenants.

Application—The bread is sanctified for us that we may remember and witness that we are willing to take the name of Jesus Christ upon us and always remember Him and keep the commandments. For this we can always have His Spirit to be with us. This is a great promise and covenant that will bless us every moment of our lives.

2. THE CHURCH:
DIVINE INSTITUTION FOR NURTURE

THEME. Baptism is the gateway to God's kingdom on earth, where individuals and families are "nourished by the good word of God, to keep them in the right way" (Moro. 6:4) through fellowship and sacred worship.

> *"And none were received unto baptism save they took upon them the name of Christ, having a determination to serve him to the end. And after they had been received unto baptism, and were wrought upon and cleansed by the power of the Holy Ghost, they were numbered among the people of the church of Christ; and their names were taken, that they might be remembered and nourished by the good word of God, to keep them in the right way, to keep them continually watchful unto prayer, relying alone upon the merits of Christ, who was the author and the finisher of their faith. And the church did meet together oft, to fast and to pray, and to speak one with another concerning the welfare of their souls. And they did meet together oft to partake of bread and wine, in remembrance of the Lord Jesus. And they were strict to observe that there should be no iniquity among them; and whoso was found to commit iniquity, and three witnesses of the church did condemn them before the elders, and if they repented not, and confessed not, their names were blotted out, and they were not numbered among the people of Christ. . . . And their meetings were conducted by the church after the manner of the workings of the Spirit, and by the power of the Holy Ghost; for as the power of the Holy Ghost led them whether to preach, or to exhort, or to pray, or to supplicate, or to sing, even so it was done" (Moroni 6:3–7, 9).*

MOMENT OF TRUTH. Moroni, in pondering what "may be of worth unto my brethren, the Lamanites, in some future day, according to the will of the Lord" (Moro. 1:4), is inspired to include the exact words Jesus used in calling and ordaining His twelve disciples and enjoining them to "call on the Father in my name, in mighty prayer" (Moro. 2:2). Besides the sacrament prayers, Moroni also includes the protocol for ordaining priests and teachers, the purpose and method of baptizing members of the Church, the manner of fellowshipping and nurturing converts after baptism, keeping the fold free of iniquity, maintaining careful membership records, and instructions for conducting all meetings "after the manner of the workings of the Spirit" (Moro. 6:9). In these short gems of Church government, Moroni confirms for modern-day readers that the Lord's program is the same in all dispensations.

MODERN PROPHETS SPEAK

Harold B. Lee:

> Your spiritual body needs nourishment at frequent intervals in order to assure its health and vigor. Earthly food does not satisfy this need. Food to satisfy your spiritual needs must come from spiritual sources. Principles of eternal truth, as contained in the gospel, and the proper exercise by engaging in spiritual activities are essential to the satisfying of your spiritual selves. Vital processes of the spirit are likewise maintained only by intelligent connection with spiritual fountains of truth. Spiritual sickness and death, which mean separation from the fountain of spiritual light, are sure to follow the severance of your connection with the spiritual nerve center, the Church of Jesus Christ. (*The Teachings of Harold B. Lee,* ed. Clyde J. Williams [Salt Lake City: Bookcraft, 1996], 121)

ILLUSTRATIONS FOR OUR TIME

Not Just Another Meeting. It is good to follow the scriptural injunction: "And now, behold, I give unto you a commandment, that when ye are assembled together ye shall instruct and edify each other, that ye may know how to act and direct my church, how to act upon the points of my law and commandments, which I have given. And thus ye shall become instructed in the law of my church, and be sanctified by that which ye have received, and ye shall bind yourselves to act in all holiness before me— That inasmuch as ye do this, glory shall be added to the kingdom which ye have received. Inasmuch as ye do it not, it shall be taken, even that which ye have received" (D&C 43:8–10).

The Spirit may be experienced like sanctifying fire in our meetings. As we meet together and feel of this spirit, we want to do good, walk humbly, do justly, and judge righteously. Our minds are enlightened, and we feel joy (see D&C 11:12–13). We experience that "the fruit of the Spirit is love, joy, peace, longsuffering, gentleness, goodness, faith, meekness, temperance" (Gal. 5:22–23). These feelings flow freely as we come to our meetings prepared to feel the Spirit.

The Spirit will direct our lives if we but yield to its enticings and put off the natural man as King Benjamin directed (Mosiah 3:19). The Spirit is the key. May we prepare ourselves in all things to be worthy of His Spirit by always remembering our Savior and our Heavenly Father, as expressed in the sacramental prayers. May we go up to the house of prayer and solemnly renew our covenants in the manner the Lord has prescribed for our benefit (see D&C 59:5–19). (Pinegar)

Likening the Scriptures to Our Lives

Moro. 6:5–6—We meet together oft to fast and pray and to speak to one another concerning the welfare of others. Why?

Application—As Saints we learn that this is what we do. We fast and pray for those who know not God (see Alma 6:6). We fast and pray to become full of the love of Christ (see Moroni 7:48). We fast and pray to become even as He is (see 3 Nephi 27:27). We fast and pray to stand as witnesses (see Mosiah 18:8–9). We fast and pray to become firm in our faith and strengthened in our humility (see Hel. 3:35). Then we covenant to do these things as we partake of the sacrament.

SUMMARY

The sacrament is the Lord's key for helping us remember our covenants. Moroni confirms in these chapters that the sacrament was administered in his day in precisely the same manner that priesthood leaders of today administer the sacrament. Similarly, we learn that the Church in Book of Mormon times provided a divine institutional environment for nurture, much as it does today. The sacramental prayers are to remind us—then, as now—of the covenants we have made with our Heavenly Father. We are to exercise our faith, repent, keep the Lord's commandments, and live by the Spirit, that we might endure to the end and prove worthy of eternal life and exaltation.

CHAPTER FORTY-EIGHT

CHARITY, THE PURE LOVE OF CHRIST ... INVITE ALL TO COME UNTO CHRIST

MORONI 7–8; 10

"May I remind you . . . of the greatness and of the goodness of this man Mormon. . . .
When he was a boy of ten the historian of the people, whose name was Ammoron,
described Mormon as 'a sober child, and . . . quick to observe.' (Morm. 1:2.)
Ammoron gave him a charge that when he reached the age of twenty-four, he was to
take custody of the record of the generations who had preceded him. . . .

"He wrote to our generation with words of warning and pleading, proclaiming with
eloquence his testimony of the resurrected Christ. He warned of calamities to come if
we should forsake the ways of the Lord as his own people had done. . . .

"Such was the goodness, the strength, the power, the faith, the prophetic heart of the
prophet-leader Mormon."
—GORDON B. HINCKLEY, *THE TEACHINGS OF GORDON B. HINCKLEY* [SALT LAKE CITY:
DESERET BOOK, 1997], 42.

THEMES *for* LIVING

Searching for Happiness in the Light of Christ
Faith, Hope, and Charity
Children Are Saved through the Atonement
Knowing the Truth of All Things through the Spirit
Come unto Christ and Be Perfected in Him

INTRODUCTION

In these concluding chapters are unfolded transcendent truths: how to find our way through life "in the light of Christ" (Moro. 7:19); how to judge between good and evil; how to infuse our lives with faith, hope, and charity; and how to come under the power and blessings of the Atonement by acting in faith on the invitation to come unto Christ and be perfected in Him. Our purpose for coming to this earth is summarized in beautiful simplicity within these final testimonies of Moroni and his father.

1. SEARCHING FOR
HAPPINESS IN THE LIGHT OF CHRIST

THEME. When we "search diligently in the light of Christ" (Moroni 7:19), we can become the children of Christ, always embracing the good and avoiding evil, exercising unwavering faith in the redeeming power of the Savior.

> *"For behold, God hath said a man being evil cannot do that which is good; for if he offereth a gift, or prayeth unto God, except he shall do it with real intent it profiteth him nothing. For behold, it is not counted unto him for righteousness. For behold, if a man being evil giveth a gift, he doeth it grudgingly; wherefore it is counted unto him the same as if he had retained the gift; wherefore he is counted evil before God. And likewise also is it counted evil unto a man, if he shall pray and not with real intent of heart; yea, and it profiteth him nothing, for God receiveth none such" (Moro. 7:6–9).*

> *"For behold, my brethren, it is given unto you to judge, that ye may know good from evil; and the way to judge is as plain, that ye may know with a perfect knowledge, as the daylight is from the dark night. For behold, the Spirit of Christ is given to every man, that he may know good from evil; wherefore, I show unto you the way to judge; for every thing which inviteth to do good, and to persuade to believe in Christ, is sent forth by the power and gift of Christ; wherefore ye may know with a perfect knowledge it is of God. But whatsoever thing persuadeth men to do evil, and believe not in Christ, and deny him, and serve not God, then ye may know with a perfect knowledge it is of the devil; for after this manner doth the devil work, for he persuadeth no man to do good, no, not one; neither do his angels; neither do they who subject themselves unto him" (Moro. 7:15–17).*

MOMENT OF TRUTH. Consider the eclipsing circumstances in which Moroni is writing at this time. His father's epistle to him about conditions in the land establishes the framework: the people "have lost their love, one towards another; and they thirst after blood and revenge continually" (Moro. 9:5). "And they have become strong in their perversion; and they are alike brutal, sparing none, neither old nor young; and they delight in everything save that which is good; and the suffering of our women and our children upon all the face of this land doth exceed everything; yea, tongue cannot tell, neither can it be written" (Moro. 9:19). Not knowing from one moment to the next whether he is to be murdered through the fomenting hatred and all-consuming anger of the people surrounding him, Moroni writes (through the words of his father) of things dear to the "peaceable followers of Christ" (Moro. 7:3), of love, and of discerning that which is good "in the light of Christ." Not knowing from whence his next meal might come, he writes of the nourishment that comes to the people from receiving "the word of Christ" (Moro. 7:31). The contrasts are poignant and compelling: anger and love, darkness and light, evil and goodness, degrading hopelessness and edifying hope. As Moroni prepares to seal up his records in the earth, he invests in them, through the Spirit, a message of urgency and appeal to the future generations who would read them: repent and exercise abiding faith in Christ, that you may not sink to the depravity of the Nephite nation at its demise, but rise in the majestic light of Christ, full of faith, buoyed with divine grace, as the sons and daughters of God. How grateful we should be to Moroni and his colleagues for preserving this record as an anchor to our testimonies and covenant honor at a time when forces of iniquity rage against the light of the restored gospel.

MODERN PROPHETS SPEAK

Gordon B. Hinckley:

> Some would have us believe that the area between good and evil is largely gray and that it is difficult to determine what is right and what is wrong. For any who so believe, I recommend this beautiful statement of Moroni found in the Book of Mormon: "For behold, the Spirit of Christ is given to every man, that he may know good from evil; wherefore, I show unto you the way to judge; for everything which inviteth to do good, and to persuade to believe in Christ, is sent forth by the power and gift of Christ; wherefore ye may know with a perfect knowledge it is of God." (Moro. 7:16)
> (*Teachings of Gordon B. Hinckley* [Salt Lake City: Deseret Book, 1997], 678)

ILLUSTRATIONS FOR OUR TIME

A Parable about Light. There is an old Sufi tale about a man who is observed searching for something beneath a street light. "What are you looking for?" asks a neighbor. "My house key," is the response. "Where do you think you might have left it?" asks the neighbor. "In the house." "Then why are you looking for it out here on the street?" "Because the light is better here."

It is a chronic human propensity to be looking for things in places where they cannot be found. We sometimes seek for happiness in worldly abundance or transitory pleasures—even those rooted in transgression. Alma cautioned his wayward son Corianton: "wickedness never was happiness" (Alma 41:10). Samuel the Lamanite proclaimed to the pridefully indulgent Nephites: "Ye have sought all the days of your lives for that which ye could not obtain; and ye have sought for happiness in doing iniquity, which thing is contrary to the nature of that righteousness which is in our great and Eternal Head" (Hel. 13:38).

Moroni, quoting from his father's moving sermon on Christian goodness, added to the final section of the Book of Mormon a beautiful statement about the nature of the true light in which we should search for eternal rewards: "Wherefore, I beseech of you, brethren, that ye should search diligently in the light of Christ that ye may know good from evil; and if ye will lay hold upon every good thing, and condemn it not, ye certainly will be a child of Christ" (Moro. 7:19). Searching for happiness "in the light of Christ" is a prudent and wise practice. The Psalmist counseled: "Blessed is the people that know the joyful sound: they shall walk, O Lord, in the light of thy countenance" (Ps. 89:15; cf. Ps. 90:8). The Prophet Isaiah added this admonition: "O house of Jacob, come ye, and let us walk in the light of the Lord" (Isa. 2:5; 2 Ne. 12:5).

By searching for the key of happiness in the illuminated precincts of covenant honor and righteousness we assure ourselves of a place nearest the Savior, for that is where the light is best. (Allen)

Likening the Scriptures to Our Lives

Moro. 7:6; 7:16—Our motives and intent make the act acceptable before God. To judge righteously the standard is set: Will it invite people to come unto Christ and persuade them to do good?

Application—Let us seek to become pure in heart, striving to bless others with no thought of ourselves, that all might do good and come unto Christ. Our reward is joy now and the opportunity to be forever with them in the kingdom of our Heavenly Father.

2. FAITH, HOPE, AND CHARITY

THEME. The essence of the gospel is to cultivate faith in the Lord Jesus Christ, through whose atoning sacrifice and mercy we can be sustained in our hope for salvation, and to confirm this hope through our own charity and works of righteousness.

> *"Wherefore, by the ministering of angels, and by every word which proceeded forth out of the mouth of God, men began to exercise faith in Christ; and thus by faith, they did lay hold upon every good thing; and thus it was until the coming of Christ" (Moro. 7:25).*

"And what is it that ye shall hope for? Behold I say unto you that ye shall have hope through the atonement of Christ and the power of his resurrection, to be raised unto life eternal, and this because of your faith in him according to the promise. Wherefore, if a man have faith he must needs have hope; for without faith there cannot be any hope" (Moro. 7:41–42).

"None is acceptable before God, save the meek and lowly in heart; and if a man be meek and lowly in heart, and confesses by the power of the Holy Ghost that Jesus is the Christ, he must needs have charity; for if he have not charity he is nothing; wherefore he must needs have charity" (Mor. 7:44).

"Wherefore, my beloved brethren, pray unto the Father with all the energy of heart, that ye may be filled with this love, which he hath bestowed upon all who are true followers of his Son, Jesus Christ; that ye may become the sons of God; that when he shall appear we shall be like him, for we shall see him as he is; that we may have this hope; that we may be purified even as he is pure" (Mor. 7:48).

MOMENT OF TRUTH. Moroni quotes his father's superb sermon on faith, hope, and charity—the qualities that would have redeemed the Nephite nation from its fate. Mormon explains that a person can "lay hold upon every good thing" (Moro. 7:25) through faith in Christ and His atoning sacrifice: "And Christ hath said: If ye will have faith in me ye shall have power to do whatsoever thing is expedient in me" (Moro. 7:33). The meek and lowly at heart will be sustained by their hope in Christ and, by prayerfully practicing charity—"the pure love of Christ" (Moro. 7:47)—they will be able to endure to the end in righteousness.

MODERN PROPHETS SPEAK

Jeffrey R. Holland:
> Faith in Christ and hope in his promises of resurrected, eternal life can come only to the meek and lowly in heart. Such promises, in turn, reinforce meekness and lowliness of heart in that believer. (*Christ and the New Covenant: The Messianic Message of the Book of Mormon* [Salt Lake City: Deseret Book, 1997], 334–338)

ILLUSTRATIONS FOR OUR TIME

The Beacon of Hope. We have a neighbor with a remarkable gift—the gift of hope. Though her physical frame is severely racked with the effects of a degenerative disease, she persists resolutely in staying the course, preserving her gracious smile, confirming her faith and trust in the Lord, and speaking nothing but uplifting and positive words at every turn. To see her walking the halls of the chapel or bearing her testimony from the podium is to see the embodiment of hope in our midst. The physicians shake their heads in wonder at her resiliency. Her friends nod their heads in admiration at her faith.

When Moroni sealed up his final testimony with the sacred records, surrounded on all sides with the most hopeless and atrocious depravity, what did he write about? Of hope. In the bleak environment of anger and hatred that characterized the prevailing conditions, he quoted his father concerning how to "search diligently in the light of Christ" (Moro. 7:19) with an eye to discovering the keys to faith, hope, and charity. Hope is a pervasive theme in the Book of Mormon. Toward the beginning of the chronicle, Nephi counseled never to give up hope: "Wherefore, ye must press forward with a steadfastness in Christ, having a perfect brightness of hope, and a love of God and of all men. Wherefore, if ye shall press forward, feasting upon the word of Christ, and endure to the end, behold, thus saith the Father: Ye shall have eternal life" (2 Ne. 31:20).

The gospel of Jesus Christ is the gospel of hope. The Book of Mormon is the handbook of hope. The history of God's people is the chronicle of hope. Hope will ultimately prevail over the forces of evil, which conspire relentlessly to undermine hope and degrade faith. But such conspiracies will not stand, because the mission of Christ is one of supreme and triumphant hope for all who receive it in the spirit of meekness and love. (Allen)

Likening the Scriptures to Our Lives

Moro. 7:44–45—We need charity. All truth seems to flow from the love of Christ. President Hunter said that charity "distinguishes both the beginning and end of the plan of salvation" (*The Teachings of Howard W. Hunter,* ed. Clyde J. Williams [Salt Lake City: Bookcraft, 1997], 99).

Application—Let us pray with all the energy of heart that we may be filled with this love.

3. CHILDREN ARE SAVED THROUGH THE ATONEMENT

THEME: The Atonement of Christ envelops little children in saving grace, for they are not capable of sinning. We are commanded of the Savior to become as little children in order to qualify to enter the kingdom of Heaven (Matt. 18:3).

> *"And their little children need no repentance, neither baptism. Behold, baptism is unto repentance to the fulfilling the commandments unto the remission of sins. But little children are alive in Christ, even from the foundation of the world; if not so, God is a partial God, and also a changeable God, and a respecter to persons; for how many little children have died without baptism!" (Moro. 8:11–12).*

"But it is mockery before God, denying the mercies of Christ, and the power of his Holy Spirit, and putting trust in dead works. . . . And the first fruits of repentance is baptism; and baptism cometh by faith unto the fulfilling the commandments; and the fulfilling the commandments bringeth remission of sins; And the remission of sins bringeth meekness, and lowliness of heart; and because of meekness and lowliness of heart cometh the visitation of the Holy Ghost, which Comforter filleth with hope and perfect love, which love endureth by diligence unto prayer, until the end shall come, when all the saints shall dwell with God. . . . Pray for them, my son, that repentance may come unto them. But behold, I fear lest the Spirit hath ceased striving with them; and in this part of the land they are also seeking to put down all power and authority which cometh from God; and they are denying the Holy Ghost" (Moro. 8:23, 25–26, 28).

MOMENT OF TRUTH. Mormon's epistle to his son Moroni condemns the practice of infant baptism. Children are alive in Christ through the Atonement and cannot sin, hence there is no need for baptism until they become accountable for their actions. Baptizing little children would be mockery before God and deny the Atonement of the Lord Jesus Christ. Mormon speaks of the blessings of the remission of sins and encourages Moroni to pray for the prideful Nephites that they might repent.

MODERN PROPHETS SPEAK

Joseph Smith:

"Do you believe in the baptism of infants?" asks the Presbyterian. No. "Why?" Because it is nowhere written in the Bible. Circumcision is not baptism, neither was baptism instituted in the place of circumcision. Baptism is for remission of sins. Children have no sins. Jesus blessed them and said, "Do what you have seen me do." Children are all made alive in Christ, and those of riper years through faith and repentance. (*Teachings of the Prophet Joseph Smith*, comp. Joseph Fielding Smith [Salt Lake City: Deseret Book, 1976], 314)

ILLUSTRATIONS FOR OUR TIME

The Greatest Mother's Day Gift. It was Mother's Day. The children, grandchildren, and great-grandchildren were gathered together in our home to honor and revere motherhood as embodied in our loveliest of family members. The meal was sumptuous, the dialogue uplifting, the stories inspiring, and the fellowship heartwarming. But the most memorable aspect came in the midst of an unexpected crisis. Just as the youngsters were walking down toward a neighborhood pavilion, our 84-year-old matriarch, the oldest of the mothers being honored in our family that day, tripped over the curb in front of our home and came crashing down against the cement sidewalk, incurring severe lacerations to her knee and face. What then happened was unforgettable. The youngest of our guests took charge, rushing back to help her in her moment of need. Especially little two-year-old Sydney, who had tenderly chaperoned great-grandma out to the sidewalk in the first place, eagerly attending every step, blossomed now as a veritable Florence Nightingale, with words and gestures of compassion and concern: "Band-Aid! Band-Aid!" she exclaimed with anguish in her voice.

The other grandchildren were equally solicitous as they rallied to help the injured one back into the house, where one of them repaired her broken glasses while Sydney helped to apply the bandages with all the consummate skill of a miniature physician. Fortunately, the wounds turned out to be less serious than at first suspected, and the air of urgency gave way gradually to a feeling of relief, and then returned once again to an ambiance of Mother's Day joy. The next day several of the grandchildren called Grandma to make sure she was well on her way to recovery.

Charity comes full-blown in the hearts of the youngest of God's children. No wonder Alma was able to declare, "Little children do have words given to them many times, which confound the wise and the learned" (Alma 32:23). Mormon wrote to his son Moroni that "all little children are alive in Christ" (Moro. 8:22). Little children partake of pristine charity by virtue of their not being assailable by the evil one, coming as they are under the full protection of Christ's Atonement. No wonder Mormon could say, echoing the feelings of all compassionate and feeling individuals, "I love little children with a perfect love; and they are all alike and partakers of salvation" (Moro. 8:17). What greater gift on Mother's Day than the gift of charity as shown in the lives of little children! (Allen)

Likening the Scriptures to Our Lives

Moro. 8:26—Through the remission of sins we become meek and lowly and invite the visitation of the Holy Ghost, which fills us with hope and perfect love. This blessing can endure if we are diligent in our prayers.

Application—We are to repent, be forgiven, and receive the blessings of the Holy Ghost through diligent prayer.

4. KNOWING THE TRUTH OF ALL THINGS THROUGH THE SPIRIT

THEME. When we ponder the scriptures and ask the Father in the name of Christ, with a sincere heart, with real intent, He will confirm the truth of His word through the Holy Ghost, who is the source for all spiritual gifts.

> *"Behold, I would exhort you that when ye shall read these things, if it be wisdom in God that ye should read them, that ye would remember how merciful the Lord hath been unto the children of men, from the creation of Adam even down until the time that ye shall*

receive these things, and ponder it in your hearts. And when ye shall receive these things, I would exhort you that ye would ask God, the Eternal Father, in the name of Christ, if these things are not true; and if ye shall ask with a sincere heart, with real intent, having faith in Christ, he will manifest the truth of it unto you, by the power of the Holy Ghost. And by the power of the Holy Ghost ye may know the truth of all things." (Moro. 10:3–5).

"And again, I exhort you, my brethren, that ye deny not the gifts of God, for they are many; and they come from the same God. And there are different ways that these gifts are administered; but it is the same God who worketh all in all; and they are given by the manifestations of the Spirit of God unto men, to profit them" (Moro. 10:8).

"And again I would exhort you that ye would come unto Christ, and lay hold upon every good gift, and touch not the evil gift, nor the unclean thing" (Moro. 10:30).

MOMENT OF TRUTH. Moroni, though he "had supposed not to have written more" (Moro. 1:1), is moved to expand his record with his own book, including the extraordinary promise that the Holy Ghost would confirm the truth of the record to all who seek earnestly to gain a testimony thereof. He exhorts his brethren the Lamanites (and by extension "all the ends of the earth"—Moro. 10:24) to remember the goodness of God and the things He has caused to be written (the Book of Mormon). If they ponder and pray, they can know the truth of all things by the power of the Holy Ghost. The gifts of the Spirit are granted to those who come unto Christ with a fervent commitment to serve and profit others through such gifts.

MODERN PROPHETS SPEAK

Gordon B. Hinckley:
> The Holy Ghost is the Testifier of truth, who can teach mankind things they cannot teach one another. In those great and challenging words of Moroni, a knowledge of the truth of the Book of Mormon is promised "by the power of the Holy Ghost." Moroni then declares, "And by the power of the Holy Ghost ye may know the truth of all things" (Moroni 10:4–5).
>
> I believe that this power, this gift, is available to us today. (*Faith: The Essence of True Religion* [Salt Lake City: Deseret Book, 1989], 26)

ILLUSTRATIONS FOR OUR TIME

"Please Show Me the Truth." Hartman Rector, Jr.:

When I returned home from Hawaii, on the first evening Connie, my wife, told me the Joseph Smith story. When she said that he had had visions and revelations it seemed so ridiculous that I laughed in her face, and this made her cry. I then saw how much the message really meant to her and I relented and said, "Well, the least I can do is read some of the material they left for you to study."

No sooner did I start to read the Book of Mormon than I knew that at last I had found that for which I had been searching.

While reading First Nephi, I remember saying to myself, "Dear God, let this be true, please let this be the truth—for if it is, it answers all the questions I have been trying to answer all my life." I hadn't finished Second Nephi when I knew it was true.

I had prayed one simple prayer to the Lord for many years: "Dear God, please show me the truth. Please lead me to the truth." I had sought truth in many places. Now here were two young men, Elders Teddy Raban and Ronald Flygare, boys really—their grammar was poor, their diction less than perfect, they had no great store of worldly knowledge—but they brought the truth right into my living room. And although they were very young, they had two great powers with them, truth and God. I could not argue against what they offered, neither did I wish to. (Hartman and Connie Rector, *No More Strangers* [Salt Lake City: Bookcraft, 1971], 7)

Likening the Scriptures to Our Lives

Moro. 10:3—We are asked to ponder the mercy of God and His goodness as part of our sincere involvement in reading and studying the Book of Mormon.

Application—Pondering God's goodness and mercy is one of the great ways to follow our Heavenly Father continually and not stray from the path. This is the way the prophets have always encouraged the faithful to hold to the iron rod and the wayward to return. Yes, remembering is the way to keep the covenants and commandments.

5. COME UNTO CHRIST AND BE PERFECTED IN HIM

THEME. The Book of Mormon is "Another Testament of Jesus Christ." It is a dynamic and vibrant witness for the mission of the Savior and the efficacy of His atoning sacrifice. It is a roadmap of security for the latter days.

"Yea, come unto Christ, and be perfected in him, and deny yourselves of all ungodliness; and if ye shall deny yourselves of all ungodliness, and love God with all your might, mind and strength, then is his grace sufficient for you, that by his grace ye may be perfect in Christ; and if by the grace of God ye are perfect in Christ, ye can in nowise deny the power of God. And again, if ye by the grace of God are perfect in Christ, and deny not his power, then are ye sanctified in Christ by the grace of God, through the shedding of the blood of Christ, which is in the covenant of the Father unto the remission of your sins, that ye become holy, without spot" (Moro. 10:32–33).

MOMENT OF TRUTH. Moroni concludes the Book of Mormon with the plea to come unto Christ and be perfected in him by denying ourselves of all ungodliness, by loving God with all our might, mind, and strength, and by becoming "sanctified in Christ by the grace of God" (Moroni 10:33), so that we are holy and without spot, ready to meet Him on the Day of His Coming.

MODERN PROPHETS SPEAK

Russell M. Nelson:

> Moroni taught how to gain this glorious objective. His instruction stands in any age as an antidote for depression and a prescription for joy. I echo his plea: "Come unto Christ, and be perfected in him, and deny yourselves of all ungodliness; . . . love God with all your might, mind and strength, then . . . ye may be perfect in Christ . . . holy, [and] without spot." (Moroni 10:32–33) (*Perfection Pending, and Other Favorite Discourses* [Salt Lake City: Deseret Book, 1998], 9)

ILLUSTRATIONS FOR OUR TIME

"What Great Things the Lord Hath Done." In his title page, Moroni made very clear, as he surveyed the breadth and scope of the entire work for which he served as the final and consummate curator, what the Lord's purposes are for the Book of Mormon: "Which is to show unto the remnant of the House of Israel what great things the Lord hath done for their fathers; and that they may know the covenants of the Lord, that they are not cast off forever—And also to the convincing of the Jew and the Gentile that JESUS is the CHRIST, the ETERNAL GOD, manifesting himself unto all nations." Great merciful acts of God in the past, great covenant honor for the present, great hope for the future (i.e., that we are not cast off forever), all on the foundation of the atoning sacrifice of Jesus Christ—that is the four-fold message of the Book of Mormon.

It is not surprising that Moroni touches on these same themes as he concludes his prophetic witness and seals up the sacred records to come forth in our day and age. First, he exhorts us to "remember how merciful the Lord hath been unto the children of men, from the creation of Adam even down until the time that ye shall receive these things, and ponder it in your hearts" (Moro. 10:3). Next, he emphasizes the need for us all—daily, in the here and now—to remember our covenant obligations: "And awake, and arise from the dust, O Jerusalem; yea, and put on thy beautiful garments, O daughter of Zion; and strengthen thy stakes and enlarge thy borders forever, that thou mayest no more be confounded, that the covenants of the Eternal Father which he hath made unto thee, O house of Israel, may be fulfilled" (Moro. 10:31; cf. Isa. 52:1–2). Continuing, he holds out eternal hope for those who are willing to deny themselves of all ungodliness and fill themselves with the love of God: "Then is his grace sufficient for you, that by his grace ye may be perfect in Christ" (Moro. 10:32). Finally, none of this magnificent plan of redeeming virtue would be possible, Moroni confirms, except it should be empowered by, and extended through, "the shedding of the blood of Christ, which is in the covenant of the Father unto the remission of your sins, that ye become holy, without spot" (Moro. 10:33).

Great merciful deeds of the past rendered by God on behalf of our forefathers, great covenant blessings for the present, great hope for the future—all on the foundation of Jesus Christ. The Book of Mormon is true, and it testifies of Him. As the Prophet Joseph Smith said, "I told the brethren that the Book of Mormon was the most correct of any book on earth, and the keystone of our religion, and a man would get nearer to God by abiding by its precepts, than by any other book" (*HC,* 4:461). (Allen)

Likening the Scriptures to Our Lives

Moro. 10:32—We have been exhorted to take up our cross and deny ourselves of all ungodliness (wickedness).

Application—"Similarly the gospel cause commands every man to take up his *cross* and follow him who carried his own cross to Golgotha. That is, the saints are to carry the cross of service and consecration, the cross of devotion and obedience. 'If any man will come after me, let him deny himself, and take up his cross and follow me,' our Lord said. 'And now *for a man to take up his cross, is to deny himself all ungodliness, and every worldly lust and keep my commandments*' (*Inspired Version,* Matt. 16:25–26)." (Bruce R. McConkie, *Mormon Doctrine,* 2d ed. [Salt Lake City: Bookcraft, 1966], 173)

SUMMARY

In the final pages of the Book of Mormon, we are presented with a banquet of spiritual nourishment: how to search for happiness in the light of Christ; how to foster faith, hope, and charity in our lives; how to become like little children (who in their innocence are saved through the Atonement); how to know the truth of all things through the Spirit; and how to come unto Christ and be perfected in Him.

This wisdom is the essence of the gospel of Jesus Christ in a succinct and illuminating summary of truth. What more can be said? The goodness of God is showered down upon His children through this glorious book. We can become perfected in and through our Savior, Jesus Christ, by virtue of the grace of God. How we ought to thank our Heavenly Father and our Savior for the words of eternal life that so many have suffered and sacrificed to bring to us, enabling us to live by "every word that proceedeth out of the mouth of God" (Matt. 4:4; Moro. 7:25; D&C 84:44; 98:11). The long sequence of prophets of the Book of Mormon: Mormon (the magnificent abridger), the beloved Prophet Joseph Smith, who translated the records by the gift and power of God; and all the rest who have made this record possible—these are the valiant servants of God who have assisted in the restoration of the gospel in its fulness through the grace and mercy of the Lord. This work can be an instrument of salvation as we live the gospel of Jesus Christ and seek to share its message with others.

ABOUT *the* AUTHORS

ED J. PINEGAR

Brother Pinegar is a retired dentist and a long-time teacher of early-morning seminary and religion classes at Brigham Young University. He teaches at the Senior MTC and has served as a mission president in England and at the Missionary Training Center in Provo, Utah. He has been a bishop twice, and is a temple sealer and stake president.

Brother Pinegar and his wife, Patricia, are the parents of eight children, and reside in Orem, Utah.

RICHARD J. ALLEN

Richard J. Allen is a husband, father, teacher, writer, and organizational consultant. He has served on several stake high councils, in several stake presidencies, and as a bishop. Brother Allen has filled many teaching assignments in the Church, including full-time missionary, gospel doctrine teacher, and stake institute instructor. He has served as a faculty member at both Brigham Young University and The Johns Hopkins University. Richard has authored or co-authored many articles, manuals, and books, and loves to study the scriptures and Church history. He and his wife, Carol Lynn, have four children and live in Orem, Utah.